COTTAGES AND VILLAS
The Birth of the Garden Suburb

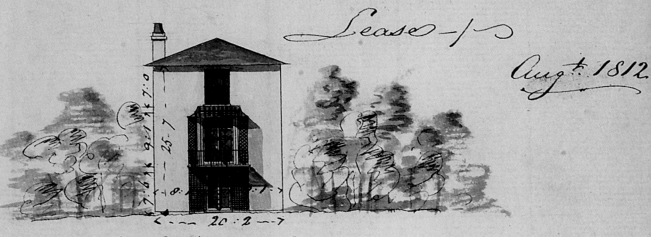

Plan and Elevation
as inserted in Mrs O'de...
Lease —/
Augt 1812

North Elevation

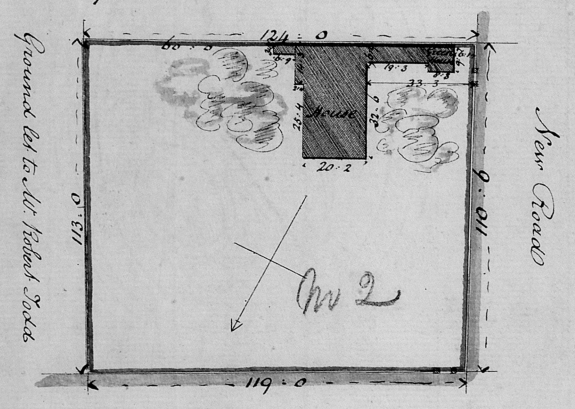

Ground let to Mr Robert Todd

Ground let to Mr Robert Todd

New Road

House

No 2

Alpha Road

60 —
6 - 9
2 - 1
22 - 8
19 - 3

Mireille Galinou

COTTAGES AND VILLAS
The Birth of the Garden Suburb

YALE UNIVERSITY PRESS
NEW HAVEN AND LONDON

The Eyre Estate

Designed by Mick Keates

Printed in Singapore

Library of Congress Cataloging-in-Publication Data

Galinou, Mireille.
    Cottages and villas: the birth of the garden suburb / Mireille Galinou.
        p. cm.
    Includes bibliographical references and index.
    ISBN 978-0-300-16726-9 (cl : alk. paper)
    1. St. John's Wood (London, England)--History.
    2. Gardensuburbs--England--London. I. Title.
    DA685.S144G35 2010
    942.1'32--dc22
    2010023281

A catalogue record for this book is available from The British Library

Frontispiece: **1** Lease drawing for one of the Alpha Cottages, dated 1812 (No. 14 on the
plan reproduced at Plate 63). It is one of around 1500 lease drawings in the archive of
the Eyre estate. It is unusually attractive and it is the only lease drawing to depict trees.
It is also the first lease to have been granted to a woman, Mrs Odell (see p. 196).
Eyre estate archive (Bk of Drawings I, 21).

Front jacket: The Eyre estate archive boasts the survival of an almost complete set of
detailed lease drawings such as the one reproduced opposite the title page (Plate 1).
These made this computer reconstruction possible. It shows the Alpha Cottages at the
southern end of the St John's Wood estate, built between 1805 and 1815, the first houses
of the very first garden suburb. For further information about the viewpoint and the
houses, see Plates 62 and 63. Eyre estate (computer reconstruction by Elliott Krause).

Back jacket: The seasons in St John's Wood – Woronzow Road, back gardens in
Ordnance Hill, Acacia Road. The Eyre estate (photos: the author).

CONTENTS

FOREWORD

Is it grossly patronising for many of us city dwellers to look down on the suburbs as representing an inferior urban form and lifestyle? Why might we think this when the reality is that they are so sought after by large sections of the population?

Suburbs have had a bad press, reinforced in our consciousness by films such as Sam Mendes's *American Beauty* or *Revolutionary Road*, with their portrayal of hopelessness and stagnation. It is time to re-examine the suburban model of living, and this book is a good place to start. *Cottages and Villas* is the story of London's first purpose-made suburb and the forebear of the Garden City concept realised (as you will see) rather later at London's Bedford Park and further with the utopian ideas of Ebenezer Howard. The development along London's Metropolitan Line (Metroland), for instance, was actually a highly sustainable model by today's standards; the train took one quickly to work and back, food was delivered by local retailers, you could grow your own vegetables and owning a car was not essential.

Condescension towards the suburbs is embedded in mainstream architectural and urbanist thinking. Somehow the semi-detached house and suburbs in general are not seen to measure up to the true ideal of city living. Without the concentration of diverse communities, jobs, cultural and commercial services, the argument runs that the suburb as a phenomenon falls short of the high-density, highly socialised city. It is claimed that city living is more civilised, with country living a close runner-up (great if you have both), and that suburbs are at the bottom of the pile.

In its own way the suburb is as interconnected and complex an organisational structure as any city – it just occupies more land. It should not be confused with the 'junkspace' of desolate dual carriageways, intersections and the sprawl of supermarkets and retail sheds. These may make up the fringes of our cities, but they serve city and suburb alike. But is it right that so many people should be considered undeserving of the luxury of their own space, forced to live in small apartments with no outside space of their own?

I have been fortunate enough to have been involved in the Eyre estate in St John's Wood as a family member and latterly as chair of the trustees for the last twenty years. I have lived in St John's Wood and nearby since 1980 and have watched the changes in that period with interest. I also happen to be an architect. As a family we knew relatively little ourselves about the detailed history of St John's Wood, but I was aware that we were sitting on a mine of information in an untapped archive. In the past the estate had been less than helpful to historians' and researchers' enquiries, and accordingly the scarcity of in-depth reliable history written about it is witness to that legacy. Even great figures such as Sir John Summerson could not get at the documentary evidence, and as a consequence his comments on St John's Wood are not always accurate.

The title of this book, 'Cottages and Villas', alludes to a shift from country to town, thereby reflecting the transition from an agrarian to an industrialised and expanded mercantile economy through the late eighteenth and on into the nineteenth centuries. London's extraordinary growth through this period brought with it the emergence of the middle classes and heralded their eventual dominance through a restructured social hierarchy. I like to think after reading this book that St John's Wood can be seen as a significant character in that narrative with its pioneering urban form and the tale of its socially and commercially vital fight to establish itself and remain as a 'respectable neighbourhood'.

When I think of cottages in the urban context contemporary with emerging plans for the estate, it is Queen Charlotte's cottage in Kew Gardens that comes to mind as perhaps a more extreme illustration of the romanticising of country living. In a era where society was bruised by the Napoleonic Wars and not long after the French Revolution, artists and writers were beginning to look at the landscape in a different way, worthy as subject matter in its own right.

That during the course of the development of St John's Wood the cottage label became interchangeable with the word 'villa' is perhaps just a product of fashion, but would seem to be consistent with the upwardly mobile aspirations of the resident population. That so many of the buildings took the form (as envisioned in the very first 1794 scheme) of joined up pairs of houses turned a classical form derived from the typology of the temple almost on its head. Sir John Summerson (a resident of nearby Belsize Park), lecturing about St John's Wood in 1958, asserted that the Italianate villa suffered the ultimate indignity by becoming two houses rather than one. A patrician viewpoint that a building form should be so demeaned or just a swipe, perhaps, at a clever innovation to create the now stigmatised physical manifestation of a suburban lifestyle – the semi-detached house?

In St John's Wood the new development was successful, despite the bankruptcies of many of the housebuilders who took on the enormous risk of developing tranches of the estate and subsequently leasing out the product of their labours. Many of the houses were taken as second homes, to be close to London but not too close to the crime-ridden stink. Like many architects I think of Andrea Palladio as the man who perfected the architecture of the second home back in the sixteenth century through his designs for the celebrated villas of the Veneto. Built for wealthy merchant families who also owned city palazzos, the villas were conceived as working farms. With their exquisite proportions and distinctive connection to the landscape (incidentally, a feature overlooked in the 2009 exhibition at the Royal Academy), an architectural form bonds with nature, romantically alluding to a simpler life.

Though Palladio's villas are grand by today's standards, they were actually relatively modest and well within the means of their patrons. Their aesthetic of austerity coincides with the start of Venice's decline as a dominant trading city. It is the exact opposite trajectory of the St John's Wood villa in the London context two and half centuries later.

London's massive growth through the period of the Enlightenment was accompanied by a strong ethos of self-improvement in the wider population. In this context the semi-detached villas of St John's Wood are a product of a pragmatic vision. Aspirational but practical, the typology straddles the worlds of town and country as well as labourer and aristocrat. The 'respectable neighbourhood' was definitively for those interested in a better life. Offering convenience, privacy and escape from the squalor of the city, the new suburb was at least the beginning of liberation from the hegemony of rural social hierarchies. That the vision as realised turned out to be a haven for artists is fortuitous for us rather than an objective of the time, but in retrospect it does not seem all that surprising that leading artists of the day were drawn to what was then an avant-garde environment. In the late eighteenth and well into the nineteenth centuries, central London was not good for one's health and was also dangerous. It is not hard to see how the innovation of this new form of living might appeal to those migrating to London or those of modest birth succeeding in business.

The built manifestation of the master plan for St John's Wood used to seem to me, a practising architect, to be a little disappointing in architectural terms. There are no grand buildings or landmarks of exceptional architectural quality, nor is there the great gesture of a green public realm landscape painting, which has turned out to be an extraordinarily important document for the world's first garden quarter.

In 2005, I duly produced, with kind help from Diana Eyre, a detailed list of the Eyre estate archive. I also prepared a report summarising its contents and encouraging the trustees of the Eyre estate to pursue the publication its chairman, Jim Eyre, had been considering for some time. In May that year, research began in earnest; as I gradually pieced together the appearance of the first houses on the estate (Plate 62) and as the new quarter mapped in the letter books slowly unfolded before my eyes, I was bowled over by the quality and vivacity of the information encountered. The chairman of the Eyre trustees had dreamed of an 'authoritative' book, and the archive would certainly provide the necessary ammunition.

The significance of St John's Wood as the first garden quarter in England was only recognised in 1958 when the architectural historian Sir John Summerson prepared an account of some of its distinctive features, although he lamented: 'the detailed history of Alpha Road [the earliest part to be developed at the south] must be presumed lost'.[1] It took almost forty years before another historian, Malcolm Brown, made another partial attempt at recovering that early history in an article published in the *London Topographical Record* in 1995. Mark Girouard also discussed the origins of the Eyre estate in his book *Cities and People* (1985) with the caveat that 'there is no adequate modern study of the estate to replace A. M[ontgomery] Eyre's gossipy *St John's Wood* (London, 1913)'.[2] Now the trustees of the Eyre estate have allowed me to make full use of its previously unpublished archive to inform this book.

Opposite: **2** This contemporary aerial photograph of north-west London, including Primrose Hill and Regent's Park on the right, shows the extent of the original St John's Wood estate, known as the Eyre estate since the late nineteenth century. Photo: Getmapping (artwork: Stephen Conlin).

The earliest publication to discuss St John's Wood dates from 1833 when its author, Thomas Smith, wrote that 'the prevailing character of the buildings is that of detached villa residences, situated in large gardens, erected in every variety of architectural elegance, and occupied by persons of the first respectability. A number of artists reside in this neighbourhood.'[3] But this story started the previous century.

The survival of a late eighteenth-century engraved master plan for St John's Wood (Plate 29) attracted the attention of various architectural historians from the 1950s onwards. The plan was not implemented, but the intention to create a cottage estate was formulated. This was the earliest conception of a 'planned suburb' of detached and semi-detached houses in the country close to a town or city, and it gradually opened the way to the development of suburbs.

This early plan, commissioned by Henry Samuel Eyre II, inspired him to develop St John's Wood into a 'respectable' neighbourhood, where fresh air and attractive gardens would be the key to commercial success. Theirs was the first example of a carefully managed city garden suburb since development started as early as 1804. The wealth of archive material allows a highly detailed reconstruction of the early character of St John's Wood. This is a crucial resource as nothing survives from the estate's first group of houses south of the Regent's Canal.

At the beginning and centre of the book are the Eyre family members who owned the estate in the eighteenth and nineteenth centuries – merchant Henry Samuel I (1676–1754); Henry Samuel II (1770–1851), an army colonel in the first half of the nineteenth century; and Reverend Henry

Samuel III (1816–90), the first member of the Eyre family to live on the estate. The most significant of all was Walpole Eyre II (1773–1856), the colonel's younger brother, who masterminded the full-scale development of St John's Wood. As a solicitor, he oversaw the legal framework of the new development and liaised with builders, financiers and lessees. He created the remarkable Eyre archive, which throws so much new light on estate development and management in the Regency and Victorian periods. Between 1804 and his death in 1856, he supervised most aspects of the estate.

His legacy is contained within the archive – detailed letter books reveal the intrigues, setbacks, solutions and pioneering decisions taken by the Eyre brothers to ensure development was successful and 'respectable'. The letter books also contain the names of the builders, architects, developers and lessees who took an active role in the process – successful or otherwise. The archive's books of drawings provide the images of the emerging estate. Each property is mapped with great precision and each elevation is carefully drawn, giving a unique visual record of a new type of urban quarter as it was being built.

The famous George Cruickshank caricature, the *March of Bricks and Mortar* (1829), comes into its own at St John's Wood. In an early example of 'sustainability', the houses there were constructed with bricks that had been made on site and the roads lined with gravel extracted from the soil. This inexorable *March* depicts the conflict between city and country on the outskirts of the capital. In St John's Wood at that time this conflict manifested itself through the clash of two powerful personalities – developer Walpole Eyre and gentleman farmer Thomas Willan. Ironically, the two men were friends, with the wealthier Willan playing a significant role in ensuring Walpole remained financially afloat. However, in the 1820s, Willan's extensive grass farm became a much reduced dairy farm, gradually making way for more villas.

The initial success of the St John's Wood estate was threatened when, in the late 1820s, large areas of land were in the hands of builders and developers who, despite their best efforts, were declared bankrupt. I recount the stories, the dangers and the solutions to this downturn. I also chronicle other threats to the integrity of the estate – for instance, the Regent's Canal and the arrival of the railway.

Walpole dominated the first fifty years of the nineteenth century. After his brother's death in 1851, he was in sole control of the St John's Wood estate until his own death in 1856. At this point it faced a difficult period of transition, and in 1858 the family, worried about the outstanding large debts, took the matter to the Chancery Court to seek authorisation to sell large tracts of St John's Wood, including landmark sites such as Lord's Cricket Ground.

The foundations laid by Walpole were solid and the estate recovered. St John's Wood remained a desirable location for many who wanted *rus in urbis*. Its social constituency was not without problems. I discuss landmark buildings – secular and religious – the lure of the area for artists of distinction who valued its mixture of town and country, and its raffish reputation in fiction and reality as a convenient place to keep a mistress. The extraordinary painting by William Holman Hunt – *The Awakening Conscience* – combined both themes in a masterly stroke, and I offer an in-depth analysis of its St John's Wood setting in the 'chronology of a house on the road to scandal' (see p. 198). The adventures of the members of the St John's Wood Clique are mentioned, as is the role of the Victorian era's two 'master dealers', William Agnew and Ernest Gambart, who created London's art market and the fortunes of many St John's Wood artists (including that of Holman Hunt).

Opposite: **3** This composition shows a selection of objects and documents from the Eyre estate archive. This book could not have been written without the data provided by artifacts such as the 1733 estate map (on the wall), the estate maps kept in tall boxes (right), or the letter books and leases (here displayed in a deed box). Eyre estate (photo: John Chase).

This detail from Stephen Conlin's 2009 pictorial map of the Eyre estate (Plate 228) focuses on Lord's cricket ground, framed by Grove End Road on the left and Wellington Road on the right. Other notable landmarks are the two St John's Wood hospitals: the stepped Wellington Hospital (right) and the St John and St Elizabeth Hospital (top right). The elongated Abbey Road studios (top left) show how deceptive the villa façade really is (façade at Plate 146). Eyre estate.

The story of St John's Wood draws tremendous strength from the quality of the Eyre estate archive. It bears witness to the genius of the brothers Eyre – the men who fought to build an idyllic neighbourhood on the edge of the big city. Unwittingly, the archive also documents a large number of urban issues which were central to Victorian cities.

The book's remit is firmly focused on St John's Wood. It dwells on what was realised there and only briefly mentions the area's links with the outside world. But it is clear that its developers, builders, architects and residents happily 'conspired' to spread the estate's winning formula far and wide through example, direct involvement or recommendation. In the first instance the concept was taken up by most of the estate's immediate neighbours – the Harrow Free School estate, the Greville estate and the Eton College estate. The Eyre archive confirms and at times reveals subtle links between these estates: the architect John Shaw junior, surveyor of the Eyre estate from 1832, also became the surveyor of the Eton College estate. The architect Decimus Burton, who had made a significant contribution to the Regent's Park project in the shape of villas, the Colosseum and the Zoological Gardens and was a close friend of the Eyres, became the surveyor of the Harrow Free School estate. The builder-developer George Pocock, whose life is so movingly evoked in his son's diary (see bibliography), was pursuing development work on both the Greville and Eyre estates, as were a number of others. After successfully completing the canal houses in St John's Wood, the builder-developer James Burton (Decimus's father) went on to create his villa town of St Leonards-on-Sea near Hastings. In his book *Cities and People* Mark Girouard described how the formula swept across the country. It is now clear that despite the financial setbacks experienced by the Eyres and their partners, the concept was a roaring success, and the craze for gardens was rapidly catered for by nurseries and gardeners who lost no time in addressing the market which had been created. In time the fashionable concept was exported – to the United States, naturally, but also to the colonies. In London it was periodically reinvented: at Bedford Park in the 1860s, during the Garden City movement at the turn of the twentieth century and in Metroland between the wars. The urban garden was here to stay.

1

THE EYRE FAMILY AND THE ESTATE OF ST JOHN'S WOOD

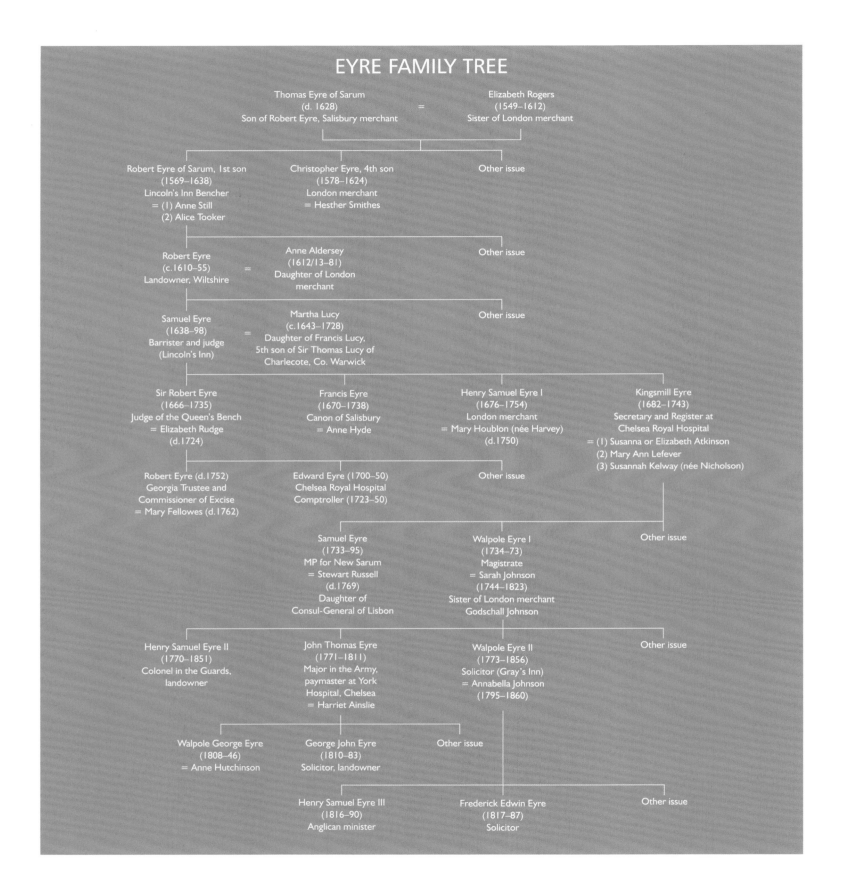

EYRE FAMILY TREE

Thomas Eyre of Sarum (d. 1628) Son of Robert Eyre, Salisbury merchant = Elizabeth Rogers (1549–1612) Sister of London merchant

Robert Eyre of Sarum, 1st son (1569–1638) Lincoln's Inn Bencher = (1) Anne Still (2) Alice Tooker

Christopher Eyre, 4th son (1578–1624) London merchant = Hesther Smithes

Other issue

Robert Eyre (c.1610–55) Landowner, Wiltshire = Anne Aldersey (1612/13–81) Daughter of London merchant

Other issue

Samuel Eyre (1638–98) Barrister and judge (Lincoln's Inn) = Martha Lucy (c.1643–1728) Daughter of Francis Lucy, 5th son of Sir Thomas Lucy of Charlecote, Co. Warwick

Other issue

Sir Robert Eyre (1666–1735) Judge of the Queen's Bench = Elizabeth Rudge (d.1724)

Francis Eyre (1670–1738) Canon of Salisbury = Anne Hyde

Henry Samuel Eyre I (1676–1754) London merchant = Mary Houblon (née Harvey) (d.1750)

Kingsmill Eyre (1682–1743) Secretary and Register at Chelsea Royal Hospital = (1) Susanna or Elizabeth Atkinson (2) Mary Ann Lefever (3) Susannah Kelway (née Nicholson)

Robert Eyre (d.1752) Georgia Trustee and Commissioner of Excise = Mary Fellowes (d.1762)

Edward Eyre (1700–50) Chelsea Royal Hospital Comptroller (1723–50)

Other issue

Samuel Eyre (1733–95) MP for New Sarum = Stewart Russell (d.1769) Daughter of Consul-General of Lisbon

Walpole Eyre I (1734–73) Magistrate = Sarah Johnson (1744–1823) Sister of London merchant Godschall Johnson

Other issue

Henry Samuel Eyre II (1770–1851) Colonel in the Guards, landowner

John Thomas Eyre (1771–1811) Major in the Army, paymaster at York Hospital, Chelsea = Harriet Ainslie

Walpole Eyre II (1773–1856) Solicitor (Gray's Inn) = Annabella Johnson (1795–1860)

Other issue

Walpole George Eyre (1808–46) = Anne Hutchinson

George John Eyre (1810–83) Solicitor, landowner

Other issue

Henry Samuel Eyre III (1816–90) Anglican minister

Frederick Edwin Eyre (1817–87) Solicitor

Other issue

'I have no cousin of the name of Robert Eyre nor indeed any relation of the name of Eyre except my Brothers & a Lady who resides in Wiltshire,' wrote Walpole Eyre in 1808.[1] This statement may now seem very surprising as we know the Eyre family to have had a long and distinguished history with branches in Wiltshire, Derbyshire, Nottinghamshire, Ireland and even the United States. However, in the early years of the nineteenth century when the St John's Wood branch of the Eyre family had barely emerged, there was a clear sense of isolation and also, as we shall see, a lack of resources. By the end of the nineteenth century, the St John's Wood branch had become 'the eldest branch of the Wiltshire Eyres'[2] and their estate was flourishing. So how did the St John's Wood branch emerge from their solitary start? How did St John's Wood become known as the Eyre estate, and who were the key family members responsible for its acquisition and subsequent development? These simple, obvious questions have led to complex and detailed research which is summarised below. This chapter will be limited to the St John's Wood branch and their immediate predecessors. It will focus on those Eyre members who moved to London from Wiltshire, thus preparing the ground for the future acquisition of the St John's Wood estate.

WILTSHIRE ORIGINS

The Eyres of St John's Wood came from a very ancient Wiltshire family (Plate 5). The four Wiltshire Visitations of 1531, 1565, 1623 and 1677 provide the most reliable source for the family's early history.[3] It starts in the mid-fourteenth century with John Eyre of Wedhampton and his wife Hellin, daughter and heir of John Crooke of Urchfont. The Heralds' Visitations of England and Wales were official surveys in the sixteenth and seventeenth centuries to establish that arms were borne with proper authority and to register the descent of armigerous families. The last Visitation was held in London in 1687 and included an entry on a Nathaniel Eyre and his descendants, with the correct Wiltshire Eyre arms, but doubt was cast on his credentials: 'Mr Eyre produced a Silver Seal (alledged to be his Fathers) but nothing met with to justify his Pretensions.'[4] Other historical accounts start with Humphrey le Heyr of Bromham, who is mentioned in a grant made by his wife Cilicia to her son Nicholas. This document is undated but appears to belong to the reign of Henry III (1216–72). However, somewhat misleadingly, tradition has described Humphrey as a follower of Richard I (1189–99) in the Crusades.[5]

The Wiltshire Eyres share their arms and crest with the Eyres of Derbyshire. Some accounts have argued that the Derbyshire branch is the most ancient, and this appears to be borne out by evidence collected by the 'Ulster King of Armes of all Ireland' from Mary Eyre, relict of the 'Seaventh Sonn of Giles Eyre of Brickworth', who was 'descended from the Noble and antient house of Hassopp in Derbishire in England'.[6] This link was mentioned in 1795 when the *Gentleman's Magazine* published a letter on the origins of the Eyre family in which the writer stated: 'he had it *from tradition* that the family of Eyre, of *Wiltshire*, was descended from a younger branch of the family of *Eyre, of Derbyshire*'.[7] The Eyre family history is discussed in great detail in Hoare's volumes on the history of Wiltshire,[8] in Burke's *Landed Gentry*, and is the subject of three books and two private family memoirs,[9] one of which, *Memorials of the Eyre Family*, contains useful footnotes which clarify the source of many facts and also of some of its most astonishing stories.[10] While many sources agree that the name derives from the words 'Her', 'Heyr' or 'Heire' meaning 'heir', the one who inherits, there is a delightful legend which can be traced back to 1835 and uses a different etymology: 'eyre' meaning the 'air' that we breathe. According to Edmund Phipps Eyre:

> The Eyres came into England with William the Norman, and their possessions at Battle arose, questionless, from gift. The first of the family was named Truelove; but at the Battle of Hastings, Oct. 14, 1066, William was flung from his horse, and his helmet beaten into his face, which Truelove observing, pulled off and horsed him again. The Duke told him 'Thou shalt hereafter from Truelove be called Air (or Eyre) because thou hadst given me the air I breathe'. After the battle the Duke, on inquiring respecting him, found him sorely wounded, his leg and thigh struck off. He ordered him the utmost care, and, on his recovery, gave him lands in Derby in reward for his services, and the leg and thigh in armour, cut off, for his crest; an honorary badge yet worn by all the Eyres in England (Plate 5).[11]

Other accounts have suggested links with France – some with the entourage of William the Conqueror, another with the south-west of France.[12] There are indeed a number of names in and around the Aquitaine region which appear based on 'Eyre' and its various spellings before becoming fixed in the eighteenth century: 'rue des Ayres' in Bordeaux, the 'Leyre' river (which should in fact be the 'Eyre' river as in L'Eyre), the 'Val d'Eyre', 'Eyres-Moncube' in the Landes, 'Eyrans', and 'Eyreville'. Those French institutions contacted about this matter have confirmed that the name could not be traced to a family name, but that in its recurrent toponymic use it had Celtic roots and signified water.[13] These associations with 'air and 'water' evoke the four elements, but there is one among those not mentioned which would be particularly appropriate to the Wiltshire Eyres – 'earth' – as land became the key to this family's success.

5 The coat of arms of the St John's Wood branch of the Eyre family. 'The quarterly arms blend the argent on a chevron sable three quatrefoils or of the Eyre family, with the gules, semy of cross-crosslets three lucies hauriant argent of the Lucy family. This coat of arms is the outcome of the 1661 marriage of Samuel Eyre (later Sir Samuel) of Newhouse in Wiltshire with Martha Lucy of Charlecote in Warwickshire. Mantling: sable and argent. *Crest:* on a wreath of the colours a leg in armour couped at the thigh proper garnished and spurred or. *Motto:* Pro rege saepe, pro patria semper.' Eyre estate (detail from College of Arms pedigree).

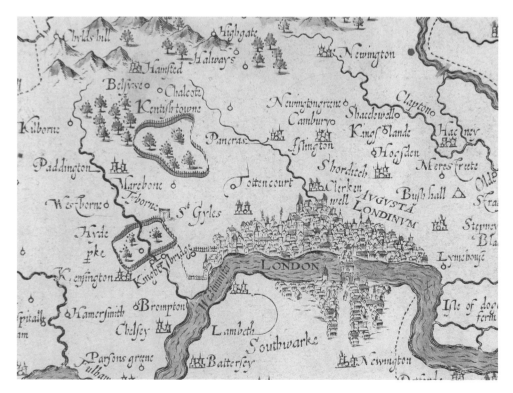

6 John Norden's map, *Middlesex Olimatibus Trinoban*, is the earliest to show St John's Wood. It was first published in 1593, but this edition dates from around 1610; unlike its predecessors it includes a representation of the three-legged structure at 'Tyborne' (Tyburn) for hanging criminals. St John's Wood is just above the word 'Marebone' (Marylebone) and next to the enclosed Crown land which became Regent's Park some two hundred years later. City of London, London Metropolitan Archives (sheet no. Dewey 912.42 MID).

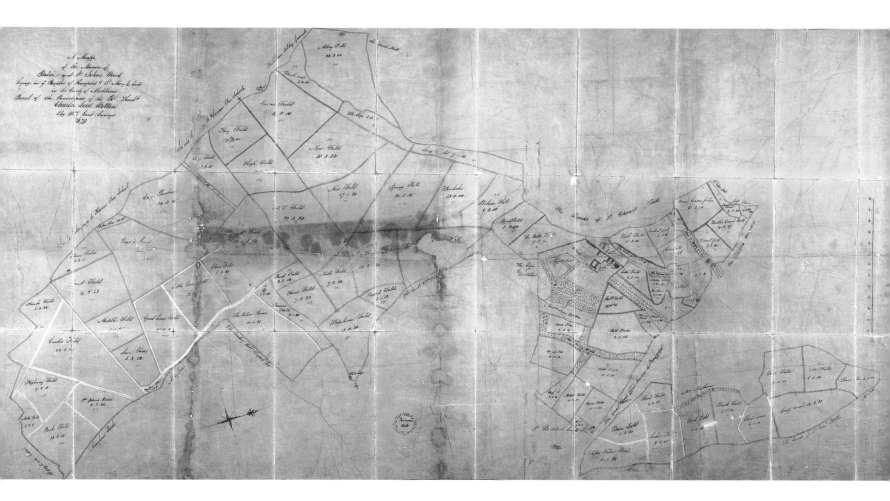

7 This appears to be the earliest survey of the St John's Wood estate. It dates from 1679 and was carried out by William Gent for the lord of the manors of Belsize and St John's Wood: the Rt Hon. Charles Lord Wotton. The map seems to be a copy of an original which has remained unlocated or perhaps has not survived. It is stored in the Holborn Library at ST2 1A./5 (formerly Hampstead Deeds 136). In the current filing system it has become separated from the written survey (Hampstead Deeds 137), which spells out the names not only of all the fields (some are illegible on the map) but also of the tenants, who were Joseph Girle (c.185 acres), Robert Lee (c.116 acres), Roger Barrett (c.94 acres), Henry Smith (c.48 acres),

Thomas Ward (c.23 acres) and Willin Crewes (c.22 acres). The 'Manor of St John's Wood' covered just over 492 acres. This map has received little attention except in an article entitled 'The Belsize Map of 1714', *Newsletter of the Camden History Society*, no. 134, November 1992. Its author, Roy Allen, cites references to preparatory versions in the Bodleian Library (Gough Maps 18, folios 18–21). Although these bear similarities to the Holborn map, they depict St John's Wood with its farms (Red Barn and St John's Wood Farm), and this suggests they date from a later period as no farm buildings are shown in 1679. Roy Allen was mistaken about the lease of St John's Wood belonging to

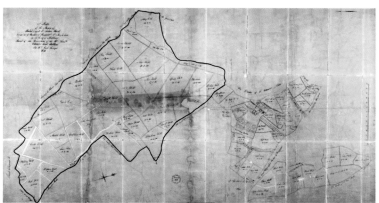

the Dean and Chapter of Westminster (see chronology under Plate 16).

Between 1679 and 1733, the date of the next survey (Plate 16), all the names of the parcels of land changed

except for the Whitehouse Field, the triangular plot which projects in the middle right. It is there that the only building on the estate was found: the White Lodge, also present on the 1733 map. Camden Local Studies.

THE MOVE TO LONDON

Records dealing with early members of the Wiltshire Eyres are of the driest kind: names but no dates. It is not until the late sixteenth and early seventeenth centuries that surviving records offer some idea of who people were and what they did. The attractive tomb of Thomas Eyre (d.1628) and Elizabeth his wife (1549–1612), in the Lady Chapel of St Thomas's Church at Salisbury, is the first memorable testimony (Plates 8 and 9). Thomas was mayor of Salisbury in 1587 and purchased the manor of Chilhampton in Wiltshire. He also owned land in Dorset which may have formed part of his wife Elizabeth's dowry. She was Elizabeth Rogers of Poole, whose brother, Robert Rogers, was a citizen of London and founder of almshouses in Cripplegate.[14] This early London connection was further developed by their fourth son, Christopher. The latter left instructions in his will to commission and pay for his parents' tomb and his own monument, which is sited opposite theirs in St Thomas's Church.[15] Both monuments have been attributed to William Wright of Charing Cross.[16]

8 General view of the Lady Chapel at St Thomas's Church, Salisbury. The wall screen which spreads across the whole width of the chapel is the monument which was erected in Robert Eyre's memory after his death in 1735. The two corner monuments are those of Thomas and Christopher Eyre erected in the 1620s. They were formerly sited in the most prestigious part of the church – the chancel – but were moved to the Lady Chapel when Robert Eyre's monument was installed. NMR.

Christopher's father was still alive when his son left instructions for his parents' monument to be made. The inscription, now barely visible, has been engraved around her sculpted outline and reads:

> ELIZABETH/EYRE WAS THE WIFE OF/THE WORSHIPFUL THOMAS EYRE ESQ:
> MOTHER/OF THESE XV CHILDREN A VIRTUOUS/MATRON A GOOD
> NEIGHBOUR. CHARI/TABLE & AN ENEMY TO IDOLATRY./IN THE FEAR OF
> GOD SHE DEP[A]RTED THIS/LIFE THE 24 OF DECEMBER 1612 AGED 63.[17]

Christopher Eyre (1578–1624) is reasonably well documented and is perhaps the first Eyre to emerge as a personality.[18] Probably guided by his uncle Robert Rogers, Christopher settled in London and set up business there. The inscription on his monument (Plate 10) contains significant information:

> IN THE PARISH CHURCH OF ST STEVENS/IN COLEMAN STREET LONDON LIES
> BURIED/THE BODY OF MR CHRISTOPHER EYRE 4TH SON/OF THE WORSHIPFUL
> THOMAS EYRE ESQ: ALDERMAN/OF THIS CITY WHO ATTAINED PROSPE/ROUSLY
> TO BE AN EAST INDIA MERCHANT/ADVENTURER & COMMITTEE OF THE
> HONORABLE/COMPANY OF THE EAST INDIA MERCHANTS &/UPPER WARDEN
> OF THE WORSHIPFUL COMPANY OF/LEATHERSELLERS & ONE OF THE
> COMMON/COUNCIL OF THE HONORABLE CITY OF LONDON/WHO LIVED
> VIRTUOUSLY & GAVE LIBERALLY/& CHARITABLY TO THE CITY OF LONDON/&

ALSO TO THIS CITY FOR THE ERECTING/OF AN ALMSHOUSE IN THIS CITY AND/MAINTENANCE THEREOF FOR EVER & FOR/A WEEKLY LECTURE IN THIS PARISH FOR EVER/& BEING OF THE AGE OF 47 YEARS DEPARTED/THIS LIFE IN THE FEAR OF GOD HATING/IDOLATRY & HIS LATE LOVING WIFE DAUGHTER/OF GEORGE SMITHES ESQ: ALDERMAN OF THE HONORABLE/CITY OF LONDON ERECTED THIS & THE OPPO/SITE MONUMENT ACCORDING TO HIS WILL.

Some details of his life are confirmed by the Court Minutes of the East India Company; on 2 July 1624 they state that he was elected a committee director for 1624–25, no doubt after serving as a committee member. Earlier, on 18 June 1622, they state: 'Eyre to go down to Blackwall today to break bulk aboard the Roebuck', and later on 1 August 1623: 'Messrs Abdy and Eyers to see the weight and tale of the ryals now to be sent in the Charles', and again on 10 September 1623: 'Messrs Garraway and Eyres to view George Bell's caskets and deliver to him "such toyes" as they shall think fit'.[19] However, these records do not corroborate the claim that Christopher was one of the original founders of the East India Company, as has sometimes been stated.[20] The inscription also claims Christopher was the Upper Warden of the Leathersellers' Company, but the records of this company state clearly he had only reached the stage of a Third Warden at his death.[21]

Christopher married Hesther, daughter of George Smithes, sheriff of London. From Christopher's will we learn that he still felt a strong attachment towards Salisbury, as he left £400 to purchase land near the Winchester Gate and a further £200 to build on this land.[22] His aim was to provide lodgings for 'six or seven poor couples, past labour and children and known to be of honest disposition and God-fearing'. Apparently no land was bought, but six almshouses – Eyre's Hospital – were eventually built on the north side of Winchester Street, the small stone tablet over the door reading: 'Donum Dei et Deo/Christopher Eyre/Anno. Dom. 1617'.[23] Another bequest funded a weekly lecture at St Thomas's Church in Salisbury, and these were still taking place in 1905 when Edmund Neville published his guide to the church.[24]

The references to Christopher 'hating idolatry' on his funerary monument and to his mother being 'an enemie to idolatry' are in keeping with the religious beliefs and practices associated with the parish church of St Stephen in Coleman Street in the City of London, the church so prominently named on Christopher's monument. During the Civil War, this poor City parish became a centre for Puritan and Parliamentary activity. Apparently, communion was only allowed to the virtuous and the repentant – thirteen parishioners and the vicar deciding who these were.[25] The inscription on Christopher's monument suggests that his personal beliefs were in accord with the practices at St Stephen's.

The City of London was a bastion of parliamentary support before, during and after the Civil Wars of the 1640s. However, there is evidence in Salisbury that other members of the Eyre family had similar views, for instance Christopher's brother Giles (1572–1655). In the church of Whiteparish outside Salisbury, a wall-mounted monument carries the following inscription:

Buried here Gyles Eyre Esqr and Jane his Wife [blank] A man much oppressed by publick power for his laudable opposition to the measures taken in the Reigns of James and Charles the first [blank] In the year 1640 (for then well known Court reasons) He was … [flogged][26] Was afterwards plundered at Brickworth by the Kings Soldiers of 2000l. value

Above left: **11** Portrait of Sir Samuel Eyre, dating from around 1675, and presented to Salisbury Corporation by Alderman Ballard in 1789. The corporation ledgers specify Samuel Eyre was Ballard's maternal grandfather, but do not name the artist of this portrait, who is sometimes thought to be John Riley. According to the catalogue *Pictures of Salisbury Corporation*, this painting was lent to a Miss Benson in 1818 to be copied. Salisbury District Council.

Below left: **12** Portrait of Martha Eyre (d.1728), née Lucy, who married Samuel Eyre of Newhouse in 1661. She was the daughter of Francis Lucy of Charlecote, Warwickshire, from whom she inherited the estate of Brightwalton, Buckinghamshire. She is buried at St Thomas's Church, Salisbury. Private collection.

Right: **13** Newhouse in Redlynch, near Downton, south-east of Salisbury. This early seventeenth-century house belonged to the Eyre family between 1633 and 1817, when it passed to the Eyre-Matcham family on the marriage of Harriet Eyre (1792–1873) with George Matcham (1789–1877) on 20 February 1817. NMR.

and imprisoned for refusing to pay the Sum of 400l. illegally demanded of him by two instruments under the privy Seal bearing date at Oxford 14th: Feb: 1643.

Recent research by C. G. Lewin has shown that Christopher's eldest brother Robert (1569–1638) was also a prominent Puritan, as was Robert's son, another Robert (c.1610–55), and his grandson, Sir Samuel, who is discussed below.[27]

Despite the significance of Christopher's career and achievements in London, it was his eldest brother Robert's descendants who provided dynastic continuity. Robert Eyre had four children with his first wife Anne, daughter of John Still, bishop of Bath and Wells. Robert was the first Eyre to choose a career in the law and to lay the foundations for a brilliant array of contributions to this field by his descendants. He was a Counsellor at Law and Bencher at Lincoln's Inn, where his arms once adorned the western window of the chapel.[28] His only son, also called Robert, became a barrister and married Anne Aldersey, daughter of London merchant Samuel Aldersey. They lived in a house fronting Salisbury Market Place (adjacent to the Cheese Cross and now 31 Cheesemarket) which has survived to this day: the fourteenth-century three-storey timber framed structure is intact behind its later eighteenth-century façade.[29] Robert and Anne Eyre suffered greatly during the Civil War and had to take refuge in the Isle of Wight, where in July 1643 Anne and two of her children survived a smallpox attack. Samuel Eyre, Robert and Anne's second son,[30] was a very important member of the Eyre family.

A SIGNIFICANT MARRIAGE

Samuel Eyre (1638–98)[31] also entered the legal profession, and his success and social mobility eventually led to rank and fortune (Plate 11). In 1653 Samuel registered at Wadham College, Oxford, paying his 'caution money' though he did not take his degree there.[32] Instead he was admitted to Lincoln's Inn in June 1654, qualifying as a barrister in June 1661; later that year, on 16 October, he married Martha, daughter of Francis Lucy, the fifth son of Sir Thomas Lucy of Charlecote in Warwickshire (Plate 12). This alliance with a well-established country gentry family considerably strengthened Samuel's status. The marriage settlement records that Francis Lucy paid £1,800 and, in addition, that Martha was given land worth £316 a year in rent revenues. The properties were the manor and manor house of Chilhampton in South Newton, the manor and farm of Choulston in Figheldean, Bonhams tenement in South Newton and land at Fisherton Anger.[33] A group of leases for various Eyre properties in Salisbury have survived, the earliest dating from 1610.[34] Samuel also acquired Newhouse or Titchbourne Park near Redlynch, south-east of Salisbury, from his cousin William in 1660 (Plate 13).[35] It had been purchased in 1633 from Edward, Baron Gorges by the Giles Eyre encountered earlier, when it was described as newly built.[36] Newhouse is a fascinating property which may still be visited: its three blocks radiate from the centre according to a plan sometimes known as 'Trinity'. With its unusual Y shape it would appear to have some connection with the triangular Longford Castle nearby, another building linked to the Gorges family.[37]

By the seventeenth century the family's relationship to London had shifted from the early merchants' connection dependent on the City towards the legal world of the Inns of Court in the 'West End' of town. Francis Lucy, Martha's father, was from the parish of St Martin-in-the-Fields; he was believed to be the confidential adviser of the first earl of Shaftesbury (Anthony Ashley Cooper,

Left: **14** Portrait of Sir Robert Eyre, the eldest son of Samuel and Martha Eyre, and a renowned judge from Lincoln's Inn. This oil painting, by an anonymous artist, may be dated c.1715. Salisbury District Council.

Right: **15** Portrait of Kingsmill Eyre, the younger brother of merchant Henry Samuel Eyre. His loyalty to his employer Robert Walpole accounts for the use of the name Walpole in the Eyre family. His keen interest in gardening may have influenced the formula of a cottage estate which his grandchildren later pursued at St John's Wood. Private collection.

1621–83), a powerful and opportunistic political figure who, after being a strong supporter of the Parliamentary regime, had turned against Cromwell and joined the Royalists. By 1692 Samuel had been made Sergeant-at-Law, and two years later he was one of the judges of the King's Bench and also knighted.

Samuel and Martha had four sons – Robert, Francis, Henry Samuel and Kingsmill – as well as two daughters – Martha and Lucy. The eldest, **Robert Eyre** (1666–1735), later Sir Robert, achieved considerable social and professional status (Plate 14). He had trained at Lincoln's Inn between 1683 and 1689 and became a recorder in Salisbury in 1696. After becoming a judge of the Court of King's Bench, he was appointed Lord Chief Baron of the Exchequer in 1723, Chancellor to the Prince of Wales and Lord Chief Justice of the Court of Common Pleas in 1725. Close to the ruling elite – Godolphin, Marlborough, Walpole and Burnet – he has been described as 'a peculiarly haughty man'.[38] Reverend **Francis Eyre** (1670–1738) became a canon of Salisbury Cathedral and is buried there. His wife Anne was daughter of Alexander Hyde, bishop of Salisbury in 1665–67.[39] They lived in the austerely beautiful house facing the main entrance to Salisbury Cathedral in the Close. It is now called Walton Canonry, but the arms above the door, now barely discernible from the closed gate, are those of the Eyre/Lucy Family.[40] The couple had no children. **Henry Samuel Eyre** (1676–1754) became a merchant who, towards the end of his life, made the shrewd acquisition of the St John's Wood estate – he is discussed in some detail below.

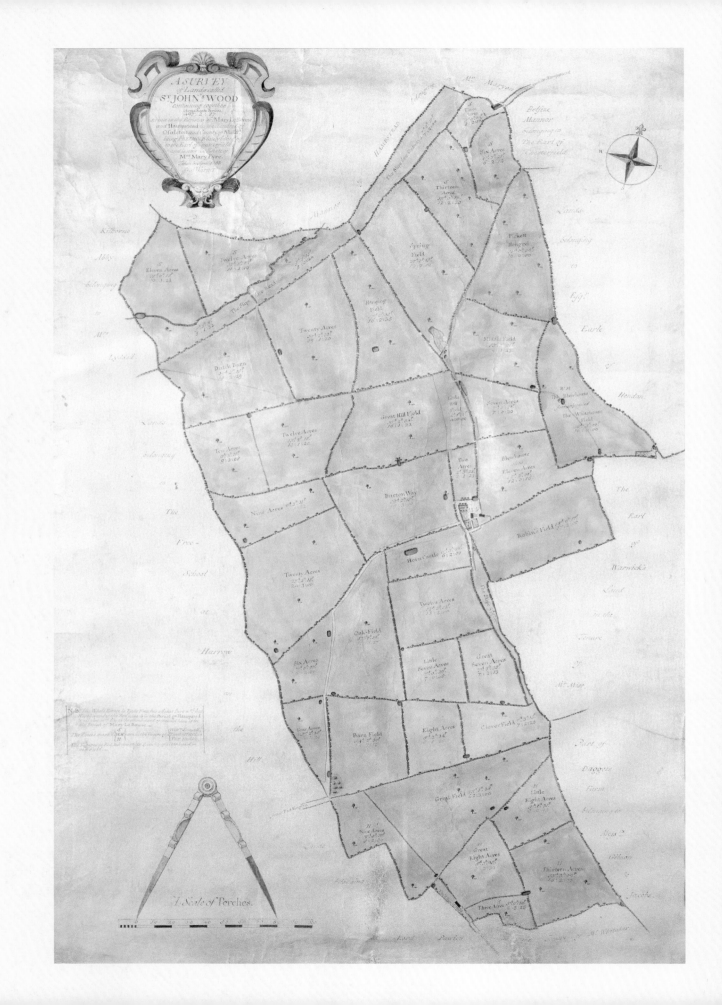

A SURVEY
of Lands called
St JOHN'S WOOD

A Scale of Perches.

16

THE ST JOHN'S WOOD ESTATE IN 1733:

'A Survey of Lands called St John's Wood, containing together 497 Acres 2 Roods 17 Perches situate in the Parishes of Mary le Bonne and Hampstead in the Hundred of Ofulston and County of Middx being FREEHOLD Lately belonging to the Earl of Chesterfield and is now the Estate of Mrs Mary Eyre taken in April 1733 S. [?] Warner'. Eyre estate archive (EE 2652/1).

Acquisition history:

Principally drawn from the St John's Wood Abstract of Title covering the period 1686–1825 (EE 2650/1/120(A)) and Bright Ashford (1965). The dates in brackets are the 'correct' Gregorian calendar dates; before 1752 the year started on 25 March. (See pp. 523–24 for abbreviations.)

11th century	Domesday survey: St John's Wood is part of the manor of Lilestone.
13th century	Otho, son of William de Lilestone, gives St John's Wood, part of his manor of Lilestone, to the Knights Templars.
1323	St John's Wood in the possession of the Knights Hospitallers after the suppression of the order of the Knights Templars.
1539	Property confiscated by the Crown at the Reformation.
1553–58	Queen Mary restores St John's Wood to the Knights of St John.
1558–59	Act reannexing all religious houses to the Crown. St John's Wood becomes part of royal hunting ground.
1581 (1582)	1 February: Queen Elizabeth grants a moiety of St John's Wood to Sir Arthur Aly, his wife and son Robert for life (Plate 6).
1675 (1676)	21 March: Charles II grants St John's Wood to Charles Henry Lord Wotton (in response to a petition and in discharge of a debt of £1,300 – see Plate 7).
1682	6 October: in his will Charles Henry Lord Wotton leaves St John's Wood to his nephew Charles Stanhope, younger son of the Rt Hon. Philip earl of Chesterfield with Jane Thacker.
1701	17 and 18 September: marriage settlement of the Hon. Charles Wotton alias Stanhope.
1730	12 December: the new earl of Chesterfield (Philip Dormer, son of above) mortgages St John's Wood to Bennett, earl of Harborough. Redemption at £12,000 plus interest. (The earl of Chesterfield fails to pay back the £12,000 on the agreed date.)
1732	The earl of Harborough makes his will and appoints Lucy dowager duchess of Rutland as his executrix and legatee.
1732 (1733)	22 March: sale of St John's Wood to Henry Samuel Eyre, James Colebrooke and James Ruck in trust for Mary Eyre (née Harvey), wife of Henry Samuel.
1750 (1751)	10 and 11 January: after Mary Eyre's death, Henry Samuel purchases St John's Wood from her trustees.

The parties in the 1733 purchase deed (WCA, 2194/3 1–6):

1 'The Right Honorable Philip Dormer Earl of Chesterfield'
2 'Henry Samuel Eyre of London Merchant and Mary his Wife'
3 'Jacob Harvey of Islington Esquire, James Colebrooke of London Esquire and James Ruck Citizen and Mercer of London'.

The price:

'For the compleat purchase of the absolute Estate of Inheritance in Fee simple':
• The earl of Chesterfield had raised a £12,000 mortgage from Bennett, earl of Harborough, which had not been paid off.
• Mary Eyre's trustees paid £23,500 to the earl of Chesterfield in 1733 (WCA, 2194/3 1–6), but also had to pay off the £12,000 mortgage to the dowager duchess of Rutland (EE 2651/358). Total: £35,500.

- Henry Samuel Eyre purchased St John's Wood from Mary's executors (her husband Henry Samuel Eyre and her nephew Samuel Clay Harvey for £22,500 in 1750 (EE 2651/172B(4).

The best document for a summary of these (complicated) transactions is the 'Assignment of Term' (attested copy) dated 24 January 1797 (EE 2651/172(6).

The size:

1679   492 acres 0 rood 15 perches (see Plate 7)
1733   497 acres 2 roods 17 perches
1750   494 acres approximately (deed of purchase by H. S. Eyre)
1794   497 acres 3 roods 20 perches (Spurrier & Phipps survey)

The tenants:

The key at the bottom left-hand corner of the 1733 map names three tenants: William Snoxhall (S), the Widow Hillier (W.H.) and Thomas Huddle (H). The surveyor has used their initials to show the tenure of the different fields. Snoxhall occupied fields at the very top of the estate, the Widow Hillier occupied 'The Blewhouse' on the east side of the estate and Thomas Huddle all the fields situated in the lower part of the estate. The latter did not hesitate to switch from rural to urban pursuits and became actively involved in building development on the adjoining Portman estate (see Bowden, 2006).

Geology:

The geology is described in some detail in VCH, but here we favour the testimony of St John's Wood resident and amateur naturalist, George Daniell from Elm Tree Road (see p. 301). In his 'Early Historical Notes and Other Notices', a typescript in the collection of Westminster City Archives, he wrote:

> heavy cold clay, interspersed with veins of course gravel, but with a considerable depth of rich mould on the surface, the natural deposit of the early forest debris, forming excellent pasture for fattening cattle, and formerly yielding remarkable abundant crops of hay.

The handwritten key found on the 1853 map of the estate (Plate 70) carefully recorded the husbandry implications of this geology by labelling each field 'Pasture', 'Meadow' or 'Arable'. Walpole Eyre was very well aware of the geology of St John's Wood and its commercial implications when he was developing the land in the first fifty years of the nineteenth century:

> The soil I apprehend is either clay or gravel (30 January 1828).

> [Mr Maidlow] is going on digging and making Bricks without any agreement & which must not be continued (24 June 1824). If the purchasars [purchasers] should make either cellars or vaults & which I do not suppose we mean to prevent them from doing they certainly will go much deeper then [than] 2 or 3 feet & might perhaps find a Considerable Quantaty [Quantity] of Gravel (3 June 1811).

> you have been … carrying the Mould into your own field without any authority from me…. The Mould is worth 10 shillings per load. I shall have what you have removed measured & you must pay 10 shillings a load for it (27 December 1823).

Kingsmill Eyre (1682–1743), the youngest of the four brothers (Plate 15), spent eight years in Holland apprenticed to Mr Chitty, a merchant,[41] before he became a protégé of Robert Walpole, now regarded as Britain's first prime minister. Robert Walpole was a close friend of Kingsmill's eldest brother Robert, and soon after Robert Walpole was appointed Paymaster General at the Royal Hospital Chelsea, Kingsmill's name appeared in the hospital's records, initially as a clerk to the Secretary and Register (1714–15), then as 'Acting Secretary' (1715) before becoming Secretary and Register in 1718.[42] Kingsmill's salary was regularly reviewed, and he also received a number of handsomely remunerated promotions, first as 'Agent to the Regiment & twenty-five companies of Invalids' (1719) and then the following year as 'Agent to an Independent Company of Foot in South Carolina'.[43] The administration of the hospital was open to many abuses, and Kingsmill was one of a number of people who routinely 'lined his pockets'.[44]

One of the scandals exposed by Kingsmill's contemporaries concerned the exploitation of Chelsea Hospital's Out-Pensioners. It has been suggested that the worry this affair created may have brought Kingsmill to his death: he was sixty-one when he complained of symptoms resembling influenza, though his death was also attributed to 'his obstinacy of not bleeding'. His will, dated barely two months before his death, was modest: 'I desire that my body may be interred in the meanest and least expensive manner practicable – having always thought expenses of that kind vain and useless, and that this article of my will may be known to prevent any reflection on my Executrix [his wife Susannah]'.[45]

Kingsmill appears to have been married three times: first to Susanna or Elizabeth Atkinson, then to Mary Ann Lefever on 26 July 1721,[46] and finally to Susannah Kelway (née Nicholson), the mother of his four children – a girl, Elisabeth or Betty born on 20 April 1728, then three boys. The first born, Robert, had illustrious godfathers – the bishop of Carlisle and Sir Robert Walpole – but he died aged one, and his father recorded his burial as being on Christmas Eve 1730. Two healthy boys followed after a short break: Samuel, on 6 April 1733, and Walpole, who would later inherit the St John's Wood estate, on 20 April 1734. Kingsmill's marriage settlement with widow Susannah Kelway has survived and is dated 22 April 1727. His keen interest in his family can be traced to a page in his account book where he listed his immediate family, recording their dates of birth or death and other personal information, such as the illustrious names of Robert's godfathers.[47] His widow Susanna opted to remain in Chelsea and took out a lease on a house in Paradise Row.[48]

One interesting aspect of Kingsmill's career is his work as a plantsman and garden designer. Although he was recently described as 'dabbling' in this field,[49] the evidence unearthed so far implies a very serious involvement. Horace Walpole, Robert's son, credited Kingsmill with the layout of his father's gardens at Houghton Hall in Norfolk, and recent scholarship suggests he may have been involved with two further gardens: Wimborne St Giles in Dorset and Chevening in Kent.[50] Kingsmill's landscape gardening expertise is clearly stated in a letter of 1718 replying to a canal cleaning enquiry: 'I remember I had some discourse with you about cleaning a Canal butt doe nott recollect that I ever heard of an instrum[en]t for itt, there is a plow used of late for breaking fresh Ground instead of a spade, which is after ye manner of other plows bute stronger, & only loosens the ground to save digging & proper for all Soils except Clay.'[51] Another letter of 1723 addressed to Hans Sloane implies that Kingsmill was negotiating with Sloane over a parcel of ground for growing fruit: 'I should hope in a short time to entertain you with some fruits from my own labour.'[52] Kingsmill's nephew, Robert Eyre (d.1752), may well have been inspired by or sought advice from his uncle for his kitchen garden at Newhouse. It was thus recorded for posterity: 'A Mapp of the kitchen Gardens Belonging to Robert Eyre Esqr in White Parish in Wilts Surveyd September 1746', surely an indication of considerable pride as such visual records were not commonplace at that date.[53] Would it be so far-fetched to suggest that Kingsmill's interest and knowledge of garden and countryside issues influenced various members of the Eyre family – certainly his children and by proxy his grandchildren including the young Henry Samuel, future owner of the St John's Wood estate? We shall see in the next chapter that the development concept of the St John's Wood estate was based on the predominance of gardens and that the early Alpha Road cottages bore a resemblance to the Houghton estate village with which Kingsmill would have been so familiar.

MARY AND HENRY SAMUEL EYRE, THE FIRST OWNERS OF ST JOHN'S WOOD

Henry Samuel Eyre (1676–1754), the third of the four sons of Samuel and Martha, was the man who purchased the St John's Wood estate. He was a merchant who specialised in the Portugal trade. His career is poorly documented, though he is listed as operating from premises in Lime Street in the Bank of England's Stock Account indexes in February 1703 (i.e. 1704). In Lime Street he was or may have become acquainted with the Delmé (or Delmey) family of merchants, as Peter Delmé had premises there.[54] Henry Samuel was one of Sir Peter Delmé's executors in 1732,[55] and the sons, Peter and John Delmé, would also later feature in Henry Samuel's will. The Delmés were prominent in the Portugal trade as were the Houblons. Both the Delmé and Houblon families were Huguenots and closely involved with the creation of the Bank of England in 1694.[56] The Portugal trade flourished after the 1654 Anglo-Portuguese treaty and received further impetus when Charles II married the Portuguese princess Catherine of Braganza in 1662.

A letter dated 26 April 1706, written from Lisbon by Henry Samuel to Ralphe Radcliffe, a merchant who had just returned to the City of London, confirms that in the early years of his career he was based in Lisbon, in a partnership known as Eyre & Watts: 'All trade this way is so much overdone at present that I cannot encourage you to ingage in anything; The Fleets lately arrived from England have brought great quantitys of Woollen Goods and Corne…. As yet no Convoy is apointed home when there is wee will look out for some of the best Wine you desire.'[57] A year later, he wrote anxiously to a Mr Burchett, deeply worried that the French fleet would intercept their ships: 'Twenty five Sayle of French men of Warr Sayl'd out of Brest, under Command of Mons.r Barbiner, and it was reported that they were to intercept our Lisbon Convoy.'[58]

Nothing else is known about Henry Samuel's early career, but he must have been back in London by 1725 when he married Mary, the widow of Samuel Houblon and daughter of Jacob Harvey of Islington. Mary Harvey was apparently under 18 when, after the death of her father in May 1706, her mother Catherine arranged her marriage to merchant Samuel Houblon,[59] son of Sir John Houblon, a prominent London citizen who was chairman of the Company of Merchants trading to Portugal. A 1701 document records Sir John Houblon's suggestion that the English merchants should petition the king of Portugal for protection against hostile local merchants.[60]

On the Harvey side, there seems to have been a distinct lack of harmony: the eldest son Jacob was left out of his father's will, the second son George was described as a lunatic, and the rest of the

nervous, felt compelled to give guidelines to his brother to ensure things got off to a good start.

> [£1,000] for which Mr Willan and I are your sureties, this is a large sum and I have therefore taken upon myself to give you one or two hints before you enter upon your new Situation, With regularity and constant attendance I conceive there can be no difficulty in keeping the Accounts of the money that passes thro your hands, This is one point that you should particularly attend to, I don't mean that you should have the drudgery of keeping the Accounts yourself but merely that you should constantly superintend them and see that the Clerk keeps them regularly posted up, and you should never allow him to quit the Office without making up the cash account of the Day, the more regularly the Accounts are kept the more easily will you understand them, You should also be cautious to make immediate entries of all Sums of money, which you may either pay or receive in the course of the day and never allow yourself to postpone these entries till the following Day,
>
> … if the Accounts are extensive and you once allow them to get in arrear you may probably never be able to set them to rights.[119]

Despite this fresh start, a year later John was dead. On 16 April 1811, Walpole wrote: 'My brother John was taken very unwell yesterday & I am sorry to say the Medical people think very unfavorable of him.' He died two days later leaving a wife and three children aged five, three and one. After his death his widow and children were 'wholly supported' by Harry.[120] As Harry never married, it was John Thomas's oldest living son, George John, who would inherit the life tenancy of St John's Wood.

By contrast to John's dispiriting military life, the career of his older brother **Henry Samuel** – Harry (Plate 20) – was very successful. The latter entered the army in 1788, joining the 11th Foot Regiment, and worked his way through the following regiments: 57th Foot in 1793, 82nd Foot in 1804, 19th Foot in 1808, 7th Regiment of Guards in 1812;[121] he retired in 1813 with the rank of lieutenant colonel. He spent many years on the island of Jersey where his mentor, General Gordon, was based. His career never overlapped that of his brother John's. Both spent time with the 19th Foot Regiment but at different periods.[122] John resigned from the army in 1805 at the end of seventeen years, a broken man. Henry Samuel, on the other hand, was in service there between 1808 and 1812, at the height of the Napoleonic Wars and immediately after he had been granted the rank of lieutenant colonel. This flattering outcome had filled his younger brother, the calm Walpole, with immense pride: 'I suppose you have seen my Brothers name in the Gazette as command[in]g the 82 in Portugal, his R.H. has promoted him without Purchase to Lieut. Colonelcy of the 19 foot, which is very handsome tho' I trust it is deservedly bestowed.'[123] A year later in 1809 came the anti-climax: Harry took part in the Walcheren expedition, when over 4,000 soldiers lost their lives, mostly to disease, and the operation was generally regarded as disastrous.[124]

For many years Harry's career was frustrated by lack of money. The training period as ADC (aide-de-camp) had been manageable, as Walpole recorded: 'I know an A.D.C. may live almost for nothing both my Brothers were A.D.C.s to Gen[era]l Gordon and one to Gen[era]l Hewitt they lived well and cheap.'[125] However, at that time military promotion was still almost entirely based upon the ability to purchase commissions. Several of Walpole's letters chart his failure in securing a lieutenancy for his brother. In September 1805 he had written to General Gordon: 'there is no getting forw[ar]d

22 *Mrs Walpole Eyre and her Children*: this was the official title of Thomas Heaphy's oil painting when it was exhibited at the Royal Academy in 1825. It depicts Annabella Eyre, née Johnson, with two of her daughters, Elizabeth Annabella (later Freeling) and Alathea Sarah (later Tooke Robinson). We know that Walpole paid £73 10s. for this painting and that it led to two further commissions: another portrait of Mrs Eyre and one of 'Miss Eyre' (LB 'K', p. 303). The artist, Thomas Heaphy, was an early tenant: first in Alpha Road, then in St John's Wood Road, where this work was painted. Collection of George Eyre and family.

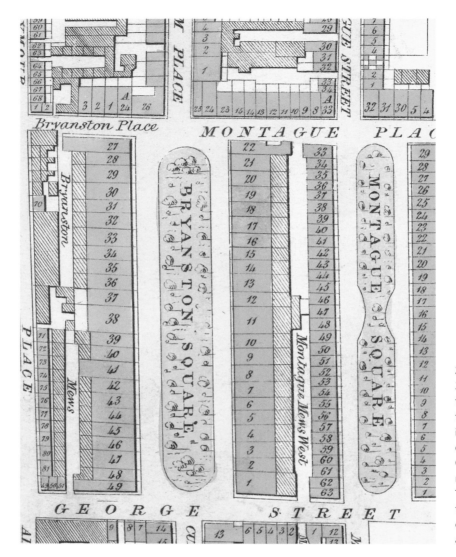

23 The Eyre house and office at 22 Bryanston Square was situated at the north-east corner of the square, at the junction with Montagu Place, and is clearly labelled on the 1846 map of Marylebone parish by the surveyor George Oakley Lucas, a Camden Town resident (see Plate 108 for full map). The estate office was at the back of the house, built on the site of the coach house and stables. Eyre estate archive (EE 2651/353).

Before renting and then buying a house near to London, the Eyres were frequent visitors to Holland Grove House in Wigan.[164] They also benefited from the hospitality of Thomas Willan, first at Farmington, near Northleach in Gloucestershire,[165] and later at Twyford Abbey near Ealing. In addition, they made regular visits to their uncle, Reverend John Johnson, at Great Parndon in Essex.

These small personal details become rare after the mid-1810s when Walpole separated 'business' and 'personal' by recording the business part in his letter books, then noting 'Remainder private', a great shame for later historians! Fortunately, however, the letter books document in great detail the Eyre brothers' domestic arrangements. The Eyres may well have been mortgaged to the hilt, but by 1830, through a series of house moves, Walpole had established the family on a very firm footing. In 1804, when he began to administer the estate, he lived in cramped and modest accommodation at Gray's Inn, and his brother would stay in a hotel whenever he took a break from the army. Walpole soon persuaded Harry to purchase a house of his own where he would have his own apartments alongside Walpole's rooms and office, and in October 1810 they took a house at 21 Beaumont Street

a noticeable change of management style. The proposed stabling at 29 Finchley Road which had been described as 'unsightly and objectionable' now obtained a licence, and the proposed Ladies School in Cavendish Road which had been previously turned down was reconsidered.[203]

The change in management style is reflected in the Eyre archive: the first sixty-five years (between 1804 and 1869) spread across twenty-three large volumes, but the next twenty-four years (between 1870 and 1894) were charted in three slimmer volumes. The figure offers a stark contrast to the first twenty-five years of estate management, which occupied twelve hefty volumes. John White only spent one day a week in the estate office: his fluent and more relaxed style of management is only partially documented, as from 1868 onwards many records would have been kept at his Bedford Row office rather than in St John's Wood. This seems to have been a constant source of frustration to the long-suffering Charles Freeth.

The development story which is detailed in this book goes up to the mid-1890s, when the southern part of the estate was lost with the arrival of Marylebone Station. The last letter book contains fragments of the action undertaken by the estate. When Reverend H. W. Maddock, vicar of All Saints at St John's Wood (Plate 193), died suddenly in 1870, his position was offered to Reverend Henry Samuel Eyre, one of the colonel's trustees. While his brother Edwin had followed in his father's estate management footsteps, Henry Samuel was apparently following his mother's wish when he became a vicar. After Eton he had gone to Christ Church in Oxford and 'took Holy Orders chiefly … to please his mother', recounted his daughter in her 1904 memoir.[204] His first curacy was at Buckland near Reigate where he met his future wife, Maria Charlotte Carbonell, the daughter of Italians who settled in England around 1700. The family moved around to follow Henry Samuel's curacies. When they were based in Newington, Kent, his daughter Mary recounted a worrying episode for the future owner of a villa estate: as their accommodation was rather small, 'My father at once decided to build another [house] and himself drew the plans for our new domicile. I don't think, poor dear, though it was a great amusement to him, that he possessed any talent as an architect, for such an ugly house as it was when finished I had never seen before and certainly never have since.'[205]

When Henry Samuel became the vicar of All Saints in 1870, he moved his family to nearby 23 St John's Wood Park (they would later move to 35 Finchley Road).[206] He was the first Eyre to live on the estate and was apparently so devoted to All Saints that his daughter recorded these words, uttered shortly before his death: 'I care more for the well being of All Saints' Church and parish than for anything in the world.' Mary added: 'His last gift was a beautiful spire which he built at a cost of £3000 in memory of my mother.'[207] Further information on his ministry can be found under All Saints in the religious chapter of this book.

At John Eyre's death in 1883 Henry Samuel Eyre became the next tenant for life. His tenancy was relatively short-lived since he died in 1890, but as one of the estate's trustees, his influence had been felt from the 1840s (see p. 339). He lived to see his son-in-law, Reverend John Richardson-Eyre, become vicar at All Saints in 1889. John Richardson adopted the Eyre surname, perhaps to please his wife; he was not alone in doing this.[208] John and his wife Mary (Plate 26) were also entirely devoted to this church. However, the ageing Henry Samuel did not live to see the destruction of his estate south of St John's Wood Road. The blow seemed a fatal one in the 1890s, but the mutilated southern end simply ceased to be known as St John's Wood and the surviving St John's Wood lived on, with renewed energy.

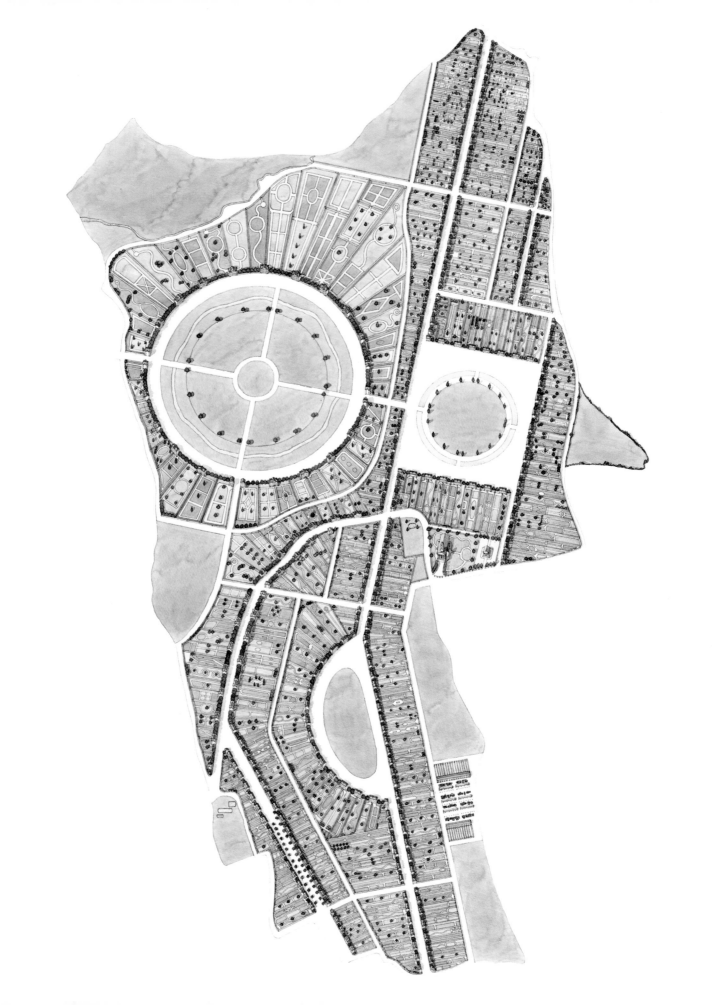

2

A MASTER PLAN FOR ST JOHN'S WOOD

A 1733 map (Plate 16) provides a concise inventory of the lands acquired by Mary Eyre, which her husband, Henry Samuel I, purchased from her executors in 1750. It was updated in 1794 when Spurrier & Phipps, a firm of surveyors, valuers and auctioneers, were commissioned to carry out a survey of the estate – a document which was thought to be lost but has now been recovered (Plate 42).[1] It is interesting that in 1794 the property listed as No. 1, which must have been viewed as the heart of the estate and a substitute for the traditional manor house, was St John's Wood Farm, described simply: 'House, Yard, Barn, Garden'.

In 1794, as well as producing a survey, Spurrier & Phipps also published *A Plan for the Improvement of a Freehold Estate call'd St John's Wood situated in the parishes of Marylebone & Hampstead* (Plate 29).[2] This plan is a significant landmark in the history not only of St John's Wood but also of London and the English suburban movement. It broke new ground, conjuring up a vision for St John's Wood which subsequently set the tone for its immediate neighbours as well as for London as a whole, the rest of the country and indeed the world.

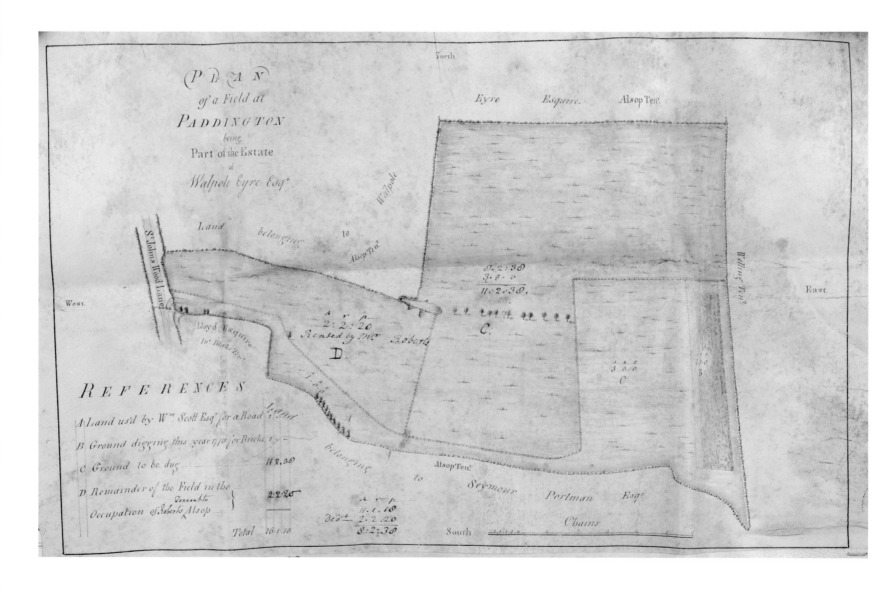

Previous pages: **27** This reconstruction shows what Henry Samuel Eyre II might have envisaged when he commissioned Spurrier & Phipps to draw up a master plan for his estate in 1794 (Plate 29). Two types of elevation have been used: one to deal with the houses in the grand circus, the other to deal with houses which had smaller gardens. In the absence of any known elevations, the appearance of the more modest houses is based on houses found in William Hall's 1810s development work at the junction of Grove End and Abbey Roads (most have not survived). The design that has been used for the circus houses was proposed twice but never built (see Plates 65 and 239). Eyre estate (reconstruction drawing by Stephen Conlin, 2010).

Opposite: **28** This plan, drawn from the 1770 'Articles of Agreement' between Walpole Eyre I and William Scott, shows in great detail how the southern tip of the St John's Wood estate was exploited for brick earth and therefore became known as the 'Brick Field'. Eyre estate archive (EE 2651/285(B)).

Right: **29** 'A Plan for the Improvement of a Freehold Estate call'd St John's Wood situated in the parishes of Marylebone & Hampstead propos'd by Spurrier & Phipps London 1794'. City of London, London Metropolitan Archives (M0008206CL).

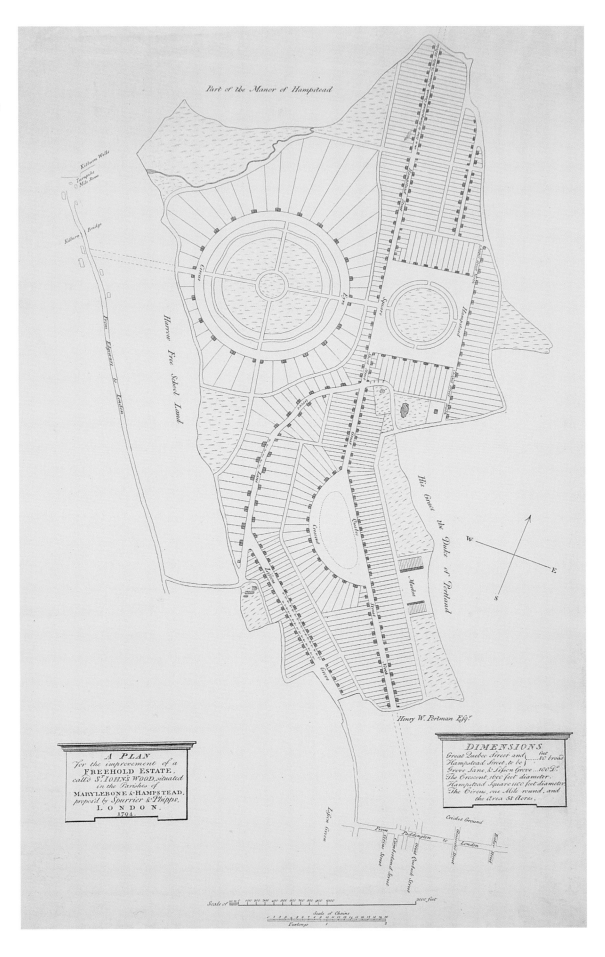

Between 1750 and 1794 the Eyres seemed content with the relatively modest income provided by leasing the land for rural use (see tenants at Plate 16), though there was a development in 1768 which indicated the shape of the future. One of the agreements with William Alsop, 'Cowkeeper', allowed the Eyres to exploit brick earth on the southern end of the estate.[3] Another agreement followed two years later, this time with a 'Brickmaker' stating that the owner 'permit[s] the said William Scott [of Grosvenor Square] to dig Brick earth and other earth ground soil and materials and to burn[,] make[,] and take away bricks in and out of thirteen acres two rood and thirty eight perches'.[4] Meadow No. 28 in the Spurrier & Phipps key was indeed the amalgamation of four parcels of land called 'Three Acres', 'Great Eight Acres', 'Thirteen Acres', and 'Little Eight Acres' and renamed the 'Brick Field' (see Plate 28).[5]

In August 1774, another agreement was made between Sarah Eyre (Walpole I had died) and the Mr Alsop previously encountered, who by now had switched to the more lucrative trade of brickmaking. On this occasion the prospect of building upon the land is clearly envisaged: 'And Whereas it may happen that the said Sarah Eyre [who is Tenant for Life] may during the said Term hereby Granted have occasion to let the said eight acres of Land or some part thereof to *build upon* after the said William Alsop shall have dug out the Brick Earth' (my italics).[6]

Spurrier & Phipps

In 1792, Henry Samuel II, eldest son of Walpole I and his wife Sarah, became the new owner of the St John's Wood estate one year after his majority. As a captain in the 57th Regiment of Foot[7] he was often away from London, and therefore delegated in 1794 the running of the estate to a firm of professionals run by John Spurrier and Josiah Phipps. Their appointment coincided with an era of renewed ambitions, which is why they had been asked to prepare the survey and master plan.

Spurrier & Phipps were based in the City at Copthall Court, Throgmorton Street, from 1793, but little has been published about them beyond their minimal entry in the *Dictionary of Surveyors*.[8] Trade directories reveal that the earliest entry for John Spurrier, auctioneer, is in the year 1780 when he was listed at 101 Leadenhall Street.[9] By the following year he had moved to Copthall Court, where he remained until around 1800. His name is also mentioned in connection with Leicester Square in 1787: he was the surveyor nominated on behalf of the mortgagees of the earl of Leicester's property there, and this implies he must have been reasonably well known.[10] He was in partnership with 'Sampson' as early as 1782, but this did not last and by 1784 he was back on his own and remained so until 1790 when he was joined by Phipps.[11]

Throughout the 1790s Spurrier & Phipps placed regular advertisements in the columns of *The Times*, which suggests business was going well, and they appear to have sold a range of goods and services including large estates, wine, single houses and annuities. In 1796 the St John's Wood Farm seems to have been central to their activities.[12] They also prepared an agreement between Captain Eyre and the farmer Thomas Willan. This early agreement with Willan was carefully phrased to allow for development of the St John's Wood estate, even referring to the 1794 master plan: 'That the Landlord shall and may at any time during the Lease take away any part of the said premises for the purpose of Building thereon and the necessary Gardens and outhouses to such Buildings according to the Plan already prepared or any other plan to be prepared for the Improvement of the said Estate by building thereon.'[13] The allusion to 'any other plan' may indicate that they had found the master plan not entirely feasible and were considering an alternative scheme. However, with the disappearance of John Spurrier around 1800, their work on the estate came to an end.[14]

John Gwynn

In the decades preceding the development of St John's Wood, the case for a rational, intelligent and organised approach to urban planning was eloquently made by John Gwynn, who published in 1766 his *London and Westminster Improved*.[15] The book spelt out many of the contemporary ideas which underpinned the Eyre master plan and also what was to follow in its wake, so it is worth examining this seminal text and its influence on the St John's Wood plan.

After lamenting the poor planning of the older parts of London, Gwynn goes on to analyse the failings of the western developments as they had been built up over the previous fifty years. Although he conceded that private property and individual taste could explain the 'perplexing irregularity' of the old city, he continued: 'surely the case is widely different in respect to that part of the town about Grosvenor Square and Mary-le-Bone. No such difficulties presented themselves in that quarter and it is certain if a well regulated plan had been consulted, so noble a spot might have been made more ornamental at least.' Gwynn deplored that

> so wretched an use has been made of so valuable and desirable an opportunity of
> displaying taste and elegance in this part of town.... It is to be wished that the ground-
> plans of all great cities and towns were composed of right lines, and that the streets
> intersected each other at right angles, for except in cases of absolute necessity, acute angles
> ought for ever to be avoided as they are not only disagreeable to the sight, but constantly
> waste the ground and spoil the buildings; indeed if it was practicable, a square or circular
> form should be preferred in all capital cities as best adapted to grandeur and convenience.[16]

The only two British cities to have taken steps in that direction were Bath (Plate 33), between 1729 and 1774, and Edinburgh, where a competition for the layout of the New Town was announced in 1766.[17] The latter echoed London's square-based developments with its emphasis on a checkerboard/gridiron pattern, but was far removed from Spurrier & Phipps's master plan, which bore affinities with Bath. Other groundbreaking developments during Gwynn's life were the first planned new towns – Londonderry in Ireland (the oldest) and Whitehaven in Cumbria. However, these were workers' towns where aesthetics and elegance mattered little, though their contribution to urban planning was significant.[18]

With hindsight it seems clear that Gwynn's detailed recommendations were so closely followed on the St John's Wood estate that the Eyres must have had first-hand knowledge of Gwynn's book or thinking. From drainage to roofing, his guidelines were adopted on the estate. He paid close attention to the hygiene of the capital, as would the Eyres: 'as cess pools are found to be very offensive and inconvenient, it is a great pity that more attention is not given to making publick drains or common-sewers, which should always be large enough for a man to walk upright, and at proper distances trap-doors be contrived of sufficient strength, in order to cleanse them without breaking up the pavements, which is the common inconvenient method now practised.'[19] He favoured the

30 This early nineteenth-century watercolour by William Frederick Wells (1762–1836) is inscribed on the verso: 'London from St John's Wood'. The composition, centred on the distant dome of St Paul's Cathedral, depicts the St John's Wood landscape, with its pleasant pasture grounds and tree-lined boundaries, prior to the building development that was soon to follow. New Haven, Yale Center for British Art.

rendering of buildings and the adoption of a slate roof: 'It is surprising that stucco-fronts are not more frequently introduced, especially in the country, as it is not very expensive, agrees well with stone, and being covered with blue slate, harmonizes in the most agreeable manner with trees and all degrees of verdure.'[20] This was firmly part of the St John's Wood style of building.

John Gwynn has been discussed and quoted in this chapter because his remarks provide the perfect setting for the St John's Wood plan of 1794. Gwynn understood what an asset the lovely landscape of Marylebone (where the Eyre estate was situated, Plate 30) really was – charming rural surroundings in a metropolitan context – and this was precisely how the Eyres 'marketed' the area. He advocated the use of a well thought-out plan before carrying out any development work – a piece of advice which was followed by the Eyres. He believed in the harmony of a geometric plan such as that devised by Spurrier & Phipps. He also recommended that great attention be paid to the infrastructure of *any* new development. Though this issue was not made explicit in the 1794 St John's Wood plan, we know the estate was equipped with a system of sewers right from the very beginning (see Chapter 7). Lastly, Gwynn understood the inherent benefits of a flourishing relationship between artists and their city, devoting a substantial section of his book to the London art scene and describing the shift of artists from early isolation to a thriving, welcoming community. St John's Wood, as is well known, would become an artists' quarter, a point to which we will return in Chapter 8.

THE PLAN AND ITS AFTERMATH

Description

The Eyre estate plan broadly sets out the land available within three areas, which are organised around three familiar geometric figures: a semicircle or crescent at the south, a circle in a square just above it on the eastern side, and a very large circle or circus on the opposite side to the west (Plate 29). Each figure is articulated along one major north–south axis, with a deviation at the northern end of the crescent. The road on the west side follows a meandering course not as a picturesque feature but because the plan retained an *existing* path, known as St John's Wood Lane (later to become Grove End Road), which led to St John's Wood Farm. This path is clearly visible on Rocque's map of Middlesex (Plate 31).

The houses in this estate are shown principally as semi-detached, each with a garden. They have not been set back as in later plans but are placed immediately overlooking the road. This decision recalls very much the arrangement of the cottages which line the road at the village of New Houghton in Norfolk (Plate 40), and we will return later to this important precedent. Rare detached houses are found on the corner sites formed by two roads. The low-density housing of this plan is in marked contrast with the high-density character of the West End (Plate 108). It is both amusing and instructive to analyse the housing hierarchy which is suggested by such a plan. There is little to differentiate between the houses themselves. Some are shown as slightly bigger than others, but the real measure of desirability here is based on the size of the garden. The lavish circus is unquestionably the central and grandest part of the estate. The more ordinary holdings are those on the eastern side, lining up the roads, while the square and the crescent provide intermediate stages in this hierarchy. This is a fascinating inversion of the usual order: we normally expect the size of a building to

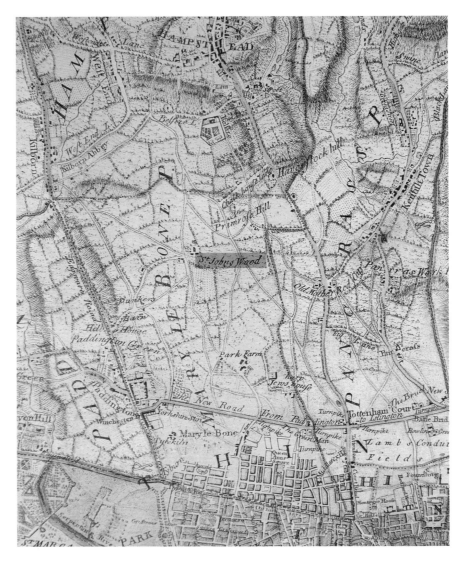

31 This detail from John Rocque's 'A Topographical Map of the County of Middlesex' shows St John's Wood in 1754, the year when the merchant Henry Samuel Eyre I died. Little had changed since 1733 – the 'St John's Wood' heading is placed next to the estate's principal farm, and Punkers Barn is also clearly marked. Edgware Road is as straight as a Roman road should be, and the lines which criss-cross the estate should be read as tracks, not roads. City of London, London Metropolitan Archives.

define the status of a scheme, but here it is the size of the garden which matters. This signifies two things – the paramount importance of nature and the appropriateness of a scheme which pays homage to it.

In the master plan, the presence of a church and a market, tucked away on the eastern side of the estate near the border with the Portland estate, is significant. It implies a notion of self-sufficiency and independence for this new part of London, though it is surprising that the author of the plan should not have given the church greater prominence. It is unusual when compared to other contemporary schemes; for instance, John Plaw proposed a church or chapel as the centrepiece of his oval green (1795, see Plate 36), and in the early 1800s Joseph Gandy suggested 'sixty-four cottages for Labourers and their families whose common centre must be a Chapel or Parish Church'.[21] Similarly, all the early nineteenth-century designs prepared for Regent's Park proposed a church on a prominent site.[22] However, this appears to confirm that the St John's Wood plan did not seek to create *architectural* landmarks.

Analysis and authorship

The two architectural historians who have contributed the greatest amount of research to, and analysis of, this plan are the late Sir John Summerson and Mark Girouard.[23] Summerson charted in detail the emergence of the villa and its semi-detached version – from large urban piles, such as those found in Kennington Park Road dating from around 1770, to the more rural type developed at St John's Wood. He concluded that the St John's Wood model was the pioneer for subsequent developments of detached and semi-detached houses in London's suburbia. Cautiously, Summerson also stated that, in the absence of elevations, we cannot know for certain to which type the proposed 1794 houses belonged: were the rectangular boxes marked on the plan intended to be large multistorey buildings or more rural habitations such as cottages? This is a question to which we will shortly return.

The advertisement in contemporary newspapers for the St John's Wood master plan offers some further clues. The following text was published in 1794 in *The Times* on 5, 8, 18, 19 September and on 1 and 4 October. It was also published in the *Cambridge Chronicle and Journal* throughout October.[24] The text is reproduced in full because it clearly defines the ideas upon which this plan was based.

FIVE HUNDRED ACRES of LAND

In the PARISHES of St. MARY-LE-BONNE and HAMPSTEAD.

To be LET, in Lots, upon Building Leases, for 99 Years,

By Messrs. SPURRIER and PHIPPS,

AN ESTATE, containing the above-mentioned Quantity of Land, situated in the said parishes, and perfectly compact.

It commences at Lisson-grove, and extends within about half a mile of Hampstead Church, leaving the Edgware-road at an agreeable distance to the westward, and into which it has a good carriage way.

The Estate forms an elevated site, commanding prospects of great extent, over a rich diversified country, including that grand Woody Scene, the lower part of Hyde Park and Kensington Gardens; and is most obviously suitable for the erection of Residences of such novel description, as will unite the beauty and pleasure of a Country-House, with the convenience and advantage of a town one.

Messrs. Spurrier and Phipps have, in conformity to this idea, laid down a plan of the Estate, in which an amplitude of Ground, for Offices and Gardens to each intended House, is set out; and in no instance is one House to be erected opposite to another.

They have likewise been constantly regulated by the propriety of not crowding the Houses, and so to arrange the situations, as to give them the tendency of forming respectable Neighbourhoods.

On a part of the Estate, a grand Circus, of 42 Houses, is intended to be built, the Area of which is to contain upwards of 57 Acres, and to be formed into Shrubberies and Pleasure-ground.

For a view of the said Plan, and information of the Prices, apply to Messrs. Spurrier and Phipps, Copthall-court, Throgmorton-street.

N.B. Brick Earth in sufficient quantity, will be allowed to each taker gratis.

The alliance of country and town in 'the beauty and pleasure of a Country-House, with the convenience and advantage of a town one' is the key to the proposed scheme. The careful balance between forming a 'respectable' community *and* securing seclusion was part of the attraction, and was achieved by positioning each house facing the gardens of the houses opposite rather than the houses themselves. In 1802 the architect John Shaw, whom we shall shortly meet, took care to retain this same idea for his 'British Circus' (Plate 32). The principle was again taken up by Nash in the planning of Regent's Park, where his villas would be 'planted out from the view of each other, so that the inhabitant of each seems, in his own prospect, to be the sole lord of the surrounding scenery'.[25] When faced with the reality of parcelling off the land, this particular idea was probably found too hard to implement and it was dropped, as is clear from the estate's working plan (Plate 53). We have no means now of judging what was meant by 'Residences, of such novel description', but we should note the intention 'of not crowding the Houses' and the resulting 'respectable neighbourhoods' (Plate 27).

The Eyres and their architect were careful not to create an isolated idyllic suburb removed from neighbouring communities. This is made quite clear in the naming of the streets on the St John's Wood estate. The continuation of key axes ensured that the new 'quarter' – part of the newly developed Marylebone parish[26] as well as the more rural Hampstead parish – would be fully integrated into adjoining neighbourhoods. Quebec Street and Crescent are linked to New Quebec Street in the West End and Hampstead Road to the village of the same name but also to the road network north of the capital, as Walpole II would later be at pains to point out when he first attempted to create what would become Finchley Road. This attention to infrastructure reinforced the very special location of the estate, poised as it was on the doorstep of both the city and the country.

The Spurrier & Phipps plan was published in 1794, the same year as Uvedale Price's *Essay on the Picturesque*. It is fair to say that there is no hint of the contemporary craze for the picturesque in the St John's Wood plan. With its attention to geometry and regularity the proposed scheme would almost certainly have been criticised by Price, the guru of all things picturesque, had he been asked for his opinion. This is what he wrote about the rebuilding of a village: 'An obvious and easy method … [would be] to place the houses on two parallel lines, to make them of the same size and shape, and at equal distance from each other. Such a methodical arrangement saves all further thought and invention: but it is hardly necessary to say that nothing can be more formal and insipid.'[27]

When the master plan for St John's Wood was published, landlord Henry Samuel was a young man of twenty-four who had already been in the army for six years. After inheriting the estate at the age of twenty-one he had mortgaged it four times in the first year (see p. 99), so it is clear he needed his land to be as financially rewarding as possible. This provided him with a powerful incentive for development, but where did the concept originate? It was novel and entirely adapted to a rural estate on the doorstep of the capital: the joys of the countryside made available to the many rather than the few. For a financially needy landlord, maximising revenue by combining his love for nature with the creation of a community for the respectable classes was a stroke of genius. Spurrier & Phipps, the surveyors who published the plan, are not known to have orchestrated any remotely similar project, so their role was likely to have been administrative only. When the Eyre brothers took over the development in the first decade of the nineteenth century, their fluid and confident handling strongly suggests that the St John's Wood concept originated with them.

The author of the St John's Wood plan is not named. John Summerson is inclined to dismiss the possibility of John Shaw (1776–1832) on the ground of age, though he miscalculated Shaw's age by two years.[28] Shaw's name has been associated with this plan, first because in 1802 and 1803 he exhibited at the Royal Academy two drawings connected with the Eyre circus, and second because he became the official architect and surveyor to the Eyre estate in 1805, an appointment which lasted until the end of his life.[29] The Royal Academy drawings of the circus are not known to have survived though we know their titles: 'Two Villas, part of a circus near Hampstead etc.', exhibited in 1802, and 'The British Circus near Hampstead etc.', exhibited in 1803.[30] This ambitious master plan does indeed appear to have been abandoned by 1800, with the exception of the circus, which survived as an idea as late as the 1820s.

The British Circus

In 1794 John Shaw would have been eighteen, perhaps not too young to visualise with aplomb Henry Samuel Eyre's pioneering scheme. The historian B. M. G. Smedley has no difficulty attributing the scheme to Shaw.[31] It is indeed tempting to favour the attribution of the plan to a young hand, as it displays a number of unresolved features which could be the outcome of youth and inexperience: the uneven size of the gardens in the circus is an awkward decision, while the closeness of the scheme to John Wood's Bath development is perhaps another sign of impressionability (Plate 33).

John Shaw's revised design for the large circus is known through a map published by Edward Mogg in May 1806. This particular map was reissued no fewer than twenty-three times between 1806 and 1846.[32] The British Circus featured on the first edition of 1806, but here we reproduce the 1809 edition (Plate 32). The 'upwards of 57 Acres' circus of 1794 has now been scaled down to forty-two acres. The name 'British Circus' is interesting for its patriotic overtones, almost certainly a reflection of the mood of the country during the Napoleonic Wars. There is another example of patriotic naming around this time. In 1808 Walpole Eyre tentatively requested Samuel Wild, the owner of the public house which opened in that year at the west end of Alpha Road, to name it 'The Spanish Patriot', clearly in homage to his brother's contribution to the Napoleonic Wars.[33] However, on this occasion, Samuel Wild evidently ignored Walpole's plea and called his pub 'The Nightingale' instead, reflecting local topography (the nearby Nightingale Lane) rather than far-flung heroic deeds.

There is one feature worth highlighting in this revised plan: the increase in the number of houses. An average builder would have regarded the 1794 circus as extremely 'wasteful' of land and therefore money. In the second plan, the curved line of semi-detached houses has been retained, but the density of houses has considerably increased and the length of gardens, amusingly irregular in the 1794 plan, has been tidied up and reduced. A second line of residences has been inserted between the circular road and the central grassed area.[34] This time the new line is made up of detached houses. Shaw continued the principle of making houses face greenery rather than other houses, but he also

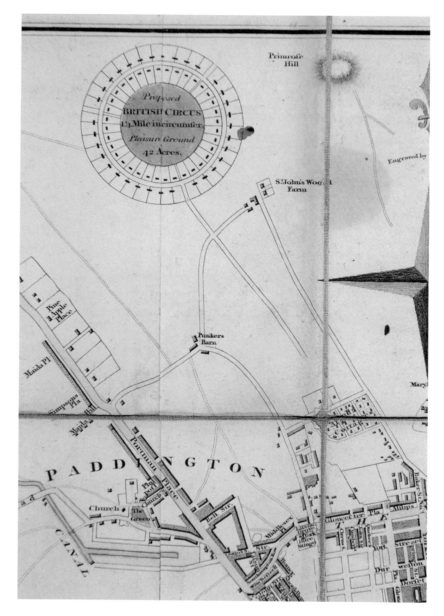

32 John Shaw's 'British Circus' at St John's Wood. Detail from Edward Mogg's map, *London in Miniature with the surrounding Villages an Entire New Plan in which the Improvements both present and intended are actually reduced (by permission) from the surveys of the Several Proprietors.* This map was first issued on 1 May 1806 when it featured the Eyre circus in splendid isolation. This particular plate comes from the 1809 edition, as by that date it also shows the development of the southern tip of the St John's Wood estate: Alpha Cottages. City of London, London Metropolitan Archives.

increased the housing density: the 1794 scheme had thirty-six semi-detached and four detached houses. The revised scheme has sixty-six semi-detached and thirty-six detached houses. All the houses are now set back from the road, most probably the fifty-foot distance stipulated in all agreements from 1805.[35] The immediate consequence of this extra row of houses was to restrict, but not prohibit, access to the green area in the centre, which could now only be reached by three footpaths created between houses. The true beneficiaries of this particular arrangement were the owners of the detached houses.

The Eyres were clearly attached to the idea of a circus. In 1810 when the War Office was building the Ordnance Barracks at the back of St John's Wood Farm, the hope of realising it still seemed possible. Walpole wrote: 'I cannot run the risk of having an inferior Building standing upon the side of a Road intended to be one of the main Entrances to the Circus.'[36] After 1810 references to the

'Coliseum' and a circus (Plate 34). This technique enabled Dance to present a strong and coherent infrastructure in contrast to the even-patterned design published by Spurrier & Phipps (Plate 29).

George Dance was no stranger to the theme of the circus as he created the first circus in London, completed in 1767 and virtually contemporary with the Royal Circus in Bath, which was its direct source of inspiration.[48] This miniature circus was sited in the City of London, in the area called The Minories near the Tower of London, and was the earliest development to pay homage to John Wood's new quarter at Bath. The new circus in the City was built alongside a crescent and a square. This group of buildings was destroyed in the Second World War but was recorded in the magnificent early nineteenth-century Rhinebeck Panorama (Plate 35). The character of the scheme was firmly urban, a mass of walls and dense elevations four storeys high, as was Dance's 'Design for a Crescent including John Howard's Monument' published in the *Gentleman's Magazine* in September 1786.[49]

By contrast, the circus George Dance proposed for the Camden estate is composed of semi-detached houses, and it is therefore the earliest design to present these types of cottages or villas within the London urban environment. The 'exploding' form of the 'Coliseum', so confidently handled, seems to take the Bath model in quite a different direction. However, the relationship between built structures and nature seems markedly different from that found in the St John's Wood plan. In St John's Wood the gardens dominate a development which aims to blend with nature and displays minimal architectural bravura. By contrast, the architectural Camden plan is made up of solidly built lines which would dominate nature.

Dance's introduction of the circus and crescent onto the London scene was followed up in the last decades of the eighteenth century by a spate of developments based on circular geometries. These predate the St John's Wood plan and include Robert Mylne's St George's Circus in Lambeth of 1767, Novosielski's crescent in Brompton of 1786 (now demolished), a half-completed circus at Great Cumberland Place of c.1790 and Michael Searles's Paragons in Lambeth and Greenwich begun in 1794 (Plate 38).[50] All of these schemes are firmly architectural and display none of the sensitivity to the countryside which is the hallmark of the Eyre plan.

John Plaw and the rural dream

Aspects of the St John's Wood plan were adopted by the architect John Plaw (1744/5–1820), who specialised in building villas but also made his name publishing designs. The latter were found among the numerous pattern books on cottages and villas to be published between 1770 and 1850.[51] The success of this genre shows that the proposed development of the St John's Wood estate into a community of semi-rural and semi-urban cottages incorporated a body of ideas connected to rural dwellings. This trend had been influenced by the writings of Jean-Jacques Rousseau and others on the moral superiority of a natural, primitive state of humankind over society's corrupt ways. This influenced the fashion for 'wealthy rustic' which inspired Queen Charlotte to build a cottage in the grounds of Kew Palace sometime in the 1770s and Marie-Antoinette to commission her rural hamlet in the park of Versailles from the architect Richard Mique (1783).[52] Plaw's designs, on the other hand, were aimed at builders of homes 'calculated for persons of moderate income'.[53] The advertisement for the St John's Wood master plan was worded in more opaque terms, but seemed to suggest a higher social level with the phrase 'forming respectable neighbourhoods'.

35 The late 1760s Minories development at Tower Hill in the City of London was a miniature version of what John Wood had planned for Bath and was the brainchild of the City Corporation architect, George Dance. The development is shown as completed in Horwood's 1792–94 map of London, but this detail from the Rhinebeck Panorama (c.1810) captures the scheme in colourful glory. This group of buildings, destroyed in the Second World War, included the first circus and crescent to be built in London. Publication No. 125 of the London Topographical Society, 1981 (the original drawing is in the collection of the Museum of London).

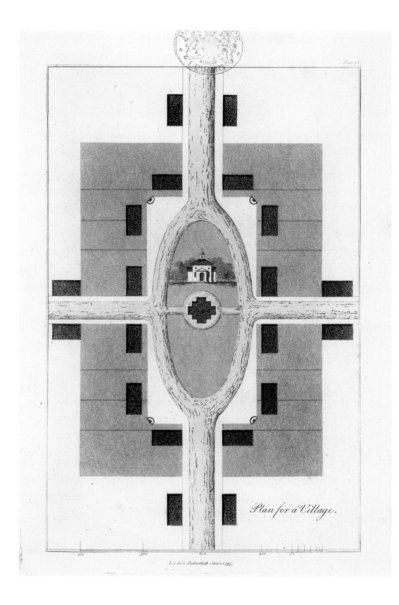

Plan for a Village.

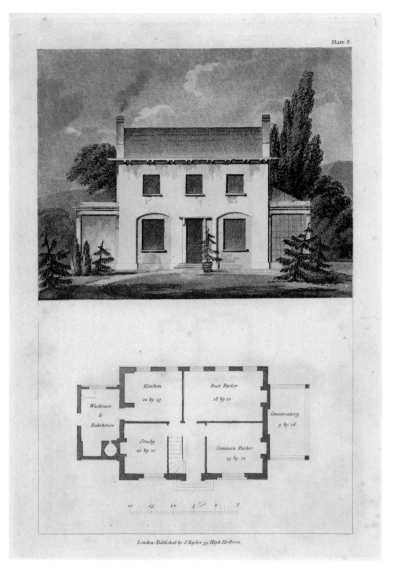

One of Plaw's publications, *Ferme Ornée or Rural Improvements* (1795), reproduced a plan for a village 'either for labourers and their families or for persons of more independent circumstances' (Plate 36). This unrealised project created a bridge between a type of design normally associated with labourers and a scheme that would be appropriate for other classes. The design, 'intended to unite symmetry and utility', was 'to have been built in the vicinity of lead mines' in Yorkshire, a small-scale project which drew much inspiration from the St John's Wood plan: detached houses on corner sites, semi-detached houses elsewhere, gardens and grouping of habitations around a geometric design. Plaw even adopted the same way of placing the houses opposite garden ground rather than another house, specifying: 'The views would thereby be preserved, and the air circulate more freely,' two tenets which guided the St John's Wood development (see, for instance, pp. 69 and 71).[54] While Plaw was in effect disseminating some of the ideas contained in the St John's Wood scheme, he was also creating his own sphere of influence.

Opposite left: **36** This unrealised plan was published in 1795 as Plate 33 of John Plaw's *Ferme Ornée or Rural Improvements*, a year after the publication of the St John's Wood plan. In this design, 'intended to unite symmetry and utility', a pleasing rhythm is achieved by alternating semi-detached and detached houses. The latter, placed on street corners, recall the arrangement found on the St John's Wood plan. The church in the middle gives a firm focus to the scheme. British Library.

Opposite right: **37** This design for a house was published in John Plaw's *Sketches for Country Houses, Villas and Rural Dwellings* (1800, Plate 8). Keats's house in Hampstead and some of Thomas Martin's houses in St John's Wood may have been inspired by such a model. British Library.

38 Michael Searle's Paragon in Blackheath (begun in 1794). The late 1780s witnessed the appearance on the London streets of large semi-detached town houses linked to one another by lower buildings which, in the case of Searle, were elegantly colonnaded. Another example, in Kennington Park Road, was described by Sir John Summerson as 'ludicrously crammed together to waste as little ground as possible while retaining some show of semi-detachment' (1995, p. 6). This type of distinctively large 'urban' double house was, in fact, planned for St John's Wood in 1813 but never built (see Plate 65). Eyre estate.

This one-time Marylebone resident had designed the nearby church of St Mary at Paddington in 1788–91.[55] The Eyres may have been familiar with his publications, and his designs quite possibly influenced what was happening in St John's Wood. In Plate 8 of his *Sketches for Country Houses, Villas and Rural Dwellings* (1800), a sturdy, simple yet decorative design is illustrated. Its caption echoes perfectly the development at St John's Wood, even down to its price of £600: 'Cottage or rural dwelling … a very comfortable residence for a family with a small independent fortune, or a retreat occasionally to relax from the bustle of business.' The main body of the house is framed by a lean-to on either side which accommodated a washhouse and bakehouse on the left and a conservatory to the right (Plate 37). There is an echo of this design in Thomas Biddle's house in Alpha Cottages[56] (see No 22 in Plate 63) and in John Bennett's more sophisticated house, also in Alpha Cottages (see No. 11 in Plate 63).[57]

TOWN HOUSES VERSUS VILLAS VERSUS COTTAGES

John Summerson's observation on the master plan was that 'we cannot know for certain if it was meant to consist of couples of town-houses like the Paragons [Plate 38] or if a "villa" character was intended.'[58] Neither the plan nor the advertisement published to accompany it gives any indication of the sort of houses that were intended, so conclusions about this important issue have to be reached by other means. As the early master plan (1794) and the subsequent development of the estate (from 1804) were carried out by the same owner, Henry Samuel Eyre II, and as the early concept presented a number of features which were retained, we should be able to assume some continuity between the two periods.

Nowadays, the houses at St John's Wood are commonly referred to as 'Italianate villas', but this description would have been alien to Walpole when he first started developing the estate.[59] There are

39 These cottages at Chippenham, Cambridgeshire, were built by 1712 alongside a church and charity school. This was the result of Edward Russell's ruthless and pioneering policy of emparking. The pairs of cottages are set well back from the road, with generous gardens at the front and back. They are linked together by service buildings. Eyre estate (photo: the author).

only two references to 'villas' in the first twenty-five years of Walpole's letter books. In 1806 he wrote: 'Mr Lewes has been with me & means to take some land at St Johns Wood for build[in]g himself a Villa,'[60] and again in 1812 he wrote: 'I have been in hopes of hearing from you naming a time for riding over the Estate with me, that you might fix upon a spot for a Villa.'[61] Despite Walpole's effort to meet these two clients on their home ground, it seems that neither Mr Lewes nor Mr Sanders became tenants in St John's Wood. Shaw's design of 1802 for houses overlooking the British Circus made use of the term 'villa', but by 1804, when development on the estate began in earnest, the guiding concept had clearly become an estate of cottages. The word 'cottage' is not found in the 1794 advertisement for the master plan, which used the words 'residences' and 'houses'. But it is the name chosen for the first houses built upon the estate: 'Alpha Cottages' (Plate 32 for map and Plate 52 for view from adjoining fields). It is also the term used in agreements with builders and in leases with tenants, and 'cottages' feature repeatedly in the estate's advertisements for building plots: 'The whole or any part of this Frontage being 300 feet in Depth to be let for building detached Cottages- For fur[the]r particulars enquire of Mr W. E. 7 Mont. Place or of Mr Shaw Gower St.'[62]

John Summerson wrote about the 'ultimate humiliation of semi-detachment' when he charted the shrinking of the noble Italian villa to its affordable miniature version for the English market.[63] In St John's Wood, however, what matters more is the development of the cottage. Amusingly, the social trajectory of the cottage is in the exact opposite direction to that of the villa. Its definition in Dr Johnson's *Dictionary* (1755) betrayed its very humble beginnings: 'a mean habitation' (it is worth noting that Dr Johnson has no entry for villa). However, by 1798 James Malton offered a much more enticing definition: 'I have led myself to conceive very differently of a cottage; which may I think, as well be the habitation of a substantial farmer or affluent Gentleman, as the dwelling of the hedger and ditcher.'[64] In truth, contemporary eighteenth- and nineteenth-century uses of the words 'villa' and 'cottage' can be astonishingly confusing, as John Archer has shown in his detailed review of the architectural literature of this period.[65] Here we will focus on the concepts which underpin the creation of the St John's Wood estate.

The reappraisal of the cottage came out of the combined influences of the agrarian revolution and the policy of 'emparking' villages by owners of eighteenth-century stately homes. Villages which found themselves in the way of sweeping estate developments were destroyed and often rebuilt in a neat and orderly fashion just outside the entrance to the parks of the great mansions. One of the earliest examples of this phenomenon, still extant, is found in Cambridgeshire in Chippenham, on the doorstep of the country estate of Edward Russell, first Lord of the Admiralty and later Lord Orford (Plate 39). Another early example is that of New Houghton in Norfolk where two lines of cottages, started in 1729, frame the road leading to Robert Walpole's Houghton Hall.[66]

Most of these early model villages use the double house – the early nineteenth-century name for two semi-detached houses – as the prime unit for development. The Eyres' insistence on describing

40 The line of 'cottages' which make up the emparked village of New Houghton in Norfolk bears a resemblance to the Alpha Cottages of St John's Wood's early days (see Plate 52). Eighteenth-century members of the Eyre family would have been aware of this development because Kingsmill Eyre worked closely with Sir Robert Walpole, the lavish creator of Houghton Hall. Eyre estate (photos: the author).

the building work at St John's Wood as 'cottages' offers a natural link to these early antecedents. This link is made even more compelling when one considers the knowledge that the Eyres had about these model villages through the work and social network of Kingsmill Eyre. The man who commissioned the St John's Wood plan, Henry Samuel II, was Kingsmill's grandson. Kingsmill had long been dead by the time Henry Samuel was born in 1770, but Kingsmill's associations were likely to have lived on through relatives, particularly his son Walpole I, who was Henry Samuel's father.

We saw in the first chapter how Kingsmill Eyre spent most of his professional life working for Prime Minister Robert Walpole and how he is recorded as Walpole's landscape architect at Houghton by Robert's own son. The lines of 'cottages' on the approach to the Houghton estate offer a striking resemblance to the Alpha Cottages of the early days of the St John's Wood estate (Plate 40). Historian Gillian Darley's description of these could have been written for the Eyres' Alpha Cottages: 'well built whitewashed cottages standing either side of the road. They are two-storeyed buildings with slate roofs, widely spaced and with particularly large gardens behind.'[67] The 'double house'[68] was completely standard in model villages from the early eighteenth century onwards, including those which were contemporary with the early development of St John's Wood, such as George Dance's East Stratton scheme (1806).[69] This applied, too, to unrealised designs of model villages like the one by Plaw we have already discussed (Plate 36).

The 'ideal cottage' found in Walpole Eyre's early nineteenth-century letter books was a well-built, comfortable dwelling which offered a modest way of life: 'I am glad to say John has at last taken a small Cottage at a rent of £18 a year and where I hope he will be able to live upon his income,' wrote Walpole. John was the middle brother who always seemed to have difficulties settling his bills.[70] Elsewhere Walpole wrote: 'I thought you had known that Godschall [Johnson] had taken a very small cottage near Guildford with 5 acres of Land at a rent of only £30 per ann[.] this appears to be remarkably cheap & I hope will prove an economical plan.'[71] Unfortunately, life in a cottage was not what Godschall Johnson really wanted, and when he finally ran away from his creditors to France, taking his whole family with him (see p. 43), we discover from Walpole's letter books that the rent of his house at Bath was in fact £200 per annum.[72] By comparison, the annual rent of a St John's Wood cottage, though much higher than that of a country cottage, seemed very reasonable. Writing to his client and friend Lady Boyd, Walpole, who was well aware of her mounting debts, suggested in 1811: 'Miss Churchall [Churchill], Miss Trevanion & myself took a walk a few days back up to my brothers new Buildings whare [where] we saw a Cottage with a Garden to it, which I think would have sueted [suited] you & Miss Boyd[.] the Rent and tax together I suppose would be about sixty pounds.'[73]

THE AVENUE OF TREES

There is one important feature in the master plan which appears to have been realised: the Avenue of Trees. Its presence is barely noticeable in the smooth pattern of gardens and houses, but it lines a section of 'Lisson Grove' and would become one of the estate's landmarks. It is included in Thomas Milne's land use map of 1800.[74] When Walpole II developed a version of this master plan in the early years of the nineteenth century, he showed a keen interest in plants, gardens and trees, and was extremely protective of this avenue. In 1810 he was appalled by the action of the Punkers Barn's tenant: 'I have just learnt that the man who holds the Slipe under you at St John's Wood has been lopping all the Trees in the Avenue. This is a great injury to my Brother's property and I will thank you to make immediate inquiry into it as I must proceed to recover the Damage done.'[75]

The Avenue of Trees is depicted in the 1853 map of St John's Wood (Plate 70), though by 1865 it no longer survived.

CONCLUSION

The vision of St John's Wood as a 'neighbourhood'[76] of houses which capitalised on the rural beauty of its surroundings predates all similar developments on the outskirts of the cities of London and Westminster. Things were different in Clapham and other villages where City merchants built houses with large gardens from the seventeenth century onwards. Clapham was indeed the first village to grow into a residential area for these merchants, but there the development was piecemeal, built on demand, and it was therefore not a planned suburb.[77]

The St John's Wood master plan brought together a variety of existing concepts and ideas, but in a unique blend suited to the spirit of the age and soon so attractive to the middle classes that the formula rapidly spread elsewhere.[78] A careful scrutiny of the Eyre archive confirms the verdict of urban historians as to the pioneering role of St John's Wood in suburban and cottage development. The next chapters will trace the early development work of the Eyres at St John's Wood which will set the scene for neighbouring developments. The estate's architect, John Shaw, directed the development of the Chalcots estate, while John White junior and Decimus Burton, both closely involved with St John's Wood, were employed by the Harrow Free School estate. The schemes of John White senior and John Nash for Regent's Park also indicate their knowledge of developments on the Eyre estate, and John White senior certainly knew Walpole, with whom he had dealings in his capacity as surveyor of the Portland estate.[79]

As this chapter deals more with vision than reality, we may go as far as suggesting that the St John's Wood master plan was the first to marry the dream of idyllic countryside with the reality of affordable housing. The Eyres were also responding to the magic of the site. Walpole, who was no poet, wrote of the environment at St John's Wood: 'The situation is Delightful.'[80] But if we now turn to a real poet, William Blake, who was a regular visitor to Alpha Road, we can marvel at the glory of his vision for that special part of London:

The fields from Islington to Marybone,

To Primrose Hill and Saint Johns Wood:

Were builded over with pillars of gold,

And there Jerusalem pillars stood....

The Jews-harp-house & the Green Man;

The Ponds where Boys to bathe delight:

The fields of Cows by Willans farm:

Shine in Jerusalem pleasant sight.[81]

3 FIRST STEPS, 1805–20

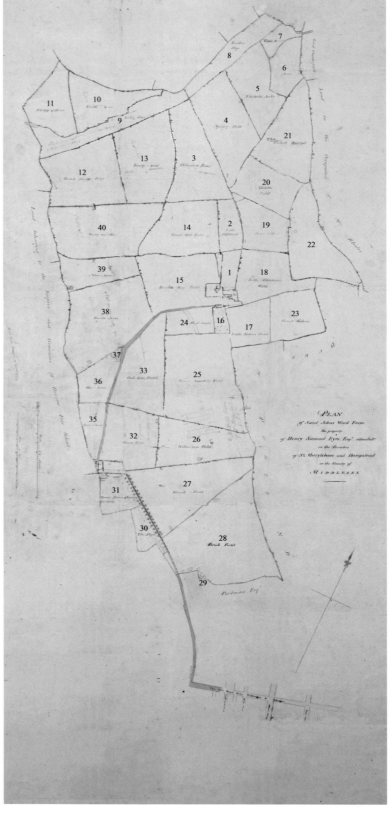

THE LANDLORD AND HIS ATTORNEY

The life of Walpole Eyre, the man effectively responsible for the development of the Eyre estate, changed forever in April 1805. Since 1 April 1796 he had been working in an agreeable partnership with a respectable lawyer, Mr Thomas Sermon. He was thirty-two when he left this partnership to set up on his own. To Walpole's credit, he successfully maintained cordial relations with Thomas Sermon until the latter's death in 1817, despite taking with him all the partnership's Eyre-related clients.[1]

Walpole's letter books are a crucial tool for understanding the difficult years of the early nineteenth century. Both brothers understood that they must exploit the St John's Wood estate in order to secure the family's future prosperity and social status. But Walpole seems to have had a much more realistic approach to business than the older Henry Samuel (Harry), the titular freeholder.

When Walpole set up his legal business in April 1805, the development plan for the estate focused, more realistically, on the southern tip and not on the whole as before. There may not have been a physical plan on paper but Walpole's general direction was very clear, as this letter to Henry Samuel shows: 'Since I last wrote to you I have been letting some land for Brick making, I have also let some more for Building & at present I have every reason to hope that *our plan will go on prosperously*' (my italics).[2] The following year Walpole also wrote: ' we have daily applicat[io]ns for Land & the Plan seems to take wonderfully'.[3] Walpole was now acting as Harry's agent on the St John's Wood estate, directing all development operations, negotiating with builders, gardeners and surveyors, and also, as a lawyer, preparing all the agreements or conveyances and later the leases that might be required.

Spurrier & Phipps: termination of contract

Quite a lot had happened prior to Walpole's close involvement with the estate in 1805. We saw in the last chapter how the firm of auctioneer-surveyors Spurrier & Phipps were appointed to look after the estate and how their plan for development had largely failed to materialise. There are no records of precisely what happened, but presumably the response to the proposed scheme had been negligible, so no action followed. One of the early tasks for the two brothers would have been to dissolve this arrangement, which was very expensive. Henry Samuel Eyre's financial records have survived for the year 1798, and between June and November he paid Spurrier & Phipps the substantial sum of £590 'on account'. During the same period in 1799, the fees had more than doubled to reach £1,265.[4] By 1801, *The Times* of 5 February advertised 'Two Ricks of remarkable fine meadow Hay' and other farm equipment for sale at St John's Wood Farm; John Spurrier's name was not in the advertisement, only that of Josiah Phipps operating from the usual Copthall Avenue address. This departure gave the Eyres the opportunity to revise the existing arrangements. The matter was settled reasonably quickly: the last payment to Mr Phipps labelled 'balance of account' was made in August 1801.[5] There is a brief, final reference to Mr Phipps in a letter to Thomas Sermon dated 11 September 1805. It confirms that by that date the Spurrier & Phipps episode had been over for some time: 'I thought all accounts between that Gentleman & us had been settled long ago.'[6]

John Shaw and early activity

The previous chapter mentioned the arrival of the architect John Shaw. His proposed circus for St John's Wood has already been described, and although he did not officially become the estate surveyor until 1805, he had been directly employed by Henry Samuel Eyre in 1802 when he received the sum of £20 – no doubt for his work on the proposed circus. He also received £150 0s. 6d. in January 1805.[7]

Shaw probably advised the Eyres in the last few months of 1804 when preparations for development actually started on the St John's Wood estate. On 2 November of that year John Webber was paid '£15.0.4 for making Road & Rect Stamp'; another, more evocative entry in the account book for that year was 'for ploughing line of Road'.[8] Webber received the same amount again on the following 3 January when a certain John Sidwell was paid 'for Boards &c for letting Est[at]e on building Leases'.[9] Walpole confirmed some of this activity when a few months later he wrote to his brother Harry, who was stationed with the 52nd Regiment in Mullingan in Ireland: 'I have now let nearly the whole of the 13 acres we took from Mr Willan for building upon.'[10]

TENANTS IN 1805

In the spring of 1805 Walpole's list of tenancies of the St John's Wood Estate showed some interesting changes. Writing again to his brother Harry in Ireland, he stated:

the amount of your present Rents exclusive of the small Rents are as follows viz

WILLAN	1077..6..8	
ABBOTT	871..8..6	
HILL	395..6..0	
JEFFERSON	92..15..6	
WALKER	88..11..8	
WEBBER	20..0..0	(part of Land taken from Willan for Build.)
HALLETT	12..0..0	
TODD for Brick Earth	21..0..0	
	£2578..8..4	

I have given you this Sketch that you may regulate accordingly & you will recollect that in addition to the paym[en]ts I have above ennumerated that in all probab[ilit]y Mr Shaw will be receiving £100 a year from you at least if the Improvem[en]ts go on as we have every reason to hope they will.[11]

Who are these people on Walpole's list? There is an extraordinary mixture of old and new guard, of St John's Wood residents and non-residents, and, most fascinatingly, of people with urban concerns and those with country interests. One way of interpreting the early years of the development at St John's Wood, as we shall see, is that of a race between town and country. For now let us discover more about the names listed above.

Willan has been mentioned already; he is the 'celebrated' **Thomas Willan** (1755–1828) from Marylebone Park Farm, a shrewd, articulate and accomplished gentleman farmer who passionately

43 Ben Marshall, *Mr Thomas Willan of Marylebone Park and Twyford Abbey*, 1818, oil on canvas, location unknown (reproduced in *Connoisseur*, June 1949). City of London, Guildhall Library.

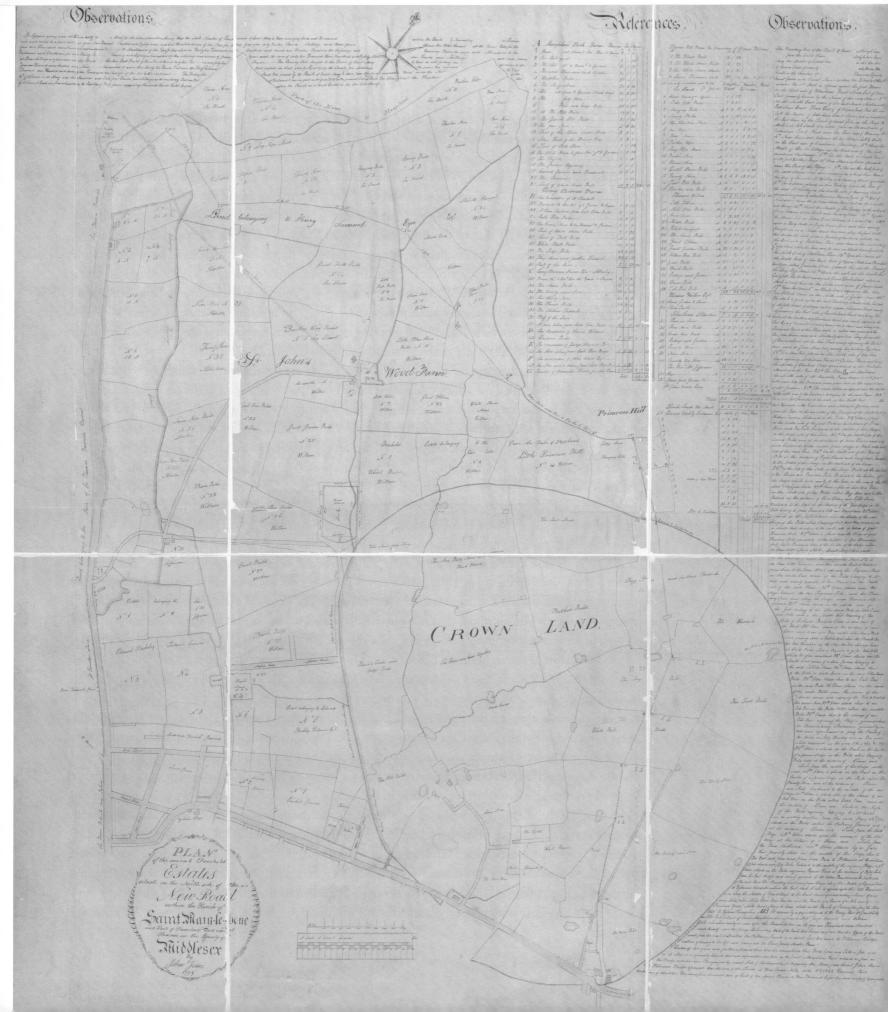

to the whole place/I observed a good many Building materials upon your premises, I hope you are not going to make any additional Build[in]gs as that cannot be allowed.'[31]

These comments bring life to the history of the early St John's Wood houses, but they also show with what care and interest Walpole was following the building work and the creation of this neighbourhood. He knew better than most that the devil is in the detail, and was very much a 'hands on' administrator with a rare attention to detail. At times this must have pleased and reassured his tenants, even if, at other times, they may have cursed their landlord's agent for his interference with their various schemes.

RURAL CHARACTER OF ST JOHN'S WOOD

John Jones's map

John Jones's map of 1799 (Plate 44) offers a unique visual record of the estate's tenants. Despite apparent anachronisms – for instance, the presence of Alpha Road and the St John's Wood chapel burial ground as both of these date from a few years later and must have been subsequent additions to the map[32] – each field on this map bears the name of its leaseholder.

As its caption suggests, the map covers a much larger area than St John's Wood. Its author, John Jones, was Marylebone's parish clerk. The layout of St John's Wood, including the numbering system used, is based on the Spurrier & Phipps survey of 1794 (Plate 42). However, the Jones document is crucial evidence as it shows exactly who occupied which field. At that time the St John's Wood Farm and surrounding fields covered an area of 67 acres 2 roods and 32 perches. They are inscribed 'in hand'. This was indeed the situation in the interregnum period between two of its farmers – William Knightley, who died in 1797, and debt-ridden John Abbott from 1800.[33] In 1799 Thomas Willan's farm in the adjoining Marylebone Park comprised a vast 182 acres 1 rood and 32 perches.[34] The Jones map, in conjunction with Willan's St John's Wood rent (see above), demonstrates that Willan had also become St John's Wood's largest tenant prior to taking over St John's Wood Farm in 1806 and Punker's Barn in 1811.

Two farms and a cottage

By 1805, despite the exploitation of brick earth by Robert Todd and the arrival of 'developers' in the Brick Field, the St John's Wood estate was entirely rural. There had been five pockets of human habitation, but Walpole that year sent a notice to quit to Thomas Jefferson, who was the Slipe's tenant, reducing the figure to four. The picture of a crumbling cottage, 'Where the Alpha Cottages now stand' (Plate 45), bears witness to the presence of a rustic residence on this site visible on the 1733 map (Plate 16, small black rectangle bottom left). The most important pocket was St John's Wood Farm (Plate 41), which was more or less in the middle of the land; just across the lane from it was St John's Wood House, an old cottage which by 1816 was considerably dilapidated but repaired.[35] Then there was Punkers Barn, also called Red Barn, at the 'old entrance' to the estate from the Edgware Road and close to the dividing line between the Eyre and Harrow School estates. A small settlement stood in the Blewhouse field on the east side of the estate which is visible on Plate 16 and named White Lodge on Plate 7.

44 'Plan of the several Freehold Estates situate on the North Side of the New Road within the Parish of Saint Mary-le-bone …', by John Jones, 1799. The names of the tenants (sometimes barely legible) have been added underneath the original inscriptions. British Library (Crace collection, XIV-42).

By 1808, the author Cyrus Redding was exhorting his friend Matthew Tearle to consider St John's Wood in these words: 'Beautiful fields – green lanes, clean air – the very place for lovers of quiet and the lovers of Nature – why don't you build a villa in the heart of St John's Wood?'[36] In the early 1820s, the developed southern part of the estate was still regarded as essentially rural, as is made clear by the painter John Constable in his diary. There he records in 1824 the visit to his friend, painter C. R. Leslie, who had just moved into premises at Lisson Grove (those of sculptor J. C. F. Rossi): 'Dressed to go to Leslie's for dinner. He has got things quite comfortable and it is a very fit house for an artist but sadly out of the way – but it is quite the country. We had salmon, and roast beef, peach pie & pudding. After dinner took a walk in the fields.'[37] Although he clearly had mixed feelings about the distance from town, he was forced to admit: 'The day passed pleasantly.'

DEVELOPMENT METHOD

Historian Donald Olsen has neatly encapsulated the role of the private estate in London town planning: 'the primary planning unit in London was the landed estate'.[38] He made this claim for the period up until 1855 but added that the process continued on after that date. Here we examine the role of the Eyre estate in that process.

Administration

Henry Samuel Eyre spent a great deal of time outside London, so a power of attorney enabling Walpole to have complete control over letting, leasing, mortgaging and collecting rents was essential. This was duly organised but almost immediately challenged by the tenants,[39] so that it became necessary to convey the St John's Wood estate to Walpole (in trust for Henry Samuel) on 2 and 3 December 1807, a landmark date in its administration which features on all Abstracts of Title for the Eyre estate as well as on early leases.[40]

Once Walpole was sufficiently steeped in the affairs of St John's Wood, it did not take too long for him to realise that as a non-Marylebone resident he was at a serious disadvantage:

> I have felt great inclination to take a small House in the parish of Marylebone and of residing in it as I might then get into the Vestry of that Parish and which I perceive, every day more & more, is very essential to the management and improvement of your Property.... Mr Portmans agents and also the Duke of Portland are both in the Vestry and of course have much more influence than I can possibly have merely as an individual living out of the Parish, Every thing I now apply to the Vestry for is considered as a favor whereas if I were in the Vestry there are many things I should be inclined to insist upon, the Expence of taking a House as far as I am individually concerned would be absurd, at the same time I think it very necessary for your Interest; and it has struck me that it wo[ul]d be a very good plan if I were to get an house in Marylebone in which I might at present reside & when you return home there would be a house for you to come to, instead of going to the expence of a lodging,/The Expence of a House for Rent and Taxes would be somewhere about £130 per annum and if you think it adviseable to make that sacrifice I should have no objection to part with my Chambers & to live in it.[41]

Six months later, in October 1810, Walpole moved to 21 Beaumont Street,[42] situated immediately south of the future Regent's Park, and soon became a full member of the Marylebone vestry. From that time onwards, the two brothers shared a home.

First auction

The single most effective tool for developing St John's Wood – selling off agreements which led to the issue of lucrative leases – was initially pursued at the auction house. At first Walpole opted to act as a developer, though he quickly realised that he would be better off treating with large-scale developers than with small-scale builders. The first auction, however, was crucial as it introduced new

45 The photograph of this anonymous pencil drawing (formerly in the Gardner Collection) is accompanied by the inscription 'Where the Alpha Cottages now stand' and is dated c.1800. With the help of the 1733 map (Plate 16), this cottage may be identified as the dwelling recorded near a pond at the south-west tip of the estate, in the Slipe, which by 1800 was in the hands of Reverend Thomas Jefferson. Walpole took away the land in April 1805 (Bill Book I, p. 13). Westminster City Archives (Ashbridge collection, 160/ALP).

TABLE 1
Partial reconstruction of the first St John's Wood Estate auction in 1804

Lot number	Agreement with	Underlessee	Source*
1 (Nightingale pub)	Thomas Martin		Bill Bk I, 1
2	Thomas Martin		Bill Bk I, 1; LB 'A', 708
3	Alexander Birnie		Bill Bk I, 1
4	Alexander Birnie		Bill Bk I, 1
5	Alexander Birnie		Bill Bk I, 1
6	? Biddle		
7	? Biddle		
8	Hallett		
9	Hallett	Thos Papworth	LB 'A', 410, 652
10	Hallett	Thos Papworth	Bill Bk I, 1; LB 'A', 410, 652
11	Robert Todd (cancelled)		Bill Bk I, 1; LB 'A', 158
	Hallett		Bill Bk I, 1; LB 'A' 581
12	Robert Todd	Thos Martin	Bill Bk I, 1; LB 'A', 581, 582, 627
13	James Biddle	Thos Papworth	Bill Bk I, 1; LB 'A', 462; EE 2651/12(A)
14	? Biddle		
15	Robert Todd	Todd's house	Bill Bk I, 1; LB 'A', 508
16	Robert Todd	Todd's house	Bill Bk I, 1; LB 'A', 508
17	Hallett		
18	Drinkwaters (cancelled)		
	Francis Fenton		
19	Thomas (cancelled)		Bill Bk I, 1
	Francis Fenton		Bill Bk I, 1
20	Robert Todd (cancelled)		Bill Bk I, 1; LB 'A', 714
	Francis Fenton		Bill Bk I, 1; LB 'A', 581, 634
21	Robert Todd (cancelled)		Bill Bk I, 1; LB 'A', 714
	Francis Fenton		Bill Bk I, 1; LB 'A', 581, 634
22	Robert Todd		LB 'A', 714
23	Robert Todd	Alexander Birnie	Bill Bk I, 1; 'LB 'A', 714
24	Webber	Alexander Birnie	Bill Bk I, 1
25	Robert Todd	Martin	Bill Bk I, l; LB 'A', 589, 708, 714
26	Robert Todd	Martin	Bill Bk I, 1; LB 'A', 158, 714, 708
27	Robert Todd	Martin	As above
28	Robert Todd	Martin	As above
30	Robert Todd	Chamberlain	
31	Webber	Waples (lease)	Bill Bk I, 1

* Bill Book (Bill Bk)/Letter Book (LB).

speculative builders to the estate, including Robert Todd, who turned out to be a key figure in the early decades of development.

This first auction took place in 1804. It is largely undocumented though a tentative reconstruction is proposed in Table 1 as lot numbers were recorded in early lease drawings, in Bill Book I and in the letter books.

Incentives

The surveyor of the Portland estate, John White junior, offers us a glimpse into early nineteenth-century urban planning:

> it is well known that no large portion of ground can be successfully covered by good buildings all at once; either the ground landlord must do much himself in making advances of money, forming roads and sewers, or by letting his ground, at a moderate price, to some man of capital, hold out a sufficient temptation to induce [him] to make an outlay of money; the doing this is impracticable on a very extended scale, because the market for buildings is never capable of taking off any very great number of good houses in one situation.

In a footnote White added: 'this is apparent from Mr Changeur's extensive scheme at Kensington which appears totally to have failed.'[43] This was a reference to the difficulties experienced by Louis Léon Changeur, who attempted to develop what would become Edwardes Square, near the Commonwealth Institute, without due caution. However, many of the landlord's incentives which John White described as encouraging successful development played a part in the planning of St John's Wood.

Walpole did make some advances of money. These would have been relatively modest sums, as we will see below that Walpole and his brother were themselves struggling to raise the necessary cash for development. When Walpole did lend money, however, as for instance to the developer William Hall, it was for a limited period only: 'And you will have to pay me the £25 I lent you in August & which was to have been immediately returned, you will also have to pay me the £15 I lent you on the 5 Instt.'[44] This particular episode took place in 1820 when finances were less tight than in the early years of the nineteenth century. There seems to have been a great deal of creative accounting between Walpole and William Hall. The letter books reveal him to have been Walpole's landlord at Montagu Place:[45] 'the Rent of the house & prem[is]es which he [Walpole] occupies was by agreement with Mr Hall to be set against the Rents he has taken at St Johns Wood'.[46] Elsewhere, Walpole also bluntly stated his lack of trust in the financial reliability of builders: 'I told Mr Levien that I should expect a Satisfactory Reference in case we came to a determination of letting him have the House.... he said he would refer me to a Mr Mayer a Builder which I begged to decline.'[47] As 'Mr Mayer' was probably the Charles Mayor who built Park Crescent for Nash but failed spectacularly in 1814, Walpole's circumspection appears to have been very well founded.[48]

Walpole was careful not to take financial risks, but there were other ways of helping builders rather than lending cash to them. As early as 1806 he wrote: 'it is my Wish that the builders who are speculat[in]g upon my Brothers Estate, sho[ul]d be put to as little expence as possible for their Leases.'[49] He also understood well that once the work on a house had progressed sufficiently, it was disastrous to keep builders waiting for their leases, which they needed to sell to earn a living and bring in money to continue the building work. Walpole was therefore prompt in issuing these, constantly hurrying architect John Shaw along for the drawings and plans that were needed for completing the task: 'you will have the goodness to get the plans drawn as they are all in want of their leases & it is our Int[eres]t to get the Houses inhabited as early as possible.'[50] Or again: 'I write to request you will get the plans done of the Leases which Mr Freeth [the office clerk] has already written for, the Builders are so much in want of them, that they cannot do without them.'[51] By way of comparison we could mention the less congenial situation on the adjoining Eton estate: 'the dilatory behavior of the Provost and Fellows [of Eton College] and particularly the bursar and registrar, with respect to the management of their London property – leading especially to delays in the execution of leases – did nothing to encourage builders.'[52]

Another incentive for builders was that in the first three years of their agreements, they were only asked to pay grass rent as opposed to the full building rent. This was a great help as the difference between the two sums was massive: 'The following are the Terms upon which I will let you the Ground Viz. Term 99 years from Midsummer last – £25 Grass Rent for the first three years – & £150 for the Remainder of the Term.'[53] Walpole revealed the very delicate balance he had to maintain between helping others and helping himself when, in May 1806, he wrote to Harry:

> In all build[in]g concerns it is usual to let the Builders have the Gro[un]d for two years at a Pepper Corn Rent, as they cannot of course turn their build[in]gs to account unless [in less] than that period, we have however endeavoured to prevent your Income from being lessened during that period by making them Pay a Grass Rent which will about equal the All[owan]ce to be made to Willan for the Land taken from him.... I don't think you can imm[ediate]ly look forw[ar]d to receiv[in]g any Increase of Income, for as you have no ready money every expence must be paid out of your Income, & when you come to calculate the money I have p[ai]d for the Road & what it must require to keep it in repair & the money we shall have to pay Mr Shaw[,] it will for the p[re]sent exhaust the Increase of Income.[54]

As this passage makes clear, Walpole had to spend enormous sums on infrastructure. The success of Alpha Cottages was made possible by the building of Alpha Road at the Eyres' expense, and there is also no doubt that the sale of land to the vestry was facilitated by Walpole's enticing terms: 'sale of some land to the Parish for the purpose of enabling them to form a Burial Ground & build a Chapel & when at last I agreed to sell them any quantity not exceeding six acres at £600 pr acre & *to make a 50 foot Road from the East end of Alpha Road up to the Gro[un]d to be sold*' (my italics).[55] To attract builders and speculators onto the estate, the Eyres had to take on the building of roads, and follow this with the provision of water, drains and sewers. In due course Walpole worked out ways of passing on these costs to tenants, but initially, at least, what must have seemed massive expenditure had to be borne by Harry. The accounts have not survived, but Walpole's letters make it clear that the sums were large: 'I hope you will be as moderate as you can & will endeavour to confine your Expences for a year or two, you have no idea of the expences of the St John Wood Improvements but time will soon bring every thing about.'[56]

When dealing with William Hall, the builder with the greatest number of acres in hand under development, Walpole's clerk, Charles Freeth, firmly showed what was due to the estate for the years 1819–22 but phrased his demand for payment diplomatically: '[I] send the Sewer Account between you and Mr Walpole Eyre and upon which there is a balance due from you of £429-13 which sum being added to the above balance upon the general Account of £469-17 makes a total balance due from you of £899-10 and which he will be glad to have put in train of Settlement.'[57]

Mortgages

We saw that as soon as Henry Samuel Eyre was old enough to inherit the estate in 1792,[58] St John's Wood was mortgaged. His military career and that of his brother John Thomas consumed considerable sums of money, and early borrowings were no doubt entirely connected with this. The borrowings were relatively modest at first: £2,000 from John Partridge on 12 December 1792, barely three weeks after Harry's inheritance, another £1,000 from John Dyneley on 18 February 1793 and a further £1,000 two months later. But the stakes increased on 24 January 1796 when a mortgage of £13,000 was set up between Harry and Samuel Moody, represented by John Askell Bucknall, George Samuel Wegg and Richard Hollingworth.[59]

Walpole inherited this arrangement and had considerable trouble with it. When, in 1806, the documents for the very first leased house on the estate (No. 5 in Alpha Cottages reconstruction, Plate 63) had to be signed by all mortgagees – and it had to be done at great speed to ensure the deal was not lost – Walpole was forced to go on an epic journey. All three mortgagees lived quite far apart – Moody near Watford, Wegg in Acton and Hollingworth near Ware (Bucknall had died by then). Walpole also had to overcome individual objections from each mortgagee.[60] Not surprisingly, at the time of the sale of the burial ground to the vestry in 1807, he desperately tried to leave the mortgagees out of the transaction, knowing it would only complicate matters a good deal more,[61] but the vestry insisted on them joining in the conveyance. So, as Walpole expected, the transaction was seriously delayed: 'I am sorry to occasion any further delay & I assure you I have done all in my power to get the Mortgagees Answer but you must be aware how difficult it is to get people to stir in Business which does not interest them.'[62]

With all the building development taking place at St John's Wood, Walpole soon contemplated a new mortgage. With the help of his friend and client Godin Shiffner,[63] he managed to kill two birds with one stone: in 1810 he obtained a new mortgage of £20,000 and switched to a much more convenient source of capital with the Sun Fire Insurance Company. Walpole's letter books record the deal, but the inspiration behind it is only revealed in his bill book: 'Att[endin]g Mr Godin Shiffner one of the Directors of the Sun Fire Office where he offered to advance me £20,000 upon the security of the St Johns Wood Estate in order to promote the Building thereon provided I wo[ul]d make the Builders insure at their office.'[64] This was a shrewd move on the part of Shiffner and one which worked, as Walpole informed Harry: ' I have lately had an offer made me of £20,000 upon the mortgage of the Saint Johns Wood Estate and which I mean to accept[.] out of this I shall pay off the present mortgage to Mr Moody of £13,000 and shall invest the remainder in the funds, I thought this a very adviseable step as occasions may occur when all the ready money may be of great service in the management of your property and it will also be a pleasant thing when you return home to this Country to have some Money at command.'[65] Mortgage negotiations were protracted as Walpole was keen for the mortgage to be raised against part of the St John's Wood estate only, giving him a free hand to develop or sell the rest as he wished: 'I understood it was Mr Sanders's intention to take the Security upon the whole of the Estate[.] there are however Premises to be excepted in the Mortgage[,] about 65 acres which are situated on the western side of the Estate.... My Motive for wishing to except these premises, is that I may have the power of selling them to enable me to pay the expences of making Sewers and Roads.'[66] The previous mortgagees were disconcerted by the sudden cancellation of a steady source of income, and negotiations with them were a little tense for a while.[67] Finally, the new mortgage was ready and dated 25 and 26 January 1811 naming the new mortgagees: Messrs Bolton, Bewick, Pole and Thornton.[68]

But despite this new arrangement, Walpole required more capital the following year, and he applied for a further £10,000 mortgage from the Sun Fire Office.[69] This must have been turned down, as it is not recorded in the Abstract of Title. Besides the estate loans recorded in the Abstract of Title, there were also a number of other loans for private use, which show that money was not flowing in that direction either. We mentioned earlier the money borrowed for Harry's proposed promotion in 1806 (see p. 47), and a further loan from the bank was also secured prior to Harry's departure for Ceylon.[70] In 1813 Walpole borrowed £4,000 from Thomas Willan (no doubt for Harry), a sum of money he would only repay in 1822 when a second mortgage was raised from the Sun Fire Office.[71]

By 1815 another strategy was needed. Walpole approached his uncle Reverend John Johnson, based at Parndon in Essex, asking for £5,000,[72] and the Sun Fire Office again, asking for a further £5,000 on the existing mortgage.[73] Walpole was partly successful: nothing seems to have come from the Sun Fire Office, but the family loan is recorded at £8,600. The respite, however, came to an abrupt end in 1819 when, somewhat unexpectedly, Johnson asked for his money back and Walpole was not ready.[74] To make matters worse, he also ran into difficulty with the Sun Fire Office repayments: 'Latterly I have not been quite so regular in my payments as usual, this arises from the large sums of money I am under the necessity of expending in the Improvements upon my brothers St Johns Wood Estate.' However, determined to give a positive picture, he added: 'These improvements are daily increasing the Income of the Estate and of course bettering the Security of the trustees of the Sun Fire Office.'[75]

Agreements and leases

Three key documents were needed as tools for development: the agreement, the lease and the conveyance. The development process has already been described in a number of publications, but the Eyre archive offers a uniquely detailed and lively picture of the important issues which arose and how they were resolved.[76]

An **agreement** was prepared when a speculator or builder was willing to take on a part of the estate for building purposes or, increasingly rarely in the nineteenth century, when farmers, gardeners or private individuals wanted land for 'grass purposes'. Willan, for instance, was the largest 'grass tenant' in St John's Wood, and we saw that his first agreement with the estate, going back to 1796, has survived.[77] Grass rent was clearly much lower than building rent (we saw above that it was £25 as opposed to £150), but this type of agreement now contained a clause stipulating the land could be taken away for building purposes. The covenants in grass rent agreements dealt principally with countryside issues, and these contrasted with covenants in building agreements, which focused on

4 EARLY RESIDENTIAL DESIGNS

Donald Olsen's perceptive study of one of St John's Wood neighbouring estates – Chalcots – left him in no doubt as to who was responsible for the architectural style of an area. It was not the landlord, and it was not the architect in charge. Olsen writes: 'no portion of [architect John] Shaw's plan was put into effect, since it proved to be … unacceptable to speculative builders.… it was the builder, and behind the builder the investing public and their estimate of the market for houses, who ultimately determined the shape and character of the expanding English town.'[1] This statement is confirmed by what happened in St John's Wood – in particular, the residential schemes contemplated by Thomas Lord as well as St John's Wood Grove, both discussed below. However, this statement should also be qualified: before the Eyres' pioneering initiative, nobody actually knew whether or not there was a market for small 'country' houses, be they main or secondary residences.

THE LONDON BUILDING ACTS

The Great Fire of September 1666 was especially destructive because the narrow City streets were densely packed with shops and homes, all built from highly inflammable timber, wattle and daub. The rate of the fire was accelerated by a strong wind, but the building materials and overcrowding were major factors in the loss of approximately four-fifths of all properties. The City of London was determined to impose strict rules to prevent any similar reoccurrence; this was the 1667 Rebuilding Act, and for the first time buildings were categorised in 'sorts', ranging from the modest 'first and least Sort' to the grandest 'fourth Sort' for 'Mansion Houses of the greatest Bigness'.[2] Subsequent London Building Acts (1707, 1709 and 1774) essentially reinforced the anti-fire regulations of the 1667 Act but also refined this system of categorising buildings, replacing 'sorts' by 'rates' and inverting the rating order, i.e. 'Buildings of the fourth Rate' were now of modest nature. By 1774 there were seven 'Rate Buildings', though still only four dealt with 'dwelling houses' – the first covering landmark public buildings and large houses worth £850 and above, the fourth covering houses worth £150 to £300, and the rest being reserved for non-residential buildings.[3]

By the early years of the nineteenth century these categories were still in loose use, enabling us to put a price on the St John's Wood houses. The cost was a reflection of the materials used, the quality of craftsmanship and, of course, the size of the buildings. From the patchy evidence that has survived for St John's Wood, the Eyres opted to cover the estate with 'buildings of the second Rate', which fell within the £300–850 bracket value. The documents sometimes specify 'second rate houses', as in the agreements drawn up with the Regent's Canal Company and Thomas Lord.[4] Later on, the actual value of the houses to be built was used: £800 for a detached house and £500 for a semi-detached house.[5]

Size mattered at St John's Wood, and Walpole fought hard against the construction of small houses people might want to build to suit their purse. Small houses simply did not fit the vision of a respectable and comfortable neighbourhood, and would have reduced the value of the estate in the long term:

> I understand that the person who has taken the corner piece of Ground at Lodge Road
> west of Mr Stevensons is building some small dwellings[.] this I cannot allow and whoever
> has taken the Ground must either build according to the terms of the agreement between

Previous pages: **51** Detail from *View of the Alpha Cottages near Paddington* (taken from the south-west, half-way up Lisson Grove). John Seguier (1785–1856) exhibited this oil painting at the Royal Academy in 1812. This work seems unique in depicting the temporary brickmaking facilities that we know accompanied all building work at St John's Wood. Its accuracy is such that we can identify Robert Todd's house, the second one from the left, framed by its two low, symmetrical outbuildings (see Plate 58). As Robert Todd was a key builder on the St John's Wood estate, it is not surprising to find that the kiln-house with tall chimney is standing on the south-east side of his ground. Private collection/ Bridgeman Art Library.

Henry Warren delt.   1818.

Alpha Cottages. Regent's Park.

52 Alpha Cottages seen from Regent's Park. This 1818 drawing by Henry Warren captures the look of St John's Wood's early development. The tall cottages line the north side of the Alpha Road (the south side is not visible in this view). The large house in the right foreground can be identified (No. 23 on the Alpha Cottages reconstruction) and was built by and for the artist Thomas Heaphy. This drawing was formerly in the collection of J. E. Gardner, a long-term resident on the estate (see p.185). Westminster City Archives (Ashbridge collection, Box 160/ALP).

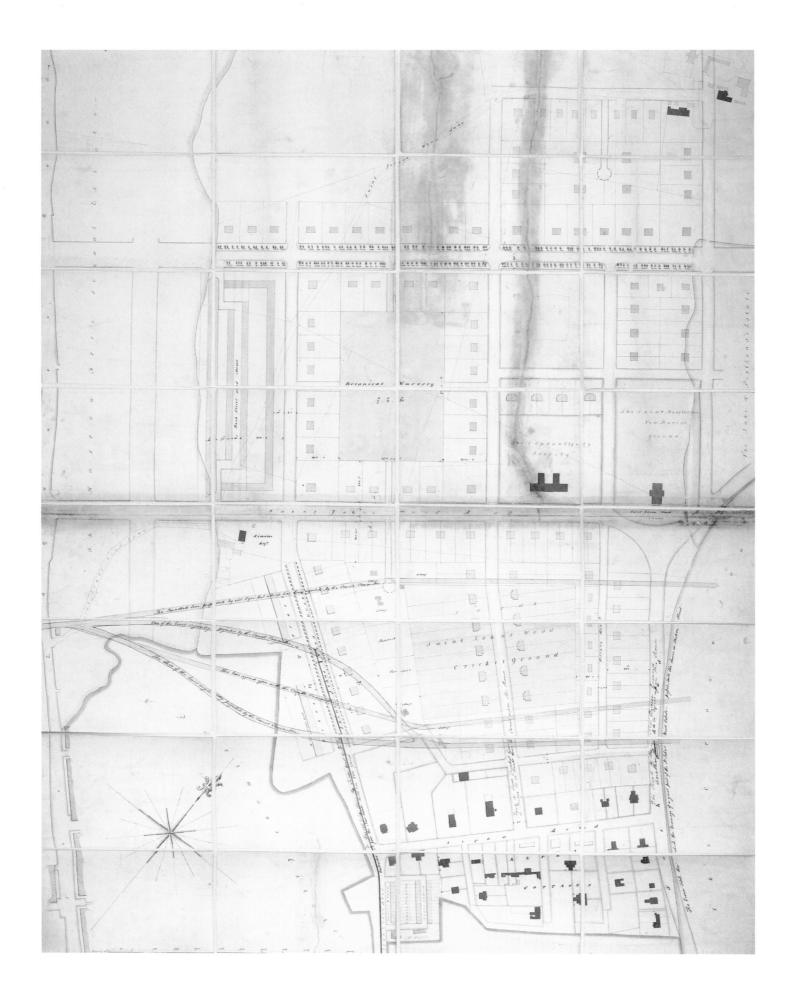

Opposite: **58** The house Robert Todd
built for himself and his family in 1806
(the lease drawing reproduced here is
dated 1809 because it was prepared
later). 'I will thank you to make out a
policy of £565 on the house £20 on
the stables £15 upon the Coach
house detached (& all brick and
slated) of Mr Rob[er]t Todd situate
on Lots 15 & 16 on the south side
of a newly made Road called Alpha
Road,' wrote Walpole on 11 May
1807 (LB 'A', p. 508). Eyre estate
archive (Bk of Drawings I, 8).

However, the architectural type which was to prevail at St John's Wood was not that of Haselar's house, but rather that of Tatham. The latter was almost a carbon copy of the house Robert Todd built for himself. There were some differences (to which we will return below), but it is important to establish which of these made its appearance first.

PIONEER ROBERT TODD

At this point it is worth revisiting another statement made by John Summerson. He mentioned that James Elmes, in *A Topographical Dictionary of London* published in 1831, wrote in his entry for Alpha Road: 'that the first site to be let [at St John's Wood] was taken by "a builder of some taste" who erected "a cottage for the residence of himself and family" and that this was promptly imitated'.[15] Summerson believed this man of taste to have been C.H. Tatham, but patient reconstruction of the Alpha Cottages points the finger in a different direction: 'the builder of some taste' had to be Robert Todd (see No. 8 on Alpha Cottages reconstruction, also Plates 58 and 59). We have already come across his name in Chapter 3 (p. 91) as he was involved from the beginning, taking numerous lots on agreement in 1804, developing some and subletting others, for instance to Edward Chamberlain (whom we saw went bankrupt) and also to Thomas Martin (see Table 1, p. 96).

Todd's influence must have been considerable as he worked closely with many developers and architects. We learn that in 1809 'Mr Todd is going to do Mr Atkinsons Brick work.'[16] Both men had connections with James Wyatt (1746–1813), the ubiquitous and fashionable architect who became Surveyor General and Controller of the Office of Works. William Atkinson had been a pupil of James Wyatt, and Walpole's bill book unmistakably linked Todd with Wyatt, first in May 1815: 'Several attendances upon Mr Todd and advising and taking Instructions relative to assignment of part of

59 The back of the house of
Robert Todd: by the time this
photograph was taken in the early
years of the twentieth century, the
house was called Walton Lodge and
the association with Robert Todd
forgotten. It had also been extended.
London Topographical Society
(see Head, 1906).

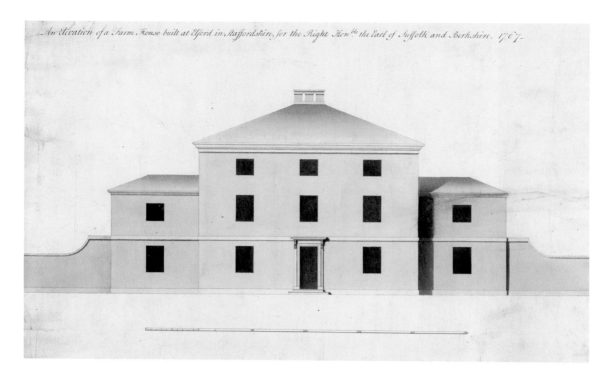

An Elevation of a Farm House built at Elford in Staffordshire, for the Right Honble the Earl of Suffolk and Berkshire. 1767.

60 This design for a farmhouse in Staffordshire is probably the work of Benjamin Wyatt I (1709–72). The pen and wash drawing is signed 'Benjn Wyatt & Sons' and dated 1767. The architect recorded in his diary in 1767 that he was making drawings for estate buildings for Lord Suffolk. Royal Institute of British Architects (SC74/Wyb (1)).

Debt owing to him from the late Mr Wyatt'. The January 1816 entry on the same page specified the debt was for £1,189 6s. 2d. and that Todd 'had agreed to take £730.11.7 and to give up the remainder in favour of Mr Wyatt's family'.[17] Given these connections, it is perhaps not surprising to find that Robert Todd's house in St John's Wood bears similarities to the farmhouse designed by Benjamin Wyatt I for Lord Suffolk in Staffordshire (Plate 60).

In Alpha Road, Todd built himself a substantial cottage, with stables and a coach house, which would become his main residence (Plate 58). His house spread across the entire width of his plot and was built by 1806, the first house on the estate, even though the lease appears to date from 1809.[18] One of Walpole's letters to Alexander Birnie, written in April 1806, clearly indicated that Todd's house was already built by that date and that it immediately acquired a model status: 'Mr Shaw has no objection to your having permission to build two more Houses upon the Lots you have taken, provided they are of equal value with the House Mr Todd has built upon lots No. 15 & 16 for his own residence.'[19]

A passage in a document dated 30 June 1818 confirms that, even after ten years, the houses of Robert Todd were still flagged by Walpole Eyre as models for other developers to follow: 'The internal finishings of the said houses to be at least equally good quality with those of the four houses last built by Mr Robert Todd.'[20] The four houses mentioned in this document would have been the two detached houses he built in Alpha Road (Plate 63) and two more (double) houses on the corner of Lisson Grove and St John's Wood Road (see Plate 213) which are visible on the 1853 map.[21]

Todd's relationship with St John's Wood was at the heart of its development. He was making bricks, roads and sewers and was permanently based at Alpha Road from 1815, attended vestry meetings, ran an ongoing account with Walpole and chose to have Walpole as his attorney.[22] What we do not know, however, is how closely Todd's house was based on the 'model' house prepared by John Shaw in 1802 (see p. 71), designed as one of the British Circus 'double houses'. Todd's design for his house combined features from two of the model villages discussed in the last chapter: the sturdy carcass was lofty and the roof hipped as in Houghton village, but the positioning of the house inside the plot and the siting of service buildings behind a screen arrangement are reminiscent of the Chippenham cottages (see Plates 39 and 40). Todd also introduced a decorative horizontal band to articulate the façade, and this soon became a standard feature at St John's Wood. His design for a detached house could easily be adapted to the double house as shown in No. 18 in Plate 61, another house built by Todd.[23]

In conclusion, the house Todd built for himself at Alpha Road was of such appeal to builders and prospective lessees alike that it was the model not only for Tatham's house, but for a very large number of houses on the estate, initially among the Alpha Cottages but soon spreading to William Hall's ground and other parts. Its endurance throughout the nineteenth and twentieth centuries gives it the status of a prototype – Todd's prototype – popular while he was alive and living on after his death (see Plate 81).

61 This double house was built by Robert Todd in or around 1810. He adapted the style of his detached house to a double house. Here some of the service buildings have been integrated into the main house with the help of an extra storey, perhaps in response to the way shown by Tatham's house (Plate 56). Eyre estate archive (Bk of Drawings I, 14).

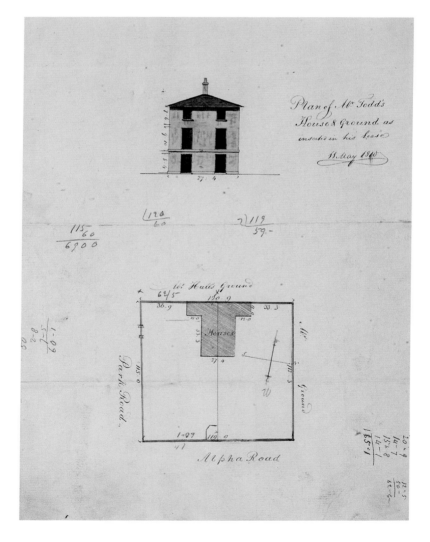

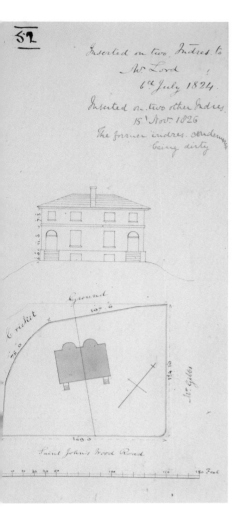

66 This double house was built by Thomas Lord in 1824. The 1813 agreement between Walpole and Lord made provision for building houses on the south and east sides of the ground, but this simple construction falls rather short of the grand plan of the earlier scheme (Plate 65 opposite). From 1828 Thomas Lord's son, a solicitor also named Thomas, resided at 28 St John's Wood Road in one of these houses (LB 'L', p. 134). Eyre estate archive (Bk of Drawings II, 52).

Wood Grove, but this is a fair assumption as Walpole's letter and bill books suggest Shaw was the main and only adviser on this scheme. The internal layout on the ground floor was very close to that of a 'typical house in Doughty Street' illustrated in Rasmussen's *London*, which the author described as a scaled down version of a Bedford Square house.[38] The St John's Wood model was scaled down even further with a two-bay façade rather than three. Yet the scheme also included a grander side to it: the central pile, framed by two-bay houses (their side entrances enabled the architect to create grander rooms), mostly consisted of three very large houses, each five bays across.

THOMAS LORD'S HOUSES

The St John's Wood Grove development of terraced houses failed to attract the attention of developers. The same fate would meet the semi-detached houses which first appeared in the 1813 agreement with Thomas Lord. This building agreement, the earliest to have survived, was issued in connection with Lord's third (and final) site for his cricket ground.[39] The agreement was primarily concerned with the use of the land as a cricket ground, but it also made provision for some building development after the first ten years of the eighty-year agreement. This meant that in 1823 when ten years had elapsed, if Lord decided to erect buildings, he could do so provided that notice was given to the Eyres in writing. The schedule for the building programme stipulated that within five years 'sixteen messuages or tenements to be second rate houses and to have and to bear the appearance of eight houses' should be erected on the spots marked 'with good and sufficient materials and in a substantial and workmanlike manner', the Eyres' perennial conditions. The agreement provided the elevation and ground-floor plan for the houses (with St John's Wood Grove, some of the earliest ground-floor plans to have survived in the Eyre archive, Plate 65). The drawing shows them to be smart dwellings of a decidedly urban style. They were to be sited on the south and east sides of the cricket ground (Plate 239).

The Eyres must have approved of Thomas Lord's houses because when the builder William Hall signed the first in a series of agreements with the St John's Wood estate, we learn from one of Walpole's letters that 'he is to pay a guinea a foot for Road & Sewer & is to build eight houses as good as those to be built by Lord'.[40] The dwellings were not simply to be 'as good as' but *the same as*, as is clear from the agreement with Hall which has survived. This promised to be a harmonious and co-ordinated move, as the ground let to Hall was on the western side of the cricket ground. As late as 1835, the scheme was still alive and featured in Mr Dark's agreement with Walpole Eyre.[41] However, neither Thomas Lord nor William Hall nor Henry Dark ever built any of those houses. The only double house Thomas Lord did build was considerably more modest (Plate 66). A lease was issued for it in 1824, and it was sited, at an angle, in the south-east corner of the ground, clearly visible on the 1853 map of St John's Wood (Plate 70).

THE ROLE OF THE ESTATE ARCHITECT

Although the landlord and his architect may not have been able to dictate the architectural style of what was built in St John's Wood, there was a great deal they could do to ensure good buildings were put up. One of the conditions for building on the estate was that all elevations be checked and approved by the estate's architect. Walpole could be quite severe if this guideline was not followed: 'Before I left town I desired that the Elevation of the House should be sent to Mr Shaw for his approbation, this I find was neglected and I think it right to apprize you that you have no right to build but according to the Elevation in Webbers Agreement unless some other Elevation be approved by me.'[42] As time went by and Shaw's practice became more and more successful, Walpole asked prospective developers to submit their elevations directly to himself: this way he could liaise with his busy architect, saving time and minimising delays.

The two schemes discussed above – St John's Wood Grove and Thomas Lord's houses – probably made Walpole realise that it was more realistic simply to ensure nothing objectionable was built on the estate. There is indeed no evidence to support the idea that, apart from these early experiments, Walpole and his architect attempted to dictate the architectural style by encouraging builders to use an agreed stock of designs. This is clear, for instance, from a letter sent to James Morgan, John Nash's associate in the development of Regent's Park, at the time the Regent's Canal agreement was being prepared: 'I have no sort of wish to fetter the Company as to the number of houses except that a sufficient number should be built to secure the rent and which we had before agreed upon[.] With respect to any additional houses All I desire is that they may be detached and ornamented according to the original Stepulation [sic].'[43] Ten years later, Walpole described the process of quality control unequivocally: 'The course I usually adopt in the first instance is to understand the intention of the parties & to see their plans, & if approved of, then to prepare a building agreement & when the buildings are completed to grant a Lease, for the remainder of the term.'[44]

Once plans and elevations had been 'passed', these would be drawn in John Shaw's office and then transferred to the agreements and leases, thus binding all original intentions to a precise contract. These detailed, and often beautiful, drawings increased the costs of documents. The Board of Ordnance turned to their official architect, William Atkinson, to find out whether 'it is the usual practice with Persons in the Neighbourhood of London letting land for building upon, to be furnished in the first Instance with Plans, showing what is intended to be Built'. In his reply Atkinson implied it was the practice generally in St John's Wood, but also added: 'in some Instances I have had an opportunity of knowing the same to be done in taking land for Building of Mr Portman and I believe it to [be] the general practice with both those Gentlemen and also Lord Grosvenor and where I have been employed it has been the same in taking land of the Crown for Building in the New Street [Regent Street]'.[45] Plans were indeed common, but what was not the usual practice was the stipulation of elevations, a precaution the estate clearly regarded as essential for guarding against last-minute savings when costs escalated.[46]

On one rare occasion, a design for a very small cottage was needed for a gardener, John Gibbs, who had taken land for a nursery garden but must have felt ill-equipped to deal with the building side of the transaction. Walpole asked Todd and Shaw for a design and settled on Todd's proposal, writing to Shaw: 'I enclose Mr Todd's Plan for a Cottage in w[hi]ch he informs me there is almost half as much more building as in the one you proposed & that he will undertake to complete it for £77.10 – the Rent to be increased to £25 – Will you fin[d] a spot for the Cottage as he wishes to begin in a few days.'[47] The sum of £77 is exceedingly modest and corresponds to a house of the fourth or fifth rate, according to the 1774 Building Act.

On another occasion, in 1817, Walpole called on Shaw for a design for a couple of lodges:

opposite side of the Avenue Road as it completing [completely] excludes the *View of the Canal and Slopes which are now becoming very beautiful*' (my italics).[69] However, in the long term, the estate would pay dearly for relaxing the rules on that part of the estate, as the properties which Burton developed were precisely those which gave rise to rumours about kept women and, later, prostitution (see pp. 197–98 and 200–02).

BUILDERS AND ARCHITECTS

The early and extraordinary 'lettings map' of the Portland estate bears the names of all of the men who built the estate,[70] but the St John's Wood archive yields an enormous amount of information about the previously unknown pioneers of this very special estate (see Appendix 9 on p. 469). Even if drawing the line between builders and architects is not always easy, a striking number of architects seem to be represented.[71] Nevertheless, it would be mistaken to imagine that the development of St John's Wood afforded an architectural opportunity. There was little that was truly groundbreaking in the design of the houses. Once Todd's prototype was found to be a winning formula, most builders were happy to follow this particular groove, which in turn led to a pleasing sense of unity; the simple, sturdy, vaguely classical style prevailed. The rendering and painting of the houses provided a striking finish: the clean white houses set like precious stones in the gloriously green setting of the trees and gardens.

Despite the Eyres' insistence on good materials and craftsmanship, modern surveyors and builders are unimpressed by the quality of nineteenth-century building at St John's Wood. Builders seemed to have had little grasp of how to turn the house's four walls into a cohesive whole, and the following disaster illustrates this particular shortcoming well. In the late 1880s, Mary Richardson-Eyre and her husband were living at 7 Marlborough Hill: 'We had about this time a very tiresome experience with our house; we woke one morning to find that daylight was showing through the walls in Patrick's dressing room and study. Both these rooms were built off from one end of our little domicile. Patrick at once sent for a builder, who came and propped it up, telling us the only thing to be done was to pull that part down and rebuild it, and that the whole of the house must be underpinned. We had taken it on a repairing lease, and our landlord would do nothing.'[72]

So the criticism which has been levelled at John Nash in Regent's Park – too quickly built, mediocre quality – also seems to have been deserved in St John's Wood. London building quality is generally considered low in the 1810–40 period, improving thereafter. Twenty-first century surveyors in St John's Wood are continually amazed to see that some of the early houses are still standing. In the words of one of them: 'the houses have assumed a habit of stability.'[73]

5 CREATING AND MAINTAINING A GARDEN QUARTER

I … strolled thoughtfully on to the Regent's Park near which I lost myself in a wilderness of cottages and villas, that had sprung up like magic since my last visit to London (*New Monthly Magazine*, vol. V, 1822, pp. 502–7, cited in Vincent, 1953, p. 142).

In 1824, Mrs Annette Hatton, the Eyre brothers' youngest half-sister, wrote a begging letter to Walpole: she needed to borrow £300. It is easy to guess from Walpole's reply that she made this request because she had run into difficulties with a building project in Ireland, where she lived with her husband General Hatton. Walpole secured the loan from his brother Harry, 'a man of good property but not a monied man', before adding: 'I must entreat of you not to dabble more in building than is absolutely necessary[.] in this country [England] unless very well managed it is ruination & I suppose it is pretty much the same thing in Ireland.' Annette died without repaying her debt.[1]

There is something prophetic in this family incident. The St John's Wood estate had certainly experienced a developers' boom after the completion of the Regent's Canal in 1820. This project had been very disruptive and had taken years to complete (1811–20), but the appearance of small and attractive houses lining the canal banks led to a surge of interest from would-be developers. Alas, this rapidly turned sour as funds for the building market began to dry up. The list of casualties is a long one, with many builders/developers going bankrupt or as good as bankrupt from the mid-1820s to the mid-1830s (see p. 142). Records show that 1830 and 1831 were still good years, with seventeen and nineteen leases per year, but by 1832 the figure had dropped to ten, from 1833 to 1835 to nine, reaching a low of seven in 1836. The figure started rising again in 1837 with eight leases issued, and in 1838 it had gone up to eleven. The lease rate reached new dizzying heights by 1839, with twenty-nine new leases.[2] It is remarkable that Walpole did not lose his nerve throughout that time, that he succeeded in maintaining high standards of development, and kept forging ahead with the back- and bank-breaking project of the Marylebone and Finchley Turnpike Road (i.e. Finchley Road), borrowing whatever money was needed to keep it going. In these dark but interesting years probably lies the ultimate success of the St John's Wood estate.

The creation of Alpha Cottages, narrated in Chapters 3 and 4, had been pursued in times of war. The Napoleon scare – 'Boney is Coming!' – traumatised a generation of children, and measures were taken to 'Drive the Devoted Armies of Bonaparte to Hell and Perdition'.[3] When at last, in 1814, Bonaparte abdicated and was exiled to the Isle of Elba, all breathed a sigh of relief. The spectre of Napoleon rose one last time, but almost immediately came the crushing defeat of Waterloo and the exile to St Helena in the summer of 1815. To commemorate that time a St John's Wood lessee named his house 'Napoleon Cottage', no doubt one of many to fall for the 'Napoleonmania' which raged for decades after the downfall of Bonaparte.[4] It reached fever pitch when Napoleon's Waterloo carriage was shipped over to England, making the fortunes of William Bullock at the Egyptian Hall and of Madame Tussaud.[5]

However, the transition from a state of war to a peacetime economy proved difficult. Was the economy too feeble to sustain London's growing population, prompting many to resort to crime for survival? Or did unemployment and the loss of a common enemy encourage people to channel violent instincts towards one another? There is evidence in the Eyre letter books that this criminal fever, real or imagined, affected the Eyres both on their estate and at home in Bryanston Square. A mild form of panic set in when the Bryanston Square house needed to be altered and was left partly unprotected during the works in 1824. Having approached Mr Howell at Marylebone Watch House, Walpole

Previous pages: **68** James Tissot's *A Convalescent* shows Kathleen Newton resting by the pool and colonnade at 17 Grove End Road. An old lady companion who appears to be reading to her is checking to see whether she is asleep. The painting dates from 1875–76, when Kathleen came to live with Tissot. She was suffering from tuberculosis and died in November 1882, leaving Tissot devastated. Sheffield Galleries and Museums Trust.

explained to the lessee: 'until the house is finished and fit for occupation it is absolutely necessary to have a watchman as the house would o[the]rwise be very much exposed and one might be robbed & murdered in our Beds.'[6] The reader might be tempted to associate these worries with the dangers of living in the West End, but there are several references in the letter books which suggest St John's Wood was apprehended in the same light. The danger found in neighbouring Portland Town was made unequivocally clear by Walpole when, in 1830, he tried (unsuccessfully) to encourage the Commissioners of Police to set up a branch at St John's Wood House: 'I need not state to you that Portland Town is principally inhabited by persons of the lowest description and as that place and the neighbouring district are not included in any system of parochial Management it is highly desireable [*sic*] that there should be an effectual Police Establishment in that quarter.'[7] Various episodes of

69 Peter Potter's map of St Marylebone, 1820, offers a good summary of the development described in Chapter 3 and should now be compared with Plate 70 to gain a sense of the formidable development masterminded by Walpole Eyre between 1820 and 1853. City of London, London Metropolitan Archives.

property damage and theft were mentioned when houses were left empty, including St John's Wood House in 1826, despite being centrally placed next to the farm and the Barracks, though of course also a stone's throw from Portland Town: 'Mr WE [Walpole] has been at St John's Wood this morning and finds that owing to Mrs Cooper's having left the house unprotected a considerable part of the Paling next St John's Wood Lane has been destroyed.' A few weeks later more damage had been done: 'the garden was broken into & there were about 50 or 60 boys destroying the trees & shrubs & the damage was very considerable.'[8]

'In the middle of the worst economic depression on record, criminal commitments in London and Middlesex rose from 2621 in 1824 to 3384 in 1827,' wrote Peter Hall in *Cities in Civilisation*.[9] Against this backdrop of increasing crime, the building market on the St John's Wood estate appeared initially to be buoyant around 1820 when the canal houses were built and completed: a record number of agreements were signed.[10] The smaller houses built by James Burton and his associates along the banks of the canal seemed to have sold well. The first sign that something was amiss came when the energetic and popular John Maidlow went bankrupt in 1826 and his large building yard in Portland Town was sold off. To offset his debts to the Eyres, he assigned to the colonel the lease of a large villa on the Portland estate, which had been built by Stephen Watkins at 9 Avenue Road, on the corner with Henry Street. Walpole spent years trying to find a tenant or indeed a buyer for this house. Eventually in 1834, having given up trying to make any profit out of it, he let it to be used as a school to a relative and friend, simply charging the annual rent of £60 that needed to be paid to the Portland estate.[11]

St John's Wood builders/developers' bankruptcies or near bankruptcies between 1823 and 1843 (in chronological order)[12]

The names with asterisks (*) have an entry in Appendix 9.

John Clemence in 1823. His partner, Henry de Bruno Austin, only just managed to avoid bankruptcy (LB 'H', p. 178).

Mr William Jeffereys in 1824 (LB 'I', p. 113).

William Hall* avoided bankruptcy in 1826 but lost control of his building empire to a trust (LB 'K', p. 555).

John Maidlow* in 1826 (see auction catalogue inside agreement at EE 2651/96).

Stephen Watkins* in 1827 (LB 'K', p. 292).

Samuel Gardner* in 1827 at EE 2650/1/119.

John Hinton* in 1827 (LB 'K', p. 347).

Mr Dowley[13] in 1827 (LB 'K', p. 277).

John White (publican)* cancelled his agreement with Walpole in 1833 and left for Australia in 1843 (LB 'Q', p. 227, and LB, 'R', pp. 400–1).

John White junior (surveyor)* avoided bankruptcy by cancelling his agreement in 1834 (EE 2651/243(B)).

William Robert Fry* in 1835 (LB 'N', p. 433).

Charles Maidlow* in 1843 (EE 2650/1/152(A)).

Henry Bundey in 1843 (EE 2650/1/168(C)).

70 'Plan of the St John's Wood Estate 1853'. The original drawing for this plan was almost certainly prepared in John Shaw's architectural practice and then lithographed by W. F. Bursill. Only two copies appear to have survived. This copy reproduces the handwritten key to the Spurrier & Phipps 1794 survey. It also shows a later stage of development on the estate than 1853: many of the properties in Belsize and Victoria Roads in the north were only leased in the 1860s. The thick blue line shows the vast area of the estate which was under mortgage while the Eyre brothers were developing St John's Wood. Eyre estate archive (EE 2652/8).

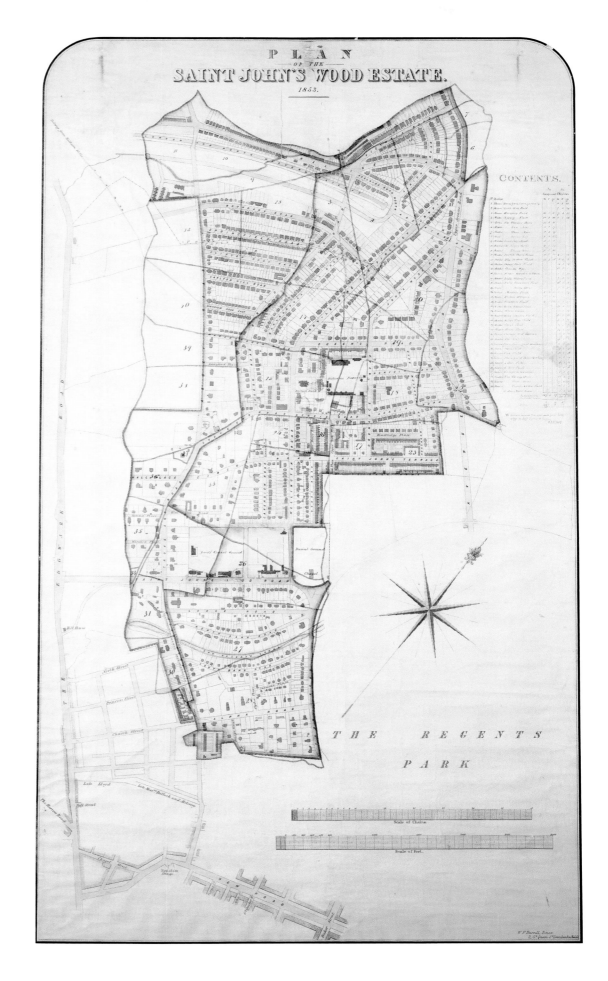

SUBURB VERSUS QUARTER

When urban historian H. J. Dyos attempted to define 'The Meaning of the Suburb' he eventually settled on: 'In essence, a suburb is a decentralized part of a city with which it is inseparably linked by certain economic and social ties.'[14] This is a useful benchmark. A glance at a map of north-west London in 1834 (Plate 71), shortly after the creation of London's first boroughs in 1832, makes it clear that St John's Wood was an integral part of the parish of St Marylebone, then of the borough of the same name. The map excludes the northern section of the St John's Wood estate which was in the parish of Hampstead (Boundary Road being the dividing line between the two parishes).

And yet the Eyre formula of 'garden houses' clearly set apart this neighbourhood, particularly as its residential formula of comfortable cottages placed in large gardens promoting healthy, 'country' living would become, towards the end of the Victorian period, synonymous with suburban living. The St John's Wood estate was recognisably a garden quarter long before the garden suburb movement was identified as such, one which pioneered the systematic use of the cottage/villa building style and with it a particular way of life. A claim has been made for Nash's development of Regent's Park: he 'had brought the picturesque to town and had created the first garden city'.[15] However, the research for this book shows that St John's Wood preceded the Regent's Park project by about a decade.

Suburb? Quarter? Neighbourhood? Which term is best suited to describe the St John's Wood estate? 'Neighbourhood', sometimes accompanied by the adjective 'respectable', first appeared in the 1794 Spurrier & Phipps advertisement (see p. 69) which described the aspirations and goals of the landlord/developer in relation to the estate. After this date, Walpole made continual use of this word, as for instance when writing to Thomas Heaphy in 1817: 'you intimated a wish of making Bricks upon your Ground[.] I have been considering the subject and it appears to me that it would be such a nuisance to the whole *neighbourhood* that I cannot comply with it' (my italics; this particular building project was opposite Lord's and the Clergy Orphan Asylum).[16] In this context 'neighbourhood' is very close to the modern notion of 'quarter'.

However, 'neighbourhood' is also used to define the considerably more general context of the outskirts of London, as for example in 1811: '[Thomas] Lord will also engage not to have any other Cricket Ground in the Neighbourhood of London,'[17] or in 1817 to Thomas Willan: 'Since my Letter of the 11th Jan[ua]ry I have made enquiries of differ[en]t persons as to the Value of Land in the Neighbourhood of London situated as my Brothers property is.'[18] This broader use of the term fits more comfortably with the notion of suburb.

Suburb, quarter or neighbourhood are all valid words to describe St John's Wood, the first planned suburb in the western world but also the very first garden quarter.[19]

FROM 'COTTAGE INDUSTRY' TO LARGE-SCALE DEVELOPMENT

George Spencer Smith, who created the Swiss Cottage Tavern and developed the triangular plot of land around it, was a friend of Walpole. In 1845, after the tavern had been in existence for just under ten years, Walpole urged Smith to develop the rest of the plot as had been envisaged from the start. When he sought clarification of Smith's development methods, he spelt out the two principal methods

71 'Topographical Survey of the Borough of St Marylebone … and Plans & elevations of the Public Buildings, 25 June 1834, F. A. Bartlett under the direction of J. Britton'. The borough comprises the parishes of Paddington (left), Marylebone (centre) and St Pancras (right). Each parish is made up of rural fields and dense urban fabric, but in different proportions. St Marylebone, though not the largest, is by far the most developed, offering within the same administrative unit the striking contrast of urban and 'airy' living. Published by the London Topographical Society, copy at Eyre estate archive (EE 2652/5).

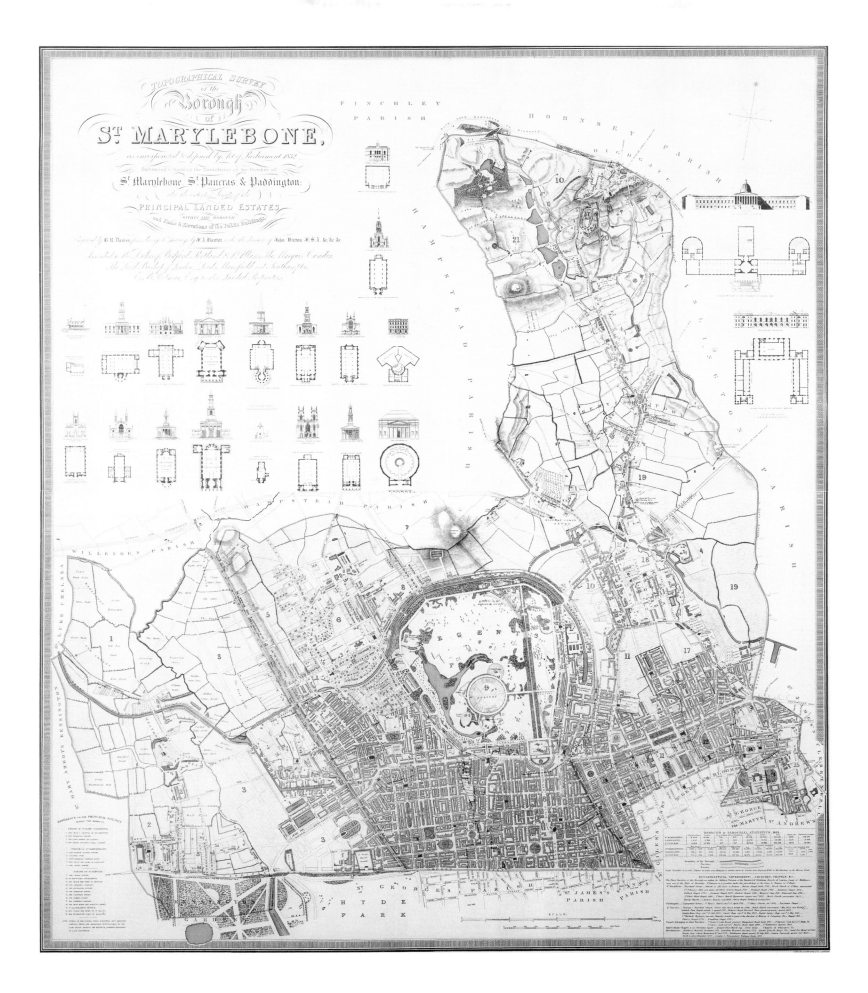

TOPOGRAPHICAL SURVEY
of the
Borough
of
ST MARYLEBONE,
as incorporated & defined by Act of Parliament 1832
Embracing & Marking the Boundaries of the Parishes of
St Marylebone, St Pancras & Paddington:
Also the entire Extent of the
PRINCIPAL LANDED ESTATES
WITHIN THE BOROUGH
and Plans & Elevations of the Public Buildings.

FINCHLEY
PARISH

HORNSEY PARISH

HAMPSTEAD PARISH

HIGHGATE

ISLINGTON PARISH

WILLESDEN PARISH

HAMPSTEAD PARISH

St LUKE CHELSEA

St MARY ABBOT'S KENSINGTON

REGENT'S PARK

HYDE PARK

St GEORGES PARISH

St JAMES'S PARISH

St ANNS PARISH

St GEORGE
THE MARTYR

St ANDREWS

SCALE.

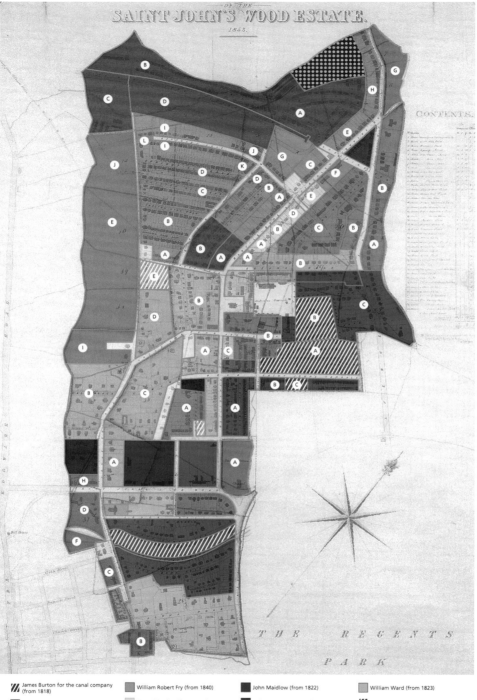

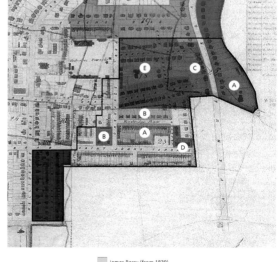

72 The St John's Wood estate: a developers' map (see Plate 70 for base map used). This map shows most of the agreements Walpole Eyre granted to developers. Some developers barely lasted a few months before going bankrupt, others withdrew just before disaster struck (e.g. publican John White), while others ploughed their course reliably and effectively (e.g. William Holme Twentyman). There were also those who at first did not succeed but then tried and tried again, e.g. Robert William Fry. Appendix 2 on p. 450 gives a breakdown of these agreements, which were often negotiated in different stages: 'A' being the earliest, followed by 'B', 'C', etc. The key indicates the starting date for each developer. Eyre estate (artwork by Damon Richardson, 2008 and 2010).

James Burton for the canal company (from 1818)

Canal company (from 1813)

Charles Claudius Cook (from 1839)

Edward Davies (from 1851)

Charles Day (from 1824)

Samuel Erlam (from 1852)

Walpole Eyre (from 1804)

Charles Freeth junior (from 1840)

William Robert Fry (from 1840)

Samuel Gardner (from 1823)

William Hall (from 1814)

John Hinton & John White (from 1823)

Thomas Johnson (from 1825)

Lewis Jones (from 1838)

The Leigh brothers (from 1838)

Thomas Lord (from 1813)

John Maidlow (from 1822)

Ophan Clergy Society (from 1810)

Pink & Erlam (from 1835)

James Salter (from 1839)

James Sharp (from 1846)

George Spencer Smith (from 1841)

John Wright Treeby (from 1840)

William Holme Twentyman (from 1839)

William Ward (from 1823)

The Watkins brothers (from 1824)

John White (victualler) & Robert Clavering Savage (1829 & 1833)

William Woolcott (from 1819)

Robert Yeo (from 1851)

Sales

James Berry (from 1839)

Charles Freeth junior (from 1840)

William Robert Fry (from 1831)

Pink & Erlam (from 1837)

John Wright Treeby (from 1840)

William Holme Twentyman (from 1839)

John White (victualler) (from 1827)

available to him: 'do you mean to let it in separate lots or altogether[?] the former I should recommend as the most profitable but will give you much additional trouble.'[20] Walpole knew all about the 'additional trouble', as it had been the method he adopted when he first started developing the estate at Alpha Cottages.

However, things had moved on since that time. The agreement with the canal company had meant that a single developer, in this case the canal company, would ensure the payment of the ground rent over a large area of land. The canal company was responsible for building the canal and for lining its banks with houses, a task which was delegated to James Burton. The method carried risks as the failure of one large-scale developer meant vast tracks of land could remain in limbo. But Walpole had endured the pettiness of mind and smallness of means of the small-scale developer for long enough, and was ready to switch to a more pain-free method of development. Between July 1813 – the date of the agreement with the canal company – and 1820, he had entered into no fewer than eight separate agreements, some covering very large areas such as Lord's and the land taken by William Hall (see Appendix 2 and Plate 72).

There were casualties, but this method of development prevailed and indeed accounted for most of the St John's Wood estate. At times the situation was more complex as various agreements could not be completed because of bankruptcy or death or for other reasons: for instance, the land allocated to Gardner on the west side of Wellington Road (bankruptcy) or the land allocated to Leigh north of Marlborough Road (death). The bankruptcy of John Maidlow must have been somewhat spectacular, as he had taken a vast number of acres through a series of separate agreements. As the area covered played a critical part in the history of the estate, a second map shows what happened to the land which had once been on agreement to Maidlow (Appendix 2 and Plate 73).

73 Detail of developers' map. John Maidlow signed several agreements with Walpole before going bankrupt in 1826. The black outline shows the extent of the land he took under agreement. This neighbourhood may be regarded as an 'architectural nursery' for the rest of the estate, and this specially commissioned map shows how the land was redeveloped following Maidlow's disappearance from the scene. Eyre estate (artwork by Damon Richardson, 2008 and 2010).

The developers were responsible for delivering the roads, sewers (partly funded by the estate) and of course the houses, whether they built them or contracted others to do so. Often the developer's role was that of grand co-ordinator – liaising with the estate, raising funds and finding buyers for the houses. The job of putting up the houses could be delegated to smaller scale builders, as was the case with the remarkable Alhambra Cottage, built by the sculptor Henry Sibson, who had taken a plot not from the Eyre estate but from one of its developers, Charles Claudius Cook (Plate 72, also see p. 419). The developers would, of course, make sure they had in hand a certain number of leases to guarantee themselves a steady flow of income. Peppercorn leases were the most desirable. They incurred no ground rent and were only issued when enough leases had been granted to cover the ground rent to the estate stipulated by the agreement. For instance, when James Burton had built and sold enough houses to cover the full amount of ground rent at £1,035 to be paid annually to the estate, he was granted a single peppercorn lease in 1823 for the remaining properties (see Plate 74). This method has been described as 'bad management' as it was assumed the peppercorn houses 'might tend to get lost to sight'.[21] A procedure of rigorous control was followed when issuing all leases, whether they were peppercorn or not, but as part of Burton's ground did later encounter problems (see p. 202), there may be some truth in this comment.[22]

Many of the St John's Wood lessees were, of course, developers, and to a large extent they determined the overall character of the development they had in hand. The contrast between those of Treeby and Fry is particularly tangible on the ground (Plate 260). The terraced houses in Treeby's development were subcontracted to Jacob Hibberd. They are classical, tasteful, elegant and on a

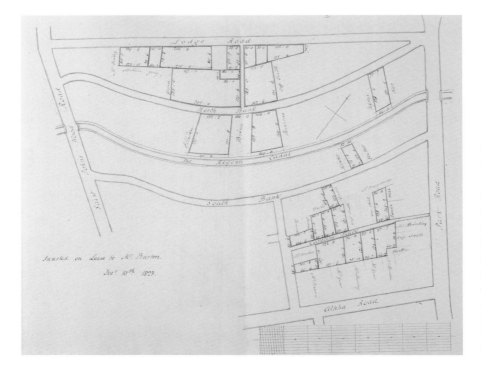

74 Drawing prepared for the peppercorn lease dated 24 December 1823 to James Burton showing all the properties he had in hand south of St John's Wood Road at the end of his contract with the canal company. Provided the properties could be let, he would have collected the rents, and these would have amounted to a substantial sum. Eyre estate archive (the lease has survived at EE 2651/297, but is in a poor condition so we are reproducing Bk of Drawings II, 12, with an earlier date than the lease).

scale which harmonises rather than clashes with the surrounding villas. It was also Hibberd who took over Erlam's agreement in the 1850s and built more elegant 'close houses' in St Ann's Terrace. His style is distinctive, invitingly attractive, quite different from James Sharp's terraces in Queen's Terrace, which have a sturdier, more monumental and also more austere appearance.

Prior to his bankruptcy in 1835, William Robert Fry was building 'novel' houses in and around Norfolk Road, creating clusters of charmingly exotic residences set in good-sized gardens. After recovering from his bankruptcy, Fry took more land under agreement from the Eyres east of Abbey Road, and was joined by his son George William. The two builders continued to construct rows of classical villas punctuated at crossroads by 'Gothic' villas in the way that they had in Norfolk Road, but the style became simplified and the repetitive output meant a more mechanical result. The plots also shrank, reducing the size of gardens, and the houses became so closely packed together as to give the illusion of terraces. Whether this change of approach was the outcome of the new partnership or whether William Robert senior was determined to be more ruthless after the earlier setback of his bankruptcy is uncertain. Although the architectural formula was the same as in Norfolk Road, the overall appearance of Blenheim Road and the parallel roads north of it is decidedly different.

Robert Yeo also cut his teeth as a developer working for Freeth and Fry in and around Acacia Road. When he 'emigrated' to the northern parts of the estate, taking on the difficult site of Belsize Road beyond the unsightly railway line, his terraced houses closed the estate in a most attractive way. The decorative vocabulary used to articulate the façades of the houses was elaborate, and may now seem even more so when compared, for instance, to the way in which John Maidlow closed the estate at St John's Wood Terrace. The twenty or so year gap between the two developments will account for certain stylistic differences, but nevertheless Yeo appeared to have created a richer formula than the Frys.

VILLAS VERSUS COTTAGES: ANTIDOTE TO A DEPRESSED MARKET?

In 1826, William Baker had built and leased two houses, one called Box Villa, the other Box Cottage (Plates 75 and 76). They stood side by side in Marlborough Road, and Baker finally found a tenant in 1829.[23] We saw in Chapter 2 how the early concept for the estate was that of a community of cottages, not of villas, as the houses in St John's Wood would later be labelled. William Baker's houses appear to provide an ideal example of the switch from one idea to the other.

At first sight the differences between the two houses seem insignificant, and if anything their distinctive features add to the confusion of their status. For instance, the grander classical porch does not belong to the 'villa' but to the 'cottage'. Instead, the villa displays ironwork on the ground-floor windows. The cottage's lack of a basement is made up by two low side wings, but otherwise the plans of these buildings are very similar. The plot of Box Villa is wider but that of Box Cottage longer. Perhaps the significant distinctive sign is the dormer window, more forcefully implying the presence of servants in the house, always a mark of higher status. If we now turn to the somewhat later building agreement between Walpole Eyre and Charles Claudius Cook (1844), it gives a further clue about the early Victorian distinction between 'villas' and 'cottages'. Cook signed up to build 'twenty six cottages within six years … either detached cottages or villa residences or attached

75 and **76** An 1829 letter from Walpole to the lessee William Baker confirms that these two houses were Box Villa (left, August 1825) and Box Cottage (right, October 1826), built side by side by Baker on the south side of Marlborough Road on the site now occupied by the American School in London. Eyre estate archive (Bk of Drawings II, 95, for Box Villa and III, 5, for Box Cottage).

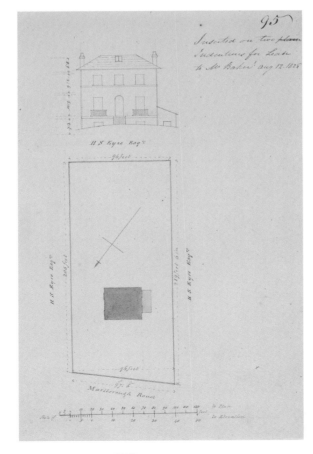
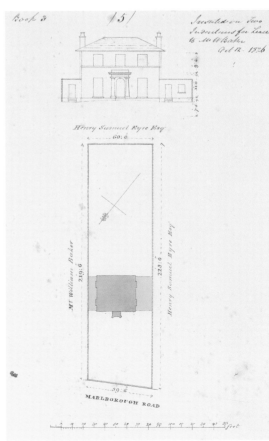

cottages or villa residences', implying a notion of permanence in the villas since they were 'residences', while cottages were likely to be understood as additional to the main place of residence and perhaps of simpler construction.[24]

The Eyre archive offers another example of the transformation of a 'cottage' into a 'villa'. In 1830, David Griffith, 'Gentleman', purchased the lease of a cottage at 12 Circus Road which, at his death, would be demolished and rebuilt as 'Franks Villa'.[25] In his will, proved on 24 June 1836, the lessee bequeathed 'to my Niece Mary Perfitt my cottage and furniture in Circus Road together with the dwelling house being No 21 in East Street Manchester Square for her and her husbands natural Life and afterwards for their children'. Here the arrangement is clear: a main residence in the West End and a 'country cottage' in St John's Wood where the lessee may very well have retired (Plate 77).[26] The transformation from cottage to villa was achieved by his niece and her husband Samuel Perfitt, hat maker of King's Cross, and thus described by Walpole in a letter to the estate's architect Shaw: 'In the year 1830 a plan was taken by you … for Lease to Mr David Griffiths of house [sic] on the North West side of Circus Road nearly opposite Elm Tree Road – his house being small and inconvenient has been taken down and a larger house built in its stead – I have to request that you will now take the plan of the new house for Mr Samuel Perfitt who has mentioned to the Tenant your intention to call for that purpose.'[27] 'Franks Villa', as the new house is described in the 'Consent to take down 12 Circus Road and building another house instead thereof',[28] had thus become the residence of a 'Tenant'.

The evolution of a cottage into a villa was not achieved overnight. It seems clear from the letter books that the 'villa' idea did not come from the Eyre office. Builder-developer Treeby's Devonshire Villa and his nearby Elizabethan Villa were frequently described as 'cottages' in letters sent from Walpole's office, and it is tempting to imagine Treeby and others having, time and time again, to correct the terminology with the office clerks of Bryanston Square.[29] At some point in the late 1820s, the builders and developers must have realised the word 'villa' was more fashionable, and therefore more saleable, than that of 'cottage', a concept perhaps deployed as an antidote to the desperately depressed building market at that time. By 1830 it would also have been clear that the original idea of harassed town dwellers in search of peace and tranquillity on the doorstep of the capital did not entirely reflect what was happening in St John's Wood, as many tenants lived there all year round.

At this point it is worth revisiting the early and subsequent use of the word 'villa'. We saw in Chapter 2 (p. 80) that the two early references noted for the years 1806 and 1812 were not only rare but unrepresentative of the favoured concept of a neighbourhood of cottages. However, from 1829 the word 'villa' makes another and more confident appearance, first with William Baker's Box Villa, mentioned above. The following year, Walpole announced he was ready to treat with Mr Bland 'for the sale of Freehold Ground on the West side of the Abbey Road for the p[ur]p[o]se of erecting detached *Villas*' (my italics); the deal came to nothing, perhaps because building development was now in difficulty.[30] In the late 1830s, with the building market fully recovered, the villa returned to resume a meteoric course. 'Riches Villa' had been leased to Jonathan Riches in 1837 but made its appearance as a named villa in 1839, followed a year later by William Holme Twentyman's building programme composed entirely of villas, starting with the 'Regents Villas' which lined the east side of the Marylebone and Finchley Turnpike Branch Road, now known as Avenue Road.

77 This cottage was leased to David Griffith in 1830 (EE 2650/1/452). In 1847, Walpole gave his consent for the house to be demolished and replaced by a larger house called 'Franks Villa'. No picture of it appears to have survived, but Walpole described the replacement as 'a larger house'. Eyre estate archive (Bk of Drawings III, 59).

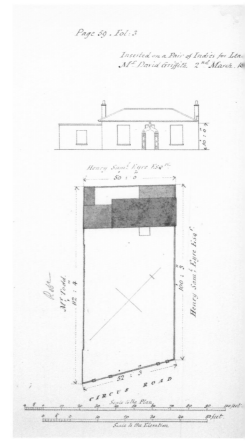

Right: **78** Charles Claudius Cook, a house painter and glazier, was responsible for the first 'Italian Villa' in St John's Wood (LB 'P', p. 256), which was leased to him in 1840. Eyre estate archive (Bk of Drawings IV, 52 right).

Far right: **79** John Wright Treeby's 'Gothic Villa', soon relabelled 'Elizabethan Villa', is taken from the lease drawing dated November 1844. It became Treeby's residence. There was a large pond in the garden which must have been regarded as a special feature. Eyre estate archive (Bk of Drawings V, 23 right).

80 Watercolour of All Saints Lodge in Wellington Road, the villa built for Reverend Edward Thompson, who masterminded the building of All Saints Church (Plate 194) as well as the controversial school next to this villa (Plate 269). The architectural vocabulary is truly eclectic, the overall baronial appearance of this mansion 'contradicting' the classical porch which faced the 'Gothic' All Saints Church. The architect of 'Gothic Villa', as it was originally known, was Thomas Little, who was also in charge of the church. Westminster City Archives (Ashbridge collection, outsize box 849).

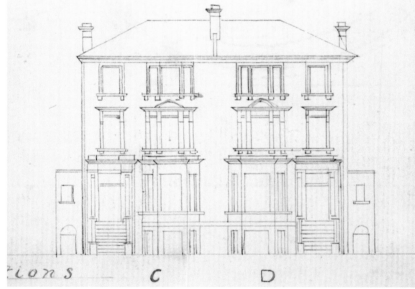

81 The endurance of the house model created by Todd was remarkable (see Plate 58). The three designs built over a period of seventy-odd years and the late twentieth-century Servite houses in Grove End Road demonstrate a lasting attachment to Todd's simple winning formula, which would later, somewhat misleadingly, be described as 'Italianate': (top left) 1831 lease to George Howell of house in Grove End Road (Bk of Drawings II, 121); (top right) 1851 lease to William Coney of a house in Belsize Road (Bk of Drawings V, 97 left); (above) 1869 lease for several houses in Alexandra Road (Bk of Drawings VII, 263). Eyre estate archive. Photo: the author

87 This country lane, inscribed 'Alpha Cott.' and signed John Linnell, 1814, seems too narrow to depict Alpha Road, which ran east to west at the southern end of the estate. This is more likely to show the future Alpha Place, which until 1813 led to Lord's second cricket ground. Martyn Gregory, London.

88 Reconstruction of the garden of James Tissot at 17, then 34 (now 44) Grove End Road. The numbers show the viewpoints adopted for some of Tissot's paintings, i.e.
1 *Croquet* (see Plate 89);
2 *In Full Sun*;
3 *In the Conservatory* (Plate 151);
4 *The Garden Bench*;
5 *La Soeur Ainee.*
Eyre estate (drawing by Stephen Conlin, 2009).

'The extent of the Gardens of the two Cottages is more than three quarters of an acre; the largest part of it belonging to Digamma Cottage is divided into four parts: Front Garden; Flower Garden; Kitchen Garden, and pleasure grounds; and planted with the choicest fruit and ornamental trees, and flowering shrubs of every kind, some of which are very rare.'[55]

Sadly, no pictures exist of Foscolo's enticing garden, although some of the best records of St John's Wood gardens come from the painter's brush. In the first half of the nineteenth century, artistic endeavours had tended to focus on the predominant 'landscape' element of this neighbourhood (see Plates 86 and 87 for Linnell and Plate 41 for Gouldsmith).[56] However, in the second half of the century, the dwindling countryside no longer offered interesting possibilities, and so the gardens, by now established, provided attractive subjects for artists living or working in St John's Wood.

One such garden, at 17 Grove End Road (now 44), is exceptionally well documented for the 1870s. Its creator was the French painter James Tissot, who produced no fewer than thirty pictures – paintings and etchings – of his garden and conservatory between 1873 and 1882 when he was living there. The house is now best remembered for the extravagance of his more famous successor, another painter, Lawrence Alma-Tadema (see Plate 166). However, Tissot's pictures conjure up an

89 James Tissot's *Croquet* dates from around 1878 and shows how spacious the gardens on land developed by William Hall really were. The pool and colonnade inspired by those in the Parc Monceau in Paris gave appealing focus to the garden. Art Gallery of Hamilton, Canada.

image of the happy garden life which a house in St John's Wood could offer. Most of them focused on the artist's beloved mistress, Mrs Kathleen Newton, and her two children as well as the friends or family who gathered around them on sunny afternoons. These paintings coupled with maps and plans of the period have enabled the reconstruction of Tissot's garden (Plate 88), which displayed several French features including the colonnade, based on that of the Parc Monceau in Paris (Plates 68 and 89), while the conservatory (Plate 151) was conceived along French lines judging by William Robinson's lament: 'We build more glass houses than any other nation but have as yet nearly everything to learn.... Abroad they are gracefully verdant at all times, being filled with handsome exotic evergreens and arranged so as to present the appearance of a mass of luxuriant vegetation, and not that of a glass shed filled with pots and prettiness with which we are all familiar.'[57]

So besotted were residents with their gardens that they drove builders to devise and erect special architectural features to indulge their enthusiasm. As early as 1826 Alexander Birnie, an early Alpha Road resident, obtained permission to create bay windows, Walpole solemnly writing: 'I hereby … authorize & empower you to throw out a Bow on the East & South sides of your house No 36 Alpha road.'[58] Conservatories would also become a popular feature on the estate. The abolition of the tax on glass in 1845 made conservatories more affordable, but they had been enjoyed on the St John's Wood estate long before that date. They are first mentioned in the letter books in 1819: 'Mr Kerr has taken a bit more land adjoining which should be added to the Plans[;] he has also built a Green or Conservatory which sho[u]ld be put upon the Plan,' wrote Walpole to John Shaw.[59] This excerpt is interesting because it also shows that the lessee had opted to increase the size of his garden, a device a number of other lessees also adopted.

Every garden would have had to fulfil not only an ornamental role but a functional one as well. The letter books make clear that Walpole's domestic arrangements in the West End did not include access to a functional garden, but he was in the fortunate position of being able to take land at St John's Wood, employing a gardener to cultivate fruit and vegetables for the needs of the family.[60] Some of the gardens in St John's Wood still contain old varieties of Victorian pear which do not ripen on the tree but do so if placed indoors – a type of fruit which was largely superseded with the introduction of the Williams pear and other tree ripening varieties.[61] There are unusually detailed data about Mrs Kipps's 'Seed an[d] Fruit Room' at 17 Grove End Road, the future Alma-Tadema house. Many houses would have had such a room, but the spotlight shone on this one because a complaint was made by the Kelk family from Circus Road, whose property backed onto Mrs Kipps's house. The latter's first lessee in 1825 was Thomas George Kipps, a coachmaker from Great Marylebone Street. By 1841 when the complaint was made, Mr Kipps had died and Mrs Kipps was in charge: 'The Windows you complained of she [Mrs Kipps] says will be close barred on the outside so that no person can look out of it & the room is only intended as a Seed an[d] fruit Room & that she intends keeping the Key in her own poss[essi]on.'[62]

The painter Frederick Goodall, who moved to 62 Avenue Road in the mid-1870s (see Plate 170), provides a good example of the utter devotion some people had to their gardens. He recorded doing gardening from five o'clock in the morning, clarifying later: 'My first and foremost recreation was gardening and the cultivation of flowers.... In due time I became known among my brethren as "the artist gardener".... Afterwards I became a member of the Royal Botanical Society.'[63]

90 and **91** These are rare photographs of a St John's Wood house and garden in the 1860s.

The house, which no longer exists, was Kent Villa at 83 Finchley Road, east side, more or less on the site of Sherlock Court, Boundary estate. It was originally leased to William Wartnaby in 1843 (Bk of Drawings, 76 left). By the time these photographs were taken, it was in the ownership of Frederick Allen, a silk mercer in the 1871 Census. The crosses on the photographs helped identify the members of the household.

The topography of the garden recalls the well-illustrated garden of the Butters family in Hackney at around the same time (see *Country Life*, 6 September 1990). Fortunately, these photographs have been partially captioned, and so we know that the onlooker in the view from the street is an 'old nurse' while the sitter in the middle ground of the garden is Mrs J. S. Allen. In the garden the cage at the front is home to love birds and the white cage to its right to chickens. Camden Local Studies.

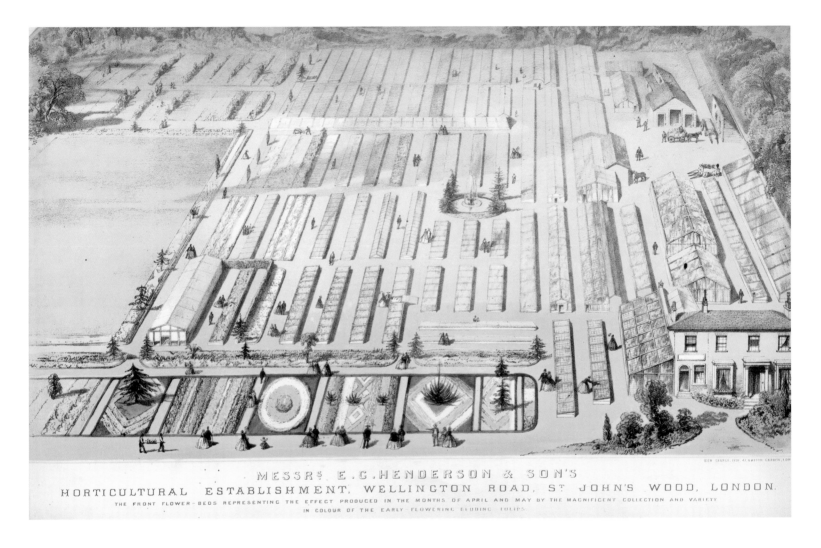

MESSRS. E.G.HENDERSON & SON'S
HORTICULTURAL ESTABLISHMENT, WELLINGTON ROAD, ST JOHN'S WOOD, LONDON.
THE FRONT FLOWER-BEDS REPRESENTING THE EFFECT PRODUCED IN THE MONTHS OF APRIL AND MAY BY THE MAGNIFICENT COLLECTION AND VARIETY
IN COLOUR OF THE EARLY-FLOWERING BEDDING TULIPS.

92 Ben George's lithograph of Henderson's Nursery in Wellington Road around 1857. Edward George Henderson took over John Gibbs's Wellington Nursery. Gibbs had operated on various sites on the estate since at least 1817. This particular site was acquired by Lord's in 1887 and is still today known as the 'Nursery End'. Westminster City Archives.

Commercial gardening

St John's Wood was a favoured site for nurseries from the early years of the nineteenth century. Had perhaps Walpole's early endeavours with planting a field of potatoes encouraged commercial gardeners to consider St John's Wood as a suitable site? He recorded in his letter book for 1805: 'I have planted between two & three acres of potatoes & which I hope will turn to good account, it was necessary to dig the Ground for the purpose of levelling it, as it was full of holes & had a very shabby & nasty appearance, & as you know I am a bit of a farmer it occur[r]ed to me that while I was digging for appearance I might as well put in a few potatoes & turn the Ground to some advantage & I hope that it will more than repay the expences.'[64]

The Eyre brothers used the services of the well-known nurseryman Thomas Jenkins (d.1832) as an early plant and tree adviser on the estate. His nursery was sited immediately south of the St John's Wood estate, on the east side of Lisson Grove.[65] In 1809, he was summoned to a meeting held at St John's Wood, as Walpole and John Shaw wanted 'to see him about some planting'.[66] A year later his name featured in Walpole's bill book, 'The Nurseryman to St John's Wood', Walpole having consulted him about 'the Injury done by Mr Davis to the Trees in the avenue by lopping them'. Jenkins's advice had been 'to plant a Tree between each of the trees in the Avenue in order to fill the space made by the lopping and to fence in the same that they might not be injured by Cattle'.[67] The relationship must have been close and trusting, as one of Walpole's relatives, Miss Harriott Hodges from Bath, lent money to Jenkins in return for a £60 annuity which Jenkins seems to have paid without fail.[68]

The Eyre archive records the presence of a number of nurseries on the estate, though John Gibbs's was arguably the most important. In 1817, he took land immediately north of the Orphan Clergy ground.[69] Gibbs subsequently expanded his empire moving into the north-east end of the Orphan Clergy ground (1826), which became the famous Wellington Nursery (Plate 92). Gardener Eli Cook took over Gibbs's original ground in 1831, while Gibbs moved to what is now the junction of Queen's Grove and Wellington Road. Eli Cook seems to have been suffering from chronic rent arrears, and so building development gradually ate all the land he had taken under agreement.[70] Gibbs's ground further north was also shrinking until it totally disappeared. Less prominent enterprises included James Gulley, who set up his nursery in 1818 at what would become Garden Road. He was succeeded by Mr Hogg (his wife took over the business when her husband died). After the collapse of John Maidlow's agreements (see Plate 73), the eastern section of Queen's Grove was occupied by a nursery run by Messrs Townsend and Kendall, florists from Wellington Road, between 1832 and 1842.[71]

These nurseries seem to have been largely utilitarian. When there was a change of lessee, plants sometimes had to be removed by the leaving party or purchased by the arriving party, and so we know for instance that Cook was growing cauliflowers, cabbages, peas, strawberries and fruit trees.[72] By the early 1840s such nurseries were disappearing, and a new type of nursery, geared to servicing the growing passion for gardening and ornamental planting, entered the scene.

Henderson's Pineapple Nursery in Maida Vale was one of the great Victorian nurseries, and they opened a branch in St John's Wood when they acquired Gibbs's Wellington Nursery in 1844.[73] Some information is found in one of the Eyre licence books: 'I hereby consent to the contemplated New erection on the premises leased by the Orphan Clergy Society to Mr Edw[ar]d George Henderson provided such Erection be built in accordance with the Plan & Specification submitted to me by Mr Philip Hardwick as Architect for the Orphan Clergy Society.'[74] Presumably the house is that shown in the 1850s lithograph (Plate 92), and the nursery was described in *The Gardeners' Chronicle* of 17 May 1856:

> a kind of winter garden has been made here by removing the partition between two houses, and thus throwing them into one, taking away the stage,[75] and arranging the plants in groups on the floor, which is traversed by a 3 feet wide gravel walk that winds in a zig-zag manner from one end of the house to the other.... In the centre is a small aquarium surrounded by a little rock-work, on which are placed numbers of the pretty Grass-like Isolepis gracilis, the bright green foliage of which falling down towards the surface of the water has a very good effect.... The above arrangement has had many admirers, and may be taken as a fair example of what may be done in this way even in common lean-to houses.

Henderson's branch in St John's Wood was deemed important enough to be regularly reviewed in *The Gardeners' Chronicle* alongside its Maida Vale premises. Other Wellington Road notices mentioned 'the Geranium-house', 'galvanised iron-wire baskets' suspended from the roof, and 'variegated plants, of which there are great numbers here'.[76]

The success of the St John's Wood's villas was such that the size of gardens steadily decreased over the first fifty years of development. They had started out very large at Alpha Cottages, but William Hall was the last developer to maintain their generous size. James Burton's canal houses must have shown that smaller houses with smaller gardens offered an acceptable and equally lucrative alternative. The gardens on Maidlow's ground assumed much more modest proportions, and by the time Messrs Fry and the Yeos developed east of Abbey Road and the northern region, gardens had shrunk further still.

These casualties were not limited to the diminishing size of villa grounds. Nursery and public gardens disappeared before the 1853 map of the estate was drawn. The Eyre Arms' famous pleasure ground was built over (see chronology on p. 208) and Marlborough Hill Gardens, which acquired its name from the ornamental plantations it boasted on the east side, became Marlborough Hill when these were sacrificed to more villa building.[77]

THE LOSS OF COUNTRYSIDE

Though the concept of *rus in urbe* was so deliberately pursued by the Eyre brothers, the building of St John's Wood still amounted to systematic loss of countryside. Some of the urban/rural battles which ensued, particularly those involving animals, may now seem trivial and even comic. For instance, in 1813, Walpole wrote a peremptory letter to the Clergy Orphan Society School: 'I understand your Cow & Horse are constantly turned upon the Roads at St John's Wood to feed[.] they do so much mischief to the footpaths &c.… I have therefore to request you will not again turn them upon any of the roads & if you do they will certainly be put into the pound.'[78] In 1827, Walpole wrote to the landlord of the Eyre Arms, John Hinton: 'I have frequently desired that you w[oul]d not allow y[ou]r fowls to be running about the yard & field lately occupied by Col[onel] Cooper [i.e. St John's Wood House] I will thank you to confine them to y[ou]r own prem[is]es as they destroy the grass & y[ou]r boy is constantly getting over the fence to feed them.'[79] Rabbits, too, formed the object of a complaint (see p. 455), and in 1833 Walpole described a field 'crowded with Donkies and horses', though the absolute scourge for a neighbourhood which attempted to become respectable was without doubt the presence of pigs (see pp. 209 [Eyre Arms] and 400 [Ordnance Mews]).

The letter books also provide evidence of the rural character of the land prior to its development, which called for rural management and activities. Todd, the estate's pre-eminent builder, was requested on 6 November 1820 'to have all the perch put <u>into the pond by the Hay Rick at St Johns Wood</u> the pond alluded to is the large one nearest the farm buildings adjoining the Land and not the one some distance in the Field' (see Plate 41). To Walpole, control was an essential requisite, and he had little patience with tenants who showed too little of it; even his friend Robert Todd would be chastised in 1822: 'Your galloping Cow has been twice into my Garden lately and ate up and destroyed a considerable quantity of my winter stock I wish you wo[ul]d either sell her or enclose the ground in such a way as to keep her in the field.'[80]

FARMS' CHRONOLOGY

(See p. 523 for key to references.)

1796   Agreement for lease (to start Michaelmas) between Thomas Willan and Spurrier & Phipps (on behalf of H. S. Eyre) for lands at St John's Wood at EE 2651/172E(A).
St John's Wood Farm itself is let to William Kightley (Knightley?), who dies the following year. His executrix gives up the farm soon after (LMA, MJ/SP/1799/02/036).

1800   John Abbott takes over the farm around this time.

1806   Willan takes over St John's Wood Farm previously in the hands of Abbott (71 acres) (LB 'B', p. 520).

1811   (Winter) Willan takes over Captain Simpson's Punkers or Red Barn (LB 'B', pp. 520 and 571). The spelling 'Punkers Barn', found on Rocque's 1754 map of Middlesex (Plate 31), has been adopted here. By the early nineteenth century the name Red Barn was more prevalent (see Plate 54).

1813   The architect William Atkinson takes over the Red Barn (LB 'C', p. 274).

1819   Willan renews the lease of St John's Wood Farm for fourteen years (EE 2651/236(A), starting 1817).

1824   William Atkinson's lease of Red Barn is renewed and the freehold sold to John Smith of Nottingham Terrace, who becomes Atkinson's landlord (LB 'I', p. 129).
Temporary falling out between Walpole and Willan over the renewal of the Barracks' lease: Willan refuses to be party to the new lease (WCA, 765/3).

1825   (June) Major John Margerum Close from Somerset Farm in Kilburn enters into negotiations with Walpole about a lease of the Homestead for the Great Westminster Dairy Company (LB 'I', p. 466). Willan assigns St John's Wood Farm to Major Close, James Henry Deacon and John Stewart, all directors of the dairy company at EE 2651/236(B).

1826   The Westminster Dairy Company runs into difficulty (LB 'K', p. 55), and William Wilberforce (eldest son of the anti-slavery campaigner, Plate 93) offers to take over the lease if the 1825 assignment could be cancelled (LB 'K', pp. 32–33). The lease did not materialise until 1831.

1828   Death of Thomas Willan (Brown, 2001, p. 4).

1830   Wilberforce interested in building houses on the farm site (LB 'M', p. 14). Finchley Road had just been finished and his brother Robert pointed out: 'St John's Wood, which is the worst part of the business, will clearly become more desirable when there is a road by it'.[81]

1831   Wilberforce brings in Richard Spooner (his uncle), then Mr Rickman of the West London Dairy (various letters throughout LB 'M'), to administer the farm (Major Close having been dropped: he owed Todd £1,400) and disappears abroad (Geneva).

1832   Spooner gives notice that Wilberforce does not wish to continue with the lease after Michaelmas 1832 (LB 'M', p. 488). Walpole orders 'four Boards to denote that the Land is to be let for Building purposes' (LB 'M', p. 536). Cleeves (sometimes spelt Cleaves) and Cottam show an interest in the farm.

93 Photographic portrait by John and Charles Watkins of William Wilberforce junior (c.1798–1879), the eldest son of the abolitionist. He succeeded Thomas Willan at St John's Wood Farm, and this led to devastating financial losses. As a result he was forced to flee abroad where he lived between 1831 and 1834, writing in 1833: 'About St John's Wood, I am extremely anxious to be freed from the responsibility, a responsibility so great that I dare not return till by some arrangement I am freed from the danger of a bill in Chancery which Eyre (who has behaved to me like a rogue) would certainly file against me did he know of my return to England' (see note 81). Hulton Archive/Getty Images.

He therefore revisited the terms of the lease, wanting fourteen rather than seven years, also expressing concern about the Eyres' power to take the land away without any notice:

> I communicated your wish to my brother of having from ten to fifteen Acres of land adjoining the buildings at St John's Wood which he should not be at liberty to take away during the Term of your new Lease[.] my brother desires me to say that he will always endeavour to consult your Convenience in taking away land, but that he cannot consent to preclude himself from taking it away as the general Improvements of the Estate may require it[.] if he were to be confined from taking away any ten or fifteen acres it might during your Term make a difference in his Income of from 300 to 400 a year.[89]

As the Eyre brothers refused to give way on many points, it was not entirely surprising that the tone of Willan's letters became that of a man utterly frustrated, as acknowledged by Walpole in the following letter:

> I cannot help lamenting that you have thought it right or necessary to express yourself in such strong and threat[en]ing language as you have done in your letter of 19th Inst. You talk of <u>resisting</u> my brothers claim to resume the Land for agricultural purposes and of <u>insisting</u> upon the power of resumption being confined to the Cases of Building or Selling – such language can only be replied to in the same tone, and I am therefore instructed by my brother to say, that he means to insist upon your taking a Lease of 14 years of the buildings and Lands with a power for my brother from time to time to take possess[io]n of the land or any part of it as he may think fit for any purpose whatever.

In the same letter it appears that Willan was also determined not to contribute a penny to the repair of the road leading to the farm, highlighting the impact of the building development on the life of a farm: 'you say you agree with me as to the state of the Lane, but differ with me as to the Causes, and you go on to say, that it appears to you that the brickmaking and Buildings erecting upon my brothers Estate have occasioned more injury to the Road than the use you have made of it for the last Seven years could possibly have done.'[90]

The relationship had reached breaking point but tempers eventually calmed down, and a new lease was granted for fourteen years from 1817, as per Willan's request.[91] Another concession the Eyre brothers had made was to enable Willan to carry on receiving the rent for the Barracks from the Ordnance. However, when in 1824 the Ordnance approached Walpole to negotiate a long-term lease with him, old wounds reopened. By that date Willan was happy to surrender his lease and live in retirement at his large home at Twyford Abbey near Ealing. A final outburst of correspondence between Walpole and Mr Law, Willan's solicitor, is instructive:

> Mr Willan must have forgotten that during our negotiation for the lease he now holds he expressly stated to me that his great object was to obtain a permanent Term in the build[in]gs in order that he might carry on his Cow keeping & seemed very indifferent about the land & indeed told me that he could bring fodder for his Cows to St Johns Wood cheaper than he could grow it there[.] Mr Willan must also have forgotten that he & I differed materially as to the value of the build[in]gs & that I proposed to treat separately with the board of Ordnance this he would not hear of.[92]

When a new lease was issued to the Ordnance dated 9 March 1824, the recital stated Willan had refused to be a party to it.[93]

Thomas Willan seems to have been the only man on record to have run St John's Wood Farm with ease (Plate 96). John Abbott before him had found it impossible to make the books balance and was in serious rent arrears, and so were the men who followed. The 'march of bricks and mortar' was made all the easier for it. The magic ingredient in Willan's winning recipe had undoubtedly been the Barracks.

Walpole described urban encroachments and the ensuing loss of countryside in lucid terms in 1845. Shaw junior, the estate's architect, must have asked his advice on the price of agricultural land around London, and the reply showed just how much times were changing:

> The last Agreement I made with Mr Biggs for letting him the Grass Land at St Johns Wood was in June 1844 & he then agreed to pay £4 per Acre per Annum but he has since complained that the Land is so Trespassed upon that he cannot afford to pay that sum.... another inconvenience to Mr Biggs is that I resume possession of the land for building at all times whenever I think fit without any previous Notice to him[.] the approaches to his ground are also very inconvenient except along the Turnpike Road and which ... [lengthen] the distance from his premises in the Edgware Road very considerably – I don't know how your land is situated but if it is not exposed to the above inconveniences I should ask at least £4 per acre for it[.]

> I am much inclined to think that the consumption of Hay in this great Town is much diminished within the last ten years & the facility of bringing that commodity to market is greatly increased and which together render the grass Lands in the immediate vicinity of London of less value[.]

> When there was scarcely any buildings North of the New Road I used to let the St Johns Wood Estate at £5.5 & £5.16.6 per acre but since the increase of buildings and the consequent decrease of Grass Land the Rent has been gradually reduced[.]

> It appears to me that there are not nearly so many horses kept in London as there were formerly[.] I allude particularly to this part of the Town and my reason for thinking so is that we have stables adjoining our house in Bryanston Square & for which I used to get £30 per annum but now cannot get more than £20.[94]

Then as now, the last refuge for wildlife could be found along the railway line. The last tenant for grass land at St John's Wood was the Gell family, initially Francis Gell, 'Cowkeeper', who ran a dairy at Blenheim Terrace off Abbey Road. He rented the railway slopes and the 'spoil bank', the result of cutting out the railway line.[95]

ENVIRONMENTAL CONTROL

The urbanisation of St John's Wood meant that more than ever the Eyres had to walk a very tight rope: to show too much inflexibility or too much leniency in the face of success could have had unpalatable consequences. To create the kind of neighbourhood they had in mind, the Eyres needed

96 This seductive aquatint by Robert Hills of cattle at Willan's Farm, St John's Wood, was published in 1825, the year that Thomas Willan ended his long association with the farm, assigning it to Major Close and two other directors of the Westminster Dairy Company. The basket on the left was probably filled with turnips. City of London, London Metropolitan Archives (M0028712CL).

to attract the respectable classes, and they in turn needed to be satisfied if they were to remain. In order to do this, the Eyres needed both quality of building and quality of environment. The success of St John's Wood depended as much upon the environment as it did upon the houses, and to fulfil the original promise of an area being 'singularly pleasant' and with a 'delightful view' (see p. 108), the Eyres needed to guard against many problems.

The image of the estate's first cab-stand, in Acacia Road (Plate 97), provides an excellent example of how attentive Walpole needed to be to ensure the quality of the environment. In 1852, he wrote to the Commissioner of Police to attempt to rectify what St John's Wood tenants had reported as being a problem:

> I have had representations made to me as proprietor of the St John's Wood Estate of the injurious effects upon property occasioned by the removal of a Cab stand from the Wall of the Eyre Arms Tavern to the centre of Acacia Rd next Wellington Road[.]
>
> I can have no doubt but that these representations are correct and I hope that you will be

pleased to cause the Cab stand to be removed to its former situation next the Blank Wall of the Eyre Arms Tavern or to some other situation where it may be less objectionable than it is at present.[96]

On this occasion Walpole's request must have been unsuccessful, as six months later we learn from a letter to Major Moore that the following drastic action had had to be taken:

I beg to say I have not heard of any intention to cut down any tree in Grove End Road [where the major lived] and no one has any power to cut down any tree with[ou]t the consent of the Freeholder – Some Trees have been recently cut down in Acacia Road at the request of some of the inhabitants and with the consent of Mr Eyre – as in consequence of the cab stand placed in that Road the Trees were used so as to become a Nuisance.[97]

Cab-drivers and enthusiastic drinkers at the nearby Eyre Arms were undoubtedly the culprits on this occasion. However, this is not an isolated case, and it would appear that despite St John's Wood's aura of respectability, certain members of the male population could not resist relieving themselves against walls or trees, as this earlier letter (1841) confirms: 'two of your neighbours … [have complained] of the great nuisance arising from the improper use of the wall at the end of Hall Place', wrote Walpole to William Scott, who lived at No. 3.[98]

Walpole had to fight many battles. He used his legal knowledge and expertise to keep a firm grip upon builders, and he also used mild – and probably necessary – blackmail to ensure he would

There was some tension between Walpole and Twentyman over the naming of St John's Wood Park, but in the end Twentyman's name prevailed. Walpole had objected to not calling a road a road.[120] St John's Wood Park is first mentioned in 1844, and its unusual layout was the brainchild of John Shaw junior.[121] The road formed a triangular plot which maximised the number of houses that could be built and also created an open space (at least initially) which, if it were to become a public garden, could partly justify the name 'Park' to which Twentyman seemed so attached.[122] The word evoked the 'villa parks' which developed all around the country in response to what was happening in St John's Wood and Regent's Park. Mark Girouard has shown the connection between the north-west London developments and these later 'villa parks', naming some of the first examples to be developed outside London: Calverley Park in Tunbridge Wells (1828), The Park in Cheltenham (1833), Prince's Park in Liverpool (1842), Birkenhead Park (1843) and People's Park in Halifax (1856). Girouard also pointed out that the 'concept of a park acquired so much prestige that "Park" began to occur in place-names even if there was no park'.[123] Twentyman's efforts in St John's Wood Park would certainly appear to fall in that category! This road, which was mostly sited in the parish of Hampstead, made history when the time came (in 1852) to hand it over to the parish, as Charles Freeth explained: 'And as we have never had occasion to apply to Hampstead Parish to take a Road I do not know the proper course to pursue with them.'[124]

The 'Manor House' which became Twentyman's main residence in 1853 dominated the street (Plate 100). It was a large detached house and had the largest garden in St John's Wood Park. Only one other house competed with Twentyman's for scale and lavishness: 28 St John's Wood Park, the largest house in the street (Plates 101–106). It was the residence of John Edmund Gardner, a 'Gentleman' with an address in the Strand, who obtained a lease from Twentyman in the summer of 1851.[125] Almost immediately Gardner applied for permission to erect a conservatory,[126] the remains of which are visible in the exterior view of the house reproduced left. Gardner purchased further strips of adjacent land, in 1854 and in 1857, to increase the size of his garden.[127] He resided there until his death in 1899, and during that time he amassed a formidable collection of prints, drawings and maps about London (see, for instance, Plate 52). The collection was kept in a room decorated in neo-Jacobean style. It was acquired by Major Sir Edward Coates, Bt, MP, in 1910 and then sold at auction in 1923. It was so extensive that the sale spread over five days.[128] Gardner's son, Edmund Thomas Gardner, continued to live at 28 St John's Wood Park, and the property was only surrendered back to the estate on 3 May 1930.

However, no amount of architectural decorum could save Mr Twentyman's houses in the twentieth century. In 1950, a journalist described their fate in depressingly graphic terms: 'The Street That Died – Ghosts with carnations in their button holes haunt silent drawing rooms carpeted with broken plaster.'[129] When the air raids started in 1940 most of the residents in St John's Wood Park left their houses, as the government had advised those who could to do so. Three of the houses were destroyed by a land mine, but 'it so happened that after the war these houses in St John's Wood Park had no owners, because the ninety-nine year leases had run out. The properties had reverted to the Eyre Estate.' The end of this strange story is narrated on page 366. The same fate awaited the school for the blind at Swiss Cottage, also on Twentyman's land: the pupils were evacuated to Dorton House during the war, never to return to their former home.

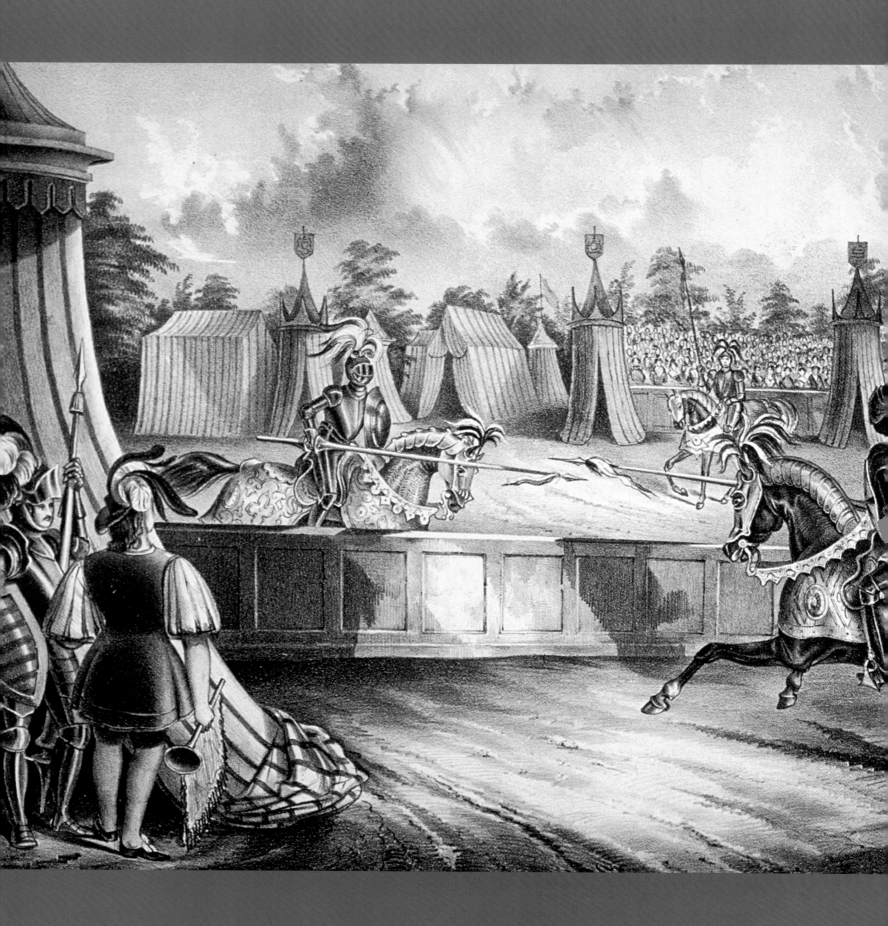

6

THE COMMUNITY AND ITS SERVICES

In the middle years of the nineteenth century the novelist and dramatist Edmund Yates (1831–94) lived at 12 Alpha Road, 'a very pretty place', where his mother had moved. His *Recollections* give us a good picture of the area's heyday and subsequent deterioration:

> The houses had large gardens, and the respectability of the locality was unimpeachable, my kind old friend, Mr Thomas Harrison, Commissioner of Inland Revenue, and the family of the late Mr Serjeant Bompas being our immediate neighbours. Our house was a cosy and comfortable one, and had nearly an acre of garden, which I need scarcely say has now been built over, but which then, despite the London 'smuts', produced a fair crop of flowers, and was always green and pleasant to look upon. The one drawback, so far as I was concerned, was the distance from the centre of London and from all places of amusement. There was a good omnibus service to the Post Office [where Yates worked], and the ride in the early morning was pleasant enough; but returning home from some festivity late at night, I constantly wished Fate had caused my mother to pitch her tent in some less remote district.[1]

12 Alpha Road is No. 10 on the Alpha Cottages reconstruction (Plate 63). It lost part of its garden in 1853 when John Palmer de la Fons (or Delafons) obtained permission to erect a studio at that address (see Plate 152).[2] The site was acquired by the estate clerk, Charles Freeth, around 1865 and a new estate office erected overlooking Alpha Road (No. 12B, later No. 3), further reducing the size of the garden. This is not an entirely atypical example of what happened to a number of properties in St John's Wood (see also Plate 178). The 'filling-in' of gardens is noticeable in the second half of the nineteenth century (see, for instance, Woronzow Road on p. 409), but the process gathered speed in the twentieth century.

By the mid-nineteenth century, the early tightly knit community of lessees along Alpha Road (see Chapter 3) had been succeeded by an increased and permanent population. As the estate developed, it became very difficult to keep track of lessees, underlessees, developers and other tenants. Letters from the estate office indicate there was plenty of room for confusion, and these are just a few examples in 1847 and 1851:

> In reply to your note of this date enquiring what Ground Rent is due for the 7th house north of Adelaide Road I beg to say I do not know by that description to what house you refer – If you will please to send me the date of Lease and the party to whom granted I will immediately send you the requested Information.[3]

> … your note wanting a duplicate receipt for gro[un]d rent stated to be paid by you for Woronzow Cottage…. I beg to say that we have not your name in the St John's Wood Estate Books & do not know which is Woronzow Cottage.[4]

> I am not able to answer questions as to houses by their numbers, but by the names of the Original Lessees & if you will inform me of that, and the purpose for which you require the information & that you are authorized to ask it, I will give it to you.[5]

The estate office would remain loyal to the system of lessees' names for many years, as it enabled them to control potentially sensitive information and its recipients; it was not until Christmas 1885

Previous pages: **107** This lithograph shows rehearsals for the famous Eglinton Tournament (held at the earl of Eglinton's seat in Scotland) in the grounds of the Eyre Arms Hotel. According to Montgomery Eyre: 'Every Tuesday and Saturday for some time before the event a distinguished company assembled there, and attempted with more or less success to emulate the skill and prowess of the mediaeval knights whose costumes they wore' (1913, p. 113). This is one from a pair of similar prints on this theme and probably shows the event held on Saturday 13 July 1839, depicted by Waterhouse Hawkins. City of London, London Metropolitan Archives.

108 'Plan of the Parish of Marylebone in the County of Middlesex, surveyed by George Oakley Lucas in 1846'. The Eyre letter books record the estate's acquisition of this map on 22 October 1850. Amusingly, the clerk wrote to Lucas on that day: 'Instead of giving Mr W Eyre a plan of the Boro[ugh] you left a roll of Blank papers- please therefore bring a plan & take away the paper.' Eyre estate archive (EE 2651/353(B)).

according to the 1810 lease (see No. 21 on Alpha Cottages reconstruction). By 1828, she was letting this semi-detached house, furnished, for £126 a year, making a gross profit of £121.[20] In 1831, the ground rent of the detached house at 9 Avenue Road on the Portland estate, which Maidlow had assigned to Henry Samuel Eyre, was worth £60, but the letting price, unfurnished, was £180 per annum.[21] Such figures suggest that only the upper strata of the middle class would have been able to enjoy many of the houses in St John's Wood. Mary Richardson-Eyre's lucid assessment of the congregation of All Saints Church in the 1890s is worth quoting here: 'The congregation consisted principally of the well-to-do tradespeople class, those who, possessing shops in London, having made more or less of a pile, thought themselves entitled to take a villa in this salubrious suburb.'[22]

This definition is implicitly challenged by Anthony Trollope in *The Small House at Allington* (1864); his realistic portrayal of struggling aristocrats such as the De Courcy family brought them to St John's Wood, a respectable and affordable part of London where they could settle their daughters. There was indeed a flavour of aristocracy (indigent or otherwise) in that neighbourhood (see box below). It may also be worth mentioning in this context the weekly rehearsals (in the summer season) for the Eglinton Tournament at the Eyre Arms Hotel (Plate 107). This event attracted many aristocrats to St John's Wood, such as the earls of Eglinton and Craven, the marquis of Waterford and even Prince Louis Napoleon.[23]

Aristocratic and/or titled tenants who held leases at St John's Wood

Source of information has been placed in brackets; see p. 523 for Key to references.

Lord and Lady Turnour from Rose Cottage, Primrose Hill, were in Lodge Road 1828 (LB 'L', p. 115). Lord Turnour became Lord Winterton in 1831 (LB 'M', p. 404). Later at 18 North Bank (LB 'M', p. 352).

Lady Ramsay from 1 Upper Seymour Street, in Grove End Road 1830 (LB 'L', p. 435).

Lord Hawkes from Wormsley, Yorkshire, in St John's Terrace 1831 (LB 'M', p. 297).

Earl Ferrers from 2 Harley Street, in Alpha Road 1831 (LB 'M', p. 340, and EE 2650/1/259(F)).

Sir William Long of Kempston House, Bedfordshire, in Grove End Road 1831 (LB 'M', p. 378, and EE 2651/313).

Sir Samuel Whalley in St John's Wood Road purchased a house from Harris in 1833 (LB 'N', p. 148).

Marquis de Robeyre considered acquiring one of Twentyman's properties in 1840 (LB 'P', p. 288).

Marquis de Villimont/Villemont at 7 Regents Villas in Avenue Road 1841 (LB 'P', p. 300).

Rt Hon. Viscount Lowther from 14 Carlton House Terrace took over Mr Crace's premises at Lennard Place 1842 (LB 'Q', p. 62, Lord Lowther on p. 140).

Lord Cottenham in Townshend Street 1843 (LB 'Q', p. 121).

Countess of Kingston in 35 Alpha Road 1843 (see 1843 Annual Report of Western General Dispensary in Lisson Grove, WCA, M Acc 320).

The earl of Lonsdale had premises in Lennard Place 1846 (LB 'R', p. 154).

Mrs William de Montmorency from 5 Bridge House in Lewisham for premises at 31 Park Road, 1846 (LB 'R', p. 293).

The Hon. Sir Frederick Stovin, Bt, in Finchley Road 1847 (LB 'R', p. 586).

Lady Frances Maria Beauclerk in 35 Finchley Road 1893 (lease EE 2650/1/282(A)).

NON RESPECTABILITY

To the eyes of most twenty-first century citizens, the subordination of women to men in the nineteenth century still seems extraordinary. The power of a husband over his wife affected any personal legacy she might inherit. For instance, in 1810 Walpole's half-sister Emily Darvall wanted such a legacy 'transferred into her own name', but 'the consequence of it I apprehend will be that the moment it is transferred into her name (she being a married woman) the Bank will not permit her to dispose of it without her husbands consent'.[24] The male hold on women was such that even a moment of female self-discovery such as that captured by William Holman Hunt in his famous painting, *The Awakening Conscience*, was channeled and shown in the picture to be physically circumscribed by a man (Plate 111).

Various mistresses are known to have lived in St John's Wood (see box below), and the scene is meticulously documented in fiction in Michael Sadleir's novel, *Forlorn Sunset*.[25] In 1853, when Holman Hunt embarked on his *Awakening Conscience*, set at Alpha Place, a factual source recorded that 'St John's Wood was once resorted to by dissipated men of affluence for the indulgence of one of their worst vices.'[26] However, one might have expected to come across veiled references to such undesirable sexual behaviour in the Eyre letter books, just as there are veiled references to men's unfortunate habit of urinating in the streets (see p. 176). Not so, not a word from the habitually frank Walpole, and this can only mean one of two things – either the subject was so taboo that it would only be dealt with in face-to-face interviews rather than put in writing, or there were no complaints from tenants and therefore Walpole would not have needed to interfere. The latter seems most likely, as there is evidence in Walpole's letters that he had perfectly comfortable ways of dealing with the most awkward and controversial situations. In this the Eyre brothers led by example when Harry generously granted Eleanor Collins a £60 annuity for life in 1806, raised to £100 the following year.[27] It appears from one of Miss Collins's letters to Walpole that she had once had a liaison with the middle brother John. The annuity was probably the honourable price paid for breaking off this relationship.[28]

In his correspondence with clients Walpole showed no squeamishness in dealing with embarrassing situations. For instance, Colonel Hart (not a St John's Wood tenant) had an illegitimate child, Mary Lawrence, renamed Mary Hungerford, and Walpole was hired to ensure her placement in a good boarding school, to ensure her well-being as well as give advice on legacy issues after her

St John's Wood 'victims of propriety' according to Montgomery Eyre (1913)

- George IV's last mistress, Jane Belmont, a house at the corner of Marlborough and Loudoun Roads (p. 148).
- Mrs Everest, a peer's daughter fallen from grace with a wealthy sugar broker called Russell who provided for her at his death, in Circus Road (p. 148).
- Lydia Rose in South Bank (p. 149).
- Miss Howard, Napoleon III's mistress from 1838, based at 23 Circus Road (pp. 150ff.).
- Molly Baker, known as Mrs Meeres (possibly the model for Thackeray's Becky Sharp in *Vanity Fair*), in Loudoun Road (p. 150).
- Countess Fretchkoff, née Kate Gillman, lived in retirement at South Bank (p. 157).

Opposite, top: **109** The property depicted in *The Awakening Conscience* started life as a most modest cottage purchased by a butcher, William George Jacomb, in 1822 (drawing marked 'B'). By 1883 the property had doubled its size but retained a decent size garden. Eyre estate archive (Bk of Drawings I, 122).

Below: **110** Detail from the 1903 estate map to show the Alpha Place property. The house imprint is the same in 1883 and 1903. Eyre estate archive EE 2652/14(J).

Right: **111** William Holman Hunt, *The Awakening Conscience*, 1853–54 (retouched 1856). The artist chose St John's Wood as his modern life setting, the work bravely depicting the relationship between a kept woman and her lover. According to the artist's daughter, Hunt hired a room at 'a maison de convenance' called Woodbine Villa, 7 Alpha Place (*The Pre-Raphaelites*, 1984, p. 121). This work was conceived as the material counterpart to Hunt's *The Light of the World*, a night painting depicting Jesus holding a light in a gesture of redemption. Here, bathed in light, is the image of the fallen woman for whom all is not lost since she may yet be saved by 'The Light of the World'. Tate London.

to Ford Madox Brown in 1853, perhaps because he had direct insight into the situation he depicted. Holman Hunt's painting was produced as a pendant to the *Light of the World*, both paintings relying on the strident treatment of light as a trigger for spiritual awareness. This was the very light which the Eyre brothers defended tooth and nail against unprincipled developers or lessees: 'this additional fence obstructs both the air and light and is extremely annoying to the Tenant of the prem[is]es in Circus Road'.[46] In Hunt's painting, the source of illumination was the garden. The tool for redemption of the fallen woman was therefore the brilliantly green haven surrounding the fallen house, its beauty suddenly perceived as the presence of God.

Holman Hunt was not simply depicting a subject central to ideas of Victorian morality; he was himself directly involved in its moral dilemma: the female model he used for the painting was Annie Miller, an artist's model he had fallen in love with and wished to marry. The battle for respectability was fought and eventually lost, as described in 1859 by one of his friends, the painter George Price Boyce: 'Miss Annie Miller called on me.... She was determined on sitting again in preference to doing anything else. All was broken off between her and Hunt.... Called on Hunt in the evening.... He said it seemed now as if she could do nothing else for she rejected (naturally enough) all his efforts to find employment through friends. Finding he could not get her to do what he wanted to make her a desirable wife for him, nor to wean herself from old objectionable habits, he had broken off the engagement, but the whole affair had preyed on his mind for years.'[47]

PROSTITUTION

There is a considerable difference between the world of prostitution and that of kept women: Mrs Newton, who seemed to have had a truly loving relationship with the painter James Tissot in Grove End Road (see p. 163), had no real connection with the world of prostitution, even if, in the mind of her contemporaries, the two things interchangeably defied social conventions. An undated pamphlet written by 'A Late Detective Inspector', probably published in the 1880s, attempted to provide evidence about prostitution in St John's Wood, though its claims appear to come straight from the world of sensationalist journalism: 'Sweet Mabel: Life in St John's Wood; A Truthful and Astounding Account of the Disgraceful Scenes and Doings of the Upper Ten Thousand in St John's Wood, in the Nineteenth Century'.[48] This poorly written document chronicles in meandering ways reprehensible occurrences in St John's Wood – gambling dens, burglaries, a pimp and his prostitutes in a house near Swiss Cottage Tavern called 'Holly Lodge', and 'kidnapping of young maidens'. The doings of 'Sweet Mabel', alias Mabel Fitzroy, recounted at the end of the article seem relatively tame by comparison: she was guilty of seducing a wealthy local youth who lived at 'Brandon Lodge' and of receiving £500 for the return of compromising letters. The article also recorded the presence of pawnshops 'which, considering the wealth of the district, are proportionately far more numerous in St John's Wood than in any quarter of the metropolis'.[49] The evidence this article claimed to provide amounts to a random and sparse catalogue of sins likely to be encountered almost anywhere and at any time. It gives only one example of prostitution.

And yet, undeniably, sometime after Walpole's death, prostitution thrived on the southern part of the estate. In its first issue, the weekly newspaper *Marylebone Mercury* reported in 1857 the concern of the great and the good in an article entitled: 'Crusade against immorality in Marylebone'.

It states how the vestry 'rose *en masse* to support any measure which might be proposed for suppressing the evil, but what was to be done? Much discussion ensued in which the Rector, the Revd Mr Eyre, and other most influential of the Vestry took part.... they directed Mr Greenwell … to authorise the parish solicitor … to indict all houses of bad repute, and at the same time, called on the police commissioners to assist them.'[50] St John's Wood was not mentioned on this occasion, the 'evil' trend thriving in Portland Place and Fitzroy Square.

The estate office was finally confronted with this unpalatable reality in 1865 when the leases of the Alpha Cottages came up for renewal. Charles Freeth discovered that the large property which had been leased to Thomas Higham in 1836 (No. 9 on Alpha Cottages reconstruction, in what would later be called Beta Place) lost its respectability sometime after it was assigned to a merchant, Thomas Flight. Freeth first described the situation to John Eyre in the following terms:

> We are brought to a dead lock by Mr Flight & his undertenants (such undertenants being infamous and unmanageable) who will not give up poss[essi]on of the property (a large quantity of land) & prevent the Terrace (for which we have a most respectable Builder) being commenced [Boscobel Gardens], some means must be at once taken to get poss[essi]on of Flights prem[is]es but I think his tenants will not leave until the houses are pulled down over their heads.[51]

This is how he briefed the estate's solicitors about the troublesome case:

> Mr Flight underlet these prem[is]es to various persons & among others to one John Clarke [*sic*] a Gardener.

> Mr Clark began to build various add[iti]onal erections.... & in par[ticu]lar a dw[ellin]g house.... After this Clark erected a perfect Rookery on his portion of the Gro[un]d – Mr Flight let [the] other portion of the Gro[un]d to one [Mr] France a railway contractor who made it a lay stall for all the broken & damaged materials connected with Railway Carriages & contractors materials while the principal house No19 belonging to Mr Flight was occupied by Prostitutes & latterly & at this time by one Sarah Lyons a woman of infamous notoriety with a house full of prostitutes – indeed the whole houses 16a 17 18 & 19 … were all of the same description & Clarke [*sic*] erected hovels on the Ground w[hi]ch were occupied by people in wretched condition-

> These prem[is]es lying principally at the end of a road no thoroughfare – & the rent being paid by Mr Flights draft their state escaped observation for some time.[52]

The estate succeeded in recovering possession of the ground, and the injurious houses were pulled down and the tidy but more ordinary terrace of Boscobel Gardens was erected on part of the land (see Plate 218). However, a few years later a chance comment in one of the letters from the solicitor John White suggested that the difficulties encountered in Beta Place were not unique. Of Hanover Cottages (formerly Caroline Place, on James Burton's land) he wrote in 1869: 'the ladies who live there do not raise its character.'[53] He attributed the deterioration of that part of the estate to the railways, and as a connection with the railways is made on both 'fallen' sites by two different people and at two different times, the idea might be worth exploring further in a more general context.[54]

It should also be noted that this second site, Hanover Cottages, was a stone's-throw from Alpha Place, where Holman Hunt set his controversial painting, *The Awakening Conscience*.

As far as St John's Wood was concerned, the unbearable reality of the 'fallen woman' may have been ushered in by Ugo Foscolo, who experienced it at first hand in his 'abode of oriental splendour' in South Bank. In November 1823, his friend Hobhouse wrote: 'I called on Foscolo at his Digamma Cottage. I found him in great distress. He had two sisters for servants, one 25, the other 17, the latter beautiful as Hebe, he told me. Both have turned out prostitutes and he read to me a letter which he had written to the youngest on her sad situation – a very good kind letter backed also by a present of £50 which he is about to put into a savings bank for her. The poor fellow burst out in tears several times whilst reading to me this letter.'[55] This affair even led to an eighteenth-century-style duel between Foscolo and the man who had compromised the younger servant.

Reparation methods changed in Victorian times, but they were not necessarily welcome on a 'respectable' estate. Miss Armytage of 34 North Bank wanted to turn her home into 'a house for fallen girls & their infants', a project which was obstructed in 1875 but may have evolved into an 'infants' school'.[56] In the same street and in the same year, another charitable resident had taken steps to create a 'hospital for incurable women'.[57] In 1878, North Bank was confirmed as an area plagued by prostitution when the Lincoln's Inn barrister J. F. Stanford wrote the following complaint:

> I cannot help expressing my opinion that the Owner in Fee of the Eyre Estate should take steps to protect a gentleman who has purchased one of the houses on the Estate from the disgusting & filthy traffick carried on by a ruffian right opposite to his house! Shouting Murder & Police continually disturbing the neighbourhood at 2 & 3 oclock in the Morning – 17 Gentlemen, Barristers[,] Clergy … Signed a Memorial to the Vestry against the Nuisance & asking help but no steps have been taken to punish the filthy ruffians and their dirty foul [illegible word].… Im [*sic*] quite sure the forfeiture Clauses in y[ou]r Leases must extend to Brothel Keepers as a nuisance.… There were no brothels when I bought my house No 5.[58]

Stanford had complained about the hospital for incurable women back in 1875, and the estate's reply expressed a determination to address the issue. Here, however, the estate's reply was not recorded in the letter books.[59] It would appear, unfortunately for Stanford, that the problem did not go away. When Charles Booth was conducting his extraordinary social survey in London, the following notes were taken by one of Booth's team members about North Bank in 1895:

> detached and semi-det[ached] Villas in gardens: those at the west end are respectable but the small semi-det[ached] villas at the east end are … inhabited by prostitutes, and have been for years, sometimes one, sometimes two in a house: things are conducted very quietly: the houses are not now used in any sense as brothels, though at one time some of the larger houses here and in Lodge Road were open brothels, but these were suppressed.… Discussing the question of prostitution with Souter [local policeman] with reference to North Bank: he said that there were many more prosecutions of disorderly houses than there used to be: but he thought if anything the number of women in the streets had increased.[60]

SHOPS

A document of 1824 categorically identified traders as the major source of non-respectability in residential areas. When Ugo Foscolo could no longer fob off his creditors, the particulars of sale prepared for his Regent's Canal 'Digamma' and 'Cappa' Cottages in South Bank were very clear about this point: 'It may however be added that the property will improve as it is yet a new neighbourhood, and the plantation very recent; – it will also remain a respectable neighbourhood, as by the original lease no shop is allowed to be opened nor any trade to be carried on in the houses of south Bank.'[61] The leases were indeed very strict from the very beginning concerning the solely residential use of the dwellings and their gardens, which could not be converted to other purposes without prior consent from the estate. The references to shops and trading which are found in the letter books confirm that any form of trading on the estate was forbidden. This was not simply a condition imposed by the estate on the lessees, but a covenant which most people would have regarded as key to maintaining a healthy and trouble-free environment, which in turn would be sought out by a respectable class of tenants. 'No trade' was a standard condition in residential leases going back to the eighteenth century. In 1833, a complaint was made to the estate about 'some process or manufacture connected with the Glove Trade … in the house … No 20 Wellington Road from which an offensive & unwholesome effluvia arises'. The complaint was repeated, but eventually Walpole was able to write: 'I saw Mr Thomas this morn[in]g upon the subject of y[ou]r complaint[.] he states that Mr Whitehead will quit on the 25th Inst the house being relet to a *respectable* Tenant' (my italics).[62]

The earliest recorded licence, to George Watkins for a baker's shop, dates from 1824, and the earliest reference to shops in the letter books occurs in 1827, when a request for an unspecified shop was sent from Capland Street, off Lisson Grove on the south-east edge of the estate. In this instance, Walpole opted for the following compromise: 'I sh[ou]d have no objection to have shops in the back St[reet] but not in the front.'[63] Only a couple of licences were granted in the late 1820s, one for a chandler's shop at 2 Upper York Street (now St Ann's Terrace), the other, in 1828, to Thomas Parker for 'a shop' at 2 York Place. The box overleaf lists the trades which Walpole allowed at that time. Neither innkeepers, bakers nor butchers appear on that list, for reasons which appear from the letter books. In 1852, Charles Freeth turned down a request for a baker's shop: 'In reply to your note as to using No 9 Portland Terrace as a Bakers, I beg to inform you that Mr Thomas made application to use that house as a Bakers some time since and was distinctly informed that it could not be permitted there being already a Bakers within a few doors the nuisance of which latter sensibly affects the neighbourhood.'[64] This was not an isolated example. In 1853, the estate's concern for unfair competition (as they saw it) drove them to turn down a chemist and jeweller's shop for similar reasons.[65]

Nowadays shops are considered desirable 'amenities' and sometimes indicate affluence, so it has become quite difficult to draw up a mental picture of the level of nuisance these could cause in the eighteenth and nineteenth centuries. Walpole's letters contain graphic details which convey how quickly an area could go downhill if trades were not monitored with a fist of iron. In 1845, he wrote: 'I am sorry I cannot consent to have a Bakers Shop erected at the corner of Ordnance Road & Henstridge Place/The smoke usually emitted from the chimney of a Bakehouse would extend over a

Trades not permitted in 1806 at Alpha Cottages

Art mistery [alchemist?] trade or business of chymist [*sic*]
Auctioneer
Broker
Vintner
Alehouse keeper
Coffee house keeper
Bagio [Bagnio?] Keeper
Washing and drying of linen
Cookshop
Victualler
Butcher
Baker
Cheesemonger
Soap boiler
Pewterer
Bell founder
Brazier
Pav[ior?]
Blacksmith
Whitesmith
Coppersmith
Flax dresser
Tallow chandler
Fellmonger
Hatter
Hosier
Catgut spinner
Dog skinner
Tripe boiler
Pig jobber
Cow keeper
Horse dealer
Plumber
Hot-presser
Distiller
Or any other dangerous or annoying or
Offensive trade or business whatsoever
Or permit or suffer the same to be let as a
Common lodging house or inhabited by
Women of the Town …

Trades permitted in 1828 for shop with licence

Chandler in the general line
Cheesemonger
Haberdasher
Linen-Draper
Hosier
Oilman
Boot & Shoe Vendor
Bookseller
Stationer
Pawnbroker
Furniture Broker
Corn Chandler
Druggist
Confectioner
Cook
Poulterer
Fishmonger
Hatter
Hairdresser
Perfumer
Fruiterer
Grocer
Plumber
Glazier

or any other trade or business to be
approved of by me & which shall not
be or become an annoyance
grievance disturbance or damage
to me Walpole Eyre …

The list of prohibited trades on the left comes from the earliest surviving lease dated 29 August 1806 at EE 2651/12(A). The list of permitted trades on the right comes from a 'License to Mr Thomas Parker' prepared on 15 April 1828 for a shop at 2 York Place (later 75 High Street). The underlined trades were forbidden in 1806 and permitted in 1828. The juxtaposition indicates a shift towards a greater tolerance of trades which were beneficial to the well-being of a community.

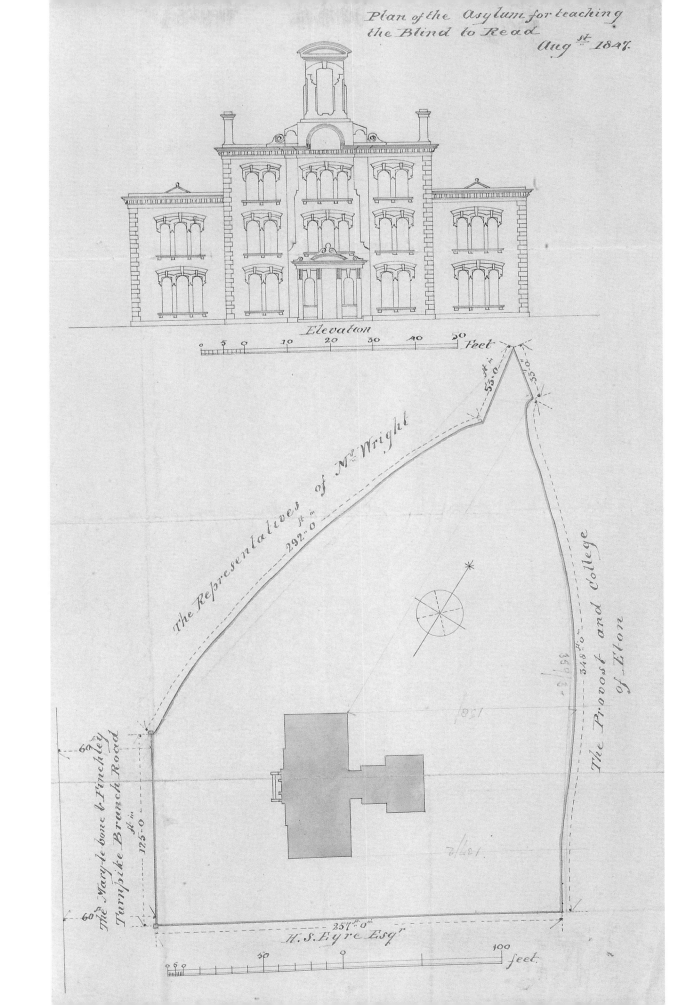

Plan of the Asylum for teaching
the Blind to Read
Aug.st 1847.

Elevation

0 5 10 20 30 40 50 Feet

The Representatives of M.r Wright

292.0

55.0

55.0

The Mary-le-bone & Finchley
Turnpike Branch Road

125.0

60.

The Provost and College
of Eton

359.3

H. S. Eyre Esq.r

257.0

50 100 feet

Some key dates in the arrival of schools on the estate

1807   Request for establishing a 'Ladies Boarding School' at Alpha Road (LB 'A', p. 599).

1809   Act of Parliament permits the foundation of the Orphan Clergy Society (Licence Book I, pp. 85ff.).
The society signs an agreement with Walpole the following year.

1810   Early proposal for a 'School for the Deaf and Blind' (not realised, see LB 'B', p. 263).

1812   Orphan Clergy School opens its doors (Simmonds, 1897).

1838   First licence for a school, at 2 Warwick Place (Licence Book I, p. 162).

1846   Henry Sibson's wife and daughter set up a small school at their new home at 9 Douro Cottages
(Sibson archive at the Tate).

1846   (November) Lease to Robert Yeo for what would become (in 1857) St John's Wood School at
43A Acacia Road (WCA, 765/59).

1846   (December) Reverend Edward Thompson proposes a Sunday school at All Saints Church (LB 'R', p. 333).

1847   (February) Application from C. Churchill to run a school from 3 Abbey Road (LB 'R', p. 374).

1847   Reverend Edward Thompson's battle with Walpole re: building a paupers' school next to All Saints
(LB 'R', pp. 336, 346, 391, 393, 398–9).

1847   (March) Proposal for a college at St John's Wood Park (not realised, LB 'R', p. 421).

1847   (June) Site of All Saints School is resolved (LB 'R', p. 485).

1847   (July) First mention of the School for the Blind (LB 'R', p. 492).

1848   (February) All Saints School completed externally (LB 'S', p. 17).

1849   Mention of a licence to knock two houses into one to create a 'Ladies Boarding School' in the
Turnpike Branch Road, e.g. Avenue Road (LB 'S', p. 430).

1851   The census for that year reveals that Annie Erlam (sister of architect John Samuel Erlam?) is running a school
in Elm Tree Road opposite the site of what would become the School of Art.

1854   (January) The Eyres are approached about a licence to use 24 St John's Wood Park (now 25) as a
'Collegiate School' (LB 'T', p. 527; Licence Book II, p. 21, 21 August 1854).

1854   (April) Estate approached re: school proposed to be built at rear of Portland chapel (LB 'T', p. 563).

1855   Licence to knock down two houses into one to create a school at Avenue Road (Licence Book II, pp. 38ff,
17 and 19 Regents Villas, dated 22 March 1855).

1855   (31 July) Licence to build new dining room and to make alterations at the 'Schools for Teaching the Blind to Read'
(Licence Book II, p. 51).

1855   'School of Industry for female Orphans' on Landseer site is completed (Plate 236 *Marylebone Mercury*, no. 47,
10 July 1858, p. 4; drainage work recorded in 1852 at LB 'T', p. 186).

1857   (13 August) Licence and consent to additions and alterations at New Place, Acacia Road, and to use the
premises as a day school (Plate 117 and Licence Book II, p. 79).

all the five districts except in Christs Church but these Schools are generally under the
management and direction of the Laity as much or more than under the Rector or
Clergymen and are supported generally by the Laity[.]

With respect to your church being singular and inefficient with[ou]t a school – your
District can have but very few Paupers in it and if your School is built and is filled with
children – they (as far as it appears to me) must be drawn from the neighbouring Districts

and particularly those of Portland Town. I will not conclude with[ou]t assuring you that I am as warm an advocate as you or any other person can be for affording religious and moral Education to the lower Orders but at the same time I cannot help feeling that National and other schools for the lower orders sho[ul]d be placed in par[ticu]lar localities & not in situations where the Neighbourhood consists of houses and inhabitants of a better Description.[99]

The last thing Walpole wanted was for All Saints to become a magnet for the poor, as he argues in a further letter: 'I am satisfied there is no permanent resident Paupers living upon Col[one]l Eyre's Estate though there may be (as I think you stated) some families living in the kitchens in houses which are in the building but generally speaking these families belong to men who are employed in and about the buildings and who have good wages and ought if provident persons to be able to support their families.'[100] As the row developed, Thompson claimed eighty children attended his school, mostly from his own district – an assertion Walpole disputed again. The site of the proposed school also created problems:

When my Brother Col[one]l Eyre consented to grant so large a portion of gro[un]d whereon to build All Saints Church it was under the distinct impression that the additional gro[un]d not actually required for the site of the Church should be kept as an open area clear from all additional Buildings so as to afford ample space for the admission of Sun and air giving an opportunity for the church itself being seen from all points and the means of providing proper walks and shrubberies round the church as shown in the Lithographed picture of the Church which has been extensively circulated [Plate 194] – and in this spirit and with this view my brother ent[ere]d into a cov[enan]t... not to suffer to be erected any house or other Buildings within 40 feet of the East side or rear of the land conveyed.[101]

The row reached its peak when, despite Walpole's strenuous opposition to the scheme, Thompson continued regardless to build his school right against the church. The clergyman had a forceful vision and a keen sense of evil:

The great fact is, then, that the deficiency of education in our country is more than startling – it is terrific. The beast has been called into being, and he is already howling in our streets; his blood is boiling for mischief. The enemy is *growing into force*. The little urchins, who a few years ago were comparatively innocent, to the amount of thousands on thousands, are issuing from our back streets, alleys, and lanes, and beginning to manifest their vice and ferocity. Our prisons are becoming filled with juvenile profligates.... *Ignorance*, and its foster-child, vice, are like two combustible engines, that only have to be touched by the flambeau, and the death of untold numbers inevitably follows.... Our metropolis and manufacturing towns are disgorging into their streets the fruit of inebriety, seduction and prostitution.[102]

Thompson proposed to build the school in the grounds of his own house, Gothic Villa, which had been built by Thomas Little, the architect in charge of the church (Plate 80). Walpole accepted this opportunity to settle the row. He put Thompson in touch with James Sharp, the developer for that

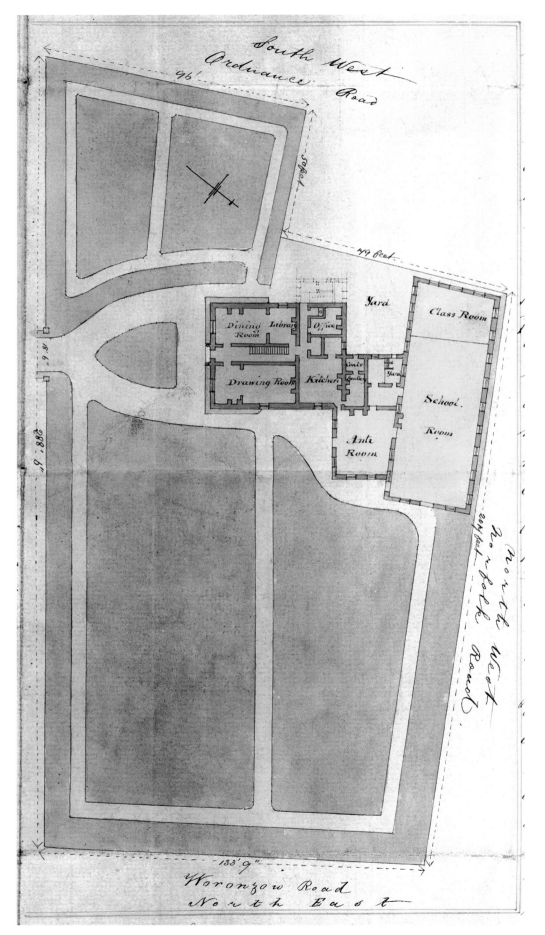

117 Licence drawing of 'New Place' at 43A Acacia Road, dated 13 August 1857. This house was sited on a large plot of land which extended to Woronzow Road, and it became a school in 1857 after a detailed evaluation was carried out to ensure it would not be disruptive to the neighbourhood. This plot still exists, reduced in size, and now 'landlocked' after the Woronzow Road frontage was developed (see p. 355). Westminster City Archives (765/59).

part of the estate, who gave up a plot of land alongside the vicarage's garden. The school was completed by early 1848 and was the first purpose-built school on the estate.[103] Amazingly, this little building has survived (see Plate 269).

This episode was exceptional in the history of the estate. There certainly were regular requests for establishing private schools, the earliest dating from 1807 for a 'Ladies Boarding School' in one of the Alpha Cottages (No. 20 in the Alpha Cottages reconstruction, Plate 63).[104] At first Walpole was very circumspect, not wishing to forbid or encourage the running of private schools in the estate houses, and as late as 1838 his position remained as follows:

> There may be[,] indeed I know there are[,] several Ladies Boarding Schools upon the Estate but I never grant Licenses for such a p[ur]p[o]se[.]

> I am not disposed to interfere with such a letting nor sho[ul]d I do so unless I found it objectionable or the Neighbours complained but the discretion must be left with me.[105]

The lessee, John Rees, who had requested a licence, must have insisted because on 19 June 1838 Walpole granted the first licence for a school, at 2 Warwick Place (now Scott Ellis Gardens), to be run by a Mrs Mary Davis.[106] The ground for making that decision would have been prepared when Walpole was canvassing hard to let a house the colonel had acquired at 9 Avenue Road (see p. 142). When it became clear ordinary tenants could not be found for such large premises, Walpole had sought to let it as a school.[107] The second licence for a school was not drafted until 1849 when two of Twentyman's houses in Avenue Road (Nos 17 and 19 Regents Villas) were altered to be used as 'Educating a limited Number of pupils as Boarders by a Clergyman'.[108] By 1853, the licence procedure seemed well established because the solicitor of Mr Cass, a builder, received the following reply regarding his 'application for permission to use a house in Carlton Hill R[oa]d as a Ladies School – I have to inform you that such permissions are given in the form of Licenses, the charge for one such being two guineas.'[109]

As with shops, the great decade for the mass appearance of schools was the 1840s. In one touching instance, the link between being on the verge of bankruptcy and setting up a school is apparent. The story of sculptor Henry Sibson, who introduced Islamic style architecture to St John's Wood, is told in a later chapter (p. 419). His financial difficulties forced him to downsize from a house in Wellington Road to one in Douro Cottages. There his wife and daughter 'commenced a Day School, which was patronized by our small neighbours', and was no doubt a vital source of revenue for the family who had lost so much to creditors.[110] The year was around 1846, the same year that Robert Yeo acquired the landlocked site at 43A Acacia Road which in 1857 would become an important school for St John's Wood, not connected with any church (see pp. 336, 405 and Plate 117). The Eyre estate, prior to granting its licence, had canvassed expert and local opinion.[111] By 1864, it was known as St John's Wood School and was being extended, mostly upwards.[112]

With the arrival of shops, schools and churches, as well as the mushrooming of stables and coach houses, the 1840s and 1850s signified a marked urbanisation of St John's Wood. Soon, too, the land was in such demand that a stream of requests flowed in for increasing the building density. Was the success of the St John's Wood estate about to engulf the original vision of a civilised semi-rural neighbourhood?

7 INFRASTRUCTURE

We have now nearly let the whole of the Land we took from Willan[.] at present the expences are very considerable as we are making *a good Road* & must now make a *Drain* (6 July 1805, my italics).[1]

The Tenants are now pressing me to make a well & I am afraid it must be done for without *Water* it will be impossible to expect the build[in]gs to go on (14 May 1806, my italics).[2]

There are signs in the early correspondence that despite John Shaw's and Robert Todd's advice on all building issues, Walpole did not fully appreciate the vastness of the task he had taken on. For instance, having set his heart on providing tenants with a well, once he realised the expense of such a project he decided to approach a water company instead: 'if the Chelsea Water Work Company do not lay on the water, a well must be sunk which wo[ul]d be an enormous expence & a continual outgoing to keep it in repair'.[3] Similarly, when he first tackled the issue of drainage, he soon realised the high costs involved, but in trying to limit the scope of this project he ran into difficulties with the Commissioners of Sewers in 1810 (see below): 'I am sorry to say have got into some difficulties about the Drainage of Saint Johns Wood, The Commissioners of Sewers have great powers under the Acts of Parliament and I think want to exercise them very arbitrarily and to which I don't mean to submit.'[4]

After Walpole recovered from the initial shock of the cost of development infrastructure, he found ways to mastermind some very ambitious schemes indeed. His drainage programme included the building of 'Colonel Eyre's Sewer' underneath the modern Lisson Grove – a major project from which Walpole drew enormous pride – while his road building programme eventually gave London its wide and fast Finchley Road (originally 'Marylebone and Finchley Turnpike Road') with its 'Branch', now Avenue Road.

ROADS

The development of a road network in St John's Wood during the first forty years of the nineteenth century coincided with the creation in England of 'much the best road system seen in the country since the fall of the Roman Empire'.[5] John Loudon McAdam and his sons contributed much fresh thinking and energy to this programme, which was channelled through the Turnpike Trusts and, in London, the Metropolis Roads Commission. Walpole's awareness of the work and influence of the McAdam family is made clear when he threatened to go to 'Mr McAdam' in 1826 (almost certainly James McAdam) when his dissatisfaction with the Wellington Road was at its height (see p. 229). (Sir) James McAdam (1786–1852), the talented son of his father John Loudon McAdam (1756–1836), was a resident in St John's Wood, first at the Villa Etruria in Grove End Road, then at 1 Finchley Road, close to the Eyre Arms Tavern.[6] The letter books record a payment of over £362 to 'Mr McAdam' (James) in 1830, almost certainly in connection with the Marylebone and Finchley Turnpike Road.[7] More generally, the archive of the Eyre estate offers a fairly detailed road building diary which highlights the problems, successes, setbacks and landmark dates in the story of road making in this neighbourhood.

By the early years of the nineteenth century, there were two main points of access to the estate:

Previous pages: **118** Although this view of the Regent's Canal was thought to show the bridge at the junction with Lisson Grove Road on the west side of the estate, the houses depicted have a far better match on the east side at the junction with Park Road. The trees in the background would be in Regent's Park, while those on the left-hand side signalled the exuberant garden of lessee C. H. B. Kerr, a conveyancer who built a conservatory in 1819 when the lease was issued. Walpole even mentioned in 1819 the presence in this garden of a 'Turf Bank' as well as the 'boundary Fence that is the Paling along the Towing path' (LB 'F', p.136), which perfectly matches what is depicted in this watercolour by William Crotch, dating from c.1830. City of London, London Metropolitan Archives (Wakefield collection, p5387713).

one qualified as a 'road', the St John's Wood Lane from the Edgware Road to St John's Wood Farm, while the other was thus described by Walpole: 'when I first began to have the managem[en]t of it [the estate], the only approach from the New Road [Marylebone Road] was up a dirty narrow lane opposite the Yorkshire Stingo' (see Plate 51).[8]

The earliest St John's Wood agreement in the Eyre archive dates from 1752, and it ensured the three-year maintenance of St John's Wood Lane.[9] It is visible on the 1733 map when it was the only road to service the estate. By 1754, the date of John Rocque's map of Middlesex, there were many paths to and from the estate's two farms (see Plate 31). The road linking St John's Wood to Lisson Green is shown as rather wide but dwindling into a path in the southern tip of the estate. The 1752 tenants – Thomas Huddle, John Pye, Thomas Stedman and Thomas Charles – agreed to keep the main road in repair.[10] It became known as St John's Wood Lane, and its contemporary trajectory roughly corresponds to St John's Wood Road (for access from Edgware Road), and then Grove End Road and Acacia Road up to the junction with Ordnance Hill, the eastern limit of the original St John's Wood Farm.

In this early document the road was divided into three sections for the purpose of maintenance: the first part from Edgware Road ('Hill House in the occupation of Mr Mason') to the entrance to the St John's Wood estate ('Thomas Huddle's Gateway'), the next section up to 'the Gate of the Greatfield', and finally the last stretch up to the 'further end … adjoining the Yards of John Pye and Thomas Stedman', presumably St John's Wood Farm. The document specified that every year, between 1 April and 1 August, Thomas Huddle should lay 'Twenty full loads of good Ballast' on the first section, John Pye thirty-two loads on the second section and thirty loads on the final section. The work had to be done 'in a good and husbandlike manner' and the loads shared between all the tenants.

Some fifty years later 'ballast' had been replaced by 'gravel', but the principle of sharing maintenance of St John's Wood Lane and laying on full loads was unchanged.[11] However, access to St John's Wood was by now being rapidly developed with a network of lanes criss-crossing the estate and a road programme which accompanied the building work. By 1825 road building was, in theory, less of a drain upon the Eyre purse, and this is how Walpole described the procedure: 'A considerable part of Col[onel] Eyres Estate is built upon and all the Roads have been made at his or his Tenants expence and they are bound by the Covenants in their Leases to pay towards the expence of repairing the Roads.'[12] In practice it was difficult to get the tenants to pay for road maintenance, and Walpole was therefore keen to hand over the roads to the parish as soon as they had been made and properly finished: 'Generally speaking the tenants upon the St John [sic] Wood Estate are bound by their Leases to make & repair the Roads opposite their prem[is]es or to pay a fair proportion of the expences[.] the former I never can get them to do & [the] latter is a difficult & unpleasant duty to perform.'[13]

First roads – Alpha and Park Roads

Road building started at the end of 1804: what was to become Alpha Road was ploughed through the fields by gardener John Webber and then turned into a proper road the following summer. Walpole referred to it as 'the great road', and he was forced, with Harry's permission, to sell stock to cover the cost.[14] He also immediately sought contributions to the cost from the men who had taken land on agreement.[15]

The Eyres had barely recovered from the expense of Alpha Road when two years later they set out to make Park Road. The making of that road was part of the agreement struck with the vestry when they purchased the land for their burial ground (see p. 106). By then the job seemed well organised, with John Shaw to measure and stake out the ground and Robert Todd to make the road, as Walpole explained:

> I am going to Ireland early in next month and in my absence I hope you will be getting forward with the road[.] The first thing to be done will be to mark out and measure the quantity of Gro[un]d to be taken from Mr Willan for the Burial Gro[un]d and the Fifty foot road from the Alpha Road up to the Burial Gro[un]d and also the space of Fifty feet which is to be left round the two sides of the Burial Gro[un]d adjoining my Brother's Property…. P.S. I have written to Todd to desire him to move his Sand Houses and to be getting things ready for us to begin the road.[16]

By March 1808 the road had been formed, using the nine acres of land taken away from Thomas Willan; by the end of July it had been completed. Walpole promptly organised for all roads made so far to be transferred to the care of the parish: 'I have now completed the Road leading from the Alpha Road to the intended Burial Gro[un]d & therefore expect that this Road as well as the Alpha Road, and that leading from the Paddington Road to the Alpha Road be taken under the imme[diate] management of & kept in repair by the Parish according to the Agreement.'[17]

The effort of making these roads had been so considerable that Walpole showed signs of anxiety when the vestry carried out no road maintenance over the summer: 'From the time I first made the Alpha Road I have been under the necessity of keeping a man constantly employed to fill in the Ruts & of occasionally filling in the holes with fresh gravel & I sho[ul]d hope the Gentlemen of the Vestry will direct their Surveyor to attend to the repair of these Roads immediately or the money I have expended in making them will be thrown away.'[18] These early concerns are illustrative of a learning process which Walpole later took for granted. Another early example is in a letter to the archdeacon of Cambridge, who had approached him for land to build a school for the Society of the Deaf and Dumb, a project which was not realised in St John's Wood: 'I cannot describe to you the Expences attendant upon the making Roads upon my brothers St Johns Wood Estate[.] the soil is principally clay and of course is ill adapted to the purpose of making Roads.'[19]

These records suggest that the Eyres had not written the cost of road making into the early tenants' agreements and that any contribution the tenants would be asked to make was 'understood' rather than a legal requirement. It was John Shaw who in 1809 took the first step towards addressing this issue, as Walpole described in his bill book: 'he [Shaw] thought it wo[ul]d certainly be advisable that we sho[ul]d undertake to make the Sewer & the Roads and take them into the calculation of the price to be given for each Lot'.[20] By 1814, the date of one of the earliest surviving agreements, road making (including 'footpaths') formed an integral part of the building contract, and was the first item on a long list of covenants.[21] From around 1810 road making would effectively be driven by building projects, and not the other way round, with one exception: the Finchley Road.

Roads could easily be damaged and needed to be protected from heavy traffic. In 1816, Colonel

Thornhill, who lived at No. 5 Alpha Cottages, requested access to St John's Wood Road from the Avenue of Trees at a time when the works of the canal company had seriously disrupted the neighbourhood:

> the Road to which you wish to have a Key is at present impassible [*sic*] from the Sewer which is now making across it[.] as soon as the Sewer is completed and the Road restored I will send you a Key to the Bar but it must be with an express understanding that you will give your Servant positive directions to lock the Bar whenever he comes thro[ugh.] I am under the necessity of making this Stipulation as my brother has been put to a very serious expence by this Bar having been left open by persons who had the Key and the Road being cut up in consequence of heavy Carts passing along it.[22]

Much later Walpole bitterly objected to the unilateral decision to put bars in Avenue Road and introduce a charge, so eager were the concerned parties to protect the road and recover part of the investment it represented: 'latterly a Bar has been placed at the end of this Road either by Mr Bromley or Mr Fry with the Duke of Portlands concurrence & a Toll demanded. This I consider very injurious to the Property in the Avenue road [Colonel Eyre was the lessee of No. 9] & I conceive no one Tenant has a right to place a Bar upon a Road & demand a Toll of ano[the]r.'[23]

St John's Wood Road

The next major building project to generate more road building was the Orphan Clergy School (1812). Walpole was immediately ready to connect it to Park Road, though he also knew that what was really needed was a major link road on that site – the future St John's Wood Road. Writing to Shaw in July 1813 he stated: 'I wish you would have the goodness to get Lords New Cricket Ground set out and also the Road from the front of the Orphan Clergy Ground into the St Johns Wood Lane[.] I should also like to have the Road opened from the Avenue of Trees thro Atkinson Ground [Lisson Grove] to meet the other Road [St John's Wood Road or Grove End Road] but this I fear we cannot do without greatly Annoying Atkinson.'[24] Walpole must have deployed an abundance of cash and persuasive arguments, because this is how he achieved the strategic crossroad at St John's Wood Road, Grove End Road and Lisson Grove.

Footpaths

Footpaths, too, had to be well regulated. They are recorded on the estate from as early as 1814, though they may well have been found earlier. In 1817, Walpole confronted the Ordnance to try to put a stop to the misuse of footpaths: 'I have to request the favor of you to give Orders to the Troops quartered at the Saint John Wood Barrack not to ride upon the Footpaths of the Road leading from Saint John's Wood Lane to the new Parish Chapel & Burial Ground [i.e. the future St John's Wood Road] – I have particularly to complain of a Soldier of the name of <u>Luke Bates</u> whom I saw riding upon the footpath and desired to go into the Road but he would not do so[.] if this request is not complied with I shall be under the necessity of stopping up the Road & the Soldiers will then have to go round by St Johns Wood Lane.'[25]

The footpaths were generally gravelled, but in 1848 there is a reference to a 'paved footway' in Charles Lane.[26] It was also in the 1840s that the Wood Paving Committee was formed and approached the Marylebone vestry for business. Its representative, Mr Virtue, must have been disappointed to read Walpole's 'private communication': 'I am afraid that the price of putting down the wood pavement is more than our Vestry will be disposed to give.'[27]

Collaboration with other estates

John White junior stated in his 1815 *Account of Proposed Improvements* that he 'believed' the Portman estate had refused to allow access to the south-east corner of the Eyre estate.[28] There is nothing in the letter books to indicate that there were any problems between the two estates; on the contrary, there seems to have been regular cooperation when necessary.

Walpole appeared to be a step ahead of everyone else, initiating the next move rather than waiting for others to do so despite financial pressures. No sooner had St John's Wood Road been formed and linked to St John's Wood Lane than Walpole was writing to the duke of Portland's surveyor to proceed with the road informally agreed around 1810, the future St John's Wood High Street.[29] At the same time Walpole was also writing to the Crown surveyor:

> Mr Portman and my brother have it in contempl[ati]on to make a Road from the
> West End of the Alpha Road to communicate with the Edgware Road [Church Street.]
> whenever this is done I conceive it would be very beneficial to the Crown Estate to have
> a Communication from the Road in the Park which runs North and South and nearly
> parallel with the Road leading up to the new Parish Chapel [Park Road] into the Alpha
> Road and so to communicate with the Edgware Road.[30]

The Harrow School estate achieved the continuation of St John's Wood Road as a straight line to Edgware Road a few years later, in or around 1817.[31] Here it is worth recording Walpole's unsympathetic comments about what would become the Harrow School estate's Hamilton Terrace as they confirm that the width of this road was most unusual:

> the ... Road you have ... set out as an hundred & twenty feet Road[.] this appears to
> me much wider than there can be necessary for any purpose whatever and is a useless
> waste of land and would very considerably increase the expence of making the Road &
> of keeping it in repair when made – I do not therefore propose to make the Road upon
> my brothers Estate above sixty feet wide.[32]

Having dealt with the western entrance to the estate, he then turned to the eastern connection with the Crown estate:

> I have lately sold an acre of Ground to the Crown w[hi]ch is partly to be made into a
> Road & the other part laid into the Regent's Park[.] this was a narrow Slip of Ground
> running along a Road side & of no use to my brothers Estate & the Road w[hi]ch is now
> made will connect the Estate with the Hampstead Road & will be a great improvement
> to it.[33]

Road schizophrenia

The dates of road making in St John's Wood can be confusing: for instance, Ordnance Road appears to have been 'made' and 'handed over' to the vestry several times from the late 1830s to the late 1840s. This is because the road was made incrementally, and the situation was complicated by two different developers having land on either side, so that each was responsible for only one-half of the carriageway. If their efforts were not properly co-ordinated, the results could be very unsatisfactory. Although guidelines were issued for road making, there were of course instances of substantial discrepancy: 'The road on the North side of the Adelaide Road has been … well made but I do not think very much has been done to the other side except making the footpaths & they have been much damaged by the cart traffic.'[34] Another case concerned a section of Boundary Road in 1845 and involved builder-developers Samuel Erlam and William Todd. Walpole wrote to Erlam: 'You stated to me that as much gravel & material was put on your side of the Road as on Mr Todd's & that Mr Todd is so much higher than yours from his having brought a Quantity of Clay out of his Garden and having placed it upon the Road previous to having put the gravel & other materials upon the Road.'

Erlam made no reply to this letter, but a few days later Walpole obtained from Todd the information that his side was '9 inches of Brick Rubbish & pickings & over that 9 inches of good screened gravel – yours of only 6 inches of each & which he says occasions the difference of level in the Road'.[35]

The need for proper collaboration between the various building parties on the estate is again highlighted in a later example (1861) in Victoria Road, at the top of the estate: 'Mr Yeo who has since my letter to you of the 8th Mar[ch] [i.e. eight months previously] built 21 houses south-westward of the portion of road alluded to … complains strongly of that piece of road not being made as most injurious to him & he informs me that he is making the road in continuation – but which is perfectly useless until the commencement of it is made by Messrs Edwards.'[36]

Finchley Road

Barely a year after obtaining a large mortgage of £20,000 from Sun Life Insurance, Walpole wrote to them again in 1812, needing more funds for a major road project: 'I wish immed[iatel]y to undertake the making a Road thro the Centre of the Estate & which will be attended with a very considerable Expence' (Plate 119).[37] Walpole must have found the estimates from Messrs Poplar and Smith for building this road quite daunting – so first he argued with the builders and then he gave further consideration to the source of materials, having just found gravel where the canal was being dug.[38]

Walpole asked Hugh McIntosh to reconsider his estimate, stating there must be 'an error', and to Mr Smith from Paddington he wrote: 'I find I can make the Road much cheaper & upon easier Terms to myself than what you ask, I want to have some parts of the Estate bored for Gravel and if you like to undertake this & will call here tomorrow at three – I will go with you & point out the places, I wish to have tried first.'[39] Gravel was a valuable commodity, and the temptation to steal it from the roads seems to have been great. Rossi, the respectable sculptor turned developer, was an

119 These four maps – the first two by Peter Potter, another by Henry Phillips, the last one anonymous – were created between 1819 and 1826. They chart the gradual transformation of the original turnpike road ambitions of the Eyre brothers. Map 1 (top left) shows the original scheme they formulated for their turnpike roads through the estate in 1819; map 2 (top right) is a watered down version of the original plan and was presented to Parliament in 1820. The opposition of Sir Maryon Wilson to the scheme proved a fatal blow, and the Eyre brothers had to abandon the idea. The final scheme, as built, was initiated by Oakley & Phillips in 1824 (map 3, bottom left), but the Eyres were more than willing to implement the project. In the face of further opposition, more adjustments were made (map 4) and the scheme, now in the hands of the vestry's solicitors (see p. 456) was finally accepted. Eyre estate archive (EE 2651/283A(1, 4, 12 and 15)).

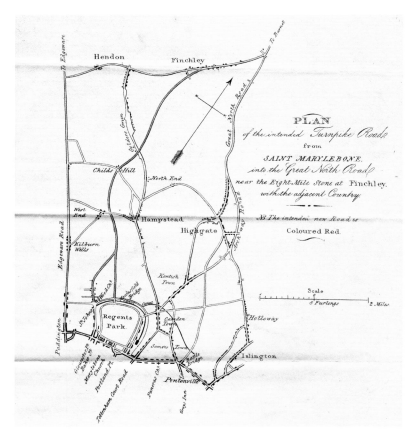

Finchley Road: a chronology

1817   (November) The future Wellington Road between the burial ground and St John's Wood Lane (i.e. Grove End Road) is formed (LB 'E', p.337).

1819   (August) Walpole contemplates a road 'into Hampstead and West End Lane' and approaches surveyor Peter Potter (LB 'F', p. 182). Potter suggests alterations and his plan is ready by September (p. 197). This plan is presumably the one reproduced on Plate 119 at EE 2651/283B(1).
(mid-December) Walpole backs down: 'likely to be so much opposition to some of these Roads and the expence of making them would have been so great, that I determined to abandon them all except the one from the Yorkshire Stingo Public House … to the North East End of Belsize Lane Hampstead' (LB 'F', p. 294). See Plate 119.

1820   (May) Bill in front of Parliament and shown to the vestry (LB 'F', pp. 405 and 418, EE 2651/283A(2)). Walpole appoints trustees for the Turnpike Road Bill: John White, Samuel Ware, William Masters, C. H. Tatham, William Davison, William Atkinson, Charles Day, J. R. Wheeler and William Key in Hampstead. 'There is a Clause in the above Bill to protect the Trustees from all personal liability' (LB 'F', pp. 408 and 414). Both the Dean and Chapter of Westminster and Maryon Wilson opposed the bill, the former presenting a petition against it (LB 'F', pp. 414 and 415).
(September) Walpole obtains road making estimates (LB 'F', pp. 514, 516).
Shortly afterwards he abandons the project (LB 'F', p. 540).

1822   (August) First mention of the name 'Wellington Road' (LB 'G', p. 476).

1823   The making of Wellington Road (according to a new method): around 1,000 feet from west corner of burial ground (LB 'H', pp. 270 and 354).

1824–25   The surveyors Messrs Oakley & Phillips sent Walpole a draft for a turnpike road proposal in May 1824 (LB 'I', p. 91). Walpole prepared Clauses to be inserted in the Bill at EE 2651/183A(7). The Bill, opposed once more by Maryon Wilson was rejected in 1824 and again in 1825 (see note 44 on p. 511).

1826   (5 May) Act of Parliament for making a turnpike road from St John's Wood Chapel at EE 2650/1/395(A3) and EE 2651/237(1).

1827   (May) 'New North Road (a Turnpike Road now making at Finchley & proceeding to London)' (LB 'K', p. 327).

1828   (Summer) The St John's Wood end of Finchley Road is delayed because Shaw has not decided on the precise line of the road (LB 'L', p. 77).

1829   (3 March) £2,773 2s. is awarded to H. S. Eyre by jury 'as compensation payable for Land required from him for the Road including Timber thereon' (LB 'P', p. 387, and LB 'S', p. 560).
(October) First mention of 'Line of Turnpike Road & Branch' (the future Finchley and Avenue Roads) (LB 'L', p. 385).

1830   (May) Opening of the 'Finchley Road' (probably the first written mention of the abbreviated form) (LB 'L', p. 507).

1850   (14 August) 'An Act for continuing the Term of … An Act for making a Turnpike Road from Saint John's Chapel', see EE 2651/283B(8).

1871   (24 July) 'Marylebone and Finchley Roads … The Turnpike Gates and Bars were removed' (see Mark Seale, *Turnpike and Toll-Bars*, London, 1930, vol. II, p. 702).

7072 WELLINGTON ROAD. ST. JOHN'S WOOD.   LONDON.

120 View of Wellington Road which becomes Finchley Road just before the steeple of All Saints. 'Wellington Road I always considered as the main key to the Estate otherwise I would not have sustained such an expence in the formation of it' (LB 'I', p. 237, dated 22 December 1824). The Eyres paid over £1,800 for this road using a new building technique, which turned out to be a great disappointment (LB 'I', p. 562). The steeple of All Saints Church is visible. Pamela E. Edwards, *St John's Wood and Regent's Park in Old Picture Postcards*, London, 1997, pl. 11.

early culprit: 'I am also informed that your men have at different times taken Gravel off the Road and carried it into your own prem[is]es, My Brother has been at a Great Expence in making the above Road, and the Gravel if carried off must be replaced at a fresh expence.'[40]

Walpole had had an early vision of Wellington Road which had to be postponed while the canal was being built. This road was formed in 1817, giving rise to another vision – linking St John's Wood and Hampstead, the future Finchley Road. The Eyres went as far as promoting a bill in Parliament (1820), but it met with considerable opposition and in the end Walpole had to withdraw: 'I am bothered to Death[,] I am more hunted about this bill, than any old fox in Essex ever was.'[41] The Finchley Road would be realised, but not until a decade later, initiated by others and with the full collaboration of the Eyres.

From time to time and when circumstances dictated, Walpole would prepare summaries of events to ensure various parties gained a proper understanding of the facts. He produced such a summary about the water supply in St John's Wood (see pp. 234–35), and he also prepared an exceptionally detailed account of the history of the Finchley Road in order to combat the stereotypical arguments used against landlords and their assumed greed. Walpole argued that in times of public penury Colonel Eyre had bailed out the Turnpike Road Trust, on the condition that the money he lent would be returned with interest. The letter reviews the history of the road between 1826 and 1850, and makes fascinating points about the different issues which sealed the fate of the Finchley Road. It is a remarkable document (see Appendix 4, p. 456).

The actual making of Wellington Road happened in 1823 (Plate 120). Because of its strategic role, Walpole strove to make it a thoroughly modern road and rejected the usual road making technique in favour of a new method pioneered by A. C. Chambers: 'The Road to be substantially made upon the principal [principle] you have discovered of burning the Clay and with such other materials as may be necessary.'[42] He was to be bitterly disappointed by this project, and wrote a furious letter to Chambers's agent:

> The Wellington road has failed generally & not merely opposite Hintons Ground – the ruinous state of that road cannot therefore proceed from the use Hinton has made of it, but from the want of hard materials, this is notorious to every body who has seen the road & understands any thing of road making…. I must now give Mr Chambers notice to put the road into immediate repair & I send you this notice as the agent of Mr Chambers & … if the Wellington Road is not immed[iate]ly put into good & substantial repair, I shall call upon his Surety to do so, & if he does not do it, I shall employ Mr McAdam or some other established Road Maker to repair the Wellington road & shall require Mr Chambers or his Surety to repay me the expence.[43]

By 1828 the cost of the Finchley Road (overall, not simply in St John's Wood) was substantial: 'you will see that £10,845 has already been paid towards making the road of which £9050 is secured by mortgages upon the Tolls and £1795 remains to be secured…. I hope your client will be induced to advance £14,000 upon the credit of these Tolls,' wrote Walpole in a vigorous fund-raising attempt.[44] Even after the official 1830 opening of the Finchley Road, the bankrupting effect of this ambitious project was very much felt by the Eyres, as the two brothers were sued by Mr Hoffman: 'claim ag[ain]st Col[one]l Eyre & me as having subscribed to the undertaking for making a turnpike Road to Finchley and Barnet'.[45] By 1841 Colonel Eyre still had not been paid for the purchase of the land and at this point no investor was receiving any money.[46] In the late 1840s another battle had to be fought following Sir James McAdam's decision to exclude the Marylebone and Finchley Turnpike Trust from the Turnpike Acts Continuance Bill. This meant that the toll income would be stopped, and Walpole, outraged, defied McAdam to suggest a way of dealing with the massive debt left to pay: over £58,000 between the mortgage debt and the interest.[47] McAdam was forced to back down. The Act which began on 1 November 1850 dictated that the management of the trust was vested in the Metropolis Roads Commissioners; at that time the debt was recorded as being around £33,000.

The presence of toll-gates between 1830 and 1871 in the vicinity of Swiss Cottage certainly boosted the business of the tavern there but was otherwise a hindrance to building development. William Holme Twentyman, the developer of the land between Finchley and Avenue Roads, seems to have struggled with this issue in 1840. This is how Walpole summed up the situation:

> I don't know under what impression you agreed to take the ground on the West side of the Branch Turnpike R[oa]d for building upon, but I am quite positive I never told you that the Toll Bar should be removed having no authority to remove this toll Bar & the removal of it dependant upon the trustees…. You were aware when you took the first & second pieces of ground on the East side of the B[ranch] T[urnpike] R[oa]d of the existence of this Toll Bar & you were equally aware of it when you agreed to take the Lot on the West side of the Road.
>
> I readily admit that at the last meeting of the Trustees when the removal of the Toll Bar was objected to by the majority of the trustees that you then stated that you should not

carry out the engagements you had entered into or build any more upon the St Johns Wood Estate. This declaration I attributed to the excitement of the moment & did not suppose that you could have any serious intention of abandoning engagements that you had previously entered into.[48]

121 This photograph records the old toll-gate at Swiss Cottage prior to it being removed in July 1871. Camden Local Studies.

In 1859, when the abolition of turnpike gates and toll bars was being discussed, the debt was under £26,000. The report prepared prior to the abolition read: 'but the actual value of the debt is probably considerably less than that sum'.[49] A nineteenth-century photograph (Plate 121) offers a last glimpse of the old toll-gate at Swiss Cottage before it was taken down in 1871.

Pricing of the land

One of the advantages of the Marylebone and Finchley Turnpike Road project was that the land needed was not 'given' but could be sold at its real value. Pricing the land was a sophisticated process which had to take into account the general context of the neighbourhood. Those who were quick to assume the Eyres were only interested in making a profit would have been humbled by their attitude towards this valuation: 'As Col[one]l Eyre is the Proprietor of so large a Property it is of importance to keep up its value but he is not anxious upon the present occasion that any attempt should be made to over rate it.' This philosophy was followed up in practice, as out of the three surveyors who were asked to value the land, the estate architect John Shaw's was, at £400 per acre, the most modest sum by a large margin. The surveyor of the Portman estate, Mr Parkinson, valued it at £500 and Edward Tilbury, a Marylebone surveyor, at £465 per acre. The three valuations were made 'without communication with each other'. As there was considerable variation in the valuations, the colonel and the trustees 'agreed to go to a reference', and 'as many of the Trustees are Col[one]l Eyres intimate friends' the decision was left to 'a Jury … summoned for Tuesday 3rd March [1829] at the Eyre Arms Tavern'.

The final outcome may have been disappointing to the Eyres as the land was purchased at just under £300 (see Appendix 4). Their contemporaries saw things differently: Colonel Eyre was being paid for the land he provided to a road that he promoted to develop his estate (Appendix 4 gives the Eyre version of this). By contrast, Henry Gore Chandless successfully speculated on the estate by reselling the land he had just bought at around the same time (see Appendix 2, sale 'E'):

> Mr Chandless before he had completed his Conveyance resold the greater part of this Land – eight acres of that part of it which is nearest to London he sold by Auction in small Lots and which produced him £6720 being at the rate of £840 per Acre – Four acres he sold by private contract to a Mr Kerslake and for which he got £2800 being at the rate of £700 per Acre…. the remaining 18 Acres he sold for £9720 being at the rate of £540 per acre – this is the lowest part of the ground and is most distant from Town and of course the least valuable part…. The Total amount of the money received by Mr Chandless for the 30 acres was £19240 and which for 30 Acres will be found to average £641.6.8 per Acre.[50]

Maintenance and lighting

In 1858, the estate's clerk, Charles Freeth senior, wrote despairingly: 'The time & trouble ab[ou]t the Roads is quite disheartening.'[51] Problems of road maintenance which had been seething in the background appear to have come to a head at about that time over two difficult cases – Abbey Road and St John's Wood Park. These two roads had not been made according to the terms of the agreement and had been left to deteriorate until they had become 'most injurious to all persons & property near it – and the subject of long continued & just complaint'.[52] In his young and energetic days Walpole probably would have financed the repair to ensure prompt action and then applied pressure upon the lessees to obtain repayment. His son Edwin recommended to the clerk a course of action which would not solve the problem of St John's Wood Park: 'It was clearly the fault of the various Lessees that by not contributing their respective portions of the expence in 1855 that the parish did not adopt the Road and in fact there is such a bad feeling between Mr Twentyman [who formed the road] and his neighbours in respect of this Road that any amicable arrangement seems hopeless,' wrote Charles Freeth on Edwin's behalf in 1858.[53] John Eyre, who by then had become the tenant for life of the estate, commissioned a counsel's opinion to determine whether or not the road should be considered as made, as this had legal implications.[54] In the event, the situation would only be resolved in April 1860 when Charles Freeth expressed gratitude to Hampstead vestry.[55]

Street lighting was the responsibility of the vestry from the start, and the earliest mention of street lighting in the Eyre archive occurs in 1829 at Grove End Road, just outside the future Alma-Tadema house. In the 1820s it was the residence of the Kipps family, headed by Thomas George, a coachmaker from Great Marylebone Street.[56] Having requested £8 towards the making of the road outside his premises, Walpole added: 'There is no difficulty remaining as to the placing [of] the Lamp near your prem[is]es.'[57]

Gas lighting made its appearance in London in 1810, and the Marylebone vestry first refused the lighting of Oxford Street by that method in 1815.[58] However by 1829, when lamps are recorded in Grove End Road, the vestry had given in to gas lighting in Marylebone after a long and bitter battle. Many parishioners presented petitions in favour of gas, and so the vestry reluctantly took the decision to adopt gas lighting in the summer of 1824.[59]

The fear which gas could generate in the early decades after its appearance is palpable in Walpole's letter books: as late as 1845 when Walpole was finally able to contemplate gas lighting inside Swiss Cottage Tavern, he still felt nervous about its danger, asking his developer friend and lessee of the tavern: 'What think you of a Gas lamp in the Hall[?] Now is the time for doing it, I think you have a Gas lamp at your Door[.] do you ever find any inconvenience from the Escape of the gas[?]'[60] This fear may have originated with the close relationship between the Eyre estate and Sun Fire Insurance, the principal insurance company on the estate as well as its mortgage holder. Their position on this issue is revealed in a letter from Charles Freeth, who doubled as a Sun Fire Insurance agent, to Shillibeer, a tenant on the Seymour estate:

> it appears that the premises you rent in Commercial Place City Road … are now lighted
> by the Patent Domestic Gas Apparatus which is manufactured therein and that the Sun
> Fire Office where the above premises are insured will not insure premises ag[ain]st any
> loss or damage occasioned by explosion & from the consequences thereof[.]/I have there
> to request that the Manufacture of Gas on the above premises may be imm[ediate]ly
> discontinued & any apparatus or fittings objectionable to the Fire Office removed &
> I must beg you to send me a Letter stating that this has been done.[61]

The manufacture of gas on the premises also took place at the Eyre Arms Tavern, an enterprise the Eyres viewed with grave concern. Walpole asked for the gas-works to be discontinued in January 1834.[62] The injunction was forcefully reiterated three months later by the clerk: 'With respect to the alter[ati]ons in the Draft Lease the only one that appears material is that as to the making [of] Gas & which Mr WE [Walpole] will not consent to on any acc[oun]t.'[63] Under these circumstances we should not be surprised by Walpole's reply to Henry Cory at the Gas Light and Coke Company in 1835: 'I have given this subject much cons[iderati]on since the meeting on Wednesday last & I must decline becoming a Director or taking any responsible part in this concern.'[64]

Nevertheless the estate's lessees clearly wished to adopt this method of lighting, as is further demonstrated by the lighting of Hall Place. In February 1831 Walpole wrote: 'the best way to get Hall Place lighted wo[ul]d be by an application to the Vestry by the inhabitants.'[65] The residents chose a more independent route as Walpole confirmed a decade later:

> The Houses in Hall Place were built in the year 1822 & 1823 & were shortly afterwards
> inhabited, from that time down to the present time the Carriage way – Footpaths of Hall

Place have been kept in repair by the inhabitants without any expence to the Parish although the inhabitants during the whole of that period have been assessed to & paid the Highway rate[.] The inhabitants have also lighted Hall Place at their own expence.[66]

Despite his early reservations, Walpole liaised directly with a gas company to arrange the lighting of Wellington Road:

With reference to the conversation I had with you this morn[in]g as to lighting the Wellington Road … it appears from the Plans in this office that the length of that Road from the North end of the P[ari]sh Burial Gro[un]d where the lights terminate to Grove End Road in front of the Eyre Arms Tavern is 1300 feet or 433 yds[.]/From the above spot to Circus Road already lighted by your Comp[an]y for the p[ari]sh is about 800 ft or 267 y[ar]ds – In the arrangement of the lights it will be requisite that a Lamp sho[ul]d be placed at the Corner of Circus Road & of Grove End Road.[67]

By the time the estate witnessed a truly massive gas explosion, the kind Walpole had dreaded so much, the year was 1866, and the house at 62 Avenue Road was that of the art dealer Ernest Gambart, but by then Walpole had been dead for ten years (see p. 307).

WATER

Be sure to build only where good water is to be had freely, and where you can as freely get rid of it (John B. Papworth in 1818).[68]

John Papworth would have been familiar with the St John's Wood estate because his brother Thomas was an early lessee at Alpha Cottages. No doubt Thomas subscribed to this wise tenet, and he may have been one of the tenants who required Walpole to bring water to the Alpha Cottages as early as 1806: 'Tenants are now pressing me to make a well.'[69]

There was plenty of natural water in St John's Wood, as Walpole repeatedly pointed out when the canal company seemed unable to complete the Regent's Canal through lack of water (see below). Several ponds were sited around St John's Wood Farm, one of which was even nicknamed the canal; others, including a large one at what would later become the junction of Finchley and Boundary Roads, were sited in the northern half of the estate: 'which ponds have never known to be dry'.[70] Walpole even proposed to establish an 'ornamental reservoir' in 1814, to be funded by the canal company, which would have elegantly combined the practical (feeding the canal) with the beautiful.[71]

The delivery of water to the homes of north-west London was fraught with many problems. Walpole attempted to persuade the Grand Junction Water Works to lay pipes at Alpha Cottages in August 1813. He also used this company to supply his own home in Beaumont Street[72] but found it unsatisfactory, as a letter of May 1814 records:

I send a Jug of Water that you may see the State it came into my house yesterday after the Engine had been working [Plate 122] I attribute this very much to the want of washing the pipes and if that is so & I have made such repeated complaints about it I hope the Turncock of this District will be discharged as he must have neglected his Business most shamefully[.]

To the Directors of the West Middlesex Water Works

When I had the honor of attending your Board on the 2nd Instant [1822], I thought we had come to a clear understanding relative to the Covenant contained in the Leases granted upon my brothers St Johns Wood Estate and the Supply of Water to be furnished by your company for the use of that property[.]

… I am aware that many persons have presented the intention and meaning of that Covenant under an impression that it has been introduced with some hostile view towards your Company,

This Covenant originated in an Agreement that was made in the year 1806 between the Chelsea Company and my brother for the supply of his St Johns Wood Estate and was intended for the benefit of that Company. This I believe was long before your Company was established[.] some time after this arrangement had been made it was discovered that the Chelsea Water Works were at that time either incapable of furnishing the property with a sufficient supply of water or it was not thought worth their while to do so, at least so I understood it, Shortly after the Grand Junction Water Works Company had obtained their Act of Parliament, The Agreement which had been entered into by the Chelsea Company and my brother was abandoned by mutual consent, and the Grand Junction undertook to supply the Estate, Previous to this alteration in the supply the Chelsea water works company had been named in the Saint Johns Wood Leases, but when the Grand Junction Company undertook the supply their names were introduced.

When the arrangement was made between the different water companies for dividing the Town into districts, and for each company having the individual service of particular parts of the Town[,] The Saint Johns Wood Estate (with other properties in that neighbourhood) seems to have been allotted to your Company[.] Your Company's name was then introduced into the Leases, but unfortunately at this period the public mind was in such a state of agitation and discontent in consequence of the proceedings of the water Companies, that the very name of any Company concerned in that arrangement became obnoxious and offensive to individuals as well as to the public, I then omitted mentioning any name in the Covenant but continued the substance and effect.

Having explained to you the origin of the Covenant, I shall now say a few words upon the language and effect of this Covenant which seems to have created an unnecessary alarm amongst some of your proprietors, The Covenant does not authorize me to call upon the Tenants to take a supply of water from any particular Company unless such Company would supply the same at as cheap a rate and

122 'Monster Soup commonly called Thames Water being a correct represent[at]ion of that precious stuff doled out to us!!!' This etching and aquatint by 'Paul Pry' (i.e. William Heath) was published in 1828: a drop of water has been magnified to show the frightening array of impurities it contains. The heading at the top dedicates the print to 'the London Water Companies'. City of London, London Metropolitan Archives (Collage 18107).

of as good and wholesome a quality as any other Company, the most therefore that can be said of this Covenant, even if I were disposed to exercise it[,] is that it is calculated to excite a fair competition between two Companies dealing in the same Article and after all I have heard about the vast sums of money that have been expended in establishing your works and the great losses that your Company have [sic] sustained in creating these works and it being confidently stated that no new Company could be established without great risk to their property[.]

Your Company ought not to be alarmed at any proceedings which hold out nothing beyond fair compe[ti]tion or at least if they are so alarmed it is not prudent to proclaim that alarm to the public, and I must say if you quarrel with my Covenant, you complain of that which cannot do more than excite fair Compe[ti]tion, I have entered into this Explanation first to show you that the Covenant was not introduced with any prejudiced illiberal or improper Motive, concerning your Company[,] next that it did not originate in the arrangements which had been made between the different Water Companies, and lastly that the Covenant cannot affect your Interests so long as you are disposed to supply the same Article upon the same terms as any other Company[.]

The arrangement which I understood to have been agreed upon the 2nd Instant, was that you should engage to extend and continue your supply upon my brothers Estate at a fair & reasonable rate and as far as your power enabled you and that I should enter into an Engagement not to exercise the Covenant to your prejudice – The only point that remained for explanation was, that you should state to me, the extent of your powers, and which by this time you are probably prepared to do[.]

On behalf of my brother I beg to state that I am willing to enter into any Agreement that may be required to prevent the Covenant being exercised to the Injury or prejudice of your Company or indeed I will waive it altogether if your Company will agree to continue to supply the Estate at a fair & reasonable rate and will extend the supply as the Buildings proceed and have sufficient power to do so[.]

I will not conclude without again assuring you that the Covenant was not introduced into my brothers Leases with any intention of injuring your property or with any hostile views to your or any other Company and after having explained to you that the Covenant was inserted in the Lease long before your Company was established, you cannot suppose that it was introduced with any improper motive or illiberal Feeling towards the West Middlesex Water Works Company.[73]

I have now submitted to use the Grand Junction Water for above six months in the most filthy and dirty state & I am constantly under the necessity of sending for other Water to boil Fish and other things in[.] if this cannot be remedied & that immediately I shall be under the necessity of applying to the West Middlesex or some other company.[74]

In 1822, Walpole wrote one of his illuminating summaries about water supply on the estate – a long document but worth quoting in full (see box). It was addressed to the directors of the West Middlesex Water Works, who had come to believe that the water covenant in the Eyre leases was prejudicial to their company. This letter gives a chronology of the different water companies which supplied the estate, each of which had laid their own pipes.

A glance at the water covenants before and after this April 1822 letter will show that the West Middlesex Company must have had a point, and Walpole, however justified he may have been in so cautiously phrasing the earlier covenant, gave in to the request of the offended water board.

1821 water covenant:

And also ... shall take or require a supply of water for the use of the said messuages or dwellinghouses and premises ... from any water Company or Water Companies ... for the time being shall and will take water from such Company as he the said Walpole Eyre ... shall or may from time to time nominate and appoint and shall and will pay the said Company a fair annual rate for such supply of water so long as the same shall be duly and sufficiently supplied and of a good and wholesome quality and at as cheap a rate as any other Company would supply the same provided that they [the lessees] ... requiring or taking the same be not made subject or liable to any expense or charge for laying on the said water[.][75]

1822 water covenant:

And also shall and will pay a fair annual rate to the Governor and Company of the West Middlesex water works and their Successors or any other company to be named by the said Walpole Eyre for the supply of water which shall or may be laid on to the said premises so long as the same shall continue to be duly and sufficiently supplied and of a good and wholesome quality.[76]

Walpole had good grounds for introducing a cautious covenant in his leases, as he explained to James Burton in 1819:

The Water Companies[,] by the arrangements they have made[,] have established so complete a monopoly that unless some steps are taken by the Legislature to Controul [sic] them they may & no doubt will in the course of a few years increase their rates and this to any amount the proprietors may judge fit[.] under these circ[cumstanc]es I think it incumbent upon every Proprietor of building ground for the protection of their tenants to insert a Clause in their Leases similar to the one I have introduced in Mr Struthers[.]

The present Directors of the West Middx Water Company profess a determination not to make an exorbetant [sic] demand for a supply of Water and as I understand them to be men of high honor and Character, I have no doubt they will act up to their profession but they may die or sell their shares, and new Directors be appointed who will be at liberty to make whatever demand they think fit[.][77]

The chronology and facts presented in Walpole's earlier summary can certainly be trusted, though such a letter would necessarily gloss over some of the more messy aspects of the estate's water adventures. There is no trace, for instance, of the special relationship between the Eyre estate and the Grand Junction Water Works (GJWW). Walpole seemed determined to support GJWW, which he joined. We mentioned earlier his efforts to encourage them to lay down pipes at Alpha Road, but they must have been reluctant to do so without some assurance the tenants would take their water. So in August 1814 Walpole tried to persuade forty-seven tenants to switch to GJWW, without much success it would appear, as few replies were received.[78] In 1816 Walpole was keen to oppose the 'principle of the bill' aiming to unite the water companies of north and west London.[79] Although the letter books do not state his reasons, he almost certainly regarded the competition between companies as a lever for obtaining a good service. In 1819 Walpole complained bitterly of the 75 per cent increase to his home bill by the West Middlesex Company.[80] However, by 1834 he must have felt reasonably content with the provision of water in St John's Wood, as he chose not to support surveyor John White junior's proposal to set up a water company in that neighbourhood, arguing: 'I fear the District is too limited for the object you have in view.'[81] The Eyres also dissented about the 'Parliamentary Notice for a projected Water Company' put forward in 1840, a project which evidently came to nothing.[82]

DRAINS AND SEWERS

Walpole confronted the issue of drainage and sewers as early as 1805 when he wrote to the different tenants along Alpha Road:

> The greater part of the Tenants who have entered into Agreements for building upon the St Johns Wood Est[a]te have applied to me to have a Common Sewer made & as this will be absolutely necessary for the Comfort & Convenience of the Inhabitants of the Houses already engaged to be built, I intend to have one made & I have accordingly had an estimate of the expence & I find that the proportion to be paid by the Tenants of each Lot will be thirteen pounds five shillings. I shall give immediate directions for making the Sewer, & mean to call upon the different tenants to pay their Proportion of this expence by quarterly Installments the first to be paid at Micha[elma]s next & which will amount to £3..6..3 for each Lot.[83]

This indicates the high standard of infrastructure the Eyre brothers wanted for their estate right from the start, despite their lack of substantial resources. Walpole was also careful to devise a fair way of making his tenants contribute without halting the project or disadvantaging the builders with large sums to pay upfront. The issue of drainage was at the forefront of Walpole's thoughts not simply at St John's Wood but within his home. Before taking his house in Beaumont Street he wrote to the Marylebone parish clerk: 'I am about taking the lease of No 21 in your Street, I wish you wo[ul]d have the goodness to inform me whether there is any objection to the Houses in Beaumont Street either from Drains or any other circumstances.'[84]

Colonel Eyre's sewer

The first sewer on the estate was built by March 1806 up Lisson Grove and along the Avenue of Trees.[85] It was soon described as 'Colonel Eyre's Sewer'. The following year, in 1807, Walpole agreed to construct another sewer, this time on the eastern side of the estate, as part of the purchase deal with Marylebone vestry of the burial ground.[86] 'Colonel Eyre's Sewer' features on the c.1811 estate working plan (Plates 53 and 54), and the Eyres were proud of its creation. At first there was some confusion between the use of terms such as 'drain' and 'sewer', Colonel Eyre's (common) sewer frequently being described as a drain.

The letter books chart the rise of the Commissioners of Sewers, powerful and at times intransigent, a group with whom confrontation and clashes seemed inevitable.[87] The Eyres were not alone in clashing with the Commissioners of Sewers. The canal company drew up a 'Statement of the Dispute between the Regent's Canal Company and the Commissioners of the Mary-le-Bone Sewers' (early 1810s):

Is it reasonable that a body of water brought to a particular spot, for a particular purpose, at the expence of a vast sum of money, should become the property of the Commissioners of Sewers, because it is brought within that District, over the natural springs and rivulets of which the law has given them dominion for the purposes of public sewage? Is it reasonable they should have any controul [sic] over that water, farther than to see that it does no injury to the sewage entrusted to their care? And yet this is the dominion which the Commissioners of Mary-le-Bone Sewers seek.[88]

While the canal company battled it out with the Commissioners of Sewers (see text below caption), Walpole was more anxious than ever to protect the drainage work which had been done at St John's Wood:

It [the Canal] also intercepts the Drainage of nearly 250 acres of Land which now drain thro' the Line of the intended Canal in a southerly direction.... The proprietor has already expended nearly £2000 in making a Sewer up to the North West Corner of his Estate which according to the Plan and Section of the Canal deposited at the Sessions House will be rendered entirely useless to this Property by the projected Canal, The whole of the Estate is within the District of the Commissioners of Sewers and from the nature of the Soil can only be drained by Sewers. The 250 Acres therefore which now drain thro' the Line of the intended Canal will be for ever destroyed as Building ground unless the projectors of the Canal furnish such Drainage as will hereafter be sufficient for the Drainage of Buildings.[89]

Walpole's worst fears did not materialise as the canal company willingly undertook the appropriate sewerage work.

Developing the network

As early as 1810 Walpole had spoken about the expansion of the sewers' network and the need to sell parts of the estate to enable such development: 'I find the Commissioners of Sewers will require main Sewers to be made thro the Estate which is an Expence the Estate can never bear without selling parts to pay for it.'[90] The Commissioners of Sewers seem to have required from Walpole an overall plan of the drainage system. Walpole complied with their request: 'I intend to submit to the Cons[iderati]on of the Comm[issione]rs of Sewers such a plan for the Drainage of the Saint Johns Wood Estate as I conceive will be adequate to the system of Buildings now carrying on.'[91] By February 1811 such a plan had indeed been submitted, though Walpole could not help the odd grumble after a meeting: 'They are a strange set,' he noted on 21 August 1811. Nevertheless, Walpole knew that strategically he needed a good working relationship with the commissioners, and by the end of that year he had applied to join the 'strange set'.[92]

However proud the Eyres may have been of the colonel's sewer in Lisson Grove, more – many more – sewers like it were needed (Plate 123). With the arrival of the canal company Walpole was quick to negotiate the making of further sewers, on both the east and west sides of the estate:

I am authorized by a person to say if the Regent Canal Company will give him a thousand pounds that he will make the Sewer from the Sewer in Baker Street north to the South East corner of the St. Johns Wood Estate. I think this offer is worth your attention.[93]

123 West London drainage plan of 1844. The imprint reads: 'Plan of the Districts Drained by Water Courses Discharging into the River Thames between the City of London and the Parish of Fulham Being that portion of the General District under the Jurisdiction of the Commissioners of Sewers for the City & Liberty of Westminster & part of the County of Middlesex'. The map, 'drawn and engraved by James Wyld, Geographer to the King', is marked 'corrected to January 1840' and 'further corrected to August 1844'. The King's Scholar Pond sewer is the thin dark blue line which goes round the west side of Regent's Park and into the Thames just west of the Millbank Penitentiary. Eyre estate archive, EE 2652/25(B)

The statement of the dispute between the Regent's Canal Company and the Commissioners of the Mary-le-Bone Sewers (early 1810s) described the drainage of that part of London: 'All the water north of the New Road drains into the King's Scholar Pond Sewer: that Sewer begins in Mary-le-Bone Park, at the north end of Baker street, and empties itself into the Thames at Millbank, Westminster, and is an arched Sewer all the way.

There are no springs or rivulets north of the New Road; all the water which enters the Sewer, at the end of Baker-street, is rain water, running over the surface of the land from the higher ground.

This surface water, accumulating in the valley, has formed itself a ravine ditch or water-course across Mary-le-Bone Park, in its way to the before mentioned Sewer, at the north end of Baker-street.

A small part of this surface water takes another course, namely, through the adjoining land of Mr Eyre (westward) into the New Road, and from thence into the King's Scholar Pond Sewer before mentioned.' (Eyre estate archive, EE 2651/141(F)).

PLAN
of
Districts
DRAINED BY WATER COURSES,
Discharging into the River Thames,
BETWEEN THE
CITY OF LONDON AND THE PARISH OF FULHAM.
Being that portion of the
GENERAL DISTRICT UNDER THE JURISDICTION
of the Commissioners of Sewers for the
CITY & LIBERTY OF WESTMINSTER
and part of the
COUNTY OF MIDDLESEX

The Commissioners have given permission to make a Sewer up the Avenue of Trees and across the Road leading from the New Parish Chapel and also to make a Sewer along that Road which is to empty itself into the Sewer up the Avenue of Trees.... I sho[ul]d be obliged by your beginning this Sewer immed[iate]ly ... that I may continue it across the Road to the Chapel.[94]

Walpole soon tested the real power of the commissioners; he was concerned that houses on the Portman estate positioned to drain into Colonel Eyre's sewer should contribute to its cost:

I sho[ul]d conceive as these Houses will have the full benefit of the Sewer I have built that you will oblige the proprietors to drain at once into it & to pay me a proportion of the Expence of making it as far as their frontage extends. This is a point of Great Consequence to my Brothers St Johns Wood Estate & I sho[ul]d therefore be glad to have the Decision of the Court of Sewers upon it, The whole of this resolves itself into this simple Question whether the Commissioners can oblige parties having drainage into an open Water Course where a Sewer is built in front of their Houses to drain into such Sewer & to pay a proportion of the expence of it.[95]

The problem would not go away and a year later, in 1813, despite the issue of a commissioners' order, the developer on the Portman estate effectively broke into the Eyres' sewer without permission or compensation, driving Walpole to utter fury.[96] Eventually, by 1816, Walpole's efforts were rewarded, the Commissioners of Sewers having devised a system which seemed to work well: clearance and guidance to drain into any sewer had to be obtained from the Commissioners of Sewers, who would only issue the correct guidelines and their permission once they had received a letter from the relevant landlord. Most of the sewers on the Eyre estate were in Walpole's name,[97] and the letter from the Commissioners of Sewers was only issued once the financial contribution had been settled and the landlord's permission granted.

Walpole described the procedure when he billed Mr Ward's solicitor in 1818: 'an Account of the charge I make for giving him permission to drain into the Sewer built by me up Lisson Grove[.] The sum I charge for this drainage is 14/6 per foot run – Mr Ward informs me he wants to drain three houses of 16 feet front each making together 48 feet – the amount of the sum to be paid for that number of feet at 14/6 per foot will be £34..16 – if you will send me a draft for that sum I will return you my receipt with a Letter to the Commissioners of Sewers to request they will give him leave to make the above drainage.'[98] From that date onwards the letter books provide a reliable record of all houses being connected to the sewerage system, this information often carrying both the names of the lessees and the builders in charge of the project.

Further improvements came in 1820 when gulley drains are first mentioned, supplied and installed by the commissioners.[99] These grids were intended to channel surface water into the sewers: 'We shall be much obliged by your causing Gulley Drains to be made from the Road called Circus Road and a Road intended to be called Leonard Place into the sewer lately built by us under the s[ai]d Lennard Place and we have to request than [sic] an early attention may be given to the doing of this work as the Roads are much injured by the Surface drainage not being carried away and they are not parochial Roads.'[100] An 1837 letter shows how well organised things would become when the Eyre estate office requested from the Commissioners of Sewers 'a dozen of the Printed

Regulations for building sewers & as many of the printed plan of the sewers of the size of 5 feet by 2.6'.[101]

A new sewer could only be built once permission had been obtained from the commissioners, and this applied equally to Walpole. When he wished to build the sewer along the southern section of the future Wellington Place, he wrote to the commissioners: 'It is my wish to make a Sewer for a length of about four hundred and Fifty Feet from the Mouth of the Sewer lately built by me between the north side of the Orphans Clergy Ground at St Johns Wood and the side of Gibbs Nursery[.]/The Sewer I am now requesting permission to build will form part of the Drainage you allowed me to make by open cutting and will drain in a southerly direction.'[102] By 1825 Walpole could dispense sensible advice to large-scale builders such as William Hall regarding some of their drainage proposals: 'you propose that the drainage which comes Eastward of the ground you have taken should be carried through Mr Challoners ground [site of Neville Court opposite Abbey Road Studios]. I am quite confident the Commissioner of Sewers will not allow this to be done & I understand it is a general rule with them that all Sewage should be carried along Roads.'[103] Walpole then recommended the preparation of a drainage plan for the part of the estate that Hall was developing.

Within a few years no roads would be contemplated without first building a sewer underneath them. At times Walpole felt this was an overly restrictive approach: 'I am sorry to say there seems to [be] a feeling in the Vestry not to take Roads under their Care unless Sewers are built under them[.] I think this extremely unreasonable and very unnecessary[.] until however this point is settled I do not think it would be advisable to make the Road along Upper York Place [now St Ann's Terrace],' he wrote to developer Charles Freeth junior in 1841.[104]

Accidents and blockages

Few sewers collapsed to judge by the evidence found in the letter books. Only a couple of instances are recorded: one in 1819 connected to the houses of the canal company and another in 1841 near the Barracks: 'The late heavy rains or some other Cause has (I fear) caused the Sewer under Ordnance Road (near Acacia Road and near the Spot where I understood Mr Jenkins to say he had directions to place a Gully drain) to fall in.'[105]

One particular incident, however, involved the very vocal Gray's Inn lawyer Mr Kibblewhite. The following extracts from correspondence between May 1830 to September 1831 show how awkward things could become prior to having adequate records of the drainage system. Building sewers was not enough; you also needed to know what precisely had been built. Kibblewhite, who purchased the lease of three houses on the north side of South Bank, experienced drain problems which went on for years. Here is a brief summary of the issues as they first arose:

> You seem to think that I have neglected your application when the fact is that … I have been frequently to the prem[is]es[,] have written to and had interviews with Mr Davis who built your house & several others Westward to learn from him the course of this drainage and I find it empties itself into the sewage in St J.W. Wood Grove…. I have also called several times upon Mr Bastin[,] Mr Neelds Agent[,] who had a hole dug near to your prem[is]es to try if we could find where the Obstruction was[.] I have since had a

Correspondence with Mr Neelds Surveyor and I am now awaiting his Answer.… it is hardly to be expected that I should destroy different Gent[lemen']s gardens to a distance of 500 ft when perhaps 20 would answer the purpose[.] (p. 21)

I will not be surprised if it turns out that y[ou]r house as well as the other houses built by Davis drain into a Cess Pool[.]/Mr Neeld has had a Cess Pool made in his prem[is]es with a flat Stone over which may at any time be removed & the Cess Pool emptied out but this will not afford such good drainage as Building a Sewer along South Bank provided the Sewer in St John's Wood Grove is deep enough to receive the drainage from it[.] (p. 55)

I went yesterday to South Bank[.] the depth of the Holes that have been opened [at the house west of Neeld] for the purpose of cleaning this drain is 12 or 14 feet & I see no good that can arise from keeping them open.… have you made the openings as suggested by me & what is the result[?] (p. 64)

After I saw you yesterday I saw Mr Burton & he informs me that he thinks the drain in front of your Cottage runs Eastward towards Park Road and empties into a regular Sewer built by him under the South Bank Road terminating on the East side of Alpha place[.] /Mr Burton seems quite of Opinion that the drain does not empty into the Sewer in St John's Wood Grove and the reason he gives for not knowing more respecting the drain is that it was made by Mr Davis contrary to his wishes (he desiring the proper Sewer under the Road) and surrepticiously [sic] introduced into some sewer[.] (p. 352)[106]

This episode demonstrates the limitations of the early sewerage infrastructure. The seven commissions which operated in London worked entirely independently, and there was no reliable overall plan for constructing sewers, no systematic record of what had been built already and no plans showing levels.[107] An 1847 royal commission concluded that the drainage of the metropolitan area should become the responsibility of a single competent body. Action was taken the following year with the formation of the Metropolitan Commission, though real progress was only made after 1855 when this commission was transferred to the Metropolitan Board of Works.[108]

THE REGENT'S CANAL

Early objections

When the canal was first proposed, Walpole had feared the worst. In those days canals were not picturesque, leisurely arteries but noisy, filthy, trade networks (Plate 124), as may be surmised from the following: 'When the Canal shall be filled with commerce; its banks lined with warehouses filled with the luxuries and necessaries of life; when thousands of the labouring classes shall have found employment …'.[109] It is not difficult to see how this description would have clashed with the Eyre brothers' ideal of a garden suburb. However, in his official list of objections, Walpole chose to focus on the tangible effects such a scheme would have on the building plans he was pursuing. This long list survives in the 'Statement as to the Injury there will be done to the St. John's Wood Estate … by the Intended Canal'.[110] The first of his objections was:

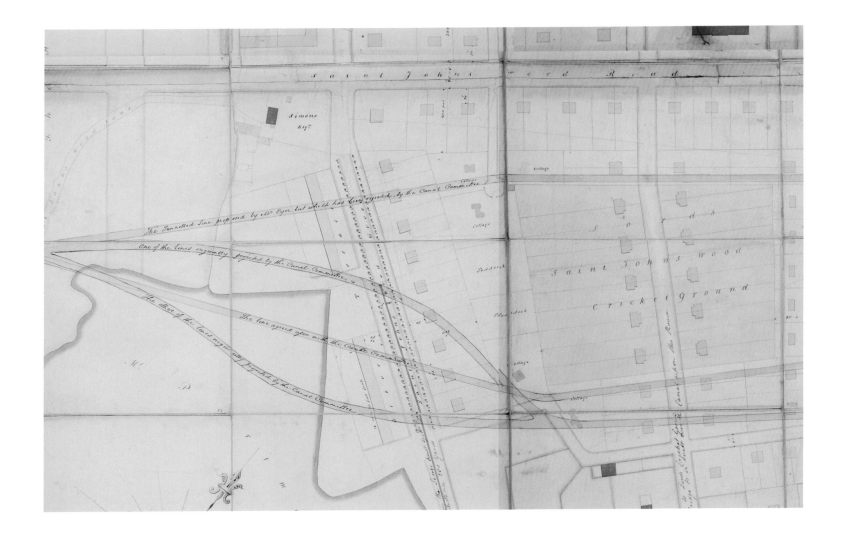

126 Detail from the working plan of the St John's Wood estate, c.1811 (full picture at Plate 53), which shows the different lines of the canal under discussion. None of these routes were adopted. Plate 127 shows the adopted route. Eyre estate archive (EE 2651/262(A)).

Lord … rather seems inclined to get rid of the whole concern, he tell[s] me he is getting old & that the Distance is to[o] great for him, he asks £500 for the ground buildings &c&c&c as they now stand, will give up the Subscription of this year of both the Marylebone and St Johns Wood Clubs which together I suppose amounts to nearly £500, Lord will also engage not to have any other Cricket Ground in the Neighbourhood of London.[120]

However, eighteen months later, he surprised everyone concerned by his demands: 'I have seen Lord[.] the value he sets upon his Lease exceeds any thing we had any Conception of, he talks of £9000,' wrote Walpole to John Nash in December 1812.[121] Eventually, in the summer of 1813 Walpole wrote to Shaw: 'I have settled Lords Agreement[.] he made many foolish objections, but I dont think there is [*sic*] any mater[i]al alterations.'[122]

It is fair to say that during the construction of the canal, the dealings with the company were often difficult. Walpole expected a swift response to his observations on the ground and ensuing requests, but the canal company (James Morgan being the main contact) seemingly ignored many of his pleas. The agreement between the two parties remained unresolved for two and a half years (see chronology, p. 245, and Plate 127): 'Since Oct[obe]r 1813 I have written above forty Letters to you upon the subject of this Agreement and of the Plans and Sections and never have been able to obtain them.'[123] In addition, the perpetual struggle to collect rent from the embattled canal company continued throughout the building works,[124] only improving when James Burton began building the canal houses, which in turn started the process of reducing the ground rent the canal company had to pay to the Eyres. Walpole also made a number of suggestions on fund raising and water supply which appear to have been largely ignored.[125]

So it is not surprising if, from time to time, Walpole could not resist the temptation of taunting the canal company: 'What have you done about water for the Canal[?] I hope you do not mean to bring it from Finchley.'[126] Or: 'why don't you begin to work the Canal[?] I hear you are waiting for water.'[127] The next incident, however, was more serious. On the south-west side of the canal facing Punkers Barn, the Eyre brothers sold a small piece of land to Marylebone vestry in 1825 to be used as a yard for depositing stone and other materials for the repair of streets and roads in the parish as well as for erecting a new watch house. The effectiveness of the canal for transporting materials was

127 Map taken from the agreement dated 29 July 1813 between Walpole Eyre and Charles Monro, John Delafield and John Nash, the directors of the canal company.

In 1812, after opposing the proposed Regent's Canal, Walpole and his brother found common ground for negotiations with the canal company which led to this formal agreement. This map is excellent for showing the actual state of road building by 1813. The southern tip of the estate was almost surrounded by roads: Alpha Road on the south side, Park Road on the east, about half of St John's Wood Road on the north and St John's Wood Grove, partially completed, on the west. In the summer of 1813 Walpole set out to complete the two unfinished roads. The Avenue of Trees is also clearly depicted. Eyre estate archive (EE 2651/141(B)).

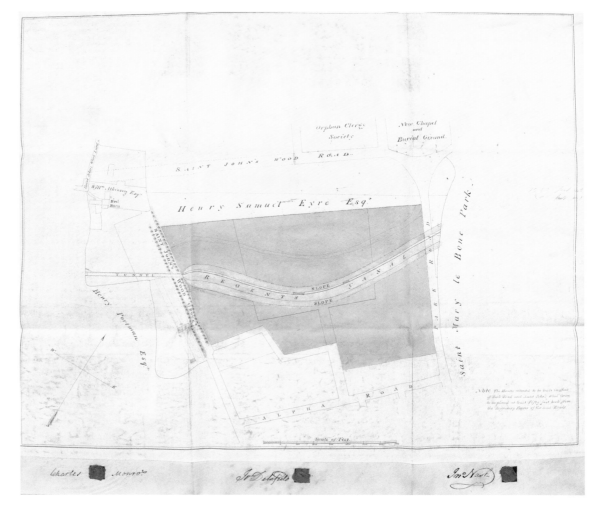

questioned by Walpole when he wrote, carping, to the canal company: 'It has been asserted by some of the Gent of the Vestry that these materials can be brought by the Thames & landed at Scotland Yard & carted from thence up to Marylebone cheaper than they can be brought from the Thames by the Regents Canal.… if this be so the Regents Canal has been made to very little purpose.'[128] Still, this did not stop him from purchasing canal shares and therefore from attending meetings of the Regent's Canal proprietors.[129]

GETTING ABOUT

The early nineteenth-century working plan for St John's Wood had envisaged blocks of stables, like those in the West End, on the west side of the estate (Plates 53 and 54). However, such a scheme was inappropriate on an estate which developed progressively over a period of sixty years or so. In time there would be small pockets of stables built among the houses. One of the earliest was built by developer William Hall on the north side of Elm Tree Road in 1820 and is clearly visible on the 1853 map (Plates 70 and 284) (we will return to this development below), while Robert Yeo on the northern reaches of the estate in the 1850s and 1860s seems to have made a successful business in leases for stables and coach houses.

Horse riding and private carriages

As a landowner, Henry Samuel Eyre owned a carriage, whereas Walpole's principal means of transport was the horse. Walpole rode everywhere – to Twickenham where his mother lived, to Bolney Court in Oxfordshire where he collected rents for William Hodges, to Parndon in Essex where his uncle Reverend John Johnson lived, to Watton (also in Essex) to visit his friend Reverend Samuel Hornbuckle – 'I will however ride over to you on Sunday (wind and weather permitting)' – and of course to St John's Wood, at times inviting others to do the same: 'I wish you wo[ul]d ride up & see how we are going on at St Johns Wood.'[130] Walpole did not have a carriage but would borrow his brother's when necessary.[131]

To run a carriage was an expensive business, as the accounts of Henry Samuel Eyre indicate. In the year 1803–4 the coachmakers Walker & Co. were paid over £220 in three instalments to settle the account to Christmas 1802. There were also the wages of a groom (£2 2s.), a livery stable keeper (£2 3s. 6d.) and a coachman (not entered). In September 1804 a black coat and waistcoat had to be purchased for the coachman (£3 16s.) when mourning clothes were required.[132] Taxes added to an already heavy bill. Those who hoped to run a carriage on a budget set themselves up for a rude awakening. Walpole successfully fought the taxman's surcharge for one of his fairly wealthy client friends, John Hall, but others were not so successful:

> I called yesterday upon Mr Brown the Tax Surveyor, who had surcharged you for an
> occasional Coachman[.] Explained to him that you had no Coachman or ever employed a
> man in that capacity, Mr Brown asked me if you did keep a Carriage and whether you did
> not occasionally job horses and have a man to drive them & who after the days work
> cleaned your Carriage – I told him certainly not & that the only way in which you used
> your carriage was with post horses & that your carriage when used was cleaned by the

man of the livery stables were [where] your horses stood[.]/Mr Brown then informed me if that was so that he sh[oul]d withdraw the Surcharge.... he ment[ione]d an extremely hard case (and which had been decided upon the opinion of the Judges) of a Lady in Herts who resided with her brother who kept his carriage but no horses or Coachman and occasionally the brothers Coachman & horses drove the Lady out in her own Carriage and for which she was surcharged for an occasional Coachman and was forced to pay the Surcharge.[133]

In a different context Walpole confirmed that the occasional borrowing of other people's facilities carried tax penalties: 'I never hired any horse for drawing the two wheeled carriage mentioned in your letter, I used this Vehicle merely for shooting purposes & when I wanted it Col Eyre lent me one of his horses & who compounds for his taxes.'[134]

The transport facilities encountered on the estate in many ways mirrored those of the two brothers – the carriage owner and the horse rider, both present in the early days of building development. For instance, the wealthy gentleman farmer Thomas Willan was both a carriage owner and a keen horseman (Plate 43), while designer-architect Charles Heathcote Tatham, who kept a large and lively house in Alpha Road as a second residence (his main address being in Mayfair), may have relied on hackney coaches (the taxis of the day) or his own two feet for travelling back and forth, as he does not appear to have added stables and a coach house to the Alpha Road property. The artist William Blake is recorded as having walked back to his home around 1825 from Tatham's rural residence in St John's Wood:

leaving late in the evening, my father [the painter George Richmond] asked Blake
to permit him to escort him on his way home. Blake, no doubt, during this journey
discoursed divinely, as was his wont, and set into flame my father's youthful adoration
and imagination. The walk continued till my father had made the whole journey from
the Regent's Park to the Strand. Upon giving an account of it later, my father said:
"I felt like walking on air, and as if I had been talking to the Prophet Isaiah."[135]

However, the greatest walker on record has to be John Pocock (1814–76), son of George Pocock, the builder who developed part of the neighbouring Kilburn estate where he also settled his family. In 1829, John wrote: 'I walked with him [his friend James Magson] to Finchley along the new road cut from St John's Wood.'[136] John's diary reveals he walked everywhere, even as far as Brighton! In 1828, he recorded a walk which started at his friend's house in the East End when they walked thirty miles in one day.[137]

Robert Todd, the successful developer whose own house in Alpha Road inspired the first phase of development at St John's Wood, built on a large scale, the pretty screen arrangement of his house hiding such facilities as a coach house and stables (Plate 58). The building of stables and coach houses was as tightly controlled as that of the houses. Walpole insisted on vetting their site and appearance which, if proper care was not taken, could turn out to be 'extremely injurious' either to neighbours or to the general appearance of the street. Licence books show there was a building spree of coach houses and stables from the 1840s onwards. However, the 1853 map (Plate 70) reveals that the great majority of houses did not have stables or coach houses, implying that Walpole's comfortable but more modest social category prevailed over the affluent group represented by his brother.

128 This painting of 1859 by William Maw Egley, entitled *Omnibus Life in London*, shows well how claustrophobic travel on an omnibus could become. A packed omnibus (here showing all levels of society) would have pleased the omnibus proprietor but also signalled discomfort for travellers. Tate London.

Opposite: **129** By contrast with Maw Egley's painting, Sidney Starr in the *City Atlas*, 1889, chose to depict the freedom and excitement afforded by travel on the roof of omnibuses. The subject is highly unusual judging by Edmund Yates's words: 'Women are never seen there, save when an occasional maid-servant going into the country for a holiday climbs up beside the coachman' (*The Business of Pleasure*, 1879, p. 269). The scene was probably located in Wellington Road, St John's Wood (the artist resided at 38 Abercorn Place). We know that in the 1850s the City Atlas ran between Swiss Cottage and London Bridge (Barker and Robbins, 1963, vol. I, app. 3). National Gallery of Canada, Ottawa.

of approach from the Railway to a populous neighbourhood might perhaps be the Case for a certain distance from the Railway[.] it however happens that the greater part of the Railway where it passes thro[ugh] my brothers Estate will be deep cutting & will be at least 40 feet below the present surface of the Gro[un]d[.] this circumstance I apprehend greatly reduces the value of the Land even for building warehouses as it would be most inconvenient & attended with great expences to land & cart away heavy goods under such circumstances[.]

The Surveyor & Engineer of the Comp[an]y in support of their opinion state that the Land along the Manchester & Liverpool Railway has greatly increased in value since the making of the Railways & perhaps it may be so to a certain extent.[152]

Walpole, at pains to demonstrate he was not against the railways per se, asked Lawrence for his candid opinion about the Manchester railway experience. Lawrence's letter has not survived, but we have some idea of its content when Walpole wrote to Shaw: 'from Mr Lawrences's letter you will

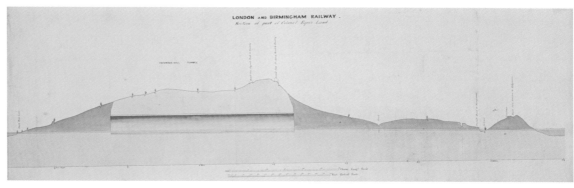

130 London and Birmingham Railway: watercolour cross-section inscribed 'Section of part of Colonel's Eyre's Land – Primrose Hill Tunnel', c.1836. Eyre estate archive (EE 2652/21).

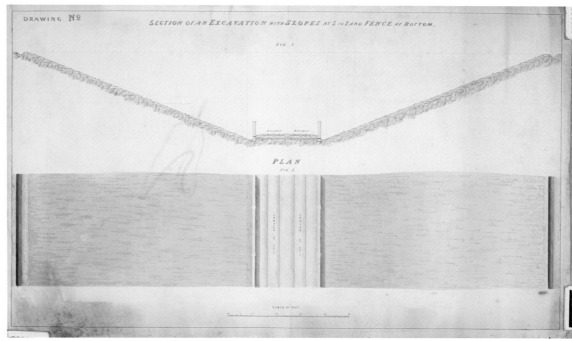

131 London and Birmingham Railway: watercolour showing a 'Section of an Excavation with Slopes at 3 to 1 and fence at Bottom', c.1836. Walpole had been particularly worried about the angle of the slopes, writing to J. W. Lyon of the canal company on 6 March 1834: 'what is the declivity of the Slopes of the Regent's Canal … [on the St John's Wood estate] … as the L[ondon] & B[irmingham] R[ailway] Comp[an]y are about to carry their Railway thro[ugh] the Est[at]e by open cutting & I am anxious to prevent if possible the Slips such as have happened at the Regents Canal' (LB 'N', p. 260). Eyre estate archive (EE 2652/22).

see that owing to the Deep Cutting it cannot be converted to building Warehouses & it will be so confined & in some parts so narrow that it will not be fit for Villas[.] it therefore appears to me that the value of this part of the Property will be greatly depreciated & I think you sho[ul]d urge this point before the Arbitrators & claim compensation accordingly.... as the Gro[un]d to be taken for the Railway is unencumbered it cannot be valued at less than £750 per acre.'[153] The land the company needed was duly measured and came to just over three acres, which they purchased for the sum of £1,040, considerably less than the £750 per acre which Walpole had wanted.[154] However, there were other benefits – such as the award granted by the company[155] and also sewer work it undertook alongside the building of the railway line.

The paperwork was completed in September 1834, but progress seems to have been too slow for Walpole, who sent a letter of complaint in January of the following year: 'you seem to be getting on very slowly at St. Johns Wood[.] I hope you will soon proceed more rapidly or the Injury to the property will be very serious.'[156] The letter books and documents chart some of this project's setbacks (Plates 130 and 131), notably the difficulty of disposing of the soil. Initially it was going to be taken away,[157] though of course the company soon realised the potential difficulty of such a task and so the issue of a spoil bank was revisited. John Shaw junior also appears to have been consulted regularly over the project, even producing a drawing for the positioning of the two bridges over the railway line.[158]

In 1846, the London and Birmingham Railway amalgamated with the Grand Junction and the Liverpool and Manchester companies, and was renamed the London and North Western Railway, 'the aristocrat of the railway business'.[159] In the 1850s the new company negotiated with the Eyre family over the widening of the former London and Birmingham line and later with developers on the estate about creating a station to serve the northern parts of St John's Wood – the future Loudoun Road Station. As early as 1851, Walpole opposed the widening of the railway line by refusing to sell the land the company wanted to buy. At that point, the company produced a new 'weapon': a compulsory order for buying the land they needed, and so Walpole registered his dissent to the project.[160] What made Walpole change his mind is unknown, perhaps the knowledge he could not win this fight or the prospect of generous compensation.[161] In any case, work started in the late 1850s, by which time Walpole had died, and the estate was now the property of the embattled George John Eyre, whose failing health meant he had to live in the country. The estate clerk, Charles Freeth senior, was powerless to intervene in the developers' negotiations with the railway company but still voiced his disapproval to builder William Ifold in 1857: 'I have rece[ive]d your note with draft of proposed memorial to Dir[ect]ors [of the railway company] to be signed by the Inhabitants – you must excuse my saying that I do not admire the matter of the memorial & particularly that portion which makes the persons signing say that the Railway would be in constant requisition by themselves & families & I do not think it right to run down the Omnibuses – however it is for you & Mr Yeo … but the sooner it is signed and sent to the Dir[ect]ors in my opinion the better.'[162] This request must have been the genesis of Loudoun Road Station, later known as South Hampstead.

The railways would eventually bring mass travel, but in the early days they were very underused as a service for daily commuting to and from work, thus explaining Freeth's objections to the arguments put forward by the developers when presenting a case for a station at the top end of the St John's Wood estate. The historian John Kellett has convincingly argued that, apart from a few exceptions, early railways tended to be main lines between towns and cities and not commuting lines between these towns and cities and their suburbs. There are no figures available for St John's Wood, but the figures for London are indicative: in the mid-1850s only some 6,000 to 10,000 travelled daily by rail, compared with 15,000 using the steamboats and some 20,000 carried by the omnibuses.[163]

When the London and Birmingham railway line was built, development on the estate was taking place much further south. However, the villa formula proved so successful that developers felt reasonably safe about taking on parts of the estate close to the railway line. Still, the severance of the estate which Walpole had feared back in the early 1830s (see p. 256) had become a real issue by the early 1860s, added to which the failure of two developers, Charles C. Cook and Edward Davis, must have raised the estate's concern. So when Robert Yeo took on agreement the land on either side of the railway (this was done incrementally), the Eyre estate breathed a sigh of relief, as is clear from this 1862 letter from the estate clerk to George John Eyre:

> I have the pleasure to inform you that Mr Yeo has made an offer to take the remain[in]g gro[un]d at St. J. Wood not let for Building.… The quantity of Land is about 20 acres – so that the ultimate Rent will be about £800 per annum – In addition Mr Yeo will take upon himself the payment of the £939.5.7 w[hi]ch is payable to Messrs Edwards for the Sewer recently built by them & he will make all other necessary Sewers & Roads at his own expense[.]
>
> The Land is what we call the Spoil Bank & the Carpet Gro[un]d – it is now in the occupation of Mrs Gell Cowkeeper (who is greatly in arrear) and the present state of the land is injurious to all property near it – I have seen Mr Shaw upon this offer & he considers it a most advantageous one for the Es[ta]te & pronounces it a 'God send' & advises it being at once accepted – & I trust that you will be of the same opinion – as if Mr Yeo makes the Abbey Road through – w[hi]ch he will do under the Agr[eemen]t it will no doubt rescue that portion of the Estate from the very bad state it is in at present – & give the inhabitants there access to a Church – w[hi]ch they can see but cannot reach for want of a road.[164]

The church the St John's Wood residents could see but not reach was St Mary's in West End Lane. This is a useful reminder that for many years Abbey Road was left unfinished, the pace of road development having become entirely the responsibility of developers.

Walpole's other concern about the railway line had been the depth of the cutting required, and it is easy to see, standing on the bridge, how correct he was. Undeterred, Robert Yeo went ahead, building villas on both sides of the railway: none of them has survived!

Metropolitan and St John's Wood Railway

In the 1840s and early 1850s the Eyres opposed several railway projects, some successfully, such as (in January 1846) the North London Junction Railway and in October of the same year the Regent's Canal railway 'to be worked with the Regents Canal'.[165] In 1852, Walpole also objected to the 'construction of a Railway or Sidings from Primrose Hill to Willesden'.[166] However, the railways were now part of London's transport system, and a parliamentary select committee in 1855 called

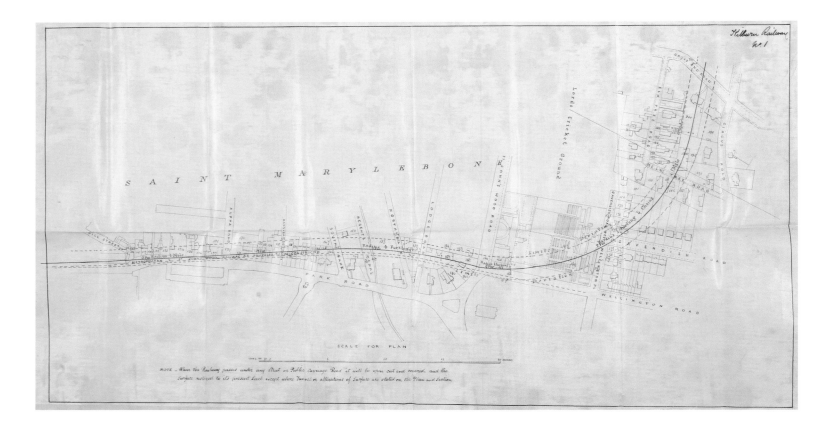

for improvements to the abundant infrastructure which had been created in just a couple of decades. Greater cohesion was needed and greater communication between the various lines of the vast network.

St John's Wood was spared further upheaval until the mid-1860s when an independent company set out to build 'The Metropolitan & St John's Wood Railway' authorised by an Act of 29 July 1864 (Plate 132). Money soon ran out and the line was supported by the Metropolitan Railway Company, which had made its name building the first underground railway in the world from Paddington to Farringdon, which opened in 1863.[167] They obtained another Act of Parliament in 1868 to be able to continue developing the St John's Wood project.[168] The extension of the line from Baker Street finally opened on 13 April 1868, branching off north towards Wellington Road, before veering west towards Kilburn and finishing 156 yards beyond Swiss Cottage Station. It provided three stations for the estate: the original St John's Wood Station on the St John's Wood Church roundabout, Marlborough Road on the corner of Queen's Road (see p. 413), and Swiss Cottage.

The financial results of the new line were apparently 'abysmal'.[169] Therefore its supporter, the Metropolitan Railway, resisted several attempts to increase the service frequency but did not give up on it altogether. Under the driven chairmanship of Sir Edward Watkin (1872–94) this once independent line would be fully absorbed by the Metropolitan on 1 April 1882,[170] and used for the extraordinary expansion of this line north-west into the Home Counties, which started in 1873 when the line was extended from Swiss Cottage to Willesden Green (opened in 1879). By 1900, it reached almost fifty miles north-west of the company's headquarters at Baker Street, eventually giving rise

132 The Metropolitan and St John's Wood Railway, also known as the Kilburn Railway: early plan showing how the Eyre estate would be affected. Eyre estate archive (EE 2651/210(B)).

8 ARTISTS' QUARTER

A great number of the larger houses upon the Eyre Estate are and have for many years been in the occupation of Artists and Authors to whom the quietude of the neighbourhood has been of considerable importance[.] They no doubt were originally attracted to the district by the fact of this quietude and by the large open spaces and the shaded and well timbered gardens with which the district abounds so that it has practically become and is recognised as the Art Centre of London. There is also throughout the Estate an entire absence of Factories, Workshops or other trade premises which in many suburbs of London are of an obtrusive and offensive Character.[1]

So Edward Tewson, senior partner in a firm of surveyors and auctioneers, described the Eyre estate in the year 1895. This extract formed part of the 'Proofs' which were gathered by the estate when it fought (and lost) the campaign to prevent the Manchester, Sheffield and Lincolnshire Railway extension (see p. 263). By that date, many of the painters associated with St John's Wood were held in high regard; the area ran a very successful art school and a new arts club had just been formed.

Contrary to what is often stated, the artistic nature of St John's Wood was born neither in the Victorian period nor with the arrival of Edwin Landseer in St John's Wood Road in 1825.[2] Artists were an integral part of the neighbourhood from the beginning. Today most people do not know that the area south of the Regent's Canal was once part of the Eyre or St John's Wood estate, and thus fail to realise that the blue plaque to B. R. Haydon and J. C. F. Rossi at 116 Lisson Grove marks the southernmost tip of the estate while commemorating its first creative community.

There is no evidence to suggest that the Eyres sought to recruit artists as developers, lessees or residents. The whole of Marylebone was popular with artists in the eighteenth century, who may have gradually moved towards the more airy parts of this large parish. This is indeed what Ann Cox-Johnson argued when she compiled her list of Marylebone artists.[3] Yet various anecdotal details suggest that Walpole Eyre had considerable respect for the work of artists, and that this was inextricably linked to the workings of the estate. For instance, Walpole must have asked Thomas Heaphy, one of the estate's lessees, to add the name 'Purrier' (Walpole's friend) to the subscription list for this painter's ambitious Wellington picture (Plate 138). In September 1815 Walpole wrote to Heaphy: 'You may if you please deduct Mr Purrier's Subscript[io]n to y[ou]r Picture from the £18,' i.e. the rent due for the artist's Alpha Road house.[4] It is also clear that for a few years Heaphy paid his way out of rent arrears by painting portraits of Walpole's family (see Plate 22).[5] Another example of 'soft evidence' for his encouragement of the arts may be found in Walpole's response to architectural excellence. His 1840 letter to architect Thomas L. Donaldson on seeing the latter's plans for Lucas's studio in St John's Wood Road was particularly encouraging (see p. 286).

What factors lead to an area being taken over by artists? Kit Wedd's *Creative Quarters* (2001) provides an intelligent summary of artists' quarters in the capital, but its wide scope does not allow it to come to grips with this tantalising issue. The development of the St John's Wood estate makes it clear that there are two dominant factors: first, there is the presence of artists with highly developed social skills who create 'circles' around them, turning their studios into influential salons; as we shall see, these operated in vertical and horizontal clusters. The presence of 'entrepreneurial' artists with a passion for building is the other influential factor, for instance J. C. F. Rossi, the first artist to make a significant impact on the estate.

Previous pages: **134**
George Frampton's studio at 32 Queen's Road was converted into residential accommodation, but his Carlton Hill studio, shown overleaf, lives on as an artist's studio. It was taken over by another sculptor, Arthur Fleischmann, who ensured its preservation. It is still used for sketching sessions organised by Arthur's widow, Joy. Fleischmann arrived in London in 1949 and was the first artist to carve in acrylic. Gabo had used sheets of acrylic in the 1930s, but 'blocks' of this material were specifically made for Fleischmann. Eyre estate (photo: John Chase).

circumstances [this business] might have been finished long ago but you take such whims and fancies into y[ou]r head accompanied with so much suspicion that it is really difficult to treat with you in the common & ordinary way of business.'[30] Heaphy seems to have so repelled his St John's Wood Road tenant, Colonel Salmond, that the latter was determined to deal not with Heaphy but with Walpole over his lease.[31] Walpole wrote of Heaphy to the colonel: 'he has behaved extremely ill & is a most extraordinary person'.[32] In the course of this correspondence Walpole, having produced a summary of the properties Heaphy had in hand, warned Heaphy he should not expect 'a continuation of the indulgence' he had been shown so far.[33] Heaphy managed to clear his debts with the estate: after 1829 he was no longer pursued for rent arrears by Walpole or his clerk.

Heaphy's Alpha Road address – given as 1 Park Road because his house was the last one in that road with an elevation on Park Road – seemed perfect for an artist who had acquired fame and wealth depicting rural genre scenes. All praised his technical excellence and his paintings commanded high prices. He painted with great energy, producing a succession of noteworthy watercolours that prompted the painter David Wilkie to write in his diary: 'Went to the Royal Academy Exhibition in the evening and looked at and liked the drawings of Varley, De Wint and Heaphy. The industry of the latter is beyond all example. When I think of the number of highly finished objects which he has in these pictures of his, and compare them with what I myself have done in the same time, my labour seems idleness. I must exert myself more' (Plate 137).[34]

However, not everyone was a fan. William Henry Pyne, for instance, recorded in 1824: 'many

137 *The Family Doctress – or The Wounded Leg* by Thomas Heaphy was exhibited at the Watercolour Society in 1809, the same year that David Wilkie painted his celebrated *Cut Finger*. *The Wounded Leg* was fiercely defended by Heaphy's contemporary Richard Redgrave, RA: 'it is not an agreeable subject to choose, but Heaphy made no compromise in representing it, and the wounded leg forms a prominent feature' (Whitley, 1933, p. 13). Victoria and Albert Museum, London.

of the compositions of his ingenious hand represented scenes in low life, or rather, vulgar life, which, although depicted with great observation of character and truth of expression, yet being destitute of that moral point which characterizes the works of the incomparable Hogarth, they were disgusting to good feeling and repulsive to delicate sentiment.'[35] *The Fish Market*, set on the strand at Hastings, was regarded as his masterpiece and sold in 1809 for the unprecedented price of 400 guineas.[36] Heaphy's move to St John's Wood was probably the result of his professional success and a wish to invest his money in a profitable investment scheme.

By far the most ambitious and celebrated painting produced by Thomas Heaphy in St John's Wood was the *Duke of Wellington Giving Orders to his Generals before the Battle of the Nivelle* (Plate 138). He had been settled in St John's Wood for a couple of years when Captain Freemantle brought to London the news of the victory of Vitoria (21 June 1813, Peninsular Wars), and eventually Heaphy accompanied Captain Freemantle back to Spain where 'he had the honour to live at the Marquis's [Wellington's] table.' There 'he became acquainted with all the distinguished officers of his staff,'[37] eventually producing fifty-two portraits which he wove into his great painting of the Nivelle battle (10 November 1813), including his own.[38] The engraving of this picture was plagued with difficulties and only completed in 1822. By then interest in the subject had waned, though the work was revived with enthusiasm in 1852 following the death of Wellington.[39]

Heaphy's success was crowned early on when he was appointed portrait painter to the Princess of Wales in 1803. He was also generally well regarded by his peers, who elected him a member of the Old Watercolour Society in 1806 and the first president of the Society of British Artists in 1824. There is no evidence that he formed a social circle on the Tatham model, though the presence two doors down from his house in Alpha Road of another member of the Watercolour Society and the

138 *The Duke of Wellington Giving Orders to his Generals before the Battle of the Nivelle* was painted between 1813 and 1816 at 1 Park Road, one of the Alpha Cottages at St John's Wood where the artist Thomas Heaphy resided. The work commemorates the battle which took place on 10 November 1813, and it is now only known through this engraving commissioned from Anker Smith but finished by Heaphy in 1822. We know that Colonel Eyre purchased a copy of this print, perhaps influencing the naming of Wellington Road. The detail, taken from the right-hand side, is a profile portrait of Heaphy. Victoria and Albert Museum, London.

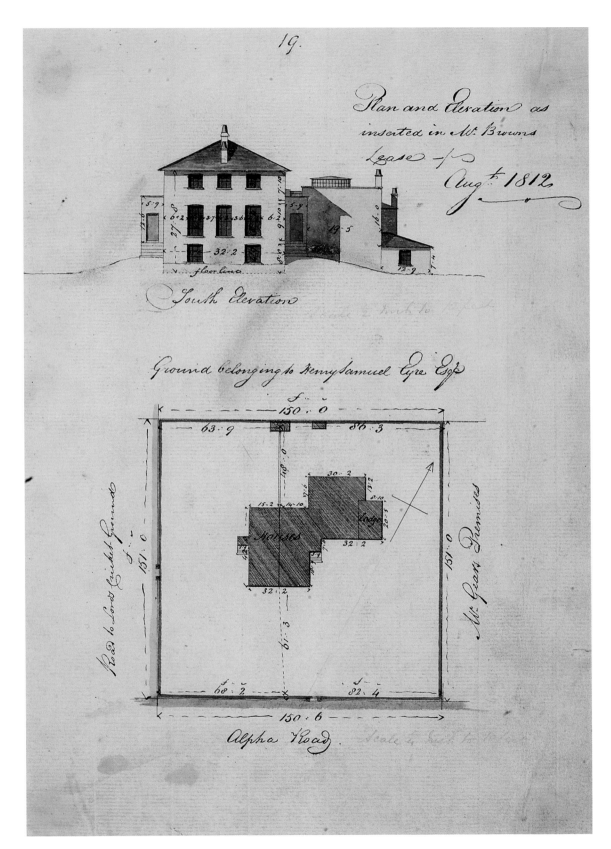

139 Lease drawing for the cottage and studio of the painter Robert Brown (No.26 on Plate 63). The lease has survived and is dated 6 August 1813, slightly later than this drawing. This is the earliest purpose-built painter's studio on the estate. Eyre estate archive (Bk of Drawings I, 19).

Society of British Artists, Harriot Gouldsmith (1786–1863, later Arnold), may not have been a coincidence.[40] She was certainly there between 1811 and 1820, though the ratepayer was Richard Gouldsmith (her father or brother).[41] As Gouldsmith was taught by William Mulready, a friend of John Linnell whom we encountered at Tatham's, she perhaps provided a possible link between Heaphy's and Tatham's circles. Gouldsmith, Mulready and Linnell are even known to have collaborated on a painting together.[42] Mulready and Linnell were taught by John Varley and are sometimes described as the Varley circle, taking Varley's motto to heart: 'Go to Nature for Everything', which was precisely what Linnell did with his 1814 watercolour (Plate 87) and Gouldsmith with her 1819 painting of St John's Wood Farm (Plate 41).[43]

The first artist whose home provides an example of a specially designed studio building was the now forgotten landscape painter Robert Brown. He exhibited at the Royal Academy between 1792 and 1821, moving to 39 Alpha Road (see No. 26 on the Alpha Cottages reconstruction) in 1812. Barely anything is known about his life or art,[44] except that he offended his Alpha Road neighbours with an inappropriately placed 'necessary' (see p. 177)! The drawing for his lease provides a very early example of a purpose-built, top-lit painter's studio, certainly the first on the estate (Plate 139).

THE LANDSEER CONNECTION

When Edwin Landseer (1803–73) (Plate 140) moved to St John's Wood in 1825, he certainly was not the first artist to do so but was following a trend which, as we have just seen, was well established, first at Lisson Grove and then at Alpha Road. He was also well connected to the creative groups discussed above: with his brothers, Edwin had been a pupil of B. R. Haydon from 1815, and they were caricatured hard at work in Haydon's workshop in 1818 (Plate 141). Edwin is also believed to have painted the donkey in Haydon's *Christ's Entry into Jerusalem*,[45] a work which we saw was painted in Lisson Grove (Plate 142). In addition, Landseer was a friend of Leslie, Haydon's successor at the Lisson Grove address. Leslie and Landseer had gone to Scotland together the previous year: Landseer, visiting for the first time, immediately fell in love with the Highlands. At Abbotsford he met Sir Walter Scott, who made a deep impression on him. The novelist recorded the encounter: 'Mr Landseer who has drawn every dog in the House but myself is at work upon me.'[46] It is probably no coincidence that the man who designed Abbotsford for Scott, William Atkinson, became Landseer's landlord in St John's Wood the following year. Atkinson had leased from Willan the large site of the former Punkers Barn or Red Barn, which was made up of three distinct plots (Plates 84 and 85). The Eyre brothers sold the lot to John Smith in 1824 but renewed Atkinson's lease(s) just prior to the sale.[47] At first Landseer was Atkinson's underlessee and since he had limited means, the small cottage was clearly the most appropriate plot;[48] Edwin leased and subsequently purchased further land as fortune smiled upon him (Plate 143). As with Rossi and a number of other artists, Landseer's connection with St John's Wood quickly turned 'dynastic',[49] with various family members opting to live close by: Thomas, Edwin's brother, an eminent engraver, at 10b Cunningham Place between 1840 and 1877 and then at 11 Grove End Road; Charles, another brother, Keeper of the Royal Academy, at 35 Grove End Road between 1861 and 1879; George, son of Thomas and Edwin's nephew, at 10a Cunningham Place between 1849 and 1858; Jessica, Edwin's sister, living with him at 1 St John's Wood Road between 1861 and 1879.

140 This 1865 self-portrait of Sir Edwin Landseer is entitled *The Connoisseurs: Portrait of the Artist with Two Dogs*. The animal painter Landseer lived at 1 (later 18) St John's Wood Road for forty-seven years from 1825 until his death. The Royal Collection.

141 Etching by John Bailey from *Annals of the Fine Arts for 1818*, London, 1819 (opp. p. 58). B. R. Haydon's pupils, including the Landseer brothers (Tom top left, Charles on the right) and William Bewick (middle), are seen copying cartoons for their master, by then well settled at Rossi's property on the southern tip of the St John's Wood estate (see Plate 234). Haydon, in the guise of a bird labelled 'Director of Public Taste', hovers at the top of the composition. British Library.

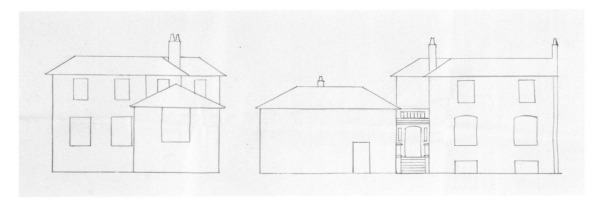

152 The estate prepared a licence to authorise the erection of this proposed studio at Alpha Cottages in 1853. It is the first such licence and was requested by John Palmer de la Fons (Delafons), the underlessee of the house. The studio was attached to the free side of a semi-detached house (side and front views shown here). The other side of this house later became the estate office when it moved to Alpha Road in 1867. Eyre estate archive (EE 2650/1/61(A), inside Fenton's lease).

The first licence 'to erect a Studio or Painting Room' was not issued until 19 March 1853. It was for one of the Alpha Cottages (No. 10 on the reconstruction, right-hand property), originally leased to Francis Fenton in 1814,[75] but at this time assigned to George Smith, Oxford Street, an undertaker. It was Smith's underlessee, the mysterious 'John Palmer de la Fons' (elsewhere spelt Delafons),[76] who was 'desirous of erecting and building a Studio or Painters Room', and he therefore provided the required drawing for the estate's approval (Plate 152).[77] The studio was built,[78] and this licence led the way to others, in particular the following month, for a 'Studio Conservatory at 4 Grove End Road' which backed onto Lord's.[79] This was duly issued to the lessee, Martha Charman, without naming the applicant artist. With the help of Ann Cox-Johnson's guide to Marylebone artists (1963), it is easy to establish that the applicant would have been Edward Armitage (1817–96), then aged 36, whose painted output was dominated by scenes from the contemporary and biblical Middle East. This appears to be the earliest record of a 'studio conservatory', and there were several instances of these in St John's Wood. Painters seemed to have relished recording these attractive structures (Plates 151 and 153). Armitage's studio extension was more elaborate than the plain room planned by de la Fons at Alpha Cottages: as well as the studio and conservatory, the licence also mentioned 'some small offices' and other alterations 'as shown on the plan', which alas has not survived. We are on the threshold of the great wave for grand studio buildings.

As with 3 St John's Wood Road, the property at 4 Grove End Road offered one of the earliest examples of artists' 'vertical clusters': once equipped with an artist's studio, it made sense for such a house to remain in the hands of an artist, and indeed that is what happened. Armitage was there until at least 1860 when he moved to nearby Hall Road; his artist daughter (?) E. Armitage was recorded there in 1858. They were followed by Henry Wallis in 1865, of *Chatterton* and *The Stonebreaker* fame, in turn followed by William F. Yeames, a member of the St John's Wood Clique who spent over twenty years there between 1866 and 1892. This is where Yeames painted the famous Civil War painting, *And When Did You Last See Your Father?*[80] Finally, Alfred East lived there from 1893 to 1895, if not longer.

The historian Giles Walkley organised topographically the detailed NW8 gazetteer in his book *Artists' Houses in London* (1994). For the purpose of the present book, it has been reorganised chronologically, incorporating supplementary evidence from the Eyre archive. This clearly reveals the rise and fall of the trend for studio building in St John's Wood in the second half of the nineteenth century: four extensions in the 1840s, six in the 1850s, five in the 1860s, forty in the 1870s

153 George Dunlop Leslie's *Five O'clock* (1874) is likely to have been inspired by one of the many conservatories which adorned houses in St John's Wood, perhaps even the artist's own at Grove End Road. Private collection (Christie's sale of the Forbes collection, 20 February 2003, Lot 268).

(with the appearance of conversions, garden pavilions and studio-houses), thirty-eight in the 1880s, thirty-seven in the 1890s but less than a dozen in the early 1900s (see Appendix 5 on p. 457).

At first the evidence contained in the estate letter books about this studio explosion seems contradictory. For instance, when painter John Faed (1819–1902) approached the estate about building a studio in 1862, his house agent was told:

Mr White has handed me your letter to him … with a gro[un]d plan of 1A Cavendish Rd upon part of w[hi]ch you state Mr Faed wishes to build a Studio & for w[hi]ch he wo[ul]d be glad of a License- The Owner of the houses North & South strongly object to the proposed or any other add[iti]on & he informs me that he has so expressed himself to

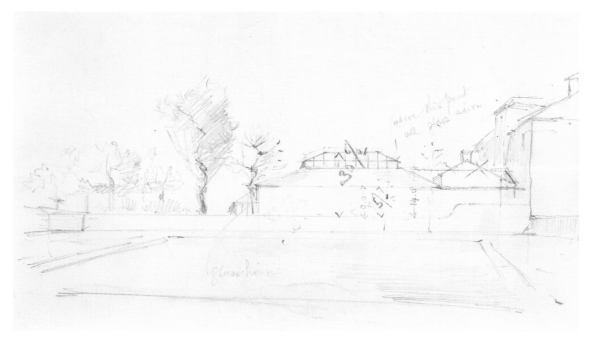

154 This sketch shows the proposed studio planned by John McLure Hamilton at Alpha House, 14 Alpha Road, the house originally built for C. H. Tatham. It almost certainly accompanied the report made by surveyor Christopher White to the Eyre estate dated October 1887. Eyre estate archive (EE 2650/1/197(A)).

Mr Tovey the Surveyor who made the sketch – & there can be no doubt but that such an add[iti]on wo[ul]d be most injurious to the whole of that neighbourhood. I must therefore decline joining in any License for making it & request that it may not be commenced.[81]

Edwin Eyre was the author of this unsympathetic letter – perhaps because the lessee north and south of the property Faed was occupying was none other than the son of the estate clerk, Charles Freeth junior (see Plate 72).

There is a second instance of non-cooperation in 1867 concerning a property which had been leased to William Holme Twentyman at 2 Regents Villas (38 Avenue Road, on the east side) and where the artist Frederick Tayler (1802–89) resided:[82] 'your Tenant wished to make an alteration at the above house & I have this day rece[ive]d a letter from Mr Taylor [*sic*] stating that such an add[iti]on is a studio &c. I am directed to inform you that Mr Eyre considers the erection of a Studio & the carrying on some profession therein will be injurious to the Interests of the Estate and declines to sanction the erection of it.'[83] However, Twentyman must have challenged this response. As a result the estate clerk sent the plans to John Shaw junior, the estate architect, with the accompanying note: 'a proposed Studio & rooms over, to be built at the above house … let to Mr Frederick Taylor an Artist'. A few days later Twentyman obtained the desired reply: 'I have the pleasure to inform you that Mr Shaw does not object to the proposed add[iti]onal building at the above house. I will prepare the new License.'[84]

These early objections in the 1860s show there was initial concern about studio development on the estate, at times emanating from the lessees themselves. Was Twentyman's challenge a turning point for studio building? We cannot be sure as his letter has not survived. But by the 1880s the professional status of artists had become respectable,[85] and the initial difficulties were largely smoothed over, as the following surveyor's report, dated October 1887, testifies. It was prepared in connection with the studio extension for John McLure Hamilton at 14 Alpha Road (Tatham's house, No. 29 on the Alpha Cottages reconstruction). As the proposed studio was planned to be built against the house and along a party wall, the surveyor Christopher White anticipated a possible objection from the neighbour on the west side, but still regarded the project as desirable and was keen for it to go ahead (Plate 154):

> This [the Studio] would interfere with the view from the back windows of 2 Grove End Road [No. 30 on Alpha Cottages reconstruction]; but, having regard to the fact both houses are on the Eyre Estate, we do not think it would be right to prevent one tenant from improving his property for the sole reason that it interferes somewhat with a view across the garden of an adjoining tenant, but that a fair and reasonable course should be adopted, and a compromise arranged to meet, as far as possible, the wishes of both tenants. We therefore consider that Mr Hamilton should be allowed to build the Studio in the position shewn subject to the following modifications....[86]

Studios were now regarded as property improvements.

Interiors

One consequence of the presence of artists in St John's Wood is the magnificent record some painters have made of life in their delightful suburban retreats. In this respect it is interesting to compare the deadpan record of Charles Purton Cooper's library in Circus Road (Plate 155) with Tissot's masterly rendering of his sitting room at 17 Grove End Road (Plate 156). The comparison illustrates perfectly the gap between document and art.

155 View of the principal library at 12 Grove End Road, the residence of the lawyer and antiquary Charles Purton Cooper on the corner with Circus Road (later 24 Grove End Road, now the site of Grove Court). This coloured lithograph dates from 1852 when Cooper wished 'to dispose, by private agreement, of 8 mahogany bookcases of the kind there represented'. Westminster City Archives (Ashbridge collection, 791–884/1851).

Opposite: **156** In *Hide and Seek*, painted around 1877, James Tissot set the scene in the comfortable studio/drawing room of his home at 17 Grove End Road. His beloved Mrs Newton is resting and reading a paper by the window. The conservatory and the garden can be glimpsed on the right and centre of this picture. Despite the full height of both window and conservatory and the vast amount of light which as a result would be expected to stream into the room, an atmosphere of soothing shade has been achieved. However, the mischievous heads of four children playing in the room bring in life to this sedate corner of the house. National Gallery of Art, Washington, DC.

St John's Wood's interiors as subject matter for painters made their appearance in the 1850s; one of the earliest and most controversial examples, which its author loaded with personal, social and spiritual meaning, was William Holman Hunt's *The Awakening Conscience*, exhibited in 1854 and discussed on p. 198. The studios of St John's Wood were lavishly recorded in paint, in the new medium of photography (see below, p. 319) and in architectural journals. An early series on artists and their studios in London was produced by the painter John Ballantyne (1815–97). It featured a number of St John's Wood artists, including perhaps the most famous (and controversial) work in the series, which recorded the involvement of Edwin Landseer with the Trafalgar Square lions (Plate 157).[87] Philip Morris (1833–1902) was photographed in his studio at 33 St John's Wood Road in a most unusually relaxed way (Plate 158). Tissot's studio along with numerous others was published in the contemporary architectural press (Plate 159). Alma-Tadema's studio, by far the most often depicted, was represented in all three media.

What painters and photographers could not make obvious in their output is the distinctive architectural brief of a house-studio. Andrew Saint reduces this potentially complex field to just two principal features: access and light. Victorian propriety called for a separate access for models and 'ceremonial' access for important visitors. The orientation of the studio to enable artists to work in an even northern light would have also dictated the layout of the entire house.[88]

Right: **157** John Ballantyne's oil painting shows Sir Edwin Landseer sculpting the lions for the base of Nelson's Column at Trafalgar Square, c.1865. For this difficult commission Landseer abandoned his own studio in St John's Wood to work in the studio of his friend and collaborator Baron (Carlo) Marochetti (see Plate 235). The work became controversial when Ballantyne exhibited the painting in 1865 before the completion of the base of the Nelson's Column (1867). Ballantyne had obtained access to Landseer and Marochetti's studio after promising not to reveal the appearance of the lions prior to their being finished. Landseer ordered and obtained the immediate withdrawal of the painting from Ballantyne's exhibition. National Portrait Gallery, London.

158 This photogravure by J. P. Mayall shows Philip Morris in his studio at 33 St John's Wood Road. Watts Gallery, Compton, Surrey (Rob Dickins collection).

159 Tissot's studio at 17 Grove End Road was commissioned from the architect John Brydon, and its design was published in the *Building News* on 5 May 1874. The illustration shows well how the studio connected with the two-storey conservatory which adorned the artist's house. The bay window is one of the rare features to have survived Alma-Tadema's extensive redesigning ten years later (but differently sited). By comparison with Brydon's lavish 1859 project at the Poplars, 18–20 Avenue Road, Tissot's studio must have seemed relatively modest. The Poplars, recorded by the Bedford Lemere photographic studio, later became the summer residence of art collector Ludwig Mond (of future ICI fame). Private collection/Bridgeman Art Library.

160 The St John's Wood Clique photographed by David W. Wynfield, c.1865. From left to right: Calderon, Yeames, Leslie, Marks, Hodgson and Storey (standing). The seated figure on the right is Wynfield. Reproduced in Marks, 1894, vol. I, p. 182. Westminster City Archives.

THE ST JOHN'S WOOD CLIQUE

The group of artists known as the St John's Wood Clique has been well researched and published.[89] The group was formed in 1862,[90] and several of its members wrote useful memoirs or articles.[91] Henry Stacy Marks (and others) named the seven original members of the St John's Wood Clique (Plate 160): Philip Calderon (1833–98), George Dunlop Leslie (1835–1921), John Evan Hodgson (1831–95), William Frederick Yeames (1835–1918), David W. Wynfield (1837–87), George Adolphus Storey (1834–1919) and of course Marks (1829–98) himself. The name 'St John's Wood Clique' seems to have stuck, though Marks believed 'The Gridirons' was the best name as it was 'descriptive of our object in forming this band, which was, while continuing to be the best of friends, to criticise each other's works in the frankest and most unsparing manner'.[92]

The decision to form a group based on friendship was reinforced by the appeal history had for all its members. By 1850, setting up 'brotherhoods' was a well-rehearsed scenario. They started on the Continent with the 'Barbus' (bearded men) who came out of Jacques-Louis David's studio in the 1790s. They were followed by the Nazarenes, a group of students from Vienna Academy who settled in Rome and were the talk of London in the 1820s.[93] The 'Ancients' (discussed above) emerged next, based in London and Shoreham in Kent. 'The Clique', different from the 'St John's Wood Clique' but close to it in spirit and practice, was formed in the late 1830s by former students of the Royal

Academy: John Philip, W. P. Frith, Richard Dadd, Henry O'Neil and Augustus Egg.[94] The Langham Sketching Club, formed in 1838, also predated the St John's Wood Clique and particularly appealed to the latter's members of the clique as it indulged their penchant for exotic historical costume.[95] But by far the most famous brotherhood was that of the Pre-Raphaelites founded in 1848.[96] All these groups were formed from the ranks of art school or studio training. The St John's Wood Clique followed the same rule, as most of the members had met at Leigh's Academy of Drawing in Newman Street.

This is the order in which the members settled in St John's Wood (the dates in brackets show when the artists were recorded at the addresses below):

From 1851   George Adolphus Storey at 12 Marlborough Place (until 1863)
            At 2 Elgin Road (1864–77)
            At 19 St John's Wood Road (1877–85)
From 1853   Philip Hermogenes Calderon at 10 Marlborough Road (until 1854)
            At 7 Acacia Road (1854–57)
            At 17 Abbey Place (1858–62)
            At Abbey Villa, Hill Road (1863–68)
            At 9 Marlborough Place (1869–75)
            At 16 Grove End Road (1876–98)
From 1857   George Dunlop Leslie at 2 Abercorn Place (until 1869)
            At 21 Abercorn Place (1870)
            At 8 Grove End Road (1871–83)
From 1858   John Evan Hodgson at 5 (now 10) Hill Road (until 1889)[97]
From 1863   Henry Stacy Marks at Camden Villa, Hill Road (until 1863)
            At 2 Elgin Road, Maida Vale (1870)
            At 15 Hamilton Terrace (1871–95)
From 1864   David Wilkie Wynfield at 3 Park Place, Maida Hill West (1864–67)
            At 14 Grove End Road (1867–87)
From 1865   William Frederick Yeames at 4 Grove End Road (until 1893)

So the first in the group to settle in St John's Wood was George Adolphus Storey (Plates 181 and 182), and by far the longest resident was Philip Calderon, who was regarded as 'the head of the Clique' (Plate 161). 'On Sunday mornings the Clique was in the habit of assembling at Calderon's studio, and, if the weather were fine, walking to Willesden, Neasden, and sometimes to Hendon. Our most frequent route was, I think, along West End Lane, then a rural solitude, now populous and covered with the abortions of the jerry-builder.'[98] The group was described as 'coming men' in 1864,[99] and a few 'honorary members' were added 'in course of time': Frederick Walker (1840–75), George du Maurier (1834–96), Val Prinsep (1838–1904) and Eyre Crowe (1824–1910), all living outside the St John's Wood area.

The members of the St John's Wood Clique are now largely forgotten. The excellent 1992 exhibition held at the Walker Art Gallery focused on the group's passion for history painting which had driven them in 1866 to 'rent a mediaeval castle to live and work in', their choice falling on Hever Castle.[100] Their close-knit community did not exclude them from St John's Wood's larger artistic community: everybody knew everybody and many indulged in the pursuit of exotic subject matter – not only history, in particular the seventeenth century, but also Scotland with Landseer and the Faed brothers, the Bible lands with Edward Armitage and Frederick Goodall, Italy with Matthew Ridley Corbet and William Linton, and Spain with John Bagnold Burgess. Yet they also recorded their domestic life, and therefore life in St John's Wood (Plate 162).[101] In some respects their paintings are comparable with those of the Dutch Golden Age painters, who recorded in detail their homes and streets. Alma-Tadema, Dutch by birth, had of course recreated a little Holland at 17 Grove End Road, alongside features evoking his love affair with Greece and Rome.

Below: **161** Philip Calderon was photographed in his studio at 16 Grove End Road by J. P. Mayall for F. G. Stephens's 1884 publication, *Artists at Home*. National Portrait Gallery, London.

Right: **162** Laura Epps (1852–1909) was the second wife of the celebrated Lawrence Alma-Tadema. Like many painters of her generation she was seduced by the exoticism of the past, but she also put her talent to translating into paint scenes of everyday life, as in this work (reproduced in *The Art Journal* in 1891, opp. p. 161), *Battledoor & Shuttlecock*, set in the entrance hall at 17 Grove End Road. Victoria and Albert Museum, London.

THE ST JOHN'S WOOD ART SCHOOLS

From Uppingham I went straight to heaven: to St John's Wood School of Art, where I was to train for the Royal Academy Schools.... I became, within half an hour, almost unrecognisable as the same character that had been at Uppingham.... What energy I had in those days! I cannot think how I packed so much work and pleasure into eighteen or twenty hours a day.... There were wild dances, student rags as they were called ... and various excursions with exquisite students, young girls and earnest boys; shouting too much laughing too often.... St John's Wood School of Art was essentially a school for academic training, and I had begun to do well. Sir David Murray awarded me a prize; Charles Sims was kind about a pastel; and other Academicians, Hacker and Sir James Lynton, had given me encouragement. For a time I had a swollen head because Sir John Clausen had praised a landscape.[102]

Here is a rare display of positive writing by the painter C. R. W. Nevinson (1889–1946). His autobiography, *Paint and Prejudice*, sometimes reads like a litany of complaints, objections and difficulties. His enthusiasm for the St John's Wood Art Schools is therefore remarkable. The school, at 7 (later 29) Elm Tree Road, was sited in the bend of Elm Tree Road on the western side (Plates 163 and 164). Most of the properties in that road had been sold by the estate in the late 1850s.[103] There is therefore no information in the Eyre archive about the creation of the school, and when exactly its founders made the decision to redevelop the site after the early residential formula had proved such a success. The 'conversion' has been dated c.1896, and its outcome was mapped in 1903 (Plate 165) when the school had started advertising.[104]

Above left: **163** The entrance to St John's Wood Art Schools in 1913, when this photograph was published in Montgomery Eyre. Appropriately, the figure standing by the gate is female, making the point that over half of the students there were women. Eyre estate archive (Montgomery Eyre, 1913, opp. p. 267).

Above: **164** Ruth Alice Hobson (later Irving) was one of the many young ladies who went to St John's Wood Art Schools. This chalk portrait by D. McLaren dates from 1913, the same year as the photograph of the school above. Private collection.

The final site of the school spread over two plots made up of two separate double houses, originally plain and of modest size. One had first been leased in 1824 to William Hall, the developer of this part of the estate, and the other, split into two leases, had gone to Mr Mahoney in 1823 and William Hall in 1824.[105] Advertisements for the school in the 1890s stated that it opened in 1878. Its early beginning, on a very modest scale, can be traced from the 1881 Census. The painter Abelardo A[lvarez] Calderon, born in Lima, Peru, aged 32 and described as an 'Artist', resided at 7 Elm Tree Road. He had a wife and two young sons and also one lodger, Bernard E. Ward, described 'Student (Sch:)', the future Headmaster of the St John's Wood Art Schools. Two further pupils were cited as 'Lodger Art Students' at No. 6 – Thomas B. Garnie and James Brownlie.[106] From such modest beginnings – three residential students – the school, not yet named in the 1881 or 1891 Census, finally became 'School of Arts' in the 1901 Census.

Elm Tree Road was transformed from an ordinary neighbourhood to an artists' enclave by the early twentieth century. There was not a single artist in sight when the census men recorded the activities of this street's inhabitants in 1851. Three principal trades dominated the neighbourhood: the omnibus (see p. 254 for disgruntled resident), a gardener/nursery further along on the north side and a 'Ladies School' in the bend, opposite what would become the art school. One-third of the households were in the hands of women. Alongside a population of comfortable residents 'living on own means', merchants and lawyers, new younger blood started to seep through. The first artist to make his appearance in the street was David Lee in 1871, who lived at No. 1, next to the omnibus yard, for around ten years. By 1881, as well as A. A. Calderon and his students, the landscape painter Ernest Parton resided at No. 8 next to the school. By 1891 he had been replaced by another artist, Ethel Wright, while Arthur May lived at No. 9. Phil May, the well-known caricaturist, briefly lived at No. 15 in 1902. Other creative professions should also be noted: the publisher Frederick Macmillan at No. 2 (1881 Census), the author Bronson Howard at No. 15 (1891 Census) and a couple of actors, Lewis Waller and his wife, at No. 10 (1891 and 1901 Census). George Henry Cowell, 'Artist Photographic', was at No. 1 in 1901 with one tenant of the same profession. Detailed research into St John's Wood's most famous house – 44 Grove End Road – also shows that it rehearses on a micro scale what was happening in Elm Tree Road and all over St John's Wood:[107] the transformation of a neighbourhood of 'shopkeepers' into a thriving artists' quarter (Plate 166).

The school was originally intended to train students for the Royal Academy Schools, as noted by Nevinson, and its reputation stemmed from its success rate in this area. In 1890 it provided statistics in *The Year's Art*: 'Since 1880, out of a total of 304 students admitted to the Royal Academy, 201 have been prepared in these Schools; and out of 66 prizes for drawing and painting awarded by the Academy during the year 1886 to 1888 inclusive 53 were taken by old pupils.' The same advertisement specified that 'All Classes are open to Ladies/There is a Studio for Ladies only.'[108] In the 1880s, 'girls outnumbering the boys by about ten to one',[109] the rules were appropriately stringent: 'Silence was the order, and we were given printed rules for observation. One, I think, ran thus: "Talking between male and female students is not allowed except in the rests, then only on matters relating to art!".'[110] From the recollections of Rex Vicat Cole, who explained that 'to enter the lower schools of the Academy a student had to submit drawings from the Antique', we also glean a forbidding schedule:

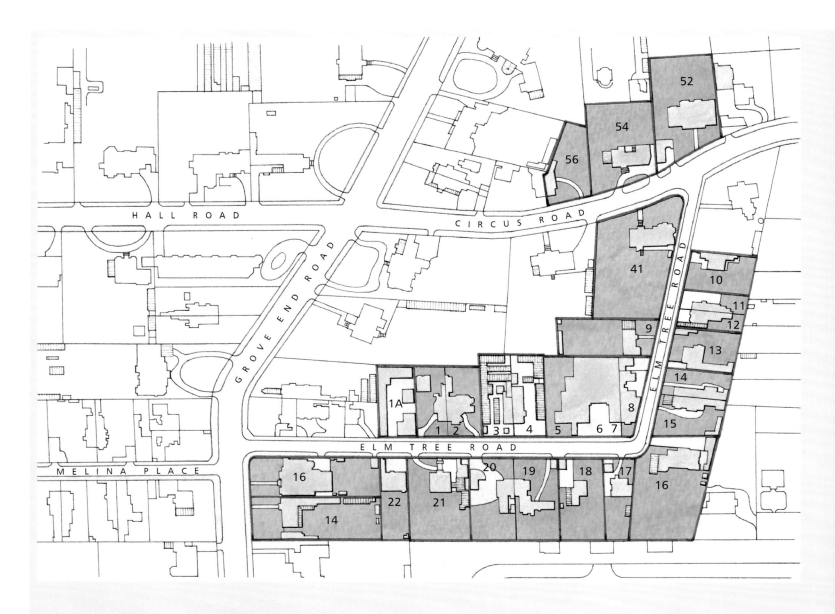

The 1851 to 1901 Census data provide fascinating insights into the residents of Elm Tree Road. The Eyre archive also contains documentation about adjoining properties in Grove End Road and Circus Road which have been added to this plan.

165 Plan of Elm Tree Road based on an estate map dating from 1903. Eyre estate (redrawn by Stephen Conlin, 2010).

1 and 1A Elm Tree Road: Omnibus yard and omnibus proprietor's home (Plate 284). David Lee, artist (1871 and 1881 Census); George Henry Cowell, 'Artist Photographic', with one tenant of the same profession (1901 Census). No. 1 is probably the house Henry James contemplated buying (see Plate 177).

2 Elm Tree Road: Frederick Macmillan, publisher (1881 Census); James H. Ince, architect (1901 Census).

3 and 4 Elm Tree Road: Gardeners, florists, nursery.

5–8 Elm Tree Road: Bernard Ward, artist painter (No. 5, 1891 Census); Charles H. Lowe, architect and surveyor (No. 6, 1871 Census); two art students (No. 6, 1881 Census); A. A. Calderon, artist (No. 7, 1871 Census); 'School of Arts' (No. 7, 1901 Census); Ernest Parton, artist landscape painter (No. 8, 1881 Census); Ethel Wright, artist painter (No. 8, 1891 Census).

9 Elm Tree Road: Arthur May, artist portrait painter (1891 Census).

41 Circus Road: John Evan Hodgson, painter (1888–90); Lilian Hamilton, sculptor (1890–99); Miss Mary Swainson, painter (1897).

52 Circus Road: Henry H. Armstead, sculptor (Cox-Johnson, 1963, gives 1898–1904, but the estate's licence for conversion of a stable into a studio at EE 2650/1/230 indicates he was there from 1883); Miss Charlotte W. Armstead, painter (1885–97).

54 Circus Road: Matthew R. Corbet, Mrs Corbet, later Mrs Arthur Marsh, painters. Cox-Johnson, 1963, gives 1892–1902, but the studio extension drawings at EE 2650/1/521(B) are dated 1891 (Plate 167).

56 Circus Road: Maurice Greiffenhagen, painter. His studio extension schedule has survived at EE 2650/1/521(C) (architect: F. M. Simpson), dated 1894. He is traditionally recorded at 12 Loudon Road (1895–1931).

10 Elm Tree Road: 'Devon Villa': Lewis Waller and his wife, both actors (1881 and 1901 Census).

11 Elm Tree Road: James Greenland, builder (1851, 1861, 1871 Census).

12 Elm Tree Road: Arthur A. Staight, civil servant (1881, 1891, 1901 Census).

13 Elm Tree Road: Thomas Williams, barrister (1871, 1881, 1891 Census).

14 Elm Tree Road: George Daniell, trunk maker and amateur natural historian (1851 Census, see p. 34).

15 Elm Tree Road: Bronson Howard, dramatic author (1881 Census); Wallace Mollison, actor (1901 Census, trade directories give the name of Phil May).

16 Elm Tree Road: Annie Erlam, schoolmistress (1851 Census).

17 Elm Tree Road: Thomas Hood, writer, was based at this house in the early 1840s (see Plate 174).

18 Elm Tree Road: Charles Wilson, egg merchant (1871, 1881, 1891 Census).

19 Elm Tree Road: Joseph Norton, Captain 3rd Dragoon Guards (1881, 1891, 1901 Census).

20 Elm Tree Road: Samuel Hyde, painter (decorator), and family (1851, 1861, 1871 Census).

21 Elm Tree Road: Charles Jarvis, glass merchant and family (1861, 1871, 1881 Census). The oldest house on the Eyre estate, now No. 8 (see Plates 49 and 50).

22 Elm Tree Road: Thomas Hall, house agent, one of the sons of William Hall, the builder who developed this part of the estate (see Appendix 9).

14 Grove End Road: David Wilkie Wynfield, painter, amateur photographer and member of the St John's Wood Clique (1867–87).

16 Grove End Road: George Dunlop Leslie, painter (1871–83), who 'almost entirely rebuilt the messuage'. Succeeded in 1883 by Arthur Graeme Ogilvie and his wife Marie Caroline, née Agnew (Plate 168).

Opposite: **166** This reconstruction drawing shows the gradual transformation of 44 Grove End Road from a tradesman's residence to that worthy of an artists' quarter. The original house (top), shown in 1825 when it was newly built, was the home of the Kipps family, coachmakers in Marylebone. By 1875 (middle) when the house was inhabited by the French painter James Tissot, it had acquired a studio and conservatory along with a magnificent garden. Finally, around 1900, it was thought of as the 'Palace of the Beautiful' and described as 'The Universally Admired Home of the late Sir Lawrence Alma-Tadema'. Drawing by Stephen Conlin, 2010. Courtesy of the artist and *Country Life*.

Right: **167** The drawings for adding a studio to 54 Circus Road for the benefit of resident painter Matthew Ridley Corbet have survived, dated July 1891 (for precise location, see Elm Tree Road map on previous spread). They were prepared by Howard Iver Architects. The extension provided lower and upper studios, lower and upper workrooms as well as a store. Here we reproduce front and back elevations only. Eyre estate archive (EE 2650/1/521(B)).

Far right: **168** The house on the corner of Grove End and Elm Tree Roads (the left-hand bay in this lease drawing) was built by William Hall in 1821 and considerably extended by George Dunlop Leslie when he took over this property in 1870. He assigned it to Arthur Graeme Ogilvie in 1883, who had married into the Agnew family of art dealing fame. This must have been a convenient platform for dealer William Agnew, who was personally connected to many St John's Wood artists. Eyre estate archive (Bk of Drawings I, 38).

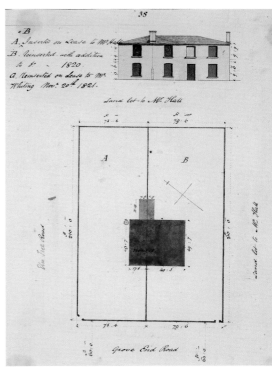

In our early days there was no Life class – that came later. Our task was to draw from the Antique for five and a half days a week, from 10 a.m. to 5 p.m. Attendance was registered and even a day off noted.... Later on, the innovation of a life-model was a great event. We trooped in and began our drawings with stumping-chalk and plumbline, as we had been taught over the Antique casts! Soon charcoal found more favour, and that led to charcoal smeared, and worked over with a dry paint brush. The phase culminated with the teaching of a new assistant-master who, finding a natural difficulty in pronouncing his R's, exhorted us to 'wub it wiv a wag'. His own dexterity with charcoal was amazing, and we all caught a trick reproducing a superficial surface remarkably like flesh, though apt to be a trifle boneless.[111]

The school's most famous pupils included Byam Shaw (who went on to found an art school of his own, which still exists); Claude Flight, a representative of the English futurist movement; and the robust and energetic C. R. W. Nevinson, who made his reputation with powerful First World War paintings but also produced strong and at times lyrical works on London.[112] Of foreign artists who were at the school, it is worth mentioning Paula Modersohn-Becker (1876–1907) from Bremen, who attended drawing classes there in 1892 while staying with an aunt in Surrey.[113]

In a clever marketing move the school devised a series of awards and invited established artists to teach. Some did not have far to come: in 1892, in *The Year's Art* advertisement, local residents Yeames and Alma-Tadema were mentioned alongside John William Waterhouse (a future resident).[114] Later, in 1902, the Principal, A. A. Calderon, was 'assisted by T. B. Kennington, S. Goetze, B. E. Ward and L. Walker'.

The school closed during the Second World War. By that date it was identified as No. 29, and when it returned after the war – if indeed it was the same institution – it called itself the 'Anglo-French Art Centre'. By 1953 it had been replaced by the 'Modern School of Flower Work', more clearly identified the following year as 'The Constance Spry Flower School'. It is last listed in Post Office Directories in 1958.

DEALERS IN THE WOOD: AGNEW AND GAMBART

Presiding over the Grove End Road entrance to Elm Tree Road stood a large semi-detached villa: 16 (formerly 8) Grove End Road. This house had started life as the diminutive 'half' of a double villa built in 1821 by developer William Hall (Plate 168). By 1870 it was in the hands of painter George Dunlop Leslie, who considerably extended the original house,[115] and in 1883 the engineer Arthur Graeme Ogilvie purchased the lease from Leslie.[116] Ogilvie had married Mary Caroline Agnew, daughter of the famous art dealer **William Agnew** (1825–1910), in 1878, and this connection must have influenced the purchase of the house.[117] George Dunlop Leslie had been part of William Agnew's circle since 1860 (Plate 169). At that time Agnew opened a London branch for the Manchester-based art dealers, Thos Agnew & Sons; 'William knew personally most of the contemporary artists and he and his sons were friendly with Poynter, Leader, Ouless, Keeley Halswelle, MacWhirter, T. S. Cooper, Farquhason, Henry Woods, Edwin Long, H. W. B. Davis, Faed, Pettie and Orchardson' (the artists based in St John's Wood have been underlined).[118]

The links between William Agnew and St John's Wood were strong and are best illustrated by an amusing anecdote which Geoffrey Agnew recounts in his history of the firm. The scene was Summer Hill, the Agnew residence near Manchester, and the date 1870:

> William [Agnew] had just built a billiard room. A party of artists including Walker, G. D. Leslie, J. E. Hodgson and Stacey [sic] Marks, was staying in the house and suggested playing pool. It was Sunday and William told them that he had a rule not to use the table on Sundays. An hour later he came out of the library to find his children burning corks to make charcoal, his butler sharpening billiard chalks; Walker was just finishing a large Mermaid on the lining papers of the walls (the Paris wallpaper had not yet arrived); Leslie had painted a landscape of the Thames; Stacey Marks had done a sketch of Fred Walker and William Agnew playing billiards, surmounted by the Agnew coat-of-arms with the motto 'Ecce Agnew Dei'; and Hodgson on another wall, had started on a Highland landscape. They worked until midnight and all the next day. The Paris wallpaper was countermanded and the drawings glazed. They survived until the First World war.[119]

This illustrates perfectly the friendship that existed between these artists, all members of the St John's Wood Clique, and the Agnew family (long before the Agnew/Ogilvie couple settled at 8 Grove End Road). The episode also predated the bout of domestic creativity at Hodgson's house in Hill Road which Montgomery Eyre documented in his book on St John's Wood (see Plates 287, 288 and 289).[120] Two years later, in 1872, William purchased Fred Walker's *Harbour of Refuge* (now known as the *Almshouses at Bray*), which he presented to the Tate Gallery in 1893. In 1875, he also bought four of Hodgson's paintings for £1,000 each.[121]

169 George Dunlop Leslie, *Pot Pourri*, 1874. The use of eighteenth-century costume in this picture should not detract the viewer from the strong contemporaneity of this subject. The light and lovely setting a garden could afford to the house within it had been first exploited by Holman Hunt (see Plate 111). Here Leslie, no doubt inspired by the artistry of his own house at 8 Grove End Road, delighted in depicting the interaction between house and garden. Private collection/Bridgeman Art Library (Christie's sale, 27 November 2002, Lot 13).

By the time William's daughter Mary Caroline married Ogilvie, the schedule attached to her marriage settlement contained a notable number of works made by St John's Wood artists: 'Oil Picture by G. D. Leslie/Watercolour Drawing by F. Walker 'The Bridge'/Drawing by G. D. Leslie R.A./Drawing by Sir E. Landseer/Drawing by H. S. Marks ARA', alongside a group of artists' proof engravings and other works by R. Ansdell (*Robin*), W. Wyld (*Venice*), sketches by G. Du Maurier and L. Sambourne, and a watercolour by E. G. Warren.[122]

These connections partly explain the substantial number of paintings made in St John's Wood which have found their way into Guildhall Art Gallery. The principal source for their acquisition was the wealthy merchant Charles Gassiot (d.1902), who bequeathed his collection to Guildhall. This Tooting-based collector had no direct links to St John's Wood, but as he purchased almost exclusively from Agnew's, this is how the connection came to feature so prominently in the City's paintings collection.[123]

Ernest Gambart (1814–1902), nicknamed 'Prince of the Victorian Art World',[124] presided over a different part of St John's Wood between the 1850s and 1882. When he moved there, probably in the late 1850s, he lived briefly in Acacia Road, but his best remembered address was 62 Avenue Road, made famous by the lavish parties Gambart held there (Plate 170).[125]

Belgian by birth, this born entrepreneur had set up his own print business in Paris by the time he was twenty. He moved to London when he was twenty-six to set up a branch for the Goupil print publishers, who were thriving in Paris. However, despite a couple of attempts at collaborative ventures, Gambart seems to have operated best on his own. He made his fortune and that of painter William Holman Hunt when in 1858 he purchased the rights to reproduce the *Light of the World*. Overlooked by most critics when it was first exhibited, the painting was championed by Ruskin in a letter to *The Times* (5 May 1854): 'one of the very noblest works of sacred art ever produced in this or any other age'.[126] Gambart picked up the project and disseminated the image through print

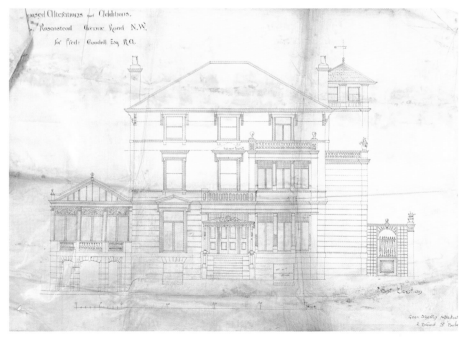

170 Elevation of 'Rosenstead', 62 Avenue Road, built in 1839 by developer W. H. Twentyman. It became famous when it was the residence of art dealer Ernest Gambart between 1862 and 1882. This drawing was produced by architect George Sherrin for the next occupant, painter Frederick Goodall, who planned the addition of a studio/conservatory wing (on the left). A licence was prepared in 1882, though the alterations do not appear to have been carried out. Eyre estate archive (EE 2650/1/256(A)).

184 The animal painter Briton Riviere in his studio at 'Flaxley', 82 Finchley Road, on the south-east corner of Adelaide Road. He was based there between 1880 and 1904. The unfinished painting on the easel is *Prometheus*, exhibited at the Grosvenor Gallery in 1889. Of his studio Riviere wrote it was 'by no means a show one, but only a workshop of a very rough description. At the present time it is, if possible, even less attractive than usual, as I am having horses in it, which add neither to its tidiness nor to its fragrance' (*The Art Journal*, 1890, p. 138). *The Art Journal*, which published the photograph by R. P. Robinson, added that Riviere 'decorates only a portion of the studio with those things that please the eye and charm the senses, leaving that quarter where the animals pose in that state of which animals approve' (p. 138). Like Landseer before him, the proximity of Regent's Park Zoo was a great incentive for living in St John's Wood. Victoria and Albert Museum, London.

185 Elevation of Riviere's house (left side only) in Finchley Road, from the lease drawing dated 1842 (also see Plate 300). Eyre estate archive (Bk of Drawings IV, 30 Left).

186 The Music Room at 27 Marlborough Hill, the residence of watercolourist Robert Little. Little obtained a licence to build a studio on 25 October 1888. He was still connected with this address in 1891 when this photograph was taken, but by 1892 he was listed at 47 Palace Court. Photograph taken by WW (from Bedford Lemere photographic studio) on 14 July 1891. NMR (red boxes, Westminster).

The editorial team of *The Art Journal* was no doubt inspired by Stephens's book when they commissioned R. P. Robinson to photograph artists in their studios in 1890. The text which accompanies the photographs is particularly informative (Plates 183 and 184).

The Rob Dickins collection, formed by the art dealer Jeremy Maas and now in the collection of the Watts Gallery at Compton near Guildford,[168] also includes a number of photographs of St John's Wood artists and studios, the most unusual showing the painter Philip Morris lying on the floor in the middle of his huge sitting room (see Plate 158). Perhaps surprisingly, the collection does not include the work of St John's Wood Clique artist David Wilkie Wynfield, an 'amateur' photographer who produced a remarkable series of close-up portraits of his artist friends including Thomas Faed, George Adolphus Storey and William Frederick Yeames.[169] Wynfield's portraits indulged the common desire among his contemporaries to return to the past and be portrayed in costumes from the sixteenth and seventeenth centuries. It was Wynfield who introduced Julia Cameron to photography.

Another woman, Adeline (Lena) Beatrice Connell, later known as Beatrice Cundy (1875–1949), made history by being the first female photographer to have male sitters. She spent most of her working life in St John's Wood by following in her father's footsteps, taking over his photographic business at 3 Blenheim Place in Grove End Road (opposite the Eyre Arms), and then moving to 50 Grove End Road (1901–19) before finally settling at 12 Baker Street (1919–22).[170] She is perhaps best remembered for her portraits of suffragettes: she became an early supporter of the suffrage for women, attending meetings and processions.[171] But the portrait which won over the judges of the Professional Photographs Association in 1912 was that of an unknown woman, and Connell was awarded the Gold Medal that year.[172] There were many more photographers working in St John's Wood and a comprehensive list is at Appendix 7.

One photographer who, alas, did not take as many photographs of St John's Wood homes as one might have expected was Bedford Lemere (1839–1911). His photographic business was vast; it operated between the 1870s and the 1940s and employed several photographers to deal with the constant flow of commissions the firm received.[173] His day books have yielded a number of references to photographs taken in north-west London, but hardly any of the relevant ones can be traced.[174] The photograph of an interior at 27 Marlborough Road is a rare example, and shows the comfortable home of an artist of independent means, Robert Little (Plate 186).[175]

THE ST JOHN'S WOOD ARTS CLUB

The St John's Wood Arts Club was born in 1894, and one may regard its creation as the culmination of St John's Wood as a creative quarter. Dubbed by Montgomery Eyre as a 'Band of brothers in art', the club took form at the house of Dendy Sadler at 44 Finchley Road on 23 December 1894 (see Plate 302). Those present were the first members of the club: J. B. Burgess (Chair), Ernest A. Waterlow, Arthur Hacker, Gordon Thompson [or Thomson?], Yeend King, George Simonds, Charles W. Wyllie, John Fulleylove, Edwin Bale, C. F. A. Voysey and W. Dendy Sadler.[176] All were painters except for Simonds, a sculptor, and Voysey, the famous architect and designer.

The club's first home was the upper room of the Knights of St John pub (Plate 267), where Voysey is recorded as carrying out 'decorations, alterations and repairs'.[177] The inaugural dinner was held there on 30 January 1895. It was attended by a substantial group of London's creative leading lights, many of them St John's Wood residents: it was chaired by sculptor Alfred Gilbert (who made *Eros* in Piccadilly Circus) and graced by Onslow Ford (whose monument still stands near Abbey Road Studios) and Lawrence Alma-Tadema. An attempt to immortalise this event was rudely whitewashed by the pub landlord: it was the silhouette of Alma-Tadema sketched on one of the walls by Arthur Hacker, RA. Barely a year later, the club moved to more spacious premises at the Eyre Arms, with the attraction of a billiard room. The club's final home was, from 1900, the house that used to be Thomas Hood's in the 1840s (see p. 416). Judging by its imprint on maps, this building must have been extended in the early years of the twentieth century. By 1900, according to Montgomery Eyre, the principal source of information about this club, membership was rigorously confined to 'architects, sculptors, painters and engravers'.[178] By then the club had 111 members. A drawing by Cecil King shows a comfortable, country-style interior with a blazing fire, a billiard table in the background and the portraits of its members arranged in a frieze around the top of the walls in the lower room (Plate 271). The overall arrangement recalls that of the Clifton pub (discussed on p. 439).

Apart from its social agenda, the club also appears to have encouraged professional collaboration between artists. A Cabinet of Works by its members was formerly in the Forbes Collection of Art. The green leather-bound wooden box was designed by C. F. A. Voysey and contained eight glazed white maple trays filled with five watercolours, one pencil drawing and an enamel plaque, all by different artists (as well as a steel copyright plaque). The inscription reads: 'to T E Scrutton/From the copyright/Committee of the/S. John's Wood Arts/Club', and was signed 'L. Alma-Tadema', 'Frank Dicksee Hon. Tres.', 'Edwin Bale Hon. Sec', 'Alfred East', 'Solomon J. Solomon', 'G. A. Storey', 'W. Reynolds-Stephens', 'George Simonds', 'John Cother Webb', 'Chas. F. Annesley Voysey', 'H. Annesley Voysey Legal Advisor'.[179]

The contribution of several of these artists to the Copyright Committee is mentioned by Montgomery Eyre: 'The Artistic Copyright Committee … was formed, with Tadema as chairman, H. A. Voysey, the club's honorary legal adviser, and Edwin Bale as secretary. I do not think that it has at all been generally recognised, by the artistic world, what is due to these indefatigable workers, especially the last-named, for the part they have played in bringing to a successful termination what is now the Copyright Amendment Act.'[180] As well as the painter-architect Alma-Tadema, both C. F. A. Voysey and Charles Harrison Townsend, two Edwardian architects, seem to have played a substantial role in this subcommittee.[181]

9

SPIRITUAL
ST JOHN'S
WOOD

When they developed their estate, the Eyre brothers were anxious to create and maintain a respectable neighbourhood. Provided residents were happy to emulate their level of civilised living (and this, of course, meant being able to finance their St John's Wood tenancy), the brothers seem to have avoided passing judgement on religious issues. For instance, when the developer William Holme Twentyman announced he needed the underlease for St Paul's Chapel (later church) (Plate 188), Walpole wrote to him: 'I will thank you to inform me of the name and description of your Lessee, the annual rent payable & from what time – and the name of the Re[li]gious worship to be used in the chapel.'[1] This open-minded approach ensured the blossoming of a varied and interesting community. However, the next generation had a markedly different approach. The tenant for life from 1856 was George John Eyre, Walpole's nephew, whose failing health forced him to live in the country. His physical disability (he was in a wheelchair for the last twenty-five years of his life) and his anxious disposition[2] meant that Walpole's eldest sons – Henry Samuel and Frederick Edwin –

Previous pages: **187** The Abbey Road synagogue replaced a temporary structure which was the first synagogue built in St John's Wood. The new building, at No. 33, was designed by a Jewish architect, H. H. Collins (1833–1905), in 1882. The site was vacated in 1965 when a new synagogue was completed in Grove End Road to replace the ageing structure. A Masorti community is now based in the Victorian synagogue. Eyre estate (photo: John Chase).

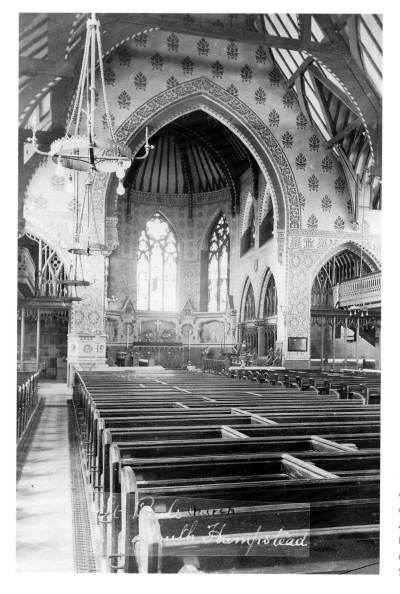

188 Interior view of St Paul's Church on the west side of Avenue Road, designed by S. S. Teulon (1812–73) and consecrated in February 1864. It was bombed in 1940 and finally demolished in 1958. Camden Local Studies (Hampstead collection, LSB).

managed the estate, the former as a trustee, the latter as the estate's solicitor. Until the mid-1840s when Walpole relinquished management to his son, estate management had been firm but creative, open and conciliatory; with the next generation it was more reactive, more closed and also less conciliatory with regard to religious issues.

ANGLICANISM

The Commission for Building Fifty New Churches in and around London was set up by Act of Parliament in 1711, but by 1811 there was only accommodation for one-ninth of the population in Marylebone and St Pancras.[3] In 1818, the Incorporated Church Building Society was founded, and in the same year Parliament voted one million pounds for the building of new churches under the supervision of the Church Commissioners. However, St John's Wood had benefited from the services of a chapel long before that date and was fortunate in acquiring it in the early years of its development.

St John's Wood Chapel (later parish church)

> Mr Shaw & I [Walpole] have lately been in treaty with the Parish of Marylebone for the sale of six acres of Ground to them for the purpose of building a handsome Chapel & making a burial ground[.] Mr Shaw & I have thought a great deal about this & we are both well satisfied that in all probability it will prove of great benefit to your Estate.[4]

The main reason for building this chapel was Marylebone vestry's need for a new burial ground. The land was acquired in 1807,[5] though the vestry did not enclose the ground for three years. Lack of money delayed the construction of the chapel, designed by Thomas Hardwick (1752–1829),

189 Front elevation of St John's Wood Chapel in St John's Wood Road, 1828, engraving from Elmes's *Metropolitan Improvements: London in the Nineteenth Century* (published between 1827 and 1830). City of London, London Metropolitan Archives.

Marylebone chapel

190 Marylebone Chapel (i.e. St John's Wood Chapel) viewed from a distance across Regent's Park a few years after it was built and consecrated in 1814. The terrace development on the left may show John Punter's houses, which have survived to this day (see p. 381). The chapel was designed by Thomas Hardwick. Watercolour by W. May, dated 1818. Westminster City Archives (Ashbridge collection, 224).

for another five years,[6] and it was eventually consecrated in 1814 (Plates 189 and 190).[7] However, the need for burial places was so pressing that permission to dig a couple of graves was immediately requested, though the episode turned into farce when the diggers dug in the wrong field: 'When the Committee go on Monday to look at the Graves that have been dug I will thank you to request they will trample the grass as little as possible, I have seen Mr Willan & he informs me that the graves having been dug upon his Ground has put him to a serious inconvenience[.] he intended to have turned his Cows into the Field which he will not now be able to do till after the Hay making.'[8]

At first Sunday services at the chapel seem to have been organised on a weekly basis using peripatetic clergy, as this 1816 letter addressed to Reverend D. Wilkinson suggests: 'I have seen Mr Balfour [Belfour] this Morning and find a friend of his has undertaken the Duty for next Sunday at St Johns Chapel[.] if you will perform it for him on the Sunday follow[in]g ... both he and I shall be much obliged to you.'[9] More struggles, this time financial, plagued the new institution, and Walpole called on the Barracks for help, writing to Colonel Thornhill in the same year:

> I underst[an]d you have the Command of Artillery quartered at the St Johns Wood Barrack[.] The Soldiers from that Barrack usually attend Divine Service at the St Johns Wood Chapel and have done so ever since it was consecrated which is now nearly two years[.] If Governm[en]t do make the above allowance I will thank you to inform me what they allow usually[.] I here [hear] Mr Belfour the Minister is to apply for it[.]
> I must apologize of taking the liberty of requesting the above Information but as the remuneration Mr Belfour receives from the Parish for the duty he performs at the Chapel

is but trifling I am desirous if possible of getting him any additional Emolument & I trust therefore you will excuse this application.[10]

By 1819 the chapel was sufficiently well established to organise a fund-raising event, and Walpole was drumming up local support from the vestry clerk George Jones: 'We are to have a Charity Sermon at St Johns Wood Chapel to morrow [sic] for the benefit of the Midd[lese]x Hospital- I hope you will be present with a pocket full of money.'[11]

Unrealised projects

By 1820 Colonel Eyre was ready to reserve land for the building of another place of worship in St John's Wood, as this letter shows:

> if there is any part of my property in St Marylebone which they [the Marylebone vestry] may think eligible for a Parochial Chapel I shall readily present the parish with a sufficient quantity of Land for that purpose[.]

> The Saint Johns Chapel is built upon my St Johns Wood Estate and from that circumstance I am apprehensive the Vestry will not think it advisable to erect another Chapel in that part of the Parish, if however the Vestry think otherwise I will give my Agents directions to attend any appointment the Vestry may make for the purpose of going over the Estate and fixing upon a site – I am fully convinced of the necessity of having additional places of Worship in this Parish and shall be glad to promote so desirable an object[.] at the same time I think it may be a question whether it will be most beneficial to the Parishioners at large to erect additional Chapels under the present parochial Act or under the Church Commissioners Acts, or whether it may not be advisable to obtain a fresh Act of Parliament for that particular purpose – If the Vestry accept of a Site upon my Estate I shall expect the Chapel to be built upon a plan & elevation to be approved of by my architect and to be completed within two years from this time – The Chapel must also be so placed as not to interfere with the improvements now carrying upon my property[.]

> I have to request an early answer from the Vestry or I shall not feel myself bound by the above offer.[12]

This document makes reference to the many different issues that needed consideration before electing to build a new chapel or church. On this occasion, however, the offer was not pursued. Neither was the informal offer Walpole made to Major Close and William Wilberforce junior (who would later become disastrously involved with St John's Wood Farm – see p. 168) for a new parish church in Hampstead where the northern end of the estate was sited: 'my brother is disposed to offer the parish a sufficient quantity of Gro[un]d for the p[ur]p[o]se of er[e]ct[in]g an add[ition]al parish Church'.[13]

Chronologically, the next place of worship to appear on the estate was the Catholic chapel (later church) in Lodge Road (1836). However, before discussing the return of a religion England had virtually banned until 1829, we should try to assess the way in which the Eyre brothers attempted to shape spiritual life on their estate.

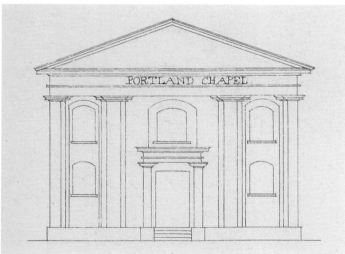

191 and 192 The Portland (Congregational) Chapel in St John's Wood Terrace, Circus Road, was originally leased to developer John Maidlow in 1841(lease drawing on the right). It survives (see far left) situated next to Robinsfield Infant School. Eyre estate archive (Bk of Drawings IV, 101 right; photo: the author).

Portland Chapel

John Maidlow's chapel in St John's Wood Terrace showed that the estate had a firm grasp on the appearance of all buildings (Plates 191, 192 and 252). Walpole wrote to estate architect John Shaw:

> The bearer of this is Mr Maidlow who wishes to build the Chapel at St Johns Terrace- I explained to him that you did not approve of the plans[.] he states to me that the walls are 18 inches thick & which he says is sufficient but this I must leave to your better judgment. With respect to the elevation- he says he is willing to make any alteration you may require[.] I will therefore thank you to suggest to him what you may think necessary.[14]

John Maidlow was an ambitious and respected builder from Portland Town who took, on agreement, vast tracts of land in St John's Wood (see Plate 72). Like many developers he must have regarded the inclusion of a chapel in his development as a desirable element. When he built this chapel he had already faced bankruptcy and was making a comeback (see Appendix 9).

The chapel was leased to him in 1841 and was described as a Congregational chapel, i.e. it ran its own affairs and was independent from the authority and hierarchy of the Church of England. Maidlow soon found a priest subtenant – Reverend Baker from Douro Cottages – who requested 'Consent to the erection of a Vestry and Offices in the rear of the Chapel'. The licence specified it should not be used as a school or for public meetings, as this was regarded as 'disconnected with the Religious character of the s[ai]d Chapel'. Exception was made for 'the Religious teaching of youth … on the Sabbath day Xmas day and Good Friday'.[15] The chapel's appearance in St John's Wood Terrace immediately had a civilising influence (see p. 400–01). It catered for the poorer end of the estate and also for the adjoining Portland Town.

William Stott's lively history of the Abbey Road Baptist Chapel describes how the core of people who would later create it held meetings at Portland Chapel between 1859 and 1862 when they were effectively 'homeless': 'For three years, daily, without intermission, Saturdays excepted, meetings have been held in the Congregational School room, where united prayers have been offered up that God would send a revival, and convert sinners.'[16]

In 1860, a further licence was issued giving permission 'to erect school rooms and [make] alterations at St Johns Wood Congregational Church Circus Road' (Circus Road being the former name of St John's Wood Terrace).[17] This modest school, which originated with the church, is clearly marked on the 1883 map of St John's Wood. By the 1890s it is labelled 'Sun School', and by 1937 the church and school blocks have merged and are labelled 'Club'. The present infant school, adjacent to the chapel and aptly called Robinsfield after the name of the former meadow, 'Little Robins Field', was created after the Second World War. Although Portland Chapel no longer functions as a chapel, it has survived to this day.

Most of the religious projects on the estate tended to be reactive; however, on one occasion in 1844 the Eyres did attempt to create an opportunity for church building on the adjacent Portland estate, but the outcome was unsuccessful. The colonel, as the lessee of a house on the west side of Avenue Road (No. 9, part of the Portland estate), was willing to waive his interest in the property if the duke of Portland agreed to redevelop the site and erect a church.[18] It was clear to the brothers that the people residing on the east side of the estate were some distance from any place of worship, so this is how Walpole tried to persuade the duke's agent: 'if his Grace the Duke of Portland would be so good as to give up the Freehold I have no doubt a Church might be built on that Ground without any additional expense to his Grace or if he were to make a Small Endowment the Church & presentation wo[ul]d belong to him'. It is interesting to note that Walpole was hoping the duke of Portland would give up the freehold when Walpole himself was so reluctant to do so in similar circumstances, as will be clear below. In any case Walpole failed to convince. The church of St Stephen on the opposite side of Avenue Road (also on the duke of Portland's estate) was eventually built in the late 1840s.[19]

All Saints Church

In 1843, when the bishop of London approached the colonel for further church projects, this was the reply: 'my Brother Col[one]l Eyre … will most readily concur in promoting the Build[in]g of one or more Churches upon his St JWE[state.] he wishes me however to add (and in which I am confident y[ou]r L[or]dship will agree) that he will not approve of the Erection of any church upon his Property unless it be of an handsome Elevation & of sufficient capacity to meet the Wants of the increasing Population in that District.'[20] In the same letter Walpole also indicated that the colonel would wish to appoint the minister, his choice on this occasion being his nephew Henry Samuel (Walpole's son). On the latter point the Eyres were unsuccessful, as Walpole subsequently clarified: 'I understand he [the bishop of London] will not allow the person build[in]g a Church or Chapel to have the nomination or appointm[en]t of the Minister unless the Church or Chapel is endowed.'[21] The 1843 date suggests that church and district were founded under Peel's Populous Parishes Act of 1843, which led to the loosening up of the ways in which new Anglican churches were built by allowing what were commonly known as 'Peel districts'.[22]

The outcome of this exchange of correspondence was certainly All Saints Church, as the following month Walpole arranged that the selected site, the Rick Yard, formerly part of St John's Wood Farm, was cleared: 'Many complaints are made to me of the offensive use that is made of the piece of gro[un]d on the East side of the Turnpike Road and near the Barrack…./I must now request that such use may be imm[ediate]ly discontinued and that the things upon the Ground may be forthwith removed[,] it being my intention to resume poss[essi]on of such piece of gro[un]d in order to a church being built there.'[23]

All Saints was built in 1846 (Plate 194) with private funds from its first minister, Reverend Edward Thompson, a passionate believer in popular education (see p. 212). On this occasion Walpole wrote to Shaw: 'the Church was to be built by Mr Thompson & at his expense & that under the circumstances I could not object to his appointing his own Architect – if The Church had been to be built by my brother or at his own expense I should most undoubtedly have put it into your hands & should have awaited [availed] myself of your Architectural Taste & judgment[.] as it is I am sure you will agree with me that I could not do otherwise.'[24] In this letter Walpole was annoyed that the church architect, Thomas Little, had bypassed him, going straight to John Shaw, particularly as Walpole had not had a chance to brief Shaw about this project. This may explain why, most unusually for Walpole, he chanced to make a joke about the architect's name: 'I think they ought not to have troubled you upon this occasion but through me & were I disposed to be facetious upon this subject – I should perhaps say Little People sometimes like to ride the High Horse.' He also added on a more sober note: 'Mr Thompson has proposed to purchased [sic] the Freehold and has offered £2000 for it but I don't think it advisable to dispose of any part of the Freehold in that Central situation.' Although the church design is credited to Little, his principal assistant at that time was the architect George Devey (1820–86), who joined his office in 1837 and who signed 'both the original design drawing on which the estimates were based, in March 1845, and the contract drawings on the 3rd June 1845'.[25]

It seems that the money available for the project (£4,000 according to Walpole's letter of 16 November 1844) ran out too soon, driving the architect and his backer to make unpalatable cuts. First the organ: 'I am much disapp[ointe]d at the Exclusion of the Organ from the furnishing – Organs are so much in use now that without one a Church cannot be considered as complete.'[26] But much worse was to come: 'I find they are not going to build the Tower at present & which I think will entirely destroy the beauty of the build[in]g.'[27] This was particularly disappointing, as Reverend Thompson had based his church building campaign on the design (Plate 194), a fact which Walpole would point out with a keen sense of frustration (see p. 215). The church was consecrated on 9 July 1846, and two years later Reverend Thompson was fundraising for a steeple for which he had the cautious support of the Eyre brothers: 'I understand there is to be a collection after dinner for the purpose of erecting a Steeple at All Saints Church – I beg to enclose my draft for Five Guineas as my donation to that purpose – I have already explained to the Revd Dr Thompson that whenever the Steeple is erected that I have my Brother Col[one]l Eyre's authority to subscribe for him £100 towards the expenses.'[28] But the project remained in abeyance, and barely four years later the All Saints' incumbent left the parish and was replaced by Reverend H. W. Maddock (Plate 193). The church must have been a great success as by 1852 Maddock was contemplating its enlargement.[29]

The Eyre brothers had intended that their son and nephew Henry Samuel should be the first minister of that church. This original plan did not work out, but in 1870 when Maddock died after a ministry of twenty years at All Saints, Reverend Henry Samuel Eyre became the new vicar, moving to London from Newington in Kent where he had worked for seven years. The move was particularly unpopular with his daughter Mary (Plate 26), who described her first encounter with this church:

193 Portrait of Reverend H. W. Maddock, the long-serving vicar of All Saints Church. He was in post for twenty years between 1850 and 1870. The gouache drawing is signed 'H Collen', probably Henry Collen (1797–1879), portrait painter and photographer. The Vicar and Churchwardens of St John's Wood.

194 Church of All Saints in Finchley Road. The commission went to architect Thomas Little of Nunhead Cemetery chapel fame, but his assistant George Devey was responsible for the design. This view was reproduced in *The Builder* in August 1846 after the consecration of the church on 9 July. The tower was part of the original design, though it was 'cut' through lack of funds and only completed in 1890 when Reverend Henry Samuel Eyre provided the funds needed for its erection. Westminster City Archives (Ashbridge collection, 241–53).

The Hindle Archt.   F. Bedford Lith.

Our new church was very ugly; it had no tower or spire.... it was without any proper chancel and had Pews up to the very Altar rails. It had galleries all the way round, and there was not a stained glass window in the church.... The congregation consisted principally of the well-to-do tradespeople class, those who, possessing shops in London, having made more or less of a pile, thought themselves entitled to take a villa in this salubrious suburb.

At that time of day [1870s] people were very good churchgoers ... : in walked Papa, followed by Mamma and all the little Master and Misses olives branches – all spick and span and well brushed up.... Alas how different things are to-day [1904]. Fathers of families slink off to golf; sons tear countryward on cycles; the mothers ... occasionally attend services and now & again a daughter or 2 will accompany them.[30]

In 1881, William Clarke's assessment of All Saints had been more positive: 'the fashionable and first ... and in the patronage of the Eyre family'.[31] However, in the mid-twentieth century Reverend E. G. Semple looked back on Henry Samuel's contribution (1870–87) in more realistic terms:

The new incumbent was a true disciple of the Tractarians.... He had the honour of leading the Catholic revival in this neighbourhood. Of course he met with opposition – that is ever the fate of the reformer. When he appeared in Church in a white linen surplice ... there was a furious rumpus at his 'Puseyite goings on', and it was loudly complained that All Saints 'had gone to Rome' when he attired his choir in the same hated vestments. Undaunted the incumbent persevered in his course.... Collections dropped steadily with each innovation.... A cross must at this time have been placed on or behind the altar ... and further protests are revealed by the records of a new drop in receipts in 1877 after a temporary recovery.[32]

In 1888, his daughter Mary married a clergyman, John Richardson-Eyre, who became minister at All Saints between 1889 and 1910.[33] The young couple threw themselves into various improvements which necessitated frequent fund-raising events. One such event was held at the large premises of 43A Acacia Road, the future Mermaid Theatre (see Plate 117 and pp. 217 and 405). The property's unusual size made it a perfect venue for parties and theatricals, and Mary Richardson-Eyre described the very successful 'Rose Fete' organised at the time of Queen Victoria's Diamond Jubilee (1897): 'it was held in the large grounds belonging to Mr Oliver's School in Acacia Road.... Over a thousand people were present, rich and poor being equally represented[;] 14 ladies provided refreshments and had tables all decorated with roses.... The Artillery here gave a musical ride ... and we had the Artillery Band from Woolwich.'[34]

The church demonstrated the patronage of the Eyre family – from the parish room (built with a gift of £1,000 from Henry Samuel III) to the tower, which was finally erected and also paid for by Henry Samuel, via stained glass windows and altar cloths embroidered by Mary Richardson-Eyre.[35] The end of All Saints is a particularly sad episode recounted by Mark Lomas, its churchwarden between about 1966 and 1976. When he started, the High Anglican priest was presiding over a congregation of around thirty or so. Numbers began to dwindle when he was replaced by a young curate who eventually retired for reasons of ill health. After his departure there was a lengthy interregnum, and eventually All Saints was partnered with St Mary's Primrose Hill. By the end of 1976 the congregation was down to eight or ten, and around £30,000 was needed for repairs. The congregation came under two bishops – the bishop of London and the bishop of Willesden (through the involvement with the Primrose Hill church) – but it seemed they were unable to come to All Saints' rescue. In the absence of guidance, Mark Lomas wrote to both bishops for the last time to explain that unless he heard from them he would simply have to close the church. He received no replies, and the church was duly closed on 9 December 1976.[36]

From around 1970 the church had hosted a Christian Armenian congregation. They had been allocated space in the Lady Chapel where they held their long, 'terrific' services (lasting three hours). They were still in occupation of the church when it 'officially' closed. Unusually for a consecrated church, no faculty was obtained before disposing of its contents, though a few items were donated to the Museum of London and others to St John's Wood church (for instance Plate 193).[37]

All Souls Church, Loudoun Road

By 1853 the St John's Wood residents in the parish of Hampstead were clamouring for a new church in the northern part of the estate, and Edwin Eyre, Walpole's son, now in charge of administering the estate, contacted Reverend Thomas Ainger at Hampstead Rectory.[38] The chosen site was at the top end of Loudoun Road by the railway bridge: the future All Souls. The original plan was very ambitious: 'We are trying if we can [to] arrange with Mr Cook [the developer] to lay out the land so as to form a Square and have the Church in the middle which would give an approach also from the Boundary Road and w[hi]ch would be very desirable if it can be carried out.'[39] The suggested site of half an acre was proposed to be sold at the top price of £1,200 an acre (the last recorded price was in 1849 when land was sold to Charles Hall for £900 an acre). The letter books reveal fund-raising was a difficult issue, and must have been one of the reasons why the Eyres were so anxious to establish beforehand whether the relevant authorities favoured the establishment of new places of worship. The principal sponsor is named in the letter books as Reverend Henry Robinson Wadmore from St John's Parsonage in St John's Wood.[40]

In the footsteps of John Maidlow, builders did attempt to encourage the building of churches and chapels on the land they were developing – for example, James Ponsford west of Abbey Road (p. 433) and Robert William Fry in Blenheim Road East[41] – though both failed in their endeavours. The Yeo family, who undertook so much development on both sides of the railway line at the north end of the estate, deployed all the tools of the trade in the 1860s, supporting the building of All Souls Church in Loudoun Road to the tune of £100 but also building a pub opposite – until they realised the combination of the two formed a combustible mixture:

> Mr John Yeo fears some opposition on the gro[u]nd of the contiguity of the Public House to the Church – He has therefore requested that you as the freeholder & your two Cousins will sign a paper to shew that the Public House was projected before the Church.… It wo[ul]d be an almost ruinous affair to Mr John Yeo if he did not obtain his License besides the blot to the neighbourhood by an unopened Public House of w[hi]ch no License had be [*sic*] obtained & once refused might not be obtained for years.[42]

This church project was made under the authority of the Church Building Acts and the lease dated 6 July 1864.[43] All Souls was made redundant in 1985 and known as Grace Chapel in the 1990s. Cherry and Pevsner note it was designed by J. F. Wadmore, the brother of the vicar.[44]

Dissenting chapels

> All the land in St. John's Wood, or nearly so, was under the ownership of a very strait churchman, who would neither rent or sell to us a yard of land at any price…. We could not get a site at all anywhere near the Eyre Arms, because the agent of the Estate said, 'Not a yard for Dissenters at any price'. Some of us will not forget that reply to our letter of enquiry respecting a nursery garden near to our meeting place [Eyre Arms].[45]

So wrote William Stott, the charismatic pastor of the Baptist chapel in Abbey Road. His history of that church is a vivid and detailed account of the life and work of a dissenting institution and of the difficulties he and his committee met when they first attempted to settle their church in St John's Wood.

It might be tempting to regard Stott's recollections as exaggerated, but the dry world of the Eyre letter books echoes the pastor's passionate story, including the episode of the 'nursery garden', the first instance of the estate's anti-Dissenters policy. It was in 1845: 'I cannot consent to have a Wesleyan Chappel [*sic*] built on the ground taken by the late Mr Rewlins [Rawlins],' a piece of land opposite the site chosen for All Saints Church.[46] And again in 1857: 'I laid before Mr Edwin Eyre

195 The ground which Dissenters tried to secure from the Eyres in the middle years of the nineteenth century was still a nursery by 1903 when this map of the estate was made. The detail shows the nursery ground originally leased to Rawlins in the 1830s, situated at the end of Waverley Place and very close to All Saints Church in Finchley Road. The site is now occupied by the American School in London. Eyre estate archive (EE 2652/14(F)).

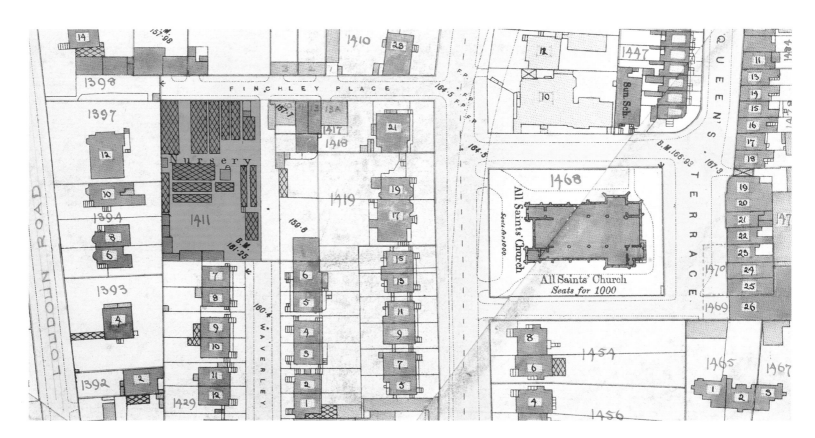

your note of the 11th as to building a chapel at the end of Waverl[e]y Place. He decidedly objects to a dissenting chapel' (Plate 195).[47] In 1861, Edwin wrote to the architect William Ifold: 'I have a letter from my brother [Reverend Henry Samuel Eyre] objecting most strongly to the Dissenting Chapel being built on the ground let to the late Mr Edwards at Bridge Road.'[48]

The 'strait churchman' responsible for this policy of intolerance was undoubtedly Reverend Henry Samuel Eyre (see Plate 25). He became one of the estate's trustees at the death of his father in 1856 and would finally become the estate's tenant for life in 1883 on the death of his cousin. Since there are no records suggesting his father Walpole or his uncle Colonel Eyre shared his aversion towards Dissenters, it is likely that Henry Samuel's influence dictated the early 1845 refusal of a site for a chapel.

His objection to Dissenters was not limited to the Methodists. In 1869, he firmly rejected the proposal of a Baptist chapel in Hanover Cottages – a part of the estate close to the canal which had been disrupted by the new St John's Wood railway line and was in severe need of spiritual guidance. In that year, the estate's trusted clerk, Charles Freeth, died, and the solicitor John Thomas White, who had been handling the leasework on the estate for some time, was appointed to manage the estate office. This experienced lawyer had not been in post for very long and was clearly unaware of Henry Samuel's distaste for Dissenters. He attempted to persuade the Eyres that such a project was a good idea:

> I send a proposal to build a Baptist Chapel in Hanover Cottages[.] You probably recollect the character & situation of this ground[;] it is one of the pieces repurchased from the Railway Co[.] The road is a narrow one running at right angles from Park Road & on the West side of the Railway so that it … has no frontage to the main thoroughfare[.] the ladies who live there do not raise its character.… I think it probable that building a place of worship there might purify the neighbourhood[.] Have you any objection to a dissenting Chapel being built there?[49]

The situation offered parallels with Portland Chapel, which had led to great improvements to the area in which it stood. But the reply to the applicant, Reverend J. Clifford, who lived at 42 Alpha Road, came immediately, a disappointing one-liner: 'Mr Eyre will not consent to the erection of a chapel on this gro[un]d.'[50]

At just this time the Abbey Road Baptist Chapel was showing what a thriving religious community could do when based in a permanent building (Plate 196). Stott's history of its early years recounts how in 1862 he was a young clergyman staying for a short while in London, before moving to Liverpool and then on to America, having already purchased his boat ticket (Plate 197). He was shocked by what he saw:

> Never shall I forget my first Sabbath in London.… In the morning hours shops were open, and men, women, and children were trafficking as if it had been a Saturday. My soul was moved, my heart beat with a quicker motion, for I had never before seen nor even heard that such Sabbath desecration was allowed in a Christian land. I went boldly up to these vendors of fish, flesh, and all sorts, convinced in my own mind, and in ignorance of London, that they only needed to be told from the Word of God that they were commanded to keep the Sabbath day holy, and they would at once shut up. But to my simple astonishment they laughed, and pushed me away, and some blasphemed.[51]

During his stay in the capital Stott had the opportunity to preach and one day was approached by 'a young gentleman from St. John's Wood, and the Secretary of the Branch of the Young Men's Christian Association [YMCA] ... to come and address the Annual Meeting of their Branch at the Eyre Arms Assembly Rooms on 1 July [1862] at 7 o'clock p.m.' Prior to the meeting the gentleman in question wrote to him: 'When you come to the Eyre Arms ... please rouse the people; speak home to their drowsy conscience; they are all asleep in an empty profession, and the devil is rocking the cradle.'[52] Stott must have been successful in his mission, as he recorded: 'many were in tears and some fell upon their knees, crying for mercy.... thus the Public Meeting ... was suddenly and unexpectedly changed into a birthtime of immortal souls.'

balance had to be raised by the St John's Wood members and loans were not the recommended option: 'the executive Committee have anxiously desired that the building may be opened free from debt, so that the St John's Wood Synagogue may from its opening join in the contributing to the relief of the ever-increasing Communal burdens'.[100] The new elaborate building was erected at the corner of Abbey Road and Marlborough Place and opened in 1883 (Plate 187).[101] The historian Judy Glasman remarked: 'the dates of foundation of suburban synagogues provide a realistic guide to Jewish demographic change'.[102] The site was not vacated until 1965 when a new enlarged synagogue was erected in Grove End Road. But it did not remain empty for long: the New London Synagogue, a member of the Assembly of Masorti Synagogues, purchased the building, and a new 'renegade' Jewish community is now thriving there. It was founded in 1964 by Rabbi Dr Louis Jacobs, blending Orthodox Judaism with the open-mindedness associated with scholarly research.

Liberal Judaism is also represented in St John's Wood by the presence on St John's Wood Road of the Liberal Jewish Synagogue or LJS (see p. 386). Liberal Judaism grew in Germany from the beginning of the nineteenth century within the context of the Enlightenment when a series of reforms were undertaken to help people connect more deeply to Judaism while stemming the tide of those who converted to Christianity as a passport to professional success. Liberal Judaism provides a framework for religious Jews who do not wish to set themselves apart from other organised worship on the grounds of tradition, but who see themselves as part of the modern world and wish to be fully engaged with it (Plate 201).

OTHER FAITHS

Montgomery Eyre could not resist quoting 'the reminiscence of an old resident of St John's Wood' who apparently witnessed outside the Eyre Arms an amusing encounter between the philosopher Herbert Spencer (1820–1903), a long-time resident at 64 Avenue Road, and Madame Blavatsky, also known as HPB, the founder of the Theosophical Society, who lived at 19 Avenue Road in 1890–91. Both were waiting for the omnibus, and it was packed when it came: Spencer, tall and thin, successfully squeezed in, while Madame Blavatsky, short and fat, was left behind on the pavement. The same author also quoted a letter from Madame Blavatsky which stated: 'I do not know Mr H. Spencer, except by sight. His person, personality, and philosophy are alike indifferent to me.'[103] However, this is what Blavatsky herself recorded in New York on 19 October 1878 when she received the visit of the future Beatrice Webb, née Potter (1858–1943): 'A Miss Potter, tall, young, intellectual daughter of a millionaire[,] came with a card of introduction from E. K. [Emily Kislingbury], London. Insisted on seeing me. Lived half her life in Herbert Spencer's family. Knows Huxley and Tyndall. Interested in Theosophy; doubts Spiritualism. She and her *eight* sisters all materialists. Herbert Spencer read *Isis* and found some beautiful and *new original ideas*.'[104] So, while HPB was 'indifferent' to Spencer, he, on the other hand, had seemingly shown interest in her writings.

Helena Blavatsky (1831–91) had founded the Theosophical Society in New York in 1875. HPB was widely travelled but had a special relationship with London, since in the middle years of the nineteenth century this was where she first experienced a notion of hell – she wanted to commit suicide at Waterloo Bridge – and then heaven – she experienced boundless joy when she first met her 'Master' in Hyde Park.[105] Perhaps this was why she chose London for the final years of her life

202 This photograph of Madame Blavatsky in her perambulator was taken at 19 Avenue Road. The Theosophical Publishing House, Adyar, Chennai – 600 020, India.

between 1 May 1887, when she arrived from Ostend, and 8 May 1891 when she died at 19 Avenue Road, St John's Wood (Plate 202).

The theosophical movement is described as having three objects:

1 To form a nucleus of a universal brotherhood of humanity, without distinction of race, creed, sex, caste or colour.
2 The study of ancient and modern religions, philosophies and sciences, and the demonstration of the importance of such study.
3 The investigation of the unexplained laws of nature and the psychical powers latent in man.[106]

203 This detail from the estate's 1903 map shows 19 Avenue Road. The rectangular shape protruding at the back of the building may have been the hall built by Madame Blavatsky. This property is just outside the Eyre estate, though this corner would have been most familiar to the Eyre brothers as the colonel owned the lease of the adjoining house, No. 17 (formerly No. 9, see p. 142). Eyre estate archive (EE 2652/14(G)).

This programme played a crucial role in the 'awakening of the East' which would eventually lead India to fight for its independence. Both Gandhi and Nehru became interested in India's great scriptures through theosophical contacts and members of the society. It is moving to reflect on St John's Wood becoming the centre for a time of a society thriving on HPB's noble ideals as recorded after her death in the *New York Daily Tribune*: 'the regeneration of mankind must be based upon the development of altruism. In this she was at one with the greatest thinkers, not alone of the present day, but of all time.'[107]

Madame Blavatsky did not immediately settle in St John's Wood when she arrived in London in 1887. For a few months her activities were based at a cottage called Maycott in Upper Norwood before she moved to 17 Lansdowne Road, North Kensington, in September that year. The final move to St John's Wood occurred in April 1890 when HPB recorded in a letter to her sister Vera:

I am awfully busy changing from one end of London to the other. We have taken three separate houses, joined by a garden, for several years; 19 Avenue Road, with building-right. I am building a lecture hall to hold 300 people; the hall is to be in Eastern style, made of polished wood, in a brick shell, to keep the cold out; and no ceiling inside, the roof being supported by beams and made also of polished wood. And one of our theosophists who is a painter is going to paint allegorical signs and pictures over it. Oh, it will be lovely! [Plate 204][108]

204 Portrait of Annie Besant in 1892 wearing the ring of H. P. Blavatsky. The Theosophical Publishing House, Adyar, Chennai – 600 020, India.

The inaugural meeting took place on 3 July 1890:

> About 500 people had assembled, nearly twice as many as it [the Hall] would hold.... The speeches were by Sinnett and others, but needless to say, no one spoke so well as Annie Besant. Heavens, how this woman speaks!... She is now my coeditor of *Lucifer* [the Theosophical Society journal] and the president of the Blavatsky Lodge.[109]

It is a tribute to Madame Blavatsky and the theosophical movement that a fiercely independent thinker, atheist, political activist and militant such as Annie Besant (1847–1933) joined their ranks (Plate 204). Besant met HPB on 10 May 1889 and recorded in her autobiography: 'From that day ... until now [1893] ... my faith in her has never wavered, my trust in her has never been shaken.'[110] Besant was the instrumental link between St John's Wood and theosophy: 'My earliest personal recollections are of a house and garden that we lived in when I was three or four years of age, situated in Grove Road St John's Wood.' This memory must have been significant: first because it is quoted in her book and also because she would return to St John's Wood later in life. She may well have influenced her great friend Charles Bradlaugh (1833–91) when he settled in St John's Wood in 1879 at 10 Circus Road, 'the headquarters of his propaganda'[111] (Plates 205 and 206). He was the colourful and controversial president of the National Secular Society, which he had founded in 1866, and Besant had espoused this cause with great gusto.

Annie Besant's faltering religious convictions led to her divorce from Reverend Frank Besant in 1873. Between 1874 and 1889 she was an atheist, a position Bradlaugh described as: 'Atheism is <u>without</u> God. It does not assert <u>no</u> God.'[112] Besant herself described her rejection of the Anglican religion in personal and moving terms: 'I went into the darkness alone, not because religion was too good for me, but because it was not good enough; it was too meagre, too common place, too little

Above left: **205** Portrait of Charles Bradlaugh by an unknown photographer in the 1860s. National Portrait Gallery, London.

Above right: **206** Charles Bradlaugh's library at 10 Circus Road, on the site of the present Tesco supermarket! While the library appears to be comfortably spacious, the description left by Mrs Bonner, Bradlaugh's daughter, suggests otherwise: 'It was a queerly arranged house. We had the top floor and the basement, with a bath-room on the first floor, the ground floor and the rest of the first floor being occupied by a firm of music sellers.... On the top floor was one large room given over to my father's study, the other rooms being quite small.' Eyre estate archive (Montgomery Eyre, 1913, p. 235).

exacting, too bound up with earthly interests, too calculating in its accommodations to social conventionalities.'[113]

Besant had had misgivings about atheism for a few years when she met HPB, so this would have made her more receptive to the ideas of the Theosophical Society. She described her encounter with theosophy as 'I found my way "Home".' Her devotion to the cause was such that she made available part of the property at Avenue Road, weaving an invisible link between her earliest childhood memory and her newly found convictions. It is not therefore surprising to find that she penned the best description of life at Avenue Road:

> Most of the staff at Avenue Road lived on the premises. Besant writes: 'HPB insisted on great regularity of life, we breakfasted at 8.00 a.m., worked till lunch at 1, then again till dinner at 7. After dinner the outer work for the Society was put aside, and we gathered in HPB's room where we would sit talking over plans, receiving instructions, listening to her explanations of knotty points. By 12 midnight all the lights had to be extinguished.'[114]

Within this group of buildings, Charles Ryan describes 'a small room with a blue glass dome ... near H.P.B.'s workroom, in which she gave instructions to her most advanced pupils.... when the house was pulled down the glass and other parts were taken to Point Loma [California].'[115]

Montgomery Eyre claimed that at Blavatsky's death the society numbered 'at least 100,000 members'.[116] It remained in St John's Wood until around 1905.[117] Nowadays it is no longer based there, although the current address is still within the old parish of St Marylebone.[118]

The status of theosophy as a religion is open to debate, but one of the world's major religions has close connections with St John's Wood: Buddhism. The Marlborough Place resident Travers Christmas Humphrey (1901–83) was influenced by Buddhism as a child. Alongside a distinguished career in the law – he trained as a barrister and was a High Court judge between 1950 and 1959 – he was a leading Buddhist. He founded the London Buddhist Lodge in 1924, which later became the Buddhist Society – now one of the oldest Buddhist societies in Europe. At his death, his home at 58 Marlborough Place, which had witnessed many Buddhist meetings, was bequeathed to the Zen Trust, the active arm of the Zen Centre, a Buddhist monastery also founded by Travers and closely affiliated to the Buddhist Society. Travers's house became 'Shobo-an' and was inaugurated as a temple on 23 July 1984. It is a registered charity and has a teacher in residence; it came under the rule of the Venerable Myokyo-ni until her death in 2007, though the person on site since 2003 has been Sochu, a Rinzai Zen Buddhist monk.[119]

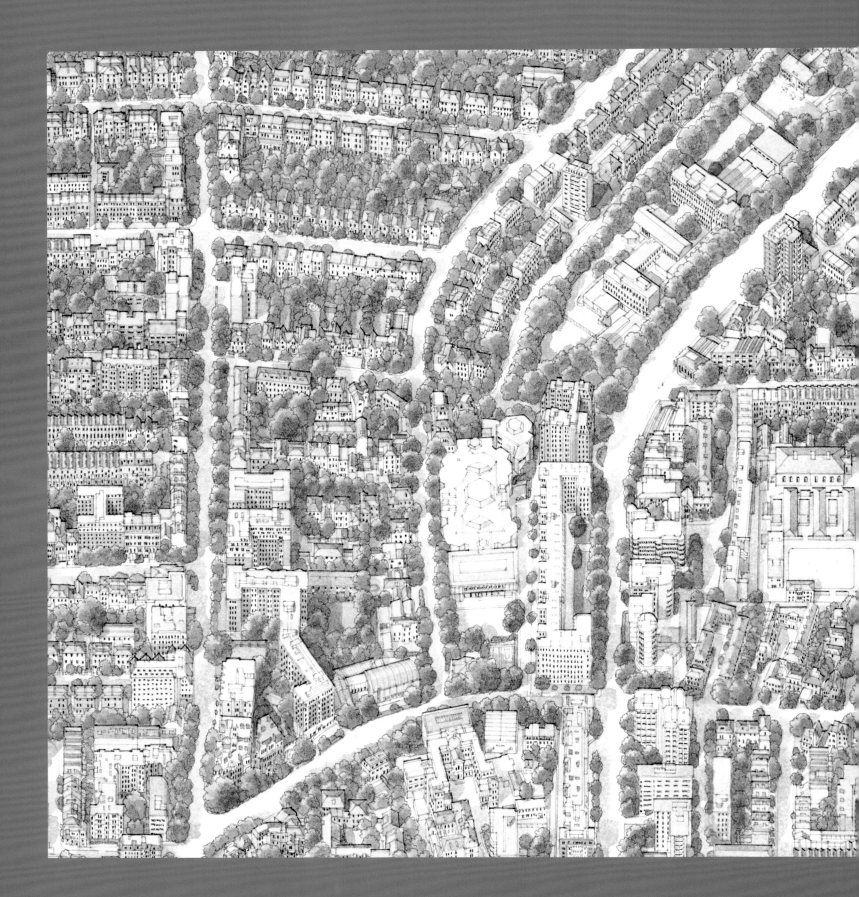

10 POSTCRIPT

St John's Wood was conceived as an ideal suburb. When and why did this picture-perfect creation turn sour? Parts of the estate undoubtedly did. The architects of ideal cities traditionally come under fire for dreaming beautiful but impractical cities or city quarters which, more often than not, take little account of the inhabitants' needs. But things were different in St John's Wood because the 'dream' was solidly anchored in reality and because idealistic schemes, such as the green circus or John Shaw's grand terrace of houses in Lisson Grove, simply did not get built.

Many ideal cities or city quarters exist only as painted or paper dreams. Of those that come to life, most do not remain ideal forever, as the 1960s creators of Auroville in India discovered when faced with ferociously vocal residents.[1] This short chapter examines how events in the nineteenth and twentieth centuries have affected the original concept – at times to endanger it, at other times to redeem it. The estate's archive for the twentieth century is vast and still in storage, so alternative sources have been used for this and other chapters' brief incursions into the twentieth century. As the Eyres sold many properties in the 1920s, further reducing the size of the estate (see Plate 285), the records on individual properties are often detailed but the overall picture is more fragmented.

PARADISE LOST

Losing control

The very tools that made St John's Wood – sale of plots of land on the outskirts for fund-raising purposes, close collaboration with the vestries of Marylebone and Hampstead as well as with the estate's lessees – turned into the instruments of its partial undoing. Walpole's early battles over road making had involved spiralling costs, disappointments with contractors who did not deliver the standards required, and the nightmare of maintenance. So he had greeted with much relief the handing over of road maintenance and lighting to the vestries of Marylebone and later Hampstead, and then, after teething problems, of sewerage to the Commissioners of Sewers. In 1855, a year before Walpole's death, the London-wide Metropolitan Board of Works (predecessor of the London County Council) was created, a supreme governing layer which further diluted the level of control each London estate had enjoyed until then. For the first fifty years of the estate's existence its architects had had the final word on all development work, but this 1857 letter to John Shaw junior from the clerk Charles Freeth reveals the weakening of past procedures: 'I send you … a Block plan of an addition which Mr Martin wishes to make at 1 Newton Villas Finchley Road (corner of Victoria Road) and on which they request your opinion[.] I don't think that such a Building could be set up against the Metropolis Local Management Act S143 without the consent of the Metropolitan Board of works who never give such consent.'[2]

A year later, in 1858, came the sale of large tracts of land to clear the debts incurred by the two brothers in the development process. Until then, sales had been discreetly kept to the western fringe, but in 1858, in consequence of the large sums needed, prime sites such as the Barracks and Lord's were put up for sale. The Barracks site was 'saved' by Reverend H. S. Eyre, who purchased it using his own money, but Lord's was irretrievably lost along with many other sites (see Plate 24). Once the freehold of a substantial number of properties had been lost, the estate could be placed in a difficult position, as Edwin Eyre's 1860 letter shows:

Previous pages: **207** Detail from the 2009 pictorial map of modern day St John's Wood commissioned by the Eyre Estate from the illustrator Stephen Conlin. See page 376.

The next landmark in mansion block building was the erection of Addison House in Grove End Road in 1920 (on the east side just before the junction with Circus Road). It was named after the social reformer Dr Christopher Addison, Britain's first health minister. Addison House was also masterminded by Abraham Davis for 'single women in the caring professions'. Davis took advantage of the 1919 'Addison Act', which offered subsidy for 'housing for the working classes'. He founded a new umbrella organisation – the Public Utility Housing Society – and contracted the work to the Central London Building Company (incorporated in 1912), another of his companies. The project was very competently delivered by Davis and judged 'undoubtedly a good one' by the London Housing Board.

Davis successfully navigated public subsidy for 'working class flats' in the waters of the Eyre estate's 'high class residential flats'. He managed this apparent contradiction very well and went on to develop the stylistically related Circus Road Mansions, separated from Addison House by Grove Court, the latter built after Davis's death by his Central Building Company.[16]

Following these early examples, the building of mansion blocks in St John's Wood was positively encouraged by the Eyre estate in the 1920s and 1930s when several substantial auctions, organised by Alfred Savill & Sons,[17] described various sites along St John's Wood Road as 'an Excellent Site … for the Erection of a Block of Middle Class Flats' or 'particularly well adapted for the Erection of a Small Block of Mansion Flats' (for a house immediately opposite Lord's at No. 32).[18] Developers took the estate's agents at their word, and the south side of St John's Wood Road is now entirely made up of large residential blocks.

South Lodge, at the junction of Grove End and Circus Roads (north side), was developed after the auction of 29 July 1929. The catalogue includes 'the form of building agreement' which is clear in its stated aims: 'the Freeholders shall permit the Lessee to enter upon the said property for the purpose of demolishing the present buildings and erecting and executing the said buildings and works[,] it being the intention of the parties that the site of the said property shall be developed in sections or blocks'. On a previous occasion, the building of apartment blocks was flaunted on the first page of the sale catalogue with properties 'forming Excellent Sites for the erection of Blocks of Residential Flats' and in the undated advertisement in *The Times* pointing out 'very suitable for a block of Family Flats'.[19]

Another of Davis's companies, the Lady Workers Homes Ltd, also successfully delivered a second scheme for women on the site adjoining the Abbey Road Studios (see Plate 149). There the former home of the painter John MacWhirter was run as a club with dining room, library and 'studio'. Davis extended it to encompass 120 hotel-style rooms as well as 26 self-contained flats.[20]

These various schemes show that Davis should certainly be credited with introducing a change in density and appearance to substantial parts of the St John's Wood estate, even if the original impulse for mansion blocks seems to have originated with the Howard de Walden estate (formerly the Portland estate, see p. 393), which built two highly noticeable blocks on its doorsteps: one in 1903 at Scott Ellis Gardens (formerly Warwick Place and part of the Eyre estate) to rehouse tenants from Portland Town, and also Northgate and Hanover House from 1903 and 1904 in the High Street alongside St John's Wood Church and churchyard. Davis's developments heralded the future to come, so it may be useful to chart one particular example of the switch from villas to blocks (Plates 212–17).

CASE STUDY: LEASE NO. 2211, FROM FIELDS TO RESIDENTIAL BLOCKS

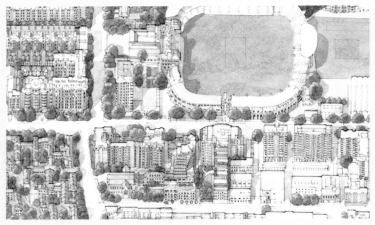

Right: **211** This detail from Stephen Conlin's pictorial map (see Plate 228) shows the site under review, immediately north of the Catholic church and almost across the road from Lord's Cricket Ground. Eyre estate.

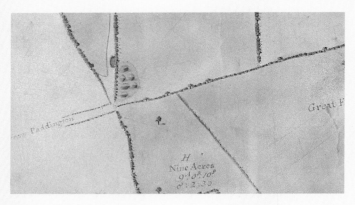

Left: **212** 1733 This detail from the estate's survey shows the site at the junction of St John's Wood Road (on the left, known as St John's Wood Lane; its eastern section, along the horizontal hedge, had not yet been formed) with Grove End Road (top, laid over the eighteenth-century St John's Wood Lane) and Lisson Grove (south, not yet built). Eyre estate archive (EE 2652/1).

Right: **213** 1817 Walpole Eyre leases to Robert Todd the two double houses he had built on a plot of land at the south-east corner of the St John's Wood Road/Lisson Grove junction (north is at the bottom). The lease for this property has survived (WCA, 765/144), also the lease drawing (reproduced here). These were archetypal Todd houses, a simplified version of his double house on the south-east corner of Alpha and Park Roads (No. 18 on the Alpha Cottages reconstruction). Like his Alpha Road house they were completely set back from the road to produce an enormous front garden but no back garden. Eyre estate archive (Bk of Drawings I, 29).

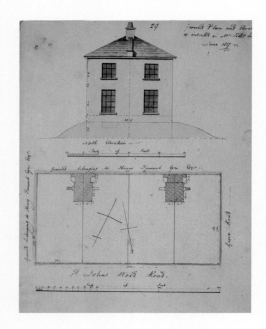

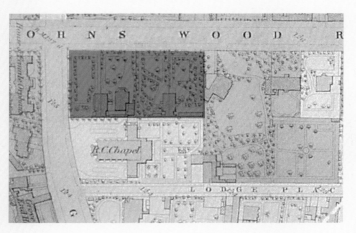

Left: **214** 1883 The spacious garden proved irresistible to the tenant of No. 22 St John's Wood Road, an artist, and a substantial studio has appeared alongside the original house on the second plot from Lisson Grove (built in 1840, see p. 286). Eyre estate archive (EE 2652/10).

Right: **215** <u>1889</u> At 20 St John's Wood Road underlessee Mary Crake obtains a licence to build a studio on 1 March 1889 (Licence Book II, p. 198, and actual licence inside the lease at WCA, 765/144). The artist recorded at that address between 1889 and 1892 was the painter Arthur Tomson. His studio is clearly visible on the 1903 map of the estate. Eyre estate archive (EE 2652/14(I)).

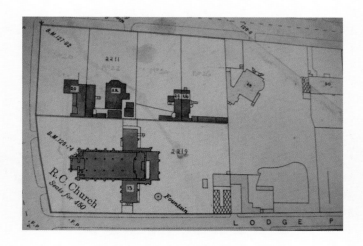

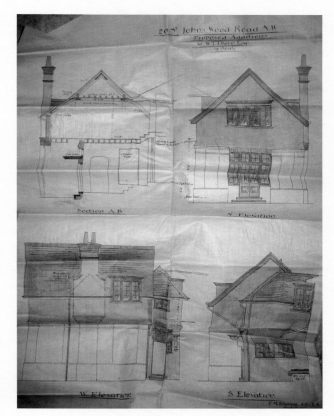

Left: **216** <u>1895</u> The drawings by the architect F. M. Elgood record the proposed additions for W. T. Thorn; we are now dealing with a completely different house, so Todd's house must have been pulled down and rebuilt. Eyre estate archive (EE 2650/1/503).

<u>1914</u> A draft building agreement with Abraham Davis has survived (WCA, 765/308). Davis is described as a builder, and the agreement proposes 'demolishing the present buildings and erecting … two separate blocks of high class residential flats'.

Right: **217** <u>1921</u> Residents move into St John's Wood Court. This is a modern photograph of the mansion block showing a 1990s height extension. Eyre estate (photo: John Chase).

PARADISE REGAINED

Regaining control

In the early 1860s, when the estate office was preparing for the reversion of leases on the south side of Alpha Road, the Eyres and their employees did not immediately realise just how 'fallen' some of the houses were, but when they did they quickly seized the opportunity of putting matters right. First of all the drainage, which had seemed so ahead of its time when the houses were first built, had proved to be inadequate in a number of cases,[21] and the vestry was now insisting on it being rectified. But other factors had also intervened, and in 1865 Charles Freeth quoted the following example at 6 Alpha Road, the premises of Sarah Garrard (No. 7 on the Alpha Cottages reconstruction):

> These premises have been let for many years to one Lowe a Gardener who removed some time since taking away all his erections & tearing the place to pieces – they have since been occupied by the lowest class of people & present the most disgraceful & ruinous appearance & their state has been most injurious to the adjoining property.[22]

One of Freeth's letters explains why the houses had not received the attention they needed:

> I am inclined to think that a strong impression has existed that at the expir[ati]on of the Leases the present houses wo[ul]d be pulled down & an entire conversion of the ground take place – & that under that impression the tenants have not done any substantial repairs to the property for some time past.[23]

The architect John Shaw junior must have been busy preparing dilapidation schedules while Charles Freeth continued to stand firm against unworthy tenants:

> Complaints are made here of the manner in which your house No. 5 Alpha Road is occupied & I therefore wish you distinctly to understand that no renewed Lease of those prem[is]es will be granted to you nor to any claiming under you.[24]

At the end of this process at Alpha Road, unacceptable tenants had been eliminated, the good houses had been repaired (one of the conditions of obtaining a new lease), the bad houses pulled down and a new street created: Boscobel Gardens (Plate 218), lined with terraced houses which shut out the difficult neighbourhood of the adjacent Portman estate (see p. 128–29).

Increase in value

In 1864, the lease of the Nightingale pub on the western corner of Alpha Road also came up for renewal. Freeth recommended to George John Eyre the proposal made by the new pub landlord: for the annual rent to jump from £2 to £200 and for the lease to contain a covenant stating the new lessee would spend £1,000 on repairs.

The letter books make it very clear that throughout the nineteenth century the value of most houses on the Eyre estate was steadily rising. Up to about 1850, Walpole regularly took stock of this to reassure his mortgage lenders, though he was always careful not to overvalue the houses.

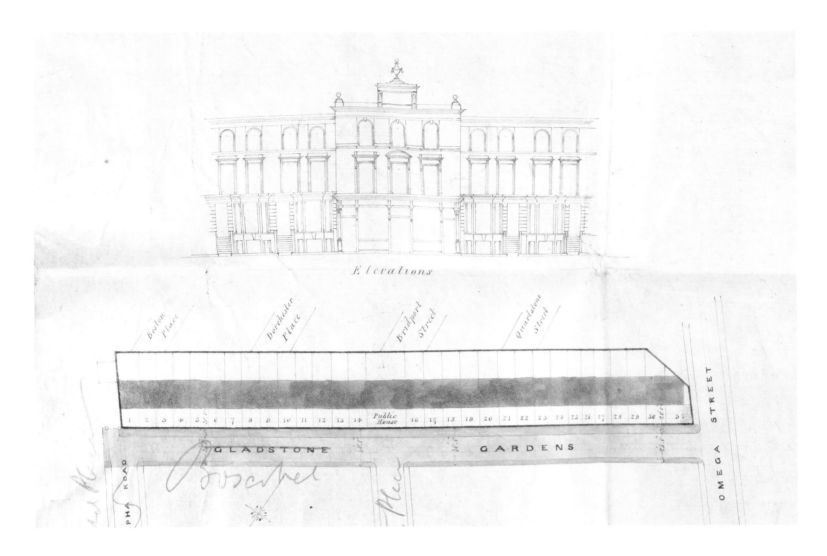

Elevations

The vestry, on the other hand, seems to have been keen to push up the value of the houses, no doubt because it increased the level of rates they could levy. This created difficulties in 1865 over the renewing of leases in Alpha Road when the practice was fully exposed. In 1868, shortly after the estate's office moved to Alpha Road, Edwin Eyre was also fighting the Inland Revenue over their inflated tax assessment (as he saw it):

> I ment[ione]d to Mr Edwin Eyre that you proposed to assess this Office to the Queen's taxes at £60 per Annum & he requests me to give you Notice of his intention to appeal against that sum thinking it too much – the Office being rated to the parish rates at £44 per annum.[25]

Local and national tax rates may in fact have reflected more accurately the true worth of the estate, because by 1868 Freeth was amazed at the spectacular results of the sale of surplus land by the Metropolitan and St John's Wood Railway:

> the R[ailwa]y Co[mpan]y sold the first portion of their surplus lands (declined to be purchased by you) on Tuesday the 18th inst by Public Auction & that some of these lands realized <u>enormous prices</u>, the effect of w[hi]ch will be that you will have to pay similar prices for the Land you have given Notice of your intention to repurchase.[26]

An interesting neighbourhood

With their litany of complaints and problems, the letter books at times run the risk of conjuring up an overly pessimistic description of the estate. But we have seen that St John's Wood was blessed, from the very beginning, with the input of energetic and dedicated entrepreneurs and with the presence of an artists' community. Montgomery Eyre was more successful than most in documenting the extraordinary range of poets, artists, journalists, novelists and philosophers who lived in St John's Wood, making it 'the abode of select spirits whose names adorn the annals of Art and Literature'.[27]

When recording the demise of this vital artistic connection in 1935, the painter Frank R. Beresford acknowledged the important role art had played in this part of London:

> No suburb had so marked a personality as the old St John's Wood…. 'Art Quarter' was written all over it, from the colour shops in the High Street and the groups of students from the School of Art strolling about in their overalls and painting coats to the numerous studios…. the distinctive character of the population has quite disappeared.[28]

The art school and the arts club may well have gone and the studios demolished or converted into drawing rooms, but we should be wary of dismissing the area's past links with the world of art. Creative genes still fuel its music studios, and Victorian ghosts have worthy rallying points in the vigorously sculpted *St George and the Dragon* by St John's Wood Church or the nostalgic monument to Onslow Ford by the famous Abbey Road pedestrian crossing.

POST-WAR: A MIXED NEIGHBOURHOOD

In the June 1949 issue of the *Architectural Review* the following intention was announced:

> a scheme is afoot, sponsored by the London County Council … to convert [St John's Wood] … into an immense flatted [*sic*] housing scheme after the familiar L.C.C. pattern. This proposal, which is the subject of a Ministerial enquiry, is being opposed by, among others, the Eyre Estate, the traditional ground landlords.

One of the areas affected, St John's Wood Park, has been discussed earlier (pp. 181–85): the impact of the Second World War (Plate 219) and the reversion of the leases had created a dilapidated blot on the estate's landscape at a time when resources were scarce. It was so concerned about the council's move that the areas which had been made the object of Compulsory Purchase Orders (CPOs) were mapped (Plates 220 and 221).

So did local government succeed in turning St John's Wood into a vast housing estate? Not quite, fortunately, but development work in the decades that followed the Second World War took the form, to an overwhelming extent, of council housing. And what Dame Henrietta Barnett could not achieve in Hampstead Garden Suburb – that is to say, a suburb which would be shared by all classes – has been achieved, strangely enough, in St John's Wood. It appears to work, with modest income-earners ready to enjoy some of the privileges that accompany life in a wealthy neighbourhood, while the wealthy classes continue to need the input of the labouring classes with their seemingly endless house refurbishment programmes as well as the vast range of domestic services they have come to expect.

219 The LCC Architects' Department used large-scale Ordnance Survey maps to record bomb damage in London between 1939 and 1945. The six-colour code ranged from yellow ('minor blast damage') to black ('total destruction'). In between these two extremes purple denoted 'damage beyond repair', dark red 'seriously damaged; doubtful if repairable', and light red 'seriously damaged but repairable at cost'. Two separate plates have been brought together to show the St John's Wood area. City of London, London Metropolitan Archives (see Saunders, 2005).

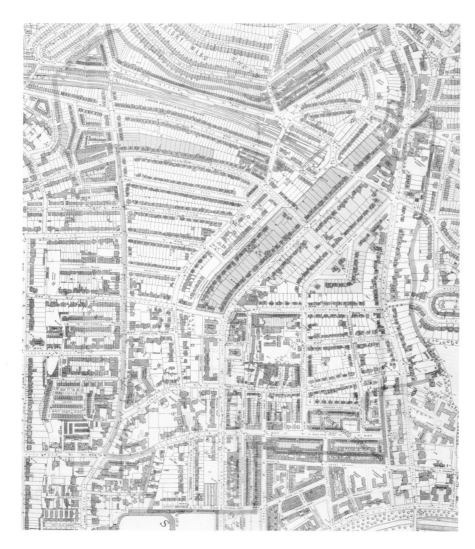

The blending of classes was not, of course, a new phenomenon. The more respectability a house commanded, the more numerous its domestic staff housed in the basements or upper floors of the neighbourhood. In addition, many of the more modest terraced houses on the borders of the estate appear to have escaped the leases' stringent rules to become service quarters, as this 1862 report by John Shaw junior on houses in St John's Wood Terrace and Charles Street made abundantly clear:

> The lease plan shows three houses in Charles Street but a fourth has been added since upon a portion of the yards of Nos 36 and 37 [St John's Wood Terrace]. This is now used for the open Trade of repairing shoes-

> The second house in Charles Street is used as a shop for the Sale of Milk – in the rear has been erected a parlour or kitchen and a Cowshed – another Cowshed has been built in the rear of the third house- and a stable and Cart shed has been built fronting into Terrace Mews – The third house is still used as a dwelling house – a wash shed having been erected at the bottom of the yard-

225 The development is viewed from the north with Eyre Court and Wellington Road on the right and Ordnance Hill on the left. Eyre estate (photo: John Chase).

226 In John McAslan + Partners's scheme for the Barracks, the historic Riding House – the oldest building on the site – becomes a leisure facility. 'It will contain a full-size swimming pool, gymnasium, changing and treatment rooms, and have a viewing gallery and lounge area' states their *Design and Access Statement*. These facilities will be planned so as 'not to affect the existing foundations and building fabric'. Eyre estate.

11

EPILOGUE

FROM FIELDS TO TOWER BLOCKS:
LANDMARKS IN ST JOHN'S WOOD

Previous pages: **227**
Top: Detail from Plate 30.
Centre and bottom: The 'Riding
House' at St John's Wood Barracks
and St John's Wood Court
in St John's Wood Road.
Eyre estate (photos: John Chase).

This chapter functions on more than one level. The evidence which came to light while researching this book is used here to clarify the shape of modern-day St John's Wood: what has survived from the nineteenth century and aspects of the twentieth-century contribution. The framework is a series of points of interest along a route organised from south to north to echo the chronological development of the estate (Plate 228). Therefore, this chapter can be read as an 'abstract' walk in two parts (walking instructions have not been included) or as a gazetteer by using the numbers on the accompanying map to focus on areas of relevance to the reader.

228 This 2009 pictorial map of modern day St John's Wood follows the contours of the 1853 map (Plate 70). It was commissioned by the Eyre estate from the illustrator Stephen Conlin. The numbers on the map correspond to the various headings in this chapter. The itinerary highlighted has been adopted to discuss St John's Wood's principal landmarks. Eyre estate.

PART ONE:
from Rossmore Road to Boundary Road

1. Rossmore Road
2. Corner of Rossmore Road and Lisson Grove
3. Lilestone Street
4. Regent's Canal (east side)
5. Regent's Canal (west side)
6. St John's Wood Road
7. Cochrane Street
8. St John's Wood High Street
9. St Ann's Terrace
10. Acacia Road
11. Ordnance Mews
12. St John's Wood Terrace
13. Woronzow Road (south) and Acacia Road
14. Ordnance Hill
15. Woronzow Road (north)
16. Queen's Grove
17. Queen's Terrace and All Saints Church
18. Devonshire Villa (Thomas Hood's House)
19. Alhambra Cottage

PART TWO:
from St John's Wood Underground Station to Swiss Cottage

20. St John's Wood Underground Station/Eyre Arms Tavern
21. Wellington Road
22. Cavendish Avenue
23. Circus Road and Hospital of St John and St Elizabeth
24. Elm Tree Road
25. Grove End Road
26. Creative junction: an artistic crossroads
27. Garden Road
28. Hamilton Gardens and panorama
29. Hill Road
30. Abbey Road (1) and Langford Place
31. Loudoun Road
32. Carlton Hill
33. Blenheim Road
34. Clifton Hill
35. Abbey Road (2) and Alexandra Road estate
36. Belsize Road and weeping willow
37. Fairfax and Harben Roads
38. Swiss Cottage

Road, immediately south of Marylebone Station, acquired its name in 1857. Prior to that date, it was known as the New Road. Built in 1756, it had been promoted by 'gentlemen of the greatest eminence and property' and was used twice a week to drive cattle to Smithfield Market, thus avoiding the congested Oxford Street.[1] For the first fifty years of its existence, this highway not only provided an easy passage between east and west, it also created a physical barrier to the expansion of the West End (despite the building of houses along the eastern section of this road). Two late eighteenth-century engravings illustrate the character of this site, showing the line of buildings which ended abruptly at the West End of that time and the sweep of countryside which

could be admired by looking the other way (Plates 229 and 230). St John's Wood, of course, was the other way.

Marylebone Station is on the site of the former Harewood Square. Designed by H. W. Braddock in 1899 for the Great Central Railway, it was the last terminus station built in London and served the London extension of the Manchester, Sheffield and Lincolnshire Railway (renamed Great Central Railway in 1899). It was not the first time that parts of the Eyre estate were invaded by railway infrastructure, but this was by far the most costly development in terms of land needed, and indeed taken, despite the estate's fierce resistance to the project (see p. 263). Harewood Square, completed in 1842, had briefly been the home of George Eliot in 1860 (at No. 10 before she moved to The Priory at 21 North Bank), and members of the Eyre family had also resided there.[2]

By 1846 when George Oakley Lucas published his map of Marylebone (see Plate 108), Boston Place – which ran along the east side of Marylebone Station – was a long, fairly narrow cul-de-sac open to traffic at the north end but with only a pedestrian exit on the south side. It was thickly lined on both sides with modest terraced houses, and some of these have survived on the eastern side. The street's main claim to fame now is that it was the setting for the wild opening scene of the 1964 Beatles film, *A Hard Day's Night*. The Beatles are seen running down Boston Place and into Marylebone Station, chased by fans.

Left: **229** and **230** These rare engravings were originally published in the first edition of Richard Horwood's map, *Plan of the Cities of London and Westminster*, 1792–99. Shortly after publication they were replaced by maps of the developing countryside (see Plates 47 and 48). The draughtsman positioned himself near the New Road (now Marylebone Road) looking north, and depicted the abrupt dividing line between city and country as well as capturing the attractiveness of the landscape. Westminster City Archives (Ashbridge collection, O.61).

231 This scene of devastation was photographed soon after 1901, when the Central Electric Supply Company purchased North Bank and Lodge Road. This shows the area in course of demolition, a sad echo to the scene which took place south of this site a few years earlier when Alpha Road and surrounding area were cleared by the Manchester, Sheffield and Lincolnshire Railway. London Topographical Society (from the *London and Topographical Record*, 1906, opp. p. 95).

PART ONE: FROM ROSSMORE ROAD TO BOUNDARY ROAD

1 Rossmore Road

This road marks the beginning of the original Eyre estate. There it is possible to measure the physical impact of the railway line – Rossmore Road was created by the railway company in the 1890s and obliterated Boscobel Gardens (formerly Gladstone Gardens), a street developed by the estate in the 1860s (see Plate 218). Boscobel Gardens had been lined with terraced houses on the south side, a standard 'walling in' device to mark the estate's boundaries. On this occasion, there is evidence that the terraced houses which replaced the original cottages on that site were regarded as blocking out undesirable tenants or streets (see pp. 118–29).

The arrival of Marylebone Station at the end of the nineteenth century created destruction in St John's Wood on an unprecedented scale. A glance at the map of the proposed railway line (Plate 133) indicates the massive amount of land which was purchased for this enterprise. It was the need for coal sheds (five acres) and goods yards (twenty-three acres) which was particularly land hungry. The Central Electric Supply Company followed suit, devastating North Bank and Lodge Road (Plate 231). Later, in the 1960s when coal sheds and goods yards were no longer needed, British Rail sold off redundant chunks out of which were created the Lisson Green estate (west) and Palgrave

233 This detail from Stephen Conlin's 2009 pictorial map shows the Palgrave Gardens private housing development situated immediately east of the railway line near Regent's Park (the development is also known as Prince Regent's Gate). The 288 flats are run on very strict leases. The first block was completed in 2001 having taken three years to build. Eyre estate.

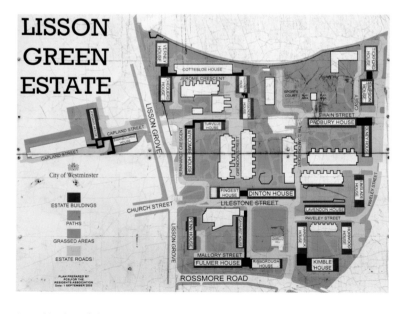

232 This plan of the Lisson Green estate, which lies south of Regent's Canal, was prepared for the Residents' Association (1 September 1982), and is displayed throughout the estate. Eyre estate (photo: John Chase).

Gardens (east) – two housing developments side by side, one public, the other private. Lisson Green estate is the older, dating from the 1970s,[3] while the site occupied by Barratt's flats was completed within the first few years of the twenty-first century.[4] Both developments have placed a strong emphasis on their garden component. Palgrave Gardens carries this connection on the ground and in its name (Plate 233), while on the Lisson Green estate the ratio between built and green environment leans heavily towards open landscaped space (Plate 232).

2 Corner of Rossmore Road and Lisson Grove

Strictly speaking, the west end of Rossmore Road was outside the St John's Wood estate, but this area was developed by Walpole as early as 1809. The land was acquired when the Eyre brothers sold a plot of their estate to the parish of Marylebone for a burial ground and chapel. As part payment for this purchase the vestry gave the Eyres a plot of ground, the Breeze Yard, now framed by Rossmore Road and Lisson Grove on the south and west sides.

In the early years of the nineteenth century Lisson Grove was the sole entrance to the southern tip of the estate, and all traffic for the chapel also had to use this entrance, turning right into Alpha Road and then left into Park Road (both roads were made by the Eyre estate). A breeze yard was not an appropriate entrance for a 'respectable' estate, so Walpole soon set out to develop this area as a grid of terraced houses around a street called Grove Street and also on the other side of Lisson Grove (Plate 234). None of the houses survive on the east side, and the terrace development standing on the west side of Lisson Grove (immediately south of Church Street) is a slightly later project. These houses and their attractive pedimented northern section date from 1819 and were leased to John Punter, a builder.[5] Walpole took a stand against these houses, writing: 'I am informed by my brothers Surveyor that the houses now erecting by you opposite Grove Place are not being built according to the Specification in your Agreement.... unless that specification is attended to I certainly shall not grant any Leases of the houses when finished.'[6] At the time of writing, these terraced houses were being restored.

The house with a blue plaque on the south corner of Lisson Grove and Rossmore Road has been identified as that of sculptor John Charles Felix Rossi (1762–1839),[7] who owned a large plot which comprised a house at the west end and also a very substantial gallery (Plate 234). We can gain an idea of the size of this plot because Rossi's gallery would have been sited where the present St Paul's Church Centre stands. The original church, designed by James W. Higgins, opened in 1839, the year of Rossi's death. Dwindling numbers forced it to shut in 1976. But whereas All Saints was quickly demolished for redevelopment, St Paul's deteriorated until Reverend Jack Maple was able, in the early 1980s, to whip up enough enthusiasm and funds (from the Church Urban Fund) to restore and reopen this church in 1986.[8]

3 Lilestone Street

The western end of Lilestone Street is on the site of the estate's first road: Alpha Road. It was lined with houses well set back from the road to give a sense of space and airiness (as shown on Plates 62 and 63). Alpha Road also led to Lord's second cricket ground. Halfway down the road was a lane leading north towards it. Thomas Lord had been forced to vacate his ground at Dorset Fields

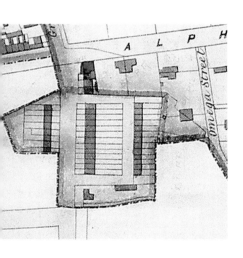

234 Detail from the 1853 map of the Eyre estate (Plate 70) showing a close-up view of the Breeze Yard once it had been developed. The main road, slightly wider, is Lisson Grove. The terraced houses are arranged in three rows, two on either side of Lisson Grove and the third one in Grove Street. At the bottom are the house and 'gallery' of the sculptor J. C. F. Rossi. Eyre estate archive (EE 2652/8).

prior to its development and had barely established his cricket ground near Alpha Road when the Regent's Canal Company selected a route for their canal which would clip his ground on the north side (see Plate 127). For the second time the cricket ground was obliged to move, to its present site further north. In 2006, two plaques were installed to commemorate Lord's second site – one at the entrance to Lilestone Street, the other in Park Road by the canal opening.[9]

4 Regent's Canal (east side)

The site of the elegant block of terraced houses planned by Walpole and designed by John Shaw in 1811 (see Plate 64) was on the west side of Lisson Grove, opposite the Church Street bus stop. The large school further up on the corner of Frampton Street marked the end of that development. Originally built as a 'School for Boys, Girls & Infants', it was a board school which may have been erected in the 1880s.[10] It is now the Gateway Primary School.

At the north-west end of the Lisson Green estate a path leads down to the south side of the canal – more or less opposite Frampton Street. The view by the water is a mixture of the picturesque and the industrial. In 1813, the land north and south of the canal was developed by the canal company not only with the view of building a canal linking Paddington and Limehouse, but also with the project of building cottages on both sides of the water, their designs to be approved by the estate architect. Although some of the cottages built were far smaller than Walpole wanted, slipping from a second rate to a third rate category of building, they were soon regarded as some of the most charming residences on the estate. They were often occupied by interesting and creative people such as Italian refugee poet Ugo Foscolo and the journalist Cyrus Redding at South Bank in the 1820s; George Eliot at The Priory, 21 North Bank, between 1863 and 1880; and T. H. Huxley, the inventor of the word 'biology', who settled for a time at the house of his brother George at 41 North Bank (George had been a St John's Wood lessee since at least 1845).[11]

By a cruel twist of fate, the commercial/industrial character which Walpole had so dreaded in the 1810s, when the canal was first proposed, now dominates in twentieth-century attire, with blots on the landscape such as the St John's Wood substation on the north side (west end) and the railway line at the east end of the site. The Eyre estate had reluctantly sold a large plot of land to the Central Electric Supply Co. Ltd in March 1901 (Plate 231).[12] The power station built on that site was known as the Grove Road Station, and it went into service in November 1902. It was designed by C. Stanley Peach and V. H. Reilly to supply 'current in bulk to the St. James' and Pall Mall Electric Light Co. and the Westminster Electric Supply Corporation'. Peach stated in 1904: 'one of the largest power houses in London will eventually be that of … Grove Road, St John's Wood'. The design of this elegant stock brick and York stone structure consisted of three blocks with two tall shafts each.[13] The electricity board went through a series of restructuring after the Second World War, and in 1986 this station was selected for closure along with a number of others.[14] It was demolished soon afterwards.

5 Regent's Canal (west side)

The drop from the bridge to the canal looks particularly dramatic at this point. The land on the south side of the canal was sold to Marylebone vestry in 1825 (see pp. 249–50), while the land on

235 Edwin Landseer's St John's Wood letterhead paper: this illustrated note from Landseer to the sculptor Carlo Marochetti is dated 4 January 1867 and reads: 'This is nasty weather for the [birds],' alluding to the shooting season. The partnership between the two men gave London a famous landmark: the lions at the base of Nelson's Column in Trafalgar Square, as shown in Plate 157. Private collection (photo: Witt Library, Courtauld Institute of Art, London).

236 This is the School of Industry for Female Orphans proposed for the south-west corner of St John's Wood Road and Lisson Grove in 1850. It was duly built and features on the 1883 map of the estate (Plate 208). Westminster City Archives (Ashbridge collection, 887.3).

the north side was one of the most idyllic spots on the estate in the nineteenth century. It had been the site of Punkers Barn (also known as Red Barn) back in the eighteenth and early nineteenth centuries, and was a constant source of aggravation to Walpole between 1808 and 1811 when it was let to a Captain Simpson, whose tenant, Mr Treble, must have run a business clearing cesspits in town and then depositing the unwelcome 'night soil' in one of the farm's fields.[15] As Treble refused to give an undertaking that this trade would stop, in 1811 Walpole approached Thomas Willan, who agreed to take over the farm.[16] Whether this grass farm was not profitable enough or Willan felt unable to resist the offer made by architect William Atkinson, we will probably never know, but by 1813 the land was occupied by the latter (see Plates 84 and 85). Atkinson built a comfortable house, Grove End House,[17] south of the farm buildings, set back from Lisson Grove, and created a spectacular garden stretching all the way down to the canal (see p. 156).

In 1825, this site became the home of one of London's best-loved artists of the nineteenth century: the animal painter Edwin Landseer (1803–73). At first Landseer lived at the far side of the plot in a cottage near St John's Wood Road, but over time (he lived there for forty-eight years) he became so wealthy that he purchased more of the original plot, extended the house and increased the size of his ground until his garden, too, reached the canal (Plate 235). The last twenty years of his life were plagued by bouts of mental illness. He died a very rich man; his will proved at £160,000, the sale of his house and studio producing a staggering £70,000. From 1852 he had shared this corner of the Wood with the 'School of Industry for Female Orphans', a 64-year-old institution looking for expansion and campaigning for funds in 1850 after acquiring the site on the corner of St John's Wood Road and Lisson Grove (Plate 236).[18]

Wharncliffe Gardens, a 1970s council estate that now stands on the Atkinson/Landseer site, replaced the late nineteenth-century housing estate of the same name,[19] which was bomb-damaged during the Second World War (Plate 237). This Victorian estate was described in moving detail in

237 Edwardian postcard, dated 1907, of Wharncliffe Gardens, the housing development built on the site of William Atkinson's and Landseer's premises in the 1890s. It was built by the Great Central Railway to rehouse over 3,000 residents who had lost their homes when the line was extended and Marylebone Station built. The group of six blocks was praised by one of the researchers for Charles Booth's poverty map and stood on that site between 1897 and 1975. Westminster City Archives (T138 (Prints), Box St Ann's Terrace–Seymour Street).

238 Detail from Charles Booth's colour-coded poverty map, 1898–99. St John's Wood is principally made up of yellow ('Upper-middle and Upper classes, wealthy') and red ('Middle class. Well to do'). The map clearly indicates where the troubled spots adjoining the estate were situated: dark blue ('Very poor, casual. Chronic want') and black ('Lowest class. Vicious, semi-criminal') are found south-west of the estate (part of the Portman estate) and in Portland Town (Portland, now Howard de Walden, estate). London School of Economics.

Charles Booth's groundbreaking *Survey of London* in the 1890s. Among the notes drafted for his famous poverty map (Plate 238), an entry explained that some of the residents displaced by the great railway works at the southern end of the estate had been rehoused here:

> they consist of six large blocks running north and south[,] the two eastern ones being rather shorter than the others owing to the school. They are of red brick and appear to be excellently built. Each work is completely detached and there is an ample asphalte [*sic*] paved space between them forming a really magnificent playground for the children. They look most cheerful and are almost the only models in London in which I conceive life as bearable.... the bulk of the inhabitants are in regular work & good wages.[20]

The estate that replaced it was designed by architects Gollins Melvin Ward Partnership for Westminster City Council and was completed in 1978. It is a mixed development of 280 dwellings.[21]

From this side of Lisson Grove there is a good view of the Catholic church on the other side; dedicated to Our Lady, it was built by J. J. Scoles as early as 1836 when the Catholic revival was gaining momentum (see p. 344). Originally the transept was made up of two houses (for the sisters Gallini, who financed the church, and the resident priest); these became chapels in 1937 after a separate presbytery was erected. The *Christ in Glory* on the east wall is by Michael Lindsey Clark (1918–90), who was also responsible for the casts of the *Madonna and Child* and *St Joseph* in the chancel aisles. The same artist also designed the reredos of the altar in the north transept chapel.[22]

6 St John's Wood Road

This junction and much of St John's Wood Road are dominated by apartment blocks. The earliest, Grove End House, at the north-west corner of this crossroads, dates from 1914 and the latest, Century Court, opposite it on the north-east corner, from the 1970s. The arrival of mansion blocks is discussed in Chapter 9 (p. 360).

In the eighteenth century the western section of St John's Wood Road was the main point of entry into the estate. St John's Wood Lane, as it was then known, ran from Edgware Road to St John's Wood Farm, near the site of the present St John's Wood Underground Station. The eastern section of St John's Wood Road, between Grove End Road and the burial ground, was formed between 1810 and 1815 to service the significant institutions which came to line the north side of the road: the Clergy Orphan Asylum (1810), Lord's (1813) and St John's Wood Chapel (1814).

Lord's Cricket Ground

Lord's Cricket Ground moved to its St John's Wood Road site in 1813 (Plate 239). It was the largest single plot on the estate at that time (bigger than the Barracks) and was attractively depicted in 1887 (Plate 240) when its size virtually doubled through the acquisition, first, of the adjacent Wellington Nursery and, second, a few years later, of the Orphan Clergy School (in exchange for allowing the Manchester, Sheffield and Lincolnshire Railway Company to build a tunnel for their extension). The Lord's site has remained the largest single plot in St John's Wood – a vast complex of facilities with its pavilion and famous Long Room, a court for real tennis,[23] a library and museum, a media centre (see p. 422), and at the 'nursery' end a practice ground with an indoor school. The early

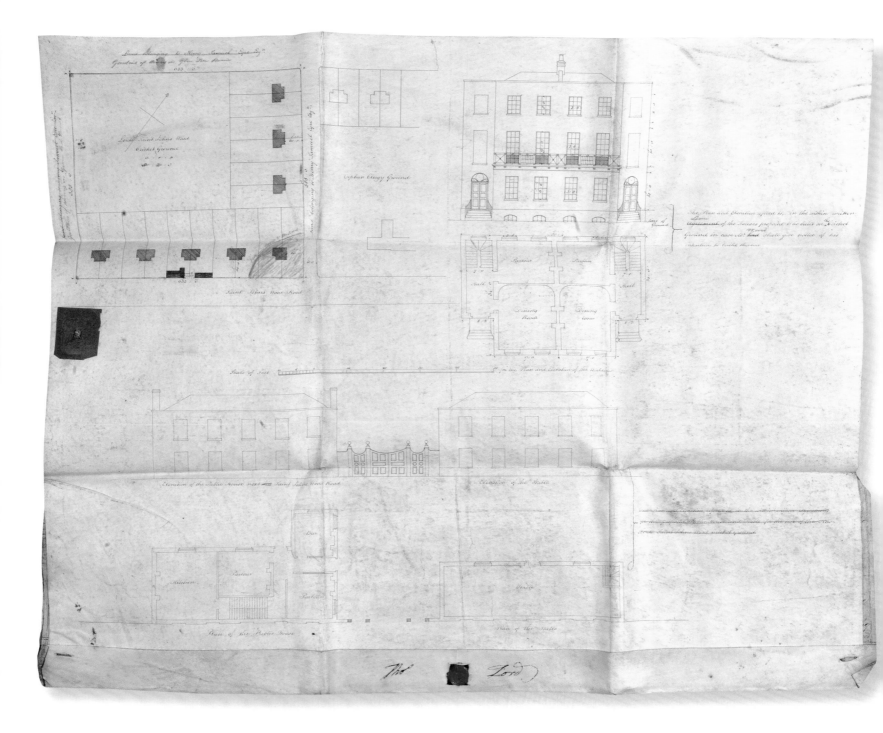

history of Lord's has been shrouded in mystery following a fire in 1825 which destroyed this institution's records up to that time. Data from the Eyre archive are therefore of significant interest, and a detailed chronology can be found at Appendix 8 (p. 467).

The Liberal Jewish Synagogue (LJS)

The first LJS was built on this site in 1925 designed by Ernest Joseph. It was damaged during the Second World War, and repaired but subsequently found to be structurally unsound. The Fitzroy Robinson Partnership, in association with Preston Rubin, won the competition to design the shell of the new synagogue, while a firm of Israeli architects, Kantor Schwartz, working closely with London-based Koski Solomon, was commissioned to design the Sanctuary. The new building was dedicated on 13 January 1991. The lofty pillars on the main façade are all that survive from the LJS's first incarnation – a large, austere building which was flooded with light and apparently very conducive to worship. The new synagogue is shaped as an octagon, and the back walls – with the sliding doors and the Ark – are lined with Jerusalem stone. Among the many works of art to be found there, two in particular should be noted: the large and serene mural in the back entrance hall on the theme of the three great pilgrim festivals (Pesach, Shavuot and Sukkot, i.e. Passover, Festival of Weeks and Feast of Tabernacles). This attractive work was made by Bill Utermohlen (1933–2007) in the 1980s for the old Montefiore Hall.[24] The other remarkable commission is the Sho'ah (or Holocaust) Memorial by Anish Kapoor, inscribed 'we have vowed to remember'. Made of black Kilkenny limestone and weighing 3.5 tons, it was dedicated in 1996. It hangs inside the doors of the main entrance, hidden from view on entering the building but in full evidence on the way out (see Plate 201).[25]

The church roundabout

On the south-west corner of this roundabout formerly stood St John's Wood's first railway station (Metropolitan and St John's Wood Railway). It was named St John's Wood Road Station, then simply St John's Wood, before finally becoming Lord's.[26] It opened in 1868 and finally closed its doors in 1939 when the Bakerloo line station was opened further north on the estate. A landmark outside the church is the magnificent *St George and the Dragon* sculpted group in the middle of the roundabout (Plate 242). It was the work of Charles Leonard Hartwell (1873–1951) and was completed in 1936. This imposing bronze group was financed by the painter Sigismund Goetze (1866–1939) and was sited immediately outside Grove House, his Regent's Park residence between 1909 and 1939 (Plate 307). Hartwell had trained in the studios of Onslow Ford and Hamo Thornycroft.[27] He later moved to 62 Acacia Road, Onslow Ford's house on the site of the Underground station.

St John's Wood Chapel and burial ground

The history of the chapel, built after designs by Thomas Hardwick and consecrated by the bishop of London on 24 May 1814, is told in Chapter 9. Despite its initial isolation it was an immediate landmark (as is suggested by Plates 125 and 190). Adjacent was the Orphan Clergy School, a national institution with a long history (see Plate 115 and pp. 211–12).

The chapel has an interesting collection of Regency funerary monuments and a substantial network of vaults in the basement, which were originally serviced by two narrow spiral staircases on either side of the porch. Bodies were lowered into the crypt by a trapdoor in the nave. These vaults would have contained the remains of various Marylebone families, but the cells and corridors now resonate with the laughter of children affiliated to the thriving St John's Wood Youth Club.[28]

St John's Wood Chapel became a parish church in 1952 to replace St Stephen's Church in Avenue Road, which had been damaged in the Second World War. The burial ground behind the chapel, purchased in 1807, was not restricted to St John's Wood residents but was used for the whole of the Marylebone parish. Smith's 1833 history of Marylebone gives 'A List of Monuments in the Chapel' as well as 'A List of Persons to whom Memorials have been erected', a useful guide now that so many tombs and memorials in the burial ground have become illegible. He also remarked that

241 and **242** St John's Wood Church, built as a chapel in 1813, became the parish church in 1952. In 1936, Charles Hartwell's striking First World War memorial was erected on the roundabout immediately outside the church, depicting St George slaying the dragon. Eyre estate (photos: John Chase).

'40,000 persons lie interred in the cemetery belonging to this chapel', adding: 'But from the comparatively small number of memorials erected, the casual visitor would not suppose there were half the number.'[29] These statistics applied to the year 1833, but this particular cemetery did not close until 1886 when the public gardens were laid out.[30]

Colonel Henry Samuel Eyre was the first Eyre landlord to be buried in the St John's Wood graveyard, but the church has been the last resting place of other Eyre family members.[31] The most famous tombs in the burial ground are those of the 'Marylebone Fanatics', Richard Brothers and Joanna Southcott, who were caught up in the millennial fever of the late eighteenth and early nineteenth centuries. Brothers, buried on the east side of the chapel, described himself as the 'Nephew of God', while Southcott, buried on the western path near the bus stop opposite Lord's, believed she was going to give birth to the second Christ in 1813, aged 64, an unusual instance of phantom pregnancy as the autopsy revealed when she died a few months later.[32] A monument inscribed with both names but only representing a praying female figure is sited in the flower garden alongside the chapel. The great watercolourist John Sell Cotman (1782–1842) is also buried there, and his tomb has been restored on the west side of the ground. A transcription of all the legible tombstones was made in 1962.[33]

7 Cochrane Street

At No. 7 Cochrane Street, just off Wellington Place, is the second oldest house on the estate dating from 1823 (Plate 244). The east side of this street is now lined with council housing well set back from the road, as the former line of Victorian terraced houses would have been. In 1945–50, the architect Louis de Soissons masterminded a development of sixty-four flats (224 people) for the St Marylebone Housing Association, a fifth housing block being added later. They include George Eyre House, which pays homage to the ground landlord, and also at the far end Cicely House, which was named after the founder of this housing organisation, Mrs Cicely Davies. The land was acquired from the Eyre estate in 1946. Cicely Davies died in 1953 just before the completion of Cicely House.[34]

243 and **244** Only one-half of this double house on the west side of Cochrane Street survives. No. 7 clings to the side of a modern 'double house' designed by David Stokes in 1936–37. The whole house was originally leased to Richard Smith in 1823 described as the '5th and 6th House from Road North end of Burial Ground'. It is the second oldest house on the estate (the oldest is in Elm Tree Road, Plate 49). Eyre estate archive (Bk of Drawings II, 34) (photo: John Chase).

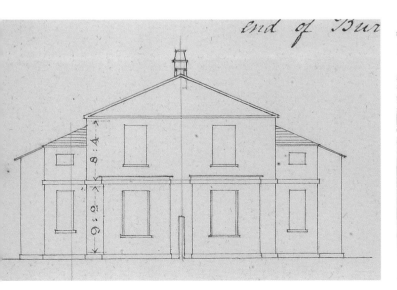

8 St John's Wood High Street

Most of St John's Wood High Street formed part of the Portland estate, which in 1879, when the fifth duke died, was inherited by his sister Lucy Bentinck. She was the widow of the sixth Baron Howard de Walden, and so from that date onwards the Portland estate has been known as the Howard de Walden estate. The street was part of an area known as Portland Town in the nineteenth century when the High Street was variously known as Portland Town Place (as shown on the Britton map – Plate 71) or York Place (on the 1853 Eyre estate map – Plate 70). The High Street was redeveloped in the early years of the twentieth century with tall blocks which replaced an area of relatively poor housing (Plate 245).

The early twentieth-century redevelopment of the High Street did not interfere with two Victorian landmarks: first, the magnificent Sir Isaac Newton public house on the corner with Allitsen Road (formerly Henry Street), a Café Rouge at the time of writing, which displays its date of construction, '1892', in a decorative cartouche at the top of the building. Further up on the right-hand side the chemist shop at No. 142 also has a long history. Its recognisable eagle can be spotted on a number of early photographs (see, for instance, Plate 246).

9 St Ann's Terrace (formerly Upper York Place)

The attractive terrace of houses on the west side of this street dates from the 1850s and was designed and built by Jacob Hibberd, who also designed Albert Terrace in Queen's Grove. Its creation was bound up with the demolition of a much loved landmark: St John's Wood House, a large and old cottage which stood opposite St John's Wood Farm (Plate 247).

The man who initially thought he was up to the task of developing the ground between the High Street and Acacia Road was publican John White, who lived and worked in this street at the Duke of York pub. The pub dates from 1826 and is the oldest surviving on the estate (see p. 206). In 1829, White signed a building agreement for the plot on the west side of St Ann's Terrace. Four years later, in 1833, no buildings had materialised, and the agreement was cancelled 'by mutual consent'.[35]

The Eyres objected to the house built by Hibberd on the site of St John's Wood House but nevertheless granted a lease. This house is still standing (2 Acacia Road): its wide façade overlooking St Ann's Terrace hides the narrow depth of the building and the small size of the garden. Edwin Eyre must have been sorely disappointed to see that what had been a landmark site was now meanly plotted ground with the ubiquitous Todd-style house on it (Plate 248).[36]

10 Acacia Road

The house at 3 Acacia Road, opposite the old St John's Wood House, was on Charles Freeth's territory (see Plate 73), and the lease was granted to him in 1840.[37] Charles Freeth junior was the major developer around Acacia Road. He was the son of Walpole's clerk, Charles Freeth senior; father and son became very involved in developing this part of St John's Wood. They had inside knowledge of the estate not only through Walpole but also because both worked for the Sun Fire Office, the estate's mortgager and the principal insurance company for the lessees. The house was

245 St John's Wood High Street was rebuilt in the early twentieth century. Its past incarnation, here in a 1904 photograph of the west side, was very modest, and this helps us realise what Walpole meant by Portland Town being 'principally inhabited by persons of the lowest description'. By 1906 J. G. Head recorded: 'It is composed chiefly of small houses, closely packed together, and occupied by a poor class of tenant. The whole of this district, the area of which is about twenty-eight acres, is now undergoing a radical change' (p. 107). Westminster City Archives (Ashbridge collection, Box 160 'S–WIG').

246 St John's Wood High Street from a photograph taken at the junction with Circus Road, looking south. This c.1910 photograph shows the section of the High Street which came under the ownership of the Eyre estate. The buildings there greatly contrast with those shown in Plate 245. The eagle above the chemist shop on the left has survived to this day, but there has been a chemist on this site since 1871 when it was in the hands of William R. Williams & Co. Westminster City Archives.

St John's Wood House: disappearance of a landmark

As early as 1816 Walpole had envisaged the development of the old St John's Wood House, as is clear from a letter to the then lessee Colonel Villiers, who wanted a new 99-year lease. Walpole said he could have it on one condition:

> we shall expect one Capital first rate house to be built on the [old] house in the course of a few years[,] you having the Materials of the present house[,] the remainder of the Ground to be converted into Garden or Pleasure Ground – You will also have the power of building 4 more houses of the second rate or of letting the Ground for that purpose.[38]

In those early days (1817) something of its situation was recorded: the house stood 'upon two acres and an half of ground beautifully laid out in shrubberys [sic] & pleasure Grounds'.[39] In 1830, this is how Walpole described it: 'a house containing many Rooms and extensive Out offices stabling and other Build[in]gs and accommodation might easily be made for 20 Horses – there is an extensive Garden well planted & enclosed with a high Wall & close paling.'[40]

In 1826, Walpole was ready to develop the site (see Plate 94), but there were setbacks, giving him the opportunity to express quite lyrical and romantic thoughts: 'the man who agreed to take it for building is off his bargain & I am not sorry for it, for it would really be a pity to destroy so beautiful a place.'[41] In 1834, when it was occupied by George Cottam, in a grand gesture St John's Wood House became the 'Manor House'.[42] But its end finally came in 1852 when Erlam was contracted to demolish it as part of his agreement. The man who landed the job, however, was Jacob Hibberd: 'Immed[iate]ly after Mr Erlam had obtained the agreem[en]t he assigned it to Mr Hibberd for £1000 (making £800 by it).'[43]

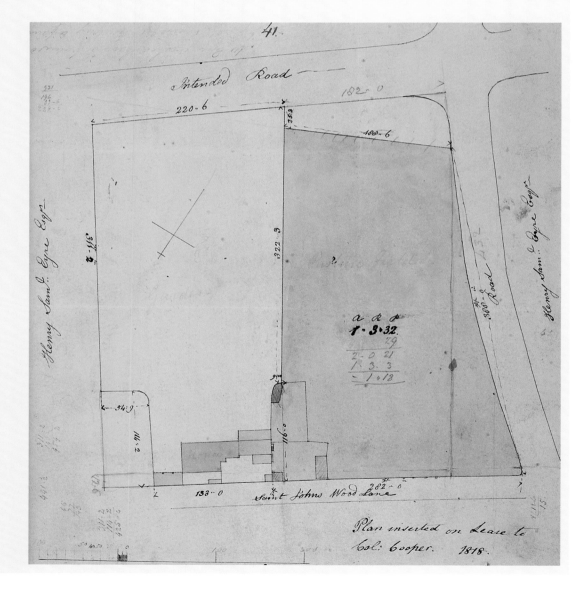

247 This is the 1818 lease plan of St John's Wood House, later called the 'Manor House'. For many years it was in the occupation of a retired 'lunatic' army man, Colonel Cooper. It was demolished in the early 1850s to make way for a development of villas and terraced housing built by Jacob Hibberd. Eyre estate archive (Bk of Drawings I, 41).

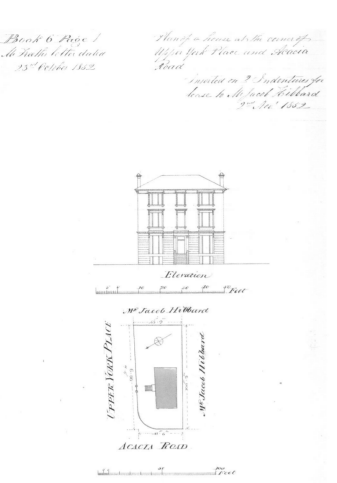

248 Jacob Hibberd, the man who built attractive terraced housing in Queen's Road (now Grove) and St Ann's Terrace, disappointed the Eyres in 1852 by building this house on the site of the old St John's Wood House. This very modestly sized plot replaced one which was two and a half acres. Eyre estate archive (Bk of Drawings VI, 1 right).

249 Although John Macallan Swan was noted for his depiction of lions and tigers, his chalk drawing, *Head of a Polar Bear*, is a particularly irresistible example of his work. Swan, like Henry Riviere (82 Finchley Road) and his near neighbour John Nettleship (35 Acacia Road), specialised in animals. Courtauld Institute of Art, London.

sited at an angle, too close to the road by the estate's usual standards; it acquired a studio around 1889 for its long-term occupant (Plate 306), painter and sculptor John Macallan Swan (1847–1910).[44] Swan, who predominantly painted and sculpted wild cats (Regent's Park Zoo providing a handy supply of sitters), was recorded at this address between 1887 and 1910 (Plate 249).

Acacia Gardens marks the western end of St John's Wood Farm, which in the 1820s was occupied by a barn, cowshed and grain pits (see Plate 94). The farm was at the top of St Ann's Terrace, and in the eighteenth and nineteenth centuries all paths led to it. The departure of its formidable tenant, Thomas Willan, in 1825 marked the beginning of the end for this early St John's Wood landmark, as subsequent tenants struggled to pay the rent and to make the enterprise a viable concern. By 1834 Charles Freeth senior had moved into the farmhouse, as the beginning of this letter testifies: 'As my private residence Viz the Farm House' (on the site of the present 56 Acacia Road).[46] His son Charles took the whole site under agreement in 1842, and Freeth senior acquired the brand new house built in 1841 on the site of the old 'Mr Willan's House' immediately east of the block of cowsheds (Plate 250 and see 'Anatomy of a robbery' box).

Most of the farm was dismantled, but it partially survived as a dairy with the block of cowsheds forming the core of what became known as St John's Wood Dairy (Plate 251). This site, too, was in

Anatomy of a robbery in Acacia Road

Two documents regarding the case, 'The Queen v John Sandlands', survive in the Eyre archive (depositions and brief for prosecution at EE 2650/1/110(C and D)). They chart in fascinating detail an aborted break-in at 56 Acacia Road in 1857. They also give real insight into social issues in this part of the Wood on the Portland Town borders.

The house is thus described: 'detached house in a garden, of modern Gothic elevation' (Plate 250). The theft apparently occurred around midnight on Monday 18 May 1857, 'the family consisting of 5 persons having gone to bed' (including husband and wife Charles and Ann Freeth, also 23-year-old daughter Annette).

Initially John Sandlands and Mary Ann Martin, who 'lived as man and wife at 16 Charles Street Portland Town', were 'charged this day before me for that they did feloniously steal take and carry away two Coats, One Dress, One Handkerchief and other articles of the value of £10 of the goods and chattels of the said Charles Freeth in his dwelling house' (also two Tablecloths and a pair of boots).

Depositions

Charles Freeth declared: 'The door of the Lobby is always left open, From the Lobby a person could get into the Water closet through the window, and from the Water closet into the house[.] On Tuesday morning I went into the kitchen and found a quantity of papers and lucifers had been burnt there – I saw footmarks in the garden – I traced them from the Wall in Acacia Road to the house, They appeared to be the footmarks of a man and woman[.] A woman that I employ as a Charwoman took off her shoe and it corresponded with the marks.' (A note in the margin reads: 'This Charwoman is nearly 70 years old and resides with her husband in a Cottage in Mr Freeth's Garden....')

Prosecution

'The Robber broke a pane of glass and attempted an entrance through a Wash house window – that window was nailed down – he then tried to get entrance through a Bottle house the door of which was broken off the hinges – failing in this – he entered through a small window about eight feet from the ground which lighted a Servants Water closet on [sic] the Basement[.] to effect this he climbed on to a wooden shelf in an outer lobby of the house which shelf he broke with his weight.'

Recent family visits had meant that 'the Family took the opportunity on this Monday to have a Great Wash.... on this particular night there was a large quantity of Linen clothes &c in the lower part of the house – the Kitchen and Lobby having great stacks of clothes and linen put up for mangling and Ironing as also loose clothes.

'The Basement floor and offices and Hall door and Dining Parlor being Gas lighted it is a rule with this family not to leave any Candles about and the key of the Gas is placed in a secret place[.]

'The Robber therefore was not able to obtain light from Candle or Gas altho' he searched the candlesticks and turned on the Gas tap – and this being the case – he resorted to obtaining partial gleams of light from Lucifer matches – from burning pieces of paper taken from the Kitchen cupboard &c – and from burning two muslin window curtains which he tore up for that purpose.... it is surprising that the house was not set on Fire[.]

'… It appeared that the Robber had entered the Kitchen – the Passage and a Breakfast parlor on the basement – he then went up a flight of stairs into a passage and from the pegs he took two coats belonging to Mr Freeth – here he must have been disturbed for he does not appear to have gone farther – although Dining room[,] Drawing room and other rooms in which there was considerable property were open – and it is supposed that this disturbance or the want of light was the reason why so little valuable property was taken when so much more was about.'

The prisoner

'The prisoner John Sandlands is supposed to be a returned convict[.] he disappeared about 6 or 7 years ago – he reappeared about 6 months since and has been since twice in custody (once had three months imprisonment and once discharged) and he belongs to a desperate gang of thieves who lurk in Portland Town and sally out to the more respectable neighbourhood of St John's Wood to rob, and where numerous robberies are constantly taking place – some time since Mr Freeth had a plate robbery (never discovered) and was more recently about to be attacked by two men and a woman on alighting from a Hansom's Cab at his own door – but a good thick stick and a determined manner prevented the attack-'.

250 This house is quite typical of the style adopted by Charles Freeth senior and junior for their houses in and around Acacia Road. This particular house, at 56 Acacia Road immediately east of the farm, no longer exists. The lease drawing is dated August 1841, and the counterpart lease, which has survived, bears the same date. It was the home of Freeth senior, Walpole's trusted clerk. This 1857 larceny case provides very detailed information about its workings. Eyre estate archive (Bk of Drawings IV, 82 right).

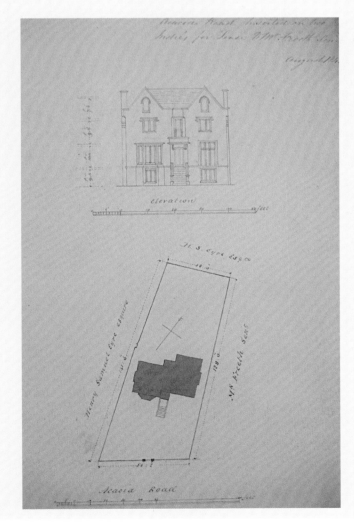

251 The St John's Wood Dairy on the site of the original farm photographed in the early years of the twentieth century. The dairy was taken over by Unigate in the 1960s and survived until shortly after 2000. Westminster City Archives.

the hands of Charles Freeth senior.[46] A remarkable document has survived which describes in vivid detail the sounds of the dairy in the 1920s following a complaint from a Mr Vincent, who claimed his rent should be reduced given the level of noise. The letter is written by a member of staff from Savill & Sons Estate Agents, who by that date were handling the affairs of the Eyre estate:

> I went to Acacia Road on the 23rd November [1927], arriving there at 4.50 a.m. They started loading the carts about 4.55. These carts are pony carts with iron tyred wheels and the milk is all in bottles and loaded into the carts in crates. There is a certain amount of noise by the loading into the carts but it is practically continuous and should not disturb anybody. The first cart came out of the yard three minutes past five. Between then and six o'clock, thirty seven pony carts came out, one hand cart and one small motor van. There is no unusual noise except when the carts pass over some granite setts. The yard itself is concrete paved but where the way out passes over the footway it is granite setts. There is a crossing about seven feet wide crossing Acacia Road to St Ann's Terrace, which is also of granite setts, and there is a long length of granite setts between the Dairy and Finchley Road. For the most part the ponies walk over these granite setts but even then there is a considerable amount of noise and when they trot of course the noise is much greater.

> I suggest that the Local Authorities be approached with a view to having these granite setts taken up. While I was there nothing came into the yard but I was informed that one motor lorry only comes into the yard about 4.30 a.m.[47]

11 Ordnance Mews

This area of garages affords a peep into the back-street workings of St John's Wood. The general feel of this hidden corner is not dissimilar to its nineteenth-century mews predecessor, though the layout now is more higgledy-piggledy: the Victorians had a horseshoe-shaped mews quarter, built in the mid-1820s.[48] This layout survived until the Second World War when a bomb caused major damage to the mews and nearby Aquila Street (formerly Edward Street).

As development was interrupted in the late 1820s and plots reverted back to being used as pasture or gardens, this area did not at first function as a mews but rather as cheap housing alongside unsociable trades. In the mid-1830s Walpole tried hard to eradicate the problem by writing firm letters to the occupants. The following letter highlights the enormous gap between the original intention for development and the reality:

> By the terms of the Lease under which these prem[is]es are held[,] the Mews[,] also the way to it[,] was to be covered with Granite 9 inches thick – the piece of Gro[un]d in the rear (enclosed with a Dwarf Wall) was to be planted with trees & shrubs so as to make an ornamental plantation or shrubbery & so to be kept – the Road in the rear was to be made with Brick Rubbish 12 inches thick & a footway 8 ft wide was to be paved & Gates at the resp[ect]ive entrances were to be put up next Upper York Place & Edward Street [now Aquila Street] with proper Locks[,] hinges & fastenings[.]

None of these matters have been performed – the prem[is]es are much out of repair – the Tenants are the lowest class of Irish – Pigs are kept upon the prem[is]es – filth of all kinds & to a great extent is deposited in the Mews & a Man named Powell under pretence of renting from you the small piece of ground which was covenanted to be laid out as plantation has taken poss[essi]on of the Road intended to be called Edward Street[,] which he has made a deposit for dung & other filth & refuses to remove the Same.[49]

It was the building of the nearby chapel in St John's Wood Terrace which eventually retrieved this part of the estate from the neglect this text describes so vividly.

12 St John's Wood Terrace

Congregational chapel

The arrival of the Congregational chapel in St John's Wood Terrace marked a turning point in the development of this area and provided Walpole with the ammunition he needed to stamp out undesirable activities. To the lessee of a property in York Place (i.e. the top of St John's Wood

252 This view of St John's Wood Terrace in the early twentieth century focuses on the Portland Chape (it is not clear when it acquired its upper structure). Beyond the chapel may be seen the original St Marylebone Almshouses (Plate 253). The terraced houses are neatly hemmed in with a dwarf wall and iron railings, while most of the façades appear to have been left unrendered except on the south-west side (right foreground). Westminster City Archives (Acc. No P210 in T138 (Prints), Box St Ann's Terrace–Seymour Street).

High Street) he wrote: 'the front being a green stall & Coal Shed & the rear a Coachmakers & the North West side has apparently various small tenements.... I have hitherto abstained from taking serious notice of these breaches of the Cov[ena]nts in the Lease but as considerable improvements are now making in that part of St J[ohn's] W[ood] I must require that the terms of the Lease be complied with.'[50]

Built by and leased to John Maidlow in 1841 on ground under agreement with James Berry, the Portland Chapel, as it was originally named, seated 600 (Plate 252).[51] It is discussed in Chapter 9.

The Star pub

This is the second oldest surviving pub on the estate (after the Duke of York further west). It was built on land under agreement with the developer John Maidlow. When he went bankrupt, his estate was sold at auction on 21 March 1826, and the building, which had probably been erected by William Robert Fry and Stephen Watkins, was thus described: 'A Plot of Ground, with a large House, intended for a Public-house, on Lease to Messrs Fry and Watkins, for a Term of 94 Years, from Christmas last [1825], at a Ground-Rent of per Annum ... 20 0 0'.[52]

The almshouses

The St Marylebone Almshouses owe their existence to an initial legacy of £500 made for the poor of Marylebone by Count Simon Woronzow (1744–1832). Four years after his death, the parish had succeeded in increasing this original sum by £2,200, making a total of £2,700. They invited a number of local architects to submit drawings and estimates, and chose John Pink and Samuel Erlam in 1836, the amount of the building contract apparently being around £3,500. Their attractive design 'in the old English domestic style of architecture' was completed mid-1837 (Plate 253). It is reminiscent of the Whittington's Almshouses in Highgate, built by George Smith in 1822 'in the pointed style of architecture'[53] – an engraving of which was published in 1827 by James Elmes in his *Metropolitan Improvements*. At around that time, P. F. Robinson was also publishing designs for almshouses in the same style of architecture.[54]

By the 1950s the maintenance bill had become so heavy that a report was commissioned from the architectural firm Louis de Soissons, Peacock, Hodges & Robertson; they suggested carrying out extensive repairs or demolishing and starting from scratch. The report pointed out that 'the Almshouses in their present form and structural condition are a financial liability'. also mentioning 'the architectural merit and charm of the Almshouse building ... a worthy example of early nineteenth century domestic architecture'.[55] The Board of Management finally decided in February 1959 to develop rebuilding proposals. Four architects were shortlisted, including David Hodges, who was involved in preparing the report quoted above,[56] but on 29 April 1959 the board appointed architect G. B. Drewitt and the quantity surveyor who had recommended him, F. Briscoe Taylor. The attempt by the LCC Historic Buildings Section to list the building was regarded as a major setback and was resisted vigorously. The almshouses were demolished and rebuilt between 1960 and 1963.[57]

The Eyre brothers had not charged Marylebone vestry any money for the land needed for the original almshouses, but Walpole declined becoming a trustee as he thought this could lead to a conflict of interest.[58] In 1926, the Board of Trustees was successful in purchasing the freehold of the site.

Inserted on one Agreement
and one sheet of paper
March 1839.

Inserted on two Indentures
November 13 1838
for Lease for the Marylebone
Alms Houses

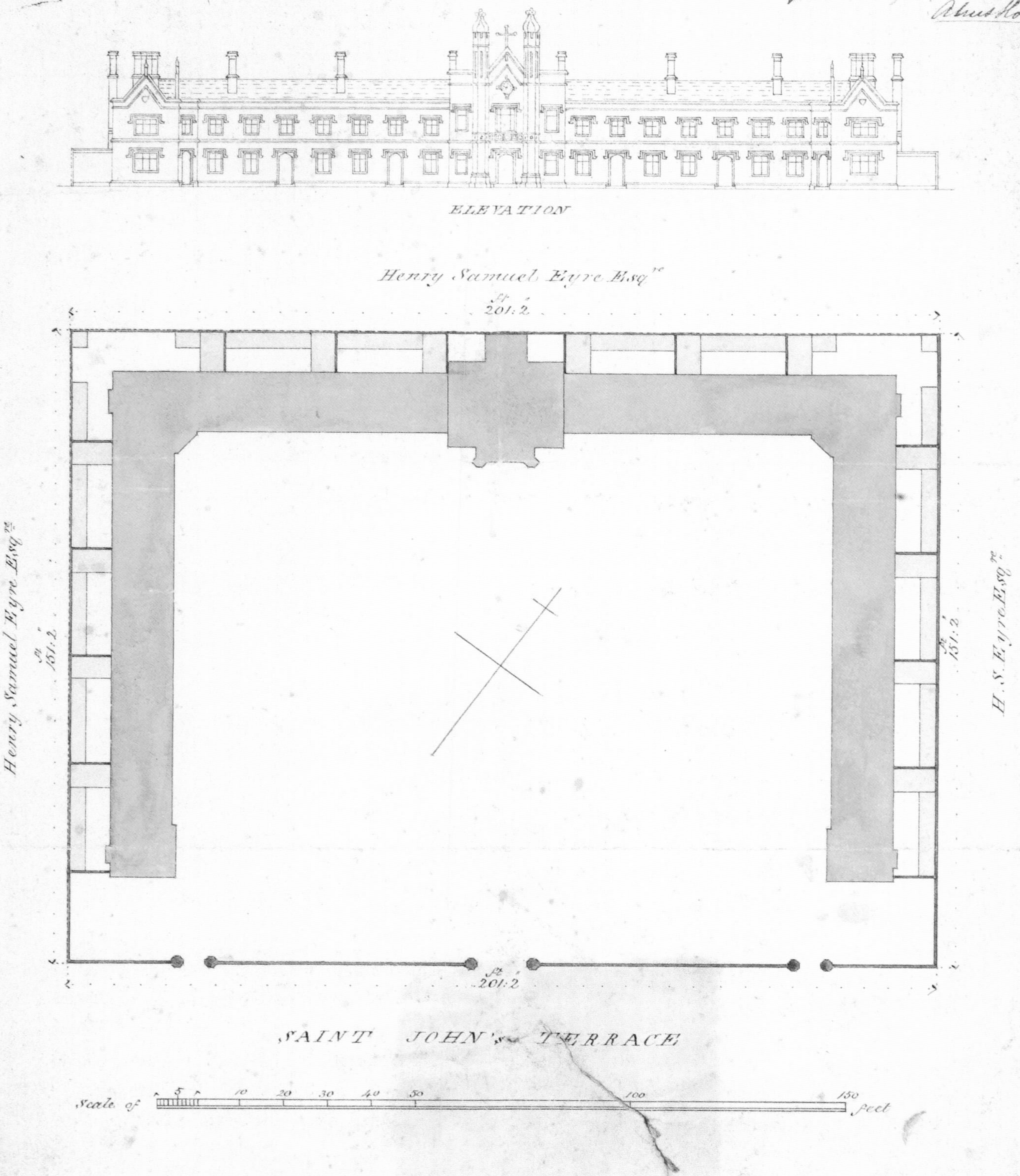

ELEVATION

Henry Samuel Eyre Esqre

ft.
201:2

Henry Samuel Eyre Esqre

ft.
151:2

H. S. Eyre Esqre

ft.
151:2

ft.
201:2

SAINT JOHN's TERRACE

Scale of 5 10 20 30 40 50 100 150 feet

Table 2 The almshouses then and now

	1849	2008
Number of residents	68 (incl. 11 couples) in 57 rooms	23 (incl. 2 couples) in 21 flats (each has 2 rooms, kitchen & bathroom)
Relief	Room rent-free	Each resident pays a 'maintenance contribution'* of £145 per week (single), £165 (couple)
	1.5 tons of coal/year Firewood 4 lb of 'best Bread' 2s. 6d./week (single) 3s. 10d./week (married)	Subsidised outings Free social events
		The majority of residents receive housing benefit from Westminster City Council
Funding	Around £800 per annum: (Voluntary) annual subs, i.e. £580 Proceeds of endowment fund, i.e. £234 p.a.	£160,420 (maintenance contributions) Bank interest & dividends

*The maintenance contribution covers the rent and includes heating, hot water and support charges.

The Townshend estate

This part of the Eyre estate was sold to Marylebone Borough Council in November 1949 by Compulsory Purchase Order (see Plate 221) and completed by 1957 when the last '42 families' moved into the final block.[59] The nine blocks of the housing estate have been named after famous artists, for instance: Turner and Cameron on the north side, Cotman, Calderon, Ramsay, Opie and Cruikshank on the other sides. Unfortunately, the one artist who actually lived on this site, opposite the almshouses, has not been included.

Between 1886 and 1905 the Dutch-born painter Matthew Maris (1839–1917) lived in near poverty at 47 St John's Wood Terrace:

> Here he passed nineteen years, living in a Spartan and most simple life. All the year round his grate was destitute of fire.... His custom of going fireless dated, I fancy, from his years in Paris, when once he and his brother James, two days without food, were driven to make use of their furniture to fill the stove.... This room in which Matthew Maris lived and worked was but a small one, its dimensions not exceeding thirteen feet each way.... It was but little more than some nine feet in height – its window not large.... Once in a

humorous smile he said to me … 'You see I am a very pious painter …' for most often to obtain the requisite lighting he would kneel upon the floor.… The only work that, to my knowledge, he completed during his last seven or eight years at St John's Wood Terrace was a very beautiful ideal head in grey Italian chalk which is now in the museum at Rotterdam.[60]

13 Woronzow Road (south) and Acacia Road

The south-east corner of Woronzow Road where Chesterfield Lodge (another sheltered accommodation for the elderly) stands was the site of a small nursery and of a separate florist which might have passed unnoticed but for the fact that they are documented and even illustrated in the estate archive (Plate 254).[61]

Walpole explained in 1842 when writing to Christopher Flood, the Marylebone clerk and also honorary secretary of the almshouses, that he was 'making a Road at the North East side of the Alms Houses & which road I have named Woronzow Road'.[62] The road is, of course, named after Count Woronzow, whose bequest to Marylebone enabled the building of the almshouses.

One of Charles Freeth junior's builders was Robert Yeo, who gained experience on the estate building houses at the east end of Acacia Road. A group of these have survived on the south-west corner of Acacia and Woronzow Roads. But things are not always what they seem in St John's Wood. The house on the corner at No. 25 is a 1970 replica of the original house, the building having been expunged of its later accretions. It was flagged as an example of 'local vigilance' and named as the City of Westminster's contribution to European Architectural Heritage Year 1975. Apparently, a member of the St John's Wood Protection Society telephoned Westminster City Hall on a Friday in 1970 to report that a contractor had started demolishing the villa. The council's response was to obtain a building protection notice on the same day. 'Later, the structure of the house was found to

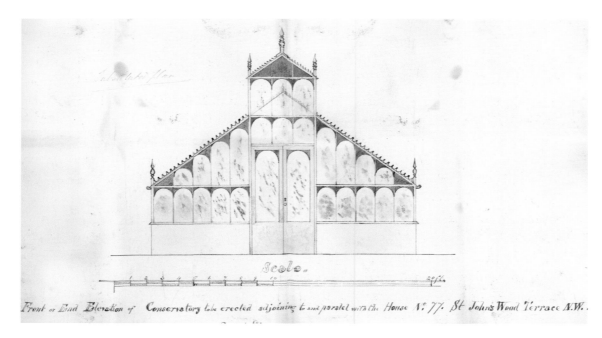

254 Design of greenhouse for Tom Smith at 77 St John's Wood Terrace (north side), adjoining the Woronzow Road nursery, 1868. The 1880 assignment of the plot from one nurseryman survives, and the deed recites the history of the site from 1826 (when it was taken over by Stephen Watkins) to 1866, the date of the deed which sealed the arrival of the nursery. This in turn attracted a florist, Tom Smith, and this drawing was produced so that he could obtain a trading licence from the estate. Westminster City Archives (765/85).

255 Lease drawing for 25 Acacia Road, built by and leased to Robert Yeo, dated 4 July 1844. The original house was demolished and replaced by a replica in the 1970s. The three adjacent houses were also built by Yeo and have survived to this day. Eyre estate archive (Bk of Drawings IV, 105 left).

Elevation.

be in poor condition and a replica building scheme was allowed, restoring 25 Acacia Road to its former glory' (Plate 255).[63]

No. 43A is well hidden, but it is worth noting because in the 1950s this unusual property became the original home of Bernard Miles's Mermaid Theatre, which subsequently became the well-loved theatre in the City of London (which survives but is no longer a theatre). This particular building plot on the north side of Acacia Road was created after every house around it had been allocated their garden, leaving a fair-sized chunk of land available in the middle. Initially this land, described as 'Garden Ground', was leased to Robert Yeo,[64] but by 1848 a single detached cottage had been erected. This cottage, which became known as New Place, was expanded in the 1850s to become one of St John's Wood's early independent schools, and a licence was granted on 13 August 1857 'to use the premises as a Day School' (Plate 117).[65] By the end of the nineteenth century it was known as 'Mr Oliver's School'. When he purchased the house in 1945, Bernard Miles had the good fortune to meet Mr Oliver's son, who had been born there in 1875, and he provided some interesting information about this school. His father was Reverend H. A. G. Oliver, and the curriculum included 'all the branches of a thorough English education together with Mathematics, Latin, Greek, French, German and Class Singing', piano and drawing being extras. He also described how Therese Tietjens, a famous soprano of the time, would come and have tea there, occasionally singing to the assembled school (she lived at Ivy Lodge on the site of the north entrance to St John and St Elizabeth Hospital).

By July 1899 Alice Buckton had renamed the property Sesame House, and the teaching now focused on 'Home-Life Training', 'planned for gentlewomen and girls having for its first object their own development, whether they wish afterwards to use the knowledge and experience they acquired in their own home, in parish or settlement work, or to gain a livelihood as lady nurses to children'.[66] Alice's pageants and mystery plays were regularly performed at Sesame House, a distant echo of the more famous Mermaid Theatre, which opened on this site in December 1949 with a packed performance of Purcell's *Dido and Aeneas*.[67]

14 Ordnance Hill

The Ordnance pub was first leased to Charles Viner in 1843, while the ground between the pub and the Barracks was leased to Charles Freeth junior.[68] By the time the Ordnance Arms opened its doors, there were already a number of public houses on the estate (see p. 206). As Viner had been based at the Duke of York pub since 1836, the area would have been familiar to him.

The main entrance to the Ordnance Barracks is sited opposite Norfolk Road. The Eyre archives have revealed that the original site for the Barracks was in a different part of the estate, in the 'Brick Field', between 1804 and 1806 (see Plate 42).[69] This early site needed to be vacated when development of the Alpha Cottages started in earnest, and so the Ordnance renegotiated their arrangement with Thomas Willan, the main St John's Wood grass tenant at that time. Ordnance Road was not made until 1843 (by William Robert Fry), and for the first thirty-seven years of the Barracks' existence by St John's Wood Farm, access was from Wellington Road (Plates 256 and 257). Despite the forbidding wall, the 'Riding House' may be glimpsed from the corner of Norfolk Road – the top just visible with its characteristic clock tower at the entrance. It is the oldest building on site, dating from 1825 (Plates 227 and 258).

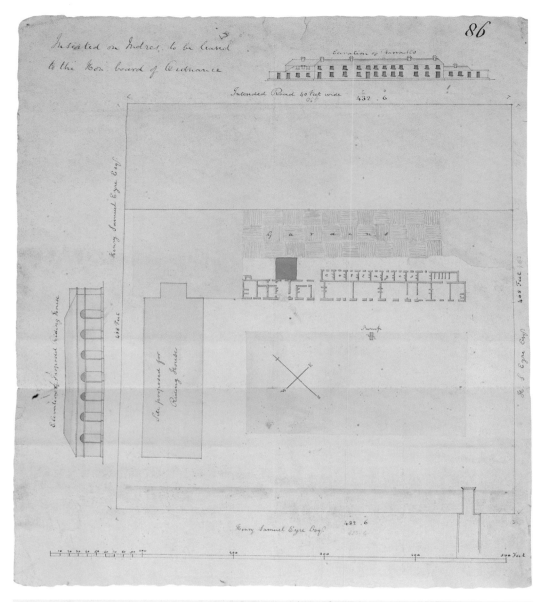

256 Lease drawing for the St John's Wood Barracks, dated 9 March 1824. The lease itself has survived (at WCA, 765/3). The riding school was envisaged in 1824 but not immediately built, judging by the inscription: 'Site proposed for Riding House'. Eyre estate archive (Bk of Drawings II, 86A).

FOOT GUARDS AT SQUAD DRILL, ST. JOHN'S WOOD BARRACKS.

257 *Foot Guards at Squad Drill, St John's Wood Barracks*, 1854. The article which accompanied this picture stated that the Barracks at that time were occupied by about 150 men of the second and third battalions of the Grenadier Guards. City of London, Guildhall Library (*Illustrated London News*, 26 August 1854).

The Riding House at St John's Wood Barracks

This 'Riding House' is the reason for the continued presence of the Ordnance in St John's Wood. At the end of the Napoleonic Wars the Barracks became surplus to requirements and were left empty between 1819 and 1823. An undated memorandum in the National Archives sums up the situation: 'In the year 1823 it became necessary to remove the Riding Establishment from the Buckingham House at Pimlico and the Commander-in-Chief determined that the most proper place to which it could be removed would be the Barrack at St John's Wood, belonging to the Ordnance.' The Riding House at Croydon had been considered but the cost of increasing its size was prohibitive, and further correspondence makes it clear that the St John's Wood site was favoured by both the duke of Wellington and the duke of York (Sworder, 2003, pp. 8ff). A memorandum signed 'W' (presumably for Wellington) firmly stated: 'We must keep St John's Wood. Let the lease be renewed and then measures taken to build the Riding House.' The cost of the operation was calculated and seemed worryingly high, so the Ordnance simply sold one of their establishments in the City Road to offset the expense. What is remarkable about this Riding House is its width. The Riding House built at the Royal Mews in the same year is as long as this one but not as wide.

258 The 'Riding House' at St John's Wood Barracks, photographed in 2009 (see also p. 374). Eyre estate (photo: John Chase).

Brief chronology of the St John's Wood Barracks

(Based on Sworder (2003) and the Eyre estate archive.)

1804–6	Barracks situated in Brick Field (Brick Field shown in Spurrier & Phipps 1794 survey, Plate 42).
1805	(December) 'we shall want to take possession of that part of the Brick Field where the Barracks stands,' writes Walpole to Thomas Willan (LB 'A', p. 154).
1806	Barracks' new site next to St John's Wood Farm, where it has remained ever since (LB 'A', p. 225).
1804–19	Royal Artillery at St John's Wood Barracks (underlease from Thomas Willan).
1819–23 (or 25)	The Barracks are empty.
c.1825–32	Cavalry riding establishment.
1832–76	Foot Guards (Plate 257).
1876–80	Household Cavalry.
1880 onwards	Royal Horse Artillery.
1947	Creation of the King's Troop, based at St John's Wood from this date.
2010	See Plates 225 and 226.

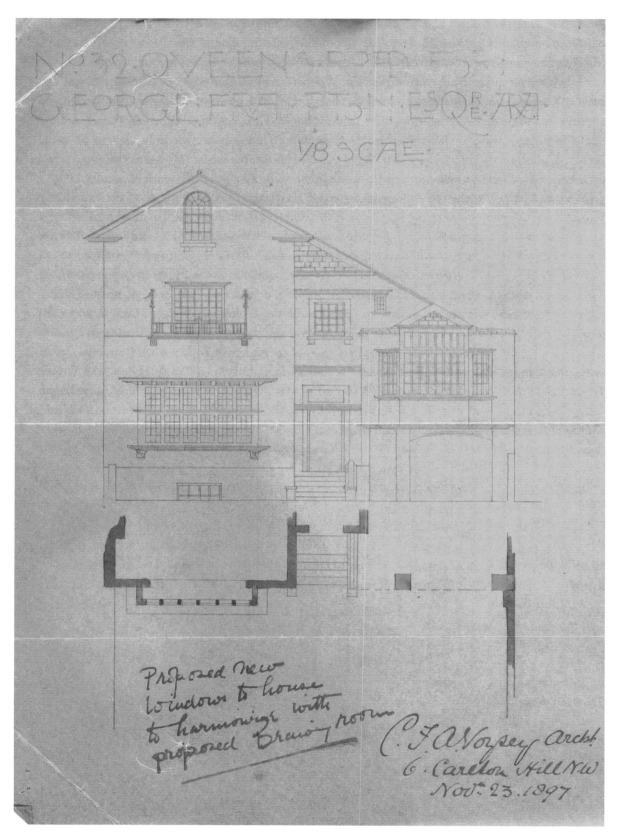

261 Building extension for the sculptor George Frampton at 32 Queen's Road. The drawing is one of a handful produced by C. F. A. Voysey in 1897. The proposed drawing room over the coach entrance on the right was certainly built but according to a much simplified design. Eyre estate archive (EE 2650/1/137(A)).

extension to the side of the house as per Voysey's drawings, but the design was considerably plainer.

In early 1909 the Framptons moved to Carlton Hill and the reasons for the move are found in one of Christabel's letters: 'We are also moving early in the New year. We have been building a house & Studio near here for the last 9 months – we are leaving here for the sake of having a nice garden & I hope my husband will make a hobby of it as he works too hard & refuses to take up golf!'.[79] The Framptons spent almost twenty years at this address (1909–28). There the studio survives in its full glory overlooking the large garden (Plate 134). The property was acquired in 1958 by another sculptor, Hungarian-born Arthur Fleischmann (1896–1990), thus safeguarding the studio from development.[80] It was in Carlton Hill that Frampton made his famous Kensington Gardens *Peter Pan* sculpture.

Queen's Grove (1)

Queen's Grove was developed in the 1840s, soon after the young Queen Victoria married Prince Albert (1841), and there was a deliberate attempt here to celebrate this event through the naming of streets and buildings. The development of Queen's Grove, formerly known as Queen's Road and prior to that as Victoria Road,[81] was the overall responsibility of John Wright Treeby. A substantial part of the original development has survived, with detached and semi-detached houses on the north side and terraced houses on the south side, the latter used as a way of 'walling in' the Barracks' site (see Plate 70). Treeby sublet the west end of the site to another builder, James Sharp, and the south side to Jacob Hibberd.

The jewel in the Queen's Grove crown is Hibberd's Albert Terrace (its 1840s name) – the elegant terraced houses on the south side of the street – which were carefully restored by the Eyre estate in the early years of the new millennium. One of Treeby's letters to Walpole survives, dated 1843; it gives insight into this building project, which had first been envisaged as taking the shape of a crescent:[82] 'Mr Hibberd wishes to know if you will allow him to build a Terrace of Close houses … in that ground where it were [*sic*] intended to build a Cres[c]ent[.] also he proposes to build the public house adjoining the barracks instead of building it, on the corner of the Queens Road & Ordnance Road.… the whole of the houses are to be as good as those that are built in Stanhope Street Camberlin [Camden] Town.'[83]

Built by Hibberd in 1844, the first public house was sited on the original agreed site at the eastern end of Albert Terrace on the corner of Queen's and Ordnance Roads. It later became known as the Prince of Wales. The estate sold it in 1925, eighteen months before the lease was due to expire. Its stables were a source of frequent complaints in the letter books. It was rebuilt in the 1960s and known as the Rossetti, now the site of Rossetti House, a modern pastiche building made to blend with Hibberd's adjacent terraced housing.[84] The second public house, built by Sharp, was the Knights of St John (see below).

St John's Wood Park

This street could be described as an early Victorian 'millionaires' row', and William Holme Twentyman presided over his creation in a house which stood opposite No. 25 and was simply but unequivocally called the Manor House (Plate 100). No. 25 has acquired an extra floor as well as bay windows but otherwise survives intact, almost the only house in the vast development work masterminded by Twentyman to have done so (Plates 262 and 263, also see pp. 181ff). Beyond the bend in the road the blocks of houses on the east side date from the mid-1930s,[85] while the neo-Georgian houses of the west side denote a more recent trend of house building in St John's Wood and elsewhere.

No. 23 St John's Wood Park is on the corner of Queen's Grove and St John's Wood Park; built in 1844, its grand appearance is deceptive as it is a fairly narrow house. It was leased to Mr James Prince, a tailor from Stoke Newington and Change Alley.[86] When Reverend Henry Samuel Eyre inherited the estate, he lived there between 1872 and 1884. His daughter Mary Richardson Eyre had a distinctively negative recollection: 'When we first came to London I can only say we disliked it intensely. My father took a house for us in St John's Wood Park No 23. To this day this road gives me the shivers and I never go through it if I can possibly avoid doing so – it is so dull, so damp and so overgrown with trees.... outside it was a patchy stucco abomination, like so many in this locality.'[87]

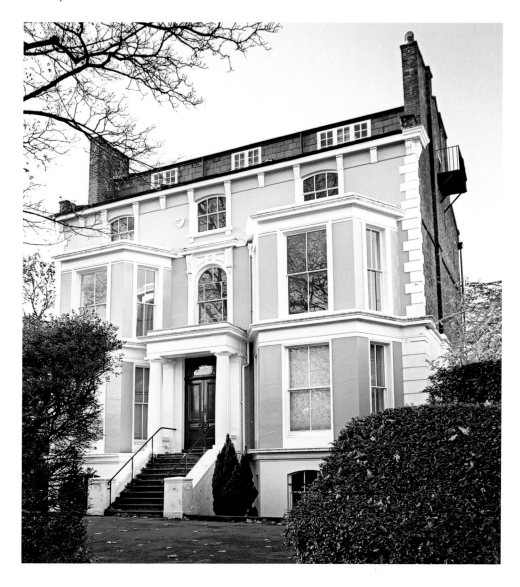

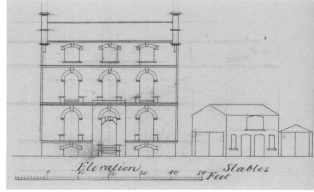

262 and **263** 25 St John's Wood Park, then and now: the lease drawing below dates from 1852. By 2005, when the Eyre estate sold this house, it had acquired an extra storey and bay windows which have considerably altered its original appearance. Eyre estate archive (Bk of Drawings VI, 20 left).

264 This faint but evocative postcard shows the façade of Marlborough Road Station in the 1910s. Before this and Lord's stations finally closed on 20 November 1939, they were subject to heavily reduced opening hours. Organised by the sculptor Sigismund Goetze, 131 local residents petitioned against this, complaining: 'Why should the St John's Wood and Marlborough Road districts be made to suffer owing to the Metropolitan Railway's policy of making systematic and sustained efforts to develop outlying districts[?]' (Connor, 2001, p. 71). Collection of Alan Irvine.

Queen's Grove (2)

At 1 Queen's Grove stands the house Jacob Hibberd, who built the adjacent Albert Terrace, devised for himself. The lease drawing has survived, dated 1844, showing how the gated area now called Walpole Mews formed part of his property, a builder's yard with a workshop (Plate 310).

The Royal China restaurant closes the north range in Queen's Grove. Who would suspect that this exotic-looking establishment was a former railway station? It is evident when viewed from the back, where there is a considerable drop which affords a glimpse of the railway line. This area was disturbed by the opening in 1868 of the Marlborough Road Station (Plate 264) built by the Metropolitan and St John's Wood Railway Company.[88] The company purchased a generous amount of land north and south of the station, and when the station was built it disposed of the surplus land, which included Tom Hood's Devonshire Villa and the extraordinarily slender triangular site opposite the station where the tiniest house on the estate stands (Plates 265 and 266).[89] The station closed in 1839 when St John's Wood Station opened further south.

The transformation from station to restaurant took place in 1970 when David Brookbank designed an Angus Steak House, turning the booking hall into a restaurant seating seventy people. The design incorporated an 'open cutting through the deserted platforms' to enable guests to view the trains hurtling down the lines beneath their feet.[90]

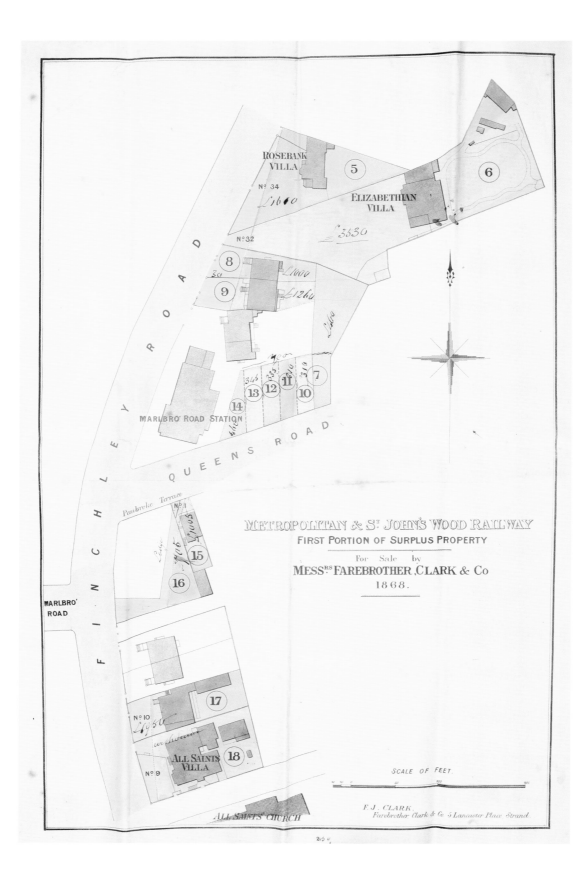

265 Map published by the Metropolitan and St John's Wood Railway showing the surplus properties they had for sale after the construction of Marlborough Road Station. This shows how the tiniest house on the estate – the pink triangle opposite the station marked '16' – came into being (Plate 266). Eyre estate archive (EE 2650/1/180(A)).

266 The tiniest house on the estate, at the western end of Queen's Grove (south side), may not survive for very much longer as plans are afoot to redevelop this part of St John's Wood. Eyre estate (photo: John Chase).

267 and **268** This is James Sharp's lease drawing for several houses on the east side of Queen's Terrace, including a public house at No. 7, the future 'Knights of St John' (see above). The lease for the latter has survived, dated 1 March 1847, made out to Sharp, who developed the land between Queen's Terrace and the Finchley Road on the north east side of All Saints Church. The pub's first-floor room was the first home of the St John's Wood Arts Club (see pp. 324–25). Eyre estate archive (Bk of Drawings V, 91 right); photo: Eyre estate.

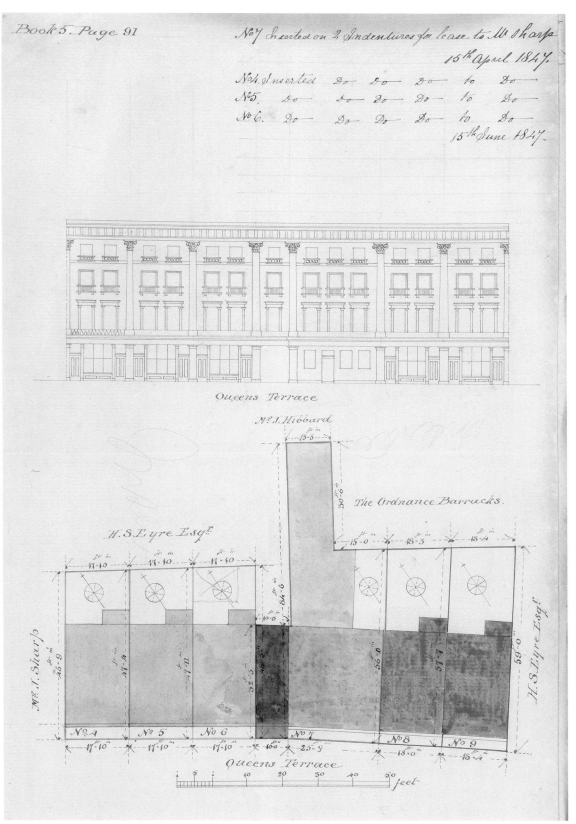

The artists' studios at 59 Queen's Grove (north side) were established in 1882 and were perhaps built by Albert E. Pridmore, who built the Woronzow Road Studios, as in both cases the site was occupied by ironmonger John Butler. John Butler appears to have exploited to good effect the trend for artists' studios in St John's Wood: he owned three of them.[91] Among the artists who were based at Queen's Grove were Harold and Laura Knight, whom we will also encounter in Langford Place below.

17 Queen's Terrace and All Saints Church

The pub which would later be known as the Knights of St John opened in 1847 and was leased to James Sharp,[92] developer of Queen's Terrace (Plate 267). It was close to the former Barracks' entrance in Wellington Road. The (later) imposing sign upon the façade has survived, but the pub itself, once popular with Lord's crowds and famous for its steak lunches, had so deteriorated when the lease expired at the end of the twentieth century that no tenant could be found. In 2002, it was gutted and turned into flats with shops on the ground floor. The façade was beautifully restored, but St George's sword went missing. The building of a council housing block opposite the Knights of St John followed the sale of this plot to Marylebone Council in 1952.[93]

The enclave at Queen's Terrace just north of St John's Wood Underground Station was the site of All Saints Church. The history of this church is given in detail in Chapter 9. The land was redeveloped in the early 1980s, making way for a block of luxurious apartments called the Terraces, built by Fairclough Building, a £5 million-plus project for London and Leeds Investment Ltd. 'The apartments are vast. Some are more than twice the size of a large detached house. The smallest, with two bedrooms, is 1800 square feet in area; those with four or five bedrooms are nearly 5000 square feet.' In 1982, when David Hoppit wrote this description, he noted there were '32 apartments in all, ranging in price between £225,000 and £775,000', and the rates and maintenance charges were estimated at £2,000 a year.[94]

The small Victorian building opposite the Terraces on the north side is a touching survival (Plate 269). Its construction led to a massive row between Walpole and the man who financed the building, Reverend Edward Thompson, who was first in charge of the congregation at All Saints Church (see p. 212). This was the church schoolhouse which Thompson had planned to build (without consultation) right next to the church. The present site was the compromise reached between two strong-willed men – a plot alongside Thompson's magnificent All Saints Lodge or Villa (see Plate 80).[95] All Saints Lodge, now demolished, was sold as surplus railway land in 1868.[96] In the twentieth century the school became known as All Saints Church Hall and was the site of St John's Wood's first library (opened in 1947).

18 Devonshire Villa (Thomas Hood's House)

No. 28 Finchley Road (Plate 270) was the last home of the writer Thomas Hood between 1844 and 1845, and the site is marked by a blue plaque.[97] This energetic man with failing health died there, barely a year after leaving his Elm Tree Road address (see pp. 428–29). The house was Devonshire Villa, built by John Wright Treeby in 1840. Treeby, who had resided there for three years, was the leaseholder and therefore Hood's landlord.[98] Treeby left Devonshire Villa to move into the now

269 Hopscotch in Queen's Terrace: the association of children with this site is a reminder that All Saints Church Hall, in the background of this lively scene, was built as an early purpose-built school by Edward Thompson, All Saints' first vicar, in the late 1840s. By the time H. Doeling took this photograph in 1951 it had become the St John's Wood Library. Westminster City Archives (T138, Queen's Terrace 4).

270 Lease drawing for Nos 26 and 28 Finchley Road. No. 28 on the left was extended sometime in the early years of the twentieth century. Eyre estate archive (Bk of Drawings IV, 68 right).

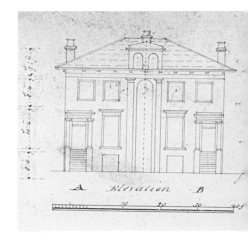

271 This drawing by Cecil King depicts the interior of the third home of the St John's Wood Arts Club at 28 Finchley Road, the house where Thomas Hood died. It was described with affection in Montgomery Eyre's book (p. 278): 'whenever I enter its cosy precincts I am warmed by the feeling of homeliness and good-fellowship. Many of the old faces whose silhouettes form the frieze of the large room will no longer meet us face to face, but there is always an atmosphere in the place which holds one and bids one stay a bit.' Eyre estate archive (Montgomery Eyre, 1913, opp. p. 278).

demolished Elizabethan Villa just north of this property and sited by a large pond (see Plate 79).

The semi-detached house contained ten rooms when it was sold as railway surplus property in 1868: 'this is a most Valuable Property for conversion to BUSINESS PURPOSES, being the High Road, close to Marlborough Station; and no Shops within a Quarter of a Mile', read the advertisement. The whole house (a double house) sold for £1,240 according to the annotated map in the Eyre archive.[99]

In 1900, the house became the third home of the St John's Wood Arts Club (after the Knights of St John and the Eyre Arms, see p. 325). Montgomery Eyre illustrated its interior in his history of St John's Wood (Plate 271).

19 Alhambra Cottage

Alhambra Cottage, 9 Boundary Road, is a most charming survival built by sculptor Henry Sibson (1795–1870),[100] who sadly had to turn the lease over to his creditors as soon as he had obtained it from Walpole in 1846 (Plate 272). He was therefore never able to enjoy this very special house. Its survival is miraculous as it is sited very close to the railway line – the London extension of the Manchester, Sheffield and Lincolnshire Railway. But like Tom Hood's house in Finchley Road, it escaped demolition and found loving owners in 1972 when the British Railways Board put it up for sale.[101]

Walpole had described Alhambra Cottage as 'the house (with round domes on the top) on the South side of Boundary Road (I think the last house on that side) built by and to be leased to Mr Henry Sibson'.[102] But the domes are no more and all the internal ceilings have been redone.[103]

Below: **272** Mauritana Villa, now known as Alhambra Cottage, at 9 Boundary Road was built by 'modeller' Henry Sibson in 1846 and is almost certainly this sculptor's masterpiece. The house has survived though the twin domes have disappeared. Eyre estate archive (Bk of Drawings 5, 71 right).

Bottom: **273** Aloe Cottage on the eastern side of Wellington Road was Henry Sibson's first home on the St John's Wood estate. The lease to Henry Bowen, the second owner, has survived, dated 1 May 1849. Eyre estate archive (EE 2650/1/440).

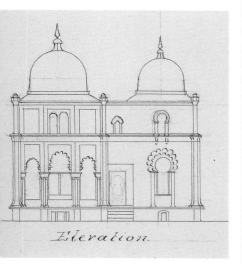

Elevation.

Elevation

Henry Sibson in St John's Wood

Sibson was a long-term St John's Wood resident who spent many years at Aloe Cottage on the eastern side of Wellington Road (Plate 273).[104] Following his change of fortune he was forced to find a smaller property in Cochrane Street (9 Douro Cottages).[105] Having described in his autobiography how the spiralling cost of Alhambra Cottage had compelled him 'to sacrifice our other little House [Aloe Cottage]', Sibson added: 'Early in November 1848 having let the little house to Mrs Rochfort we removed to the corner of Douro Cottages and Wellington Terrace having lived in our small house 18 years.'[106]

Sibson had also built Aloe Cottage, which was considerably more modest than Alhambra Cottage, though it, too, displayed exotic modelling work around the main entrance mildly evocative of Egypt rather than Spain. These early Islamic designs are interesting in relation to the craze for all things Egyptian which had swept Britain from the 1820s.[107] In St John's Wood, however, they are quite unique and judging by Sibson's 'Autobiography', 'Mauritana Villa' (as he then described Alhambra Cottage) cost him a fair amount of abuse:

> the scoffs of the insensate vulger [*sic*] well-to-do visitors during the day, their twaddling impertinent questions, and remarks…. in mitigation of my reputed folly in building such a house I may reply that had no one ever ventured from the beaten path what sort of houses should we now have again, the English and American people who are restless, and travelling peoples had grown in a measure tired of France, and even Italy, for the most beautiful things satiate in time, and therefore the desire to see the actual scenes of Oriental and ancient history, had already commenced and has now become a mania, and one or two families having this feeling have already inhabited the house to my chagrin and the Lucas's profit.[108]

He left a diary which gives a moving account of his life with its joys and difficulties. It was written for his son in 1869–70, after he had left London to settle in Stamford.[109] It records Sibson's career in great detail, from his apprenticeship to John Bacon, his brief period of work for Francis Chantrey (who hated 'cocknies'), his travels to France (he was employed to work on Notre Dame de Paris) and Switzerland, and his return to England. He found stability working for silversmiths, Benjamin Smith first and then Garrard's. Aloe Cottage was built with money he inherited from an aunt, but his financial troubles began when he lost his job at Garrard's: 'I shall never forget this period of my life, I could not find rest for my soul…. unfortunately at this time there existed one of those infamous commercial panics (the year 1846) spreading ruin everywhere.' Sibson attempted to sell the Boundary Road house, but 'there was not a single bidder the consequence was that Mr Lucas's Attorney took possession of the keys, and all documents, there and then'. Subsequently, Sibson worked on the Crystal Palace at Sydenham and also for Barry at Dulwich College. The final words of Sibson's candid account mixed lucidity and sadness: 'You have now an Outline of the life of an obscure Artist, one who has studied hard to gain excellence in his profession.'

PART TWO: FROM ST JOHN'S WOOD UNDERGROUND STATION TO SWISS COTTAGE

20 St John's Wood Underground Station/Eyre Arms Tavern

On 1 July 1933 the Metropolitan Railway was forced to amalgamate with the Underground group and others to form the London Passenger Transport Board. As a result of this a number of new stations were created when the Bakerloo line was extended from Baker Street to Finchley Road in 1935, making use of the line built by the Metropolitan Railway. On this site the station was first named Acacia Road because there was already a St John's Wood Station opposite Lord's 'nursery' end. When the latter's name changed to Lord's in June 1939, the Acacia Road Station was renamed St John's Wood. However, by the end of November 1939, the decision to close both Lord's and Marlborough Road stations was implemented, leaving this Underground station as the main transport provider.[110]

The station was built on the site of the house and garden of one of the Wood's most celebrated sculptors: Edward Onslow Ford (1852–1901). He moved here in 1887, extending the original 1841 property (see p. 462).[111] But there is another, earlier, layer of association which connects this site to the great Victorian chef, Alexis Soyer (1810–58). Westminster City Council recently unveiled a plaque at his last home at 28 Marlborough Place,[112] but the Acacia Road site is arguably where the perfect Victorian housewife, the 'Modern Ménagère', was born. There, at Bifrons Villa, lived Mrs Baker, a

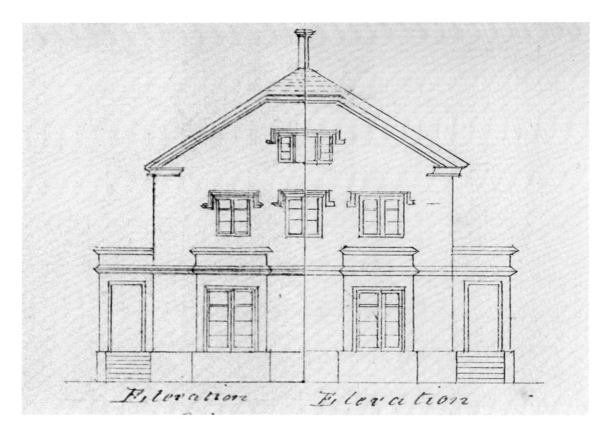

274 Charles (or George) Leigh's charming double house stood on the site of Birley Lodge in Acacia Road opposite St John's Wood Station. The two lease drawings (one for each semi-detached house) are both dated June 1839. Eyre estate archive (Bk of Drawings IV, 13 right and 14 right).

'The Modern Housewife or Ménagère'

In this book by Alexis Soyer, the author sets out an epistolary dialogue between a perfect hostess, Hortense or Mrs B[aker], from Bifrons Villa, St John's Wood, and her young friend Heloise or Mrs L. from Oatlands Cottage outside London: 'I, "Mrs B.", and you, "Mrs L.", humble but domesticated women, have had a friendly correspondence respecting housewifery in all its branches.' The key to the book's success is 'extravagant lifestyle on a budget', as one of its reviewers put it. Hortense writes that the neighbours 'flattered me with the appellation of the "Model Housekeeper", and admired the comforts of our table, but would leave with the impression that I must be the most extravagant of wives' (p. ix). Mrs B. dispels this incorrect impression and, like Heloise, the reader is expected to adopt Mrs B.'s 'system of management as closely as possible'. Early on in the book (p.xi) the special culinary requirements of an average middle-class family are summarised by the head of a family:

> there are ten of us in the family – viz., myself and wife, three children, two female servants, and three young men employed in my business, and including our usual Christmas party … two separate birthday parties of twenty each, and three juvenile petits-soupers and dances for the children upon their natal anniversaries, besides a friend dropping in occasionally, which is never less than once or twice a week[.]

The book's 1850 edition has been used above. But in 1853 Mrs B.'s change of circumstances as the result of a 'too bold speculation' was duly noted in the preface. Mrs B. was no longer at Bifrons Villa, St John's Wood, but at Camelia Cottage, Rugby. In the narrative Mrs B. tells her younger friend Mrs L.: 'Mr B. has obtained a situation as head clerk on the Railway. Though our position,

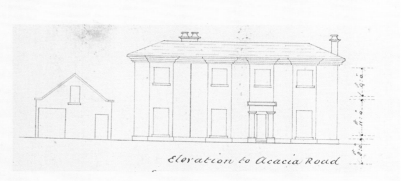

Elevation to Acacia Road

dearest, is far from being so flourishing as it has been for the last ten years, I assure you we are quite as happy and more settled in mind. The comforts of a little cottage have easily made me forget the beautiful, but troublesome elegance of Bifrons Villa.'

Above: **275** Lease drawing for Bifrons Villa which was built in 1841 and stood at 62 Acacia Road now the site of the underground station. The Eyre estate (Bk of Drawings IV, 78 Right).

This 'Soyer relish' bottle is decorated with the portrait of the famous chef Alexis Soyer. His relish was sold by Crosse & Blackwell between 1849 and 1929. The Reform Club, London.

good friend of Alexis and from their passionate discussions about food was born Alexis Soyer's bestseller book: *The Modern Housewife or Ménagère*, first published in 1849.[113] The book, reprinted many times and with an American edition, sold 30,000 copies between 1849 and 1853.[114]

Across Acacia Road, where Mr Leigh's picturesque double house once stood (Plate 274), is the towering Birley Lodge (1971–75, Sanders & Westbrook). Leigh's 1839 houses survived until 1920 when the painter Sir Oswald Birley (1880–1952) acquired the site. He took the decision to demolish them and commissioned Clough Williams-Ellis to build a brand new studio-house.[115] He lived there for twenty-nine years, and his presence is commemorated in the name 'Birley Lodge'.

Across Wellington Road stood the Eyre Arms Tavern with its sparkling assembly rooms and pleasure gardens, a significant landmark in St John's Wood which has totally disappeared. The last manager, H. M. Willing, apparently salvaged the 'series of rare lithographs & engravings of scenes and characters from Dickens after well-known artists, which hung on the walls of the saloon'. Everything else was sold in January 1929 prior to the demolition of the Regency coaching inn.[116] On the site of the Eyre Arms stands Eyre Court, aptly described as 'monstrous' in Pevsner.[117] However distinguished the architecture by T. P. Bennett & Son, its scale is quite intimidating and completely at odds with the houses which formerly stood on this site. In his autobiography Bennett pointed out: 'Almost for the first time a block of West End accommodation was devoid of internal areas, its great open courtyard was a feature. It dispensed with external railings giving a more intimate appearance. It provided parking spaces for cars.... The property world rated it as a landmark and so did the Architectural Association. I was told that the AA staff put a ban on any students' design which showed a plan for flats, more than two features of which were recognisable as "Bennett's flats".'[118] The Czech painter Oskar Kokoschka (1886–1980) took a flat there with his wife, at No. 120, around the same time as he became a British citizen in 1947. They lived there until 1953 when they moved to Lake Geneva, although they apparently retained the flat until at least 1980.[119] In Great Britain Kokoschka is perhaps best known for the panoramic views of the Thames he produced in the 1950s and 1960s.

On the other side of Grove End Road, the slightly smaller Wellington Court stands on the last corner of this disfigured crossroads. Less intimidating than Eyre Court it, too, defies the original scale of St John's Wood 'villadom'.

21 Wellington Road

Surprisingly, a small number of the original houses have survived on the east side of Wellington Road: for instance, Nos 18 and 20 as well as Nos 6 and 8 – the main double houses dating from 1830 were first leased to the surveyor John White. Even the strange mixture of styles at Nos 14 and 16 seems to have been applied over the original small double house, which was also leased to John White in 1826.[120] No 24 – with its blue plaque to celebrate Madame Marie Tussaud (1761–1850) (see Appendix 10) – is another example of survival of the original building.[121]

The approach to Lord's Cricket Ground from this side affords a good back view of the seemingly 'suspended' pod which was designed to house 250 sports journalists. This strikingly original creation, the Natwest Media Centre, was built to meet the demands of the 1999 World Cup. Made of aluminium, it was designed by Future Systems and won that year's Stirling Prize for architecture.

22 Cavendish Avenue

For just over twenty years, between 1817 and 1839, this part of the Wood formed the site of a very large nursery run by John Gibbs. When Gibbs moved to another part of the estate, the ground was eventually taken over by another nurseryman, Eli Cook, in 1839. However, Cook was immediately in difficulty over the rent and the ground was gradually taken over by building developers. Cavendish Avenue, originally known as Lennard Place and then Cavendish Road, was formed around 1840 and handed over to the parish in 1841.[122]

276 and **277** 19 Cavendish Road, then and now: the drawing dates from 1843 when No. 19 and surrounding houses were leased to developers Newton & Kelk. The photograph on the right was taken by Cluttons in 2007 when the house was sold. Eyre estate archive (Bk of Drawings IV, 66 left).

The houses on the west side of the road have mostly survived unscathed, whereas a number of the houses on the east side have been demolished and rebuilt. The three main developers at work in this part of the Wood were Newton & Kelk on the east and west sides (including Cavendish Close), James Salter on the east side (south end) and Charles Freeth junior on the east side (north end). The grandest of the houses built by Newton & Kelk in 1843 survives at No. 19 on the corner of Cavendish Place and Cavendish Close (Plates 276 and 277).[123]

At 24 Cavendish Avenue the house on the present site is a modern pastiche which gives little idea of the lavish studio-house which once stood on this plot (Plates 279 and 281), that of painter Thomas Faed (1826–1900). The original property is well documented from its origins in 1843 when it was leased to the Oxford Street solicitor William Joseph Thrupp (from Burgoynes Thrupp & Clark), who was developing the first four houses on the corner of Wellington Place and Cavendish Avenue (east side).[124]

Although the architectural drawings of 1876 are all in Faed's name and he was described as 'proprietor' in this studio project, he was an ordinary tenant (with an underlease).[125] Faed's death gave the lawyers of his executors six full years of work, but the property was eventually taken over in 1906 by another Scottish artist, James Dick-Peddie (exh. 1885–1918).[126]

Thomas Faed and his brother John must have had a soft spot for this road. Thomas had been based at 1 Cavendish Road for nearly ten years (Plate 278), followed by John (listed at 1a Cavendish Road), the latter only moving to 38 St John's Wood Road when the estate refused to grant a licence for building a studio (see p. 289).

On the east side of Cavendish Road are two blocks made up of three houses each. This cross between a double house and a terrace was peculiar to Cavendish Avenue, although there are one or two other examples to be found on the 1853 map. The houses at Nos 4, 6 and 8 date from around 1840 and were built by Newton & Kelk.[127]

No. 3 Cavendish Avenue on the west side was a later infill built by Hibberd (presumably Jacob, of Queen's Grove and St Ann's Terrace fame) as late as 1862.[128]

23 Circus Road and the Hospital of St John and St Elizabeth

Circus Road commemorates the 'British Circus' which had been planned by Henry Samuel Eyre for the north-west of the estate as early as 1794. Its story is related in Chapter 2. There is nothing circular about Circus Road,[129] and it is positioned too far south to be connected to the site of the gigantic green circus which had then been conceived. Nevertheless, the project was very dear to the Eyres, and though not realised, it is commemorated here in a symbolic way.

The main entrance to the Hospital of St John and St Elizabeth is now in Grove End Road on the site of the former Loudoun Hall, which replaced Ivy Lodge, the estate's largest house in the early days of development (this house was leased to George Barratt Lennard, sometimes spelt Leonard, in 1822, who clearly gave his name to Lennard Place before it was renamed Cavendish Road). In 1848, the state of this road was rendered problematic by the actions of lazy gardeners: 'I understand this Road is used by the different Gardeners who look after the Gentlemens Gardens in the neighbourhood as a Deposit for the Rubbish they collect from the different Gardens and amongst others I am informed that the person who looks after the Gardens and Ground at All Saints Church makes use of this Road for that purpose,' wrote Walpole.[130]

This hospital was originally conceived to be approached from Circus Road. The institution started life at 47 Great Ormond Street on a site adjacent to the famous children's hospital of that name which had opened in 1852. A Catholic dispensary attached to a convent opened there on 18 November 1856 (the feast day of St Elizabeth of Hungary). Indirectly supported by the resurrected Order of Malta and run by the Sisters of Mercy, who had distinguished themselves at Scutari during the Crimean War (working alongside Florence Nightingale), the establishment grew slowly: within two years the original twenty beds had increased to twenty-five, 106 patients having been treated in 1858.[131] The Catholic hospital acquired a splendid permanent chapel in 1863; financed by Sir George Bowyer, who was closely involved with the revival of the Order of Malta, it was designed by George Goldie and built 'in the Italian baroque style particularly favoured by Anglican converts to Rome'.[132] This chapel was moved stone by stone from its original site in Great Ormond Street to Circus Road, to become the centrepiece of the new hospital after the decision was taken to move the cramped institution to enlarged premises at St John's Wood. The foundation stone of the new hospital, usual. The nursery sited at the far end of the road is visible on the 1883 map (see Plate 208) and also on the 1903 estate map. The original lease for land on the southern side of Garden Road went to 'Mr Chandless' in 1823, and as if to labour the point, its drawing records a strip of land next to Garden Road in the hands of a Mr Gardener![141] There are early references in the letter books to two nurseries which were side by side, one headed by James Gulley (see p. 156), the other by James Whitton.[142]

28 Hamilton Gardens and panorama

Although this land formed part of the original St John's Wood estate, it was developed by James Ponsford, a Paddington architect-builder who in the early 1840s purchased the plot bounded by Garden Road, Abbey Road, Hill Road and the Harrow School estate.[143] At first the formula for development seems to have been based on that of the Eyre estate (Plate 286), but builders subcontracted by Ponsford clearly settled for a more modest appearance. Closely knit three-storey houses of low height were built with virtually no gardens, front or back, the name of the narrow road – Hamilton Gardens – making up for this deficiency. Nevertheless, the area is now very pretty with its colourful planting and façades; a resident has used the cul-de-sac area on the south-west corner of Hamilton Gardens for the pavement display of potted plants. That corner also has a panoramic view looking towards Hamilton Terrace (Harrow School estate). It offers no spectacular features

286 This drawing comes from a mortgage deed dated 15 December 1858 between James Ponsford, Reverend John J. Saint and Charles Harrison. It shows the houses that were built by Ponsford in Hill Road and Abbey (now Abercorn) Place between 1842 and 1846 (described as 'seven messuages'). They formed part of an ambitious scheme which aimed to cover the south side of Hill Road (top) with villas and was the object of a mortgage of £14,060 in 1846. Twelve years on, none of the other houses had materialised and the mortgage was still outstanding. However, all of these houses have survived. Private collection.

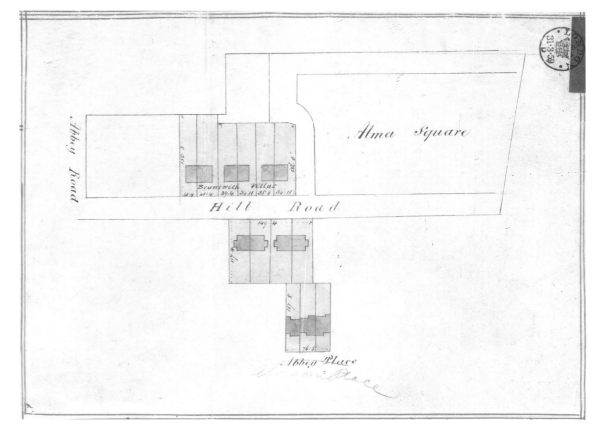

Left: **287** Members of the St John's Wood Clique are shown decorating Hodgson's house in Hill Road 'one winter season', probably in the 1860s or 1870s. The central figure may be George Dunlop Leslie, who 'painted the duel scene from *Twelfth Night*', with George Storey above, wearing glasses and painting Katherine and Petruchio. W. F. Yeames, who tackled a scene from *As You Like It*, may be at the back smoking a pipe, while Calderon is on the right (see Plate 288); the faint figure in the left background could be H. Stacy Marks, who had chosen a scene from *The Tempest* and was probably the self-effacing author of the drawing, which was first reproduced in his 1894 volume, *Pen and Pencil Sketches*, as 'chronicler' of the clique's 'social acts'. Eyre estate archive (Montgomery-Eyre, 1913, opp. p. 188).

but is refreshingly green, as is the nearby Alma Square, a communal garden for the benefit of the residents in lieu of back gardens.

There was an attempt on the part of Ponsford to build a church fronting Abbey Road in the early 1850s.[144] However, in order to carry out this scheme, permission was needed from the estate, since one of the sale's covenants stated the land should only be developed building *residential* houses. On this occasion the Eyre estate were particularly unhelpful, arguing they had no power to change the covenant and implying they might sue Ponsford for breach of covenant. A letter stated that the parties interested in the estate 'do not appear to think that the erection of the Chapel will be a great benefit to the neighbourhood, but rather injurious to the adj[oinin]g property than o[the]rwise'.[145] James Ponsford was forced to back down.

Nugent Terrace

A booklet, 'Remember Nugent Terrace St. Johns Wood', traced the arrival of shops on that site to 1867.[146] It was written in memory of Harry Mark Jordan (1883–1990), who set up his boot repair shop at No. 1a in 1919; the family business lasted until 1990 when a street party was organised to mark its closing.

29 Hill Road

As previously mentioned the land on either side of Hill Road originally formed part of the estate. Unlike the 'close houses' of Alma Square, the villas of Hill Road are, in spirit, very similar to those of St John's Wood. They were built by James Ponsford, who was well connected with the Eyre estate since he had worked there with developers Leigh and Treeby (see Appendix 9). Ponsford was responsible for a group of houses which included the following:[147]

- 11 Hill Road (formerly 6 Brunswick Villas), the home of the engraver Thomas Lewis Atkinson (1817–c.1890), a regular exhibitor at the Royal Academy, who was based at this address for at least seven years (1877–84) but lived in the neighbourhood for longer still.
- 10 Hill Road (formerly 5 Hill Road), a favourite haunt for the St John's Wood Clique (see below).
- 12 Hill Road (formerly 6 Hill Road), where Mary Hervey lived with her sister, 'la mystérieuse' Mrs Newton, who so attracted painter James Tissot when they first met in 1875 or 1876.[148] Mrs Newton subsequently went to live with Tissot at 17 Grove End Road.

10 Hill Road was the home and studio of John Evan Hodgson, a member of the St John's Wood Clique, for just over thirty years between 1858 and 1889. The walls of Hodgson's painting room ('two ordinary rooms knocked into one') were decorated by members of the clique with murals of near life-size figures mostly on Shakespearean themes (Plate 287). This is how Stacy Marks described the project:

> The walls were covered with paper and coloured in distemper of a uniform greenish-grey tint. On this ground the decorations were painted in oil colour, in flat tones, with the least possible amount of shadow and a definite outline. Leslie painted the duel scene from *Twelfth Night*: Storey, Katherine and Petruchio. A scene from *The Tempest*, and

Far left: **288** This work by Philip Calderon is from a series of (destroyed) mural paintings by the founder members of the St John's Wood Clique at Hodgson's house in Hill Road. Calderon's painting 'occupied a space over the fireplace with portraits of Hodgson and Mrs Hodgson in Elizabethan costume', explained Montgomery Eyre. Eyre estate archive (Montgomery-Eyre, 1913, opp. p. 182).

Left: **289** *Touchstone and Audrey*, painted by Stacy Marks, is a work from a series of (destroyed) mural paintings by the founder members of the St John's Wood Clique at Hodgson's house in Hill Road. Eyre estate archive (Montgomery-Eyre, 1913, opp. p. 195).

Touchstone and Audrey fell to my share. The most elaborate composition, Rosalind, Celia, and Orlando, after the wrestling in *As You Like It*, was by Yeames. Calderon occupied a space over the fireplace with portraits of Hodgson and Mrs Hodgson in Elizabethan costume [Plates 288 and 289]. It is a long time since I saw these works.... Hodgson eventually built a studio adjoining his house, and the decorated room was devoted to domestic requirements; but when I last saw them, some years after they had been executed, they were in excellent condition.[149]

The murals have now disappeared, and the only visual records are the photographs taken in 1913 for Montgomery Eyre's book on St John's Wood.

30 Abbey Road (1) and Langford Place

The Baptist chapel on the east side of Abbey Road was built by W. G. Habershon and Pite and opened its doors in 1864. It cost just over £6,000 to build after the ground was purchased for £2,000.[150] It is discussed in some detail in Chapter 9, but this is how Reverend William Stott, its first pastor and guiding light, described choosing the architectural style: 'there is no architecture more suited to our wants than the Elizabethan and Italian styles of building; or such design as gives the preacher full command over, and unbroken view of, his audience.' The final outcome was this chapel: 'planned for us, in the Byzantine style, and capable of seating one thousand persons, with schoolroom underneath'. The pastor and his committee attracted vast crowds by inviting the famous Baptist preachers of the day to come to their meetings – C. H. Spurgeon, Sir Morton Peto[151] and Dr Angus from the Regent's Park Baptist College. They even boldly wrote to Napoleon III, remembering that 'he was once a refugee and lived in St. John's Wood … [and] asking for a small donation'. The diplomatic reply was that 'the portion of money which he annually devoted to religious institutions was exhausted, or he would have been pleased to send a contribution to St John's Wood'.[152] However, the crowds of eager chapel-goers disappeared a long time ago, and the chapel was turned into flats in 2007–9.

Langford Place

In the days of the developer William Hall, whose land it was, Langford Place was a cul-de-sac. Hall succeeded in building two houses on the north side and one on the south by the mid-1820s. When he was in financial difficulty the properties were assigned to various parties, one of these being Richard Powell, who succeeded in purchasing the freehold of a substantial section of Langford Place in 1841.[153] Walpole made two attempts at opening up the east end of Langford Place: first in 1828, then in 1844, but he was unsuccessful.[154] Richard Powell was apparently determined not to pay a penny towards the cost of road making. It is unclear how or when the situation was resolved; in 1846, the road was still unfinished,[155] but by the mid-1850s Langford Place had been opened up to Loudoun Road (see Plate 70).

Perhaps the most interesting group of houses in Langford Place is Nos 12–16 on the north side. William Hall's 1825 house, later known as 'Sunnyside', has survived at No. 14, having acquired a striking glazed bay window on the main floor; it originally stood in a very large garden with its own

290 Laura Knight painted *Spring in St John's Wood* in 1933 from the home she and her husband Harold shared at Langford Place. The view, looking south, depicts the gardens of houses fronting Abbey Road on the east side. The twin towers of Abbey Road Chapel (taken down and re-erected in 2009) are clearly visible in the right background. The house on the right was leased to the developer William Hall in 1825, and the tennis court shows off the generous size of gardens in this development. Walker Art Gallery, Liverpool.

stable, but after the sculptor John Adams-Acton moved in with his St John's Wood-based wife Jeanie (also known as Hering), things started changing. He lived at this address from summer 1882 and immediately commissioned Joseph Tall to build a spacious studio alongside Sunnyside (where No. 16 now stands).[156] In the book of Jeanie Hering's recollections, its unusual fabric is recorded:

> Mr Tall, the architect,[157] was deputed to build the new studios, while in contradistinction the man to whom was entrusted the planning of the garden was a Mr Short. A little ceremony was performed when laying the foundation-stone of the new buildings. Under it Adams-Acton buried a great stone pot in which was placed an account of his family together with their portraits, and a little piece of carving done by him as a young boy.... Subsequently the studios for carving and painting rose rapidly, being constructed of concrete; above them was erected a sculpture gallery eighty feet long by thirty feet wide, reaching high into a glass dome. Even after the completion of these buildings, there remained, besides the large house and stables, a spacious and well-stocked garden with an arbour on one side for the adults and one opposite for the children, so that in summer-time all meals could be taken out of doors under the cool shade of the trees, while a large conservatory, with casements opening to the lawn, afforded a sheltered sitting-room in colder weather.[158]

Whether this studio was demolished or incorporated into the fabric of No. 16 is hard to tell. No. 16 has acquired a blue plaque to record the residence of another couple of distinguished artists – Harold and Laura Knight. Laura produced a most vibrant painting from the upper floor of this house (Plate 290).

But by far the most striking building of this group is No. 12, a Gothic folly which appears to have been built in the early years of the twentieth century. It stands on the site formerly occupied by the stables and may have been the brainchild of Mrs Edith Pigott, who moved here in January 1909.[159] This is how John Betjeman referred to it:

> Amidst all this frivolity,
> In one place
> A sinister note is struck –
> In that helmeted house where, rumour has it
> The Reverend John Hugh Smyth-Pigott lived,
> An Anglican clergyman
> Whose Clapton congregation declared him to be Christ,
> A compliment he accepted.[160]

31 Loudoun Road

15 Loudoun Road is remarkable because it has not been modernised in the way most St John's Wood houses have been. It was originally leased to James Jones in 1848,[161] an ironmonger in Oxford Street, and was clearly squeezed into the back gardens of the present 13–15 Blenheim Road.[162] No. 15 was the home of the poet Sir Stephen Spender (1909–95) between 1945 and 1995.[163] His widow, Lady Spender, has embarked on the massive task of editing her husband's journals. A former concert pianist, she has been a lessee of the Eyre estate for well over sixty years.

Across the road stands a group of 'Gothic' houses which were originally leased to the architect Samuel Erlam in 1846, suggesting he was responsible for their design. Indeed they recall, in a simplified manner, the style he and his partner John Pink had adopted when designing their landmark building in St John's Wood: the original St Marylebone Almshouses in St John's Wood Terrace (see Plate 253).[164]

32 Carlton Hill

When this road was first made in the late 1840s, it was known as Wotton Road. The Blenheim public house (occupied by Café Med at the time of writing) was built by and leased to Messrs Fry in 1851, and appears to have been the first building leased in that road, closely followed by two double houses in 1852, of which half of one survives at No. 36.[165] It is very tall and sets a different scale for building which seems to have influenced what was built in this street.

At No. 6 is a plaque commemorating the presence of architect C. F. A. Voysey (Plate 291).[166] He lived at this address between 1895 and 1899, after spending five years at 11 Melina Place.

291 This photoprint shows the study of C. F. A. Voysey at 6 Carlton Hill, the architect's second St John's Wood residence in the 1890s. RIBA Library Photographs Collection.

substantial tracts of land on either side of the eastern section of Boundary Road were sold to become large council estates.

The highly original council estate which replaced the villas on the south side of the railway line is the Alexandra Road estate. It has resolutely turned its back on the railway line, with the highest blocks 'shielding' the development from the noise of the trains: they are fully insulated and anti-vibration pads have apparently been incorporated into the foundations.[178] The Alexandra Road estate is a Grade II building (since 1993) designed by a team from the Architects' Department of the Borough of Camden, led by Neave Brown. It was built between 1972 and 1979 and was in full occupation by the latter date. It is unusual in being low rise and high density: 1,660 people in 520 dwellings on a site of just fourteen acres. The estate is made up of five six-storey blocks nearest the railway, facing three four-storey blocks across a pedestrian street, and another three blocks of terraced town houses complete the scheme on the south side beyond a public park (this arrangement is clearly visible in Plate 228). In 2006, a two-bedroom maisonette occupying the two upper storeys of a unit in one of the four-storey concrete terraces was open to the public as part of Open House Weekend. It is designed 'upside down' to give the living/kitchen/dining rooms the best light and panoramic views (an exhilarating decision), the bedrooms being placed on the lower floor. The maisonette has retained many of its relatively high specification features, including colourful tiling in the kitchen, wooden cupboards and window frames (the estate was spot listed in 1993 to stop their replacement with UPVC, among other issues).[179]

At the eastern end of the Alexandra Road estate in Rowley Way stands All Souls Church in Loudoun Road, which seated 585 in its heyday, less than half the capacity of the Baptist church. Its design is credited to J. F. Wadmore (the brother of the vicar). It became redundant in 1985 and by the late 1990s was recorded as Grace Chapel (Celestial Church of God).[180] At the time of writing it is being converted into flats, in the footsteps of Abbey Road Baptist Church (also see p. 337).

36 Belsize Road and weeping willow

This difficult part of the estate, a fairly narrow strip squeezed between railway line and estate boundary line, was ably developed by Robert Yeo. The presence of terraced houses does not show a drop in building standards, as has sometimes been argued,[181] but is consistent with the 'walling in' policy which was exercised on parts of the estate close to the boundary line (see p. 128). However, despite Yeo's elegant device, over the years this neighbourhood suffered from similar social ills to the 'walling in' at St John's Wood Terrace near Portland Town or that at Lisson Grove near the Portman estate. In the mid-1950s the Communist party described the Belsize Road area as overcrowded crumbling houses where apparently 2,372 people were living in 369 houses.[182] The villas which overlooked the railway line have long been demolished, replaced by fourteen blocks designed by A. Clarke and built between 1932 and 1936;[183] however, Yeo's terraced houses on the north side have been restored to their former glory.

The magnificent willow in the middle of the roundabout thrives on that site because its need for water is almost certainly met by the former presence of a pond and river. They are marked on the 1733 map of the estate just beneath the dip in the north-western boundary (the river is clearly depicted on Plate 27). The other large street willow on the estate which benefited from a similar situation was that found at the end of Acacia Place on the south side of the Barracks wall; the tree drew its water from the farm pond so attractively depicted by Harriott Gouldsmith in 1819 (see Plate 41).[184]

37 Fairfax and Harben Roads

The original villas and terraced houses of Fairfax (formerly Victoria) Road were developed in the 1850s and 1860s and destroyed a hundred years later in the 1960s. By September 1962 most of the housing blocks on the south side were built or under construction (Elgar House, Newton and Gladstone Courts) and the demolition of the terrace on the north side was announced, stating that by summer 1963, 'three quarters of the road will have been rebuilt, by Leonards (Builders) Ltd, with new shops, flats and houses'.[185]

By far the largest Victorian villa in this road was at No. 11, just opposite Harben (formerly Albion) Road, originally leased to Admiral Lord George Paulet in 1862.[186] The lessee in the 1880s was J. R. Clayton, of Clayton & Bell, the stained glass firm, who applied to the estate for permission to insert bay windows in 1881.[187] Five years later Clayton commissioned the photographic firm of Bedford Lemere to make a record of his library, dining and drawing rooms, though alas the photographs cannot now be traced.[188] At 8 (later 16) Albion Road lived the famous architect Richard Norman Shaw (1831–1912), who is briefly mentioned in the Eyre letter books over a rent mix-up.[189]

The Harben estate was designed by a private firm of architects, Norman and Dawbarn, between 1954 and 1959 but not built until the 1960s. Just under 200 flats are spread across five blocks. It was regarded as a 'showpiece' estate in the 1960s and entered for a Ministry of Housing 'Good Design in Housing' competition (alongside the Goldsmith Place estate designed by Hampstead Borough Council's own architect, C. E. Jacob).[190]

38 Swiss Cottage

Just as the southern part of the estate is no longer regarded as being in St John's Wood, the same is true of the northern section. Yet Swiss Cottage and neighbouring streets fell well within the estate, and the creation of the Swiss Cottage Tavern by George Spencer Smith, a friend of the Eyre family, seems to have been close to Walpole's heart (see p. 210). The inn which gave its name to this part of the estate has gone through a number of different incarnations (as is clear from Plates 293–96). The present inn was refurbished in 1965, and its then owners, Chef and Brewer Houses, claimed it would be 'the largest pub in England' with no fewer than thirteen bars and four restaurants.[191] At the time of writing, Ye Olde Swiss Cottage, refurbished in the mid-1980s, is a Samuel Smith pub.[192] It was at Swiss Cottage that the writer Wilkie Collins, son of the landscape painter William, first came across 'the woman in white' whom he would much later turn into the famous novel of the same name (see p. 314).

The area drew its vitality from the presence of a toll-gate at the apex of the Swiss Cottage triangle on the Finchley Road, formerly called the Marylebone and Finchley Turnpike Road (Plate 121 records the appearance of this toll-gate prior to its dismantling). While it created difficulties to the developer of the area, William Holme Twentyman (see pp. 229–30), it also created opportunities

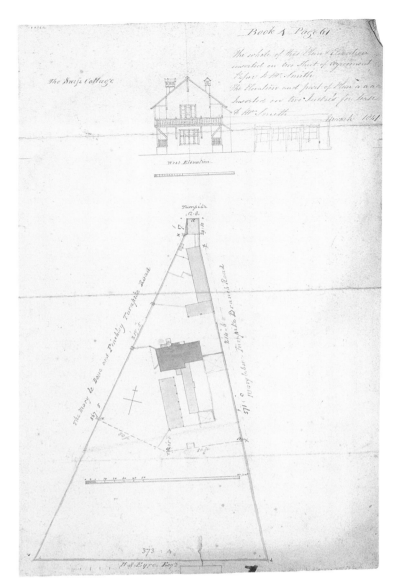

293 The lease drawing for the Swiss Cottage Tavern is dated 1841, but there is evidence the tavern was open by at least 1837 (see p. 210). This picture records the first incarnation of this establishment and its siting on the triangular plot. Eyre estate archive (Bk of Drawings IV, 61 right).

Top: **294** This picture of the Swiss Cottage was reproduced in *The Pictorial Times* of 12 April 1845. It is a more atmospheric rendering of the tavern's first design, including its most distinctive features, the balcony and overhanging roof. Camden Local Studies (LSQ).

Above: **295** By about 1900 the ground floor of the Swiss Cottage had been remodelled, but it was still essentially the building of the 1830s. Camden Local Studies (N5911, LSQ).

since the Swiss Cottage Tavern quickly became a favourite resort. In 1852, a licence was granted for various modifications to the tavern, including that 'the small building at the North end of the s[ai]d piece or parcel of ground … may be used and occupied as a Dairy or shop for the sale of Milk by retail and of such other things as are usually sold by a Dairyman or Milkman'.[193] These premises were taken over by a wine merchant in 1871, and plans to build a large hotel on that site in 1886–87 seem to have come to nothing.[194]

Although some fairly large buildings were erected all around the tavern in Victorian times – notably the School for the Blind (Plate 297), New College (immediately outside the Eyre estate), New College Chapel (Eyre estate) and 'Sunnyside' beneath the School for the Blind, which was the largest house on the estate and became a 'Home for Invalids' around 1893[195] – the present building scale still looks gigantic in comparison with its past incarnation. The enormous and intimidating road interchange perhaps dictates the size of the twentieth-century contribution, which may be divided into two parts: before and after the war.

War damage is often evoked to justify the presence of the twentieth century on the streets of St John's Wood. However, judging by the recently published war damage maps of the London County Council (see Plate 219), the impact of bomb damage seems to have been often overestimated. Direct hits on Swiss Cottage and St John's Wood Park resulted in the destruction of fewer than a dozen houses, the rest of the damage being less serious.

Already in the 1930s, at the northern tip of the estate and beyond, New College and most of College Crescent were pulled down and replaced by Northways, two concrete blocks of flats built by London & City Real Estate.[196] Most of the Swiss Cottage triangle was also redeveloped at that time, with the building of a cinema (the 1937–38 Swiss Cottage Odeon was designed by Harry Weedon) and Regency Lodge (1938–40), a large block of 107 flats by Robert Atkinson which has been described, perhaps unfairly, as 'good, but a trifle stodgy'.[197]

The top part of Belsize Road only recently became a cul-de-sac (see Plate 296). The area was described as 'decrepit' in 1962, but the decision to shut the road seems to have drained this section

Below: **296** When this photograph was taken in the twentieth century, the 'restaurant' at the apex of the triangular plot looked more Chinese than Swiss. It was no doubt the converted dairy which first appeared in 1852. The photograph also records the original size of Finchley Road (behind the lamppost in the middle of the road) and Avenue Road (left-hand side). These were the original turnpike roads at St John's Wood. The opening on the right, now sadly blocked, is Belsize Road. Camden Local Studies (N5379, LSQ).

of all its life. This was the price to pay for the enlargement of Finchley Road into a six-lane highway and the erection of a 'modern 10-storey block of shops, offices and flats, more than 100 feet high … to go up on the corner of Finchley Road and Belsize Road'. The development was masterminded by Arthur B. Blomfield of Aral Investments Ltd, who confidently announced that he wanted 'to build it [the area] up into a wonderful place far better than either Kensington or Knightsbridge'. He added that Sir Basil Spence had seen the plans of the first phase of the development by Douglas Stephen & Partner and was 'very impressed'. By the mid-1960s the complex was ready with 'seven shops (one of supermarket size), five floors of offices covering more than 20,000 square feet, and, above them, about 40 one and three bedroom flats and penthouses, all with their own balconies'.[198]

These large-scale developments seem to have set the tone for a new giant scale at this junction, which was espoused by architect Basil Spence (1907–76) when he designed his scheme for a civic centre in 1959 on the site of the 1847 School for the Blind, St Columba's Hospital (the latter housed in the former 'Sunnyside' house originally leased in 1850) and New College Chapel.[199] Only part of Spence's original scheme was carried out: the library and adjoining swimming baths, which were opened in 1964.[200]

297 This lithograph of the School for the Blind at Swiss Cottage, by E. T. Dolby, was published by Day & Son, c.1860. Designed by H. E. Kendall junior, the school was a major landmark in that part of the estate for almost a hundred years between 1847 and 1941 (see Plate 116 and p. 211). Its site is now 100 Avenue Road and part of the Swiss Cottage Park. City of London, London Metropolitan Archives.

After Spence more developments followed suit with Centre Heights by Douglas Stephen (1961–64), Cresta House at 133 Finchley Road by J. S. Bonnington Partnership (1970–75) and 100 Avenue Road by Levy Benjamin Horvitch (1986).

In 1998, Camden Council decided to redevelop Sir Basil Spence's library and leisure centre to provide new community facilities including a theatre. The following year the council invited tenders for the leisure centre and housing (including 25 per cent affordable units) and also staged a competition for the public park and leisure centre site. The favourite, Terry Farrell & Partners, was chosen as lead architect with S & P Architects for the leisure centre interiors and Gustafson Porter for the open space. Restoration of the baths was not viable and they had to be demolished, while the library was refurbished in 2001–4 by architects John McAslan + Partners, who were careful to preserve the essential features of the original scheme during restoration. The housing is provided by a bold tower – the Visage – designed by Terry Farrell. The open space, Swiss Cottage Park (2003–6), was praised in the *Building Design* review: 'the Anglo-American practice's work should be warmly applauded as it goes some considerable way to transforming an ad-hoc assembly of pretty low-wattage buildings into a convincing place.... Gustafson Porter's scheme wisely doesn't ask the surrounding elevations to work too hard. Extensive tree planting around the perimeter will, once matured, partially obscure the facades, creating a space of grove-like intimacy at the development's heart. It is here that we find the water feature that so agitated Conservative councillors after the closure of the Diana Memorial Fountain.'[201] The redevelopment scheme was completed in 2007.

The rising building scale that can be observed at this particular junction is now symbolically 'embedded' in the sport centre's 'theatrical' climbing wall, which is described by Terry Farrell and Partners: 'The main Adelaide Road façade is dominated by a climbing wall – with all the colour and paraphernalia that goes with the sport.... The theatrics of the climbing wall will create a striking night display, with a show of colour, changing floodlights, fluorescent lights, UV cannon lights on fluorescent painted climbing wall and LED lights embedded in the climbing surface.'

APPENDIX 1
Key to the Alpha Cottages reconstruction: archival information

The reconstruction and the plan are at Plates 62 and 63.
The lessees' names which are <u>underlined</u> were ratepayers in 1815.

1 PUBLIC HOUSE 'The Nightingale'. Original agreement with Messrs Hemming & Gymm, who subcontracted to builder William Storey, who went bankrupt. *Built* by Samuel Wild. *Lessee*: Samuel Wild. The lease for 53 years from Michaelmas 1811 is missing but mentioned at LB 'C', p. 50. Bk of Drawings I, 4.

2 DOUBLE HOUSE. Original agreement with William Atkinson. Probably *built* by James Davis. *Lessees*: William Atkinson, architect, and <u>James Davis</u>, builder. Lease dated 25 August 1812 for 57¼ years from summer of 1811 at EE 2650/1/250(I) and EE 2650/1/249. Rent: £10 per semi-detached house. Bk of Drawings I, 17.

3 DOUBLE HOUSE. Original agreement with Thomas Papworth (15 October 1804). *Built* by Thomas Papworth, plasterer. *Lessee*: <u>Charles Clifford</u>, shoemaker in Oxford Street. Lease dated 16 November 1807 for 58 years from Michaelmas 1807 at EE 2650/1/259(A and B). Rent: £6 per semi-detached house. Bk of Drawings I, 3 and 12.

4 DOUBLE HOUSE. Original agreement with Thomas Papworth (15 October 1804). *Built* by Thomas Papworth, plasterer. *Lessee*: Thomas Papworth. Lease dated 1 March 1810 for 56 years from Michaelmas 1809 at EE 2650/1/457(A). Rent: £18 per year. Bk of Drawings I, 12.

5 SINGLE HOUSE. Original agreement with James Biddle, tallow chandler (8 October 1804). *Built* by Thomas Papworth. *Lessee*: <u>Alexander Haselar</u>. Lease dated 29 August 1806 for 59 years from Michaelmas 1806 at EE 2651/12(A and B). Rent: £6 6s. per year. Not in Bk of Drawings.

6 DOUBLE HOUSE. Original agreement with Robert Todd (1 September 1804). *Built* by Thomas Martin. *Lessee*: Thomas Martin. Lease dated 2 May 1808 for 57½ years from Lady Day 1807 – counterpart lease at EE 2650/1/250(A). Rent: £12. Bk of Drawings I, 1A.

7 SINGLE HOUSE AND DOUBLE HOUSE. Original agreement with George and James Biddle. *Lessees*: George and James Biddle (counterpart lease at EE 2650/1/520 dated 17 November 1809; also see LB 'A', p. 802). Bk of Drawings I, 10.

8 SINGLE HOUSE. Original agreement with Robert Todd. *Built* by Robert Todd for his own residence. *Lessee*: <u>Robert Todd</u>. Bk of Drawings I, 8, October 1809, though the house was built by April 1806 (see LB 'A', p. 249). The lease is missing.

9 DOUBLE HOUSE. Original agreement with Robert Todd. *Built* by Thomas Hallett, gardener. *Lessee*: Thomas Hallett. Lease dated 7 December 1809 for 56 years from Michaelmas 1809 at EE 2650/1/186(A). Rent: £24 a year. Bk of Drawings I, 11. One of the houses sold a year later; see lease of 13 October 1810 at EE 2650/1/250(C). New lease dated 1 February 1836 at EE 2650/1/480(A).

10 DOUBLE HOUSE. Original agreement with Robert Todd (1 December 1804), sublet to Messrs Thomas and Drinkwater, then Francis Fenton. *Lessee*: Francis Fenton, hotel keeper in St James's Street. Lease dated 30 July 1814 for 52 years from Michaelmas 1813 at EE 2650/1/61(A). Rent: £24 a year. Bk of Drawings I, 2, August 1807.

11 SINGLE HOUSE. Original agreement with Robert Todd, then Francis Fenton (6 June 1805). *Lessee*: John Bennett, merchant from Welbeck Street. Lease dated 14 June 1817 for 48½ years from Lady Day 1817 at EE 2650/1/259(C). Rent: £12 a year. Bk of Drawings I, 30. New lease dated 9 May 1866 at EE 2650/1/40 (lessee: James Blyth).

12 SINGLE HOUSE. Formerly George Treble's premises. Original agreement with Robert Todd, then Francis Fenton (28 March 1806). *Lessee*: John Bennett, merchant from Welbeck Street. Lease dated 12 December 1818 for 47 years from Michaelmas 1818 at EE 2650/1/259(D). Rent £12 12s. a year. Bk of Drawings I, 36.

13 DOUBLE HOUSE. Original agreement with Robert Todd (1 December 1804). *Lessee*: Cornelius Dixon, printer in Berwick Street. Lease dated 10 November 1808 for 57 years from Michaelmas 1808 at EE 2650/1/250(B). Rent: £24 a year. Not in Bk of Drawings.

14 SINGLE HOUSE. Original agreement with Robert Todd (18 December 1805). *Built* by Thomas Papworth, plasterer. *Lessee*: <u>Mrs Eleanor Odell</u> (first female leaseholder). Lease dated 28 August 1812 for 53½ years from June 1812 at EE 2650/1/263(C). Rent: £12 a year. Bk of Drawings I, 21.

15 DOUBLE HOUSE. Original agreement with Robert Todd (18 December 1805). *Built* by Edward Smith, bricklayer from Mortimer Street. *Lessee*: Edward Smith. Lease dated 25 July 1817 for 48½ years from Lady Day 1817 – lease at EE 2650/1/442(A) and counterpart at EE 2650/1/275(B). Rent: £36 a year. Bk of Drawings I, 28.

16 DOUBLE HOUSE. Original agreement with Robert Todd (1 December 1804). Probably *built* by John Garner, carpenter from Berners Mews. *Lessee*: John Garner. Lease dated 16 November 1812 for 53 years from Michaelmas 1812 at EE 2650/1/434. Rent: £12 a year. Bk of Drawings I, 22. Alse see lease dated 31 July 1822 at EE 2650/1/456.

17 DOUBLE HOUSE. Original agreement with John Webber, gardener (1 November 1805). *Built* by Mr East? (See LB 'C', p. 313.) *Lessee*: Charles Blachford Rule, Esquire, from North Crescent, Bedford Square, and William Dalgleish, timber merchant from Limehouse. Dalgleish's lease dated 28 January 1815 is at EE 2650/1/275(A) and Rule's of the same date at WCA, 901/73. Robert Todd purchased the freehold in 1830 (LB 'M', p. 97). Bk of Drawings I, 27A.

18 DOUBLE HOUSE. Original agreement with Robert Todd (18 December 1805). *Built* by Robert Todd. *Lessee*: Robert Todd. Lease dated 12 June 1810 for 56 years from Michaelmas 1809 at EE 2650/1/286(A). Rent: Peppercorn. Todd's tenants in 1815: <u>Stanway</u> and <u>Francis Adolpho</u>. Bk of Drawings I, 14.

19 DOUBLE HOUSE. Original agreement with Robert Todd (8 December 1805), who subcontracted to John Hall. Probably *built* by John Hall, painter of Upper Berkeley Street (brother of William Hall: see Plates 72 and 73 in Chapter 5). *Lessee*: Philip James Meyer, a 'Gentleman' from Queen Charlotte Row, New Road. Lease dated 31 October 1809 for 56 years from Michaelmas 1809 at EE 2650/1/524(A). Rent: £12 a year. Tenants in 1815: James Tanner and Miss E. Blackie. Bk of Drawings I, 9.

20 SINGLE HOUSE. Original agreement with Robert Todd (8 December 1805). *Built* by Edward Chamberlain, a bricklayer from Marylebone, who was unable to finish the house and asked Robert Todd to do so. *Lessee*: Edward Chamberlain. Lease dated 4 November 1807 for 58 years from Michaelmas 1807 – lease at EE 2650/1/516(A) and counterpart at EE 2650/1/519(A). Rent: £12 a year. Assigned to William Norfolk Johnson in 1811. Tenant in 1815: Captain Bolton. Bk of Drawings I, 1.

21 DOUBLE HOUSE. Original agreement with John Webber (1 December 1805). Probably *built* by Francis Waples, carpenter. *Lessee*: Francis Waples. Lease dated 1 February 1810 for 56 years from Michaelmas 1809 at EE 2650/1/517(A and B). Waples subsequently sold the lease for half of this house to George Jones. Rent: £5 per semi-detached a year. Bk of Drawings I, 6.

22 THREE HOUSES. Original agreement with Thomas Biddle (26 September 1804). *Lessee*: Thomas Biddle. Lease dated 20 December 1814 for 51 years from Michaelmas 1814 at EE 2651/360. Rent: £15 4s. a year. Biddle's tenants in 1815: George Ross, William Knight, John Poole. Bk of Drawings I, 26. Also lease of 5 July 1864 at EE 2651/360(O).

23 DOUBLE HOUSE. Original agreement with Thomas Heaphy (1810, LB 'B', p. 278). *Lessee*: Thomas Heaphy, artist, formerly of 76 Great Titchfield Street in Marylebone. Bk of Drawings I, 15, July 1812. The lease is missing.

24 DOUBLE HOUSE. Original agreement with Benjamin Benson (18 August 1809), carpenter of Allsops Place in Marylebone. Probably *built* by Benjamin Benson. *Lessees*: Thomas Gear, 'Gentleman of Alpha Cottages', and Benjamin Benson. Leases dated 30 July 1812 for 69¼ years from September 1811 – counterpart at EE 2650/1/248(A and B). Rent £10 a year. Bk of Drawings I, 25.

25 DOUBLE HOUSE. Original agreement with George Mawbey (6 November 1811). Probably *built* by Benjamin Benson. *Lessees*: Hannah Mawbey and Thomas Gear. Leases dated 30 July 1812 for 69 years from September 1811 – Mawbey's counterpart at EE 2650/1/73 and Gear's at EE 2650/1/248(A). Rent: £10 a year. Bk of Drawings I, 20.

26 DOUBLE HOUSE. Original agreement with Robert Brown, landscape painter (December 1809). *Lessee*: Robert Brown. Lease dated 6 August 1813 for 67 years from Michaelmas 1812 at EE 2650/1/72. Rent: £16 a year. Bk of Drawings I, 19.

27 SINGLE HOUSE. Original agreement probably with Alexander Birnie, oilman. Possibly *built* by Thomas Martin, builder/architect. Lease for 73½ years unwillingly extended to 99 years on payment of £100 (LB 'A', p. 423). Lessee: Edmund Waters, part proprietor of the Italian opera house. Lease missing but probably dated 1807. The stable block above was apparently shared between Messrs Waters and Birnie. Bk of Drawings I, 23, not dated.

28 SINGLE HOUSE. Original agreement probably with Alexander Birnie, oilman. Possibly *built* by Thomas Martin, builder/architect. Lease for 73½ years unwillingly extended to 99 years on payment of £100 (LB 'A', p. 423). *Lessee*: Alexander Birnie. Lease missing but probably dated 1807. The stable block above was shared between Messrs Waters and Birnie. Bk of Drawings I, 24, not dated.

29 SINGLE HOUSE. Original agreement with Alexander Birnie. Possibly *built* by Thomas Martin, builder/architect. *Lessee*: Charles Heathcote Tatham, architect residing at Queen Street, Mayfair. Lease missing but dated 2 May 1808. Lease drawing at LMA, MDR/1809/1/265 (Plate 56).

30 DOUBLE HOUSE. Original agreement with Thomas Martin, builder/architect. Probably *built* by Thomas Martin. *Lessees*: Thomas Martin and Mr Thompson. Bk of Drawings I, 18, July 1812. The lease is missing.

31 SINGLE HOUSE. Original agreement with Thomas Martin. *Lessee*: [James] Hakewill, perhaps the artist who would later publish *Zoological Gardens* (1831). Bk of Drawings I, 16, dated July 1812. The lease is missing.

32 SINGLE HOUSE AND GALLERY. *Owner*: Charles Rossi purchased the freehold of this ground from the Eyres in August 1808 and paid £800 for it. No elevation of buildings available. Bk of Drawings I, 5 only shows a plan.

APPENDIX 2
Key to developers' maps

ADDITIONAL KEY TO PLATE 72

This complementary key lists the documentary sources which have been used to create the developers' map. The entries are organised alphabetically, and within each entry the documents are in chronological order. When agreements are known to have been cancelled, interrupted or transferred, this has been noted.

The names with asterisks (**) have an entry in Appendix 9.

James BURTON** for the canal company
Agreement dated 30 July 1818 at EE 2651/39.

The lease for all the properties which were retained by James Burton is dated 24 December 1823 and is at EE 2651/297(A) (Plate 74). It is damaged, but the drawing for it can also be found in Bk of Drawings II, 12. This document shows that although the 1818 agreement (above) was for land on the north side of the canal, Burton most certainly masterminded the building development of the whole of the land taken by the canal company.

CANAL COMPANY
Agreement dated 29 July 1813 at EE 2651/141(B). A copy is at EE 2650/1/141(A), where the text is much easier to read (see Plate 127).

Charles Claudius COOK**
(A) Agreement dated 25 July 1839 at EE 2651/127, for land on the west side of the Marylebone and Finchley Turnpike Road (now Finchley Road). This agreement was first arranged between Walpole Eyre and Pink & Erlam, but within months it was transferred to Charles Claudius Cook (see letter attached to the agreement dated 21 November 1839).
(B) Agreement dated 4 March 1840 at EE 2651/13(A), for land on the west side of plot above. Will later be transferred to John Edwards; see agreement dated 11 December 1851 at EE 2651/37.
(C) Agreement dated 30 October 1840 at EE 2651/17 (also Bk of Drawings IV, 55 right), for land on the west side of Marylebone and Finchley Turnpike Road.
(D) Agreement dated 30 November 1840 at EE 2651/13(B), for land on the west side of plot above. Will be transferred to John Edwards; see agreement dated 11 December 1851 at EE 2651/37.
(E) Agreement dated 28 February 1842 at EE 2651/31, for land on the west side of Marylebone and Finchley Turnpike Road.
(F) Agreement dated 1 March 1842 at EE 2651/125, for land on the east side of the Marylebone and Finchley Turnpike Road, just south of Adelaide Road.
(G) Agreement dated 30 December 1844 at EE 2651/5(A), for land immediately south of the Birmingham railway line. This was mortgaged to John Edwards in 1846 and subsequently surrendered.
(H) Agreement dated 19 September 1846 at EE 2651/17A(1) (also Bk of

Drawings V, 73(1) right), for land on the west side of the Marylebone and Finchley Turnpike Road at the northern end of the estate. Cook ran into difficulty a few months later. In February 1847 he attempted to transfer the agreement to William Wartnaby (see letter attached to agreement). Walpole Eyre may have vetoed this choice, as by June of that year John Edwards had stepped in. The latter would only formally take over the land in 1851 (see EE 2651/85).
(I) Agreement dated 14 August 1850 at EE 2651/48 (also Bk of Drawings V, 62 left), for land on either side of Boundary Road.
(J) Agreement dated 14 August 1850 at EE 2651/241 (also Bk of Drawings V, 64 left). Development of terraced housing with shops including pub called the Prince Arthur on the north-west corner of Boundary Road and Bridge (now Loudoun) Road.
(K) Drawing for (missing) agreement in Bk of Drawings V, 65 left, dated 20 July 1850, for more terraced housing above site at the south-west corner of Boundary Road and Bridge Road.
(L) Drawing for (missing) agreement in Bk of Drawings V, 63 left, dated 20 July 1850, for the western end plots of Boundary Road.

Edward DAVIES
Agreement dated 28 June 1851 at EE 2651/60 (also Bk of Drawings V, 94 left), for land at the very top of the estate on either side of Victoria Road and along the top part of Albion Road.

In his agreement Edward Davies is described as a builder living at 19 St John's Wood Terrace. He defaulted on his agreement, forcing the Eyre estate into legal proceedings which went on until 1858 when the land was finally recovered. In 1860, Robert Yeo took over this land on agreement (LB 'V', p. 271 and EE2651/19).

The DAVISON brothers**
Sale agreement dated 21 March 1840 at EE 2651/177, for land at the west end of St John's Wood Road (see Sales 'H' below and Plates 209 and 210).

Charles DAY**
Agreement dated 5 May 1824 at EE 2651/54, which replaced the collapsed agreement of 1821 with John Clemence and Henry de Bruno Austin at EE 2651/76.

Samuel ERLAM**
Agreement dated 10 December 1842 at EE 2651/35, for land on the north side of Boundary Road just east of the Turnpike Road. This agreement was first taken by Pink & Erlam in 1839 (see EE 2650/1/54(D) under that name) and surrendered.

Agreement dated 20 January 1852 at EE 2651/86(A), for development of terraced houses. On this plot, situated across the road from St John's Wood Farm, stood the old St John's Wood House. The agreement specified its demolition. Erlam assigned his agreement to Jacob Hibberd eleven days later on 31 January. Hibberd was therefore responsible for the two most glamorous terraces in St John's Wood – Queen's Grove and St Ann's Terrace.

Walpole EYRE

No agreements survive for the period 1804–12. The Alpha Road cottage development deserved its name not simply because it was made up of 'cottages' but also because of its modest size, a prudent move that was soon forgotten. See Table 1 (p. 96) for the allocation of land following the 1804 auction, and see Plate 62 for a reconstruction of this early community. Walpole acted as developer for the following plots:

• Alpha Cottages along the Alpha Road, from 1804
• Breeze Yard in Lisson Grove, from 1807 (see Sales 'B')
• St John's Wood Grove, also in Lisson Grove, from 1811 (see Sales 'C')
• The land immediately south of Lord's final site was also developed by 'jumping over' the land taken by the canal company.

Charles FREETH junior**

(**A**) Agreement dated 28 March 1840 at EE 2651/66, for land on either side of Cavendish Road (not the full length), the eastern plot taken from ground formerly let to bankrupt Samuel Gardner (EE 2651/52, 1823).
(**B**) Agreement dated 12 June 1840 at EE 2651/97 (the plan in Bk of Drawings IV, 22B left, shows the plot taken by Freeth as well as the adjoining Berry's 1842 plot). In May that year a sketch was prepared for an agreement with Mr Veal, the man occupying the dairy farm (Bk of Drawings IV, 33 right, and LB 'Q', p. 82), but this is the arrangement which prevailed.
Subsequent development work has also been charted separately on the map at Plate 73 (EE 2651/53).

William Robert FRY**

See detailed map at Plate 73 for pre-bankruptcy development work.
(**A**) Agreement dated 28 November 1840 at EE 2651/68 and agreement dated 28 January 1842 at EE 2651/33. William Robert's return to building development after his 1835 bankruptcy is cautious with two small plots on the north side of Marlborough Road.
(**B**) Agreement dated 30 April 1845 at EE 2651/84 (also Bk of Drawings V, 37 right), for land framing Blenheim Road East and Carlton Hill Road.
(**C**) Agreement dated 14 October 1850 at EE 2651/61 (also Bk of Drawings V, 75B left). On this occasion William Robert and his brother took out the agreement together for land on either side of Clifton Road East. This project had first been contemplated by William Robert in 1846 when the road was named Blandford Road East (See Bk of Drawings V, 75A left).
(**D**) Agreement dated 15 June 1853 at EE 2651/55 and 2651/56 (also Bk of Drawings VI, 44A left). This piece of land is immediately above land developed by the two brothers. However, this particular agreement was surrendered in 1860, William Robert being unable to pay his rent; the road, sewer and a handful of houses had been built. A year later the land had been redistributed between Parkins, Foulger and Bettinson (LB 'V', pp. 380–81).

In 1842, Fry also took over land which had been let to Pink & Erlam at EE 2650/1/54(D) and EE 2651/129(A). This fresh agreement dated 7 December 1842 is at EE 2651/32. In 1846, he took over the land which was on agreement to George Leigh, deceased (EE 2651/11(A) dated 1841).

Samuel GARDNER

Variously described as a plasterer or bricklayer, Gardner's main claim to fame is that his house in Elm Tree Road has miraculously survived to the present day and may now be regarded as the oldest house on the estate (Plate 49).

Agreement dated 4 October 1823 at EE 2651/52, for land part of Gibbs's Nursery ground on the west side of Wellington Road. This agreement was interrupted by Gardner's bankruptcy and was therefore not performed.

William HALL**

(A) Agreement dated 25 October 1814 for plot immediately west of Lord's Cricket Ground at EE 2651/123 (houses to be the same as those shown on Lord's agreement).
(B) Agreement dated 7 February 1818 at EE 2651/80 (Also Bk of Drawings I, 59A). Houses based on Todd's model (Plate 58).
(C) Agreement dated 1 October 1818 at EE 2651/87 (Also Bk of Drawings I, 59B). Houses based on Todd's model (Plate 81).
(D) and (E) Bk of Drawings I, 42, dated 30 October 1819. (D) is described as 'Mr Hall's Brick Field', while (E) is 'Ground proposed to be taken by Mr Hall' (will be taken by Thomas Johnson below).

John HINTON and John WHITE junior**

When victualler John Hinton went bankrupt in 1826, John White, the District Surveyor of St Marylebone, took over the project, but he, too, had to surrender the land shortly afterwards (see EE 2651/243(B) below).
(**A**) Agreement dated 12 February 1823 at EE 2651/1(A and B): land between Circus Road and Grove End Road. The scheme comprised houses made up of three units (other examples of this on east side of Cavendish Road and west side of Douro Road). Some were built on the corner of Grove End Road and Wellington Road, on the south side, known as Blenheim Terrace.
(**B**) Agreement dated 10 November 1823 at EE 2651/2(A and B). This substantial plot is immediately above the previous plot and includes the Eyre Arms Tavern between Marlborough Road and Grove End Road. Same type of houses as above.

Assignment and surrender dated 4 March 1834 at EE 2651/243(B). This useful document mentions all the builders/developers subcontracted by John White for work on this ground: George Caton (June 1828), Charles Freeth (October 1828 and July 1829), John Penning (December 1828), William Baker (March 1829), Thomas Lothian (March 1829), William Ifold (May 1829), Thomas Pearson (June 1831) and Henry Crace (September 1832). William Baker built Box Villa and Box Cottage side by side in Marlborough Road (Plates 75 and 76).

Thomas JOHNSON**

For ground labelled William Hall 'E':
Agreement dated 1 March 1825 at EE 2651/40 and 2651/41; this agreement was surrendered on 13 March 1830 (EE 2651/42).

Lewis JONES

A developer based at Wellington Terrace.
Agreement dated 19 February 1838 at EE 2651/70, for land on the south side of Circus Road, at the top of Cavendish Road, then called Lennard Place.

The LEIGH brothers**

(**A**) (Charles Frederick) Agreement dated 1 October 1838 at EE 2651/47 (also Bk of Drawings IV, 2 right), for land on the west side of the Marylebone and Finchley Turnpike Road just above Marlborough Road. In April 1844 James Ponsford** paid the rent arrears on this agreement and in 1846 received his leases. Walpole Eyre queried the line of responsibility between the two men at the time of issuing the leases (LB 'R', p. 202).
(**B**) (George) Agreement dated 30 August 1841 at EE 2651/11(A) (two more copies at EE 2651/165 and drawing in Bk of Drawings IV, 86 right), for land on the east side of Bridge Road (now Loudoun Road). At Leigh's death the ground was taken over by William Robert Fry (1846).

Thomas LORD**

Agreement dated 7 August 1813 at EE 2651/88(A); also the assignment dated 1 January 1824 from Thomas Lord to William Ward is at EE 2651/88(B). The drawing for Ward/Dark's lease in 1835 is in Bk of Drawings III, 106 see Lord's chronology at Appendix 8).

The MAIDLOW and WATKINS brothers**

Both John Maidlow and Stephen Watkins had brothers and all worked closely together, but their 'empire' collapsed and had to be redistributed when John Maidlow and Stephen Watkins went bankrupt (see Plate 73).

John Maidlow

(**A**) Agreement dated 20 June 1822 for the plot east of Wellington Road at EE 2651/89(A), almost immediately assigned to Messrs [William] Fry & [George] Watkins, timber merchants from Limehouse, and Charles Malpas from the Inner Temple for a sum of just under £2,000 (see EE 2651/90 dated 7 August 1822).
(**B**) Agreement dated 29 October 1822 at EE 2651/96, for St John's Wood Terrace (south side).
(**C**) Agreement dated 13 November 1824 at EE 2651/3(A and B), for the plot between the Barracks and the Eton College estate. This last agreement was revised (EE 2651/3A(1 and 2) dated 30 August 1825) when the square block of land immediately east of the Barracks was taken over by (Stephen) Watkins (see EE 2651/26 below).

Stephen Watkins

(**A**) Agreement dated 15 November 1824 at EE 2651/92(A and B), when Watkins took over the land on the north side of St John's Terrace, mostly for a development of terraced houses (the central plot in this scheme is left blank).
(**B**) Agreement dated 20 August 1825 at EE 2651/26 shows the plot of land Watkins took over from Maidlow's (C) agreement.
(**C**) Agreement dated 30 October 1830 at EE 2651/75, when Stephen and his brother Charles took over a section from St John's Terrace south: seventeen houses west of Charles (now Charlbert) Street.

ORPHAN CLERGY SOCIETY

The Orphan Clergy Asylum school project is first mentioned in the letter books in 1810, the date of the agreement with the St John's Wood estate, a document which alas is no longer in the archive. A brief history of the school is on p. 211. Like its neighbour the cricket ground, the Orphan Clergy Society's agreement technically enabled them to do some building development on their site. However, as with Lord's, this was never taken up. In 1826 market gardener John Gibbs, who was slowly being squeezed out of his site north of Wellington Place, moved into the school ground (Plate 92). From then on the society would benefit from Gibbs's rents and produce.
See Book of Licences I, pp. 85ff, and Plate 115.

PINK & ERLAM**

(**A**) Agreement dated 11 December 1835 at EE 2651/9 (also Bk of Drawings III, 133), for a plot of land next to Elizabethan Villa on the east side of the Marylebone and Finchley Turnpike Road. This is the earliest agreement taken for land along this road. It will be followed by Cook's in 1839 and Treeby's in 1840.
(**B**) Agreement dated 16 June 1837 at EE 2650/1/54(A), for land immediately north of above.
(**C**) Agreement dated 29 July 1837 at EE 2651/131, for land fronting Wellington Road (east side) just south of Acacia Road.
(**D**) Agreement dated 26 February 1839 at EE 2650/1/54(B), for land along same eastern side of the Marylebone and Finchley Turnpike Road, just under Boundary Road. This agreement was surrendered on 6 December 1842.
(**E**) Agreement dated 26 July 1839 at EE 2650/1/54(D), for land still on the eastern side of Marylebone and Finchley Turnpike Road, just above Boundary Road. This agreement was surrendered on 6 December 1842. A few days later on 10 December, Samuel Erlam alone entered into an agreement with Walpole for this plot (EE 2651/35).

James SALTER

A builder from 6 Great Titchfield Street.
Agreement dated 15 November 1839 at EE 2651/26, for land on the east side of Cavendish Road, just above the Clergy Orphan Asylum. The land is part of Gibbs's garden, and the market gardener's house is shown at the top of the drawing.

James SHARP**

Agreement dated 1 July 1846 at EE 2651/82 (also Bk of Drawings V, 87 right), for land on the south-east corner of Queen's Road and Wellington Road.

George Spencer SMITH**

The actual agreement for the triangular site at Swiss Cottage has not survived, but the drawing prepared for it is at Bk of Drawings IV, 61 right, dated March 1841.

APPENDIX 5
Studio explosion

This chronology focuses on studio building in St John's Wood. The data have been drawn from published sources, primarily Walkley (1994), supplemented by data from the archive of the Eyre estate.[1] In his gazetteer Walkley opted to arrange the data in street order, which is useful if you are working from the ground outwards. Here, however, a chronological approach has been adopted to show the increasingly fashionable trend for studio building. The chronology leaves out artists who did not operate from purpose-built studios, but this is compensated by the fact that all artists known to have been based at the listed addresses are mentioned.

The artists who commissioned the original studios are underlined when the information is known. They may be assumed to be painters unless otherwise specified. The house numbers in brackets are for properties which no longer exist.

When the date of a studio licence clashes with Giles Walkley's data, I have made a note of it, but I have retained Walkley's chronology as a licence does not necessarily mean a studio was actually built.

In a small number of cases studios outside the boundaries of the Eyre estate have been included. It seemed misleading to omit such important studios as those of Alfred Gilbert in Maida Vale or George Frampton in Carlton Hill.

Multiple studios have not been included, and for these Giles Walkley's gazeteer remains the best source of published information.

Early years

1808   J. C. F. Rossi purchases enough land to build a house, a studio and a gallery at the southern end of the estate in Lisson Grove (Plate 234).

1812   Robert Brown moves to (39) Alpha Road after he erects the first purpose-built painter's studio on the estate (Plate 139).

1840s

1840   (3) later (22) St John's Wood Road. Reference to Lucas's plan for 'proposed painting room'; architect: Thomas L. Donaldson (see LB 'P', p. 260). Members of the Lucas family based at this address – John, John Templeton and William. Other artists at this address: Edward Deanes, Christabella Deanes, Edmund Havell, James Macbeth, Edith Evelyn, Matthew Wood, Marshall Wood, T. G. Duvall.

1840   (12) later (4) Alpha Cottages. First licence application for an 'Additional Room' for John Palmer de la Fons (also spelt Delafons).

---

[1] The information was also cross-referenced with Cox-Johnson (1963), Morris and Milner (1993), Montgomery Eyre (1913) and Hitchmough (1995) for Voysey projects. I am particularly grateful to Giles Walkley for revising and clarifying his studios' gazetteer for my benefit. He used rate books, Cox-Johnson (1963), Graves (1905–6), Post Office directories and *The Year's Art* (an annual published by *The Art Journal*), and wished Wendy Hitchmough's *C. F. A. Voysey* (1995) had been available to him.

Licence dated 18 March 1840 has survived inside original lease, though it appears the work may only have been carried out in 1853 (EE 2650/1/61(A) and Licence Book I, p. 190).

1844 and 1850 (1) later (18) St John's Wood Road. Extension for a studio-house for Edwin Landseer; architect: Henry Ashton; built by Cubitt & Co. Other artists at this address: Jessica Landseer, Henry W. B. Davis.

1849   10A, 10B Cunningham Place. First extension for Thomas Landseer and second for George Landseer. Other artists at this address: C. Adloff, Downard Birch, William S. Burton, Henry W. B. Davis, John Cother Webb, Emily Osborn.

1850s

c.1850s   (45) Grove End Road. Extension for Mr and Mrs George Edward Hering. Garden studio is built at early stage of occupancy; house extension comes later. Both are replaced by mansion block in 1899. Other artists at this address: Edith Courtauld (niece of the Herings, later Mrs Arendrup), Ernest Crofts.

1851   (19) St John's Wood Road. Extension for proprietor John Lucas. Other artists at this address: William Q. Orchardson, George A. Storey, Heywood Hardy.

1853   (12) later (4) Alpha Cottages (also see 1840). Draft for a licence to build a studio (LB 'T', p. 389) for John Palmer de la Fons (also spelt Delafons). This licence was drafted over the 1840 licence mentioned above. Was the 1840 'additional room' ever built or was it the much awaited studio built in 1853? A drawing was submitted in 1853 (see Plate 152) (EE 2650/1/61(A) and Licence Book I, pp. 472–74).

1853   (4) Grove End Road. Licence to build a studio and conservatory (Licence Book I, p. 480) is granted to lessee Martha Chapman; architect: Horace Field. Artist not named in licence but 'Armitage', i.e. Edward Armitage, in LB 'T' p. 412. Other artists at this address: Miss E. Armitage, Henry Wallis, W. F. Yeames.

1856   (21) St John's Wood Road (formerly 7 Grove End Place). Extension for the Herbert family (John Rogers, Arthur John and Wilfred Vincent). Other artists at this address: John Frederick Lewis, Robert J. Longbottom, John Pettie, Reginald Arthur, Oliver Rhys, Ethel Wright, Jan Chelminski.

1856   (32) later (12) Alpha Road. Extension for sculptor John Thomas (LB 'U', pp. 219, 255, 378; also see licences at EE 2650/1/249 (with detailed plans of workshop but sculptor is not named, see Plate 179) and Licence Book II, pp. 59 and 97). Other artists at this address: sculptors Frederick Anstey (extended again in 1869 when the lease is renewed, see LB 'X', pp. 316–17, see Plate 298) and Hugh Purves.

1860s

c.1861   (6) Waverley Place. Extension for John O'Connor. Other artists at this address: Thomas M. Hemy, Florence Westfield (Nesfield?), William Eden Nesfield, Heywood Hardy.

1865   (4) Grove End Road. Extension for William Yeames. Other artists at this address: see 1853.

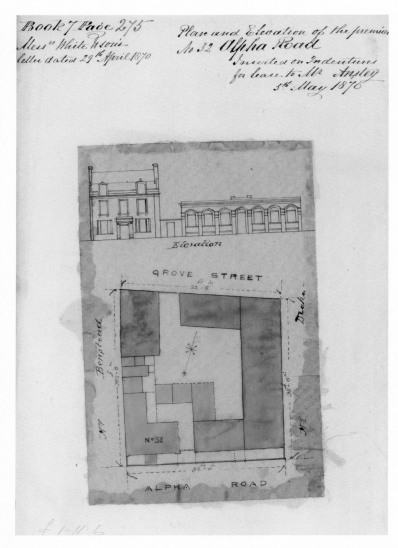

Book 7 Page 275
Messrs White & Souie –
letter dated 29th April 1870

Plan and Elevation of the premises
No 32 Alpha Road
Inserted on Indentures
for lease to Mr Anstey
5th May 1870

298 This lease drawing depicts the premises of sculptor Frederick Anstey at 32 Alpha Road in 1870. In 1857, the sculptor John Thomas was successful in obtaining a licence from the estate to carry out a massive building extension to this modest semi-detached house (Plate 179). Eyre estate archive (Bk of Drawings I, 17, and VII, 275).

1867 (38) Avenue Road, formerly 2 Regents Villas. Attempt to obtain a licence for building a studio for Frederick Tayler (see LB 'X', pp. 99, 101, 104, 129). Estate refuses at first, then agrees, but no licence is issued (see c.1878–87 below).

1868 (5) Marlborough Road. Extension for Henry and Kate Holiday (Licence Book II, pp. 87 and 168 – the double entry is a mistake – and p. 113 re: alterations for ?Arden in 1874). Other artists at this address: Briton Riviere, Henry Arden, Miriam Davis.

c.1869 9 now 21 Marlborough Place for Philip Calderon. Other artists at this address: Laslett J. Pott, Guido Bach, Herbert A. Olivier.

1870s

c.1870 15, now 36 Hamilton Terrace. Garden pavilion for Henry Stacy Marks. Other artists at this address: Nathaniel Palmer, Henry Yeend King, Lily Wrangel, Archibald Christie, Robert Christie, V. Ormsby.

1870 (8) later (16) Grove End Road. Extension for George D. Leslie (Plate 168). Other artist at this address: William Quiller Orchardson.

1870 Queen's Terrace: 'License to Mr Richd Nation to build two studios on a piece of Ground on South West side of Queens Terrace' dated 30 December 1870 (Licence Book II, p. 182).

c.1870 (14) later (28) Grove End Road. Extension for David W. Wynfield. Other artist at this address: Vincent Yglesias.

c.1870 (42) Grove End Road. Extension for Heywood Hardy. Other artists at this address: Arthur Stark, Thomas Hemy.

c.1870 (58) Queen's Grove. Garden pavilion for Frank W. W. Topham. Other artists at this address: Gordon Thomson, Arthur D. McCormick.

c.1871 (17) Titchfield Terrace, Prince Albert Road. Conversion for Lawrence Alma-Tadema; architects: Alma-Tadema and George Aitchison. Other artist at this address: Emily Williams.

c.1873 72 Hamilton Terrace, formerly 8 Upper Hamilton Terrace. Extension. Artists at this address: the Gurneys, the Josephs.

1873 (35) Grove End Road. Extension, presumably for Charles Landseer. Other artists at this address: Tom Landseer, Carl Schloesser.

c.1873 (3) Hall Road, formerly 2 Hall Place. Extension for Edward Armitage.

1873–74 17, later 34, now 44 Grove End Road. Conversion by architect John Brydon for James Tissot (Plate 159). Brydon's work has mostly disappeared; see also 1884–86.

1875 (19) Marlborough Hill. Garden pavilion built for Edwin Long which is let separately after 1885 and known as 1A Carlton Hill (Licence Book II, p. 114). Other artists at this address: Charles C. Seton before Edwin Long; at 1A Carlton Hill: Robert Walker Macbeth, Talbot Hughes, Horace H. Stanton, John Longstaff, Robert Smith, John Dawson Watson.

1875 (6) Marlborough Road, Garden pavilion for John MacWhirter (Licence Book II, p. 118). Other artists at this address: Agnes Eliza MacWhirter, George Lawson (this sculptor's workshop was photographed by Mayall and reproduced in F. G. Stephens's *Artists at Home*).

1875 (1) Titchfield Road (presumably the same as 1 Titchfield Villas). Extension for John MacWhirter. Other artists at this address: William J. Webb, Agnes MacWhirter, Charles B. Barber.

c.1875 5 now 10 Hill Road. Extension for John Hodgson. Other artists at this address: William Eden, Jessie Macgregor, Edwin Calvert, William Reynolds-Stephens. Also see 1894.

c.1875 (6) Abercorn Place. Extension. Artists at this address: C. Deschamps, Edward Gregory.

c.1875 20, then 24, now 26A Greville Road. Extension. Artists at this address: Otto Weber, E. Roscoe Mullins, William Goscombe John.

c.1875 and 1878 (8) Elm Tree Road. Conversion and extension. Artists at this address: J. G. Brown, Ernest Parton, Ethel Wright, Sophia Smith.

1875–76   61A Carlton Hill. Garden pavilion for <u>Colin Hunter</u>. Other artists at this address: John N. Flatow, Benjamin Head, Charles E. Marshall, Chevalier A. Tayler, (Sir) George Clausen.

1875–76   (33) St John's Wood Road, Aber House, formerly 1 Grove End Place. Extension by architect Thomas H. Watson, presumably for <u>Philip R. Morris</u> (Plate 158). Other artist at this address: John H. Bacon.

1875–85?   (11) Grove End Road. Extension for <u>John Charlton</u>. Other artist at this address: Tom Landseer.

1876   (1 Lennard Place). Extension. Artists at this address: Rodney Fennessy, Rudolf Blind, William H. Margetson, Ada Chevalier.

1876   (32C) then (30A) then (36) Marlborough Hill. Extension. (Licence Book II, p. 123, records an 1875 Waiver of Breach of Covenant for a studio building in Marlborough Hill. Could it be this one?) Artists at this address: Robert Ponsonby Staples, George Barrable (Plate 240), Henry Yeend King, Richard W. Halfnight, John M. Bromley, Henry Pegram.

1876   (15) Avenue Road. Garden pavilion for <u>Jerry Barrett</u>. Other artist at this address: Frederick Wallen.

1876   (16) Grove End Road. Extension for <u>Philip Calderon</u>. Other artists at this address: John Jackson (in 1825), W. Frank Calderon, Charles E. Stewart. See Licence Book II, p. 129, which specifies: 'to pull down existing buildings & to erect a studio & carry on the profession of an artist on the above premises'. The licence is dated 23 March 1876 and survives inside the lease dated 29 March 1819 at EE 2651/360.

1876–77   (24A) Cavendish Road, now Avenue. Studio-house for <u>Thomas Faed</u> (see archive file at EE 2650/1/130(A and B)). Other artists at this address: John Francis Faed next door at No. 24 and James Dick-Peddie at 24A.

1877   (15) later (30) Grove End Road. See 1880.

300 House and studio of Briton Riviere at 82 Finchley Road, now demolished. Pencil drawing by Ernest Stamp (1869–1942), undated. Museum of London (Acc. No. 38.176/16).

1877   28 Abercorn Place. Studio-house by Thomas W. Cutler for <u>John O'Connor</u> (Plate 299). Other artists at this address: Friedrich William Keyl (1849–51), Rudolph Lehmann.

1877   30 Abercorn Place. Studio-house by Thomas W. Cutler probably for <u>James Whittet Smith</u>. Other artist at this address: James William Garrett Smith.

1877   23 St Edmund's Terrace. Extension probably for <u>John Hayes Williams</u>. Other artist at this address: Harry Furniss.

1877   Licence to erect a studio at (26) later (58) Circus Road: Mr and Mrs <u>Samuel Edmund Waller</u> (EE 2650/1/234(B) and Licence Book II, p. 150). Waller's name not mentioned in the document but found in Cox-Johnson, 1963.

1877   Licence to 'Sophia Mary Winfield [i.e. Wynfield], widow and underlessee of (14) Grove End Road to maintain and keep a Studio of corrugated iron' (EE 2650/1/513 and Licence Book II, p. 151); studio is next to Agnew's, see p. 301. <u>David Wilkie Wynfield</u> recorded there between 1867 and 1887 (the lessee is Chandless, the same as 26 Circus Road above).

c.1877–87   (12) Loudoun Road. Extension probably for <u>Harry Johnson</u>. Other artists at this address: Lilian Hamilton, Vereker Hamilton, Maurice Greiffenhagen.

c.1878   (6 and 7) Elm Tree Road. Conversion: St John's Wood Art Schools. Artist-proprietors: A. A. Calderon, Bernard E. Ward, Leonard Pownall.

c.1878   (8a) Elm Tree Road. Unspecified building activity. Artists at this address: Jessie and Archie Macgregor, Arthur Ash, King, John M. Bromley, Charles W. Wyllie.

c.1878   22 Greville Road. Unspecified building activity, presumably for <u>Lucy Parsons</u>.

299 The studio-house commissioned by the painter John O'Connor from the architect Thomas W. Cutler at 28 Abercorn Place. The painter's initials are sculpted over the main entrance. Eyre estate (photos: author).

1878   46 Queen's Road (now Grove). One-storey garden pavilion for <u>Charles Knighton Warren</u> (Licence Book II, p. 159). Also see 1886.

1878   (2 Lodge Place). The Eyre estate issues a licence for a studio at that address (Licence Book II, p. 161, otherwise unrecorded as a studio building or as an artist's residence).

1878–87   (38) Avenue Road. Garden pavilion probably for <u>Frederick Tayler</u> (see 1867 above). Other artist at this address: Charles Napier Kennedy.

c.1879   57 Abbey Road. Garden pavilion. Artists at this address: Edward A. Smith, John H. Henshall, Thomas W. Cafe, James N. Forsyth.

44 Finchley Rd
The Studio & Residence of W Dendy Sadler

E Stamp
1934

1880s

c.1880   17 now 40 Hamilton Terrace. Extension for <u>Henry Stacy Marks</u>. Marks's extension covers twice the area of the house and includes an aviary. Other artist: Mrs Mary Harriett Marks. Formerly on this site: Louis N. A. Megret, sculptor (1865–66).

1880–90   (1) Waverley Place. Extension. Artists residing at this address: Ernest Crofts, Carl Wunnenberg, Ernst Hermann. The pavilion at the rear is connected to the main house by a glasshouse.

c.1880   (82) Finchley Road. Conversion for <u>Briton Riviere</u>; architect: Frederick W. Waller (Plate 300). Studio first discussed in January 1879 (see LB 'Y', p. 20; licence dated 31 January 1882 to lessee John Baker in Licence Book II, p. 203). Further alterations in 1887 (LB 'Y', p. 499).

1880   (15) later (30) Grove End Road. Extension, presumably for <u>Guido Bach</u> (Walkley, 1994, gives the date of 1880 but Licence Book II, p. 157, records a licence in 1877). Other artist: Andrew C. Gow (in Licence Book II, p. 201, permission to build a studio is granted to E .J. Barron and A. C. Gow on 15 May 1890).

1880   (44) Grove End Road. Licence to Marr (lessee) to build a studio, presumably for <u>Edwin Bale</u> (see Cox-Johnson, 1963) (Licence Book II, p. 188).

c.1881   (58) Circus Road. Garden pavilion for <u>Mr and Mrs Samuel Waller</u>.

c.1881   28 Finchley Road, the house where Tom Hood died in 1845, and where the St John's Wood Arts Club met from 1900. Conversion, presumably for <u>Walter D. Sadler</u>. Other artists at this address: Herbert A. Olivier, Arthur J. Elsley.

c.1881–82(1) Abbey Road. Conversion for <u>John MacWhirter</u> (Plates 149 and Plate 303). Other artist at this address: Charles Sims.

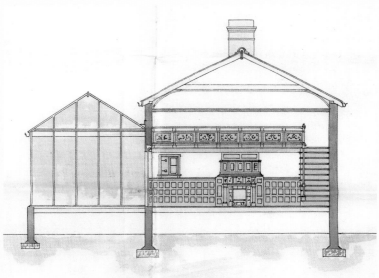

Top: **301** The house and studio of Walter Dendy Sadler at 44 Finchley Road. Pencil drawing by Ernest Stamp, undated. Museum of London (Acc. No. 38.176/19).

Above: **302** Interior of Walter Dendy Sadler's studio at 44 Finchley Road. Detail from an architectural drawing by Frederick Lewis, November 1892. Eyre estate archive (EE 2650/1/377(B)).

The Studio & Residence
of J MacWhirter R.A. abbey Rd, S' Johns wood, corner of Grove End Rd

E Stamp

303 House and studio of John MacWhirter at 1 Abbey Road, now demolished. Pencil drawing by Ernest Stamp, undated. Museum of London (Acc. No. 38.176/43).

c.1882   (9) Elm Tree Road. Extension, presumably for <u>A. A. Calderon</u>. Other artists at this address: Arthur D. May, Ralph Bailey.

1882   (44) Grove End Road, south corner of Melina Place. Extension for <u>Edwin Bale</u>.

1882   (3) Acacia Gardens. Licence (with drawing) to Thomas Trinder (lessee) and <u>Henry Thomas Schäfer</u> (underlessee 'artist' of 4 Waverley Place) to erect a studio (EE 2650/1/88(G) and Licence Book II, p. 193).

1882   12–16 Langford Place. Extension of 'Sunnyside', formerly No. 8, for sculptor <u>John Adams-Acton</u>; architect: Mr Tall. The gingerbread cottage next to it (No. 12) appears to be a conversion, perhaps c.1910, of the original stables.

1882   (62) Avenue Road: 'Rosenstead', formerly Gambart's residence, licence granted to <u>Frederick Goodall</u> to build a studio conservatory and wing (EE 2650/1/256(A and B)). See Plate 170.

1883   (52) Circus Road. Licence to <u>H. H. Armstead</u> to convert stable/coach house into a studio (EE 2650/1/230 and Licence Book II, pp. 199 and 209).

1883   (56) later (60) Finchley Road. Extension for <u>John B. Burgess</u>. Licence to Burgess to build a 'studio conservatory glasshouse and other erections' at Bruntsfield House (EE 2650/1/150(B) and Licence Book II, p. 208); architect: John Edward Pownall. Elevation of the house at EE 2650/1/151(C). Other artist at this address: Solomon J. Solomon. Also see 1901.

c.1883   (2) later (41) Circus Road, south-west corner of Elm Tree Road. Extension. 'Licence to build a studio' for <u>John E. Hodgson</u> dated 17 April 1890 (possibly retrospective licence, in Licence Book II, p. 201). Artists at this address: John E. Hodgson, Vereker Hamilton, Lilian Hamilton, Mary Swainson, Burgess Marriage.

c.1884   38 Abercorn Place. Conversion, presumably for <u>Sidney Starr</u> (Plate 129). Other artists at this address: Charles W. Wyllie, Hugh Riviere.

c.1884   11 now 25 and (12) Marlborough Road. Extension. Artists at this address: Alice Havers, Alfred Hitchens, J. Bernard Partridge, Joseph Hatton (author). The addition may date from Hatton's arrival in 1899.

1884   35 Acacia Road. Extension, presumably for <u>John Nettleship</u>. Other artists at this address: Ernest Parton, George P. Gaskell. Extension still in situ at 35A but has been rebuilt.

1884   (50) Circus Road. Studio for <u>G. F. Munn</u>; architect: Leonard Stokes (EE 2650/1/229(A) and Licence Book II, pp. 199 and 209).

1884–86   (17) later (34) now 44 Grove End Road. Conversion for <u>Lawrence Alma-Tadema</u>; architects: Lawrence Alma-Tadema and Alfred Calderon (Plates 166, 304 and 305). Artists at this address: Alma-Tadema family (Lawrence, Laura and Anna), Emily Williams, Giambattista Amendola. Also see 1873–74 for James Tissot.

c.1885   3 Hill Road. Extension, presumably for <u>James Carrington</u>. Other artists at this address: Frederick Bodkin, Walter Urwick.

c.1885   (12) Melina Place. Extension, presumably for <u>Allen C. Sealy</u>. Other artists at this address: Alfred E. and Rosalie Emslie, Frank Ogilvie. Significant artists and architects live in the other houses, especially

Top: **304** The house and studio of Lawrence Alma-Tadema at 44 Grove End Road. Pencil drawing by Ernest Stamp, undated. Museum of London (Acc. No. 38.176/4).

Above: **305** The apse in the studio of Lawrence Alma-Tadema at 44 Grove End Road, from the 1925 Hampton & Sons auction catalogue. Eyre estate archive (EE 2651/341).

Nos 9, 10 and 11, from the mid-1880s onwards. Giles Walkley (1994) suggests that this may have been the site of C. F. A Voysey's 'Studios for a London Street' project of late 1892 (reproduced in David Gebhard, *Charles F. A. Voysey*, Los Angeles, 1975, Plate 39).

c.1885   (10) Abbey Road. Extension. Artists at this address: John Varley the Younger, Heywood Hardy, Nina Hardy, Stewart Gwatkin, Arthur Vernon, E. Phillips Fox.

306 The studio of John Macallan Swan has survived at 3 Acacia Road. Eyre estate (photo: the author).

c.1885 (80) Finchley Road. Extension. Artists at this address: Arthur Hopkins, Gordon F. Browne.

1885 6 Melina Place. Extension for Henry Macbeth-Raeburn now numbered 6A (see licence to erect a studio at Melina Place, Grove End Road, inside lease at WCA, 765/177, and Licence Book II, p. 195). Other artists at this address: Charles E. Stewart, Harrington Mann.

1885 5 Melina Place. 'Conversion of stable', now 5A, presumably for John and Ellen Parker (Licence Book II, p. 195). Artists at this address: John and Ellen Parker, Phil May, Tom Mostyn. Prior to extension: William A. Brunning (1841).

1886 46 Queen's Road, now Grove. Garden pavilion for the Warren family (Charles K., Gertrude and Elizabeth); plan and elevation by Thomas Edward Pryce at EE 2650/1/509. Also see 1878.

c.1886 (1) Hill Road. Garden pavilion, presumably for Thomas Blinks. Other artists at this address prior to this addition: Mr and Mrs Charles Rossiter (1866–72).

c.1887 (34A) Finchley Road. Garden pavilion. Artists at this address: Henry Leask, Alfred E. Emslie, Clarence Bird, William Goscombe John, Helen Franck.

1887 (62) Acacia Road. Extension for the Onslow Ford family of sculptors (Edward, Rudolph and Wolfram). Other artists at this address: C. L. Hartwell (also a sculptor), Leonard Campbell Taylor. Prior to extension: art dealer Ernest Gambart (1859–62).

1887 Lodge Place, now Road. George Simonds (sculptor) took over The Priory, George Eliot's house at 21 North Bank, from Wilson Barrett, actor-manager.

c.1888 59A Abbey Road. Extension. Artists at this address: Charles Smith, Emily Holman.

1888 (Alpha House, 14 Alpha Road): licence (to Wilson) for underlessee John McLure Hamilton for building a studio (at EE 2650/1/197(B), No. 29 on Alpha Cottages reconstruction). With small sketch showing elevation from Alpha Road (Plate 154).

1888 (27) Marlborough Hill. Extension for Scottish watercolourist Robert Little (Plate 186) possibly by William Flockart, including built-in organ (Licence Book II, p. 198).

1889 (13) later (26) Grove End Road. Garden pavilion for Frederick Raymond Lynde, 'artist' (licence and plans at EE 2650/1/512(C); also recorded in Licence Book II, p. 198).

1889 (21 North Bank). Licence to build a studio granted to Francis Gooden (Licence Book II, p. 198, not otherwise recorded). Also see 1887.

c.1889 3 Acacia Road. Extension for John Macallan Swan (Plate 306).

1890s

c.1890 (21) Grove End Road. Extension for Charles P. Downing (Plate 25).

c.1890 (51) Ordnance Hill. Extension. Artist at this address: Clarence Hailey, photographer (see Appendix 7).

c.1890 (14) St John's Wood Road. Garden pavilion, presumably for Gordon F. Browne. Other artist at this address: Cecil Hew Brown (sculptor).

1890 (15) later (30) Grove End Road. See 1880.

1890 (15B) Eaton Terrace (now Kingsmill Terrace). Extension. Artists at this address: Herbert Lyndon, William R. Colton (sculptor).

1890 17 now 24 Marlborough Road. Extension for John A. Lomax.

1890 33 Queen's Road, later 1 and 2 Woronzow Studios, now 25–27 Woronzow Road. Licence to erect two studios (Licence Book II, p. 202, otherwise unrecorded). Artists at this address: William Goscombe John (Plate 180), Clement Skilbeck, Aston Knight, Herbert Ward, Flora Lion, Clare Sheridan.

c.1891 30 Abbey Gardens. Extension. Artists at this address: Joshua Glidden, Henry K. Ayliff.

1891 (54) Circus Road. Extension for Mr and Mrs Matthew Ridley Corbet. Extension drawings at EE 2650/1/521(B) (Plate 167 and Licence Book II, p. 202). Also see 1894.

1891 10 Hall Road. Extension at the back of semi-detached 1 Hall Place, presumably for Harry Bates (sculptor). Other artist at this address: John W. Waterhouse.

1891 6A Abercorn Place, now 2A Nugent Terrace. Studio-house possibly by Thomas H. Watson or Sidney Tatchell, the architect of Goetze's Grove House. Artists at this address: L. de Kerval, Sigismund Goetze.

c.1892 (1A Lennard Place). Extension. Artists at this address: Walter S. Paget, Maude Wear, Amy Drucker.

1892 (40) Acacia Road. Garden pavilion for Alfred Powell (Walkley, 1994, but in Licence Book II, p. 201, permission given to build 'a studio with covered way & passage' on 13 September 1889).

1892 7 Hill Road. Studio for Reynolds Stephen by C. F. A. Voysey.

1892–93 87A Clifton Hill. Miscellaneous work, presumably for Bertram Mackennal (sculptor). Other sculptor at this address: Albert Toft.

1892–93 (44) Finchley Road. Extension by architect Frederick J. Lewis for

Walter D. Sadler (Plates 301 and 302). Other artist at this address: James D. Penrose.

1893 (16) Maida Vale. This studio-house for Alfred Gilbert (sculptor) is outside the Eyre estate but is included because it was such a major landmark: 'The biggest private studio in London at the time' (Walkley, 1994, p. 252). Other artists at this address: Herbert Hampton (sculptor), Walter Allward (sculptor), William Reid Dick.

c.1894 (61) Acacia Road. Garden pavilion for Edgar Anderson.

1894 (54) Circus Road. Veranda for M. R. Corbet by C. F. A. Voysey. Also see 1891.

1894 5 now 10 Hill Road. Repairs and alterations for W. Reynolds Stephens by C. F. A. Voysey.

1894 (56) Circus Road. Extension by architect F. M. Simpson for Maurice Greiffenhagen (EE 2650/1/521(C)).

1894 (10 and 12) Marlborough Hill. Additions and general repairs for Arthur Lucas by C. F. A. Voysey.

1894 (3) Blenheim Place, later (50) Grove End Road. Extension to accommodate a glass studio (licence and drawing at EE 2650/1/515(C)) (for painter Julius Mendez Price?).

1895 38 Abbey Road. Garden pavilion by Inman & Jackson, presumably for Charles P. Downing. Other artist at this address: James Faed (1902).

1895 9 Melina Place. Architectural drawing for new studio and alterations by architects Inman & Jackson for lessees Lancelot Fletcher and Charles Seaton. Perhaps for painter Francis Barraud, recorded there between 1902 and 1904 (WCA, 765/176).

1895 (62) Acacia Road. Gallery for studio, for Edward Onslow Ford by C. F. A. Voysey.

c.1895 18A Cunningham Place. Extension for architect James William Wild. Other artists at this address: Ellen Wild and prior to extension: F. W. Keyl, animal painter, pupil of Edwin Landseer. No. 16 next door housed the junior Constables c.1845–55.

c.1896 (5) Elm Tree Road. Conversion and part of St John's Wood Art Schools with Nos 6 and 7. Artists at this address: Bernard Ward, L. Joshua Cowen, A. A. Calderon.

1897 32 Queen's Road, now Grove. Garden studio for George Frampton (sculptor) and Christabel Cockerell (Lady Frampton) by C. F. A. Voysey (draft licence dated 1898 at EE 2650/1/32(B) and drawings at EE 2650/1/137(A) – see Plate 261).

c.1897 7 Hill Road. Garden pavilion for Hans Schadow.

c.1897 (8) Greville Place. Conversion for Edward Gregory.

c.1897 (18) Grove End Road. Extension for Miriam Davis. A polygonal addition to the north-east corner of the house.

1898 (78) Finchley Road. Extension for Charles F. Cleverley by C. F. A. Voysey (Licence Book II, p. 204, records a licence for building a studio dated 13 April 1894).

1898 (15) Abbey Road. Garden pavilion for Herbert J. Draper.

c.1898 41A now 17A Grove End Road. Extension for Owen Owen, the owner of No. 41 in 1900.

1898 3 Greville Place. Extension for the Dicksee family (Frank, Margaret

and Herbert). See The Art Journal (Christmas 1905) for pictures and descriptions.

1900s

c.1900 1 Melina Place. Extension for Herman and Henrietta Hart.

1900 26 Queen's Road. Extension for Arthur John Elsley (licence at EE 2650/1/32(A and B) and Licence Book II, p. 205).

1900–1 6 Carlton Hill, where Voysey lived until 1900 (Plate 291). Garden pavilion for former clergyman Clement Skilbeck. Other artists at this address: Harrington Man and prior to addition: Henry Macbeth-Raeburn (1886–92), Charles E. Stewart (1893–1901).

1901 (60) Finchley Road. Alterations to Bruntsfield House. See licence to widow Mrs Sophie Burgess (of 44 St John's Wood Park) and Solomon Joseph Solomon (of 60 Finchley Road) (EE 2650/1/150(C) and EE 2650/1/151(C)). Also see 1883.

Early 1900s 3A Greville Place. Extension for the Dicksee family (Frank, Margaret and Herbert). Lewis Baumer occupies No. 5.

c.1908 92–96 Carlton Hill. Studio-house for Sir George Frampton (Plate 134). Other artists at this address: Lady Frampton, Meredith Frampton, Arthur and Joy Fleischmann.

1909 Prince Albert Road. Conversion of Grove House/Nuffield Lodge (also known as Grove Lodge) for Sigismund Goetze (Plate 307); architect: Sidney Tatchell.

1920–21 (62) Wellington Road. Studio-house for Osward Birley; architect: Clough Williams-Ellis. Directly opposite Onslow Ford's 62 Acacia Road.

c.1926 31 Grove End Road. Garden pavilion for William Reid Dick. Later the home of Thomas Beecham (see p. 279).

c.1930 4 Greville Place. Extension for Gilbert Bayes (sculptor), the recipient of a blue plaque. Other sculptor at this address: John Angel.

Studio and Residence of
Sigismund Goetze Grove Lodge St Johns Wood corner of Albert Rd

307 Grove Lodge, the house and studio of Sigismund Goetze in Albert Road, opposite St John's Wood Church. Pencil drawing by Ernest Stamp, undated. Museum of London (Acc. No. 38.176/34).

APPENDIX 6
Sculptors' chronology

This chronology, which goes up to the 1920s, has been prepared using Cox-Johnson (1963), Walkley (1994), Morris and Milner (1993), and supplemented by data from the Eyre estate archive. I am also grateful to Ian Leith at the National Monuments Record (English Heritage) for his advice.

Please note that the dates below are for guidance only. They are often drawn from the list of Royal Academy exhibitors, but sometimes artists would have lived several years at a particular address prior to or long after exhibiting at the Royal Academy. For instance, this is the case with H. H. Armstead: listed in Cox-Johnson as residing at 52 Circus Road between 1898 and 1904, the licence for a studio extension which the artist requested from the Eyre estate in 1883 proved he was at that address fifteen years earlier than realised (see p. 461).

1810s
1809–17	J. C. F. ROSSI	21 Lisson Grove
1817–20	Henry ROSSI	21 Lisson Grove

1820s
1822–24	Henry ROSSI	41 Lisson Grove (probably the same as 21 Lisson Grove)
1823–29	J. C. F. ROSSI	41 Lisson Grove (probably the same as 21 Lisson Grove)

1830s
1830	Frederick TATHAM	20 Lisson Grove
1830	F. O. ROSSI and Ellenor ROSSI	Grove Street, Lisson Grove
1830–34	J. C. F. ROSSI	Grove Street (Acte House). Probably the same as above
1832–34	Edgar George PAPWORTH (the Elder)	29 Alpha Road (Thomas Papworth had been at this address from 1804)
1833–46	Henry SIBSON	Wellington Road and Cochrane Terrace
1837–38	Nathaniel PALMER	15 (now 36) Hamilton Place
1838–40	James FILLANS	12 South Bank
1838	F. O. Rossi and Ellenor ROSSI	12 Cochrane Street
1838–44	Edward Jones PHYSICK	16 Park Terrace (Road)

1840s
1841	Hamilton and Carlton MACCARTHY	6 Hayes Place, Lisson Grove
1847–48	Henry J. RICHTER	86 Lisson Grove
1848	F. O. Rossi and Ellenor ROSSI	44 St John's Wood High Street

1850s
1850	James WESTMACOTT	1 St John's Place (Rossi's site)
1854	Marshall WOOD	3 (later 22) St John's Wood Road
1856	Frederick ANSTEY	32 Alpha Road
1856–58	Edward H. BAILY	11 York Place
1857	Brother WILLIS	5 Douro Cottages
1858–61	John THOMAS	32 Alpha Road

1860s
1860–62	Edward H. BAILY	3 Ordnance Villas
1862–70	F. S. POTTER	1 and 12A Grove Place
1863–70	Charles MABEY	103 then 108 Lisson Grove
1864	R. PURVES	32 Alpha Road
1865–66	Louis Nicholas A. MEGRET	17 Hamilton Terrace
1866–70	Charles B. BIRCH	12 Alpha Road

1870s
1871–72	Charles B. BIRCH	10 Boscobel Place
1873–76	Thomas BROCK	10 Boscobel Place
1875	William Charles MAY	3 St John's Wood Studios, Queen's Road
1875–80	Ferdinand JUNCK	32 Grove Road
1875–1904	W. R. Reynolds STEPHENS	10 Hill Road
1876?	Henry PEGRAM	36 Marlborough Hill
1878–80	Henry Thomas SCHÄFER	62 Park Road and 7 Park Road Studios
c.1879	James N. FORSYTH	57 Abbey Road
1879	Edgar Bertram MACKENNAL	55 Abbey Road

1880s
1881–98	Ferdinand JUNCK	27 North Bank
1882	Henry Thomas SCHÄFER	4 Waverley Place
1882–1906	John ADAMS-ACTON	8 Langford Place
1883	George A. LAWSON	6 Marlborough Road
1883–97	Henry Thomas SCHÄFER	3 Acacia Gardens
1883–1904	H. H. ARMSTEAD	52 Circus Road
1885	Henry BAIN-SMITH	Park Studio
1886	Giambattista AMENDOLA	17 Grove End Road
1887–1901	Edward Onslow FORD	62 Acacia Road
1888–1903	George SIMONDS	Priory Studios, Lodge Place
1889	Lilian HAMILTON	12 Loudoun Road
1889	E. Roscoe MULLINS	24 (now 26A) Greville Road
1889–1904	John Macallan SWAN	3 Acacia Road

1890s
1890–92	Henry BAIN-SMITH	29 Cochrane Street
1890–99	Harry BATES	10 Hill Road

Above: this replica of a muse by Edward Onslow Ford forms part of the sculptor's memorial at the junction of Grove End and Abbey Roads (see p. 429). Right: detail from Charles Hartwell's monument outside St John's Wood church (see p. 390).

1900s

1900–4	Arthur WHITE	93 Clifton Hill
1901–4	G. Gilbert WALKER	19 St John's Wood Terrace
1902–4	John Henry BACON	33 St John's Wood Road
1903	Herbert HAMPTON	16 Maida Vale
1904	William Goscombe JOHN	24 (now 26A) Greville Road
1904	Albert TOFT	87 Clifton Hill
1905–9	Edgar Bertram MACKENNAL	38 Marlborough Hill
1908–12	John ADAMS-ACTON	17 Abbey Road
1909–28	George FRAMPTON	90 Carlton Hill

1890–99	Lilian HAMILTON	41 Circus Road
1890–1904	William Robert COLTON	Eaton Studios, Eaton Terrace (now Kingsmill Terrace) or St John's Wood Studios in Queen's Terrace?
1891–93	John Henry BACON	43 St John's Wood Park
1891–93	Theodore TUSSAUD	53 Carlton Hill
1892	Emily GRIFFITH	1 Acacia Road
1892–94	Frank BOWCHER	6 Clifton Hill Studios
1893–1908	George FRAMPTON	32 Queen's Road
1894–1900	Alfred GILBERT	16 Maida Vale
1894–1904	William Boscombe JOHN	Woronzow Studio
1895–1903	Edgar Bertram MACKENNAL	87 Clifton Hill
1896–1902	Henry PEGRAM	26 Norfolk Road
1896–1904	George Henry COWELL	1 Elm Tree Road
1899	Hibbert C. BINNEY	5 Clifton Hill Studios
1899–1903	Cecil BROWN	14 St John's Wood Road

APPENDIX 7
Photographic studios in St John's Wood

Compiled by David Webb.

Maximilian Wolfgang ARNDT born 1846 in Trier, Germany; lecturer at Regent St Polytechnic 1884–98; 10 Nugent Terrace 1893–98.

Alexander BASSANO with studio in the West End 1882–91
Rented 18 Alpha Road to be able to expose his plates in the garden (see p. 319).

John BEER born 1823 in St Pancras, died 1876 in Kensington; specialised in microphotographs, e.g. £1,000 banknote micro-photographed and mounted in scarf pin; 30 Alpha Road, Lisson Grove 1863–64.

Frank (Francis) BRIGGS 1858–63 born 1824 in Corfe, Dorset, died 1888 in St Marylebone;
15 High Street aka St John's Wood School of Photography;
40 High Street 1869–1903 aka St John's Wood School of Photography;
10 Queen's Terrace 1900–3; Last two studios managed by widow Harriet after husband's death.

Frederick BROWN born 1840 in Bisham, Berkshire, died 1924 in St Marylebone; 10 Blenheim Place 1889–90.

Thomas BROWNE born 1812 in Sunderland, died 1876 in St Pancras; Browne was in brief partnership with Alexander Bassano; 21 Springfield Road 1863–64.

Thomas (Tom) John COLLINS born 1853 in St Pancras, died 1890 in St Marylebone; 56 Cochrane Street 1878–84.

Adeline (Lena) CONNELL born 1875 in Bloomsbury, died 1949; photographic assistant to her father F. H. Connell (below) in 1891; 3 Blenheim Place 1900–1; 50 Grove End Road 1901–19.

Frederick Henry CONNELL born 1839 in Camberwell, died 1911 in Cricklewood; 69 Abbey Road 1891–92; 3 Blenheim Place 1893–1901; 50 Grove End Road 1901–11.

Adeline (Lena) CUNDY see CONNELL Adeline Connell married Jack Arthur Cundy in May 1914.

Alfred Paul DE WITT pornographer born in Paris in 1846; court case 22 October 1879 regarding extremely obscene photos; De Witt skipped bail and fled to Paris, where he had a secondary studio (Marylebone Mercury, 25 October 1879); 103 St John's Wood Terrace 1875–79.

Hermann Wilhelm T. ERNST born 1856 in Hanover, Germany, died 1933 in Hackney; 1 Waverley Place 1890–1902; 14 Finchley Road 1902–11.

Charles James FOX born 1826 in Westminster, died 1894 in Hendon; 30 Finchley Road 1871–73; 34 Finchley Road 1873–74.

William Row FROST & Co. 69 Abbey Road 1872–75.

FROST & THOMAS i.e. William Row Frost & (?) Thomas; 69 Abbey Road 1874–75.

Edmund Gilbert GANLEY born 1843 in Ireland, died 1895; 4 Eaton Terrace, Acacia Road 1888.

George GARET-CHARLES born 1850 in France, first husband of Regent's Park photographer Lallie Charles; The Nest, 49 Acacia Road 1899–1906.

William Gough GUBBINS born 1840 in Limerick, Ireland, died 1914; 103 St John's Wood Terrace 1864–65.

Thomas Clarence HAILEY born 1867 in Clare, Suffolk, died 1949 in Aston Rowant, Oxon; specialised in photographing horses, later owned a thoroughbred racing stud; 51 Ordnance Road 1888–1903.

Heath John HAVILAND born 1872 in Bath, died 1949 in Gerrards Cross, Bucks; 7A Elm Tree Road 1899–1900.

Thomas Wood HOLGATE born 1869 in Oldham, died 1954 in Truro, Cornwall; 2 Clifton Hill 1899–1900.

Ellen LINDELL born 1836 in Bristol, died 1901 in Cricklewood; 10 Queen's Terrace 1865–66.

Lawrence LOWE born 1833 in Westminster, died 1909 in St Marylebone; 10 Queen's Terrace 1867–93; 8 Abbey Gardens 1897–1909.

John Templeton LUCAS born 1836 in Lambeth, died 1880 in Whitby, North Yorkshire; 3 St John's Wood Road 1862–63.

LUCAS BROS i.e. Arthur and John Templeton Lucas; 3 St John's Wood Road 1863–65.

Frederick William MUNCEY born 1858 in Islington, died 1944 in Hove, Sussex; 80 Boundary Road 1896–98.

George William ROBERTS born 1844 in Chelsea, died 1909 in Kingston upon Thames; 6 Henstridge Place 1883–84.

William J. Beaumont WATSON born 1838 in Clerkenwell, died 1932 in Camberwell; 103 St John's Wood Terrace 1872–73.

APPENDIX 8
Lord's Cricket Ground: a chronology

This chronology focuses on the history of the site rather than cricketing events. It traces the arrival of Thomas Lord at St John's Wood and lists the main landmark dates which led to the acquisition of the freehold of the site by the Marylebone Cricket Club. I am grateful to the staff of the Lord's museum and archive for enabling me to search discrete parts of their archive. The Eyre estate archive fills some of the gaps left by the disappearance of the club's early records in the fire of 1825.

1808   (April) first mention of Thomas Lord in the Eyre letter books (LB 'A', p. 723). In the same year Homerton Cricket Club is also in negotiation with Walpole Eyre, who concludes: 'I fear the land I have to let will be at too extravagant a price for you' (LB 'A', p. 793).

    Agreement for ten acres of land between Lord and Eyre, south of the future Regent's Canal. 'Lord says (and I think rightly) that he cannot be tied down to keep this a Cricket Gro[un]d the whole term and he therefore wishes to have the privilege of Build[in]g & to this there can be no object[io]n if the spots and sort of Buildings are agreed upon at the time of granting the Lease' (LB 'A', p. 797). Lord wants to build twenty houses, but Walpole insists it should be half that amount (LB 'A', p. 801). The formal agreement for eighty years dated 15 October 1808 has not survived but is recorded in the agreement with the canal company at EE 2650/1/141(A), p. 2.

    Lord opens up his lodge as a public house: 'I had no conception you me[a]nt to turn the Lodge into a Common tap room/I cannot allow this to go on without your entering into some very special Agreement' (LB 'B', p. 521).

1812   (December) After the news of the projected Regent's Canal, Walpole proposes to Lord to pass on his lease to a 'Gentleman' (John Nash) since Lord expresses the wish to sell. Lord takes everyone by surprise by putting a huge valuation on the land: £9,000 (LB 'C', p. 111).

1813   (Early) Lord then suggests he will hand over the lease for an annuity paid to him and his wife for their lives (LB 'C', p. 160). Lord eventually settles for the purchase of his right and interest years (EE 2650/1/141(A) – see p. 2 of copy agreement with canal company, dated 29 July 1813). The land reverts back to Walpole, who issues a new 99-year agreement to the canal company.

    (7 August) A new agreement is prepared between Eyre and Lord for the club's present site (EE 2651/88(A) for eighty years).

1824   (1 January) Assignment of the ground from Lord to William Ward (EE 2651/88(B)) for the sum of £5,400.

    (July) Lease for Lord's two semi-detached houses at the south-east corner of the cricket ground ready (Plate 66).

308 Portrait painting of the celebrated cricketer John Wisden (1826–84) at Lord's by William Bromley (1835–88). John Wisden is now best remembered for his almanac, *Wisden's Cricketers' Almanack*, started in 1864 when he retired from first-class cricket. The house in the background on the right is that of Tom Hood in Elm Tree Road. Marylebone Cricket Club.

1825   (29 July) Lord's Pavilion (classed as temporary building) burnt to the ground. No mention of this dramatic event in the Eyre letter books.

1826   (May) Starting date of MCC Committee minute books.

1827   (June) Benjamin Aislabie elected secretary to the club (MCC Committee minute books, vol. I, pp. 12 and 15).

    (August) Walpole disapproves of the planned display of fireworks and says so to B. Dark, presumably Benjamin (LB 'K', p. 382).

1832   (13 January) Death of Thomas Lord (no mention in the Eyre letter books).

1833   First mention of James Dark in the 'Members of the Marylebone Club' (early pages under C: 'John Congreve Esq 34 Wilton Crescent Resigned in July 1833 to James Dark'; the book kept in the basement store of the MCC archive).

1835 (Summer) Decision to replace the 1824 assignment from Lord to William Ward by a lease made out to William Ward (see LB 'N', letters to Madeson). The lease survives in the MCC archive, dated 30 June 1835, between Walpole Eyre, Thomas Lord junior and William Ward. (According to Stephen Green, the recipient of the lease was James Henry Dark; the lease drawing in Bk of Drawings III, 106, features both names 'Ward' and 'Dark'. However, following the 1858 auction – see below – the 1859 conveyance to Moses stipulated the lease was in the name of William Ward.) Lord's pub at the main entrance to the ground sublet first to William Ward's sisters on 1 July 1835 (form of mortgage) and then to James Henry Dark on 3 July 1835 (Licence Book I, pp. 119 and 121).

1836 Ward assigns the lease to J. H. Dark, who pays £2,000 for it (mentioned in 1843 in the MCC Committee minute books, vol. I, p. 229).

1838 The MCC records show that the first 'real tennis' court is built on the site of the present Mound Stand (not mentioned in Eyre archive but see 1848 below).

1842 (16 May) First mention of 'Mr Dark' in the MCC Committee minute books (vol. I, p. 206).
(13 June) Death of Aislabie (MCC Committee minute books, vol. I, p. 217).
(20 June) MCC Committee minute books, vol. I, p. 220: 'that Mr James Dark, the lessee of Lords Ground having offered his services to the Club in any capacity in which they may be thought useful be requested to continue his valuable assistance to the Hon[orar]y Secretary'.

1843 397 members (MCC Committee minute books, vol. I, p. 227). MCC Committee minute books, vol. I, p. 228: 'indebted to the Tennis Court Committee for the great increase in our numbers no fewer than 98 candidates having been admitted in the year 1839–40'.

1847 (May) 520 members (MCC Committee minute books, vol. I, p. 271). Dark gives up the benefit of his ground on 26 July.

1848 (14 March) Extension of 'Raquet Court' using garden of 28 St John's Wood Road (Licence Book I, p. 344).

1849 Erection of 'offending' privies in the north-west corner of the site leads to complaints (LB 'S', p. 484).

1850 Generosity of Dark: he had 'undertaken the whole trouble and expence of draining the ground' (MCC Committee minute books, vol. I, p. 313). On p. 314 Dark refuses to be paid for this job.

1853 (19 February) Dark's proposal: 'to take on himself the expence of any Matches made by the Committee on receiving the whole amount of the Subscriptions and Entrance Money as well as to give £5 annually to the "Cricketers Fund"' (MCC Committee minute books, vol. I, p. 344). This proposal is adopted for 1853 and then renewed yearly until Dark's retirement.

1858 (21 June) Three days before the sale of Lord's ground the committee 'resolved that a General Meeting of the Club be held at 5pm on Monday July 5th 1858 to omit in Rule No:16 the words "or under

the Verandah"' (MCC Committee minute books, vol. I, p. 401). No mention anywhere that year or the following year of the change of ownership of the ground.
(24 June) Lord's sold at auction (Lot 19 in catalogue at EE 2651/340): 'Freehold Ground Rent of £150 per Annum, arising out of property for many years known as "Lord's Cricket Ground", the St John's Tavern Public House, and three dwelling houses Nos 31, 32 & 33 St John's Wood Road ... occupying an area of nearly eight acres, with the Reversion in Fee. Let on Lease to Mr William Ward, for a term of 59 years from Midsummer, 1834, at a Ground Rent of £150 per annum.' It is purchased by Isaac Moses – copy of conveyance dated 9 February 1859 at EE 2651/172E(11) – who pays £5,910 for it.

1860 640 members (MCC Committee minute books, vol. I, pp. 415–16).

1863 (16 November): 'A proposal was read from Mr Dark to part with his interest in Lords Ground & the Tavern for the sum of £15,000 being 15 years purchase on £800 income of ground[,] £200 income of Tavern[.] Mr Dark's interest in Lord's Ground being an unexpired term of 29½ yrs' (MCC Committee minute books, vol. I, p. 458). Committee recommends approaching a 'Valuator', who turns out to be Messrs Norton & Hoggart at 62 Broad Street (the auctioneers who handled the sale of the ground to Moses).

1864 Dark sells his lease to Lord's (see printed report for that year in the MCC Committee minute books, vol. I, p. 462). He receives £11,000 plus £1,500 for fixtures and fittings.[1]

1866 Moses (who had changed his name to Marsden) sells the freehold to the MCC for the price of £18,333 6s. 8d.[2]

1869 Eyre estate sells adjacent Guy's Garden (i.e. Henderson's nursery) to the earl of Sefton, the earl of Dudley and others (EE 2650/1/417(C)). The purchase money is £1,750 plus interest.

1887 3216 members. Purchase by the MCC 'from the Clergy Orphan Corporation, of Henderson's nursery, for £18,500', of 43 St John's Wood Road, and of 17 and 21 Elm Tree Road (Montgomery Eyre, 1913, p. 104).

1898 Purchase by the MCC of 22 Elm Tree Road and of 3 Grove End Road. Demolition of 43 and 45 St John's Wood Road (the numbers may have changed but otherwise the houses shown in Plate 66, Montgomery Eyre, 1913, p. 105).

1 I am grateful to Keith Mayer, a descendant of Isaac Moses, for this information.
2 Green, 2003, p. 59.

APPENDIX 9
Builders, developers and architects of St John's Wood

The names of solicitors have been included when known, as many deeds and documents would have been deposited at solicitors' offices rather than kept by individual builders. This information may prove helpful in future searches.

Francis ARMSON

He developed Greville Road and Clifton Hill (west) in 1843, which in part formerly belonged to the Eyre estate but was sold prior to development in the 1840s. On the Eyre estate he was at work making a section of Abbey Road in 1845,[1] and that same year obtained leases for two houses in Blenheim Road. These have survived to this day (Plate 292). One, a corner double house at the junction with Abbey Road, is in a classical style (44 Abbey Road and 29 Blenheim Road); the other, adjoining it, is in a 'Gothic' style (28 Blenheim Road) and very similar to the corner houses found in that part of the estate.[2] Armson was working with the Frys in the mid-1840s. By 1849 his properties on the Eyre estate, i.e. east of Abbey Road, must have been significant as they were described as 'Mr Armson's Estate'.[3]
Solicitor: John Chapple (addresses: Aldermanbury and Great Carter Lane).
Bibliography: Cherry and Pevsner, 1991.

William ATKINSON

William Atkinson (c.1773–1839) is best remembered for remodelling Abbotsford in Scotland for the writer Sir Walter Scott. Evidence for Atkinson's presence in St John's Wood dates from 1808 when he took over part of the ground which had been let to Messrs Hemmings & Gymm, and which wrapped around the Breeze Yard on the south-west corner of the estate. The rest of the plot had gone to Mr Storey, who went bankrupt. This led Thomas Martin to take over the ground, notably the public house.[4] Atkinson would have assumed responsibility for developing that part of the estate. The only document which survives in connection with this episode is Atkinson's lease for [half] a house overlooking Alpha Road on the south side (see No. 2 in the Alpha Cottages reconstruction, Plate 63).

By the summer of 1813 Atkinson had decided to take a large piece of ground on the corner of St John's Wood Road and Lisson Grove, the former site of the Red Barn or Punkers Barn, although with the disruption caused by the canal, it took several years before Walpole was able to finalise the paperwork. There, Atkinson built a substantial home, which sadly appears not to have been recorded in pictures,[5] as well as a lavish garden, which was immortalised in writing by John Thomas Smith, the first keeper of the British Museum collections (see p. 156). A plan of the site has survived (Plates 84 and 85), and the house (the highest rent) stretched across the ground in an arrangement which recalled that of Todd's house in Alpha Road (Plate 58).

Atkinson was well acquainted with Thomas Willan of St John's Wood Farm, for whom he designed the Manor House at West Twyford near Ealing.[6] Atkinson also replaced James Wyatt (1746–1813) as architect to the Board of Ordnance in 1813.[7] Wyatt's and Atkinson's style was either classical or 'Mixed Gothic', as Loudoun first described the irregular castellated style in 1806.[8] Bibliography: Colvin, 1995, pp. 75ff; Brown, 1996b.

Benjamin BENSON

Benjamin Benson, a carpenter by trade, was so modest a developer that he would not normally be expected to feature on this list. However, a copy of his will, dated 23 February 1814 and proved a few weeks later, is in the Eyre estate archive (EE 2651/278).

Benson must have built the double house at No. 24 on the Alpha Cottages reconstruction, a project probably financed by Thomas Gear. He kept the eastern half.[9] His estate consisted of the St John's Wood semi-detached house which he rented (the landscape painter Harriot Gouldsmith lived there between 1811 and 1820), his residence at 9 Allsop Place in Marylebone and his workshop (leased) at West Street, Seven Dials.

James BERRY

His earliest mention in the Eyre estate archive is in 1839 when he was described as a 'Gentleman' from Hammersmith in the agreement of that year.[10] He was connected to the firm of solicitors Berry and Gray, who were based at the southern end of St John's Wood at 12 Grove Place in the redeveloped Breeze Yard. This firm represented a number of the estate's builders including the trustees of the surveyor John White and John Maidlow.[11] James Berry's ground was on the north side of St John's Wood Terrace and also on the north side of Henstridge Place. The builder in Henstridge Place was a Mr Holland,[12] who

---

1 See LB 'Q', pp. 573 and 591.

2 The lease drawings for Armson's houses in Blenheim Road are in Bk of Drawings V, 40 right and 46 right. Also see LB 'R', pp. 62 and 74 for links with Fry and p. 204 for proposed agreement to take land which appears not to have been pursued.

3 See LB 'S', p. 447.

4 The eight lots for Hemmings & Gymm are mentioned in LB 'A', p. 91. In the absence of plans, it is extremely difficult to reconstruct exactly what happened in that corner of the site. Most of the evidence comes from LB 'A'.

5 From the attested copy of the release document (for twenty-one years from 25 June 1811) in the Eyre archive, it was agreed Atkinson would build a 'second rate house' which 'shall front Saint Johns Wood Grove Road' (now Lisson Grove) spending

'Eight hundred pounds at the least' (EE 2650/1/169(C), dated 4 August 1818).

6 This house still exists; it is very dilapidated and, at the time of writing, faces an uncertain future. VCH, *A History of the County of Middlesex*, vol. 7: *Acton, Chiswick, Ealing and Willesden Parishes*, 1982, p. 173, states that Willan rebuilt the Manor House c.1806.

7 David Watkin, *Thomas Hope and the Neo-Classical Idea*, London, 1968, p. 167.

8 Watkin (as above), p. 167.

9 The original lease has survived at EE 2650/1/248(B).

10 At EE 2651/15.

11 See, for instance, LB 'R', p. 371, for John White and LB 'P', p. 447, for John Maidlow.

12 Andrew Saint suggests he might have been a partner in a firm called Winslow and Holland.

unfortunately gave Walpole many opportunities to complain – poor materials, poor workmanship and delays. While Walpole kept up the complaints with Berry and Holland, a letter he wrote to Shaw suggests he had low expectations for the Henstridge Place development: 'we need not be very particular about the Elevation as the houses are in an inferior Situation but the material point is whether these houses will be worth £600 each when completed that is £1200 the pair or for each pile of Building – Mr Holland who is to build these houses states to Mr Berry & me that they will be worth £1200 the pair.'[13]

John BETTINSON

He was the foreman of William Robert Fry and first acquired a lease for a property in Clifton Road East in 1854.[14] In or before 1858 Fry sublet to him his building yard at the bottom of Ordnance Hill (see Plate 309). Bettinson was very keen to retain it as a working building yard, even when permission was granted in 1858 to develop the rest of the site as houses.[15] In 1861, he took over a substantial part of the Springfield Road site which Fry surrendered. At that time he was described as 'a respectable man … backed by Mr Nation a Sol[icito]r'.[16] He succeeded in obtaining about a dozen more leases in that road.

Alexander BIRNIE

Alexander Birnie (d.1835), oilman, is first mentioned in April 1806.[17] We subsequently learn that he acquired five lots from Walpole and that Edmund Waters was already lined up as a leaseholder.[18] Walpole and Birnie seem to have been constantly bickering: Birnie arguing with him over money, Walpole having to send numerous rent reminders and to drive a hard bargain with Birnie, who appears to have been keen to extend his foothold in St John's Wood at the least possible expense. Birnie's cows were a regular source of aggravation, trespassing onto Lord's Cricket Ground and forcing Walpole to ensure Birnie's ground was fenced. There was a dispute between them in connection with the lease covenants, and on this occasion Birnie invoked the form of Mr Portman's leases; this may suggest he had been involved with the Portman estate in some way.[19] Some of the Wood's most glamorous residents were found on land let to Birnie: for instance, architect C. H. Tatham as well as Edmund Waters, manager of the King's Theatre, Haymarket. Birnie himself must have been a man of considerable means as he apparently guaranteed a £10,000 loan for the building of Hanover Terrace in 1823.[20] He died in 1835.[21]

James BLYTH

This plumber by trade purchased a substantial number of the Alpha Cottages when the leases came up for renewal in 1865. In 1863, he had tentatively acquired two houses in Park Road, but in 1864 he acquired another five leases, and this was subsequently followed by further nineteen leases.[22] The estate clerk thought well of him in 1865: 'Blyth whom we know so far as a man who fulfils his engagements'.[23] However, this glowing report was soon undermined by great difficulties over the rents. In the end it would appear that James Blyth seriously overstretched his resources.

James BURTON and sons

James Burton (1761–1837), the successful developer of the Foundling, Skinners' and Bedford estates, is first mentioned in the Eyre archive in 1817. He was chosen by the canal company to implement on their behalf the building programme they had agreed in 1813 with the Eyres. An 1818 agreement between the canal company, Walpole Eyre and James Burton has survived which specifically relates to the north side of the canal.[24] However, Burton would go on supervising construction on the south side as well, as is made clear by the lease he obtained from the Eyre estate in 1823 (see Plate 74).

The villa Burton built for himself – The Holme in Regent's Park – was designed by his son Decimus and is well documented.[25] It aspired to considerably more grandeur than the houses being built in St John's Wood.

His sons Decimus and Septimus were also involved with their father's work and became friends of the Eyre family. Septimus was a lawyer who dealt with the legal side of the Burton family's business. Decimus was the architect of several developments in the Regent's Park including the Zoological Gardens (1828) and the famous Colosseum for panoramic entertainments (1829). By 1826 Decimus had become the surveyor of the adjacent Harrow Free School estate, which eased further practical discussions between the Eyres and their westerly neighbour.[26] Bibliography: Manwaring Baines, 1956; Britton and Pugin, 1825–28.

Charles Claudius COOK and son

He is described as a house painter and glazier from North Audley Street in 1839, when he took over the agreement for land along the west side of the Marylebone and Finchley Turnpike Road (i.e. Finchley Road) from architects Pink & Erlam. Later he described himself as a builder.[27] Cook took out many more agreements: three in 1840, two in 1842, one in 1844, another in 1846, three more in 1850. He ran into difficulty in the mid-1840s and mortgaged several agreements to John Edwards, subsequently losing the Marlborough Hill development and the northern plot along the Finchley Road. He made a comeback in 1850 by taking land on either side of Boundary Road, asking for an extension in 1854 (or could it be his son? see below). Architecturally, Cook worked in all genres – classical in Boundary Road next to Alhambra Cottage,[28] and often 'Gothic', most notably

13 Letter dated 8 July 1845 in LB 'Q', p. 615.

14 Bk of Drawings VI, 111 right.

15 LB 'U', p. 582.

16 LB 'V', p. 381.

17 Letter to Birnie dated 16 April 1806 in LB 'A', p. 249.

18 Letter to Birnie dated 16 February 1807 in LB 'A', p. 466.

19 Letter to Birnie dated 13 August 1807 in LB 'A', p. 584.

20 Saunders, 1981, p. 118.

21 LB 'N', p. 473.

22 See Bk of Drawings VII.

23 LB 'W', p. 367.

24 At EE 2651/39.

25 Britton and Pugin, 1825–28, vol. I, pp. 83–88 and plate.

26 He was acting surveyor from 1826 (LB 'K', p. 77) and was surveyor by 1831 (Harrow School archive: Governors' Minutes, vol. II, 9 March 1831, p. 1).

27 See, for instance, the 1845 mortgage at EE 2651/5(C).

28 Bk of Drawings IV, 81A left.

the large and elaborate semi-detached houses on the east side of Finchley Road.[29] He was also responsible for the first 'Italian Villa' in St John's Wood,[30] which was leased to him in 1840 (see Plate 78). By 1850 Cook's address in the letter books is given as Pier Hotel in Chelsea. His name features prominently in the list of lessees, the earliest lease dating from 1840 and the last from 1855.

The Eyres complained on a number of occasions about his misuse of the land (without specifying what it was), and he also ran large rent arrears. Eventually, in 1866, the estate's solicitors, Messrs White & Son, brought an action against Cook to recover the land in his possession.[31]

His son, also known as C. C. Cook, took out two leases in Boundary Road in 1864; this suggests that leases to C. C. Cook could involve father and son, and distinguishing between the two can be quite difficult. The legal action described above may have been against Cook junior, who would most likely have been his father's executor.
Solicitor: E. G. Randall.

James DAVIS and sons

Builder James Davis senior (d.1825) took land on agreement with architect William Atkinson on the south side of Alpha Road around 1811. A year later he was a St John's Wood lessee. He must have resided there as he was a ratepayer in 1815. He died in January 1825, and his executors were his sons James Davis junior and Charles Davis (who built Ugo Foscolo's houses in South Bank) as well as James Price and William Thomson. In 1857, James Davis junior was the lessee of the family home at 32 Alpha Road, which was taken over by the sculptor John Thomas (1813–62) and lost its garden to this artist's studio and workshop (see p. 315). Most of this information comes from the licence that was granted to Davis for transforming his house into accommodation for a sculptor and his studio.[32]
Solicitor: E. G. Randall.

The DAVISON brothers

William Davison was the architect and his brother John the wealthy backer of his elegant St John's Wood Road project. The original agreement for this scheme has not survived, but the sale deed has, giving considerable detail about the history of this development.[33] The lease drawing for a group of four houses and a pavilion is dated 1818 (see Plate 209). In 1837, John succeeded in purchasing the land and its buildings from the Eyre brothers,[34] although the conveyance was not ready until three years later. The 1853 map, normally so reliable, does not show all the buildings erected by the Davisons, but the sale document includes a detailed plan (see Plate 210). In 1862, a Miss Davison sold part of this property.[35]

William Davison is first mentioned in the archive in 1817 when he resided at Prospect Place, Edgware Road. He exhibited at the Royal Academy in 1797 and 1798, and a volume of his designs, dating from about 1825, survives in the Avery Library of Columbia University. John resided at Grove End Place, the name of his brother's development when he purchased the freehold. Solicitor: Messrs Whishaw, in and prior to 1862.[36]
Bibliography: Colvin, 1995.

Charles DAY

Charles Day (d. c.1833) was an early St John's Wood lessee: the lease drawing for a property in Grove End Road on the west side of Lord's has survived, dated 1819. As the property stood on land under agreement with William Hall, Day is likely to have been connected to him. This is confirmed when we next encounter Day working, like Hall, on the Portman estate. He appears to have been the architect in charge of the Eyre brothers' final home, acquired in 1823 and situated at 22 Bryanston Square.[37] The following year Charles Day, described as a surveyor, entered into agreement with Walpole for a plot of land situated opposite his home at Grove End Road.[38] There had been a previous agreement for this land with carpenter John Clemence and bricklayer Henry de Bruno Austin, which had to be cancelled as 'Henry de Bruno Austin hath fallen into difficulties and embarrassments.'[39] The houses on that agreement were designed according to Todd's model. From a sketch inside the deed, we learn that the road later known as Warwick Place had already been made by Austin. Charles Day seems to have delivered the houses on that agreement and retired to Worcestershire in 1829, presumably living off the revenue from his properties. By October 1833 he is described as the 'late Mr Day'. His wife Anna received leases as late as 1835 and died on 18 January 1837.[40] The executors of the Day estate were Charlotte Frances Day and John Rees. Walpole sold the freehold of Charles Day's estate in 1839 to John Pepys to settle the late Robert Todd's bill, which his executors wanted to be paid without any delay.[41]

John EDWARDS

John Edwards (d.1858) is the man who bailed out Charles Claudius Cook in 1845 when he was in difficulty over his development work at St John's Wood. Edwards subsequently took over a large part of Cook's land, leading him to surrender Cook's original agreements in order to enter into fresh agreements with Walpole. Described as a 'Gentleman', Edwards employed William Ifold as an architect and surveyor, and one of the latter's drawings has survived.[42]

When writing to Shaw in 1849, Walpole judged: 'from enquiries I have made about Mr Edwards I have every reason to believe that he is fully competent

29 Bk of Drawings IV, 30 left.
30 LB 'P', p. 256.
31 LB 'W', p. 456.
32 Licence Book II, p. 59. Also licences at EE 2650/1/249.
33 At EE 2651/177.
34 Letter dated 29 July 1837 in LB 'O', p. 328.
35 LB 'V', p. 493.
36 LB 'V', p. 493.

37 There are very detailed descriptions of the teething problems experienced by the Eyres when they first moved into Bryanston Square. The other person they discussed these problems with was Colonel Graham, the original lessee or the financial backer. See LB 'I'.
38 See EE 2651/54.
39 See EE 2651/76 dated 23 March 1821.
40 Licence Book I, p. 162.
41 EE 2651/183.
42 See inside EE 2651/37.

to carry out this arrangement'.[43] However, Edwards died in 1858[44] having only partly fulfilled his agreements.[45] In 1862, Edwards's sons were eager to dispose of their father's concern in St John's Wood.[46]
Solicitors: E. G. Randall, Messrs Burgoyne & Milne.

John Samuel ERLAM (see PINK & ERLAM)

Charles FREETH senior and junior

Charles Freeth senior (d.1869) was Walpole Eyre's trusted clerk. He was appointed in May 1816, and Walpole described him in 1829: 'a Confidential Clerk and who has been with me many years he is also a housekeeper in this Parish, and has been so for several years'.[47] Freeth senior worked in the Eyre office up to the deaths of Henry Samuel (1851) and Walpole (1856) and then went on to serve the next Eyre generation. In addition, he was employed by the Sun Fire Insurance Company, the estate's mortgagors. He was also the clerk to the trustees of the Marylebone and Finchley Turnpike Road Trust.[48]

It is likely that Charles Freeth senior cut his teeth in the development business with surveyor John White as early as 1828 and 1829 when a Charles Freeth was entering into agreements with White (see John Hinton and John White in Appendix 2). The lease granted on 29 May 1837 for a property on the corner of Grove End Road and Loudoun Road would have been the outcome of this agreement.[49] Back in 1834 after the lease had fallen in, Charles senior also announced he had moved into St John's Wood 'Farm House' (see p. 395).[50] Charles and Walpole would probably have regarded direct involvement with the development of the estate as leading to a conflict of interest. So Charles senior's involvement was once removed by subletting from other developers – John White initially and later his own son.

Charles senior had two sons who both became involved in developing parts of the estate in different capacities – Thomas as a solicitor and Charles junior, also employed by the Sun Insurance Company in Welbeck Street, as a developer. The letter books chart a falling out between Charles senior and Charles junior and also between Walpole and Thomas. The Acacia Road scheme ran into all sorts of difficulty. Nevertheless, father and son seem to have patched up their differences and turned their troubled projects into a working concern.

Charles Freeth senior was appointed vestryman in Marylebone in 1858.[51] He died on 26 January 1869,[52] and his death marked the end of Walpole's era.

William Robert FRY and son

William Robert Fry's first appearance on the St John's Wood estate was in 1822. At that time he was in partnership with George Watkins, and both men were described as timber merchants from Commercial Road in Limehouse. They were

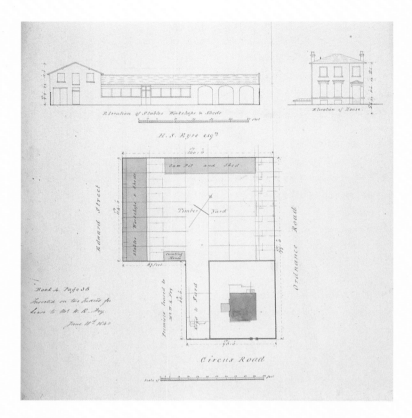

309 William Robert Fry's house and workshop at the north-western corner of Ordnance Road and St John's Wood Terrace. The drawing is dated 11 June 1840. On 6 April 1850 Walpole wrote to the estate's architect, John Shaw junior, about this plot: 'Mr Fry has not built any house but has laid the ground into his Timber Yard and Mr Futooye the tenant of No 8 (late No 6) Acacia Rd … complains of the ground being used as a Timber Yard.' Eyre estate archive (Bk of Drawings IV, 36 right).

put in charge of John Maidlow's Wellington Road development (eastern block), which came to a standstill when George Watkins was declared bankrupt in 1830. A year or so later Fry took out land on agreement in the Marylebone and Finchley Turnpike Branch Road (i.e. Avenue Road),[53] a risky strategy which led to his own bankruptcy in January 1835.[54] By that date Fry had acquired a considerable reputation for his brickmaking, and Walpole alerted his builder friend George Spencer Smith to this excellent supply when Fry was going under: 'I am told Mr Frys bricks are very good,' he wrote on 17 January 1835, but alas the popularity of Fry's bricks meant he had to write on the same day: 'I have been to St John's Wood this Evening[.] I fear Wm Frys bricks are nearly all gone.'[55]

43 LB 'S', pp. 473–74.
44 LB 'U', p. 579.
45 LB 'V', p. 34.
46 LB 'V', p. 439.
47 The first letter signed by Freeth is at LB 'D', p. 539. The quote comes from a letter dated December 1829 in LB 'L', p. 427.
48 See LB 'S', p. 559.

49 Lease at EE 2650/1/361(A) or Bk of Drawings III, 103.
50 LB 'N', p. 337.
51 *Marylebone Mercury*, no. 37, 1 May 1858, p. 3.
52 LB 'X', p. 290.
53 Bk of Drawings III, 79.
54 LB 'N', p. 433.
55 LB 'N', p. 435.

Fry was back in action by 1840, having been forced to sell his interest in the Avenue Road agreement to a Mr Saunders in 1839.[56] He set up his workshop in Ordnance Road (Plate 309) and took on various plots of land from Walpole. Initially these were in the vicinity of his workshop, but later, between the 1830s and 1850s, in partnership with his son George William,[57] he successfully developed large tracts of land on the east side of Abbey Road (see Plate 72 and Appendix 2), with the help of occasional mortgages.[58] By 1854 Fry's son appears to have taken the lead in the business,[59] but he died on 17 November 1856. His wife Elizabeth Green Fry inherited his estate and a few years later that of the father, William Robert Fry, who died on 2 October 1862.[60] A letter from Charles Freeth dated June 1857 makes it clear that the firm was in a great deal of trouble: 'the persons who ought to have made the above Road [Clifton Road East] were the Messrs Fry Father & Son – but the son is dead and the Father under restraint and in embarrassed circ[umstanc]es therefore they are out of the question.'[61] The rent arrears at that date were well over £250.[62] The land left undeveloped by the Frys was in Springfield Road, and the plot was taken over by Joseph Parkins in 1860.[63]
Solicitor: Stephen Garrard (from 1851); Richard Nation (from 1857).

Samuel GARDNER

A developer, though a plasterer and bricklayer by trade, who had built houses in Elm Tree Road (working for William Hall) and took a plot on agreement situated on the west side of Wellington Road.[64] Alas, like many others, he went bankrupt in 1827 before he was able to complete his project.[65] His house in Elm Tree Road has survived – a landmark since it is the oldest surviving house on the estate (see Plate 49).

William HALL and family

William Hall (d.1832 or 1833) was probably the brother of John Hall, house painter from Upper Berkeley Street, who worked for Robert Todd and built one of the Alpha Cottages (No. 19 on the Alpha Cottages reconstruction).

The 1814 agreement with William Hall is one of the earliest agreements to have survived. William Hall built the house in which the Eyres resided in Montagu Place between 1814 and 1823. Hall was therefore a builder of experience since he had been involved in development work on the Portman estate. He was recorded on the St John's Wood estate between 1813 and 1826 when, either a bankrupt or on the verge of bankruptcy, Hall assigned all his interests to trustees.

Described as a house painter, then a builder, he was based at Upper George Street near Montagu Square from at least 1813; he moved to St John's Wood (Elm Tree Road) in 1830 and died a couple of years later. His sons continued some of their father's development work, and this suggests that the story of William Hall dying destitute at the workhouse (see Brown, 1995) is probably incorrect. Thomas lived at Elm Tree Road (see pp. 254–55 for some colourful correspondence); William junior, Charles and Caleb acquired the lease of two stable buildings in Ordnance Mews in 1826,[66] which led to further colourful correspondence when Walpole tackled the terrible neglect into which the place had fallen by 1834 (see p. 399). Charles seems to have been based at the original home address in Upper George Street, and was wealthy enough in 1846 to buy a substantial chunk on the north-west side of the St John's Wood estate for the sum of £5,490. The final sale only came through in 1849, which suggests raising the money could not have been easy.
Solicitor: Mr Springall.

Thomas HARDWICK

A pupil of William Chambers, Thomas Hardwick (1752–1829) exhibited at the Royal Academy between 1772 and 1805. Colvin judges him 'a competent designer in a conservative neo-classical manner which he inherited from Chambers. But unlike Chambers, he never became a fashionable designer of houses for the wealthy, and he made a living chiefly as a surveyor and as a designer of churches and minor public buildings.' He was the surveyor of the marquis of Salisbury's London estate (from 1804) and of St Bartholomew's Hospital (from 1809), as well as being the Clerk of Works at Hampton Court (from 1810). In 1815, he added Kew Palace and its gardens to his 'portfolio'. He built St John's Wood's first chapel (see Plate 189) and the Orphan Clergy Asylum alongside it (see Plate 115). He was the surveyor of this school, a position inherited by his son from around 1843.
Bibliography: Colvin, 1995.

Jacob HIBBERD

He was described as a carpenter in the earliest surviving agreement he entered into in 1841, with the builder Charles Maidlow.[67] By 1853 he was called a builder.[68] He built two remarkable terraces of houses, one in Queen's Grove under agreement with John Wright Treeby, and another in St Ann's Terrace under agreement with Samuel Erlam. By 1847 the Eyre estate office referred to 'Hibberds Estate' in Norfolk Road.[69]

He ran into serious difficulty with the St Ann's Terrace scheme by taking various liberties with his 1852 agreement, notably building one extra house.[70]

56 LB 'P', p. 364.
57 For example, EE 2651/61.
58 For instance, Mr Cartwright in 1851: see LB 'T', p. 270.
59 LB 'T', p. 569.
60 These dates come from 'Abstract of Administration of G. W. Fry's Estate and of Will of W. R. Fry', a document filed inside the 1845 agreement at EE 2651/84.
61 LB 'U', p. 452.
62 LB 'U', p. 473.
63 LB 'V', p. 172.

64 See EE 2651/52.
65 See EE 2650/1/119.
66 LB 'K', p. 68.
67 At EE 2651/130, see inside the 1837 agreement with Pink & Erlam.
68 At EE 1651/63.
69 LB 'R', p. 570. What this phrase meant is clarified much later in LB 'S', p. 20, i.e. 19, 21 and 22 Norfolk Road.
70 Agreement at EE 2651/86(A and B). The liberties are described in a letter to Shaw dated 11 September 1852 in LB 'T', pp. 290 and 293.

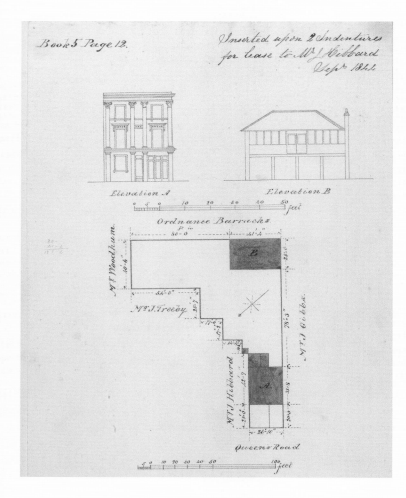

310 The house and workshop of Jacob Hibberd in Queen's Road (now Queen's Grove). The lease drawing is dated September 1844. The house and premises are still there, as is the imprint of the workshop, which has been rechristened 'Walpole Mews'. Eyre estate archive (Bk of Drawings V, 12 right).

Edwin Eyre insisted at first it should be pulled down. With the calming intervention of John Shaw, a compromise was reached which is described in one of Hibberd's leases. Despite this incident, Hibberd seems to have been determined to acquire respectability, and by 1862 he was a member of the vestry, having purchased 67 Avenue Road from W. H. Twentyman.[71] However, according to the letter books his rent-paying record was rather poor, needing endless reminders and threats. The last reminder was sent to him in 1871, which suggests he may have died shortly after.[72]
Solicitor: Edward Lambert, Gray's Inn.

71 LB 'V', pp. 453 and 497.
72 LB 'X', p. 373.
73 See recital in surrender dated 1 January 1829 at EE 2651/1(C).
74 See LB 'L', p. 192.
75 EE 2651/40 and EE 2651/41.
76 EE 2651/42.

John HINTON

This victualler ran the Vernons Arms Coffee House in North Audley Street when he entered into two agreements with Walpole Eyre in 1823 (12 February and 10 November). Overall the project meant building 127 houses, most arranged in groups of three to look like one house. On 25 October 1826 John Hinton, who had tried to keep this ambitious project going by taking out various mortgages (see p. 208), was declared bankrupt.[73] Both agreements were duly surrendered on 1 January 1829, and the surveyor John White junior acquired Hinton's concern shortly afterwards, soon to relinquish all his engagements except for a handful of properties, which included the prize possession of the Eyre Arms and its assembly rooms.

Thomas JOHNSON

Thomas Johnson, described as a carpenter from Stafford Place in 1825, was one of the many 1820s casualties on the St John's Wood estate. His development project was connected to the Hall family,[74] as he had taken land formerly used by William Hall for brickmaking. Johnson had optimistically entered into agreement with Walpole in 1825.[75] However, five years later, like his contemporaries William Ward, John Maidlow, Stephen Watkins and William Robert Fry, he had to surrender his ground.[76] On 17 December 1829, Walpole wrote: 'I very much fear Mr J[ohnson] is in a very bad way.' By the time Johnson surrendered his agreement the following year, he was residing at Abbey Road on the site of his development.

The LEIGH brothers

Charles Frederick is the first of the two brothers to appear in the Eyre archive. In October 1837 he was laying drains into the sewer from a house at 25–26 Grove End Road, and the following October he signed an agreement with Walpole for a plot on the west side of Finchley Road.[77] George Leigh's agreement followed in 1841, though he was recorded as working on the estate from at least 1838.[78] Walpole complained about the brothers' 'inferior houses' on a couple of occasions,[79] and yet Charles Frederick's house on Grove End Road[80] was put forward as a model house in the following agreements: EE 2651/131 (1837, wrongly labelled George) and EE 2651/32 (1842).

By 1845 George Leigh was dead, and Fry told Walpole that 'there was a judgement against Mr G. Leigh', suggesting he had been in difficulty.[81]

Thomas LORD

This pillar of the cricket world makes a surprising entry in the list of developers of the St John's Wood estate. Thomas Lord (1755–1832) cunningly anticipated possible development work on the fringes of his cricket ground, and his 1813 agreement with Walpole Eyre made provision for the building, after ten years

77 EE 2651/47.
78 LB 'O', p. 555.
79 LB 'Q', p. 12, for George and LB 'P', p. 229, for Charles Frederick.
80 Bk of Drawings III, 108.
81 Letter to Springall & Thompson dated 27 August 1845 in LB 'R', p. 25.

from the date of the agreement (i.e. 1823), of sixteen houses to have the appearance of eight houses (see Plate 65).[82] Lord's initial proposal had been for twenty houses but was judged excessive and reduced.[83]

Thomas Lord is first mentioned in the letter books in 1808, the date of the original agreement for his cricket ground south of the Regent's Canal (this document has not survived). When he assigned the ground to William Ward in 1824 (see Appendix 8 on p. 467), he retained the east corner and built there a modest double house (see Plate 66) which his son, a solicitor, inherited.

Thomas LOTHIAN

Thomas Lothian (d.1842), a carpenter from Princess Street, Cavendish Square, later of Chester Place, Regent's Park, made his appearance on the estate in 1826.[84] In 1830, he 'mopped up' with Mr Churchill part of 'bankrupt' William Hall's land around Langford Place. By 1838 he had secured a lease for a double house on the corner of Grove End and Kilbourne (now Loudoun) Roads (subsequently assigned to James Russell) and lived in one of the semi-detached houses.[85] This house still exists, now numbered 47–49 Grove End Road. Lothian was one of the builders named in John White's surrender document of 4 March 1834.[86] A year later he took over the ground surrendered by bankrupt Hinton on either side of Loudoun Road.[87] He died in 1842, but his executors, C. C. Black and his widow, continued the work mapped out on the agreement, securing various leases in the 1840s, including in 1845 leases for eight houses built by the architect Mr Taylor in Loudoun and Marlborough Roads and Langford Place (Plate 311).[88]

Solicitor (in 1852 to Mrs Lothian): Mr Millar, 4 Wellington Road.

John MAIDLOW

The Maidlow brothers – William, John and Charles – were troubled but important figures in the development of the estate. In the early 1820s when the houses of the Regent's Canal Company were nearing completion and the St John's Wood estate looked inviting to builders and speculators, John Maidlow boldly took on agreement three large blocks of land in 1822 and 1824 before going bankrupt in 1826.

The developers' map (Plate 72) shows the size of the original plots: the strips of land north and west of Portland Town where he had his workshop (1822) and most ambitiously the substantial plot of land between the Barracks and the Eton College/Portland estates. Maidlow's assignees put up for sale all his assets on 21 March 1826 at the Auction Mart opposite the Bank of England.[89] Henry Samuel Eyre was assigned the Portman estate lease of a house built for Maidlow at 9 Avenue Road, often described in the letter books as the

'Regent's Park house'.[90] After signing the agreements with the St John's Wood estate Maidlow immediately brought in various builders as well as a wealthy solicitor, Charles Malpas from the Inner Temple. The builders included Messrs Fry and Watkins, timber merchants from Limehouse, for the Cochrane Terrace development, Richard Roots and the Watkins brothers for St John's Wood Terrace. This series of unrealised agreements took years to iron out: Walpole was only able to complete the issuing of leases for block 'A' in the late 1840s.

John Maidlow made a comeback in 1840 to develop the north side of St John's Wood Terrace, including the building of the Portland Chapel (see Plate 191). As late as 1845 he was approached by the builder-developer George Spencer Smith, a friend of the Eyres, to build houses south of Swiss Cottage, a job he seems to have immediately delegated to Richard Thomas.

Thomas MARTIN

Early evidence for Thomas Martin's contribution to the development of St John's Wood is of such a humble nature that it is difficult to reconcile it with this architect's entry in Colvin's *Dictionary of Architects*. There are a couple of references to him in 1808 as the estate's 'fence man': 'I sho[ul]d be glad if you wo[ul]d make immed[iatel]y about half a dozen Oak Posts and paint them white with the letter P in black on the one side and the letter E on the other side, they are intended to make the Boundary between Mr Portmans and my Brothers Estates and sho[ul]d be about a foot or a foot and a half out of the Gro[un]d.' And some time later: 'I shall be at St Johns Wood on Wednesday next about 12 o/c & sho[ul]d wish you to be there with a man to dig the holes & put down the Posts I begged you to have made and painted for me with a P & E[.] How many have you got done[?]'[91] However, his involvement with fencing the Eyre estate seems to have run alongside building houses, first a house on the south side of Alpha Road on the 'Todd model' (see No. 6 Alpha Cottages reconstruction), followed by others, moving north with the estate's development (see Plate 63). The letter books also record that Thomas Martin was arrested in 1814, and this suggests he was having cash flow problems.
Bibliography: Colvin, 1995.

Richard NATION

One of a number of solicitors who seems to have been seduced by property development on the estate when their clients struggled to keep their projects afloat.[92] He is first mentioned as the solicitor of the developer James Sharp in 1845.[93] He became a developer in his own right, probably by financing Sharp's project, and he finally acquired peppercorn leases in 1847 for 10, 11 and 12 Queen's Terrace.

82 EE 2651/88(A).
83 LB 'A', p. 801.
84 LB 'K', p. 115.
85 LB 'O', p. 534, and Bk of Drawings III, 128.
86 At EE 2651/243(B).
87 Southern part of Loudoun Road, document at EE 2651/50.
88 LB 'R', p. 10.
89 Catalogue inside agreement at EE 2651/96.
90 See letter to William Todd dated 30 August 1826 in LB 'K', p. 140. Also letter to Cory

in LB 'M', p. 450. George Watkins was paid for work on this house in November 1830: see LB 'M', p. 133.
91 LB 'A', p. 769 for first quote and p. 781 for second quote, letters dated 6 and 21 July 1808. The address for Thomas Martin in the letter books corresponds to that given in Colvin, 1995, i.e. George Street, Portman Square.
92 Others which have been noted were Charles Malpas with bankrupt John Maidlow (1822) and Frederick Elijah Thompson with bankrupt Charles Smith (1849).
93 LB 'Q', p. 534.

NEWTON & KELK

The full names of these two builder partners were William Turton Newton and John Kelk of Margaret Street. Their houses on the south-west side of Cavendish Road were built in the 1840s to a single formula: a classicised version of Todd's archetypal house with distinctive rusticated ground floors (see Plates 276 and 277 for a more detailed look at No. 19). The builders' names appear in the letter books as early as 1841 when they were hired by Charles Freeth junior to develop part of Cavendish Road. The letter books record a competitive feud between them and the developer James Salter (on the east side of Cavendish Road) over sewer work.[94] Sir John Kelk (1816–86) served his apprenticeship with Thomas Cubitt before going into partnership with William Newton.

He later became an important figure in the Victorian building trade. In the 1850s and 1860s he was responsible for the early buildings of the Victoria and Albert Museum, followed by the Albert Memorial, inaugurated in 1872. His wealth came from the construction of railways and docks – including Victoria Station and Pimlico Railway. He collected art – he is recorded as buying works by John Constable and Peter Tillemans – and purchased Tedworth House in Wiltshire in 1876. He is buried in Kensal Green Cemetery.

Solicitor: Messrs Clarke Fynnmore & Co.
Bibliography: *DNB*.

Thomas PAPWORTH

Thomas Papworth (1773–1814) was the son of John Papworth (1750–99), master-plasterer to the royal palaces and brother of the well-documented John Buonarotti Papworth, a prolific author and architect. Thomas owned 'the last stucco and plastering business carried on in London on a large scale', first from Portland Place, then from Newman Street, and he regularly exhibited at the Royal Academy between 1794 and 1815 (there is a discrepancy between this date and the published date for his death). His only son, Edgar George Papworth, sent works to the Royal Academy from 29 Alpha Road between 1832 and 1834, which was one of the properties built by his father (see No. 3 on the Alpha Cottages reconstruction).

Bibliography: Gunnis, 1968, pp. 289–90; *DNB*; Graves, 1905–6.

PINK & ERLAM, architects

There appear to be two Erlam generations at work on the estate: first, Samuel Erlam, followed – after a gap of almost ten years – by John Samuel Erlam, the man who would form a partnership with John Pink. In 1801, a Samuel Erlam was apprenticed to a Paddington surveyor, Henry Cooper, who was later engaged in speculative building on the Grosvenor estate. Perhaps born in the mid-1780s, he may be identified with the Samuel Erlam who first appeared on the estate in 1827 when he purchased a lease for a house in Elm Tree Road immediately north of Lord's Cricket Ground.[95] At that time he was a surveyor

from Lees Mews off Grosvenor Square.[96] A year later he made an offer for land at the back of his premises (probably part of Gibbs's nursery ground) but Walpole refused.[97] It is difficult to know whether he built his own house, but it was built according to Todd's prototype as per Hall's agreement.

John Samuel Erlam was a 44-year-old architect in the 1851 Census, so he would have been born c.1807. Colvin suggests he may have been the son of Samuel. He is first encountered on the estate in 1835 when he took land on agreement with his partner John Pink. By the following year he had built and leased a property in Finchley Road (see Plate 83). Confusingly, the letter books sometimes refer to him as Samuel Erlam.

John Pink is encountered in more complicated circumstances. In 1829, he apparently occupied a house in Wellington Road which had been built by Mr Tovey and was to be leased to a William Toone.[98]

By December 1835 Pink and Erlam had formed a partnership, and their business premises were at Upper Seymour Street. This was the year when the Eyres were approached for a site for the St Marylebone Almshouses, a project which would be masterminded by Pink & Erlam and must have put their partnership to the test. Their design for the almshouses was in the Gothic style, just as it was becoming fashionable. The building was apparently erected in 1836 though the lease was not ready until 1838.

The partnership probably dissolved in 1842 when Pink & Erlam surrendered two of their agreements.[99] Erlam immediately took over in his own name the land in the 1839 agreement. John Pink seems to disappear from the St John's Wood scene, but Erlam was living at 49A Queen's Road in the 1851 Census, and in 1852 he took a further agreement for the plot on which stood the very old St John's Wood House, which was demolished shortly afterwards. By that date he was described as 'parish surveyor'.[100] He was still alive in 1854.

Bibliography: Colvin, 1995; Graves, 1905–6.

James PONSFORD

James Ponsford is described as 'an important developer in Tyburnia' in the *Survey of London* (vol. 40, 1980, p. 225). He seems to have been careful to describe himself as an 'architect' in deeds and documents. Today's architectural historians, however, occasionally dispute this claim, preferring to regard him as a builder (*Survey of London*, vol. 40, 1980, pp. 99 and 262). Ponsford was involved with Charles Frederick Leigh's development work on the west side of Finchley Road in the late 1830s and early 1840s, taking over some of the ground in 1844.[101] After two years' delay in his negotiations with Walpole Eyre, he purchased land on the west side of Abbey Road in 1844.[102] It is possible to gain some insight into this development from deeds in private hands for one of the Hill Road properties (see Plate 286). In 1845, he fell out with developer John Wright Treeby over the estate of William Austin, a bankrupt (Austin had taken out an agreement with Treeby). The matter was resolved when Austin assigned

94 LB 'P', pp. 297–98 and 305.
95 Bk of Drawings III, 32.
96 LB 'K', p. 423.
97 LB 'L', p. 14.
98 LB 'L', p. 339.

99 One dated 1837, the other 1839, both at EE 2650/1/54(A and B).
100 EE 2651/86(A).
101 LB 'Q', p. 313, and LB 'R', p. 202.
102 See draft agreement for sale at EE 2651/281 (1842) while the final conveyance for the property is at EE 2651/178 (1844).

his assets to Ponsford, who went on to obtain seven leases on the west side of Finchley Road.[103] In 1846, Walpole described Ponsford as 'a rich man'.[104] In the mid-1840s he was handling development work on the Grosvenor estate in Upper Brook Street (No. 41), North Audley Street, Park Street (Nos 7, 9 and 62) and Upper Grosvenor Street (Nos 10 and 11). In the same year that he had purchased land in Abbey Road (1844), he had also purchased Clarendon House, which he demolished to erect several houses in North Audley Street (*Survey of London*, vol. 40, 1980, p. 99).

In a more anecdotal vein, he seems to have been perennially ticked off by residents for his carelessness over gravel: 'Bad complaints were made at the Vestry on Saturday by the Inhabitants in Hill Road on account of the heap of gravel you had deposited on the Hill Road' or 'Mr Treeby … complains of your carting a Quantity of Gravel along the Queens Road & thereby cutting up & destroying the Road.'[105]

Solicitor: Messrs E. and C. Harrison; also Mr Heman (1840s).

Bibliography: *Survey of London*, vols 39 and 40 (1977 and 1980).

John PUNTER

Despite being severely criticised by Walpole for not following the specification in his agreement (see p. 381), John Punter's 1817 development of terraced houses on the west side of Lisson Grove has miraculously survived when all other buildings dating from the early years of the Eyre estate have been destroyed. John Punter's other notable contribution to the estate was to introduce his wealthy solicitor Thomas Chandless to the Eyres.[106] Thomas purchased some of Mr Punter's leases, and his brother Henry Gore Chandless bought land at Abbey Road which he resold almost immediately, making a considerable profit.

John Charles Felix ROSSI

Rossi (1762–1839) was born in Nottingham, the son of a Sienese doctor. He studied sculpture under Locatelli. He first attended the Royal Academy Schools in 1781 and started exhibiting there the following year. At the Royal Academy he won a gold medal in 1784 and a travelling studentship in 1785, which enabled him to spend three years in Rome. On his return he took on various jobs at the Derby China Works, with Vulliamy the clockmaker, and with the Lambeth firm of Coade, manufacturers of artificial stone, where he gained considerable experience in modelling. He then went into partnership with J. Bingley, a move which apparently cost him a great deal of money. In 1798, he was elected an Associate of the Royal Academy, becoming a full member in 1802.

His association with rural north-west London started in 1800 or 1801 when he set up in Marylebone Park next to the Queen's Head and Artichoke pub; there he had 'A Cottage, Artificial Stone Manufactory and Stables &c.'.[107] The looming reversion of the lease (1811) made him look for alternative

premises in St John's Wood, just as Thomas Willan, the local gentleman farmer, was doing. In 1808, he purchased from Walpole a large plot on Lisson Grove to include a 'gallery'.[108] From that time he became very involved in development work at St John's Wood (see p. 267). Rossi was much in demand during his lifetime, securing numerous important commissions, though at times he was criticised for bad design and poor craftsmanship. Like Tatham he fell on hard times towards the end of his life; he sought – and obtained – the help of the Royal Academy.

Solicitor: Blake & White.

Bibliography: Gunnis, 1968; Saunders, 1981.

James SHARP

Sharp made his debut in Albert Terrace in the 1840s with the developers Treeby and Hibbert.[109] He seems to have been a cautious, small-scale developer who worked well within his modest perimeter delivering terraced housing with shops – the earliest on the estate (1847), including the elegant Queen's Terrace. His landmark tavern, later known as the Knights of St John, was very strategically positioned in Queen's Terrace next to the Barracks, which at that time had their entrance in Wellington Road. Despite his caution Sharp went bankrupt, and his solicitor Richard Nation took over his 1846 development barely a year after Sharp took out the agreement with Walpole Eyre.[110] In 1850, Walpole threatened not to grant licences to some of the shops when he discovered an 'illegal' slaughterhouse at the back of 6 Queen's Terrace.[111]

Solicitor: Richard Nation from Messrs Nation & Neale.

John SHAW senior

Born in Bexley, Kent, John Shaw (1776–1832) made his apprenticeship with George Gwilt the Elder. Shaw started practising in 1798. He was a regular exhibitor at the Royal Academy between 1799 and 1820, with a final entry in 1831 for the church of St Dunstan in the West. He was appointed architect of the Eyre estate in 1805 (and not 1803 as sometimes stated, see p. 88), a post he maintained until his death in 1832. Apart from vetting all construction work on the estate and advising the Eyres on all architectural and planning issues, Shaw also designed classical terraced housing (Lisson Grove and Boscobel Gardens), both schemes proving too ambitious to be built as planned. In 1816, he was appointed architect and surveyor of Christ's Hospital where he was responsible for extensive additions in the Gothic style. He moved his architectural practice from Gower Street to Christ's Hospital. In March 1827 he prepared a building scheme for Chalcots, the Eton College estate, adjacent to the Eyre estate on the north-east side. The plan proved too ambitious despite being scaled down in 1829. He died unexpectedly in 1832 and was succeeded by his son, also John, in his many duties.

Bibliography: Colvin, 1995; Olsen, 1973, pp. 347–48.

103 LB 'Q', pp. 543, and LB 'R', pp. 93, 97.

104 LB 'R', p. 201.

105 Letter dated 10 March 1845 in LB 'Q', p. 530, and letter dated 31 July 1845 in LB 'R', p. 9.

106 Letter dated 15 October 1819 in LB 'F', p. 222.

107 The detailed plan records its location – there is a reproduction of this plan in the Conway Library, Courtauld Institute of Art, Rossi's box.

108 Bk of Drawings I, 5.

109 See EE 2650/1/291(A and B) (1844) and EE 2650/1/469 (1843).

110 LB 'S', p. 684, and LB 'X', p. 270.

111 LB 'S', p. 603.

John SHAW junior

Shaw junior (1803–1870) was the son and pupil of John Shaw senior. At the death of his father, he succeeded him as architect and surveyor for the Eyre estate and for Eton College, overseeing, among other things, the development of their Chalcots estate. This dual role ensured smooth communication between the two estates. He also succeeded his father as architect to Christ's Hospital and therefore continued to be based at that address. He built for the Church Building Commissioners of London and also exhibited at the Royal Academy between 1825 and 1846. He is buried at Kensal Green Cemetery.
Bibliography: Colvin, 1995; Olsen, 1973, pp. 348ff.

Henry SIBSON

Henry Sibson (1795–1870) described himself as a modeller and moved to St John's Wood in 1830. He was responsible for two of the most unusual house designs on the estate (he took out leases for both houses in the mid-1840s): first, a small classical house with an Egyptian-style entrance called Aloe Cottage or Villa at 18 Wellington Road which has not survived (site of Barclays Bank on the corner of Circus Road). More lavish still was his later named 'Mauritana Villa' (now Alhambra Cottage) at 9 Boundary Road, which he built and leased from the estate in 1846 (see Plate 272). Three years later he assigned his Wellington Road property to a Mr Bowen,[112] downsizing to a property in Douro Cottages (later Cochrane Terrace, then Street). He was still there in 1863. His 'Recollections', written in 1869–70, have survived and are now in the Tate Britain archive (see p. 419).
Solicitor: G. F. Hudson, 23 Bucklersbury.
Bibliography: Gunnis, 1968; Tate Britain archive (TGA, 9919).

George Spencer SMITH

George Spencer Smith was the developer of Swiss Cottage, a surveyor and a friend of the Eyre brothers. His name was added to the list of trustees for the Marylebone and Finchley Turnpike Trust in 1826, and in 1842 Walpole asked him to survey a house in Bayswater for one of his clients.[113] There is a reference in the letter books suggesting that Smith had had a plan prepared by a Mr Clutton: perhaps the John Clutton who set up the London branch of this family's estate agent business in 1835 and took over the affairs of the Smith's Charity estate in Brompton in 1845, the year of this particular reference.[114]

Charles Heathcote TATHAM

The influence of this significant figure in the early days of the St John's Wood estate is discussed in Chapters 3 and 8. As a young man Tatham (1772–1842) went to Rome, helped by his employer, the architect Henry Holland. Influenced by what he saw there, he developed a form of severe neo-classical architecture and also made his name through a series of publications on the antique which rapidly became sourcebooks. He was an important furniture designer, very

involved with the family firm of Tatham Bailey & Sanders.

He purchased the lease of a house in Alpha Road in 1808, but as all estate correspondence to him was sent to 1 Queen Street, he was probably not a full-time resident there. The relationship with the Eyres was a little rocky at times, yet Tatham was approached to become a trustee of the turnpike road bill in 1820, suggesting he was regarded as an ally rather than an enemy.[115] His brother John Tatham, a solicitor, dealt with the legal side of Tatham's transactions.[116] Around 1830 Charles's practice declined, leaving him in financial difficulty. From 1831 the Queen Street address is not found in the letter books; from then on all correspondence to Tatham is sent to his Alpha Road address.[117] Despite this downsizing Tatham built up rent arrears.[118] An 1835 rent account shows that Tatham's premises were back in the hands of Birnie, the original developer of this part of the estate.[119] Tatham was rescued from this difficult situation by Thomas Greville, the duchess of Sutherland and others who in 1837 secured for him the post of Master of Holy Trinity Hospital in Greenwich. There he died peacefully.
Bibliography: Colvin, 1995; David Watkin, *Thomas Hope and the Neo-Classical Idea*, London, 1968.

John TATTERSALL

Like John Bettinson, the builder John Tattersall was connected to William Robert Fry, 'mopping up' the plots Fry had been forced to surrender in Springfield Road. He is also recorded in Carlton Hill and Alpha Road. He acquired leases between 1852 and 1869 (see books of drawings).

George Ledwell TAYLOR

The name of this architect has been tentatively included. According to records in the Eyre archive we know that a 'Mr Taylor' was responsible for a group of large Italianate villas at the junction of Marlborough Road (now Place) and Loudoun Road (see Plate 311): 'a plan & elevations of 8 houses & gardens at Langford Place Loudoun Rd & Marlb[o]ro[ugh] Rd on Ground let by Agreement to Mr Thomas Lothian dece[ase]d & built by Mr Taylor Architect who resides in Langford Place in the house No1 on the plan', wrote Walpole Eyre to John Shaw junior in August 1845.[120] Could 'Mr Taylor' be the architect George Ledwell Taylor (1788–1873)? These houses mark a clear departure from the Todd prototype or the 'Gothic' houses which were also fashionable in that decade. They may de described as truly 'Italianate' (see p. 79), perhaps as a homage to Italian prototypes from the well-travelled Taylor? They were also contemporary with the more famous Italianate building of this period: the royal Osborne House, designed by Prince Albert and built between 1845 and 1851. We know that between 1843 and 1848 Taylor was laying out the nearby bishop of London's estate in Paddington. The 1851 Census had him living at Westbourne Terrace Road on the bishop's estate.
Sources: *DNB* and Eyre estate archive.

---

112 EE 2650/1/440 and LB 'S', p. 194.
113 LB 'K', p. 31, for Smith as a trustee and LB 'Q', p. 9, for the house survey.
114 LB 'R', p. 54.
115 LB 'F', pp. 408–9.
116 For instance, LB 'I', p. 467.

117 See list of St John's Wood tenants in January 1831 in LB 'M'.
118 For instance, six quarters are due in LB 'M', p. 335, in August 1831.
119 LB 'N', p. 473.
120 LB 'R', p. 10.

311 Could the houses of 'Mr Taylor' in Loudoun Road have been built by the architect George Ledwell Taylor while he was working on the Bishop of London estate in Paddington? Eyre estate (Bk of Drawings V, 44 right).

Griffith THOMAS

Griffith Thomas (d.1838), a carpenter of High Street, Portland Town, made his appearance on the Eyre estate in 1832 when he purchased for £265 a plot lying between Circus Road, Cochrane Terrace and Wellington Road (from the surveyor John White junior). Four years later he obtained a lease for what would become 40 and 42 (formerly 2) Wellington Road and 51 Cochrane Street.[121] We learn from an 1868 licence for 42 Wellington Road that Thomas died on 20 March 1838, after he appointed his wife Elizabeth, Thomas William Todd and John King his executors.[122] At his death the executors assigned the lease to a James Russell.

Richard THOMAS

In 1846, the builder John Maidlow, who had made a comeback after going bankrupt in 1826, assigned to the builder Richard Thomas, of Circus Road, the plot he had taken on at the back of the Swiss Cottage.[123] At first Walpole objected to Thomas's plan; he judged Thomas greedy when he increased the number of houses and stables to build and when he pushed the rents over the recommended figures.[124] However, Thomas's work seems to have gone smoothly after that, and his name was regularly recorded in lease deals. From the mid-1850s he was also employed in Upper Avenue Road by the developer William Holme Twentyman.[125] There is an intriguing reference in 1850 to 'the dissolution of partnership' between Thomas and his mother.[126] In 1851, he entered into an agreement with William Todd to build on a vacant plot.[127] He was described as a bankrupt in 1865.[128]

Another Thomas, William Thomas, described as 'Dairyman and builder', was operating from 16 Queen's Terrace and working under Sharp in the 1850s.[129] Perhaps he was related to Richard Thomas?

David TILDESLEY

We learn from the Eyre letter books that this builder, based at 2 Iron Gate Wharf, Paddington, was Robert Yeo's son-in-law, and he first made his appearance on the estate working on Yeo's ground north-west of Abbey Road (1863). He built terraced houses and a pub in Albert Road, renamed Holtham Road, all razed to the ground to make way for the Abbey Road estate. Unfortunately for Tildesley, his next large-scale project at the south end of the estate – the building of terraced houses at Gladstone (renamed Boscobel) Gardens from 1865 – was also demolished, this time to make way for railway development. He is recorded as being bankrupt in 1882.[130]

Robert TODD

Robert Todd (d.1836) made his appearance on the St John's Wood estate in 1804 when he purchased several lots from the first auction organised by Walpole. He was sometimes described as a builder, sometimes as a bricklayer.[131]

Robert Todd and Walpole Eyre struck a real and lasting friendship, as the letter books testify on a number of occasions: 'Why cannot you & Mrs Todd come to us at Weybridge on Tuesday & pass the day with us, we can give you a bed & you can proceed to town on Wednesday,' wrote Walpole on 12 August 1829.[132] We also learn from Robert's will that his eldest son was called Robert Eyre Todd, and there is a reference in the letter books to Walpole being the godfather of Todd's son.

Robert Todd married twice. His first wife Hannah died on 6 January 1819 (*The Times*, 8 January 1819), and his second wife Elizabeth survived him and

121 1832 agreement and 1835 lease at EE 2650/1/333(A and B).
122 Also EE 2650/1/333(K).
123 LB 'R', p. 225.
124 LB 'R', pp. 224 and 229.
125 LB 'T', p. 359, and LB 'V', pp. 41 and 42.
126 LB 'S', p. 663.
127 LB 'T', p. 104.

128 LB 'W', p. 317.
129 LB 'T', pp. 600, 651 and 661.
130 LB 'Y', p. 172.
131 Agreement dated 6 February 1808 at EE 2651/207 (builder) and counterpart lease dated 12 June 1810 at EE 2650/1/286(A) (bricklayer).
132 LB 'L', p. 352.

died on 19 August 1844. He must have felt particularly close to his first wife, as his will instructed his executors to bury his body with hers, at Cobham in Kent. Todd's will is dated 23 May 1835,[133] and he died on 26 October 1836 leaving detailed instructions about which family member should get what from the long list of leased and freehold properties he owned at his death. He left his Alpha Road properties to his wife (and executrix) Elizabeth in trust for his son Robert or if deceased for his daughters Elizabeth and Mary Ann. His nephew George Todd, a builder, seems to have been the main benefactor, no doubt because he knew how to care for and handle property. The portfolio was large and varied, with properties in St John's Wood but also in the West End, Chelsea and Cobham, as well as a country residence in Datchet and a farm near Chertsey (Halwick Manor Farm).

When Todd died the Eyre brothers owed him money for work done on the estate: the sum was substantial at just over £2,800 and recorded in a bond prepared in 1827.[134] The brothers had been hit hard by the building recession of the 1830s and asked for extra time to settle the amount. This the executors refused to do, which had the effect of souring the once flourishing relationship between the two families. After some difficulty, Walpole found a purchaser for the Charles Day estate,[135] Mr Kersey: 'at (Im sorry to say) the reduced price of 25 yrs p[ur]chase for the Sole purpose of paying the Bond owing to the late Mr R. Todd & which I will do imm[ediate]ly the p[ur]chase is completed'.[136] Solicitors: Walpole Eyre; James Griffiths, 6 Raymond Buildings, Gray's Inn.

William TODD and son

We learn from Robert Todd's will that William was also his nephew. The relationship between William Todd senior and Walpole seems to have been fraught. Although no agreement survives indicating William Todd was developing parts of the estate, he was certainly involved in varied development work, perhaps most notably the land which had been taken on by John White junior and then abandoned shortly afterwards. After a series of clashes with Walpole,[137] there was a falling out between the two men in May 1836: 'I shall not condescend to notice the offensive style of your letter of the 21st [May] further than to say – that in whatever language you may think to address me, it will have no influence on me in the discharge of my Duty between my Brother and his tenants.'[138] William Todd had a son, also called William, who was dealing with his father's estate from September 1855, probably because his father was by then quite old.[139]
Solicitor: James Griffiths, 6 Raymond Buildings, Gray's Inn.

Henry TOVEY

In 1830, Henry Tovey was described as a plasterer, late of Regent's Park (Albany Street) and now of Wellington Road. By 1842 when he was working

for wealthy St John's Wood leaseholder Thomas Carr, he had graduated to the title of 'architect'. Walpole Eyre seems to have had much respect for him, and the house Tovey built in Wellington Road was put forward as a model for detached houses in Pink & Erlam's agreement.[140]

He appears to have been the lessee Thomas Carr's favourite architect and built for him a picture gallery at his house in Lodge Place (see p. 286).

John Wright TREEBY

Treeby was probably introduced to the St John's Wood estate by Paddington builder Jonathan Riches, who took land from Pink & Erlam in the 1830s. His first lease is dated 1839 for a house in Finchley Road, stylistically close to Robert Todd's prototype and sited just above his (later) Elizabethan House. Treeby's first agreement with Walpole Eyre dated from 30 March 1840.[141] He was then described as a builder from Dorset Street. Despite setbacks, Treeby successfully fulfilled his contract, subletting the south side to James Sharp and building two memorable houses for himself on the north side: Devonshire Villa, which has miraculously survived (26–28 Finchley Road, see Plate 270), and the splendid Elizabethan Villa, which has not (see Plate 79). In 1842, he took on agreement a much larger plot of land bordering Queen's Grove (which had to be made) on the north and south sides and running all along it from Finchley Road to Avenue Road. This included the attractive Albert Terrace sublet to Jacob Hibberd, who built it as well as the plush villas on the north side of the road. This agreement was surrendered in 1844.[142] Treeby was clearly a well-organised and reliable builder although he may have been of an inflexible character, as several disputes/feuds between him and other developers are recorded in the letter books: with Ebbs & Brown, James Ponsford and William Holme Twentyman.

William Holme TWENTYMAN

The son of a trader, William Holme Twentyman (1802–84) was born in Liverpool. He was sixteen when he went out to the Cape with his older brother Laurence on inheriting money from a great-uncle. There William was apprenticed to Laurence, who has been described as 'the most prolific and famous of Cape silversmiths' of the period. After ten years William left his brother to go to Mauritius and set up there his own business as watchmaker and jeweller. His great store in Port Louis was doing well by 1831, and when he sold it to Farquhason & Co. in 1837 before returning to England, his fortune was made. Almost immediately he became involved with development work on the St John's Wood estate while also becoming connected with the City of London, culminating with his appointment as Sheriff in 1861–62 (see Plate 98).

He is first mentioned in the letter books at the end of 1838 when he resided at 1 Hamilton Terrace on the adjacent Harrow Free School estate. Within weeks

133 It has survived at EE 2651/294.
134 Letter dated 31 September 1838 in LB 'O', p. 536.
135 On the west side of Grove End Road, LB 'O', p. 550.
136 Letter to Griffith dated 21 February 1839 in LB 'O', p. 618.
137 LB 'O', pp. 19 and 23; LB 'N', p. 283; LB 'M', p. 3.
138 LB 'O', p. 67.

139 LB 'U', p. 204.
140 Bk of Drawings III, 57, for Wellington Road house and EE 2651/131, dated July 1837, for Pink & Erlam's agreement.
141 At EE 2651/69.
142 See EE 2651/93.

he was signing his first agreement with Walpole Eyre, and within the next few years he would colonise the large triangle of land framed south by Queen's Grove, west by the Turnpike Road and east by the Eton College estate.

He moved house to reside on his patch, first at No. 5 Regents Villas, which was used as a model for the large-scale 1843 development (B) on the developers' map (see Plate 72), switching to 11 Regents Villa in around 1844, 14 Regents Villas in 1846, then 6 St John's Wood Park in 1851–52 before reaching his final destination in 1853: the 'Manor House' on the east side of St John's Wood Park corner (No. 47 in the 1890s, opposite the surviving No. 25 at Plate 100).

He was a developer on a grand scale, choosing to build large and expensive mansions which would only appeal or be affordable to a very wealthy class of tenants; he had, for instance, dealings with the marquis de Robeyre.[143]

Twentyman seems to have handled the legal side of his development work by himself, but one of Walpole's letters suggests he was not always familiar with the English way of things. Walpole returned to him a Memorandum of Fixtures 'as it is not in the form in which it can be added as a Schedule of Fixtures'.[144] There is also a mention, not entirely positive, which implies Twentyman had lived in Calcutta: 'I have had a letter from Messrs Rogers informing me that they have found a judgment entered up against W. H. Twentyman late of Calcutta for £4000 & costs at the suit of Alexander Colvin & others.'[145] This was almost certainly a relative, as we know his parents, brother Laurence, himself and no doubt others from this Liverpool family all had very large families of ten and above.

The relationship between Walpole and Twentyman hit a low in 1847 when Twentyman seems to have sided with Reverend John Fletcher from All Saints against Walpole. Walpole wrote to Fletcher: 'that Gentleman [Twentyman] intimated to you that I had treated him unhandsomely[.] he sho[ul]d at the same time have had the candour to inform you of the very offensive manner in which he had conducted himself towards me.'[146] As Twentyman also clashed with builders Ponsford and Treeby, he may have been a tricky negotiator. Nevertheless, it is clear from the letter books that Walpole had total confidence in Twentyman's abilities. After Walpole's death it seems that the special relationship between Twentyman and the Eyre estate deteriorated – first in the unpleasant exchange over the making of the St John's Wood Park road (see p. 231) and later in 1862 over the undeveloped ground by New College Chapel at the junction of Avenue and Adelaide Roads.[147] Bibliography: Burke's *Landed Gentry*, 1952 edition; *Dictionary of Mauritian Biography*, Société de l'Histoire de l'Ile Maurice 2, January 1977, no. 36, p. 1080; *African Biographical Index*, F.389, 250–153 (British Library); for son William Laurence, see French Internet site 'La Sigoise – Saint-Denis du Sig' (Algeria).

William WARD

He may have been introduced to the St John's Wood estate by James Burton, as he was a lessee at South Bank on canal company ground. He is first encountered in 1823, described as a builder living in Grove Road. His main achievement there was building a block of houses on the west side of Lisson Grove between Church Road and Princes Street on the edge of the Eyre estate. He attempted to develop ground on the north-west side of Lodge Road, but his 1825 agreement was cancelled in 1832, freeing the site for the Catholic chapel.[148]

This is probably the same William Ward as the builder who was living in Abbey Road in 1837,[149] after purchasing land from Thomas Chandless, and who was generally very active in that part of the estate building sewers and roads. The full extent of his early 'empire' is spelt out in 1828 when he owed the sum of £253 for rent: as well as his two agreements there were three leases for properties in Grove Terrace, and at the corner of South Bank and Park Road.[150]

N.B. There are several William Wards in the letter books and a baffling number of possibilities for 'Mr Ward', making correct identification very difficult at times. There was the William Ward who took over Lord's Cricket Ground. There was another William Ward who was the solicitor of the surveyor John White.

The WATKINS brothers: Stephen, George and Charles

Stephen Watkins seems to have started work on the estate making bricks and building roads and sewers; for instance, he is recorded when he was about to make the road at St John's Wood Terrace in March 1826.[151] The letter books also mention he had been delivering bricks to Robert Todd when he went bankrupt in 1827,[152] no doubt as a result of taking several plots of land on agreement from John Maidlow. Stephen and a Mr B. Broadbridge were John Maidlow's assignees when Maidlow had gone bankrupt the previous year. Stephen wrote to Walpole on 7 April 1827: 'we have not taken possession of the ground let by you to Mr John Maidlow a Bankrupt – to which you refer – nor do we intend to do so.'[153] But this desperate attempt to distance himself from bankrupt Maidlow was in vain; within weeks Stephen himself was treading the same path. When the news reached Walpole of the proposed auction of Stephen's goods on the estate, he vigorously vetoed it.[154] Later he would recap on the unfortunate event: 'In the year 1825 I granted a Lease of various houses then in Building in St Johns Terrace … to Mr S. Watkins who (I am informed) afterwards assigned the Lease to the Metropolitan Loan Company and is since Bankrupt.'[155] However, in due course Stephen returned to develop the estate in partnership with brother Charles in 1830.

His other brother, George, in partnership with W. R. Fry, was also brought on to the estate by John Maidlow in 1822, to develop the south-eastern block

143 LB 'P', p. 288, dated 30 December 1840.

144 Letter to Twentyman dated 4 May 1840 in LB 'P', p. 204.

145 Letter to Twentyman dated 7 February 1843 in LB 'Q', p. 57.

146 Letter to Fletcher dated 21 April 1847 in LB 'R', p. 437.

147 See Charles Freeth's letter to Twentyman dated 24 December 1862 in LB 'V', p. 531.

148 See EE 2651/27(A and B) for the block of houses in Lisson Grove. See the 1825 agreement at EE 2651/43 for the cancellation of the Lodge Road agreement.

149 LB 'O', p. 329.

150 Ward's estate is described in LB 'L', p. 103. Also see Bk of Drawings I, 68, and III, 47.

151 LB 'K', p. 8.

152 LB 'K', p. 292.

153 Letter attached to document at EE 2651/96.

154 LB 'K', p. 292.

155 Letter dated 16 July 1829 in LB 'L', p. 325.

between Wellington Road and the Portland estate. George was described as a timber merchant from Commercial Road, Limehouse. With John Maidlow he was also involved in developing land on the Portland estate, and at the time of going bankrupt in 1830 George was paid for work at 9 Avenue Road.[156] This house had been acquired by Henry Samuel Eyre – no doubt in part payment for John Maidlow's debts to the estate. This substantial house, leased from the Portland estate, stood on the west side of Avenue Road on the north corner with Henry Street, now Allitsen Road, and the letter books record how difficult it was to find a tenant when the housing market was depressed. The Eyres never made a penny out of it.

John WHITE senior, surveyor

John White (c.1747–1813) was laying out the Portland estate in Marylebone from about 1787, and Colvin describes him as 'an able and successful surveyor who made a fortune out of property development in London'. A decade or so later his involvement with the Portland estate was put on a more official and lucrative footing through an agreement dated 26 February 1796 which set out the terms of his 'partnership' with the third duke of Portland. He was a leading vestryman in St Marylebone parish, designed a new workhouse for St Marylebone (1775), designed his own house in New Road, where his son John resided until at least 1844,[157] and was also involved in a number of architectural projects outside London (see Colvin, 1955). By 1809 he had sent in three designs for the development of Marylebone Park to the Crown estate, publishing his *Explanation* for one of them in 1813. His dealings with the Eyre brothers, primarily over setting out boundary lines between the Portland and St John's Wood estates, seem to have been cordial.[158] He apparently proposed the forming of the road on the eastern side of the burial ground.
Bibliography: Colvin, 1995; James Anderson, 'John White Senior and James Wyatt: An Early Scheme for Marylebone Park and the New Street to Carlton House', *Architectural History*, vol. 44, 2001, pp. 106–14; John White, *Explanation of a Plan for the Improvement of Mary-le-bone Park, Submitted to John Fordyce Esq., in 1809*, 1813 (copy in Crace Collection, British Museum); John Summerson, *John Nash: Architect to King George IV*, London, 1935, pp. 104–6.

John WHITE junior, surveyor

John White junior (d.1850), the son of John White senior, trained in his father's practice based at his large home on the outskirts of Regent's Park, at Devonshire Place, North New Road. Colvin states he was appointed District Surveyor for St Marylebone parish in 1807. Walpole later recorded that around that time 'Mr Whites Son … was … acting as Agent to the Harrow Free School'[159] and was

party to the arrangements made around the sale treaty for the burial ground between the three estates – Eyre, Portland and Harrow School. In November 1810 Walpole wrote to White, as agent to the Harrow School estate,[160] because the former was keen to implement the forming of St John's Wood Road from the chapel and burial ground to Edgware Road.

White became involved with development work on the Eyre estate through James Burton and his canal houses project: on 7 December 1822 Walpole was taking instruction for a lease from John White, 'by the direction of Mr Burton, to Mr John Russell of two houses at North Bank', suggesting he was, along with Charles Davis and others, a small developer on that site.[161] When in 1826 John Hinton needed a (further) mortgage to pursue his two agreements with the estate, White obliged along with Henry Campbell White and Henry Down.[162] White continued his association with the estate, becoming a lessee in 1826 with a house on the east side of Wellington Road.[163] This dwelling, of very modest appearance, clearly suggests a financial investment rather than an architectural project. Other leases to 'John White' were issued according to the books of drawings, but we do not know whether they relate to 'surveyor' or 'publican' John White.

In 1826, John Hinton went bankrupt and John White took over his agreements.[164] He is recorded as having made the section of Grove End Road lying between Abbey and Wellington Roads in 1827 and a section of Circus Road in 1830.[165] He soon found himself with massive debts, owing Walpole alone just under £1,000 by 1833, a sum White had no immediate means of discharging.[166] John White's 'embarrassments', as Walpole noted in a letter dated 7 November 1833, eventually made him backtrack, surrendering most of the land but managing to retain his interest in the Eyre Arms and a handful of neighbouring properties in Cochrane and Blenheim Terraces.[167] Montgomery Eyre and Colvin state White designed the Eyre Arms and its assembly rooms – the tavern ready in 1824 and the assembly rooms soon after – but while this may be true, there is no supporting evidence in the Eyre archive. In 1833, John White was also chairman of the Hampstead Water Works Company,[168] and the following year he attempted to set up a water company (see p. 237).

In 1845, John White took steps to sell by auction his properties in Cochrane (sixteen houses) and Blenheim (three houses) Terraces.[169] From that year onwards, some of the Eyre letters were addressed to him at Storey's Gate, Westminster. Otherwise he appears to have lived all his life in his father's house at the New Road.

John WHITE, publican

John White is first mentioned in 1822 as the publican who ran the Portland Arms,[170] but he seems to have been connected with other pubs – the

---

156 See letter of 16 November 1830 in LB 'M', p.133.
157 Letter to John White dated 14 December 1844 in LB 'Q', p. 469. At that date John White was still at the New Road address.
158 Summary of dealings and road decisions in LB 'C', pp. 259ff and 262ff.
159 LB 'D', p. 259.
160 LB 'B', p. 355.
161 LB 'H', p. 66.
162 See surrender of 1 January 1829 at EE 2651/1(C).

163 Bk of Drawings III, 8, and LB 'I', p. 553.
164 Culminating in the assignment/surrender dated 1 January 1829 at EE 2651/1(C).
165 LB 'K', p. 539, for Grove End Road and LB 'L', p. 453, for Circus Road.
166 LB 'N', p. 84.
167 See, for instance, LB 'O', pp. 472–73.
168 LB 'N', p. 54.
169 LB 'Q', p. 585.
170 LB 'H', pp. 36 and 350.

Duke of York in Salmond's Lane in Stepney and the Red Lion in Parliament Street.[171] In 1824, he was living at 8 Portland Terrace.[172] He briefly contemplated taking over the land where the old St John's Wood House stood in order to redevelop it, but he decided against it.[173] He settled at the Duke of York on the corner of St John's Wood Terrace (this pub still exists), and by 1830–32 his 'empire' consisted of properties in Wellington Road, Cochrane Terrace, part of the large garden of the old St John's Wood House, and of course the Duke of York.[174] However, at that time he seems to have fallen into rent arrears and eventually left to settle in Australia in 1843.[175]

William WOOLCOTT

He was first recorded on the estate in 1818, and his agreement with the Eyres dated from 1819.[176] The letter books also record that he had entered into an agreement with his son Henry.[177] He died two years later in 1821, leaving his son to continue the work. He was described as a carpenter and builder from Upper Thames Street in the City of London. At the time of his death he was living in Lodge Road on his ground at the estate (Park Road side). In 1823, Robert Todd purchased 'Mrs Woolcott['s] Estate and interest in the two houses and premises built by you [John Early] on the North side of Lodge Road'.[178]

Robert YEO

Robert Yeo is first mentioned in the letter books in 1840 in connection with houses in St John's Wood Terrace.[179] He was probably introduced to the estate by Pink & Erlam, who had taken a plot in St John's Wood Terrace.[180] He then worked in Acacia Road for Charles Freeth and William Robert Fry, building and leasing various houses including a group of four on the south side, west of Woronzow Road – three have survived and one was rebuilt (see p. 405). By 1845 the Fry brothers sublet ground to him which had formerly been under agreement with George Leigh.[181] In 1846, he took a lease of the large site of 43A Acacia Road (see Plate 117), probably where he lived and had his building yard for a while. He should also be credited with introducing shops in the heart of St John's Wood in 1847 by converting some of the St John's Wood Terrace houses, a move which Walpole described as 'much wanted'.[182] Finally, in 1851, after working for a number of different developers on the estate, he took on agreement for himself a substantial amount of ground at the far end beyond the railway line – a difficult site which was divided into eight sections. In this agreement Robert Yeo was described as of Acacia Road, builder. This was followed by further agreements, in 1860 and 1863, for land in the parish of Hamsptead (see Plate 72).

He became a friend of Samuel Cuming, the devoted developer on the Chalcots estate, who arranged 'to hand on the [Chalcots] developer's baton' to him in the 1850s.[183] Yeo was a Hampstead vestryman from November 1855.[184] In 1858, he was granted a lease for four shops and a public house in King's College Road on the Chalcots estate. Later, in 1866, he is described as living in Victoria Terrace, an easier location for his development work in the parish of Hampstead.

He had at least two brothers: Samuel, who built 5–8 Albion Road, and John, who was a lessee on the estate. He also had at least two sons: Richard, who worked with him in the northern parts of the estate, and Thomas, no doubt a lawyer since he was based at Erskine Chambers in Lincoln's Inn Fields. The Yeo firm was going strong in the early 1870s when they developed the Kilburn end of the Maryon Wilson estate.

Solicitors: Messrs Jones & Dunster in Great Marylebone Street; T. M. Vickery (Richard Yeo).

Bibliography: Olsen, 1973, p. 350; Thompson, 1974.

---

171 See LB 'K', p. 90, for the Duke of York and LB 'K', p. 173, for the Red Lion. He was connected with the Watkins brothers, no doubt via the East End connection.

172 LB 'I', p. 209.

173 In June 1826, see LB 'K', pp. 90 and 97.

174 See recap in LB 'M', pp. 108 and 171, also LB 'N', p. 18. An Abstract of Title for White's estate, dated 1883, is at EE 2650/1/77(C), pp. 13ff.

175 LB 'Q', p. 227, and LB 'R', pp. 400–1.

176 At EE 2651/62.

177 LB 'G', p. 233.

178 Letter to Early dated 17 May 1823 in LB 'H', p. 223.

179 LB 'P', p. 254.

180 LB 'P', p. 257.

181 Marlborough Hill, see EE 2651/11(D).

182 LB 'R', pp. 412 and 532.

183 Thompson, 1974, p. 243.

184 Thompson, 1974, p. 244.

APPENDIX 10
Distinguished residents

There are occasional entries in this gazetteer which have benefited from information found in the Eyre archive. By and large, however, this section predominantly draws on material found in Montgomery Eyre (1913) for the early period and Richard Tames (1998) for the twentieth century, supplemented by *DNB* entries. When it was being compiled the grouping of creative professions clearly seemed to fall in broad but distinct geographical areas: musicians around Abbey Road Studios (long before its existence as sound studios), theatre professionals in Avenue Road and painters in Grove End Road.

John ADAMS-ACTON (1831–1910), sculptor
Born John Adams, he added 'Acton' to his name in 1869. He won a Royal Academy scholarship to Rome where he studied under John Gibson and established his reputation as a competent portrait sculptor. His portraits included 'local' artists Frith and Landseer. He lived at 17 Abbey Road and 8 (now 14) Langford Place.

William AGNEW (1825–1910), art dealer
Discussed in the text – see index for the relevant pages.

Marietta ALBONI (1826–94), Italian contralto opera singer
She trained in Bologna where she met Rossini and became his pupil. She is known to have stayed in St John's Wood while on tour in London when she sang at Covent Garden and Her Majesty's Theatre.

Sir George ALEXANDER (1858–1918), actor-manager
He steered the fortune of the St James's Theatre and was keen to promote new British authors, including Oscar Wilde. He was involved with a number of charitable organisations including the Order of St John of Jerusalem. In 1882, he married into the Théleur family (Florence Jane Théleur, daughter of Edward Théleur), who had a house at the corner of Alpha and Park Roads (Montgomery Eyre, 1913, p. 287, and *DNB*).

Mary Frances ALLITSEN (1848–1912), composer
She is commemorated in Allitsen Road (formerly Henry Street). She adopted Allitsen as a pseudonym (she was the daughter of bookseller John Bumpus) and lived at 20 Queen's Grove.

Sir Lawrence ALMA-TADEMA, RA (1836–1912) and Laura ALMA-TADEMA, née Epps (1852–1909), painters
Discussed in the text – see index for the relevant pages. Lawrence is the recipient of a blue plaque at 44 Grove End Road (see Cole, 2009, p. 487).

Edward ARMITAGE, RA (1817–96), painter
He studied in Paris under the history painter Paul Delaroche, and this set the tone for his painted output, which often dealt with historical subjects, including biblical narratives. In 1855, he was sent to Crimea by the dealer Ernest Gambart and encouraged to paint history in the making, though the outcome was not entirely successful. After living eight years at 4 Grove End Road (1853–61), he spent the rest of his life in Hall Place (now Road).

Henry Hugh ARMSTEAD, RA (1828–1905), sculptor
In London this major Victorian artist is best remembered for the eighty or so figures he carved on the Albert Memorial in Kensington Gardens and for his work at the Foreign Office. He was based at 52 Circus Road between at least 1883 and 1904 (see Appendix 5).

William ATKINSON (c.1773–1839), architect
See p. 469 in Appendix 9.

W. H. AUDEN (1907–73), poet
Auden was briefly based in St John's Wood when he was staying with his friend, the poet Stephen Spender, at 15 Loudoun Road in 1963 and 1972.

Edwin BALE (1838–1923), painter
He was based at 44 (later 11, now demolished) Grove End Road on the corner with Melina Place from 1881. He was one of the founder members of the St John's Wood Arts Club.

Sir Squire BANCROFT (1841–1926), actor-manager, and Marie BANCROFT, née Wilton (1839–1921), actress
Squire Bancroft courted success in the provinces before he appeared in London (1865) at the Prince of Wales Theatre, managed by his future wife (1868). Husband and wife developed a new form of drama – the drawing room comedy. They later moved to the Haymarket Theatre and retired in 1885. They lived at 11 Grove End Road, an address associated with the engraver Thomas Landseer and the painter John Charlton.

Wilson BARRETT, actor-manager
The Barretts took over The Priory at 21 North Bank shortly after George Eliot vacated the property. Wilson Barrett and his wife (Miss Heath) were based there for five years from 1882, the year he achieved a massive success in Henry Arthur Jones's *The Silver King*.

Alexander BASSANO (1829–1913), portrait photographer
Bassano opened his first studio in Pratt Street, Camden Town, in 1851, subsequently moving to premises in Regent Street and Old Bond Street as his firm's fortune improved. He was appointed photographer to Queen Victoria in 1890. The National Portrait Gallery holds a large number of his photographs. Discussed in the text – see index for the relevant pages.

Harry BATES, ARA (1850–99), sculptor
Despite his early death, Bates was a major exponent of the New Sculpture movement. He was based at 10 Hall Road from 1891 and was involved with the Art Workers Guild.

Sir Thomas BEECHAM (1879–1961), musician
Recipient of a blue plaque at 31 Grove End Road.
Discussed in the text – see index for the relevant pages.

Sir William Sterndale BENNETT (1816–75), musician
Influenced by Mendelssohn (whom he met), Bennett was described as the most

musical of all English musicians by Robert Schumann. He spent the last two years of his life at 66 St John's Wood Road.

Sarah BERNHARDT (1844–1923), actress
This famous French actress made numerous sojourns in London, and during one of them she was based at 14 Alpha Road.

Annie BESANT (1847–1933), activist and theosopher
Discussed in the text – see index for the relevant pages.

Madame BLAVATSKY (1831–91), founder of the Theosophical Society
Discussed in the text – see index for the relevant pages.

BLONDIN (1824–97)
His real name was Jean François Gravelet, but he achieved celebrity status as Blondin, the tightrope walker who endlessly crossed the Niagara Falls – blindfold, pushing a wheelbarrow or carrying a man on his back. In London he performed at Crystal Palace in 1861 and 1862. He first resided in Finchley Road (at No. 71 west side, second house down from Boundary Road and suitably named 'Niagara Villa', and later at No. 36). In March 1868 he approached the estate for permission to build a stable and coach house at No. 71. Blondin later moved to Boscobel Gardens (Plate 218), a more modest address.

Léon Paul BLOUET (1848–1903), journalist and writer
His pen name was Max O'Rell. He was based in London for many years writing, lecturing and holding the post of French master at St Paul's School between 1876 and 1884. His first book, *John Bull and his Island* (1883, written in French and translated by his wife), was a considerable success and led Blouet to leave London. He lived in Acacia Road.

Thomas Shotter BOYS (1803–74), watercolourist
He travelled extensively to produce views of European cities, but is perhaps best remembered for the series of lithographed views published in 1842: *London As It Is*. He lived in Acacia Road.

Charles BRADLAUGH (1833–91), politician and activist
Discussed in the text – see index for the relevant pages.

A. M. BROADLEY (1847–1916), lawyer and journalist
This noted correspondent to *The Times* was counsel to the Egyptian ruler (or Khedive) Ismail Pasha (1830–95) and defended the Egyptian rebel Urabi Pasha (1841–1911). He was based at 'Cairo Cottage', 2 Beta Place (off Alpha Road), from 1887. In 1885, he also became a regular contributor to *The World*. His entertainments at Cairo House were famous (Montgomery Eyre, 1913, pp. 283ff). His voice and that of Edmund Yates were recorded on 5 October 1888 (Dinner with Colonel Gouraud, Crystal Palace Recordings found on www.webrarian.co.uk).

Sir Thomas BROCK, RA (1847–1922), sculptor
He was the first president of the Royal Society of British Sculptors and is perhaps best remembered for his statue of Queen Victoria outside Buckingham Palace, which earned him his knighthood. In the 1870s he lived at 10 Boscobel Place, close to St John's Wood's first sculptors' quarter.

Robert BROWN, painter
Discussed in the text – see index for the relevant pages.

John Bagnold BURGESS, RA (1830–97), painter
This enthusiast for Spain specialised in Mediterranean subjects and converted to Islam. He was based in and around St John's Wood from 1864. From 1883 he settled at 60 Finchley Road, where he died. He was the first treasurer of the St John's Wood Arts Club.

Philip Hermogenes CALDERON, RA (1833–98), painter and member of the St John's Wood Clique
Discussed in the text – see index for the relevant pages.

Neville CHALLONER (1784–c.1854), musician
Discussed in the text – see index for the relevant pages.

Sir George CLAUSEN, RA (1852–1944), landscape painter
Pupil of Edwin Long (see below), he moved to St John's Wood in the 1880s. He was based at 61 Carlton Hill between 1905 and 1941.

Charles F. M. CLEVERLEY (fl. 1893–1907), painter
An early member of the St John's Wood Arts Club, he was based at 78 Finchley Road in the 1890s. In 1903, Maurice Greiffenhagen exhibited a portrait of him at the Royal Academy.

George COLMAN the Younger (1762–1836), actor-manager
Lived at 4 and 5 Melina Place in the 1820s.

Charles Purton COOPER (1793–1873)
He was elected a fellow of the Society of Antiquaries in June 1825. By 1834 until his death he was queen's serjeant for the duchy of Lancaster, and he was a king's counsel in 1836. He was a bencher of Lincoln's Inn from 1837 and donated to this institution his vast collection of legal books (see Plate 155) (*DNB*).

Thomas Sidney COOPER, RA (1803–1902), painter
Described as a painter of 'contented cattle', he lived at various addresses in St John's Wood between 1833 and 1852. He once resorted to painting horses for a scene from the battle of Waterloo cavalry charge and hired a cab horse: 'the man whose horse was thus engaged was also hired to ride it at a full gallop up and down Wellington Road, Mr Cooper sitting on the wall rapidly sketching them as they came by. The man was no rider and it is a wonder he did not break his neck. His mates used to stand on the other side of the road and roar with laughter. The horse was pretty badly knocked up and we tried to get the artist to buy him, but the attempt did not succeed' (Montgomery Eyre, 1913, p. 254).

Frederick George COTMAN (1850–1920), painter
Frederick was the nephew of John Sell Cotman. His most famous painting was acquired by the Walker Art Gallery in 1880: *One of the Family*. He lived for at least twenty years at 10 Boscobel Place (1876–96).

John Sell COTMAN (1782–1842), watercolourist and leader of the 'Norwich School' of watercolour painters
He was based in London in the first decade of the nineteenth century and then between 1834 (when he was appointed Professor of Drawing at King's College

School) and his death. He never resided in St John's Wood, but his main connection with the area is his burial place at St John's Wood Church. See p. 391.

Eyre CROWE, ARA (1824–1910), painter
Like Edward Armitage, Crowe was a pupil of Paul Delaroche in Paris. According to Montgomery Eyre, he was a late recruit to the St John's Wood Clique, quipping on his name being known as 'Eyre Arms' Crowe (p. 181). He was a regular visitor to St John's Wood but not a resident.

James Henry DARK (1795–1871), cricketer and one-time leaseholder of Lord's
He was the son of a saddler and the brother of Benjamin Dark, the cricket bat maker of St John's Wood Road. Much of his life was spent at Lord's, starting at the age of ten until 1864 when he sold the remaining lease to the MCC (see Lord's chronology, Appendix 8).

Emily DAVIES (1830–1921), suffragette
She was raised in Gateshead and came to London with her mother on the death of her father. She lived for nearly twenty-five years (1862–86) at 17 Cunningham Place, only just outside the Eyre estate and now the recipient of a blue plaque (see Cole, 2009, p. 481). She actively campaigned for women's rights and in 1869 founded (with Barbara Bodichon) Girton College, now part of the University of Cambridge.

Henry William Banks DAVIS, RA (1833–1914), painter and sculptor
This successful landscape painter, based at 10A Cunningham Place from 1866, took over Landseer's property soon after his death, remaining there until 1892 prior to its demolition.

Sir William Reid DICK, RA (1878–1961), sculptor
Recipient of a blue plaque at 95A Clifton Hill (see Cole, 2009, p. 491). He is also associated with two other addresses, 31 Grove End Road (where Beecham lived) and (after 1938) 13 Maida Vale, Alfred Gilbert's grand studio residence.

Herbert DRAPER (1863–1920), painter
The Lament for Icarus, exhibited at the Royal Academy in 1898, is arguably Draper's most famous painting and is in the collection of the Tate Gallery. Turning his back on Impressionism, he favoured mythological or literary subjects. He lived for over twenty years at 15 Abbey Road (1898–1920), but his property no longer exists.

Dunham DUNLOP, writer
The wealthy Dunlop was, from 1873, the penultimate editor of the *Dublin University Magazine*, which flourished between 1833 and 1882. He lived at 7 Alpha Road where he apparently built a lavish Turkish bath (Montgomery Eyre, 1913, p. 291).

George ELIOT (1819–80) pen name of Mary Ann Evans, novelist
Discussed in the text – see index for the relevant pages.

Maxine ELLIOTT (1868–1940), American actress
She made a fortune on the stage, courtesy of her numerous admirers (including Edward VII), and settled at 20 Abbey Road in 1914.

The FAED brothers, Scottish painters
John Faed (1819–1902) and Thomas Faed (1826–1900) have been discussed in the text – see index for the relevant pages.
Thomas Faed's best-known work is probably the *Last of the Clan* (1865) in the Kelvingrove Gallery in Glasgow.

Herbert FARJEON (1887–1945), writer
This Shakespeare scholar (he produced a definitive edition of Shakespeare's plays) also wrote for the theatre. He lived at 34 Loudoun Road.

John FARQUAR (1751–1826), gunpowder entrepreneur
As a boy he went to India where he gradually worked his way to running a gunpowder factory, later becoming the sole contractor to the government. He returned to England a rich man and purchased the extravagant Fonthill Abbey in 1822. He subsequently behaved as a miser, ending his life in Park Road in seemingly deprived circumstances. He was buried in the nearby St John's Wood Chapel.

Charles Albert FECHTER (1824–79), actor-manager
A close friend of Charles Dickens, he was described as 'the Hamlet of the blond wig' when he gave a stirring rendering of that play in 1861 (Montgomery Eyre, 1913, p. 275). He lived at 11 Marlborough Place and 30 Park Road. Bilingual (English and French) he had great stage presence despite speaking English with a strong French accent. He was also a gifted theatre manager, revolutionising the workings of the Lyceum Theatre when he took over its management.

Allan James FOLEY (1835–99), alias Giacomo Foli, opera singer
He originally trained as a carpenter but switched to singing, receiving training in Italy. He was discovered by Mapleson (see below), and agreed to Italianise his name for promotional reasons. He lived at St Michael's Villa in Abbey Road between 1868 and 1873.

Edward Onslow FORD, RA (1852–1901), sculptor
Discussed in the text – see index for the relevant pages.

Ugo FOSCOLO (1778–1827), poet and scholar
Discussed in the text – see index for the relevant pages.

George FRAMPTON, RA (1860–1928), sculptor
Discussed in the text – see index for the relevant pages.

Meredith FRAMPTON, ARA (1894–1984), painter
He was the son of the sculptor George Frampton and was based at his father's address in Carlton Hill.

William Powell FRITH, RA (1819–1909), painter
Discussed in the text – see index for the relevant pages.

Emil FUCHS (1866–1929), Austrian painter and sculptor
This social high-flier catered for the royal family and the aristocracy. He lived at Abbey Lodge in Park Road between at least 1903 and 1914, and was patronised by Queen Victoria and King Edward VII. He left for New York in 1915 where he settled and died.

John FULLEYLOVE (1847–1908), painter
He regularly exhibited at the Royal Academy between 1873 and 1906, but no St John's Wood address is recorded for him in that context. Montgomery Eyre, however, recorded his involvement with the St John's Wood Arts Club (1913, p. 269).

Ernest GAMBART (1814–1902), art dealer
Discussed in the text – see index for the relevant pages.

James Louis GARVIN (1868–1947), newspaper baron
He is best remembered for taking over the editorship of the failing *Observer*, turning it around and revolutionising Sunday journalism. In 1908, he moved to 9 Greville Place and remained there until 1922 when he moved to Beaconsfield (David Ayerst, *Garvin of the Observer*, London, 1985, pp. 74ff; also Katharine Garvin, *G. L. Garvin: A Memoir*, London, 1948).

Sir Alfred GILBERT, RA (1854–1934), sculptor
He was the major exponent of the New Sculpture movement. His iconic *Eros* sculpture at Piccadilly Circus is the most famous of his works. Strictly speaking he was based outside St John's Wood and the Eyre estate, but this influential sculptor had close links with the community of sculptors in St John's Wood.

Hannah GLUCKSTEIN, later known as GLUCK (1895–1978), painter
She was eleven when her family moved to 73 Avenue Road, and she subsequently attended the St John's Wood Art Schools. When she changed her name to Gluck, she adopted a short haircut and started wearing men's clothes.

Sigismund GOETZE (1866–1939), painter and sculptor
Known as 'Siggie' among his friends, he entered the Royal Academy Schools in 1885 and is now best remembered for the decorative paintings which adorn the Foreign Office and were executed between 1912 and 1921. Described as 'a man of exceptional culture' (William Reid Dick's introduction to *Sigismund Goetze 1866–1939: Memorial Exhibition 15th Sept. to 7 Oct. 1948 at the Royal Society of British Artists*, London, 1948), he was unusually active in local issues, often in the role of benefactor. He lived in Grove House opposite St John's Wood Chapel: 'he has established here one of the finest studios in St John's Wood, ranking next to that of Sir L. Alma-Tadema in Grove End Road,' wrote Montgomery Eyre (1913, p. 227).

Sir Laurence GOMME (1853–1921), administrator, historian and author
He was clerk to the London County Council between 1900 and 1914 and was a 'vital figure' in the early history of the Blue Plaque scheme (Cole, 2009, pp. 12–13). He was also instrumental in setting up the Victoria County History and the Folklore Society. Although he is the recipient of a blue plaque at 24 Dorset Square in Marylebone (Cole, 2009, p. 413), he is also recorded at 20 Marlborough Place (Tames, 1998, p. 124).

Frederick GOODALL, RA (1822–1904), painter
An orientalist, he was based at Rosenstead in Avenue Road (see Plate 170) from 1883 until his death.

Andrew Carrick GOW, RA (1848–1920), painter
He favoured history subjects along the lines of the St John's Wood Clique and was principally based in Grove End Road (1881–1902).

Sir Francis GRANT, RA (1803–78), painter
This successful portrait painter must have been a Regent's Park devotee, first settling at 12 Village Park West (from 1835) and then in Sussex Place only just outside the Eyre estate (from 1841 until his death). He was president of the Royal Academy between 1866 and 1878.

Maurice William GREIFFENHAGEN (1862–1931), illustrator and painter
Known as 'Griffin' among his friends, he astounded everyone by taking up a teaching post at Glasgow School of Arts (1906–29) while remaining based at 12 Loudoun Road. He was a prolific illustrator contributing to several magazines, but best known for his illustrations of the novels of Rider Haggard. Also discussed in the text – see index for the relevant pages.

Arthur HACKER, RA (1858–1919), painter
He painted some very atmospheric pictures of London (night time and fog). Although he is not recorded as living in St John's Wood, he, too, was involved with the St John's Wood Arts Club (Montgomery Eyre).

Clarence HAILEY (1867–1949), photographer
He was described in 1897 as 'of St. John's Wood and Newmarket, the famous photographer of race horses' ('Photographing Race-horses: An Afternoon with Mr Clarence Hailey', *Windsor Magazine*, 1897, pp. 331–37). See Appendix 7.

John McLure HAMILTON (1853–1936), American portrait painter
Montgomery Eyre claimed that his portrait of Gladstone was said 'to be the best ever painted of that statesman' (1913, p. 261). He subsequently became the official painter to William Gladstone. Six out of seven of his portraits in the collection of the National Portrait Gallery are of St John's Wood residents. He was associated with 'Alpha House' (see Plate 154) and 6 Grove End Road (at least 1899–1900).

Sir Cedric HARDWICKE (1893–1964), actor
He was Matheson Lang's neighbour in Avenue Road and devoted his early career to George Bernard Shaw. He emigrated to New York in 1939.

Alfred HARMSWORTH (1865–1922), press baron
He started, among other projects, the *Daily Mail* and *Daily Mirror*.
He was brought up in Boundary Road in the 1870s and 1880s, neighbours of the Robinsons (maternal grandparents of Sir Basil Bartlett). Montgomery Eyre states several generations of the Harmsworth family were based in the Wood and owned various properties there (1913, pp. 285–86).
See Sir Basil Bartlett, *Jam Tomorrow*, London, 1978, p. 46.

Sir Augustus Henry Glossop HARRIS (1852–96), theatre manager
Much of his short career was spent at the Theatre Royal, Drury Lane. He became Sheriff of London and was granted a knighthood. He lived at The Elms in Avenue Road.

Charles HARTWELL, RA (1873–1951), sculptor
Between at least 1911 and 1934 he was based at 62 Acacia Road, the former home and studio of Onslow Ford.
Discussed in the text – see index for the relevant pages.

Joseph HATTON (1841–1907), journalist and author
A contributor to *Punch*, he accompanied the actor Edward Smith Willard on his American tour (1890, see below). He was based at 9 Titchfield Terrace, 1 Grove End Road, and 11 Marlborough Road (formerly the house of his friend Bernard Partridge).

Benjamin Robert HAYDON (1786–1846), painter
Recipient of a blue plaque (shared with Charles Rossi) at 116 Lisson Grove. Discussed in the text – see index for the relevant pages.

Thomas HEAPHY (1775–1835), painter
Discussed in the text – see index for the relevant pages.

Charles HENGLER (d.1887), circus proprietor
He founded Hengler's *Grand Cirque* in 1871, formerly on the site of the London Palladium. Lived in St John's Wood Park.

John Rogers HERBERT, RA (1810–90), painter
Herbert converted to Catholicism and therefore tended to specialise in biblical scenes. He lived at 7 Grove End Place (later 21 St John's Wood Road), opposite the house of his friend Landseer. They often played billiards together. Montgomery Eyre recounts how Herbert always affected to behave and speak in the French manner to very comical effect. His sons – Arthur, Cyril and Wilfred – also became painters.

George Edwards HERING (1805–79), painter
This landscape painter drew much inspiration from Italy and the Isle of Arran where he had a house. He lived at 45 Grove End Road between 1853 and 1856 and between 1863 and his death. Also see Jeanie Hering.

Jeanie HERING (1846–1928), Scottish novelist and playwright
Jeanie Hering was the literary pseudonym of Marian Adams-Acton, the illegitimate daughter of the duke of Hamilton. She was adopted by the landscape painter George Hering (1805–79) and his wife, who resided at 45 Grove End Road for over twenty-five years (see Appendix 5). She married the sculptor John Adams-Acton in 1875.
Also discussed in the text – see index for the relevant pages.

Dame Myra HESS (1890–1965), pianist
She was bombed out of her home in Carlton Hill and moved to Cavendish Close.

Ivon HITCHENS (1893–1979), painter
Studied at St John's Wood Art Schools in 1911 before going to the Royal Academy. Between 1919 and 1940 when his studio was destroyed, he was based at 169 Adelaide Road.

John Evan HODGSON, RA (1831–95), painter, member of the St John's Wood Clique
Discussed in the text – see index for the relevant pages.

Jefferson HOGG (1792–1862), barrister and biographer
He was a friend of the poet Shelley and in 1826 married the widowed Jane Williams, who had been Shelley's muse. They first came to live in St John's Wood in 1830. They subsequently settled in Clifton Road where Jefferson wrote his biography of Shelley (Montgomery Eyre, 1913, pp. 161ff).

John HOLLINGSHEAD (1827–1904), theatre manager
He switched from being a freelance contributor to periodicals such as *Household Words*, *Punch* and *Cornhill Magazine* to managing the Gaiety Theatre with John Laurence Poole. The Gaiety was the first London theatre to have a bar and restaurant within its main building. Hollingshead lived at 14 North Bank.

Thomas HOOD (1799–1845), writer
Recipient of a blue plaque at 28 Finchley Road.
Discussed in the text – see index for the relevant pages.

William HOWITT (1792–1879) and Mary HOWITT (1799–1888), authors
Montgomery Eyre states they lived at Avenue Road between 1848 and 1852 (1913, p. 38).

Travers Christmas HUMPHREY (1901–83), lawyer, judge and Buddhist campaigner
Discussed in the text – see index for the relevant pages.

Thomas Henry HUXLEY (1825–95), scientist
A close friend of Charles Darwin, T. H. Huxley was his great supporter and the first to popularise science in this country. With his beloved Australian wife, he lived at various addresses in St John's Wood before settling, in 1872, at 38 (formerly 4) Marlborough Place where they remained for eighteen years, now the recipient of a blue plaque. The philosopher John Fiske declared the house was 'the nearest to an earthly paradise of anything that I have seen', and was also overwhelmed by 'seven of the loveliest children that ever live' (Tames, 1998, p. 68; also see Montgomery Eyre, 1913, pp. 169–180, and Cole, 2009, p. 489).

W. W. JACOBS (1863–1943), civil service clerk and writer
He wrote many humorous short stories including 'The Monkey's Paw' in the 1902 collection *The Lady of the Barge*. Between 1898 and his death, Jacobs had an arrangement to publish his stories in *The Strand Magazine*. He is the recipient of a blue plaque at 15 Gloucester Gate near Regent's Park (Cole, 2009, p. 85), but between 1937 and his death he was based at Elm Tree Road Mansions in Elm Tree Road (Tames, 1998, p. 83).

John JACKSON, RA (1778–1831), portrait painter
In the 1820s he lived, and then died, at 16 Grove End Road and is buried in St John's Wood churchyard.

Henry JAMES (1843–1916), novelist
Discussed in the text – see index for the relevant pages.

Jerome K. JEROME (1859–1927), actor and writer
He wrote his acclaimed book *Three Men in a Boat* (published in 1889) at 7 Alpha Place. He fought the London extension of the Manchester, Sheffield and Lincolnshire Railway over the pitiful amount of compensation he was offered but lost.

Douglas JERROLD (1803–57), dramatist and journalist
He lived in Circus Road before moving to Kilburn in 1856. He was a compassionate and generous man, a trait of character that was apparently abused by some. He is perhaps best remembered for his regular contributions to *Punch*.

Joseph JOACHIM (1831–1907), Hungarian violinist
This child prodigy was probably the greatest violinist of his age. He was immensely popular in London as a soloist and leader of a string quartet. He made annual visits to London from 1862 and was at one time based in Grove End Road. Brahms wrote his violin concerto for Joachim, and he in turn conducted its first English performance (Tames, 1998, p. 92).

Sir William Goscombe JOHN, RA (1860–1952), sculptor
Between 1894 and 1904 his studio was based at 2 Woronzow Road (now No. 25). After this he was based at 24 Greville Road.
Discussed in the text – see index for the relevant pages.

John Henry Yeend KING (1855–1924), painter
According to Montgomery Eyre he was a founder member of the St John's Wood Arts Club. He was connected to various addresses in St John's Wood, in particular 36 Marlborough Hill (1885–93) and 103 Finchley Road (1894–1907).

Melanie KLEIN (1882–1960), psychoanalyst
She was the first psychoanalyst to carry out research on children. She is best known for her 1932 publication, *The Psychoanalysis of Children*. She moved to 42 Clifton Hill in 1935 and remained there until 1953.
Recipient of a blue plaque (see Cole, 2009, p. 491).

Dame Laura KNIGHT, RA (1877–1970) and Harold KNIGHT, RA (1874–1961), painters
Laura was a landscape painter now best remembered for her ballet studies, while Harold was a portrait painter. They are the recipients of a blue plaque at 16 Langford Place.
Discussed in the text – see index for the relevant pages.

Richard Brinsley KNOWLES (1820–82), journalist
He was the son of the dramatist John Sheridan Knowles, and after an early and successful theatrical venture (producing a comedy, *The Maiden Aunt*, at the Haymarket Theatre), he became a newspaper editor. He lived and died at 29 or 30 North Bank.

Oskar KOKOSCHKA (1886–1980), painter
Recipient of a blue plaque at Eyre Court, Finchley Road.
Discussed in the text – see index for the relevant pages.

Alexander KORDA (1893–1956), Hungarian film-maker
He lived at 81 Avenue Road between 1933 and 1939. He was the first film-maker to be knighted (in 1942). He founded London Films in 1932, which led to the construction of Denham Studios, 'Hollywood on Thames'. *The Private Life of Henry VIII* (1933) opened the road to popular success in this country. Subsequent 'blockbusters' included *The Four Feathers* (1939), *The Thief of Bagdad* (1940), and *The Third Man* (1949). His ashes are at Golders Green Crematorium.

Mary LAMB (1764–1847), writer
Discussed in the text – see index for the relevant pages.

Sir Edwin LANDSEER, RA (1803–73), painter
Discussed in the text – see index for the relevant pages.

Matheson LANG (1879–1948), Canadian actor and dramatist
This Shakespearean actor had a house in Avenue Road. We owe to him the Old Vic's long association with Shakespeare.

Charles Robert LESLIE, RA (1794–1859), painter
He painted history and literary scenes, but also made his mark as an author with his biography of Constable published as early as 1843 and his autobiography published in 1860 after his death. He is recorded as living at St John's Place in the mid-1820s (the former Breeze Yard) but then settled at 10 Pineapple Place, Edgware Road (1835–47), followed by 2 Abercorn Place from 1848 until his death.

George Dunlop LESLIE, RA (1835–1921), painter, member of the St John's Wood Clique
Son of the painter Charles Robert Leslie, his style of painting was different from that of other members of the St John's Wood Clique, but his friendship with Marks and Storey (see below) going back to the 1850s made him a central figure in the group. He spent over twenty years at 2 Abercorn Place, the family home, and at least thirteen years at 8 Grove End Road (1870–83).
Discussed in the text – see index for the relevant pages.

George Henry LEWES (1817–78), literary critic and philosopher
The best known of his writing is *Life of Goethe* (1855), and his last work, *The Problems of Life and Mind*, was written in St John's Wood and published posthumously.
He lived with George Eliot in North Bank.

Robert LITTLE (1854–1944), Scottish painter
The son of a wealthy Glasgow shipping merchant, this oil and watercolour painter specialised in landscape and genre. His stay in St John's Wood was relatively brief but vividly documented (see Plate 186).

John Gibson LOCKHART (1794–1854), Scottish writer and editor
He was Walter Scott's son-in-law and is best remembered for his authoritative *Life of Sir Walter Scott* (in seven volumes), which has been described as the best ever biography after Boswell's life of Dr Johnson. He died, suitably, at Abbotsford, Walter Scott's former home, but he is also recorded as living in Abbey Road (Tames, 1998, p. 78).

John A. LOMAX (1857–1923), painter
This narrative painter is recorded as living at 39 Alma Square (1889), but he settled in earnest at 17 Marlborough Road where he is recorded between 1891 and 1914.

Edwin LONG, RA (1829–91), painter
He specialised in scenes from ancient Egypt. His most memorable painting is arguably the *Babylonian Marriage Market* (1875) in the collection of Royal Holloway College. He lived for ten years at 19 Marlborough Road.

Thomas LORD (1755–1832), cricketer and founder of Lord's
Discussed in the text – see index for the relevant pages and in particular Appendix 8.

The LUCAS family

John Lucas (1807–74) was a successful and fashionable portrait painter who regularly exhibited at the Royal Academy and is well represented in the National Portrait Gallery. His sons John Templeton (1836–80), a genre painter, and William (little known, no dates available) followed in their father's footsteps and were based at 3 (later 22) St John's Wood Road. According to Arthur Lucas's book on John Lucas (*John Lucas, Portrait Painter 1828–1874: A Memoir of his life*, London, 1910), both sons were involved in training the future Royal Academician John Seymour Lucas (John's nephew – pp. 91 and 94). The address is linked to the Lucas family between 1841 and the mid-1870s. Also discussed in the text – see index for the relevant pages.

Sir James Nicol McADAM (1786–1852), surveyor of the metropolitan turnpike roads

Son of John Loudon McAdam (1756–1836), who revolutionised the road system in Britain. James followed in his father's footsteps in improving and co-ordinating road making and became head of the Commissioners of Metropolis Roads. In 1843, he bought a house in St John's Wood – Villa Etruria in Grove End Road (LB 'Q', p. 206).

Sir Paul McCARTNEY (born 1942), musician

The Liverpool singer, former member of the Beatles, has been based in St John's Wood for a number of years. He purchased his house there as early as 1966 but did not immediately adopt it as his residence.

Sir George MACFARREN (1813–87), composer

Born in Ealing, he trained at the Royal Academy of Music where he later taught. His poor eyesight (he became totally blind in 1860) forced him to concentrate on composing rather than interpreting works. He founded the Handel Society and is associated with Marlborough Hill and 13 Blenheim Road.

Arthur MACHEN (1863–1947), Welsh actor and journalist

He came to London at the age of seventeen, and his first job – cataloguing occult books – seems to have made a lasting impression on him since he eventually made a name for himself writing tales of the supernatural. He lived at 12 Melina Place, where he translated the memoirs of Casanova. Also discussed in the text – see index for the relevant pages.

Sir (Edgar) Bertram MACKENNAL, RA (1863–1931), sculptor

He was born in Melbourne to a Scottish father who was a mason, and came to Europe to study in London and Paris, eventually making his home in England. He lived at 87A Clifton Hill and 38 Marlborough Hill where he stayed just over twenty years (1904–c.1925). Two of his works stand prominently on the streets of London: the statue of Edward VII in Waterloo Place and the *Horses of the Sun*, the quadriga over Australia House in Aldwych.

Louis MACNEICE (1907–63), Irish poet and playwright

He belonged to the generation of 'thirties poets' including Stephen Spender, W. H. Auden and Cecil Day Lewis, who all met at Oxford. After working as a university lecturer, he joined the BBC in 1941. He wrote plays and programmes and was also sent on assignments to countries such as India, Egypt and Ghana. His 1944 play, *Christopher Columbus*, was apparently written from his home at 10 Wellington Place (Tames, 1998, p.77).

John MACWHIRTER (1839–1911), painter

He specialised in mountainous scenes. He spent thirteen years at 6 Marlborough Road before moving to 1 Abbey Road where he lived for twenty-three years (1888–1911). Discussed in the text – see index for the relevant pages.

Katherine MANSFIELD (1888–1923), writer

Born in Wellington, New Zealand, she moved to London at the age of fifteen. This *enfant terrible* led a tumultuous life which involved a great deal of travelling. In London she favoured a bohemian lifestyle, and she is recorded at 15 Acacia Road in 1915. She is regarded as the best short story writer of her time.

'Colonel' James Henry MAPLESON (1830–1901), opera impresario

He trained as a singer and violinist, but soon discovered his talent as an impresario (he lost his voice in the mid-1850s). In 1856, he founded the first musical agency in London. He also managed the Haymarket, Lyceum, Her Majesty's and Drury Lane theatres. In the 1870s he attempted to build a 2,000 seat national opera house on the Embankment, but he ran out of money and was forced to abandon the project (now the site of Scotland Yard). Mapleson published his memoirs in 1888. He lived at 62 Avenue Road, the house of art dealer Ernest Gambart (see above) and Frederick Goodhall (see Plate 170).

Henry Stacy MARKS, RA (1829–98), painter, member of the St John's Wood Clique

Discussed in the text – see index for the relevant pages.

Sir John MARTIN-HARVEY (1863–1944), actor-manager

He is best remembered for *The Only Way*, an adaptation of Charles Dickens's *A Tale of Two Cities*, which was first performed at the Lyceum in 1899 and which he claimed, apparently unrealistically, to have performed 3,000 times. He is recorded as living at 30 Avenue Road in 1912.

Edna MAY (1878–1948), American actress and singer

Her career straddled the cities of New York and London, but her first big success was in London. She eventually settled in England when she married the millionaire Oscar Lewisohn and retired from the stage. She is recorded as living in Boundary Road (Montgomery Eyre, 1913, p. 278).

Phil MAY (1864–1903), illustrator

This well-loved pen and ink illustrator is best remembered for his 'Guttersnipes' drawings and for his contributions to *Punch* magazine. He has a blue plaque at 20 Holland Park Road (Cole, 2009, p. 206), but died at 5 Melina Place and is also briefly recorded at 15 Elm Tree Road (1901–2).

Bernard MILES (1907–91), theatre impresario

Discussed in the text – see index for the relevant pages.

St George Jackson MIVART (1827–1900), biologist and philosopher

This ardent Roman Catholic tried and failed to reconcile Darwin's doctrine of the evolution of the species with his religious beliefs. His initial friendship with Huxley and Darwin made way for enmity after a long controversy. He lived at 7 North Bank.

Ludwig MOND (1839–1909), German chemist
He worked in chemical plants in Germany and the Netherlands before settling in Britain in the 1860s. He was a noted art collector, having made a fortune manufacturing products such as nitrogen, sulphur and ammonia. He lived in the southern end of Avenue Road at The Poplars (designed by Brydon, who also designed Tissot's studio – see Plate 159), a property which was only just outside the Eyre estate.

Louis NAPOLEON (1808–73), French statesman
He was both the first president of the French Republic and France's last monarch. His uncertain status meant that he spent virtually the first half of his life living abroad – educated in Switzerland and Germany, living in Italy for a time, taking refuge in America and England. Montgomery Eyre describes in some detail his affair with Miss Howard: she lived at 23 Circus Road in the 1840s, and the address became the couple's love nest (1913, pp. 151ff).

Lilian NORDICA (1857–1914), opera singer
She was known as the 'Yankee Diva' and lived at 27 Finchley Road.

John O'CONNOR (1830–89), Irish painter
Born in Londonderry, he came to London in 1848. He received no formal training but learned the painting trade by working as a scene painter in Belfast and Dublin and at Drury Lane theatre in London. He was the principal scene painter at the Haymarket Theatre between 1863 and 1878. He also produced striking topographical paintings which he exhibited at the Royal Academy between 1860 and 1888. He lived almost ten years at 6 Waverley Place before moving to 28 Abercorn Place, which has survived to this day and bears his initials on the façade (Plate 299).

Sir Bernard PARTRIDGE (1861–1945), actor and cartoonist
Multi-talented Bernard Partridge was a gifted actor who developed his drawing skills working for architects (including Philip Westlake) and stained glass designers. In 1892, he joined *Punch* magazine as an illustrator, and by 1901 he had become their chief illustrator. He resided at 11 Marlborough Road.

Henry PEGRAM, RA (1862–1937), sculptor
This versatile artist sculpted portraits as well as narrative and mythological subjects. He is connected with 26 Norfolk Road followed by 36 Marlborough Road (or Hill).

John PETTIE, RA (1839–93), Scottish painter
He was adopted by the St John's Wood Clique as an honorary member and was as devoted as they were to depicting historical subjects. When John Rogers Herbert (see above) moved out of 21 St John's Wood Road in 1869, Pettie took over his house and stayed there until 1882.

Sir Arthur Wing PINERO (1855–1934), actor, stage director and playwright
After studying law he went on stage, working in Edinburgh and Liverpool before joining Henry Irving's Lyceum Theatre. He wrote many plays which were very successful in their day but are now hardly ever performed. He is recorded as living in Finchley Road (Montgomery Eyre, 1913, p. 276).

James and John POPE-HENNESSY, authors
James (1916–74) and Sir John (1913–94) were brothers and grew up at 74 Avenue Road. James was based there when he wrote his first (and landmark) book, *London Fabric*, in 1939. He subsequently made his reputation writing biographies and travel books. His murder in 1974 so traumatised his brother John, then director of the British Museum, that the latter soon left his post and moved to Italy. This Renaissance scholar and writer headed the Victoria and Albert Museum between 1967 and 1973 and had a second career in New York when he subsequently led the European Paintings Department of the Metropolitan Museum of Art.

Ferdinand PRAEGER (1815–91), German pianist and critic
He settled in London in 1834. He was a friend of Berlioz (two letters of his survive dated 1856 and 1867), but he is best remembered for championing the German composer Richard Wagner. He lived at 22 Portland Terrace (Wellington Road). This was Wagner's pied-à-terre in London from 1855, the year of his first visit. Praeger's book, *Wagner as I Knew Him* (1885), apparently made extravagant claims about the great man and was rudely exposed by Houston Stewart Chamberlain.

Cyrus REDDING (1785–1870), journalist and writer
He lived at South Bank in the 1820s when he was editing the *New Monthly Magazine*. He was a neighbour and a friend of Ugo Foscolo, and is still remembered for his book on the history of wine. Between 1846 and 1870 he lived in Hill Road.

Robert REECE (1838–91), writer of farces
He was successful in his day and lived at 58 Adelaide Road.

Dorothy RICHARDSON (1873–1957), writer
Her masterpiece, the *Pilgrimage* novels, started with *Pointed Roofs* (1915), which some see as the first complete stream of consciousness novel. Between 1916 and 1938 she spent her summers at 32 Queen's Terrace.

Briton RIVIERE, RA (1840–1920), painter
Discussed in the text – see index for the relevant pages.

George ROBEY (changed from Wade) (1869–1954), actor and music hall artist
He is recorded at 35 Circus Road (1908) and 70 Finchley Road (1924), and is appropriately described as 'a master of large and unruly audiences' (Tames, 1998, p. 120).

John Charles Felix ROSSI, RA (1762–1839) sculptor
Discussed in the text – see index for the relevant pages and Appendix 9. Recipient of a blue plaque, shared with Benjamin Haydon (see above) at 116 Lisson Grove (see Cole, 2009, p. 481).

Walter Dendy SADLER (1854–1923), painter
He is connected with three Finchley Road addresses: No. 34 (1878–81), No. 28 (1881–94) and No. 44 (1894–96, see Plates 301 and 302). Discussed in the text – see index for the relevant pages.

Sir Charles SANTLEY (1834–1922), opera singer
Described by George Bernard Shaw as 'the best baritone singer with whom the London public is familiar', he was born in Liverpool and trained in Italy. He was a committed St John's Wood resident, living twenty years at 5 Upper Hamilton Terrace (1872–92), at 4 Grove End Road, Carlton Hill and Blenheim Road. Recipient of a blue plaque at 13 Blenheim Road where he was based between about 1911 and his death (see Cole, 2009, p. 490, and Tames, 1998, p. 90).

Sophia SCALCHI (1850–1922), opera singer
A member of Mapleson's company, she toured the United States and settled in New York until her retirement in 1896. She is known to have resided at Finchley Road.

Henry Thomas SCHÄFER (1854–1915), painter and sculptor
He exhibited at the Royal Academy between 1875 and 1915, and was involved with the St John's Wood Arts Club, according to Montgomery Eyre (1913, p. 270). From 1882 until his death, he was based in St John's Wood at Acacia Gardens (Plate 224) and Abercorn Place. The plan and elevation of his studio there survive (EE 2650/1/88(G)).

Clement William SCOTT (1841–1904), journalist
He was associated with *The Daily Telegraph* between 1871 and 1898 and became their principal dramatic critic. He is recorded as living at 44 Clifton Road East.

George Gilbert SCOTT (1811–78), architect
For about ten years from 1835, Scott and his assistant (later partner) William B. Moffatt built over forty workhouses. After that he came under the influence of Augustus Pugin and the Gothic Revival. He ended up running the largest architectural practice in England. He is best remembered for his St Pancras Station Hotel and the Albert Memorial. He is recorded as living at 23 (then 12) Avenue Road.

Clare SHERIDAN (1885–1970) sculptor and writer
Discussed in the text – see index for the relevant pages.

Clement King SHORTER (1857–1926), newspaper baron
He founded *The Sphere* magazine in 1900 (ran until 1964) and *The Tatler* a year later. He lived at 16 Marlborough Place.

Henry SIBSON (1795–1870), sculptor
Discussed in the text – see index for the relevant pages and Appendix 9

George SIMONDS (?1847–1929), sculptor
'Brewer, banker, sculptor, master of the Art Workers Guild' (Walkley, 1994, p. 229), he was the last occupant of 21 North Bank before it was demolished by the Central Electric Supply Co. around 1900. He then moved to 65 Hamilton Terrace.

Solomon J. SOLOMON, RA (1860–1927), painter
He was based in St John's Wood from 1892 until 1907 or 1908, his time there being split between 2 St John's Wood Studios and 60 Finchley Road. He was particularly friendly with Arthur Hacker (see above), with whom he travelled on the Continent. He exhibited a portrait of this friend at the Royal Academy in 1895.

Alexis SOYER (1810–58), cook
Although Soyer's death certificate states he died at 15 Marlborough Hill in August 1858, the rate books confirm that his address in 1858 was in fact 15 Marlborough Road, an understandable mistake.
Discussed in the text – see index for the relevant pages.

Herbert SPENCER (1820–1903), philosopher
Montgomery Eyre describes in great detail his domestic arrangements at St John's Wood (1913, pp. 241ff). Although Spencer coined the phrase 'the survival of the fittest' in his *Principles of Biology* (1864) after reading, ahead of publication, Darwin's *Origin of the Species*, his own philosophy differed from Darwin's evolution theory.
Discussed in the text – see index for the relevant pages.

Stephen SPENDER (1909–95), poet
Discussed in the text – see index for the relevant pages.

Sir Bernard SPILSBURY (1877–1947), pathologist
The founding father of forensic pathology, he lived in Marlborough Hill between 1912 and 1940. After testifying at Dr Crippen's murder trial, he was involved in countless criminal prosecutions. He committed suicide in his laboratory at University College London.
Recipient of a blue plaque at 31 Marlborough Hill (see Cole, 2009, p. 492).

Sergius STEPNIAK (1851–95), Russian writer
His full name was Sergei Michaelovitch Kravchinski. At the age of twenty-seven his revolutionary ideas led him to assassinate Russia's head of the secret police on the streets of St Petersburg. He fled Russia and lived in various countries including England. In London he published *Underground Russia* in 1882. Montgomery Eyre records he was based at South Bank (1913, pp. 290–91).

Florence ST JOHN (1855–1912), singer
She drew crowds to the Gaiety Theatre, notably for her performance in *Faust up to Date*, and lived at Villa 'Favart', 57 Finchley Road. Her ashes rest at Golders Green Cemetery.

Antoinette STERLING (1843–1904), American opera singer
Her popularity rose rapidly after her first appearance at Covent Garden in 1873. She is recorded as living at 24 Marlborough Place with her American singer husband, John Mackinlay.

George A. STOREY (1834–1919), painter, member of the St John's Wood Clique
Discussed in the text – see index for the relevant pages.

Eugene STRATTON (1861–1918), American actor and music hall artist
He became famous as a 'black-face' impersonator. He lived at 59 Wellington Road.

John Macallan SWAN (1847–1910), painter and sculptor
Discussed in the text – see index for the relevant pages.

Charles Heathcote TATHAM (1772–1842), architect
Discussed in the text – see index for the relevant pages and Appendix 9 (p. 478).

34 The group comprises seven leases including properties in Brown Street, Milford Street and the house at the Cheese Cross: Wiltshire RO, 1369/4/18/12.

35 See Wiltshire RO: Articles of Agreement dated 25 June 1660 and sale document of 30 November 1660 at 1369/1/1. William Eyre was the grandson of the Giles Eyre who purchased the property. Giles gave the property to his second son Ambrose when he married in 1635 (see 1635 document at 1369/1/1). William, son of Ambrose, inherited the property at his father's death (see deed dated 27 December 1660 in the same batch of documents) and sold it to Samuel.

36 1633 from the purchase deed by Giles Eyre in Wiltshire RO (1369/1/1). Cherry and Pevsner, 2002, records the same statement of 'newly built' for the year 1619.

37 The architectural styles of Longford and Newhouse are very different. Two other examples of Trinity houses are Sir Thomas Tresham's Triangular Lodge of 1593 at Rushton in Northamptonshire and Newhouse Farm near Goodrich in Herefordshire of 1636. The label 'Trinity' fits comfortably a house with Catholic occupants, for instance Rushton, but this was not so for Newhouse. Cherry and Pevsner, 2002, names the examples of Trinity houses on pp. 303–8 and p. 572.

38 *DNB*, in the 1967 reprint of the 1885–1901 edition.

39 See Burke, 1937.

40 Cherry and Pevsner, 2002, p. 433. The name Walton comes from Izaac Walton (1651–1719), son of the author of *The Compleat Angler*. Walton junior had a clerical career and he, too, is buried in Salisbury Cathedral. As the house bears the Eyre arms and is dated c.1720, its connection with Walton seems tenuous.

41 At the end of Kingsmill's apprenticeship with Mr Chitty, who 'served the Navye Office with Considerable Storess', his mother Martha Eyre wrote to the philosopher John Locke on 31 January 1702 for help in finding Kingsmill employment. See E. S. de Beer (ed.), *The Correspondence of John Locke*, vol. 7, Oxford, 1982, letter no. 3081. I am grateful to Diana Eyre for drawing my attention to this reference.

42 Captain C. G. T. Dean, *The Royal Hospital Chelsea*, London, 1950, p. 313, and therefore not treasurer as stated in a number of publications. Andrew Eburne's article ('Charles Bridgeman and the Gardens of the Robinocracy', *Garden History*, vol. 31, no. 2, 2005, pp. 193–208) clearly makes the point that on his arrival at Chelsea Hospital, Walpole surrounded himself with friends and allies (p. 201).

43 See Dean in note 42, pp. 198, 204, 212–13. Also Eburne in note 42, pp. 200–201.

44 See Dean in note 42, Introduction, p. x.

45 TNA, Prob 11/725 dated 9 January 1742 (1743) and proved 15 April 1743.

46 The birth of a son named Walpole is recorded for 1712, but he must have died very young. The second marriage is recorded in Joseph Foster, *Marriages [of the Nobility and Gentry], 1650–1880*, n.p., 1881; Mary Ann of St James's Westminster was twenty-one and single, and the marriage took place at St Martin-in-the-Fields.

47 Wiltshire RO, 1369/6/1/2. This is a correction to a previous assumption that Robert Walpole was the godfather of Kingsmill's youngest son Walpole Eyre (1734–73). This list also corrects Walpole's year of birth which was 1734 and not 1735 as previously recorded.

48 Wiltshire RO, 1369/4/51.

49 David Yaxley, 'Sir Robert Walpole's Garden at Houghton', *The Norfolk Gardens Trust Journal*, Spring 2000, pp. 18–23.

50 See Eburne in note 42, p. 208, n. 21.

51 Letter dated 18 September 1718, from the papers of the Gell family of Hopton Hall in Derbyshire: Derbyshire RO, D258/52/1/57.

52 Sloane Ms 4047, f. 56, British Library Manuscripts Department.

53 This plan is not mentioned in the standard work on kitchen gardens by Susan Campbell, *A History of Kitchen Gardening*, London, 2005, and she confirmed in an e-mail that she was not aware of it. Robert Eyre's kitchen garden would have been situated at Newhouse, discussed above. A photocopy of this manuscript plan is in Wiltshire RO at 1369/4/23/5, the original having remained at Newhouse.

54 See *The London Directory of 1677: The Oldest Printed List of the Merchants and Bankers of London, London*, 1878 (reprint). It is also possible that Henry Samuel was based at the Delmés in Lime Street when he was in London.

55 Bank of England archive, Henry Samuel's stock account for 1732–39: AC27/447. Henry Samuel Eyre is recorded as having a stock account in 1703, then in 1718–19 and from 1746 until his death.

56 See *The Quiet Conquest*, Museum of London, 1985, cat. no. 412, p. 276, and following entries.

57 Hertfordshire archives and local studies, D/ER B96, dated 26 April 1706. This Lisbon connection was clear in Henry Samuel's will as a Mr Mawman of Lisbon was named to receive a mourning ring.

58 Extract from a letter written by Samuel Eyre to J. Burchett, dated 23 February 1707, Blenheim Papers Ms 61582, f. 118, British Library Manuscripts Department.

59 See Alice Frances Archer Houblon, *The Houblon Family: Its Story and Times*, London, 1907, pp. 359–60. This volume mistakenly labels Samuel Houblon as unmarried. The Houblon family papers are in the Berkshire RO and were uncatalogued when I consulted them. In D/EAH/acc 6073.1, there is a letter starting 'Revd Sr' with a pencil inscription '?1772', which states clearly the descendants of the first Houblon (Peter) in England: 'he had issue two sons Peter who has one grand son Liveing vizt. Samuell an eminent Merch.t marryed to [blank] Harvey of London.' As Samuel Houblon was 'living', the document predates December 1723, the time of his death. Another document at LMA mentions the will of Samuel Houblon dated 3 March 1714 in relation to the properties he gave to St Thomas's Hospital. His wife and her second husband, Henry Samuel Eyre, are mentioned (HO1/ST/E/066–1).

60 TNA, SP89/18, dated 29 November 1701.

61 The details of this case are revealed in TNA, C11/2727/68, undated document but probably soon after July 1714 when Jacob Harvey's mother died and Jacob sought compensation from the Chancery Court against his mother's 'voracity', as he described it.

62 Eyre v Colebrooke, TNA, C11/257/45, dated November 1727 (top of document). The document describes how Sarah Perry, wife of Richard Perry, one of Mary's trustees, refused to sell stock which would have benefited Mary.

63 This is confirmed by trade directories from 1736 onwards.

64 See chapter on merchants' houses in Mireille Galinou (ed.), *City Merchants and the Arts 1670–1720*, London, 2004.

65 His will made no provision for the poor of his City parish; he preferred to cater for those in Southgate (£50) and in Newhouse near Salisbury (£100).

66 James Colebrooke was one of Mary Eyre's trustees when St John's Wood was acquired in 1733, and he was still around in 1750–1 when Henry Samuel I purchased this land.

67 The property is virtually identical to Henry Samuel's and the indenture with the City of London, dated 24 October 1729, is kept in the same box as Henry Samuel's. See COL/CC5/RM16/36/17–18 at LMA.

68 It has now become a care home called the Westminster Beaumont. It rarely opens to the public but was open for the 2006 Open House Weekend when the Lanscroon 1723 murals could be seen in their full glory: an optimistic depiction of Julius Caesar's triumphant entrance into Rome and his Apotheosis. See Cherry and Pevsner, 1998, p. 460. The latest publication on Arno's Grove is Ruby Galili's *Arnos Grove and the Walker Family, Book One: Isaac Walker the Founder of the Family at Arnos Grove*, Southgate District Civic Trust, London, 2008; see pp. 17–18 and bibliography.

69 See F. G. Hilton Price, *A Handbook of London Bankers*, London, 1876, pp. 40–41 and 113–14. Hilton Price states that the earliest business date for Colebrooke is 1721, but Ian Doolittle, *The Mercers Company 1579–1959*, London, 1994, p. 119, says he is first recorded as early as 1706. Nowadays, James Colebrooke's main claim to fame is his son, Sir George, who has a substantial entry in the *DNB*.

70 LMA, MJ/SP/1732. The petition itself is not dated but is accompanied by another document – affidavit – where Henry Samuel swore he had no freehold or copyhold lands or tenements in Edmonton. This document is signed by James Colebrooke and dated October 1732.

71 I am most grateful to Graham Dalling from Enfield Local History Unit for his help in tracing Henry Samuel Eyre in Southgate.

72 See Daniel Lysons, *The Environs of London*, 2nd edn, 4 vols, 1811, vol. II, part 2, County of Middlesex (Edmonton), p. 166 (first published 1792–96).

73 The date on the purchase deeds is 21 and 22 March 1732. At that time the Gregorian calendar was not yet in use and the first three months of the year were regarded as part of the previous year, so the correct year was in fact 1733.

74 Jacob Harvey of Islington, her brother, as well as banker James Colebrooke and James Ruck, in Attested Copy, lease for a year, dated 21 March 1732, EE 2651/172B(1).

75 Abstract of Title, EE 2650/1/120(A), p. 7, and WCA, 2194/3.

76 Brown, 1995, is the only author to give a correct description of the purchase scenario. Other authors incorrectly state that Henry Samuel bought the land in 1732. The relevant Eyre estate deeds are EE 2651/358(D): 'Bargain and Sale of St John's Wood Lands' between Jacob Harvey and James Colebrooke, Mary's executors, and Henry Samuel Eyre I, dated 11 January 1750. Related documents at WCA, 2194/3/1 (lease for a year, 10 January 1750) and WCA, 2194/1–3/2 (Release of 11 January 1750 and Settlement of St John's Wood of 7 March 1750).

77 The best account of this arrangement is found at EE 2651/172C(6) in the 'Assignment of Term' (Attested Copy) of 24 January 1797 from 'Sir George Colebrook Bart by the Direction of Jeremiah Hodges Esqr to Brook Allen Bridges Gent.'.

78 See VCH, T. F. T. Baker (ed.), *A History of the County of Middlesex*, vol. 8: Islington and Stoke Newington, 1985, p. 63. Like St John's Wood, the land originally belonged to the Hospitallers.

79 Harvey v Houblon, TNA, C11/2727/68, not dated, after 1714? Also Eyre v Colebrooke, TNA, C11/257/45, dated (at top of document) November 1727.

80 EE 2651/172B(7). Will dated 7 March 1750 with a codicil dated 7 August 1751 and another dated 20 December 1752. Will proved 16 September 1754.

81 The will mentions that his body should be taken to Upholders' Hall and then taken in procession to Uxbridge, where he wished to be buried next to his wife (the link with Uxbridge came from Mary's mother, Catherine Baker, daughter of Matthew Baker of Uxbridge). Henry Samuel was not a member of the Upholders Company, but by the mid-eighteenth century Upholders' Hall was used by members and non-members for funeral arrangements. If there was an Eyre monument in Uxbridge church it has not been recorded or survived. (I am grateful to Carolynne Cotton, Local Studies, Archives and Museum Manager at Uxbridge Central Library.)

82 H. E. S. Fisher, *The Portugal Trade: A Study of Anglo-Portuguese Commerce 1700–1770*, London, 1971, pp. 79–80. There is no mention of Henry Samuel Eyre in this book or in the standard work by André Simon, *The History of the Wine Trade in England*, 3 vols, London, 1964.

83 EE 2651/172C(1), p. 3: 'excepting one diamond ring with one single large stone now in my possession which I gave some years ago to my said dear husband'.

84 This name reactivates the wine connection. The earliest eighteenth-century London directory lists Gilbert and Anthony Malcher, wine merchants operating from Lime Street, Henry Samuel's old address. After 1740 Anthony disappears and Gilbert is listed on his own. From 1752 a Samuel Malcher is operating from Bury Street.

85 EE 2651/172B(5): will dated 3 April 1751.

86 From 1738 trade directory, *The Intelligencer or Merchants Assistant* (Guildhall Library).

87 These two portraits were first painted in 1728 but have come down to us through 1749 copies by the same artist at Shotesham Park near Norwich; see Frederick Duleep Singh, *Portraits in Norfolk Houses*, 2 vols, Norwich, n.d. [1928], vol. II, pp. 288–89. Another large portrait still hangs at Newhouse and records the complete family (see Plate 19).

88 Wiltshire RO, 1369/6/1/3/4. Not dated but may have been compiled at his death in 1795 (the latest publication date on the list is 1791).

89 Documents relating to this suit have survived: TNA, C12/1893/8.

90 See Doolittle in note 69, p. 104.

91 See note 80 for the will of Henry Samuel Eyre I. His nephew Samuel married Stewart, daughter of John Russell, Consul General of Lisbon and Envoy to the Barbary Powers. This suggests John Russell was part of the mercantile circle of Henry Samuel I, making Samuel's decision not to consult him over his wedding even more mortifying.

92 See note 47 for revised dates.

93 The best published information on the Johnson family will be found in Vere Langford Oliver, *The History of the Island of Antigua … from the First Settlement in 1635 to the Present Time*, 3 vols, 1894–99. Walpole and Sarah's Marriage Settlement is at EE 2651/172B(8) and EE 2651/358.

94 There was a considerable Eyre presence in Burnham from the fifteenth to nineteenth centuries, as is chronicled in George Lipscomb, *The History and Antiquities of the County of Buckingham*, vol. III, London, 1847. However, they had different coats of arms and should not be confused with the Wiltshire Eyres.

95 Intermarriage of the Johnson and Warner families resulted in Godschall Johnson senior's purchase of Antigua plantations – see Assignment of 21 July 1771 at EE 2651/257B(2). Godschall, however, appears to have remained based in the City of London and Putney (see Dorian Gerhold, *Villas and Mansions of Roehampton and Putney Heath*, Wandsworth Historical Society, 1997, pp. 60, 76-77). After Godschall's death in 1800, overall management of the estate in Antigua fell to the executors, who included Henry Samuel II. Godschall junior inherited a portion of these estates.

96 Angerstein was one the trustees of Godschall Johnson's settlement: see letter to Angerstein dated 19 July 1813 in LB 'C', p. 60. In June 1814 Angerstein had queried the presence of Walpole II's name in his (famous) little loan book and Walpole had thus replied: 'How my name ever came into your List I don't know unless it was that my late Uncle Mr Godschall Johnson always having put it down in his list[.] You (from your Connection with him and the obligation I beleive [sic] I may say you are under to him from the great Abilities he shewed in contracting loans …) thought fit to continue it' (LB 'C', p. 564).

97 Both regularly borrowed money from the Eyres. Ralph Boteler seems to have been particularly unreliable at paying it back. Walpole II also spent a great deal of professional time attempting to sort out their debts and to curb their spending, to very little effect it seems. Walpole often became exasperated with the Johnson brothers. When Godschall junior finally ended up in prison in March 1831, on hearing that his son Ralph had been appointed bank clerk, Walpole II wrote: 'I don't know what emolument may arise from this app[oin]tm[en]t of Clerk in the Bank, but I think you sho[ul]d impress upon y[ou]r son the necessity of his living within his income' (LB 'M', p. 231).

98 See Montgomery Eyre, 1913, pp. 28–31.

99 See 'Case relative to Mrs Eyre's Younger Children with Mr Madocks Opinion' inside the 1789 Declaration of Trust at EE 2651/172G(1).

100 Oliver is also the best source of information for this family (see note 93). The Hodges pedigree includes the names of Sarah's 'new' children: Jeremiah, William, Frederick Richard, and a blank for the daughter. From Walpole's letter books we learn the daughter's name was Sally and that Jeremiah senior had in fact married twice: 'Jeremiah the Son was of the first marriage and I understand was born at Toulouse and died in the West India' (LB 'D', p. 397).

101 A descendant of Anthony Hodges of Montserrat (d.1699), Jeremiah inherited Apps Court from his father, Anthony Hodges from Montserrat and Bolney Court in Oxfordshire (1728–83). See Oliver, vol. 2, pp. 80–81 (see note 93).

102 Hancock, 1995.

103 Letter dated 31 July 1811 addressed to Manning and Anderson, the bankers of the Boyd family, from Danson House, Bexleyheath, in LB 'B', p. 476. In an earlier letter addressed to Strachan on 19 July 1809, the full circumstances of the Boyd family and their interest in the West Indies are explained in detail (LB 'B', p. 105).

104 Ruth Hutcherson, *The History of Danson*, London, 1996 (published by Bexley Leisure Services Department); Chris Miele is also preparing a detailed publication on the same subject.

105 For instance, Knuston Hall in Northamptonshire where Godschall junior resided in the early years of the nineteenth century.

106 In prison Mr Trevanion is described as being 'at times quite delirious' (letter dated 10 March 1809 in LB 'B', p. 78). James Trevanion showed signs of 'derangement'

before dying in October 1811 (LB 'B', pp. 524 and 529), and Lady Boyd had a
'paralytic attack' in 1809 (LB 'B', p. 101).

107 Godschall fled to St Omer as early as 1821 (LB 'F', p. 703) but was arrested in 1830 or
1831 on a visit to London (LB 'M', pp. 66 and 222), while his brother Ralph found
himself arrested in February 1821 (LB 'F', p. 624) but by 1824 he had fled to America,
never to return (letter addressed to Grote & Co. dated 20 May 1824, LB 'I', p. 91). As
Godschall left England in great haste and secrecy, his great uncle, Walpole II, brought
over his nine children on 27 April 1821. The epic scene is thus recorded: 'I am just
leaving town with your nine little ones and will see them on Board the Cumberland
packet and I will not leave them until they Sale [sail], I shall be at Greenwich just at
the Top of the Tide & I hope the Captn will weigh anchor & sail immediately'
(LB 'F', p. 703). As time passed, Godschall was prepared to run the risk of visiting
London, which eventually led to his arrest.

108 Letter addressed to Messrs Slack in Bath and dated 9 May 1821 in LB 'F', p. 712.
The letter book reveals on p. 721 that Messrs Slack had in fact acted honourably and
tried to protect the household from the harsh treatment of others.

109 Like his father, John Thomas died in the month of April (1811) and at approximately
the same early age of 40. We know the circumstances were tragic because Walpole
says so in his letter book. He was so upset that, most unusually for him, he implored the
return of his brother Henry Samuel from India, where he was stationed
(letter to Captain Leblanc dated 25 April 1811 in LB 'B', p. 416). However, the
archive does not reveal the full circumstances of John's death.

110 See R. L. Arrowsmith, *Charterhouse Register 1769–1872*, London, 1974, p. 213 for
John Johnson and p. 133 for the Eyre brothers. Henry Samuel was there between
January 1779 and April 1787, John Thomas between July 1781 and December 1787,
Walpole between January 1782 and December 1789. Their stepbrother, Jeremiah
Hodges junior, was also sent there.

111 See Oliver, vol. 2, for the pedigrees of the Hodges and Johnson families (see note 93).
We know from Walpole that Jeremiah Hodges junior was the son of Jeremiah Hodges
senior by a previous marriage (LB 'D', p. 397).

112 At his death in 1806 General Andrew Gordon was lieutenant general and colonel of
HM 26th Regiment of Foot and lieutenant governor of the island of Jersey (his will is
at EE 2651/172G(2)). The general was Godschall Johnson junior's great uncle, as stated
in a letter to Captain Gardner dated 25 April 1806 in LB 'A', p. 257. See LB 'A', p. 812,
for the information on ADCs.

113 Case presented to Mr Morgan, with reply dated 10 May 1805 at WCA, 765/189.

114 See letter dated 12 September 1805 in LB 'A', p. 115.

115 Letter dated 20 September 1805 in LB 'A', pp. 118 and 162.

116 Letter to Harry dated April 1806 in LB 'A', p. 245.

117 Letter to Willan dated 4 June 1810 in LB 'B', p. 280, who had agreed to become a
surety for £500 which John had borrowed to take up his appointment. York Hospital
was a temporary hospital near the present Graham Street (see Dean in note 42, p. 254).

118 George John (1810–83). Letter to Milles dated 5 March 1810 in LB 'B', p. 245, and to
Harry dated 24 March 1810 on p. 249 of the same.

119 Letter to John Thomas Eyre dated 4 June 1810 in LB 'B', p. 281.

120 Letter to Warren dated 4 November 1814 in LB 'C', p. 688.

121 *Charterhouse Register* (see note 110) states it is the 1st Foot Guards, but it is clearly
named as the 7th Regiment of Guards in Walpole's letter to Mr Hoare dated 11 January
1813 in LB 'C', p. 128. The switch to the Guards probably cost £2,200, money Harry
did not have, so he gave a bond to Lieutenant Colonel Rainsford dated 29 September
1812 (see letter dated 24 April 1813 in LB 'C', p. 213).

122 *Charterhouse Register* states John was there between 1795 and 1805 and Henry
between 1808 and 1812.

123 Letter to Captain Boyd, dated 17 September 1808 in LB 'A', p. 812.

124 Richardson-Eyre, 1897, p. 8.

125 Letter to Captain Boyd, dated 17 September 1808 in LB 'A', p. 812. Probably
Sir George Hewitt/Hewett, likely to be another relative on the Johnson side as the

126 Letter to General Gordon dated 12 September 1805 in LB 'A', p. 115.

127 Letter to Major Eyre dated 6 March 1806 in LB 'A', p. 271.

128 EE 2651/139(I): Draft brief related to the Regent's Canal negotiations between the
Canal Committee and the Eyres. Not dated, but probably from early 1812 when the
agreement reached between Mr Nash and Walpole failed to be recognised by the Canal
Committee. Untitled document starting: 'Notwithstanding the reference by the Canal
Committee to Mr Nash'. Henry Samuel cut short his Ceylon stay after the death of
his brother John Thomas in April 1811; he was back in London by May 1812
(LB 'B', p. 655).

129 The 'taking of Copenhagen' was on 2 September 1807, the battle of Vimiero on
21 August 1808.

130 Letter addressed to Mrs Johnson and dated 9 March 1809 in LB 'B', p. 76.

131 EE 2652/43(A); Bill Book I, p. 72, 2 March 1809. Harry left London for Ceylon in
April 1809 (LB 'B', p. 98). George Grote (1762–1830) was the father of the historian
and politician George Grote (1794–1871). George Grote senior placed his son at the age
of fifteen in the family banking business where he remained for thirty-three years. The
Eyre brothers therefore both knew Grote very well; like the Eyres he had been schooled
at Charterhouse (see *DNB* entry on George Grote junior).

132 Letter to Mr Milles dated 8 October 1812 in LB 'C', p. 30. On p. 55 Walpole confirmed
the new position had been purchased.

133 Details found in a letter to Harry dated 14 February 1806 in LB 'A', p. 196.

134 John Timbs, *Clubs and Club Life in London*, London, 1872, pp. 69ff, and Bryant
Lillywhite, *London Coffee Houses*, London, 1963, pp. 163ff.

135 Richardson-Eyre, 1897, p. 8. Unusually for a consecrated church, All Saints was
demolished in 1978 without a faculty (authorisation prior to demolition and/or
disposing of the church's contents). In 'Poor Mary' (1904), Richardson-Eyre described
all the monuments in the church.

136 However, the money for these marriage settlements was only paid in 1858, after
Walpole's death, when the family decided to sell parts of the estate to settle all
outstanding debts, including the £10,000 dowries.

137 He made the land available at no charge for the almshouses and the church and
volunteered £100 towards erecting the church steeple (letter to Twentyman dated
30 October 1848 in LB 'S', p. 187).

138 Henry Samuel's diary starts on Thursday 22 July 1802 and ends on Tuesday 22 March
1803. It is at EE 2651/172I(3).

139 The connection between the Francis and Eyre families was via the Johnson family.
Godschall Johnson (d.1800), the Eyre brothers' uncle (brother of their mother), had
married Marie Francis, his second wife and daughter of Sir Philip Francis. Philip,
Elizabeth and Harriet Francis were Marie's brother and sisters.

140 Last page of Henry Samuel's diary.

141 The first visit was on 10 August 1802. The 'villa' is likely to have been the park
Monceau, which at that time was just within the city wall of Paris. In this property
could be seen various buildings including a Greek temple, a Dutch mill, a pyramid, a
Chinese pavilion, a ruined castle as well as a 'grand pavillon', slightly smaller than the
'petit Trianon'. I am grateful to Jean-Marie Bruson, curator at the Carnavalet Museum,
Paris, for this information.

142 On 4 and 10 August 1802.

143 The letter books regularly mention his attendance at meetings there.

144 Letter to R. Maughan dated 1 October 1843 in LB 'Q', p. 219. According to Joseph
Foster, *The Register of Admissions to Gray's Inn, 1521–1889*, London, 1889, Walpole
was admitted there on 7 November 1794 (p. 399).

145 By 1835, when it is mentioned in his son Frederick Edwin's articles of clerkship at
EE 2651/172E(7).

146 For the clerkship of Walpole with Messrs Pearson & Loggen, see for instance his
signature at the end of the 1792 mortgage for £2,000 in EE 2651/172C(4). The new
account book which was started when Walpole and Sermon formed a partnership has

survived. It is labelled 'Ledger of Sermon & Eyre commencing 1st April 1796' (EE 2652/42). Thomas Sermon is mentioned in family documents prior to that date, for instance in a 1789 assignment involving Thomas Fauquier and the Hodges (mother and stepfather of the Eyre brothers) in EE 2651/323(E).

147 See Deed Poll dated 19 June 1805 at LMA, MDR/1806/3/318 and Power of Attorney at WCA 901/163.

148 To move to No. 7 at the same address in LB 'A', pp. 1–2.

149 As with other trade directories, the information contained in the Law List, the annual directory for the legal profession, is for guidance only rather than being absolutely dependable. For instance, we know from Walpole's letter books that he left 1 Gray's Inn Square in April 1805, but this information does not appear in print until 1808.

150 The first mention of 'Messrs W. Eyre & Wilson of 2 Holborn C[our]t Gray's Inn' I could find is in a letter to Simmons dated 20 July 1825 in LB 'I', p. 419.

151 Letter to Wilson dated 9 June 1824 in LB 'I', p. 103.

152 Letter to Wilson dated 20 July 1825 in LB 'I', p. 416.

153 Letter to Wilson dated 22 July 1825 in LB 'I', p. 419.

154 Letter to Wilson dated 18 November 1826 in LB 'K', p. 185.

155 For Fletcher see letter to Shaw dated 24 June 1817 in LB 'E', p. 151, and for Seymour see LB 'H', p. 19.

156 Shillibeer was then operating from Commercial Place, City Road. Various references in LB 'Q' on pp. 12, 14, 112, etc.

157 Letter to Willan, addressed to St John's Wood, dated 31 December 1816 in LB 'D', p. 758.

158 Letter to William Hodges dated 14 August 1806 in LB 'A', p. 353.

159 Letter to John Hall dated 24 December 1818 in LB 'E', p. 809.

160 Letter to Mrs Wilkie dated 1 May 1806 in LB 'A', p. 263.

161 The wedding was at All Saints Wigan on 21 October 1813. I am grateful to Chris Watts at the History Shop in Wigan for this information.

162 After Alathea's marriage to William Tooke Robinson, the young couple were living at 9 Harewood Square where they are recorded in the 1851 census (I am grateful to Henry Phythian-Adams for this information). They were close neighbours of Alathea's uncle, George John Eyre, who was living at No. 1 in 1851 (see LB 'T', p. 34).

163 Richardson-Eyre, 1904, ch. I, p. 2. Annabella Eyre, was the daughter of the merchant Robert Johnson and his wife Anne (née Taylor, also known as Nancy). After Robert's death in 1825, Nancy Johnson moved to 9 Avenue Road known as Regent's Park House (its lessee was Colonel Eyre). Basic information about the family is at EE 2651/223, particularly in the 'Case for the opinion of Mr Finney, 1843'.

164 This is where the Eyre brothers' half-sister Sarah – known as 'Sally' – Hodson (née Hodges) lived.

165 LB 'D', p. 670.

166 LB 'B', p. 334, for Beaumont Street and LB 'C', p. 680, for Montagu Place.

167 Sun Insurance Policy records at GL Manuscripts (11936/466 No. 904968).

168 LB 'H', pp. 341ff. The wine is moved first and Walpole allows a whole day for this exercise, which suggests the amount of wine was significant.

169 William Smith wrote of Bryanston Square that it was made up of fifty 'handsome uniform houses' and 'with Montagu Square said to be the best examples of well constructed town residences' (Smith, 1833, p. 201).

170 The twenty-one-year lease for these, in Bryanston Mews, has survived and is dated 26 August 1825. It consisted of a double coach house and five-stall stable: EE 2650/1/240.

171 Letter to Col. Graham dated 16 October 1823 in LB 'H', p. 359.

172 Chancellor, 1926, p. 49. This author mentions that Fauntleroy was one of the development lessees. See also RCHM, *Annual Review*, London, 1988–89, pp. 25–27.

173 The Eyre purchase is recorded in LB 'T', p. 365. The Eyres paid £4,050 for it. For the execution of Henry Fauntleroy, see the Museum of London painting, cat. no. 72, p. 195, in Galinou and Hayes, 1996.

174 In particular, the Hodson household at Holland Grove, near Wigan. Sally (= young Sarah) Hodges, one of the Eyre brothers' half-sisters, had married the MP James Alexander Hodson (LB 'B', p. 266), and their home appears to have been used for family gatherings. Holland Grove, now demolished, became a laundry in the early years of the twentieth century, and there is a 1930s photograph of it in the Wigan archives.

175 Letter to Augustus Thesiger dated 22 August 1820 in LB 'F', p. 490.

176 Letter dated 21 November 1826 in LB 'K', p. 189.

177 See LB 'L', pp. 125 and 161–2.

178 Walpole paid £2,260 for it. Letters to Robert Todd dated 26 June and 1 July 1829 in LB 'L', pp. 312 and 315. Walpole subsequently attempted to purchase neighbouring land, a couple of cottages and even a pub, the Lincoln's Arms; see LB 'L', pp. 316 and 366, and LB 'M', p. 237. Dorney House was demolished in 1936 and replaced by Dorney Grove, a bungalow development.

179 Dorney House was sold to Captain Prescott from the Royal Navy (see letter dated 26 July 1841 in LB 'P', p. 390). Letters in LB 'R' continue to mention Weybridge, and Richardson-Eyre, 1897, p. 8, also mentions a house at Weybridge.

180 Letter to Hornbuckle dated 6 August 1808 in LB 'A', p. 792.

181 Letter to Shaw dated 29 June 1821 in LB 'G', p. 35.

182 Letter to Lieutenant Colonel Johnson, son of Reverend John Johnson of Parndon in Essex, dated 30 August 1815 in LB 'D', p. 284.

183 Richardson-Eyre, 1904, ch. I, p. 2.

184 At EE 2651/172E(7).

185 See EE 2652/44(D) from p. 96.

186 Letter to Messrs Lee & Pemberton dated 24 May 1861 in LB 'V', p. 321.

187 See 30 October 1856 assignment to 'Sir J. Clarke Jervoise Bart' at EE 2650/1/268(B).

188 His name disappears from the Law List in 1852 but the letter books are more specific: Messrs White & Co. are described as John Eyre's 'late partners' in December 1851 (LB 'T'. p. 159).

189 See for instance LB 'T', p. 155, when in December 1851 he was abroad and did not return until the following spring.

190 See LB 'T', pp. 250–51, 14 July 1852.

191 Letter to Samuel Garrett dated 9 April 1857 in LB 'U', p. 424.

192 'In Chancery, 17 April 1868' at WCA, 765/219.

193 Note to the 'Schedule to exemplify the annexed Account' (13 May 1855) at EE 2651/172G(11).

194 This compromise reads: 'That each of the said Defendants [Walpole's children and their spouses] ... should have the sum of £2000 over & above the s[ai]d sums of £10,000 settled upon them ... on their respective marriages.'

195 This was the outcome of the petition John filed on 14 July 1857 which sought permission to sell parts of the estate to meet the compromise. This extract comes from the conveyance to Isaac Moses, one of the principal bidders at the 1858 sale, and is dated 9 February 1859, at EE 2651/172E(11), p. 11.

196 A report 'by Mr Shaw & Messrs Norton Hoggart & Trist on the proposed sale of Ground Rents' was mentioned in a letter to A. Howard dated 18 May 1857 in LB 'U', p. 443. By the summer of that year tenants and builders were aware of this development. See for instance the letter to R. Yeo dated 18 August 1857 in LB 'U', p. 483, where Charles Freeth reassured him by saying, 'it is not intended to sell any part of the ... Estate which is held by the Tenants at a pepper corn rent'. The sale took place over five separate days on 27 and 28 May, on 24 and 25 June, and finally on 22 July. Auction catalogues at EE 2651/340. The first sale had eighty-five lots, the second eighty-four lots and the last fifty-seven lots.

197 The will of Colonel Henry Samuel Eyre is at EE 2651/354(A); also WCA 765/209 and 210.

198 The legal case was seemingly in the hands of Messrs John White when John Eyre gave instructions for the case to be reviewed by a different solicitor, Alfred Howard, who masterminded the sale of parts of the estate and its aftermath in 1858–59.

199 The letter books record a considerable number of addresses for John Eyre, implying he moved around a great deal.

200 It became 3 Alpha Road from October 1873; see LB 'X', p. 431. A copperplate survives for printing the estate receipts which gives the 3 Alpha Road address, at EE 2651/352.

201 See letter to Messrs Burgoyne dated 13 July 1868 in LB 'X', p. 257.

202 In a letter to Ravenscroft dated 28 September 1868 in LB 'X', p. 272.

203 Both anecdotes are in LB 'X', p. 292.

204 Richardson-Eyre, 1904, ch. I, p. 3.

205 Richardson-Eyre, 1904, ch. III, p. 1.

206 Some time after the vicar's death the house was acquired by Lady Beauclerk in 1893 and was known as 'Bishops Lodge'; see 1893 lease at EE 2650/1/282(A).

207 Richardson-Eyre, 1904, ch. I, p. 5.

208 See Richardson-Eyre, 1897, pp. 27–28.

Chapter 2 A master plan for St John's Wood

1 The key to this survey was added by hand to one of the 1853 estate maps and captioned as follows: 'This table was copied from a plan made from a survey in 1794 by Messrs Spurrier & Phipps' (reproduced at Plate 70).

2 Several copies of this plan exist – three in Sir John Soane's Museum, one in the Crace Collection at BL, one at WCA, and one in the collection of LMA which is reproduced as Plate 29.

3 'Provided that if the said Walpole Eyre ... should be minded and desirous at any time during the term thereby granted to dig Earth for Bricks in and upon any part of the closes or fields thereby demised it should ... be lawful ... and whereas the said Walpole Eyre ... agreed to lease to William Scott of Grosvenor Square Brickmaker for the term of twenty years.' The original agreement has not survived but is quoted in the agreement with William Scott at EE 2651/285(A) dated 10 December 1770.

4 EE 2651/285(A).

5 It is so described in the 1794 Spurrier & Phipps survey (No. 28). This name is confirmed in a 1796 deed; see Abstract of Title, EE 2650/1/120(A), p. 25.

6 EE 2651/218(B), Articles of Agreement dated 19 August 1774.

7 EE 2651/172E(1) and WCA, 765/229.

8 See Bendall, 1997, vol. II. The first names of these two partners have been established from a document in the Eyre archive at EE 2651/172E(1).

9 On microfilm at Guildhall Library or WCA.

10 In May 1787 the lord chancellor established a commission to prepare the partition of the estate of the first earl of Leicester (d.1743), and John Spurrier was among the five commissioners, alongside Sir Robert Taylor; Charles Alexander Craig, architect and surveyor, a pupil of Taylor; Robert Golden, surveyor; and John Willock, gentleman: see F. H. W. Sheppard (gen. ed.), Survey of London, vols 33–34: The Parish of St Anne Soho, London, 1966, vol. 34, p. 421.

11 Both names feature in an advertisement in The Times of 4 June 1790, and they are listed together in trade directories from 1791.

12 The farm itself was to be let on 13 and 22 September 1796, and on 26 October 1796 building materials from a large barn to be taken down and brick earth were for sale.

13 A second agreement was prepared for Jonathan Alderton along the same lines. Both documents have survived at EE 2651/172E(1 and 2) dated 10 February 1796 (Willan) and 20 February 1796 (Alderton).

14 It was tempting to assume John Spurrier had died around that time, but an assignment of 9 June 1802 at EE 2651/323(F) involving a John Spurrier of Yardlesbury in the County of Hertford perhaps suggests otherwise.

15 See Colvin (1995) for a summary of this architect's career.

16 Gwynn, 1766, p. 6.

17 Colin McWilliam, New Town Guide, Edinburgh, 1998 (published by Edinburgh New Town Conservation Committee); for Bath see Christopher Woodward, The Building of Bath, Bath, n.d. [1990s] (published by the Building of Bath Museum).

18 Londonderry was rebuilt by the City of London, a colonising project which began in 1613 (the walls were ready by 1618). It was the first planned city in Ireland. Whitehaven in Cumbria has been described as the most complete example of planned Georgian architecture in Europe. Both cities adopted a grid pattern, and both claim to have influenced the layout of American cities. For Whitehaven, see Sylvia Collier, Whitehaven 1600–1800: A New Town of the Late Seventeenth Century; A Study of its Buildings and Urban Development, London, 1991 (published by the Royal Commission on Historical Monuments (England)).

19 Gwynn, 1766, p. 20.

20 Gwynn, 1766, p. 116.

21 From Joseph Gandy's Designs for Cottages, London, 1807, reproduced in Darley, 1975, p. 23.

22 See White, 1815.

23 Summerson, 1995 and 1977; Girouard, 1985, devotes a whole chapter to 'London and the Growth of the Suburb', where the Spurrier & Phipps plan is discussed in some detail.

24 Smedley, 1997, p. 21. Smedley was the first to quote from this important text. The source given for the advertisement, however, is not quite correct: it is not the Cambridgeshire Journal but the Cambridge Chronicle and Journal for October 1794. The advertisement appeared four times in this weekly newspaper on 4, 11, 18 and 25 October. I am most grateful to Christopher Jakes at the Cambridge Central Library for his help in clarifying the matter.

25 Girouard, 1985, p. 282.

26 Sheppard, 1958, p. 81, notes: 'whereas in 1756 there were fewer than six hundred houses in the parish, by 1770 there were "upwards of two thousand".' The growth of Marylebone in the eighteenth century is clearly charted on the maps of John Rocque (1741–45 and 1761) and Richard Horwood (1799).

27 Darley, 1975, p. 8.

28 Summerson, 1995, p. 17. This author says Shaw would have been sixteen in 1794 when in fact, being born in 1776, he was actually eighteen.

29 The date in Colvin's Dictionary (1995, p. 861) is given as 1803, but this is incorrect; see EE 2650/1/395(A5), 'Brief for claimant Henry Samuel Eyre, Esqre', a late 1820s document produced in connection with the building of the Marylebone and Finchley Turnpike Road (p. 6). The Eyre/Sermon Account Book offers further proof (see p. 102).

30 See entry on Shaw in Graves, 1905–6.

31 Smedley, 1997, p. 21.

32 Howgego, 1978, pp. 182ff. I have used the annotated copy formerly in Guildhall Library's Prints and Maps section.

33 Letter to Samuel Wild dated 14 October 1808 in LB 'B', p. 1.

34 It may be worth pointing out that Gwynn had criticised the disordered look of the sides and backs of buildings at the Bath circus. He advocated instead the use of a double row of buildings to overcome this aesthetic difficulty. Shaw, when he increased the density of the Eyre circus, may have remembered Gwynn's double circus.

35 The earliest agreements to have survived were Lord's in 1813 and William Hall's in 1814. As time went on, this ideal distance would be revised: Davison's houses in St John's Wood Road would only be set back thirty feet (LB 'E', p. 216). Henry Gore Chandless's houses would be set back twenty-five feet; see letter to Henry Chandless dated 22 September 1823 in LB 'H', p. 337.

36 Letter to R. H. Crew dated 28 September 1810 in LB 'B', p. 332.

37 Letter to Jack Trevanion dated 29 January 1812 in LB 'B', p. 580.

38 Letter dated 15 November 1821 in LB 'G', p. 158.

39 Letter to George Law dated 14 November 1822 in LB 'H', pp. 37–38; also TNA, WO 44/557.

40 See letter of 13 August 1823 in LB 'H', p. 308.

41 Letter to Shaw dated 28 April 1824 in LB 'I', pp. 73–74.

42 See White, 1815, p. 7.

43 I used the 1792 edition in the British Library.

44 This is suggested by the title of the book but also by the introduction, which specifies

that the idea for this publication stemmed from a conversation with 'Gentlemen' in the summer of 1777.

45 (1) 'dry and healthy', (2) 'warm and chearful' (3) 'convenient', (4) 'not be more than 12 Feet wide', (5) 'should always be built in pairs; either at a little distance the one from the other; or close adjoining so as to appear as one building, that the inhabitants may be of assistance to each other in case of sickness or any other accident', (6) 'should be built strong, and with the best materials [as a piece of oeconomy]'. Wood went on to 'recommend regularity, which is beauty', (7) and 'a piece of ground for a garden should be allotted to every cottage.'

46 Lever, 2003, p. 375.

47 Lever, 2003, p. 133.

48 Stroud, 1971, pp. 84–87.

49 See Helen Rosenau, *Social Purpose in Architecture: Paris and London Compared 1760–1800*, London, 1970, p. 44.

50 Cherry and Pevsner, 1991, p. 40.

51 Early publications on cottage or villa building are discussed in Blutman, 1968. She counted 'thirty books containing designs for country houses … published in England between 1780 and 1815', James Lewis's *Original Designs in Architecture* being the earliest (1780) and Robert Lugar's *Plans and Views of Buildings* the latest (1811). The following may be useful: John Crunden, *Convenient and Ornamental Architecture*, 1770; Nathaniel Kent, *Hints to Gentlemen of Landed Property*, 1775; John Wood, *A Series of Plans for Cottages or Habitations of the Labourer*, 1781; John Plaw, *Rural Architecture or Designs from the Simple Cottage to the Decorated Villa*, 1785; Charles Middleton, *Picturesque and Architectural Views for Cottages, Farm Houses and Country Villas*, 1795. Also see the encyclopaedic Archer, 1985.

52 For the date of Queen Charlotte's cottage, see Ray Desmond, *Kew: The History of the Royal Botanic Gardens*, London, 1995, pp. 75 and 78.

53 John Plaw, *Sketches for Country Houses, Villas and Rural Dwellings*, London, 1800.

54 John Plaw, *Ferme Ornée or Rural Improvement*, London, 1795, pl. 33.

55 See Cherry and Pevsner, 1991, p. 675.

56 Lease dates from 1808. Counterpart lease at EE 2650/1/250(A), also Bk of Drawings I, 1A.

57 Leases date from 1817 and 1818, EE 2650/1/259(C) and (D). Lease drawings in Bk of Drawings I, 30 and 36.

58 Summerson, 1995, p. 7.

59 See Chapter 5 for the mid-1830s shift towards using the word 'villa'. In 1833, a contemporary account described St John's Wood's houses as 'detached villa residences': see Smith, 1833, p. 222.

60 Letter to Shaw dated 5 August 1806 in LB 'A', p. 341.

61 Letter to Sanders dated 13 August 1812 in LB 'C', p. 7.

62 The wording for this advertisement is found in a letter to Todd dated 22 March 1815 in LB 'D', p. 78.

63 Summerson, 1995, p. 11.

64 Malton, 1798, p. 4.

65 Archer, 1985: see the section entitled 'Picturesque Retreats for Country and Suburb: Designs for Villas and Cottages', pp. 59ff. He noted on p. 68 that 'the first British architect to discuss formal differences among dwelling types was Daniel Garret, who considered the cottage in particular in his *Designs, and Estimates, of Farm Houses* (1747).'

66 Darley, 1975, p. 3.

67 Darley, 1975, p. 3.

68 Walpole Eyre's terminology is a far more accurate description than semi-detached house, which shifts the emphasis away from the concept of the appearance of a single house.

69 Lever, 2003, pp. 291–96, for East Stratton. John Nash's famous Blaise Hamlet outside Bristol (1804) is essentially made up of detached houses with just one house comprising two (very different) halves.

70 Letter to Henry Samuel Eyre dated 24 March 1810 in LB 'B', p. 249.

71 Letter to Warren dated 26 May 1809 in LB 'B', p. 123.

72 Letter to Godschall Johnson dated 15 June 1821 in LB 'G', p. 20.

73 Letter dated 4 April 1811 in LB 'B', p. 408. Walpole's suggestion was not taken up.

74 Thomas Milne's 'Land Use Map of London and Environs' in 1800, published by the London Topographical Society in 1975–76 (No. 118–19).

75 Letter to Simons dated 6 January 1810 in LB 'B', p. 291. The solution to the problem is spelt out in full in Walpole's Bill Book I, p. 95, and reproduced on pp. 165–66.

76 The word is repeatedly used in Walpole's letter books.

77 Mark Girouard provides an excellent general summary of the birth of the suburbs in Girouard, 1990, ch. 17, 'The Suburbs'.

78 Spiro Kostof, *The City Shaped*, London, 1991, pp. 70ff.

79 See LB 'B', p. 354, for John White senior in 1810 when the boundary line between the two estates is discussed; also p. 410 re: sewers. Letters to John White junior are in LB 'D', and they recap on the arrangements made in 1808–10.

80 Letter to Mr Stevens dated 11 June 1811 in LB 'B', p. 443.

81 Extract from 'Jerusalem: The Emanation of the Giant Albion', 1804, published in David V. Erdman (ed.), *The Complete Poetry and Prose of William Blake*, New York, 1988, pp. 171–72.

Chapter 3 First steps, 1805–20

1 The Eyre/Sermon Account Book has fortunately survived, and it is easy to identify the names of those who later became Walpole's clients. They were Henry Samuel Eyre (Walpole's brother and the rightful owner of the St John's Wood estate); Lieutenant General Andrew Gordon; Captain Jeremiah Hodges and his father's executors; William Hodges; Reverend Samuel Hornbuckle; Francis Hodson; Godschall Johnson and his father's executors; Matthew Raper and Godin Shiffner; the Trevanion family.

2 Letter dated 11 April 1805 in LB 'A', p. 6.

3 Letter dated 14 May 1806 in LB 'A', p. 278.

4 This precious slender volume covers the period 1 April 1796 to 31 March 1805. The entries relating to the Eyre estate are found under the client's name 'Henry Samuel Eyre' in Sermon/Eyre Account Book, pp. 14 and 68.

5 Sermon/Eyre Account Book, p. 88. The sum was £78 15s. 10d. Several payments by 'Phipps' were made to Henry Samuel Eyre between December 1800 and May 1801. Only one of them on p. 86, for the sum of £200, is unequivocally from Josiah Phipps. The others are simply labelled 'Phipps' – in all they amount to £800. The interpretation of these entries should be cautious as Walpole Eyre's broker was also a Mr Phipps operating at Messrs Wood & Sons in Castle Alley, Cornhill, and there was a family friend or relative called Phipps who was based in Wiltshire (LB 'A').

6 LB 'A', p. 114.

7 The entry in the Sermon/Eyre Account Book for 3 January 1805 (p. 102) reads: 'To Balance of Mr Shaw the Surveyors Acct'.

8 Sermon/Eyre Account Book for 3 January 1805, p. 102, left and right.

9 Sermon/Eyre Account Book for 3 January 1805, p. 102, left. The sum paid to Sidwell was £23 1s. 8d.

10 Letter dated 4 June 1805 in LB 'A', p. 59.

11 Letter, undated, between 17 and 19 June 1805 in LB 'A', p. 66. It is interesting to compare this list to an 1803 list of tenants found on a 'Certificate Of The Contract For The Redemption Of Land Tax' where only the following names are featured: Willan, Abbott, Alderton, Walker and Jefferson (EE 2651/356(1)).

12 See Brown, 2001, and Saunders, 1981.

13 Spurrier & Phipps placed an advertisement in *The Times* on 13 September 1796 in connection with St John's Wood Farm: 'TO BE LET … consisting of about 188 Acres of rich Land, Tythe free, almost the whole of which is Meadow, with a roomy, convenient Dwelling-house, Garden, Huge Barn, good Granary, Stables'. However, Willan's agreement for land, prepared by Spurrier & Phipps on behalf of Henry Samuel Eyre, seems earlier than the advertisement as it is dated 10 February 1796. The agreement was

for twenty-one years. It has survived and is in the Eyre archive at EE 2651/172E(1). Malcolm Brown, in his article on Thomas Willan (2001), misleadingly stated that the farm was in the hands of Willan's father from 1777. In fact, Thomas only acquired it in 1806, as is clear from Walpole's LB 'A', p. 238.

14 Letter to Harry dated 14 February 1806 in LB 'A', p. 196.

15 Letter to Harry dated 3 April 1806 in LB 'A', p. 238.

16 See letter to Hill dated 26 February 1807 in LB 'A', p. 469, for the tenancy of the house. Presumably Hill never recovered from the accident which took place in February that year; see Mrs Hill's letter to Walpole in LB 'A', p. 675.

17 Letter dated 26 February 1807 in LB 'A', p. 469.

18 Letter to Northwood dated 17 September 1808 in LB 'A', p. 810.

19 Letter to Wilson dated 16 January 1812 in LB 'B', p. 571.

20 His name is usually given as Mr Walker but features in full in the key to John Jones's map (Plate 44).

21 Letters to Brick Field tenants dated 23 July 1805 in LB 'A', p. 91.

22 Letter to Webber dated 14 June 1810 in LB 'B', p. 287.

23 Letter to Rule dated 1 October 1813 in LB 'C', p. 313. Webber's death is mentioned on p. 635.

24 Some of the lots would be subcontracted, for instance to Chamberlain (this transaction is explained on p. 103).

25 EE 2651/294.

26 LB 'E', p. 19: Shaw and Todd each produced a design for Gibb's cottage in March 1817. In August of the same year, having failed to obtain a quick response from Shaw about the correct depth for the basement of Thomas Heaphy's house, Walpole turned to Todd (p. 249). Walpole's Bill Book I (pp. 75 and 99) also reveals that Shaw and Todd were both involved with the drainage system at St John's Wood.

27 Letter dated 5 October 1809 in LB 'B', pp. 182–83.

28 The very detailed conveyance of Grove End Place dated 21 March 1840 certainly confirms (on p. 2) the presence of James, George and Thomas Biddle by 1807 (EE 2651/177).

29 Letter dated 18 October 1805 in LB 'A', p. 127.

30 Letter dated 13 May 1808 in LB 'A', p. 730.

31 Letter dated 26 May 1808 in LB 'A', p. 741.

32 Work on Alpha Road started in late 1804 and continued well into 1805, while negotiations for the burial ground started in March 1807 and the deal was closed in December that year.

33 See LMA, MJ/SP/1799/02/036 file for the short-lived tenancy of William Knightley and the petition by Henry Samuel Eyre against the vestry's extortionate rates when the farm was 'in hand'. William Knightley probably responded to the 1796 Spurrier & Phipps advertisement in *The Times* (see note 13) and succeeded Jonathan Alderton at St John's Wood Farm; see letter to Harry dated 2 June 1810 (entered on 28 June) in LB 'B', p. 295. The agreement for a lease between Spurrier & Phipps (for Henry Samuel Eyre) and Jonathan Alderton survives in the archive and is dated 29 February 1796 at EE 2651/172E(2). John Abbott's lease has not survived but is recorded in a 'Schedule' found in 'Attested Copy Surrender of Term Giles Templeman to Charles Bell Ford' dated 12 February 1816 and at EE 1651/172C(11). The lease to Abbott was dated 27 November 1800.

34 See LMA above.

35 For instance, letter to Villiers dated 16 August 1816 in LB 'D', p. 639.

36 Montgomery Eyre, 1913, p. 34.

37 6 July 1824: see R. B. Beckett (ed.), *John Constable's Correspondence*, Ipswich, 1962–78, vol. III, p. 4.

38 Olsen, 1964, p. 7.

39 In summer 1807: Bill Book I, p. 38.

40 The 'Schedule', which lists the key dates in the legal history of the St John's Wood estate, makes its appearance in St John's Wood leases for the first time in November 1808, in the lease prepared for Cornelius Dixon: EE 2650/1/150(B).

41 Letter to Harry dated 24 March 1810 in LB 'B', p. 249.

42 LB 'B', p. 334. Incidentally, Beaumont Street was also where the clerk for Marylebone vestry, Mr Greenwell, lived.

43 White, 1815, p. 21. The Edwardes estate, owned by the earl of Kensington, is situated west of Earl's Court Road (see Hermione Hobhouse (gen. ed.), *Survey of London*, vol. 42: *Kensington Square to Earl's Court*, London, 1986). It was developed from 1811, which is contemporary with Walpole's largely failed attempt to develop St John's Wood Grove Terrace (1811, see 'Selling the estate' in this chapter). This indicates that it was a difficult time for building development.

44 In a letter dated 10 October 1820 in LB 'F', p. 519.

45 Walpole moved to Montagu Place in October 1814, presumably as the Beaumont Street house became too small after he married Annabella Johnson in 1813; letter to Hall dated 29 December 1817 in LB 'E', p. 385, and letter to Hall dated 5 August 1820 in LB 'F', p. 468.

46 Letter to Greenwood dated 12 August 1823 in LB 'H', p. 305.

47 Letter to Charles Green dated 16 February 1813 in LB 'C', p. 161. This particular transaction did not take place on the Eyre estate.

48 See Saunders, 1981, pp. 79–84. I am grateful to Andrew Saint for making that connection.

49 Letter addressed to Samuel Moody, one of the mortgagees, dated April 1806 in LB 'A', p. 235.

50 Letter to Shaw dated 7 August 1807 in LB 'A', p. 581.

51 Letter to Shaw dated 4 July 1822 in LB 'G', p. 435.

52 Olsen, 1973, p. 345.

53 Letter to Mr Simmonds, surveyor, dated 29 July 1811 in LB 'B', p. 473.

54 Letter to Harry dated 14 May 1806 in LB 'A', p. 278.

55 Bill Book I, p. 33, July 1807.

56 Letter to Harry dated 23 July 1807 in LB 'A', p. 563.

57 Letter to William Hall dated 26 August 1822 in LB 'G', p. 515.

58 The correct indenture is dated 23 and 24 November 1792 and recorded in the Abstract of Title found at EE 2650/1/120(A), p. 20.

59 John Partridge and John Dyneley were duly reimbursed when the new mortgage came through. A good summary of these borrowings is found in the St John's Wood Abstract of Title EE 2650/1/120(A), under the correct dates (pp. 20ff). Partridge's mortgage document has survived (WCA, 2194/5) and Dyneley's too (WCA, 2194/1–3/3).

60 Letters to various parties in LB 'A', pp. 358–59. The lease itself is dated 29 August 1806 at EE 2651/12(A and B).

61 Letter to Greenwell dated 24 August 1807 in LB 'A', p. 612.

62 Letter to Greenwell dated 9 October 1807 in LB 'A', p. 621.

63 Various letters in LB 'A' make it clear that Walpole and Shiffner were friends. Godin Shiffner was a London merchant who in July 1808 became a partner in the firm Shiffner & Ellis based in Old Broad Street (LB 'A', p. 768). Shiffner was forced to retire from this set-up, probably in 1809, under a cloud (LB 'B', p. 313), though luckily for him by early 1810 he had become a director of the Sun Fire Office (Bill Book I, p. 95, 17 February 1810).

64 Bill Book I, p. 95, 17 February 1810.

65 Letter dated 24 March 1810 in LB 'B', p. 249.

66 Letter to Mr Goodeve, solicitor of the Sun Fire Office, dated 18 October 1810 in LB 'B', p. 346. The description of these sixty-five acres is: 'The Slipe 4.0.6, House & Barns &c. 6.3.36, Piece in Saint Johns Wood Lane 0.0.19, Four Acres 5.3.31, Seven acres 6.1.16, Cottage & Garden 0.1.37, Twenty acres 25.1.17, Barn Field 14.0.4.'

67 LB 'D', pp. 301, 303, 307 and 315, before a settlement was reached in September 1819, on p. 366.

68 The mortgage has survived and is at WCA, 901/105 and 114. The transaction is also mentioned in the Abstract of Title at EE 2650/1/120(A), pp. 45ff.

69 Letter to Goodeve dated 11 June 1812 in LB 'B', p. 675.

70 Bill Book I, p. 72, 2 March 1809: 'to fit himself out for the East Indies'.

71 Letter to George Law (Willan's solicitor) dated 16 June 1813 in LB 'C', p. 242, and letter to Willan dated 2 July 1822 in LB 'G', p. 430. The 1813 letter implied there had been other loans prior to the £4,000.

72 The brother of Walpole's mother and also one of Walpole's clients. See Abstract of Title, EE 2650/1/120(A), pp. 65ff. Also LB 'D', p. 181, which shows that initially Walpole asked for £5,000.

73 Letter to Goodeve and Ranken dated 23 May 1815 in LB 'D', p. 183.

74 Letter dated 22 October 1819 in LB 'F', p. 231.

75 Letter to Sun Fire Office dated 11 March 1819 in LB 'F', p. 12.

76 For instance, Sheppard, 1971; Olsen, 1964 and 1973; Watson, 1989.

77 EE 1651/172E(1) dated 10 February 1796.

78 EE 2651/207 document dated 6 February 1808.

79 LB 'B', p. 279, and EE 2650/1/516(B).

80 Letter to Shaw dated 31 October 1806 in LB 'A', p. 382.

81 There are various spellings for the second name in LB 'A' – Gynn, Glynn, Gymm – but in Walpole's Bill book on p. 1 it is 'Gwynn'.

82 Letter to Storey dated 4 July 1806 in LB 'A', p. 307.

83 EE 2650/1/120(B): the earliest agreement to have survived was drawn up in 1752: 'ARTICLES OF AGREEMENT between the Tenants of St John's Wood for the Repair of St John's Wood Road', dated 22 November 1752. Also see p. 221 in Chapter 7.

84 Letter dated 12 May 1806 in LB 'A', p. 277. Lewis was a prospective buyer at St John's Wood. Despite the very unfavourable terms he requested, Walpole was willing to compromise and wrote: 'I must however confess that we are anxious that the Build[in]gs should be began upon the part of the Estate you have fixed upon & it would afford us great satisfact[io]n if we can let that land to you as we feel fully assured that whatever you undertake you will do handsomely & will of course benefit my Brother's property': LB 'A', p. 349, 12 August 1806.

85 Bill Book I, p. 45, December 1808, for the 'Japan Box'; for the strong room, letter to Charles Day dated 12 March 1824 in LB 'I', p. 25.

86 Letter to Hertslet dated 10 January 1822 in LB 'G', p. 205.

87 Letters to Shaw dated 25 April 1811 and 19 May 1811 in LB 'B', pp. 418 and 430.

88 There is an amusing anecdote in a letter to Mr Warren dated 30 October 1805 in LB 'A', p. 130, where Walpole has repeated altercations with a Mr Walter Scott at the Old South Sea House where Godschall Johnson's executors have their counting house. Walpole's *cri de coeur* is: 'I think you must dismiss Scott.' Scott was eventually dismissed but the episode dragged on, as clearly Mr Warren could not see Walpole's point immediately.

89 Letter to Greenwell dated 25 July 1807 in LB 'A', pp. 565–66.

90 Bill Book I, p. 77, dated 11 November 1809 for Mrs Eyre's will, and p. 99, dated 20 July 1810 for the Heralds Office.

91 Bill Book I, p. 38, December 1807.

92 WCA, 901/103 – this release document stated that the annuity was 'chargeable upon' the lots on either side of Alpha Road only.

93 Letter to Turner dated 18 January 1813 (date should read 1814) in LB 'C', p. 405.

94 Letter to Goodeve dated 12 February 1816 in LB 'D', p. 415.

95 Letter to Birnie dated 1 January 1807 in LB 'A', p. 423.

96 The lease is at WCA, 765/3. Also see letter to Smith dated 26 June 1823 in LB 'H', p. 265.

97 Letter to Birnie dated 24 August 1807 in LB 'A', p. 584.

98 Lease between Charles Clifford and Henry Samuel Eyre dated 16 November 1807 at EE 2650/1/259(A).

99 See, for instance, the lease between John Bennett and Henry Samuel Eyre dated 12 December 1818 at EE 2650/1/259(D).

100 Letter to Todd dated 25 January 1812 in LB 'C', pp. 584–85. The letter to Willan is on p. 588.

101 Letter to Goodeve dated 12 February 1816 in LB 'D', p. 415.

102 Letter dated 19 April 1806 in LB 'A', p. 250.

103 Bill Book I, p. 73, 4 and 5 April 1809.

104 Bill Book I, pp. 77 and 78 (7 and 16 November 1809).

105 Letter to Harry dated 7 October 1810 in LB 'B', p. 337.

106 WCA, 765/199.

107 1796 is the date given in Sheppard (1958, p. 251). Walpole's letters implied the date was in fact 1791. There was some uncertainty about the boundaries, and we learn this information when he wrote to a couple of attorneys in search of the original plan; see LB 'A', p. 751, and LB 'B', p. 77.

108 Sheppard, 1958, p. 251. In this book Sheppard gives a lively blow-by-blow account of this protracted project first formulated in 1791 and which took eighteen years to complete. The associated project of redeveloping Marylebone church took even longer.

109 Letter to James Stone dated 14 May 1808 in LB 'A', p. 731. Barker bought several lots at auction.

110 This Breeze Yard was sold in 1791 in seventy-nine lots; see letter to Messrs Strong dated 3 June 1808 in LB 'A', p. 751, and Arthur Ashbridge, *The Little Manor of Lisson Green*, p. 7 (no date, reprinted from the *Marylebone Mercury*, copy at WCA).

111 This 'dirt' included town ash for which a trade existed: brickmakers commonly incorporated ash into the local clay used for London stock brickmaking. This distinctive practice was curiously labelled 'Spanish' and apparently dated back to the Great Fire, when bricks were made from clay fields where large amounts of ash had been deposited (see Hobhouse and Saunders, 1989, p. 4).

112 Letter to Harry dated 9 April 1807 in LB 'A', p. 492.

113 One of the obstacles was finding a missing 'Assignment of the Term' from the St John's Wood title deeds. Another was thus described by Walpole in his bill book: 'perusing long Act of Parliament of the 35 George 3rd under which the Parish of Mary le Bone purchased the Breeze Yard[,] when it did not appear to me that they had any power of Purchasing Prem[is]es of such description'. A summary of these difficulties is found in Bill Book I, pp. 39ff. For the final possession of the Breeze Yard, see LB 'A', p. 722.

114 In Bill Book I, p. 77, dated 5 October 1809, Walpole stated thirty lots were sold. Six remained unsold (LB 'B', p. 327).

115 Letter to Harry dated 20 July 1806 in LB 'A', p. 327.

116 Letter to Harry dated 20 November 1806 in LB 'A', p. 395.

117 Letter to Harry dated 5 April 1808 in LB 'A', p. 713.

118 Letter to Harry dated 2 June 1810 (entered 28 June) in LB 'B', pp. 295–96.

119 Bill Book I, p. 97, 5 May 1810. The letter of 24 September 1809 has not survived.

120 Bill Book I, p. 97, 8 May 1810.

121 Letter to Harry dated 2 June 1810 (entered 28 June) in LB 'B', pp. 295–96.

122 Letter addressed to the subtenant Mr Simons (other spellings: Simmons and Simmonds) dated 21 December 1810 in LB 'B', p. 369. Also Bill Book I, p. 102, 18 December 1810.

123 Letter dated 25 April 1811 in LB 'B', p. 418.

124 *The Times*, 11 June 1811.

125 Letter dated 13 July 1811 in LB 'B', p. 466.

126 Two plots on the south-west side of the Avenue of Trees to bricklayers William and Edward Smith in February 1812. Another plot went to stonemason William Miles in July that year; and Robert Todd also made purchases in February 1816 and August 1818. William Smith purchased another, much larger plot in May 1817, and William Atkinson bought £200 worth of land in August 1818; in 1819, Emerson Dowson and William Smith are recorded as the last buyers. In Abstract of Title at EE 2650/1/120(A) as follows: pp. 56 and 58 for the Smiths, p. 60 for William Miles, p. 70 for Robert Todd, p. 76 for William Smith and Todd and Atkinson, p. 86 for Emerson Dowson, and p. 88 for William Smith. The sums involved were (in the order shown above) £109 14s. (W. Smith); £98 14s. (E. Smith); £98 14s. (Miles); £196 7s. and £417 12s. (Todd); £800 (W. Smith); £200 (Atkinson); £210 (Dowson); £220 10s. (W. Smith).

127 Letter to Shaw dated 23 July 1812 in LB 'B', p. 720.

128 Letter to Grote dated 22 July 1812 in LB 'B', p. 721.

129 Letter to Shaw dated 8 November 1820 in LB 'F', p. 535.

130 Bk of Drawings I, 96, dated 24 July 1821 and lease dated 4 December 1834 at EE 2651/95.

131 Letter to Shaw dated 11 July 1821 in LB 'G', p. 47.

132 Letter to Shaw dated 6 November 1821 in LB 'G', p. 147. Also Bk of Drawings I, 101.

133 Gardner's property was on the south side of Elm Tree Road, just above Lord's (north-west corner). The property is shown on the St John's Wood lease map, No. 1976. It is now 8 Elm Tree Road.

134 Bill Book I, p. 44, 30 October 1808.

135 Bill Book I, p. 45, 27 December 1808. Walpole first encountered William Seymour in February 1808 when he became the solicitor of Lady Boyd. In May of the same year he was handling the building leases of Birnie '& the others' (LB 'A', p. 749). Walpole noted in LB 'A', p. 792, that Seymour was 'professionally known to most of the builders upon my Brothers property'.

136 Bill Book I, p. 72, 20 March 1809.

137 Letter sent from Twickenham dated 8 October 1819 in LB 'F', p. 215.

138 LB 'F', p. 218.

139 Letter dated 4 November 1819 in LB in 'F', p. 241

Chapter 4 Early residential designs

1 Chalcots estate was developed by the Provost and College of Eton. See Olsen's contribution in Dyos, 1966, p. 348.

2 See Mireille Galinou (ed.), *City Merchants and the Arts*, London, 2004, p. 29.

3 I have used William Weymott's *An Abridgment of such part of the Building Act as will be useful to all persons who have either Freehold or Leasehold Houses or Buildings*, London, 1774.

4 Agreement with Monro, Delafield and Nash (for the canal company), 29 July 1813 at EE 2651/141(B). Agreement with Thomas Lord, 7 August 1813 at EE 2651/88(A).

5 Agreement with Thomas Lothian dated 9 October 1835 at EE 2651/50. Around sixty years had elapsed since the Building Act, and inflation may account for these figures, almost at the top of the second rate category.

6 Letter to Henry Woolcott, son of the late William Woolcott, dated 27 September 1823 in LB 'H', p. 345.

7 Summerson, 1995, p. 23.

8 EE 2651/262(A). The print version of this plan is inside the canal company agreement at EE 2651/141(B) and also in the WCA collection.

9 Efforts to locate this particular work (with the kind help of Marijke Booth at Christie's) were unfortunately unsuccessful. The painting was sold at Christie's on four separate occasions from the 1970s: on 18 June 1976 (23), on 26 June 1981, on 17 November 1989 (102) and on 12 April 1991 (54).

10 Lease and counterpart at EE 2651/12(A and B).

11 See Colvin, 1995, pp. 908 ff.

12 The lease has not survived but is recorded at LMA, MDR/1809/1/265. Its date is also mentioned in the preliminary recital of an 1887 licence at EE 2650/1/197(B).

13 Alison Kelly, *Mrs Coade's Stone*, Upton-upon-Severn, 1990, p. 391.

14 Letter to Papworth dated 13 August 1806 in LB 'A', p. 351.

15 Summerson, 1995, pp. 1–48. The quote by James Elmes is on p. 18.

16 Letter to Wild dated 20 July 1809 in LB 'B', p. 149.

17 Bill Book I, p. 206.

18 There are several instances when leases were issued some time after the house was built, but they would normally be backdated. This lease, dated 1809 rather than 1806, was adjusted to reflect the Eyres' debt of gratitude towards Todd (they offered to extend his lease free of charge: see p. 91). The lease itself has not survived, only the lease drawing at Bk of Drawings I, 8.

19 Letter to Birnie dated 16 April 1806 in LB 'A', p. 249.

20 EE 2651/39 discussed in the section on James Burton below. The reference to Robert Todd's houses is found on the page with the plan.

21 The plan and elevation of these houses are recorded in Bk of Drawings I, 29, dated June 1817.

22 For the extension of the first sewer built on the estate 'up the Avenue of Trees' (Lisson Grove), see LB 'C', p. 710. For leases issued to Todd, see for instance LB 'F', pp. 18, 152, 161, 578 (1819–21). For vestry meetings see letter to Todd dated 7 November 1817 in LB 'E', p. 347. For Todd as one of Walpole's clients, see Walpole's bill books.

23 Bk of Drawings I, 14.

24 Brown, 1995, p. 54.

25 See letters to Martin dated 19 and 31 March, 6 July 1808 in LB 'A', pp. 702, 708, 709. Tatham's lease registration states Martin had sublet part of his premises to Tatham (LMA, MDR/1809/1/265).

26 Letters to Tatham dated 11 and 15 April 1823 in LB 'H', pp. 187 and 190.

27 The original site is described in a letter to Tatham dated 11 March 1819 in LB 'A', p. 12. Also see Bk of Drawings I, 75, for elevation and plan of the house built by Tatham on St John's Wood Road.

28 Letter to Gurney dated 20 September 1823 in LB 'H', p. 333.

29 Letter dated October 1815 in LB 'D', p. 334.

30 In 1812 he used Alpha Cottages as his address on the lease to Mrs Odell at EE 2650/1/263(C).

31 Girouard, 1990, p. 283. He quotes as early examples the Thornton family of City of London merchants in Clapham and the Liverpool banker William Roscoe in Islington.

32 Letter to John Smith dated 3 April 1837 in LB 'O', p. 252.

33 Letter to John Eyre from Charles Freeth dated 3 March 1865 in LB 'W', p. 288.

34 The final number of lots was thirty-nine as listed in the auction particulars of 5 October 1809 at WCA, 765/199. An extra fifteen lots were added to Walpole's original estimate of twenty-four (see Bill Book I, p. 75). He also recorded that thirty lots were sold at auction (Bill Book I, p. 77).

35 Bill Book I, p. 76.

36 Letter to Burton dated 11 November 1809 in LB 'B', p. 191.

37 Letter to Messrs Burgoyne & Davies dated 30 November 1809 in LB 'B', p. 207.

38 Steen Eiler Rasmussen, *London: The Unique City*, London and Toronto, 1937, pp. 232ff.

39 EE 2651/88(A) dated 7 August 1813.

40 Letter to Shaw dated 1 August 1814 in LB 'C', p. 621. The agreement, EE 2651/123, is dated 25 October 1814.

41 Bk of Drawings III, 106.

42 Letter to Rule dated 1 October 1813 in LB 'C', p. 313.

43 Letter to James Morgan dated 16 July 1813 in LB 'C', p. 269. The original list of conditions has survived and is discussed under James Burton below.

44 Letter to J. Smith dated 26 June 1823 in LB 'H', p. 265.

45 Letter to R. H. Crew dated 3 July 1823 at TNA, WO 44/557.

46 For instance, they were not in use at the Portman or Portland estates. I am grateful to Richard Bowden, archivist to both estates, for confirming this (with the proviso that a large percentage of the Portman archive has not survived).

47 Letter to Shaw dated 6 March 1817 in LB 'E', p. 19.

48 Letter to Shaw dated 14 February 1817 in LB 'D', p. 806. A few years later there was an attempt to turn one of the lodges into a house, to which Walpole objected fiercely: 'I observe they are building a Story over the Lodge at the Corner of Lodge road[.] as a Lodge it had a very pretty effect but if it is to be converted into a house it will be very objectionable and will be destruction to Messrs Duppas premises, I have therefore to request that you will not allow this building to be proceeded with' (letter to James Burton dated 4 June 1823 in LB 'H', p. 242).

49 Breeze Yard sale, Walpole's Bill Book I, p. 95, for February 1810.

50 See Rasmussen (p. 202) in note 38.

51 Colvin, 1995, p. 174.

52 See his agreement with the canal company and Walpole Eyre at EE 2651/39.

53 Letter to Shaw dated 23 December 1817 in LB 'E', p. 382.

54 EE 2651/39 dated 30 July 1818.

55 Both documents to be found at EE 2651/141(B and C).

56 Letter to Monro, Delafield and Nash dated 16 July 1817 in LB 'E', p. 179.

57 The leases have not survived, but plans and elevations have been recorded in Bk of Drawings I, 50 (dated 24 February 1819) for Bristow and p. 53 (dated 30 October 1819) for Anderson. Bristow's dwelling is an uneven double house with a 'granny flat'. Both houses faced Regent's Park in Avenue Road and are mentioned in LB 'F', p. 36 for Mrs Bristow and p. 229 for Mr Anderson.

58 Letter to Burton dated 17 March 1819 in LB 'F', p. 20.

59 Letter to Burton dated 15 September 1819 in LB 'F', p. 205.

60 Letter dated 23 November 1819 in LB 'F', p. 262.

61 Letter to James Burton dated 10 March 1821 in LB 'F', p. 651.

62 Letter to Septimus Burton dated 19 January 1822 in LB 'G', p. 216.

63 Letter dated 14 August 1821 in LB 'G', p. 74. William Ford Burton's house was on the south side of North Bank. Its plan and elevation are recorded in Bk of Drawings I, 98, and the lease dated 15 August 1821 has survived at EE 2650/1/258(A).

64 Letter dated 19 October 1821 in LB 'G', p. 129.

65 Letter dated 23 December 1823 in LB 'H', p. 440.

66 The lease at EE 2651/297(A) is dated 24 December 1823 but was not executed until January 1824, as mentioned in the letter to James Burton dated 24 December 1823 in LB 'H', p. 441.

67 Letter dated 31 July 1823 in LB 'H', p. 297.

68 Manwaring Baines, 1956, p. 17.

69 Letter to J. W. Lyon dated 1 October 1821 in LB 'G', p. 113.

70 The 'John White' plan of the Portland estate, which dates from 1796–99, has been indexed by Richard Bowden. It is inscribed 'A Large Plan of the Duke of Portland's Estate as Let to Different Tennants to Build upon. Surveyed by John White 1797, 1798 & 1799'. A section is reproduced in Bowden, 2001.

71 Thomas Martin, Thomas Papworth and Robert Todd belonged to the building trade. Thomas Martin rose to the position of architect during his years at St John's Wood, while William Atkinson, James Burton, John Shaw and C. H. Tatham were described as architects when development started.

72 Richardson-Eyre, 1904, ch. V, p. 13.

73 I am grateful to Patrick Hanlon from Cluttons for sharing this insightful comment, which was coined by the engineer Michael Hurst.

Chapter 5 Creating and maintaining a garden quarter

1 Letter to Mrs Annette Hatton, Newbays, Wexford, Ireland, dated 30 August 1824 in LB 'I', p. 166. The loan had not been repaid by 1832, two years after Annette's death, when the matter is mentioned in LB 'M', p. 463. Annette Hatton, née Hodges, was the daughter of Sarah Hodges – the Eyre brothers' mother – by her second husband, Jeremiah Hodges.

2 These figures are based on the drawings prepared for leases and kept altogether in the Eyre archive books of drawings.

3 The line comes from a poster 'Rise' dating from this period and reproduced in Barker and Jackson, 1979, p. 242.

4 The house was in Wellington Road. See letter dated 27 November 1844 in LB 'Q', p. 459. Also see note by Montgomery Eyre (1913, p. 160), who placed it at the corner of Wellington and Circus Roads.

5 Altick, 1978, pp. 240–41.

6 Letter to Colonel Graham dated 1 May 1824 in LB 'I', p. 76.

7 Letter to Colonel Rowan dated 27 May 1830 in LB 'M', p. 18.

8 The first quote comes from a letter to Mrs Cooper dated 10 July 1826 in LB 'K', p. 98; the second quote from a letter to Appleyard dated 3 August 1826 in LB 'K', p. 117.

9 Hall, 1998, p. 659.

10 The 1818 agreement with James Burton was followed by those signed with William Davison (probably in the same year), William Woolcott (1819), John Maidlow (1822), William Ward (1823), Samuel Gardner (1823), John Hinton (1823), Charles Day (1824), the Watkins brothers (1824) and Thomas Johnson (1825).

11 See Abstract of Lease dated 2 April 1825 and subsequent assignment from Maidlow to Eyre at EE 2651/202(A). The assignment is recorded at LB 'K', p. 140. From 1829 the Eyres tried to sell the house (LB 'L', p. 233, and LB 'M', p. 306). By February 1832 Walpole admitted he had never been able to let it (LB 'M', p. 450). He eventually succeeded in letting it to Mrs Blacker, one of the daughters of his mother-in-law, Mrs Johnson (LB 'N', pp. 291–92).

12 The bankruptcies' records at the Public Record Office have not been consulted, but Sheila Marriner's excellent article on 'English Bankruptcy Records and Statistics before 1850' (1980) has. If commissioners were involved in a bankruptcy, a file would be opened per bankrupt, and the greatest number survives for the period 1780–1842. Marriner adds that 'even for these years there are no known files for about 95 per cent of bankruptcies' (p. 361).

13 This is likely to be John Dowley, surveyor to the Westminster Commissioners of Sewers and a big speculator in Kensington. See Hermione Hobhouse (gen. ed.), *Survey of London*, vol. 42: *Kensington Square to Earl's Court*, London, 1986, pp. 268–71.

14 Dyos, 1966, pp. 19ff.

15 Saunders, 1981, p. 72.

16 Letter to Thomas Heaphy dated 21 August 1817 in LB 'E', p. 243.

17 Letter to Shaw dated 19 May 1811 in LB 'B', p. 430.

18 Letter to Thomas Willan dated 24 February 1817 in LB 'E', p. 5.

19 The issue of St John's Wood's divided status between city (quarter) and country (suburb) finds an echo in our modern world. The London newspapers *Metro* and the *Evening Standard* do not appear to agree on the status of the Odeon cinema at Swiss Cottage. *Metro* lists the Odeon Swiss Cottage in its 'West End' section, while the *Evening Standard* has classified it as a 'local' cinema. The price of the ticket is most definitely West End!

20 Letter to Smith dated 8 July 1845 in LB 'Q', p. 609.

21 Thompson, 1874, pp. 249–50.

22 This concession is tentative as difficulties with tenants did not occur only with peppercorn leases (see pp. 201 and 357).

23 Box Villa was leased to Baker on 16 May 1826 and Box Cottage on 1 September 1826 (LB 'L', p. 303); Alexander Cowie was Baker's tenant at Box Villa in 1829. Baker presumably kept Box Cottage for himself.

24 The agreement dated 30 December 1844 is at EE 2651/5(A and B).

25 LB 'L', p. 465, and EE 2650/1/452.

26 David Griffith is described as 'of Circus Road' in his 1830 lease (at EE 2650/1/452).

27 LB 'R', pp. 588–89, December 1847. A licence was subsequently granted.

28 Dated December 1847, inside the 1830 lease to David Griffith at EE 2650/1/452. 'Franks Villa' inscribed in pencil is likely to be a later name.

29 Treeby's house is 'Devonshire Villa' on 13 August 1842 in LB 'P', p. 490, and 'Devonshire Cottage' on 22 October in LB 'P', p. 625. Similarly, his 'Elizabethan Villa' (Bk of Drawings V, 23 right, 1844) is reduced to being a 'Cottage' on many occasions, for instance on 7 May 1845 (LB 'Q', p. 565).

30 See letter to Mr Bland junior dated 16 November 1830 in LB 'M', p. 134.

31 These names do not always feature on the official deeds, and many here have been collected from the letter books: the Regents Villas in LB 'P', p. 207; St John's Villas in LB 'P', p. 171; St Ann's Villas in LB 'Q', p. 285; and Stanley Villas in Bk of Drawings V, 64.

32 It is mentioned in a letter to the Commissioners of Sewers dated 11 November 1843 in LB 'Q', p. 206. By that date, following Baker's death, it had been taken over by

165 The North London Junction Railway is mentioned in LB 'R', p. 121, and the Regent's Canal railway in LB 'R', pp. 304 and 334.

166 Letter to Messrs Swift & Wagstaff dated 14 December 1852 in LB 'T', p. 333, where it is described as 'Regents Canal Comp[an]y Paddington and Limehouse Railway & Branch'.

167 C. Baker, *The Metropolitan Railway*, South Godstone (Oakwood Press), 1951, p. 3; Barker and Robbins, 1963, vol. I, pp. 104ff.

168 See the December 1867 notice at EE 2650/1/121.

169 Jackson, 1986, p. 44.

170 Jackson, 1986, p. 45. Jackson devotes ch. 3 to 'The St John's Wood sideline'.

171 Barker and Robbins, 1963, vol. I, p. 211.

172 EE 2651/304A(8) but also see the other documents in Box 2651/304A.

173 Richardson-Eyre, 1904, ch. V, p. 28.

174 *Daily Graphic*, 14 November 1894, p. 8.

Chapter 8 Artists' quarter

1 WCA, 963 (3 of 4), loose document marked 'Proofs' re: Manchester, Sheffield and Lincolnshire Railway, 1895, pp. 14–15.

2 See Montgomery Eyre, 1913; Walkley, 1994; and Wedd, 2001.

3 Cox-Johnson, 1963, p. ii.

4 Letter to Heaphy dated 12 September 1815 in LB 'D', p. 289.

5 Letter to Heaphy dated 24 April 1827 in LB 'K', p. 303.

6 The best account of his life and career is in Gunnis, 1968.

7 This is sometimes described as St John's Place, and the north end of Lisson Grove was also known as Nightingale Lane. The names and numbering for Rossi's premises are particularly confusing: 21 Lisson Grove in Cox-Johnson, 1959; 41 Lisson Grove North in Graves, 1905–6, who also lists Acte House, Grove Street; 22 Lisson Grove in Pope's commentary in Haydon's *Diary* (George, 1967, p. 115, who also recounts the following amusing anecdote. In 1817, Haydon had written to Charles Lamb to invite him to come to his new address. Lamb replied: 'I will come with pleasure to 22 Lisson Grove, North, at Rossi's half-way up, right hand side, if I can find it'). Rossi is listed at 21 Lisson Grove from 1809, but we know he purchased the plot in 1808 (see Bk of Drawings I, 5). Also see Cole, 2009, p. 481.

8 Bill Book I, p. 45.

9 Bill Book I, p. 77.

10 Pope, 1963, vol. II, p. 375, 9 August 1822.

11 Gunnis, 1968, p. 327.

12 Gunnis, 1968, p. 327. There is a brief reference to this sale in the Eyre letter books: letter to Messrs White Blake & Co. (solicitors) dated 5 October 1834 in LB 'N', p. 391.

13 Pope, 1963, vol. V, p. 395.

14 Pope, 1963, vol. II, pp. 131 and 176.

15 George, 1967, p. 114.

16 See Vincent, 1953, pp. 189–90.

17 Quoted in Brown, Woof and Hebron, 1996, p. 37.

18 Quoted in Montgomery Eyre, 1913, p. 252.

19 This was John Landseer (1763/69–1852), father of the painter Edwin Landseer.

20 Brown, Woof and Hebron, 1996, say Joseph Ritchie (1788?–1819), who was to travel to Africa as far as Timbuktu.

21 Quoted in Brown, Woof and Hebron, 1996, p. 35.

22 Pope, 1963, vol. II, p. 392.

23 Stirling, 1926, p. 24.

24 Vaughan, Barker and Harrison, 2005, pp. 17ff, 105.

25 Stirling, 1926, pp. 32ff.

26 Stirling, 1926, pp. 98–99.

27 Stirling, 1926, p. 32. Tatham's entry in Colvin's *Dictionary* (1995, p. 808) describes his falling out with the owner of Castle Howard. Walpole also implied he could be a troublemaker on the estate (see p. 111).

28 Kenneth Garlick and Angus Macintyre (eds), *The Diary of Joseph Farington*, New Haven and London, 1978, 2–6 November 1797. The members were 'Cockerell – Treasurer & President/Wyatt/Brettingham/Mylne/Lewes/Dance/Paine/Hardwick/Tatam [*sic*]/Holland/Bonomi/Yenn'.

29 See LB 'H', pp. 302, 367, 470.

30 Letter to Heaphy dated 18 April 1827 in LB 'K', p. 297.

31 Letter to Springall dated 30 June 1839 in LB 'L', p. 314.

32 Letter to Colonel Salmond dated 27 April 1827 in LB 'K', p. 307.

33 Apart from 1 Park Road (No. 23 in Plate 63), Heaphy had acquired Dalgleish's share of No. 17 on the reconstruction (south of Alpha Road), another lease dated 30 November 1821, as well as land taken in St John's Wood Road for three houses, one of which was at No. 7. See letter to Heaphy dated 24 April 1827 in LB 'K', p. 303.

34 Whitley, 1933, p. 18.

35 Whitley, 1933, p. 13.

36 See Whitley, 1933, pp. 16–17, for a description of the painting and other comments. Whitley notes that in 1809 forty guineas was regarded as a high price for a picture sold by the Watercolour Society. Current whereabouts of the painting is unknown.

37 Whitley, 1933, pp. 20–21.

38 A copy of the key for this painting is in the Victoria and Albert Museum Library, Press Mark 40.F.Box 111. Also see Richard Walker's catalogue entry for the preparatory portraits made for this painting in the National Portrait Gallery (*Regency Portraits*, 2 vols, London, 1985, vol. 1, pp. 630–31).

39 The key to the engraving (mentioned in note above) explains how the publisher James Gilbert succeeded in locating the plate. It had been sold in 1836, along with the painting itself, at the auction sale which followed the death of Thomas Heaphy (copy of this catalogue at the Victoria and Albert Museum Library, Pressmark 11.RC.DD.30–Picture Sales 1834–41). Mortifyingly for Heaphy, the work 'painted expressly for his late Majesty George IV' was turned down by Wellington when the artist eventually attempted to secure his due of 1,400 guineas (see Whitley, 1933, pp. 20–23 and 27–28).

40 Heleniak, 2005, is the best source on this artist.

41 See, for instance, the 1815 rates for Alpha Cottages at WCA, where he lived at 43 Alpha Cottages (No. 24 in the Alpha Cottages reconstruction).

42 Heleniak, 2005, p. 26 and n. 24.

43 See Peter Brandon, 'John Linnell and his Changing Metropolis', *Camden History Review* 14, 1986–87, pp. 24–27.

44 Grant reproduced a landscape to accompany his short entry about this artist (1957, vol. 6, p. 503 and accompanying plate).

45 Ormond, 1981, p. 4.

46 From Scott's *Letters*, 1932–37, vol. 8, p. 392; quoted in Ormond, 1981, p. 6.

47 See letter to Atkinson dated 20 April 1824 in LB 'I', p. 70.

48 Ormond (1981, p. 6) says he was lent the money by a dealer called William Mayor.

49 The following artistic 'dynasties' have been identified, i.e. when more than one family member lived and worked on the estate: Alma-Tadema, Faed, Hakewill, Heaphy, Leslie, Lucas, May, Palmer, Riviere and Smallfield.

50 Bk of Drawings I, 43.

51 Bk of Drawings II, 74, 116 and 120.

52 In Grove's *Dictionary of Music* his date of death is unknown but listed as being 'after 1835'. The Eyre estate records suggest it was c.1854 when the rent account mentions 'Challoner Ex[ecut]ors' for the first time in a letter to W. L. Banks from 12 Melina Place in LB 'T', p. 618. The following year, in 1855, W. L. Banks also settled Challoner's rent (LB 'U', p. 102).

53 Cole, 2009, p. 487; Charles Reid, *Thomas Beecham: An Independent Biography*, 1962, London, pp. 226ff.

54 Ground purchased in 1825. Beecham's house would have been built within the next few years. See Bk of Drawings II, 74 (plan of ground with one elevation only – Challoner's).

55 The sale catalogue is in the Eyre archive at EE 2650/1/102(D) along with correspondence dated 1912, 1915 and 1929–31.

56 Watson, 2004, p. 77.

57 Walkley, 1994, p. 249.

58 The scheme was carried out under the umbrella of the Lady Workers Homes Ltd, founded in 1914. The development was later known as Abbey Road Mansions. See Watson, 2004, p. 74.

59 See note 55 above and Southall, Vince and Rouse, 2002, p. 17. The latter publication has a fairly detailed history of 3 Abbey Road (pp. 15ff).

60 The purchase price was £3,600 and the sale document is at EE 2651/281.

61 Edward Morgan, 'Prokofiev's Recording of his Third Piano Concerto, June 1932', *Three Oranges Journal*, no. 11, May 2006 (published by the Serge Prokofiev Foundation). I found the full text online at www.sprkfv.net/journal/three11/thirdconcert.html.

62 The original lease drawing, for Mr Sylvester, dates from June 1820 and is at Bk of Drawings I, 56.

63 Alfred W.: see Plate 147.

64 Letter dated 16 April 1884 and addressed to J. T. White Esq. at EE 2651/344(D). The reply to this letter has not been found.

65 Cole, 2009, p. 487; Becker et al., 1996; Barrow, 2001.

66 Montgomery Eyre, 1913, p. 273.

67 Cordova, 1902, p. 615.

68 From the Hampton & Sons *Catalogue of the well-known and interesting collection of Antique Furniture and Objects d'Art formed by the late Sir Lawrence Alma-Tadema, O.M., R.A., including Valuable Pictures and the Archaeological Library*, June 1913, when the whole collection was sold.

69 Matyjaszkiewicz, 1984, pp. 40–41.

70 Hamburg Art Gallery organised an exhibition around this bequest in 1970 and published the following catalogue: Werner Hofmann and Tilamn Osterwold (eds), *Ein Geschmack wird untersucht: Die G. C. Schwabe Stiftung*, Hamburg, 1970. I am grateful to Dr Jenns E. Howoldt from Hamburger Kunsthalle for this information.

71 Goodall, 1902, p. 170.

72 Letter to Thomas L. Donaldson dated October 1840 in LB 'P', p. 260. Colvin (1995, pp. 315–16) describes Thomas Leverton Donaldson (1795–1885) as 'the most distinguished member of the Donaldson family.... In 1842 he became the first Professor of Architecture at University College London,' also pointing out he was 'the virtual founder of the R.I.B.A.'

73 Out of courtesy Walpole also wrote to leaseholder Mrs Todd (Robert's executor) on 15 October 1840, stating the plans met with his 'full approbation', in LB 'P', p. 260.

74 See Licence Book I, pp. 197–98, 7 December 1841. The name of the architect is known because he was sent the licence on 6 January 1842; see LB 'P', p. 484. The licence was issued to non-resident lessee Thomas Carr without naming his subtenant (which is named in Cox-Johnson, 1963, for that address). Carr seemed to have much favoured Tovey as an architect. The licence reveals the house was originally leased (1821) to Peter Swinton and is in Bk of Drawings I, 93. The 1883 map of the estate shows clearly how the property (on the south side of Lodge Road, second house west of Oak Tree Road) doubled in size with this addition (Plate 208 and pp. 362–63).

75 12 Alpha Cottages, later 4 Alpha Road.

76 This may have been the name not of the artist requesting the studio but that of the lessee. However, the dates for the artists known to have been based at 12 Alpha Cottages (Charles B. Birch, S. G. Pollard and Nathaniel H. J. Westlake) do not match that of the studio drawing.

77 Licence Book I, pp. 472–74. The original lease to Fenton has survived at EE 2650/1/61(A), and the drawing of the proposed studio, reproduced here, was filed inside it.

78 The 1883 map of the estate at Plate 208 shows the extension to the original property recorded in Bk of Drawings I, 2.

79 Licence Book I, pp. 480–82. The licence is dated 29 April 1853. The lease and the lease drawing are not in the Eyre archive. An 1823 agreement between the builder who originally took the ground, William Hall, and Robert Todd survives at EE 2651/209; it states that Robert Todd was taking the ground and building the house thereon.

80 See Morris and Milner, 1993, for an in-depth history of this painting.

81 Letter to Millar dated 6 February 1862 in LB 'V', p. 400.

82 This artist specialised in painting hounds and horses, either in contemporary or historical (eighteenth-century) settings. He was aware of and interested in the work of the French painter Gericault.

83 Letter to Twentyman dated 23 July 1867 in LB 'X', p. 99.

84 Letter to Shaw dated 26 July 1867 in LB 'X', p. 101, and letter to Twentyman dated 31 July 1867 on p. 104. There were further complications with a complaint from the adjoining property on p. 129. No licence could be found so perhaps the studio was not built at that time. See Appendix 5, 1878–87.

85 Caroline Dakers documents and analyses well this change of status in her book, *The Holland Park Circle: Artists and Victorian Society*, New Haven and London, 1999.

86 Letter to Thomas White & Sons from Christopher White, dated 20 October 1887, in EE 2650/1/197(A).

87 See Richard Ormond, *Early Victorian Portraits, National Gallery*, London, 1973, vol. I, cat. no. 835, p. 254.

88 Andrew Saint discusses these issues in his book, *Richard Norman Shaw*, 2nd edn, New Haven and London, 2010, in the section entitled 'Painters' Houses', pp. 175–83. Although Shaw lived in St John's Wood (see p. 441), none of the examples used come from that part of London. However, the arguments developed would have been exactly the same in St John's Wood.

89 Montgomery Eyre, 1913; Morris and Milner, 1993.

90 Walkley, 1994, p. 121.

91 G. A. Storey, G. D. Leslie, J. E. Hodgson, H. S. Marks; see Morris and Milner, 1993.

92 Marks, 1894, vol. I, p. 147.

93 Vaughan, Barker and Harrison, 2005, p. 18.

94 Morris and Milner, 1993, p. 3; Bills and Knight, 2006, pp. 5 and 57. These two sources differ on the date of formation: 1837 in the former and 1840 in the latter.

95 Morris and Milner, 1993, p. 4. Two members of the St John's Wood Clique were also members of this club: G. A. Storey and H. S. Marks.

96 *Pre-Raphaelites*, 1984.

97 According to Graves, 1905–6, Hodgson is at 5 Hill Road until 1889. However, Morris and Milner, 1993, and Walkley, 1994, have a two-year stay at 41 Circus Road.

98 Marks, 1894, vol. I, pp. 147 and 155.

99 A journalist for *Fraser's Magazine* reviewing the Royal Academy exhibition in 1864 (quoted by Marks, 1894, vol. I, p. 147).

100 Marks, 1894, vol. I, pp. 162ff.

101 One of Yeames's paintings (location unknown) is a family scene close to those Tissot was painting, and entitled *James Lambe, Louisa and Mary Yeames in the House of the Artist*, 1879 (reproduced in Morris and Milner, 1993, p. 88).

102 Nevinson, 1937, pp. 14–15 and 17.

103 Except two: Nos 17 and 21, which were later purchased by Lord's (Montgomery Eyre, 1913, p. 104, and LB 'Y', pp. 34 and 347).

104 The date of the conversion comes from Walkley, 1994, p. 250. Also see file in WCA, 832 (St John's Wood Art Schools cuttings in envelope), which contains a copy of the earliest advertisement in *The Year's Art*, dated 1890.

105 See Bk of Drawings I, 87, and II, 16 and 60.

106 The name 'Garnie' may have been wrongly deciphered. The age of both students was recorded but it is difficult to read.

107 Galinou and Conlin, 2010. Unfortunately, *Country Life* introduced a last-minute

picture to the ones the authors selected, and Fig. 2 shows Alma-Tadema in his Townshend House near Regent's Park rather than in Grove End Road.

108 WCA, 832, cuttings collection.

109 Cole, 1932, p. 23; repeated by Macdonald, 1970, p. 34.

110 Nevinson, 1937, pp. 14–15 and 17.

111 Cole, 1932, pp. 23, 25–26.

112 See Galinou and Hayes, 1996.

113 *Paula Modersohn-Becker und die Kunst in Paris um 1900*, exhibition catalogue, Kunsthalle Bremen, 2007, pp. 285–86. I am grateful to Professor Michael Kauffmann for drawing my attention to this fact.

114 J. W. Waterhouse is recorded at 10 Hall Road between 1901 and 1917 (amalgamation of dates given in Graves, 1905–6, and Morris and Milner, 1993).

115 Walkley, 1994, p. 251. The 1884 Ogilvie settlement (WCA, 901/178) specifies that G. D. Leslie 'almost entirely rebuilt the messuage'.

116 The history of this house is given in the recital of the 1884 settlement when Ogilvie assigned the property to his children (WCA, 901/178).

117 It should, however, be noted that Ogilvie was already a St John's Wood lessee when he married Miss Agnew. His addresses in the marriage settlement were given as Great George Street and Carlton Hill.

118 Agnew, 1967, p. 27.

119 Agnew, 1967, p. 29.

120 Montgomery Eyre, 1913, pp. 188ff.

121 Agnew, 1967, p. 27.

122 Marriage settlement, 4 June 1878, of 'Arthur Graeme Ogilvie, Engineer, Great George Street and Carlton Hill[,] with Miss Mary Caroline Agnew of Summer Hill, Pendleton, County of Lancaster' (WCA, 901/175).

123 For information on Gassiot's collection, see Vivien Knight's article 'Collecting for Pleasure', *The Antique Collector*, February 1985, pp. 44–49.

124 By Jeremy Maas in the title of his book on Gambart (1975).

125 Maas, 1975, pp. 163 and 189–99. The house in Avenue Road was on Twentyman's territory, and the lease drawing survives in Bk of Drawings IV, 24 right.

126 *Pre-Raphaelites*, 1984, p. 119.

127 Maas, 1975, p. 199.

128 Maas, 1975, p. 193. Chapter Nineteen recreates the events with great precision and fascinating detail.

129 Both quotes come from Maas, 1975, pp. 18 and 43.

130 She married the sculptor John Adams-Acton, and they set up home in Langford Place (see p. 434).

131 Stirling, 1954, pp. 84–86.

132 The Satis House of *Great Expectations* is now generally thought to be Rochester's Restoration House. Although Stirling has a reputation for exaggerating, it was difficult not to include this passage as it almost certainly describes a real house and real events in Abbey Road, however romanticised the story may have become. This is confirmed by an earlier reference to this event found in Montgomery Eyre (1913, p. 177), which appears to quote from a letter by T. H. Huxley's son: 'the Huxleys [at 4 Marlborough Place] were faced by "a long garden full of blossoming pear trees in which thrushes and blackbirds sang and nested, belonging to a desolate house in Abbey Road, which was tenanted by a solitary old man, supposed to be a male prototype of Miss Havisham in *Great Expectations*".'

133 Mentioned in Tames, 1998, p. 78. They lived there between 1848 and 1852. See also both *DNB* entries on Mary and William. The Kensington Society was a discussion group formed in 1865 by eleven women. In time it led to the suffragette movement.

134 See Joanne Shattock, *The Oxford Guide to British Women Writers*, Oxford, 1994.

135 WCA, B/Pen-B/Rys 1712 and 1713 for portraits, one of which is a reproduction of the National Portrait Gallery oil painting.

136 In 1859, in the collection of the Victoria and Albert Museum, London. See Bills and Knight, 2006, pp. 28, 29 and 33.

137 Ormond, 1981, p. 12.

138 Lady [Mary Elizabeth] Herbert, *The Priory of Kilburn*, London, 1882 (cited in Colloms and Weindling, 2007, pp. 10–11). As Atkinson designed Abbotsford, it is strange that his contribution is described as 'helping' with the decoration. However, the context is unmistakably Atkinson's with the garden, the friendship with Scott, the relationship with Lord Mulgrave, the interest in stones and the shipping of cement.

139 Montgomery Eyre, 1913, p. 125.

140 For Richard Redgrave's painting after Hood's 'The Song of the Shirt', see Fox, 1987, p. 193. Also see 'The Centenary of Thomas Hood's Birth' published on 24 March 1899, at WCA, Ashbridge B/Hoo (2126).

141 James S. Olgilvy, *Relics and Memorials of London*, London, 1911, pl. XL, p. 240, and associated text.

142 Montgomery Eyre, 1913, p. 137. Tom Landseer was Edwin's brother and lived at 10a Cunningham Place, a stone's throw from his more famous brother.

143 With the help of Lucas's map (Plate 108), No. 40 is identifiable on the Alpha Cottages reconstruction as No. 25 (original 1812 lease at Bk of Drawings I, 20).

144 Montgomery Eyre, 1913, p. 142.

145 St John's Wood Society Newsletters: Spring 2006 for the Austins, Autumn 2006 for Dornford Yates, Spring 2007 for Alice Beckton, and Spring 2008 for Arthur Machen.

146 A Swedenborgian who lived at 24 Finchley Road.

147 James and Macmillan first met in August 1877 (Moore, 1993, pp. xvii ff). Frederick became the main contact between the author and the publishing firm. Frederick Macmillan's name appears on the 1881 Census (see Plate 165).

148 Brown, 2007, p. 21.

149 Brown, 2007, pp. 20–23. Brown thought the Elm Tree Road house, which was photographed by Alvin Langdon Coburn in 1906, might be No. 8, but No. 8 is a detached house and the house in the photograph is one-half of a double house. See Helmut and Alison Gernsheim (eds), *Alvin Langdon Coburn Photographer: An Autobiography*, New York, 1978 p. 58.

150 See David McWhirter, 'Photo-negativity: The Visual Rhetoric of James's and Coburn's New York Edition Frontispiece', *English Language Notes*, Fall/Winter 2006. In an e-mail dated 8 April 2009, McWhirter stated that the photographs in the 1905 edition 'have unannounced or undeclared autobiographical evidence'.

151 The photograph is reproduced as fig. 8 in Ralph F. Bogardus, *Pictures and Texts*, Ann Arbor, 1984, and also in McWhirter above. The evidence for identifying it as 1 Elm Tree Road is circumstantial and historical. It shows a semi-detached house, its style consistent with the house shown in the original lease drawing for a house and a range of stables at Bk of Drawings I, 81 (1820). The original other half of this house has been replaced by a protruding building, and this is consistent with the plan of No. 1 at Plate 165. The 1871 and 1881 Census records show the resident as David Lee, 'artist' (Henry James states the house had belonged to a painter).

152 The lease drawing is at Bk of Drawings I, 116. It was originally going to be leased to Tovey, but his name was subsequently crossed out in favour of Bailey.

153 Licence Book II, p. 198. It was granted to Francis Goo…? (I could not decipher the rest of the name). No artist of that or any other name has been recorded at that address.

154 Like his father, Charles Allston Collins (1828–73) was a painter who lived on the edge of the estate at 17 Hanover Terrace and produced in 1851 a memorable painting of Regent's Park: *May. In the Regent's Park*. The Wilkie Collins website has very detailed information about Wilkie Collins, and it casts doubt on the story, which was published in 1899, almost fifty years after the event: see www.wilkiecollins.com, in particular 'Where Wilkie lived, 17 Hanover Terrace'. Also see Sarah Wise, 'A Novel for Hysterical Times', in *History Today*, August 2010, pp. 46–52.

155 Wilkie Collins, *The Woman in White*, London, 1860, bk I, ch. 4.

156 Licence Book II, p. 59, dated 15 January 1857.

157 Letter to Shaw dated 9 November 1855 in LB 'U', p. 219. Also entry on James Davis and Sons on p. 471 of this book.

158 Letter to Samuel Stoddard, 34 Alpha Road, dated 7 February 1856 in LB 'U', p. 255.

159 Licence of 16 June 1890 granted to Messrs L. Walter and William Walter junior: see Licence Book II, p. 202. Walkley, 1994, p. 235, describes a different scenario: proprietor John Butler commissioning Albert Pridmore to design these studios; this is not necessarily incompatible with the Eyre archive.

160 See Walkley, 1994, p. 235, and Morris and Milner, 1993, p. 32. There is some confusion about the numbering: 9a and b in Walkley, 1 and 2 in Cox-Johnson (1963) and Morris and Milner. John's studio may have been next to Frampton's, but their situation was different: Frampton's studio was at the bottom of his garden, while John's studio with its independent entrance in Woronzow Road was not associated with a home.

161 Useful summary of her life at www.trotskyana.net: the website is run by Wolfgang and Petra Lubitz and focuses on Leon Trotsky, Trotskyism and Trotskyists. Also see David Stafford, *Churchill and the Secret Service*, London, 2001 (first published in 1995) pp. 121ff.

162 I am very grateful to Steve Cavalier for talking to me at his lovely Hertfordshire cottage in Sarratt outside Chorleywood on 5 June 2007.

163 Cole, 2009, p. 494.

164 I am grateful to Dr Peter Urbach for bringing my attention to this document: Christabel Frampton's letter to Lady MacDonnell, dated 18 November 1908, in the archive of the Reform Club (Box 47).

165 Letter to Bettinson junior dated 24 November 1863 in LB 'W', p. 103.

166 Letter to H. R. Little, re: 6 Belsize Road, dated 4 June 1885 in LB 'Y', p. 348.

167 Letter from the office of the Eyre estate to John White dated 3 January 1882 in LB 'Y', p. 150. The work of Alexander Bassano is well represented in the collections of the National Portrait Gallery and includes portraits of St John's Wood residents Lawrence Alma-Tadema, Briton Riviere, Phil May and Thomas Henry Huxley.

168 See Bills and Webb, 2007.

169 Hacking, 2000, pls 7, 8 and 20.

170 The article 'Lena Connell, St John's Wood, London' in *Professional Photographer*, February 1913, reproduces several pictures of the interior of 50 Grove End Road, including Connell's studio (pp. 34–39).

171 See entry on Adeline Beatrice Connell in the excellent website www.photolondon.org.uk, 'Gateway to London's public photographic collections', i.e. GL, LMA, MOL, NMR, WCA.

172 Reproduced in *Professional Photographer*, February 1913, p. 34.

173 See www.photolondon.org.uk.

174 Bedford Lemere day books are at NMR in Swindon.

175 See Walkley, 1994, pp. 136–37.

176 Montgomery Eyre, 1913, p. 269.

177 Hitchmough, 1995, p. 233, under 'The Knights of St John Tavern'.

178 Montgomery Eyre, 1913, p. 270.

179 Christie's, *The Forbes Collection of Victorian Pictures and Works of Art II: Battersea-6747*, 20 February 2003, Lot 124.

180 Montgomery Eyre, 1913, p. 271.

181 Harrison Townsend was clearly a key figure according to the Members Book of the St John's Wood Arts Club at WCA in Box MAcc 247.

Chapter 9 Spiritual St John's Wood

1 Letter to Twentyman dated 25 January 1853 in LB 'T', p. 353.

2 This is suggested by the tone of Charles Freeth's letters to him, always seeking to explain and reassure him in response, no doubt, to the concerns G. J. Eyre would have raised.

3 Sheppard, 1958, p. 245.

4 Letter to H. S. Eyre dated 9 April 1807 in LB 'A', p. 492.

5 In December 1807 when Henry Samuel signed the agreement and conveyance (Bill Book I, p. 38). Also see letter to Shaw dated 9 December 1807 in LB 'A', p. 649.

6 Sheppard, 1958, p. 252, says that initially there was a shortage of bricks. The Eyre archive does not mention the shortage of bricks, but there certainly were administrative delays as the sale involved an exchange of land, the Breeze Yard (see pp. 106–07). The estate also had to build the road from the east end of Alpha Road to the burial ground before the vestry would take possession of the land (see letter to Greenwell dated 17 March 1808 in LB 'A', p. 701, which incidentally specified the bricks were to be made on site and not brought in). However, by July 1808 all these issues had been settled (see letter to the vestry dated 30 July 1808 in LB 'A', p. 787).

7 See Sheppard, 1958, p. 264, and letter to Colonel Thornhill dated 5 February 1816 in LB 'D', p. 424.

8 Letter to Thomas Hardwick dated 9 May 1807 in LB 'A', p. 506.

9 Letter dated 23 January 1816 in LB 'D', p. 413.

10 Letter to Colonel Thornhill dated 5 February 1816 in LB 'D', p. 424.

11 Letter dated 22 May 1819 in LB 'F', p. 95.

12 Letter from H. S. Eyre to Greenwell (the vestry clerk) dated 21 April 1820 in LB 'F', p. 393.

13 Letter to Major Close dated 16 March 1828 in LB 'K', p. 544. Major Close seemed concerned that the parish was envisaging enlarging the old parish church.

14 Letter to Shaw dated 21 January 1841 in LB 'P', p. 295.

15 See letter to Reverend Baker dated 12 February 1842 in LB 'P', p. 498. Also see Licence Book I, p. 199.

16 Stott, 1887, p. 7.

17 Licence Book II, p. 104.

18 Letter to Skynner dated 20 August 1844 in LB 'Q', p. 402.

19 It was consecrated in 1849 and became a parish church in 1856 (see Oliver and Bradshaw, 1955, p. 35), when it is mentioned in a letter to R. Hollond dated 13 June 1856 in LB 'U', p. 309.

20 Letter to the bishop of London sent to Tunbridge Wells dated 16 September 1843 in LB 'Q', p. 173.

21 Letter to Messrs Taylor & Collisson dated 26 August 1844 in LB 'Q', p. 406.

22 Port, 2006, p. 261.

23 Letter to Biggs dated 13 October 1843 in LB 'Q', p. 187.

24 Letter to Shaw dated 26 February 1845 in LB 'Q', p. 523.

25 Jill Allibone, *George Devey Architect, 1820–1886*, Cambridge, 1991, p. 19.

26 Letter to G. F. Hudson dated 29 April 1845 in LB 'Q', p. 559.

27 Letter to Shaw dated 18 May 1846 in LB 'R', p. 200.

28 Letter to Twentyman dated 30 October 1848 in LB 'S', p. 187.

29 Letter to Maddock, the next incumbent, dated 4 August 1852 in LB 'T', pp. 265 and 447.

30 Richardson-Eyre, 1904, ch. IV, pp. 1–2.

31 Clarke, 1881, p. 429.

32 Semple, n.d. [1946], pp. 17–18.

33 Semple, n.d. [1946], p. 5.

34 Richardson-Eyre, 1904, ch. V, p. 27.

35 Richardson-Eyre, 1904, ch. V, p. 15.

36 I am most grateful to Mark Lomas for piecing together the last moments of All Saints Church.

37 The Museum of London group of objects are under the accession number 74.17: lamp bracket, wooden bench, two pews, a hymn number board, white and red church candles. These objects entered the collection in 1974, two years before the church's closure.

38 Letter to Reverend Thomas Ainger dated 11 May 1853 in LB 'T', p. 421.

39 Letter to Reverend Thomas Ainger dated 13 December 1853 in LB 'T', p. 512.

40 Letter to George John Eyre dated 8 February 1866 in LB 'W', p. 460.

41 Letter to Reverend I. Irving dated 21 February 1857 in LB 'U', p. 405.

42 Letter to George John Eyre dated 8 February 1866 in LB 'W', p. 460.

43 Counterpart lease at EE 2651/144 and also see recital in deed of appropriation of All Souls, 1913–14, at WCA, 963 (1 of 4).

44 Cherry and Pevsner, 1998, p. 200.

45 Stott, 1887, pp. 17 and 31.

46 Letter to Messrs Taylor & Collisson dated 3 February 1845 in LB 'Q', p. 509.

47 Letter to J. Haines dated 14 November 1857 in LB 'U', p. 505.

48 Letter to Ifold dated 31 January 1861 in LB 'V', p. 290.

49 Letter to George John Eyre dated 18 November 1869 in LB 'X', p. 329. A similar letter was sent to Reverend Henry Samuel Eyre.

50 Letter to Reverend J. Clifford dated 22 November 1869 in LB 'X', p. 330.

51 Stott, 1887, p. 2.

52 Stott, 1887, p. 6.

53 Stott, 1887, p. 8.

54 Stott, 1887, p. 88.

55 Stott, 1887, p. 34.

56 Lot 10 in auction catalogue of 27 May 1858 at EE 2651/340(C). The plot numbered 14 on the plan was 45 Abbey Road, known as 'The Hermitage' and 'Let on Lease to Mr N. B. Challoner, for a term of 99 years from Michaelmas, 1818, at a Ground Rent of £10 per annum'. The plot at that time appears to have been purchased by John Augs Tulk (WCA, 2194/13/2).

57 Stott, 1887, p. 32.

58 Stott, 1887, p. 39.

59 Stott, 1887, pp. 41, 48–50. Charles Haddon Spurgeon (1834–92), who founded the Metropolitan Tabernacle in Southwark, was one of the great Baptist preachers of his day, while Sir Samuel Morton Peto (1809–89) had achieved public prominence as entrepreneur and builder extraordinaire (his firm built many well-known landmarks such as Nelson's Column and the Reform Club before he became a railway contractor).

60 Stott, 1887, p. 14.

61 Stott, 1887, pp. 170 and 172 (for the men) and p. 176 (for the domestic service).

62 Stott, 1887, p. 22.

63 Whitley, 1928, p. 46.

64 Stott, 1887, p. 79.

65 Stott, 1887, p. 93.

66 I am most grateful to Jenny Hall, Curator of Roman Collections at the Museum of London, for trying to make sense of this particular passage in Stott's book (e-mail dated 25 April 2008).

67 There are a number of bibliographical sources recorded in the Sites and Monuments Record (English Heritage) for this Roman road. I am grateful to Krysia Truscoe for bringing this to my attention.

68 Whitley, 1928, p. 288. The 1903 map of the Eyre estate says it could seat 1,300.

69 Stott, 1887, p. 71.

70 Letter to Thomas Creswick at 9 Abbey Place dated 23 May 1861 in LB 'V', p. 321. Mrs Gell's land was situated by the railway at the north-west side of the estate.

71 Letter to John Thomas White dated 9 May 1881 in LB 'Y', p. 115. The licence of 1 December 1870 described 'a Lecture Hall & Dwelling House': see Licence Book II, p. 180.

72 Stott, 1887, pp. 121–24. When his book was published in 1887, Stott was still based in Abbey Road, but by 1900 he is described in one of the Eyre documents as living at 11 Chatsworth Road in Norwood, Surrey – see 1900 assignment of 28 St John's Wood Terrace at EE 2650/1/173(G).

73 McLeod, 1974, p. 33.

74 Clarke, 1881, p. 429. New College Chapel at the junction of Avenue and Adelaide Roads was designed by J. T. Emmett (VCH, 1989).

75 See letter to Maddock dated 25 May 1858 in LB 'U', p. 591, for Maddock's objections and letter to Shaw dated 19 November 1858 in LB 'V', p. 78, for crediting the church to Teulon. I am grateful to Matthew Saunders, who confirmed that S. S. Teulon was meant, not W. M., and who provided basic data about this church. See his article, 'The Churches of S. S. Teulon', for the Ecclesiological Society, 1982.

76 See Evinson, 1998, pp. 57–58.

77 This Act lifted the heavy restrictions affecting Roman Catholics in the United Kingdom. See LB 'M', p. 591, for Walpole's letter to Scoles re: his architectural drawings.

78 This is suggested in an article published in *The Mirror* on 19 December 1835 – see newspaper cutting at WCA, Ashbridge collection.

79 Letter to Ranken & Co. dated 27 November 1841 in LB 'P', p. 457.

80 Evinson, 1998, p. 56.

81 Letter to Commissioners of Sewers dated 19 January 1833 in LB 'N' p. 48.

82 The lease is in the Eyre archive at EE 2651/360 and the counterpart lease at WCA, 765/145. The agreement survives at EE 2651/73. For the assignment to Watts, see LB 'P', pp. 337 and 362, dated 19 April and 2 June 1841.

83 Rottmann, 1926, p. 256. The passage specified that 'the church contains 800 persons, 500 standing places and 300 subscription seats. Sixpence admission for Low Mass, sixpence for High Mass back seats, one shilling for front seats.' The estate's 1903 map records '450 Seats' for the Roman Catholic chapel.

84 McDermott's reminiscences are quoted in Rottmann, 1926, pp. 255–56.

85 Letter dated 17 September 1858 in LB 'V', p. 61.

86 Newman, 1976, p. 25.

87 Brown, 1996a, p. 142. Brown suggests Joshua may have been the father of David de Pinna, Chiswell Street, Finsbury, an artificial flower and feather manufacturer. Perhaps there is a link with the 1922 Bedford Lemere photograph: 'Lisson Grove Showroom Artificial Flowers', neg. no. 25958 in the Bedford-Lemere archive at the National Monuments Records in Swindon.

88 For instance, that of Lionel Goldsmid, who took a villa at 11 Lodge Road in 1839: Brown, 1996a, p. 142.

89 See receipt dated 18 July 1855 in LB 'U', p. 9.

90 Mrs Joseph is recorded on the Eyre estate in May 1868 in LB 'X', pp. 225–26. Also letter to Levy Bros dated 20 May 1881 in LB 'Y', p. 117.

91 See WCA, 901/154, for a 'List of the Lots purchased by my Father Henry Moses – in his own handwriting – which will serve to identify the respective lots with the numbers marked on the plans', signed J. H. B. for John H. Beddington. This document proves that John H. Beddington (who changed his name from Moses in 1868) was the son of Henry Moses; this information is not recorded in Doreen Berger's *The Jewish Victorian* (see note 93 below). Also see website of the Jewish Genealogical Society, in particular 'A Study of the Jewish Population Living in Britain in 1851'.

92 See WCA, 901/148.

93 See Doreen Berger (ed.), *The Jewish Victorian: Genealogical Information from the Jewish Newspapers 1871–1880*, Witney, 1999, entries on Henry Moses, Edward Henry Beddington and John Henry Beddington, and its companion piece published in 2004 – same title but for the period 1861–70. I am grateful to Malcolm Brown for this reference.

94 See Berger (1999, pp. 43 and 411) in note above.

95 See *DNB*.

96 Green, 2003, p. 69. I am grateful to Isaac's descendant, Keith Mayer, for his help with the Moses family.

97 Newman, 1976, pp. 68–69.

98 Newman, 1976, p. 26.

99 In 1824 to Chandless: see Plate 72.

100 Newman, 1976, p. 26.

101 The articles of Judy Glasman give excellent information on the context of this and other synagogues. See 'London Synagogues in the Late Nineteenth Century: Design in Context', *The London Journal*, vol. 13, no. 2, 1987–88, p. 145; also 'Assimilation by Design: London Synagogues in the Nineteenth Century', *Immigrants and Minorities*, vol. 10, March/July 1991, p. 178. Unfortunately, Glasman gives contradictory dates for the Abbey Road synagogue: 1880 in the former, 1888 in the latter.

102 In 'Assimilation by Design' (see above), p. 174.

103 Montgomery Eyre, 1913, p. 238.

104 Cranston, 1993, pp. 161–62.

105 Cranston, 1993, p. 44, for the suicide – 'the muddy water of the Thames seemed to me a delicious bed' – and p. 45 for the 'day I saw my blessed Master'.

106 Cranston, 1993, pp. 146-7.

107 Cranston, 1993, p. 414.

108 Cranston, 1993, p. 398.

109 Cranston, 1993, p. 398.

110 Besant, 1999, p. 314.

111 Montgomery Eyre, 1913, pp. 234–35. This author gives a vivid description of his house and habits at that address. Prior to that date Bradlaugh lived in considerable modesty at 29 Turner Street near Commercial Road: 'a wee room overflowing with books' (Besant, 1999, p. 118).

112 Besant, 1999, p. 124.

113 Besant, 1999, p. 13.

114 Cranston, 1993, pp. 398–99.

115 Charles J. Ryan, *H. P. Blavatsky and the Theosophical Movement*, Pasadena, CA, 1975, ch. 19. There is also a pen and ink illustration of the house's main elevation in this chapter. The room arrangement at 19 Avenue Road is described in *The Esoteric World of Madame Blavatsky: Insights into the Life of a Modern Sphinx*, collected by Daniel Caldwell, Wheaton, IL, 2000, pp. 383ff.

116 Montgomery Eyre, 1913, p. 240.

117 This is based on the Post Office Directories. Between 1901 and 1905 the society is listed as 'Universal Brotherhood Organisation & Theosophical Society' and prior to that simply as 'Theosophical Society'. The property is not listed between 1906 and 1911. From 1912 Miss/Mrs Tetley is listed as residing there: Miss Tetley in 1912 and Mrs Tetley the following year.

118 The society is at 50 Gloucester Place, W1.

119 Tames, 1998, p. 75. For the Buddhist connection, see the biography of Christmas Humphrey compiled by Robert Kitto on the website of the Blavatsky Trust (www.blavatskytrust.org.uk) and Damien P. Hougan, 'A Buddhist Judge in Twentieth Century London', *Korean Journal of Comparative Law*, vol. 24, pp. 1–16, which I found on the Katinka Hesselink.net website. The short article 'Zen Centre' in Wikipedia has the best information about the St John's Wood house.

Chapter 10 Postscript

1 Auroville in South India is an ideal township which strives to achieve human unity. This universal project was first conceived in the 1930s and implemented in the 1960s with the backing of the Indian government and UNESCO. It was inaugurated on 28 February 1968 with representatives of 124 nations. There is a vast literature on this subject, but see especially the moving article written by Toby Butler for the magazine *Art & Cities*, Spring–Summer 2003 (copy in British Library). The tension between the architects' galaxy plan and the residents' perception and needs is explicitly described.

2 Letter to Shaw dated 12 March 1857 in LB 'U', p. 414. On this occasion, however, consent was obtained (see p. 448 of same).

3 Letter to Frederick Marshall dated 20 February 1860 in LB 'V', p. 168. There is no further correspondence about this issue, suggesting this strong objection was successful.

4 Between 1847 and 1849 in LB 'R', p. 579, and LB 'S', pp. 179, 381, 388, 503.

5 Letter from Walpole to Bailey Shaw & Smith dated 7 November 1842 in LB 'Q', p. 3: 'The Trustees [of the Turnpike Road] have made an applic[ati]on to the Vestry of St Marylebone to repair the Road and which they come [*sic*] to a Resolution on Saturday not to do altho' they have rated the Property upon these Roads to the Highway Rate for the last 3½ yrs 1840, 41 & 42 at 2/6 1/6 & 1/6 in the pound– We had a long discussion on this subject at the Vestry on Saturday and I am sorry to say the decision was ag[ain]st the Trustees by a Majority of 18 to 16.'

6 Letter to J. Mortman dated 29 May 1873 in LB 'X', p. 424.

7 Letter to Dr John Harvey dated 13 November 1879 in LB 'Y', p. 49.

8 Letter to G. Wilkinson dated 26 January 1880 in LB 'Y', p. 58.

9 Letter to Shaw dated 13 August 1864 in LB 'W', p. 216.

10 Letter to Edward James Smith dated 15 June 1865 in LB 'W', pp. 338–39.

11 Letter to Bowker dated 13 April 1875 in LB 'X', p. 457.

12 John Davison senior died in 1821, a year after he had purchased the lease of Grove End Place from his brother William. The lengthy history of the site is described in the conveyance document dated 1840 (EE 2651/177). Inexplicably, only half of the houses on this site are shown on the 1853 map (Plate 70).

13 The earlier Wharncliffe Gardens, discussed on pp. 383–85, falls into the category of a housing estate rather than a mansion block.

14 Watson, 2004, p. 71.

15 Abraham pioneered the use of passenger lifts and patented 'a design for service flats based on clusters of service points around appropriately distributed lift shafts, from which meals prepared in a central kitchen on the highest floor of the building could be delivered to individual flats': see Watson, 2004, p. 73. The height of St John's Wood Court was increased by a floor in 1998 which yielded five penthouses. I am most grateful to penthouse resident Louise Brodie for her help with the history of this building.

16 See Watson, 2004, p. 83, n. 113. Davis owned a 99-year lease of the whole site, but his attempt to secure the freehold from the Eyre estate failed (see Watson, 2004, pp. 75–76).

17 Catalogues are in the Eyre archive at EE 2651/341.

18 EE 2651/341(D), sale of 31 March 1925, pp. 8 and 10.

19 Auction on 30 June 1925, catalogue at EE 2651/341(E).

20 Watson, 2004, p. 74.

21 This is how the problem was described by Charles Freeth in a letter to George John Eyre dated 28 November 1861 in LB 'V', p. 383: 'I have got the Vestry of this Parish to direct their Surveyor to inspect & report on the drainage of the Alpha Rd and Park Road property[.] he informs me that he fears there must be a more comprehensive work than at first imagined & that we must wait some time for particulars.'

22 Letter dated 8 September 1865 in LB 'W', p. 377.

23 Letter to George John Eyre dated 26 October 1861 in LB 'X', pp. 365–66.

24 Letter to Mr Steward dated 3 February 1865 in LB 'W', p. 278.

25 Letter to Mr Knight dated 15 February 1868 in LB 'X', p. 174.

26 Letter to George John Eyre dated 26 May 1868 in LB 'X', p. 231.

27 Montgomery Eyre, 1913, from the introduction written by Beckles Willson, p. vi.

28 Extract from an article published in the *Evening News*, cited in Tames, 1998, p. 137.

29 John Shaw's report on premises leased to Mr Berry, 26 February 1862, at EE 2650/1/278(C).

30 John Shaw's report on General Macdonald's houses in lease to James Berry, 21 April 1865, at EE 26501/278(D).

31 J. Ronald Andrew, *The Wharncliffe Gardens Story: Life in a London Village*, n.d. (1960s?); copy at WCA: 'My father and mother were the first tenants of the ground floor flat (No 531) to which they moved from 415 Edgware Road' (vol. I, p. 11).

32 Instone Bloomfield was known on the estate as a developer. Having bought the St John's Wood site, he most probably did not develop it himself and sold it on (to Wates). He was also a City banker and committed spiritualist who funded the Arthur Koestler Foundation.

33 See Cherry and Pevsner, 1998; VCH, 1989; Barnes, 1972.

34 Bright Ashford, 1965, pp. 6–7, for both quotes in this paragraph.

35 Agreement for lease to Thomas Willan, dated 10 February 1796, clause 10, at EE 2651/172E(1).

36 Letter to the vestry dated 11 July 1828 in LB 'L', p. 36.

37 Letter to W. Booker dated 28 November 1856 in LB 'U', p. 358.

38 The tree had been damaged in a bad storm. Letter to Reverend Tayler dated 21 October 1881 in LB 'X', p. 140.

Chapter 11 Epilogue: from fields to tower blocks – landmarks in St John's Wood

1 *Survey of London*, vol. 47, 2008, pp. 340ff.

2 William Tooke Robinson and his wife Alathea (née Eyre) lived at No. 9 in the 1850s, and the household was recorded in the 1851 Census (I am grateful to Henry Phythian-Adams

for pointing this out to me), while her uncle George John Eyre was recorded at No. 1, also in 1851 (LB 'T', p. 34).

3 A brochure produced by Westminster City Council and Taylor Woodrow-Anglian Ltd (probably in 1969) provides a useful summary of the landmark dates and setbacks of the Lisson Green housing development. I am grateful to Citywest Homes, which runs the Lisson Green estate (for Westminster City Council), for sending me a copy of this report.

4 On land sold to Sainsbury's and subsequently acquired by Barratt. I am most grateful to Richard Ross from Peverel OM Ltd, the estate manager at Palgrave Gardens, for providing access and information about this development.

5 This builder is also recorded as making roads for developer William Hall: letter to Hall dated 16 October 1819 in LB 'F', p. 224.

6 Letter to Punter dated 13 November 1818 in LB 'E', p. 730.

7 See Cole, 2009, p. 481. It is difficult to reconcile its current site with that shown on the estate's nineteenth-century maps. For Rossi, see Gunnis, 1968, pp. 326ff.

8 St Paul's Church Centre pamphlet, preface by Reverend Graham M. Buckle in June 2006.

9 This plaque was unveiled in June 2006. A booklet to commemorate this event and the history of Lord's was prepared by David Rayvern Allen and published simultaneously: *The Second Lord's Cricket Ground: Home of the MCC, 1811–1813*.

10 The school does not feature on the 1883 estate map (Plate 208) but is shown on Edward Stanford's 'Library Map of London and its Suburbs' (1891). For the difficulties of using maps made for the School Board of London, see Ralph Hyde, *Printed Maps of Victorian London 1851–1900*, Folkestone, 1975, pp. 38–39 and cat. no. 168.

11 He is first mentioned in the Eyre letter books when he wrote to Walpole to ask permission to make an addition to his house. See letter to G. K. Huxley dated 17 October 1845 in LB 'R', p. 58. No licence is recorded.

12 The rough document that survives (at EE 2651/310) indicates the sale was first contemplated in 1897 to 'The St James [*sic*] & Pall Mall Electric Light Company Limited'. The land was purchased for the sum of £50,000 and comprised 'Nos 7 to 22 North Bank, 4 to 8 including 6A Lodge Place, 12 to 16 including 14A Lodge Road, 1 and 2 Oak Tree Place, and 3 Oak Tree Road'.

13 See *The Builder*, 10 January 1903 (cutting at WCA, Ashbridge 374). By that date one of the shafts had already been built and the foundations for the second were also ready. The full scheme is illustrated and described in C. F. Peach, 'Notes on the Design and Construction of Buildings Connected with the Generation and Supply of Electricity known as Central Stations', *Journal of the Royal Institute of British Architects*, vol. XI, third series, 1904, pp. 295ff.

14 LMA, 4278/02/110, 1985–86 Annual: map on p. 11 showing 'London power station closures'. Both St John's Wood and St Marylebone feature on that map.

15 Letter to Simpson dated 24 September 1811 in LB 'B', p. 516.

16 Letter to Willan dated 10 October 1811 in LB 'B', p. 520, and letter to Wilson dated 6 January 1812 in LB 'B', p. 571.

17 This name was in competition with that of Punkers Barn and Red Barn, but is recorded as in use during Atkinson's time, for instance in LB 'E', p. 39 (17 March 1817).

18 WCA, Ashbridge 887.3. The school would have been partially built by 1852, since early that year Walpole addressed a letter to the Commissioners of Sewers to enable them to drain this building into the Grove End sewer: letter dated 20 February 1852 in LB 'T', p. 186.

19 The name 'Wharncliffe' was after the earl of Wharncliffe, chairman of the Manchester, Sheffield and Lincolnshire Railway. His photograph is reproduced in the *Daily Graphic* of 14 November 1894, p. 8. The countess of Wharncliffe is shown in the same article 'cutting the first sod' of the new railway line.

20 Charles Booth Online Archive (1886–1903) at http://booth.lse.ac.uk, original survey books, B357, pp. 232–33. This particular walk took place on 12 December 1898.

21 This development is discussed in detail in Graham Rimmer, 'High Cost of Inner London Housing', *Surveyor*, vol. 150, no. 4444, 12 August 1977, pp. 9–11.

22 Evinson, 1998, pp. 56–58.

23 The game originated in France where it was called 'Jeu de Paume'. The first court was

built in 1838 on the site of the Mound Stand. The present court is behind the pavilion and was opened on 1 January 1900.

24 Bill Utermohlen was the subject of a film called 'Telling It Like It Is'. It is worth consulting the website of its production company, OPW (Open Wings Productions), at www.openwingsproductions.com.

25 Recent security concerns have altered this original concept. The principal doors are now rarely used as the back entrance is more discreet and offers a better screening process in times of terrorist activity.

26 See Connor, 2001, pp. 64ff.

27 See *The Sphere*, 30 May 1936 (copy at WCA, T137.1 Prints). For Goetze, see Dakers, 1997, p. 63.

28 No one now knows when the bodies were removed. Martin Aldred set up the St John's Wood Youth Club in the crypt in 1974. Reverend Anders Bergquist tells me that the church was used as an air raid shelter during the Second World War and that one of the vaults is still bricked up. The church hall was opened in 1977.

29 Smith, 1833, p. 140.

30 Oliver and Bradshaw, 1955, p. 35.

31 Walpole George Eyre (d.1846); Henrietta Mary Annette Eyre (d.1847) and her husband Robert Dashwood (d.1839); Colonel Henry Samuel Eyre (d.1851); Harriet Margaret Eyre, née Ainslie (d.1856), wife of John Thomas Eyre; Walpole Eyre (d.1856); his wife Elizabeth Annabella Eyre, née Johnson (d.1860).

32 See James K. Hopkins, *A Woman to Deliver her People: Joanna Southcott and English Millenarianism in an Era of Revolution*, Austin, TX, 1982.

33 This complements the work of Smith, and may be consulted at the Westminster City Archive. At the time of writing the newly formed St John's Wood History Society has raised money to embark on an inventory project of St John's Wood Church.

34 See *St Marylebone Housing Association 1926–1986*, published in London in 1996 to celebrate this association's seventieth anniversary. There is a copy at WCA. The development was also reviewed in *Building* magazine of September 1951.

35 EE 2651/57 and EE 2651/58 dated 20 February 1829.

36 Jacob Hibberd ran into serious difficulty with the estate because he took various liberties with his agreement, including building an extra house. One side of the agreement narrates the unpleasant episode when Edwin Eyre refused to grant leases as a consequence of Hibberd's actions. It is also described in great detail in Edwin's letter to John Shaw dated 11 September 1852 in LB 'T', p. 288. The matter was eventually settled by raising Hibberd's annual rent.

37 Bk of Drawings IV, 50 right (drawing dated 27 October 1840).

38 Letter to Villiers dated 20 November 1816 in LB 'D', p. 719.

39 Letter to Cochran dated 16 August 1817 in LB 'E', p. 229.

40 Letter to Colonel Rowan dated 27 May 1830 in LB 'M', p. 18.

41 Letter to Shaw dated 19 July 1826 in LB 'K', p. 106.

42 Letter to George Cottam, the tenant of the St John's Wood House from 1830, dated 11 February 1834 in LB 'N', p. 243. Throughout 1852 the letter books refer to it as the Old Manor House.

43 Letter to Shaw dated 11 September 1852 in LB 'T', p. 290.

44 Walkley, 1994, p. 249.

45 Letter to Messrs Few & Co. dated 18 June 1834 in LB 'N', p. 337. There is no doubt this was 'Mr Willan's House'.

46 As shown by the surviving counterpart lease dated 20 October 1843 at EE 2650/1/448.

47 Letter to Messrs Lee & Pemberton (from Messrs Savill & Sons) dated 8 December 1927 at EE 2650/1/87(D).

48 The mews had two lessees: Joseph Gardener (see Bk of Drawings III, 3) and Charles and Caleb Hall, the sons of developer William Hall (Bk of Drawings III, 2).

49 Letter to Charles Few dated 9 April 1834 in LB 'N', p. 278.

50 Letter to Clark dated 18 November 1841 in LB 'P', p. 453 (one of three letters he wrote on that day to address breaches of covenants in that part of the estate).

51 A late nineteenth-century map of the estate specifies its capacity.

52 See auction catalogue inside John Maidlow's 1822 agreement at EE 2651/96.

53 The best accounts for the almshouses are the untitled summary document prepared by C[hristopher] Flood, honorary secretary of the almshouses, at WCA, Ashbridge 667 (undated but probably 1840s), and the anonymous article published in *The Mirror of Literature, Amusement and Instruction*, 18 June 1836, p. 782.

54 See P. F. Robinson, *Rural Architecture*, London, 1823, design nos 12 and 15.

55 Report dated 2 June 1958 at EE 2651/352A. The management board of the almshouses kindly donated a copy of this report to the Eyre archive after discovering the almshouses' archive in the course of redecorating this institution's lounge.

56 The shortlisted architects were D. Hodges, G. B. Drewitt, Arthur Kenyon and J. M. Austin.

57 A 'Mayor's Reception' was held on 9 March 1965 to celebrate the rebuilding of the almshouses. The recent history of the almshouses has been drawn from their Board of Management minutes. I am grateful to Diana Eyre and Jane Leaver for allowing me access to the correct documents. Diana Eyre also kindly provided the modern data for drawing a comparison between the almshouses then and now.

58 Letter to Christopher Flood dated 29 December 1835 in LB 'N', p. 605.

59 WCA, Cuttings T138, Townshend estate article (anon.) dated 17 October 1957. The date 1949 is recorded on the c.1960 map at Plate 222, but the plot also features on the 1952 CPO map at Plate 221. I have not been able to resolve this apparent contradiction.

60 Ernest D. Fridlander, *Matthew Maris*, London, 1921, pp. 11–13. Also see comments collected by B. B. Falk (originally published in the *Weekly Dispatch* on 26 August 1917), in *Matthew Maris: An Illustrated Souvenir*, arranged by D. Croal Thomson, the French Gallery, London, 1917. The Boijmans Van Beuningen Museum in Rotterdam stated they had no works by Matthew Maris (e-mail Jacqueline Rapmund, 31 July 2008).

61 The assignment (Adams to Green) is dated 29 July 1880 at EE 2650/1/437. The licence is recorded in Licence Book II, p. 169.

62 Letter to Christopher Flood at Marylebone courthouse dated 15 April 1842 in LB 'P', p. 538.

63 WCA, T138 Cuttings 'A' Box.

64 Lease dated 30 November 1846 at WCA, 765/59. The land was technically on agreement to W. R. Fry, but he sold his right and interest to Yeo for £100. Also see Bk of Drawings V, 75 right, dated 24 June 1846.

65 The plan of the site, house and school is at WCA, 765/59, inside the original lease. Also see Licence Book II, p. 79.

66 St John's Wood Society Newsletter, Spring 2007; see cover pictures and the article by Malcolm Brown on p. 8.

67 Bernard Miles, *The Mermaid Theatre*, n.d. [1951], copy in Guildhall Library.

68 Lease of Ordnance Arms to Charles Viner, by direction of Charles Freeth junior, is mentioned in LB 'Q', p. 127 (9 June 1843). Lease drawing at Bk of Drawings IV, 60 left.

69 'Mr Willan had afforded the accommodation … to a Detachment of the Corps of Royal Artillery Drivers attached to the Battalion Guns of the Guard since November 1804': TNA, WO 44/299 (extract from minutes dated 9 July 1806). Barracks were erected in the Brick Field as confirmed by a letter to Willan dated 18 December 1805 in LB 'A', p. 154. Sworder's well-researched texts (1971, 2003) are by far the most reliable accounts for the Barracks, though this author did not realise that the Barracks had started life on a different site.

70 Sworder, 2003, p. 15.

71 EE 2651/51 dated 11 May 1844.

72 Woodhams took out a lease on 6 Albert Terrace dated 28 December 1843: see EE 2650/1/472.

73 The letters to Fry in LB 'Q', pp. 532, 533 (March 1845), also clarify the relationship between the three men: Woodhams was brought in by Charles Maidlow, who was working for Fry.

74 See news article by Jane Picken in the *Ham & High* newspaper of 6 December 2002.

75 EE 2650/1/411(A, B, C).

76 See Licence Book I, p. 470. Charles Maidlow obtained a licence retrospectively, and Walpole stated in his licence that he would 'not take advantage of the breach of stipulation in such Lease in regard of a Chimney & flue being in such Coach House'.

77 At EE 2650/1/411(A).

78 At EE 2650/1/137(A).

79 Christabel Frampton's letter to Lady MacDonnell, dated 18 November 1908, is in the archive of the Reform Club. I am grateful to Dr Peter Urbach for bringing my attention to this document.

80 I am most grateful to Joy Fleischmann, Arthur Fleischmann's widow, for her hospitality and kindness.

81 For Victoria Road see EE 2651/93 (1842).

82 EE 2651/93 and Bk of Drawings IV, 23 left.

83 Letter dated 26 May 1843, inside Treeby's agreement of 5 April 1842, at EE 2651/93. When Walpole was sent the drawings for this development, he responded positively, provided the houses were set twenty feet from the road (letter to Treeby dated 21 October 1843 in LB 'Q', p. 195).

84 Auction sale by Alfred Savill & Sons on 31 March 1925, catalogue at EE 2651/341(D). The description in the auction catalogue lists a saloon bar, public bar, bar parlour, bottle and jug department as well as a bagatelle room and kitchen on the ground floor, a billiard room, sitting room, store and bathroom on the first floor, five bedrooms on the second floor and extensive cellarage in the basement. The original lease to the Prince of Wales pub has survived at EE 2650/1/479, dated 10 February 1844. It does not mention a pub, but Walpole's letter to Shaw is unmistakably clear about this matter: see LB 'Q', p. 220, dated 9 December 1843.

85 VCH, 1989, p. 62.

86 The shape and position of this house are reminiscent of 2 Acacia Road (Plate 248), the house built by Hibberd on the site of old St John's Wood House. This may suggest Hibberd also built 23 St John's Wood Park. The lease drawing is at Bk of Drawings IV, 93 left.

87 Richardson Eyre, 1904, ch. IV, p. 1.

88 See Connor, 2001, pp. 70–73.

89 See EE 2651/262(D), sale by Messrs Farebrother, Clark & Co., 1868.

90 At 24 Finchley Road. The cutting through the floor no longer exists. See article in *Building*, 27 November 1970 (copy at WCA, T138 Cuttings F-Go).

91 See Walkley, 1994. The sites are 28 Finchley Road (c.1881 conversion), 59 Queen's Grove (1882) and Woronzow Studios (1890). This data may clash with evidence found in the Eyre archive, see note 159 in Chapter 8.

92 See the letter from James Sharp to Walpole dated 1 March 1847 and attached to the 1846 agreement between the two men at EE 2651/82. The elevation of No. 7 and adjoining houses is at Bk of Drawings V, 91 right.

93 Sale information noted on a 1960s wall map of the Eyre estate.

94 Information on this development came from two newspaper cuttings at WCA, T138 dated 1981 and 1982.

95 Both the names Lodge and Villa have been used to describe this property. The plot of land was first leased to developer James Sharp in July 1856. The schoolhouse, however, had been built long before that date in the late 1840s from evidence provided by the letter books. Agreement on a site dates from 1847 (LB 'R', pp. 413–14) so the school would have been built shortly afterwards. Reverend Edward Thompson had left by 1850, when Reverend H. W. Maddock was in post.

96 The 1868 sale catalogue has survived at EE 2650/1/180(B) giving a full description of All Saints Villa. The 1856 lease drawing for the school (and adjoining terrace) is in Bk of Drawings V, 60 left. It shows that at some point the rectangular façade windows were turned into a large Gothic window.

97 Cole, 2009, p. 493.

98 See, for instance, LB 'P', pp. 590 and 625, when it is sometimes described as Devonshire Cottage and sometimes as Devonshire Villa.

99 See auction catalogue, 4 August 1868, Lot 10, at EE 2650/1/180(B) and EE 2651/262(D) for the map.

100 See Gunnis, 1968, p. 351.

101 The current owners purchased the property in 1979, and I am extremely grateful to

102 Letter to Shaw dated 16 May 1846 in LB 'R', p. 200.

103 The ceilings are now quite plain, but in the room overlooking the garden on the ground floor there are remnants by the fireplace of a very elaborate pattern which probably would have covered the entire ceiling.

104 Approximately on the site of Barclays Bank. See Bk of Drawings V, 30 left, dated 11 November 1848, and EE 2650/1/440, the lease to James Bowen dated 1 May 1849.

105 The leaseholder was William Todd, and the property, which is recorded in Bk of Drawings V, 50 left, was extremely plain. The correct address is given in the Royal Academy exhibitors in 1863 when he exhibited the half-sized model of a statue: *Lord Bacon Meditating Corrections in his Great Work, 'The Novum Organum Scientiarum'*.

106 Tate archive, TGA, 9919/7, Sibson's 'Autobiography' (Ms), Notebook VII.

107 Nicholas Tromans traces the beginning of Egyptomania to the successful outcome of Giovanni Battista Belzoni's 1817 excavation of the Valley of Kings at Thebes. See *The Lure of the East: British Orientalist Painting*, London, 2008, pp.103–4. But Alex Werner traces the roots of Egyptomania to the late eighteenth century in his chapter, 'Egypt in London: Public and Private Displays in the Nineteenth Century Metropolis', in Jean Marcel Humbert and Clifford Price (eds), *Imhotep Today: Egyptianising Architecture*, London, 2003, pp. 75–104.

108 Tate archive, TGA, 9919/7, Sibson's 'Autobiography' (Ms), Notebook VII. The house was financed by Mr Phillips, who would have lent the minimum £600 required for a house on the estate. A further £200 was advanced, but Sibson ran out of money again before the house could be finished. At Phillips's death his son-in-law, a surgeon called Mr Lucas, inherited the project.

109 Tate Archive, TGA, 9919/7, Sibson's 'Autobiography' (Ms), Notebook VII. All extracts used here have been drawn from Notebook VII (the pages of this manuscript are not numbered).

110 Connor, 2001, p. 69.

111 Walkley, 1994, p. 249. The original property, leased to Mr Bicknell, is recorded in Bk of Drawings IV, 78 right, dated July 1841.

112 The unveiling of the green plaque took place on 14 October 2008. Soyer died here on 5 August 1858 when it was known as 15 Marlborough Road, since renumbered No. 28. Soyer moved to St John's Wood in 1857 so only lived at this address for a year. See Ruth Cowen, *Relish: The Extraordinary Life of Alexis Soyer, Victorian Celebrity Chef*, London, 2006, p. 315.

113 The correct site of Bifrons Villa has been worked out using the letter books. It is in Acacia Road in LB 'U', p. 270, and the numbering and site are also confirmed in LB 'V', pp. 93 and 104.

114 This is mentioned in the *Modern Housewife*'s 1856 preface.

115 See 'A Lesser Town-house of Today, 62 Wellington Road NW', *Country Life*, 21 October 1922, pp. 521–23.

116 From newspaper cuttings framed in the Eyre estate archive, one of them dated 14 January 1929 at EE 2652/27AA. The pictures apparently went with Mr Willing to the Royal White Hart Hotel at Beaconsfield (presumably Buckinghamshire).

117 Cherry and Pevsner, 1991, p. 665. The working drawings of the architects T. P. Bennett & Sons are in the London Metropolitan Archive.

118 Quoted in the notes to a Twentieth Century Society Walk, 'South through St John's Wood', led by Ian McInnes (2009).

119 Cole, 2009, p. 493.

120 The original lease drawings for Nos 18 and 20 are at Bk of Drawings III, 64; for Nos 6 and 8 at Bk of Drawings III, 63; for Nos 14 and 16 at Bk of Drawings III, 8.

121 The lease drawing is at Bk of Drawings II, 53A. For Madame Tussaud, see Cole, 2009, p. 486.

122 See LB 'P', p. 437.

123 The first lease drawing shows that No. 19 was slightly smaller than the rest of the houses in Cavendish Place (see Bk of Drawings IV, 66 left, dated 1 August 1843). The lease for No. 19, dated 3 August 1843, is at EE 2650/1/218. Another Newton & Kelk property, 25 Cavendish Close, was discussed in a *Country Life* article of 1 October 1948 (pp. 682–83), entitled 'A Converted London House'; the 'conversion' meant 'the house has been converted for running without resident, or indeed any, domestic staff … while retaining the character of a "gentleman's house"'.

124 Builder James Salter was party to the lease at EE 2650/1/443(A) as he was developing this section of Cavendish Avenue. Therefore, he probably built Thrupp's houses.

125 Faed is described as proprietor in Walkley, 1994, p. 250. Also see EE2650/1/130(A, B). But the property was still in the hands of the Thrupp family, and it was the lessee, Miss Adelaide Thrupp, executor and beneficiary of William Joseph (who had died in March 1873), who applied for permission to do the extension work. The plan which accompanied the licence makes clear that there was no garden at the back of 24–24A and that the garden acquired in 1845 was no longer part of the estate by the time Thomas Faed built his studio. The original lease dated 11 November 1843 is at EE 2650/1/443(A). The subsequent annexing of a garden (by David Oliver Owen in 1845, presumably the tenant at that time) is described in the 1906 underlease to James Dick-Peddie at EE 2650/1/511. The 'missing' back garden was repurchased by the Eyre estate under the 'reign' of Revd H. S. Eyre: see Abstract of Title, 1884–1939, at EE 2651/354.

126 The underlease of 25 June 1906 survives giving a blow-by-blow account of the many tribulations suffered by Faed's executors: see EE 2650/1/511. The landscape painter James Dick-Peddie exhibited principally at the Royal Scottish Academy.

127 The lease drawings are at Bk of Drawings IV, 56 left, 76 right, 100 right.

128 See letter to Shaw dated 9 April 1862 in LB 'V', p. 427.

129 In Walpole's day the roads now known as St John's Wood Terrace and Townshend Road, which are the continuation of Circus Road, were also known as Circus Road.

130 Letter to Lomax dated 11 October 1848 in LB 'S', p. 173.

131 Marteau, c.1992, p. 9.

132 See 2004 leaflet, 'The Conventual Church of St John of Jerusalem at the Hospital of St. John and St. Elizabeth', written by Fra Matthew Festing. This well-written leaflet unfortunately confuses this hospital with the famous Great Ormond Street Hospital for children. Marteau remarked that the church was identical to that dedicated to the Lorrainians in Rome (c.1992, p. 10).

133 Marteau, c.1992, p. 22.

134 Marteau, c.1992, p. 95.

135 See the 'Abstract of the Title of the Assignees of Mr Samuel Gardner a Bankrupt to a Leasehold dwelling house situate No. 1 Wellington Terrace' (EE 2650/1/119).

136 Letter to Harry Fellowes dated 21 May 1885 in LB 'Y', p. 347. On p. 34 of this letter book the Eyres had turned down his offer to purchase No. 17.

137 Montgomery Eyre, 1913, p. 104.

138 'Conservation Area Appraisals' and 'Conservation Area Management', in *Conservation Area Audit*, London (Department of Planning and City Development, City of Westminster), 2007.

139 The phrase is engraved on the monument itself. The words 'by subscription' come from Montgomery Eyre, 1913, p. 268.

140 See Lord Edward Gleichen, *London's Open-Air Statuary*, London, 1928, p. 189.

141 Bk of Drawings II, 13, for Chandless. Bk of Drawings I, 78, for the plot acquired by Gardener in 1820.

142 See LB 'G', pp. 491, 492, 584. Also EE 2651/216(A and B).

143 This sale generated the money needed to extricate Colonel Eyre from a very tricky suit regarding the financing of the Finchley Road: 'Capt[ai]n Randall has brought an action of Ejectment for getting poss[essi]on of the Tolls of our M[arylebone] &F[inchley] T[urnpike] Road,' wrote Walpole in a letter to Stone dated 1 November 1840 in LB 'P', p. 268. Randall was successful in his action.

144 See correspondence with Charles Harrison in LB 'T', pp. 438, 448, 450, 451, 454.

145 Letter to Harrison dated 20 July 1853 in LB 'T', p. 451.

146 This booklet was compiled by Rufus Segar and published privately by the MacSegar Press (1990). I am grateful to James and Rosemary Bevan for drawing my attention to this publication.

147 I am grateful to James and Rosemary Bevan for allowing me access to their documents.

148 Matyjaszkiewicz, 1984, p. 50; also see David S. Brooke, 'James Tissot and the "ravissante Irlandaise"', *The Connoisseur*, vol. 168, 1968, pp. 55–59.

149 Montgomery Eyre, 1913, p. 188.

150 Stott, 1887, p. 85.

151 A layman and famous builder who went bankrupt around 1866.

152 Stott, 1887, pp. 97–98.

153 See LB 'P', pp. 331, 332, and the property purchased is spelt out in LB 'R', p. 130.

154 See LB 'L', p. 91, and LB 'Q', p. 293.

155 See letter to Ranken & Co. dated 17 February 1846 in LB 'R', p. 151.

156 The rateable value of the property jumped from £109 in 1882 to £134 in 1883, indicating the house had been enlarged. I am most grateful to Richard Bowden for bringing this fact to my attention. Also see Walkley, 1994, p. 252.

157 Joseph Tall, a patentee of concrete construction, was not an architect.

158 Stirling, 1954, p. 168.

159 I am grateful to Richard Bowden, former librarian at Marylebone Library, for his help over this issue. His detailed notes about the properties are at WCA, Marylebone envelopes 160/Langford.

160 From Richard Bowden's notes, as above, credited to 'The Best of Betjeman Metro-land', p. 219.

161 The lease drawing is at Bk of Drawings V, 17 left.

162 This was done in a manner entirely reminiscent of what Fry had done at 42 Ordnance Hill which had earned him a severe reprimand from Walpole. See Walpole's letter to Fry dated 31 January 1846 in LB 'R', p. 136. For James Jones's lease see Bk of Drawings V, 17 left, and LB 'S', pp. 69 and 97.

163 See Louise Baring, 'How We Met: Stephen and Natasha Spender', *The Independent on Sunday*, 10 January 1993. I am grateful to Professor Xavier Baron for this reference.

164 The lease drawing for the 'Gothic' houses is at Bk of Drawings V, 69 right, while the lease drawing for the almshouses is at Bk of Drawings III, 130.

165 Bk of Drawings V, 76 left for the pub and 88A left for the two doubles houses, which were leased to George William Braess in 1852.

166 See Cole, 2009, p. 490.

167 For Todd-style houses, see Chapter 4, in particular 'The Two Alpha Houses'.

168 The lease drawing for this plot is at Bk of Drawings V, 22 A and B left, dated 5 January 1853.

169 The lease drawing for this plot is at Bk of Drawings V, 43 right, dated 28 March 1853.

170 The land taken by Cook in 1850 is labelled I, J, K, L on Plate 72.

171 Colloms and Weindling, 2007, pp. 17 and 20. There are a couple of 1819 letters in the letter books addressed to George Pocock, the developer working immediately next to the estate, which deal with road making (LB 'F', pp. 132 and 199).

172 Cherry and Pevsner, 1991, p. 667.

173 See Bills and Knight, 2006, pp. 26–27; Cole, 2009, p. 492.

174 Undated auction catalogue at WCA, M Acc.320.

175 Walkley, 1994, p. 234.

176 Letter to George John Eyre dated 28 November 1861 in LB 'V', p. 383.

177 Letter to George John Eyre dated 21 November 1861 in LB 'V', p. 380. The rent arrears amounted to just over £364. The land covered by that agreement was redistributed between Messrs J. Parkins, George Foulger and John George Bettinson (1861).

178 'New Housing in Camden', *The Illustrated London News*, November 1977, pp. 26–27 (with good photographs by Roger Jones).

179 See notes for Open House London, 2006 (Open House, RIBA and AA libraries); Cherry and Pevsner, 1998; and VCH, 1989, p. 62. Anthony Minghella made effective use of the striking appearance of this development in his film *Breaking and Entering* with Jude Law (2006).

180 Cherry and Pevsner, 1998, p. 200.

181 Thompson, 1974, pp. 248–49.

182 VCH, 1989, p. 62.

183 VCH, 1989, p. 62.

184 This tree, growing between the Barracks wall and a villa, was removed in 2009 despite a campaign to save it. See St John's Wood Society Newsletter, Spring 2009, p. 5.

185 *Hampstead News*, 14 September 1962, and another anonymous newspaper cutting in Holborn Library, Hampstead Collection, LT.

186 Lease drawing at Bk of Drawings VI, 266 left.

187 At EE 2650/1/368. Clayton was a friend of St John's Wood Clique painter Henry Stacy Marks, who charted the beginning of the partnership between Clayton and Bell in his book (1894, vol. I, pp. 62–65).

188 National Monuments Record, Bedford Lemere Day Books, 4 and 8 November 1886, photos taken by WW. I am most grateful to Ian Leith for his invaluable help over this archive. The negative number for this material was 6746.

189 LB 'W', p. 454, in January 1866 and LB 'X', pp. 255, 259, in July 1868. The numbering of the road changed around 1867: it was No. 8 in 1866 and No. 16 in 1868. The Shaw family were based at that address from 1849 to 1876. They appear to have been subtenants of the Raynsfords, the family Edwin Eyre married into. The lease drawing of 16 Albion Road is at Bk of Drawings V, 64A right.

190 The information provided by VCH (1989) and a cutting in the Hampstead collection (L. T. Harben estate) in Holborn Library are partially contradictory. This development apparently cost £900,000.

191 *Hampstead News*, 20 August 1965, newspaper cutting at Holborn Library, Hampstead Collection LT.

192 See Application No. 8500248, Camden Council Planning Department. Date registered 24 April 1985.

193 Licence Bk I, pp. 74–77. Also see Bk of Drawings V, 37A right.

194 See LB 'X', p. 392, for the wine merchant and LB 'Y', p. 412, and EE 2650/1/416(B) for the unrealised hotel project.

195 See 1893 licence at EE 2650/1/380.

196 VCH, 1989, p. 62.

197 VCH, 1989, p. 62. The building leases at the Swiss Cottage triangle expired at Michaelmas 1933 (see letter to Reverend H. S. Eyre dated 16 April 1886 in LB 'Y', p. 412).

198 *Hampstead & Highgate Express (Ham & High)*, 9 February 1962, newspaper cutting at Holborn Library, Hampstead Collection LT.

199 The lease drawings for the School for the Blind and Sunnyside are at Bk of Drawings V, 11A left and 49 left. For the chapel see Bk of Drawings VI, 27B right and 26A and B left.

200 VCH, 1989, p. 62.

201 This extract from the project's review in *Building Design* is quoted in the notes to a Twentieth Century Society Walk, 'South through St John's Wood', which was led by Ian McInnes (2009, p. 3). With the 2008 notes, 'Swiss Cottage, St John's Wood and Regent's Park', these documents provide valuable data on post-1900 developments in St John's Wood. They may be purchased from the Twentieth-Century Society. For the Visage and Swiss Cottage Cultural Centre, see the website of the Commission for Architecture and the Built Environment or CABE at http://www.cabe.org.uk/case-studies/visage-and-swiss-cottage-cultural-centre (one of their case studies).

202 This quote originally came from Terry Farrell's website at http://www.tfpfarrells.com. Unfortunately, the project page entitled 'Swiss Cottage, London 1999–2005' has now been removed from the website, presumably to make space for newer projects.

ABBREVIATIONS AND SOURCES

Abbreviations

Bk of Drawings	Book of Drawings (see overleaf)
BL	British Library
Cat.	Catalogue
DNB	*Oxford Dictionary of National Biography* (all *DNB* references are to the 2004 edition of the *Oxford Dictionary of National Biography*, ed. H. C. G. Matthews and Brian Harrison, unless stated otherwise)
EE	Eyre estate
GL	Guildhall Library, City of London
LB	Letter books (see below)
LMA	London Metropolitan Archives
MCC	Marylebone Cricket Club
MDR	Middlesex Deeds Registry (kept at LMA)
MOL	Museum of London
NMR	National Monuments Record
PG	Pemberton Greenish, the solicitors of the Eyre estate
RCHM	Royal Commission for Historical Monuments
RO	Record Office
TNA	The National Archives
V&A	Victoria and Albert Museum, London
VCH	The Victoria History of the Counties of England (see bibliography)
WCA	Westminster City Archives

Eyre Archive

The reader will find some general background information about the Eyre archive in the Introduction. Over the last few decades, discrete parts from the Eyre estate archive were transferred to Westminster City Archives by the estate's solicitors – the references to these are prefaced by WCA, with the exception of WCA, M: Acc. 320, which came from a different source. However, now that the estate trustees have agreed to transfer the rest of the archive to Westminster City Council, this means that the whole archive is going to be under one roof and accessible to the public. The material referenced 'EE' followed by the numbers 2650 and 2651 for leases and documents, and 2652 for other material, is this latest large deposit. Certain parts of the archive have been used heavily for this volume, and I have listed below what have been key documents for the research.

Letter Books

There are twenty-five volumes of letter books organised alphabetically, each bearing a different letter of the alphabet (the only letter not to have been used is J). Hence the following abbreviation: LB for letter book followed by a letter (which identifies the volume) followed by the page number. The letters cover the period 1 April 1805 to 20 April 1894. Each volume has an index at the front.

EE 2652/37(A)	Letter Book 'A'	1 April 1805 to 13 October 1808
EE 2652/37(B)	Letter Book 'B'	14 October 1808 to 7 August 1812
EE 2652/37(C)	Letter Book 'C'	8 August 1812 to 8 December 1814
EE 2652/37(D)	Letter Book 'D'	9 December 1814 to 20 February 1817
EE 2652/37(E)	Letter Book 'E'	20 February 1817 to 25 February 1819
EE 2652/37(F)	Letter Book 'F'	25 February 1819 to 26 May 1821
EE 2652/37(G)	Letter Book 'G'	26 May 1821 to 7 October 1822
EE 2652/37(H)	Letter Book 'H'	7 October 1822 to 25 February 1824
EE 2652/37(I)	Letter Book 'I'	25 February 1824 to 23 February 1826
EE 2652/37(K)	Letter Book 'K'	24 February 1826 to 4 June 1828
EE 2652/37(L)	Letter Book 'L'	5 June 1828 to 10 May 1830
EE 2652/37(M)	Letter Book 'M'	10 May 1830 to 10 September 1832
EE 2652/37(N)	Letter Book 'N'	11 September 1832 to 23 February 1836
EE 2652/37(O)	Letter Book 'O'	13 February 1836 [*sic*] to 2 March 1839
EE 2652/37(P)	Letter Book 'P'	2 March 1839 to 9 November 1842
EE 2652/37(Q)	Letter Book 'Q'	2 November 1842 [*sic*] to 19 July 1845
EE 2652/37(R)	Letter Book 'R'	21 July 1845 to 20 January 1848
EE 2652/37(S)	Letter Book 'S'	20 January 1848 to 23 January 1851
EE 2652/37(T)	Letter Book 'T'	24 January 1851 to 29 August 1854
EE 2652/37(U)	Letter Book 'U'	31 August 1854 to 3 July 1858
EE 2652/37(V)	Letter Book 'V'	3 July 1858 to 20 April 1863
EE 2652/37(W)	Letter Book 'W'	20 April 1863 to 3 January 1867
EE 2652/37(X)	Letter Book 'X'	4 January 1867 to 18 April 1878
EE 2652/37(Y)	Letter Book 'Y'	18 April 1878 to 22 February 1889
EE 2652/37(Z)	Letter Book 'Z'	26 February 1889 to 19 April 1894]

Books of Drawings

There are seven volumes of lease drawings that cover most of the properties on the Eyre estate between 1807 and 1874. Each drawing consists of a plan and main elevation, and they have been pricked to facilitate the transfer on to the leases. These drawings have been annotated, and they usually state that they have been inserted in the original leases for these properties with the date and name of the lessees (these dates do not always match the dates on the leases).

The references to the books of drawings give the volume number followed by the drawing number, which is based on the page number but is not the page number. In later volumes, each page may be associated with three or four separate drawings. Also note that the periods for each volume are for rough guidance only. There are idiosyncrasies: for instance, vol. 4 goes up to 1841 on the right-hand pages and up to 1844 on the left-hand pages.

EE 2652/36(1)	Volume 1 covers the period 1807 to 1823 and has 127 drawings.
EE 2652/36(2)	Volume 2, which has a separate index, covers the period 1822 [*sic*] to 1826 and has 144 drawings.
EE 2652/36(3)	Volume 3 covers the period 1826 to 1839 and has 156 drawings.
EE 2652/36(4)	Volume 4 covers the period 1839 to 1844 and has 214 drawings.
EE 2652/36(5)	Volume 5 covers the period 1844 to 1851 and has 232 drawings.

| EE 2652/36(6) | Volume 6, with index (Roads and Lessees), covers the period 1852 to 1863 and has 309 drawings. |
| EE 2652/36(7) | Volume 7, with index (Roads and Lessees), covers the period 1863 to 1874 and has 397 drawings. |

Account Books

1 'Ledger of Sermon & [Walpole] Eyre commencing 1st April 1796' (EE 2652/42). This is the earliest account book, when Walpole Eyre was in partnership with Thomas Sermon. It goes up to 1804 when Walpole Eyre set up his own practice.

2 There are four large volumes of 'bill books' which cover Walpole Eyre's career at EE 2652/43(A to D). They form a very detailed diary of his activities as a solicitor, organised in client order (each volume has an index of names at the front). Walpole used the data to prepare appropriate invoices for his customers. The first two volumes contain important information about the estate under the heading 'Henry Samuel Eyre', Walpole's brother and one of his clients. These entries disappear in the third and fourth volumes. Much of the legal work undertaken by Walpole on behalf of the Eyre estate can be examined by looking up clients' entries connected with the development work in St John's Wood: Robert Todd, Robert Yeo, John Maidlow, etc. (see Appendix 9).

3 The set of account books which record the financial activities of various members of the Eyre family in relation to the estate (EE 2652/42 and 44).

Licence Books

There are two volumes inscribed 'License Books'. The first one (I) covers the period 1823–53 (EE 2652/40); the second one (II) the period 1852 [sic] to 1908 (EE 2652/41). The first volume is very detailed and reproduces in full the text of the licence; the second volume is a shorthand record. A number of actual licences have also survived, often (but not always) kept inside the counterpart leases of the relevant properties.

Rent Books

There are many rent books in the archive (EE 2652/45 to 50), but the addresses of properties are only listed from 1871. Until that date what mattered to the estate was the name of the leaseholder. Some leaseholders held more than one property.

Maps

These are key maps for the Eyre estate, and they come from the estate's archive.

1733	Reproduced on p. 32 (EE 2652/1)
1853	Reproduced on p. 143 (EE 2652/8)
1883	Reproduced on p. 358 (EE 2652/10)
1903	Details from this map have been used on pp. 198, 278, 300, 338, 350 and 363 (EE 2652/14(A to J))
2009	A special commission for this book from the artist/illustrator Stephen Conlin, reproduced on p. 376

Use of 'Marylebone' versus 'St Marylebone'

Readers will notice that both forms are used throughout the text. The form 'Marylebone' has been largely adopted and is now in common usage, with names such as Marylebone Station or Marylebone Road. However, when the text deals with the original parish of St Marylebone or the Borough of St Marylebone created in 1900, the prefix 'St' has been retained.

BIBLIOGRAPHY

Maurice B. Adams (with Messenger & Co.), *Artistic Conservatories*, London, 1880.

Maurice B. Adams, *Artists' Homes*, London, 1883.

Geoffrey Agnew, *Agnew's*, London, 1967.

N. W. Alcock, *Documenting the History of Houses*, London (British Records Association), 2003.

Richard D. Altick, *The Shows of London*, Cambridge, MA (Harvard College), 1978.

John Archer, *The Literature of British Domestic Architecture 1715–1842*, Cambridge, MA, 1985.

Felix Barker and Peter Jackson, *London: 2000 Years of its Story and its People*, London, 1979 (first published 1974).

T. C. Barker and Michael Robbins, *A History of London Transport*, 2 vols, London, 1963 and 1974.

William Barnes, *A Century of Camden Housing*, London, 1972.

R. J. Barrow, *Lawrence Alma-Tadema*, London, 2001.

Mavis Batey, *Regency Gardens*, Shire Garden History, Princes Risborough, 1995.

Edwin Becker et al., *Sir Lawrence Alma-Tadema*, exh. cat., Amsterdam (Van Gogh Museum) and Liverpool (Walker Art Gallery), 1996.

Sarah Bendall (ed.), *Dictionary of Land Surveyors and Local Map-Makers*, 2nd edn, 2 vols, London, 1997 (based on first edition edited by Peter Eden).

Annie Besant, *An Autobiography*, Adyar, India, 1999 (first published 1893).

Mark Bills and Vivien Knight (eds), *William Powell Frith: Painting the Victorian Age*, New Haven and London, 2006.

Mark Bills and David Webb, *Victorian Artists in Photographs: The World of G. F. Watts – Selections from the Rob Dickins Collection*, Compton, Surrey (Watts Gallery), 2007.

Sandra Blutman, 'Books of Designs for Country Houses, 1780–1815', *Architectural History*, vol. II, 1968, pp. 25–33.

Richard Bowden, *Marylebone & Paddington*, Stroud, 1995.

Richard Bowden, 'Oxford Street Two Hundred Years Ago: The Portland Estate Block Plans, c.1805–1870', *London Topographical Record*, vol. XXVIII, no. 157, 2001, pp. 79–89.

Richard Bowden, '"Silly Prejudices", "Peevish Obstinacy" and "Knavery": A Survey of Marylebone in 1738', *London Topographical Record*, vol. XXIX, no. 165, 2006, pp. 108–26.

David Boynes, *The Metropolitan Railway*, Stroud, 2003.

E. Bright Ashford, *St John's Wood: The Harrow School & Eyre Estates*, St Marylebone Society Publication No. 8, London, 1965.

J. Britton and A. Pugin, *Illustrations of the Public Buildings of London*, 2 vols, London, 1825–28.

Judith Bronkhurst, *William Holman Hunt: A Catalogue Raisonné*, 2 vols, New Haven and London, 2006.

Malcolm Brown, 'St John's Wood: The Eyre Estate before 1830', *London Topographical Record*, vol. XXVII, no. 149, 1995, pp. 49–68.

Malcolm Brown, 'The Jews of Early St John's Wood', *Jewish Historical Studies*, vol. 35, 1996–98 (1996a), pp. 141–52.

Malcolm Brown, 'William Atkinson, F.G.S., F.H.S.: A Versatile Architect', *Archives of Natural History*, vol. 23, no. 3, 1996b, pp. 429–35.

Malcolm Brown, 'The Fields of Cows by Willan's Farm: Thomas Willan of Marylebone (1755–1828)', *Westminster History Review 4*, London (Westminster City Archives), 2001, pp. 1–5.

Malcolm Brown, 'Henry James and Family in and about St John's Wood', *Westminster History Review 5*, London (Westminster City Archives), 2007, pp. 20–23.

David Blainey Brown, Robert Woof and Stephen Hebron, *Benjamin Robert Haydon 1786–1846: Painter and Writer, Friend of Wordsworth and Keats*, Wordsworth Trust, Grasmere, 1996.

Burke, 1937, see Pirie Gordon.

John Burnett, *A Social History of Housing 1815–1985*, London, 1986 (first published 1978).

Edwin Beresford Chancellor, *Wanderings in Marylebone*, London, 1926.

Bridget Cherry and Nikolaus Pevsner, *The Buildings of England – London 3: North West*, London, 1991.

Bridget Cherry and Nikolaus Pevsner, *The Buildings of England – London 4: North*, London, 1998.

Bridget Cherry and Nikolaus Pevsner, *The Buildings of England – Wiltshire*, New Haven and London, 2002.

William Spencer Clarke, *The Suburban Homes of London: A Residential Guide*, London, 1881.

Emily Cole (ed.), *Lived in London: Blue Plaques and the Stories Behind Them*, New Haven and London, 2009.

Rex Vicat Cole, *The Art and Life of Byam Shaw*, London, 1932.

Marianne Colloms and Dick Weindling, *The Greville Estate: The History of a Kilburn Neighbourhood*, Camden History Society Occasional Paper No. 6, London, 2007.

H. M. Colvin, *A Biographical Dictionary of British Architects 1600–1840*, 3rd edn, New Haven and London, 1995.

J. E. Connor, *London's Disused Underground Stations*, London (Capital Transport), 2001.

Rudolph de Cordova, 'The Panels in Sir Lawrence Alma-Tadema's Hall', *The Strand Magazine*, December 1902, pp. 615–30.

Ann Cox-Johnson, *Handlist to the Ashbridge Collection on the History and Topography of St Marylebone*, London (Borough of St Marylebone), 1959 (later Ann Saunders – see below).

Ann Cox-Johnson, *Handlist of Painters, Sculptors & Architects Associated with St Marylebone 1760–1960*, London (Borough of St Marylebone), 1963 (later Ann Saunders – see below).

Sylvia Cranston, *HPB: The Extraordinary Life and Influence of Helena Blavatsky*, Santa Barbara, CA, 1993.

Caroline Dakers, 'Sigismund Goetze and the Decoration of the Foreign Office Staircase: "Melodrama, Pathos and High Camp"', *The Decorative Arts Society Journal*, no. 21, 1997, pp. 54–66.

Gillian Darley, *Villages of Vision*, London, 1975.

Ida Darlington, *The London Commissioners of Sewers and their Records*, Chichester, 1970.

H. J. Dyos, *Victorian Suburb: A Study of the Growth of Camberwell*, Leicester, 1966.

Denis Evinson, *Catholic Churches of London*, Sheffield, 1998.

Alan Faulkner, *The Regent's Canal: London Hidden Waterway*, Burton-on-Trent (Waterway World Ltd), 2005.

Celina Fox, *Londoners*, London, 1987.

Mireille Galinou, 'Green Finger Painting', *Country Life*, 13 July 1989, pp. 120–23 (a reconstruction of the garden of James Tissot at 17, now 44, Grove End Road).

Mireille Galinou (ed.), *London's Pride: The Glorious History of the Capital's Gardens*, London, 1990.

Mireille Galinou and Stephen Conlin, 'Artist's Treasure House', *Country Life*, 3 March 2010, pp. 70–73.

Mireille Galinou and John Hayes, *London in Paint: Oil Paintings in the Collection at the Museum of London*, London, 1996.

Eric George, *The Life and Death of Benjamin Robert Haydon 1786–1846*, 2nd edn, Oxford, 1967.

Mark Girouard, *Cities and People*, New Haven and London, 1985.

Mark Girouard, *The English Town*, New Haven and London, 1990.

Frederick Goodall, *The Reminiscences of Frederick Goodall RA*, London and Newcastle-on-Tyne, 1902.

Colonel Maurice Harold Grant, *A Chronological History of the Old English Landscape Painters (in Oil): From the XVIth Century to the XIXth Century*, 8 vols, Leigh-on-Sea, 1957–61 (first published 1926).

Algernon Graves, *The Royal Academy of Arts: A Complete Dictionary of Contributors and their Work from its Foundation in 1769 to 1904*, 8 vols, 1905–6 (also see Royal Academy).

Stephen Green, *Lord's: The Cathedral of Cricket*, Stroud, 2003.

Rupert Gunnis, *Dictionary of British Sculptors 1660–1851*, rev. edn, London, 1968.

John Gwynn, *London and Westminster Improved*, London, 1766.

Juliet Hacking, *Princes of Victorian Bohemia: Photographs by David Wilkie Wynfield*, London (National Portrait Gallery), 2000.

Peter Hall, *Cities in Civilisation*, London, 1998.

David Hancock, *Citizens of the World*, Cambridge, 1995.

J. F. C. Harrison, *The Second Coming: Popular Millenarianism 1780–1850*, London, 1979.

J. G. Head, 'Changing London Marylebone', *London Topographical Record*, vol. III, 1906, pp. 94–109.

Kathryn Moore Heleniak, 'Money and Marketing Problems: The Plight of Harriot Gouldsmith (1786–1863), a Professional Female Landscape Painter', *The British Art Journal*, vol. VI, no. 3, Winter 2005, pp. 25–36.

Wendy Hitchmough, *C. F. A. Voysey*, London, 1995.

Richard Colt Hoare, *The History of Modern Wiltshire*, 6 vols, London, 1822–44.

Hermione Hobhouse and Ann Saunders (eds), *Good and Proper Materials: The Fabric of London since the Great Fire*, The Royal Commission on the Historical Monuments of England with the London Topographical Society, Publication No. 140, 1989.

James L. Howgego, *Printed Maps of London, circa 1553–1850*, Folkestone, 2nd edn, 1978 (first published 1964). (The copy formerly kept at Guildhall Library Print Room, now at LMA, has been used here. It has many invaluable additions and annotations.)

W. H. Hunt, *William Holman Hunt and his Works: A Memoir of the Artist's Life, with Description of his Pictures* (by F. G. Stephens), London, 1860.

Alan Jackson, *London's Metropolitan Railway*, Newton Abbot, 1986.

John R. Kellett, *The Impact of Railways on Victorian Cities*, London, 1969.

Vivien Knight, *The Works of Art of the Corporation of London: A Catalogue of Paintings, Watercolours, Drawings, Prints and Sculpture*, Cambridge, 1986.

Jill Lever, *Catalogue of the Drawings of George Dance the Younger (1741–1825), and of George Dance the Elder (1695–1768)*, Oxford, 2003.

David W. Lloyd, *The Making of English Towns: 2000 Years of Evolution*, n.p. [London], 1984.

London County Council, *List of the Streets and Places within the administrative county of London*, 3rd edn, 1929.

London County Council, *Names of Streets and Places in the administrative county of London*, 4th edn, 1955.

Pedro Lorente and Claire Targett, 'Comparative Growth and Urban Distribution of the Population of Artists in Victorian London', in Peter Borsay, Gunther Hirschfelder and Ruth Mohrmann (eds), *New Directions in Urban History: Aspects of European Art, Health, Tourism and Leisure since the Enlightenment*, Münster (Waxmann), 2000.

Jeremy Maas, *Gambart: Prince of the Victorian Art World*, London, 1975.

Stuart Macdonald, *The History and Philosophy of Art Education*, London, 1970.

Hugh McLeod, *Class and Religion in the Late Victorian City*, London, 1974.

James Malton, *An Essay on British Cottage Architecture*, London, 1798.

J. Manwaring Baines, *Burton's St Leonards*, Hastings (Hastings Museum), 1956.

Henry Stacy Marks, *Pen and Pencil Sketches*, 2 vols, London, 1894.

Sheila Marriner, 'English Bankruptcy Records and Statistics before 1850', *Economic History Review*, 2nd ser., vol. XXXIII, 1980, pp. 351–66.

Canon Louis Marteau, 'Hospital of St John and St Elizabeth 1856–1992', n.d. [c.1992] (copy in the Eyre estate archive kindly obtained from the Presbytery of the Church of Our Lady, St John's Wood, another copy at WCA).

Krystyna Matyjaszkiewicz (ed.), *James Tissot 1836–1902*, exh. cat., London (Barbican Art Gallery), 1984.

Alan Montgomery Eyre, *Saint John's Wood: Its History, its House, its Haunts, its Celebrities*, London, 1913. (The index to this book is particularly poor, but readers may find useful the detailed index that was compiled by Stuart Woolf in 1951. The typescript is on open shelves at WCA.)

Rayburn S. Moore (ed.), *The Correspondence of Henry James and the House of Macmillan, 1877–1914*, Baton Rouge, 1993.

Edward Morris and Frank Milner, '*And When Did You Last See Your Father?*', exh. cat., Liverpool (Walker Art Gallery), 1993.

Simon Morris, 'London's Privately Financed Roads and Bridges, 1725–1885', PhD thesis, Birkbeck College, 2005 (unpublished, copy at Senate House Library, University of London).

Museum of London, *The Quiet Conquest: The Huguenots 1685 to 1985*, exh. cat., London (Museum of London), 1985.

Lynda Nead, *Victorian Babylon*, New Haven and London, 2000.

C. R. W. Nevinson, *Paint and Prejudice*, London, 1937.

Aubrey Newman, *The United Synagogue 1870–1970*, London, 1976.

John Oliver and Peter Bradshaw, *Saint John's Wood Church 1814–1955*, London, 1955.

Donald J. Olsen, *Town Planning in London: The Eighteenth and Nineteenth Centuries*, 1964.

Donald J. Olsen, 'House upon House: Estate Development in London and Sheffield', in H. J. Dyos and Michael Wolff (eds), *The Victorian City: Images and Realities*, vol. 1, London, 1973, pp. 333–57.

Richard Ormond, *Sir Edwin Landseer*, London, 1981.

Fiona Pearson, *Goscombe John at the National Museum of Wales*, Cardiff, 1979.

Edmund Phipps Eyre, *Memorials of the Eyre Family*, Liverpool, 1885. (Copies of this home-published history are rare; the Eyre estate archive only possesses a photocopy of the original.)

H. Pirie-Gordon (ed.), *Burke's Genealogical and Heraldic History of the Landed Gentry*, London, 1937.

Tom Pocock (ed.), *Travels of a London Schoolboy 1826–1830: John Pocock's Diary of Life in London and Voyages to Cape Town and Australia*, London, 1996.

Willard Bissell Pope (ed.), *The Diary of Benjamin Robert Haydon*, 5 vols, Cambridge, MA, 1963.

M. H. Port, *600 New Churches*, 2nd edn, Reading, 2006.

The Pre-Raphaelites, exh. cat., London (Tate Gallery), 1984.

Mary E. F. Richardson-Eyre, *A History of the Wiltshire Family of Eyre*, London, 1897.

Mary E. F. Richardson-Eyre, 'Poor Mary', 1904 (copy at Westminster City Archives, D.Misc 164).

Alexander Rottmann, *London Catholic Churches: A Historical and Artistic Record*, London, 1926.

Royal Academy Exhibitors 1905–1970: A Dictionary of Artists and their Work in the Summer Exhibitions of the Royal Academy of Arts, 6 vols, Wakefield, 1973–82 (also see Graves).

Ann Saunders, *Regent's Park: A Study of the Development of the Area from 1086 to the Present Day*, 2nd rev. edn, London (Bedford College), 1981.

Ann Saunders (ed.), *The London County Council Bomb Damage Maps 1939–1945*, with an intro. by Robin Woolven, London (London Topographical Society and London Metropolitan Archives), 2005.

E. G. Semple, *All Saints Church St John's Wood Centenary 1846–1946*, n.d. [London, 1946].

F. H. W. Sheppard, *Local Government in St Marylebone 1688–1835*, University of London Historical Studies, London, 1958.

Francis Sheppard, *London 1808–1870: The Infernal Wen*, London, 1971.

Mark John Simmonds (ed.), *Register of the Clergy Orphan School for Boys 1751–1896*, Canterbury, 1897.

B. M. G. Smedley, *Norfolk Road, St John's Wood: Celebrating the First 150 Years*, London, 1997.

Thomas Smith, *A Topographical and Historical Account of the Parish of St Mary-le-bone*, n.p. [London], 1833.

Brian Southall, Peter Vince and Allan Rouse, *Abbey Road*, London, New York and Sydney, 2002 (first published 1982).

Herbert Spencer, *London's Canal: An Illustrated History of the Regent's Canal*, London, 1961.

A. M. W. Stirling, *The Richmond Papers, from the Correspondence and Manuscripts of George Richmond RA and his son Sir William Richmond RA, KCB*, London, 1926.

A. M. W. Stirling, *Victorian Sidelights from the Papers of the late Mrs Adams-Acton*, London, 1954.

William Stott, *A Ministry of Twenty-Five Years in London: Being a History of the Baptist Church Abbey Road St John's Wood*, n.d. [London, 1887].

Dorothy Stroud, *George Dance Architect 1741–1825*, London, 1971.

John Summerson, 'The Beginnings of Regent's Park', *Architectural History*, vol. 20, 1977, pp. 56–62 and plates 18–35.

John Summerson, 'The Beginnings of an Early Victorian Suburb', *London Topographical Record*, vol. XXVII, no. 149, 1995, pp. 1–48 (paper based on two lectures given in February 1958).

Virginia Surtees (ed.), *The Diaries of George Price Boyce 1851–1875*, Norwich, 1980.

Survey of London: vol. 39, *The Grosvenor Estate in Mayfair, Part 1*, London, 1977; vol. 40, *The Grosvenor Estate in Mayfair, Part 2*, London, 1980; vol. 46, *South and East Clerkenwell*, and vol. 47, *Northern Clerkenwell and Pentonville*, New Haven and London, 2008.

John Sworder, 'The Riding School at "The Wood"', *Country Life*, 1 July 1971, pp. 14–15.

Lieutenant J. C. C. Sworder, RHA, 'The Wood, a Short History: The Barracks at St John's Wood London NW8', first prepared in 1956 and repackaged as a private publication in 2003. Unpublished typescript (copies in Eyre estate archive and WCA).

Richard Tames, *St John's Wood and Maida Vale Past*, London, 1998.

Colin Thom, *Researching London's Houses*, London, 2005.

F. M. L. Thompson, *Hampstead: Building a Borough, 1650–1964*, London and Boston, MA, 1974.

William Vaughan, Elizabeth E. Barker and Colin Harrison, *Samuel Palmer: Vision and Landscape*, exh. cat., 3rd edn, London (British Museum Press), 2005.

VCH (The Victoria History of the Counties of England): C. R. Erlington (ed.), *A History of the County of Middlesex*, vol. 9: *Hampstead and Paddington Parishes*, 1989.

Francesco Viglione, *Ugo Foscolo in Inghilterra*, Catania, 1910.

E. R. Vincent, *Ugo Foscolo: An Italian in Regency England*, Cambridge, 1953.

Giles Walkley, *Artists' Houses in London 1764–1914*, Aldershot, 1994.

Isobel Watson, *Gentlemen in the Building Line: The Development of South Hackney*, London, 1989.

Isobel Watson, 'Rebuilding London: Abraham Davis and his Brothers, 1881–1924', *London Journal*, vol. 29, no. 1, 2004, pp. 62–84.

Kit Wedd, *Creative Quarters: The Art World in London from 1700 to 2000*, London, 2001 (with contributions by Lucy Peltz and Cathy Ross). NB: the hardback has a different title: *Artists' London: Holbein to Hirst*, also 2001.

Michael Wentworth, *James Tissot*, Oxford, 1984.

John White, *Account of Proposed Improvements …*, 1815 (first published 1814, republished 1815 with additions; the 1815 edition has been used here).

William Thomas Whitley, *The Baptists of London 1612–1928*, London, 1928.

William Thomas Whitley, *Thomas Heaphy*, London, 1933.

Edmund Hodgson Yates, *Fifty Years of London Life: Memoirs of a Man of the World*, New York, 1885 (original title: *Edmund Yates: His Recollections and Experiences*, 1884).

Elizabeth [and Wayland] Young, *London's Churches*, London, 1986.

PHOTOGRAPHIC ACKNOWLEDGEMENTS

Every effort has been made to trace the source of the pictures reproduced in this book. In the event of an omission or a mistake, please inform the publishers. The illustrations may not be reproduced without permission from the copyright holders listed below.

Art Gallery of Hamilton, Canada: Plate 89.

The Athenaeum of Ohio/Mt St Mary's Seminary, Cincinnati: Plate 142.

© The author and the Eyre estate: Plates 38; 39; 40; 49; 81; 135; 146; 192; 223; 299, 306 and page 465.

2010 © The British Library Board: Plates 36; 37; 44; 57; 141.

© Camden Local Studies: Plates 7; 90; 91; 102; 103; 104; 105; 106; 121; 188; 294; 295; 296.

Cardiff Museum, © National Museums of Wales: Plate 180.

Center for Southwest Research, University Libraries, University of New Mexico: Plate 177.

City of London, London Metropolitan Archives: Plates 6; 17; 18; 29; 31;32; 33; 47; 48; 56; 69; 96; 98; 107; 118; 122; 149; 176; 189; 219; 297.

Collection of Alan Irvine: Plate 264.

Collection of Mrs Diana Eyre: Plate 4.

Collection of George Eyre and family: Plates 22; 25.

Courtauld Institute of Art (Witt Library): Plate 235.

© Crown copyright. NMR: Plates 8; 9; 10, 13.

Reproduced by permission of English Heritage. NMR: Plates 186; 279; 282.

© Eyre estate: Plates 1; 3; 5; 16; 20; 23; 24; 27; 28; 42; 46; 50; 53; 54; 55; 58; 61; 62; 63; 64; 65; 66; 67; 70; 72; 73; 74; 75; 76; 77, 78; 79; 81; 82; 83; 84; 85; 88; 94; 100; 101; 108; 109; 110; 112; 114; 116; 119; 123; 126; 127; 130; 131; 132; 134; 139; 144; 145; 144; 145; 150; 152; 154; 163; 165; 167; 168; 170; 172; 173; 178; 179; 185; 187; 195; 198; 199; 200; 203; 206; 207; 208; 209; 210; 211; 212; 213; 214; 215; 216; 217; 218; 220; 221; 222; 225; 226; 227; 228; 232; 233; 234; 239; 241; 242; 243; 244; 247; 248; 250; 253; 255; 256; 258; 259; 260; 261; 262; 263; 265; 266; 267; 268; 270; 271; 272; 273; 274; 275; 276; 277; 280; 281; 283; 284; 285; 287; 288; 289; 292; 293; 298; 302; 305; 309; 310; 311.

Getmapping: Plate 2.

Brian Girling: Plate 224.

Guildhall Library, City of London: Plates 43; 97; 197; 257.

Hulton Archive/Getty Images: Plate 93.

The London Topographical Society: Plates 35; 59; 71; 231.

London School of Economics: Plate 238.

Martyn Gregory, London: Plate 87.

Marylebone Cricket Club: Plates 240; 308.

© Museum of London: Plates 300; 301; 303; 304; 307.

Chester Dale Fund. Image courtesy of the Board of Trustees, National Gallery of Art, Washington: Plate 156.

National Gallery of Canada, Ottawa: Plate 129.

© National Portrait Gallery, London: Plates 157; 161; 182; 205.

New Haven; Yale Center for British Art: Plates 30; 125.

Photo: Stephen White, London. By courtesy of the Liberal Jewish Synagogue and the artist: Plate 201.

Private Collection: Plates 4; 12; 15; 19; 21; 41; 95; 120; 124; 164; 286.

Private Collection/Photo © Christie's Images/The Bridgeman Art Library: Plates 51; 151; 153; 159; 169; 175.

RIBA Library Drawings and Archives Collections: Plates 60; 291.

Reproduced by permission of Salisbury District Council: Plates 11; 14.

© Museums Sheffield/The Bridgeman Art Library: Plate 68.

By courtesy of the Trustees of the Sir John Soane's Museum: Plate 34.

The Royal Collection © 2010 Her Majesty Queen Elizabeth II: Plate 140.

© The Samuel Courtauld Trust, The Courtauld Gallery, London: Plates 235; 249.

Scottish National Portrait Gallery: Plate 278.

© Stephen Conlin, reproduced by kind permission of the artist and *Country Life*: Plate 166.

© Tate, London 2010: Plates 86; 111; 128; 148.

The National Archives: Plate 147.

The Reform Club: Plate 275.

© The Theosophical Publishing House, Adyar, Chennai – 600 020, India; http://www.ts-adyar.org: Plates 202; 204.

© The Trustees of the British Museum: Plate 136.

© Towneley Hall Art Gallery and Museum, Burnley, Lancashire/The Bridgeman Art Library: Plate 171.

© V&A Images/Victoria and Albert Museum, London: Plates 137; 138; 162; 183; 184.

The Vicar and Churchwardens of St John's Wood: Plate 193.

Walker Art Gallery. © National Museums Liverpool: Plate 290.

Watts Gallery, Compton, Surrey (Rob Dickins Collection): Plates 158; 181.

Westminster City Archives: Plates 26; 45; 52; 80; 92; 99; 113; 115; 117; 133; 143; 155; 160; 174; 190; 194; 196; 229; 230; 236; 237; 245; 246; 251; 252; 254; 269.

INDEX

Note: Titles such as Col., Revd, Sir are ignored in the alphabetical ordering of names. Page numbers in italics refer to illustrations and their captions; those underlined refer to text boxes.

For the purposes of this index the word 'tenant' has been used to denote agricultural tenancies and the word 'lessee' to denote residential tenancies.

Index compiled by Meg Davies
(Fellow of the Society of Indexers)